AF581318

Heaven, Hell and Somewhere In Between

Portuguese Popular Art

ANTHONY ALAN SHELTON

Heaven, Hell and Somewhere In Between

Figure.1
Vancouver / Berkeley

MOA at the University of British Columbia
Vancouver

15 16 17 18 19 5 4 3 2 1

Cataloguing data available from Library and Archives Canada
ISBN 978-1-927958-24-7 (hbk.)

Editing by Scott Steedman
Copy editing and indexing by Lana Okerlund
Design by Jessica Sullivan
Layout by Ingrid Paulson
Maps by Eric Leinberger
Jacket images: *Front*: Artist unknown, *Angels* (wall mural), 2009, Rua da Alfândega, Lisbon. *Back*: David Gomes, *Portugal*, 2009.
Frontispiece image: Wall above David Gomes's workbench at 23a Rua do Anjo, Braga, 2011.
Printed and bound in China by 1010 Printing International, Ltd.
Distributed in the U.S. by Publishers Group West

Figure 1 Publishing Inc.
Vancouver BC Canada
www.figure1pub.com

MOA at the University of British Columbia
6393 N.W. Marine Drive
Vancouver BC Canada V6T 1Z2
www.moa.ubc.ca

"We can see life as an art, not simply as an obligation or boundless freedom.... This art makes it easier for men and women to change between birth and death ... In death we all become strange creatures, pale and floundering in the nets of memory ... The dead lie in the earth and their bones strengthen the old ruins. The proud construction of the modern world rests on them ... The dead repeatedly return to the world through the words of the living. We only recognize the people we spend time with through our dreams and in the pattern of what we say."

THOMAS HAUSCHILD, *Power and Magic in Italy*

"Memory is a sort of anti-museum; it is not localizable. Fragments of it come out in legends. Objects and words also have hollow places in which a past sleeps, as in the everyday acts of walking, eating, going to bed, in which ancient revolutions slumber ... There is no place that is not haunted by many different spirits hidden in silence, spirits that can 'invoke' or not. Haunted places are the only ones people can live in ..."

MICHEL DE CERTEAU, *The Practice of Everyday Life*

"The speed of a cinema film is twenty-five frames per second. God knows how many frames per second flicker past in our daily perception. But it is as if, at ... brief moments ..., suddenly and disconcertingly we see *between* two frames. We come upon a part of the visible which wasn't destined for us ... Our customary visual order is not the only one: it coexists with other orders."

JOHN BERGER, *The Shape of a Pocket*

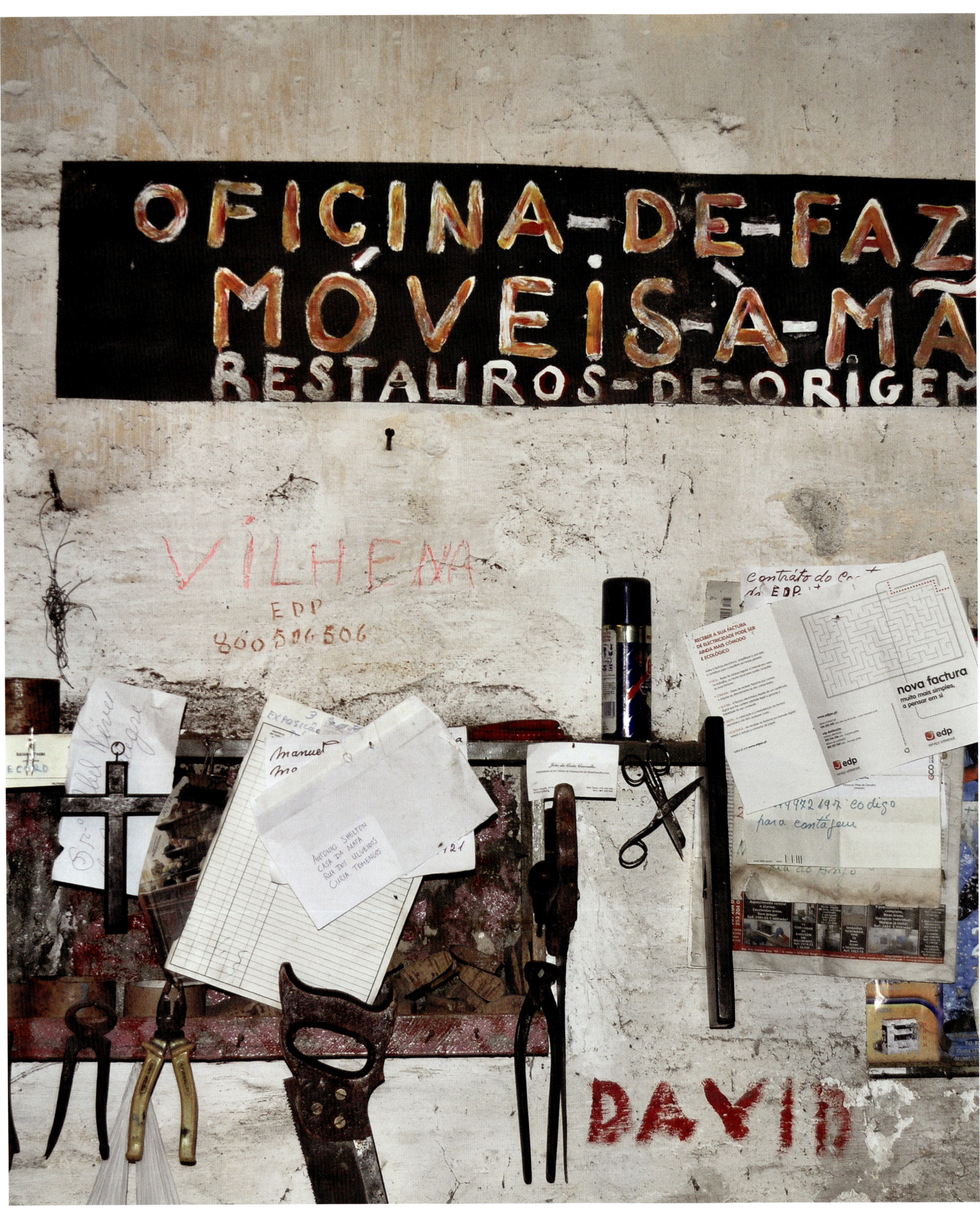
OFICINA-DE-FAZ
MÓVEIS-À-MÃ
RESTAUROS-DE-ORIGEM
VILHENA
EDP
800506506
nova factura
muito mais simples,
a pensar em si
edp
DAVID

Contents

Preface

IN THIS THOUGHTFUL and erudite collection of essays, popular art is the starting point for unfolding Portuguese cultural history and identity. The uniqueness of the country caught between its past grandeur and its present economic crisis is rendered by means of intertwined stories, things and museologies. Such an insightful analysis of the imaginaries of Portuguese identity could be carried out only by someone located both inside and outside Portugal. It is not surprising that Anthony Alan Shelton considers this book as "a sort of album" in which texts dialogue with visual images; he invites us to reflect on the past-present connections weaving cultural history and politics, popular art and religion, museums/exhibitions and puppet theatre into a tapestry full of intuitions. Yet *Heaven, Hell and Somewhere In Between* can also be envisaged as a personal album—like all albums—in which experiences, affinities and above all fortuitous meetings determined both the order of the chapters and the line of the argument running throughout the book. Thus, the album starts with "The Kingdom of the Marvellous"—in fact the shop of cabinetmaker David Silva Gomes, located in a street named Rua do Anjo (Angel Street) in Braga, which appeared "like an apparition" to Shelton the first time he entered it. Gomes's shop, with diverse objects pertaining to distinct historical periods, somehow encapsulated the different layers of Portuguese stories, a kind of "museum of Lusitania," in Shelton's words, a place "where things were taken apart, reassembled, classified and reclassified and new things were invented."

This essay can also be read as an argued defence of popular art. By extending the category of popular art to contemporary cultural expressions such as murals and graffiti, Shelton aims to demonstrate both the vitality of this form of art and its potential for disruption, to the extent that it can be considered as "an outsider art." Shelton's contention that popular art "does not blandly reflect the forces that produce it but mediates them through its own specific visual strategies and technologies" challenges the current assumptions about the presumed relationships between popular art and the community or social context. Individual artists mediate and create new universes, new mental spaces located somewhere between the imagination of Heaven and Hell.

That popular art in Portugal was "discovered" first by ethnographers and then by modernist artists undoubtedly shaped the ways in which it was perceived and its contexts of reception and display. The implicit and/or explicit parallels between popular art and the so-called primitive art that pervaded these approaches tended to circumscribe the sphere of popular art to sculpture, mainly ceramic sculpture. Popular art was thus equated with the lament for a vanishing rural past as illustrated (throughout Chapter 8) by the several attempts to create a museum dedicated to Lusitania.

In 1995 the Museu Nacional de Etnologia (Lisbon) curated an exhibit, *Onde mora o Franklin? Um escultor do acaso*, entirely devoted to the work of Franklin Vilas Boas (1919–68). It was the first time a sculptor was detached from the category of popular art—as a presumed homogeneous field—and exhibited as an individual artist. The next exhibit dedicated to a popular artist was a retrospective of Rosa Ramalho's work held in 2007 at the Museu de Olaria (Barcelos). The time span between these two exhibits highlights the problematic status assigned to popular art within Portuguese museology, as illustrated by the current situation of the Museu de Arte Popular in Lisbon, which is now devoted to contemporary art exhibits. As the product of a historical process of categorization of objects related to rural European societies, the notion of popular art has been equated with other categories such as folk art and traditional arts. Gradually the notion of popular art was extended both to other geographical regions and to different social groups with their diverse cultural manifestations, an inclusion that contributed to the blurring of the boundaries between popular art and urban art, outsider art and popular culture. Thus, the distinction between functional objects and artistic ones as well as the distinction between artisans and artists became problematic. Although popular art has been and somehow continues to be marginalized in museums, some of its manifestations have been recently promoted to the status of intangible cultural heritage.

The recent inscription of the black ceramics from Bisalhães in the Portuguese National Inventory is deemed to be a step for its further inscription in UNESCO's List of Intangible Culture Heritage in Need of Urgent Safeguarding. The supposedly endangered status of black ceramic is based on the imminent physical disappearance of its five producers and their technological skills associated with an archaic practice. Faithful to the 2003 UNESCO Convention for the Safeguarding of Intangible Cultural Heritage, black ceramic is presented both as a social practice involving a community producing utilitarian objects and as a singular practice of a sculptor fabricating decorative pieces. Black ceramic from Bisalhães illuminates the tensions somehow inherent to popular art, struck between the recognition of the individual creator and the role of the community that supposedly generated him or her. It also highlights the ambiguities and the contradictions underlying the appropriations of popular art either by museums or by national and international organizations dealing with heritage.

In 1930 Georges-Henri Rivière, vice-director of the Musée de l'Homme, published an article provocatively entitled "Religion et 'Folies-Bergère'" in *Documents*, the surrealist art magazine edited by Georges Bataille. Rivière suggested that music hall and its ritual ceremonies be considered equivalent to a religious manifestation, thus worthy of being studied by ethnologists. For the future founder of the Musée National des Arts et Traditions Populaires (Paris), the borders between the religious and the profane were porous, like the boundaries between high culture and popular culture. As mediators between official religion and popular religion, the saints and devils, as well as the supernatural and marvellous creatures of Rosa Ramalho's sculptures beautifully analyzed in *Heaven, Hell and Somewhere In Between*, remind us of the persistences and transience of social life.

Professor Nélia Dias
Department of Anthropology,
ISCTE-Lisbon University Institute

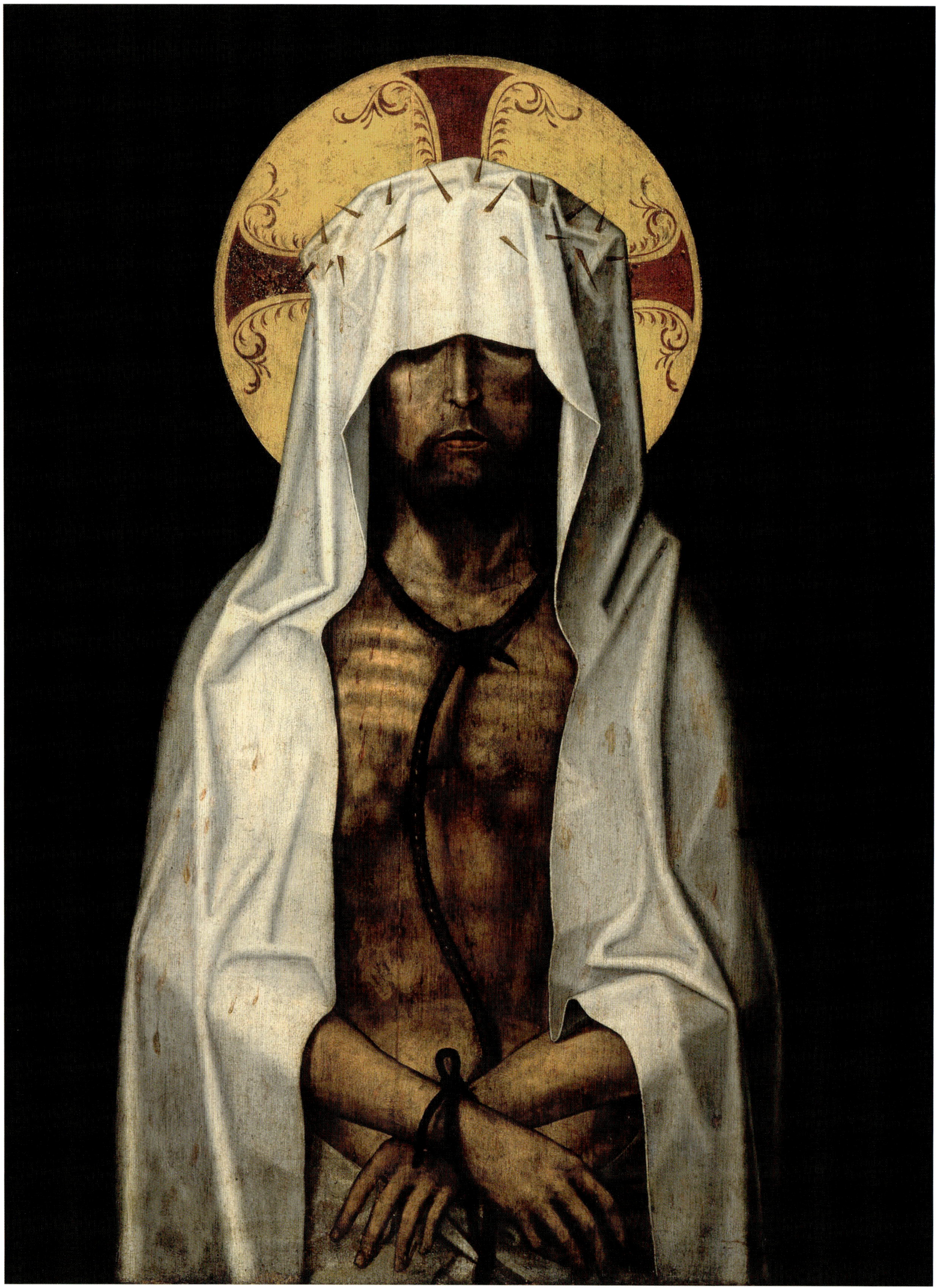

Introduction

HOW DO IMAGES AND words embalm the ghosts of the past, incessantly resurrecting them for the souls of the living? How does time become arrested, drawn out, made to double back on itself? How do a people gain the protection of God and the saints without entirely waking from the pagan enchantments cast by the ancient sea nymph Calypso? What is the effect of so much metaphysically suffused history on an inchoate identity balanced precariously on the threshold between ancient and different Christian worlds, when a modern age has been imposed on cultural productions nourished by a much older one? These questions have never been more relevant for understanding the Portuguese people as they are at the advent of the twenty-first century, especially since the economic and political crisis that has afflicted the nation since 2011.

History, metaphysics and myth are produced through the manipulation of images and texts across different genres of literature, photography, film, popular and high art, and academia. These manipulations may be conscious or unconscious, accidental or deliberate. They involve aesthetic and instrumental agencies and may be deployed by the state, corporations, universities, religious institutions, museums, communities and individuals. The rich assemblages of texts and images that permeate Western societies provide the weaponry for a veritable battlefield of discursive strategies that lie at the heart of competing world views and constructions, deconstructions and reinventions of social and national identities.

This book—which I consider to be a sort of album—opens varied perspectives and provides glimpses into the diverse aspects of the rich and complex visual and textual sources that at different times have been used to evoke particular imaginaries of Portuguese identity and notions of national essences. Each chapter juxtaposes different aspects of religion, politics, popular arts and culture, and museum and exhibition history to evoke partial and particular mappings of aspects of Portugal's cultural landscape. These texts had their origin in research based on the collection of popular art I assembled for the UBC Museum of Anthropology from 2010 to 2011 and further elaborated while collecting the images assembled in the following pages. They refer to one socially constructed imaginative world that exists side by side with many others.

Folk art—or what I term "popular art"—most clearly reveals its meanings, qualities and intentionalities when it is contextualized within the changing political, economic and cultural circumstances in which it is mediated and developed. Popular art, I shall argue, does not blandly reflect the forces that produce it but mediates them

facing
FREI CARLOS
Ecce Homo, C. 1570
Museu Nacional de Arte Antiga

through its own specific visual strategies and technologies. The ten chapters presented here share the conviction that such work should not be treated as an inferior, rustic category of art but rather as sets of diverse personal practices and responses to wider historical movements and changes in market conditions and political and religious situations. Far from being traditional or frozen in time, popular art—which includes contemporary forms of expression like murals and graffiti—has a history of its own, intimately bound with texts, photographs, exhibitions and discourses that frame it and provide it with a dynamism that is too often obscured by a descriptive vocabulary of traditionalism, rusticism and antiquarianism.

Popular art has received renewed attention in the last few years. In the United Kingdom, folk art was admitted into the Tate Gallery of British Art only towards the end of the 1990s. This led in 2009–10 to a series of workshops entitled *Folk Art and the Art Museum*, organized with Compton Verney and the American Museum in Britain. Since then a number of artists, often curating installation-style exhibits, have represented folk art to the British public: *Folk Archive* by Jeremy Deller and Alan Kane as part of the Tate's *Intelligence* exhibition (2000); Vladimir Arkhipov's *post-folk archive* (2002–3); Grayson Perry's *The Charms of Lincolnshire* (2006); Compton Verney's *What the Folk Say* (2011); and Ruth Kenny, Jeff McMillan and Martin Myrone's *British Folk Art*, curated at Tate Britain (2014). These were complemented by a retrospective archival exhibition on the groundbreaking 1951 popular art show *Black Eyes and Lemonade*, which was held at the Whitechapel Gallery in 2013.

In the United States, folk art has a longer history of aesthetic recognition that goes back to the 1930s with exhibitions like *American Primitives: An Exhibit of the Paintings of Nineteenth Century Folk Artists* (Newark Museum, 1930), *American Folk Art: The Art of the Common Man in America, 1750–1900* (Museum of Modern Art, 1932) and *Contemporary Unknown American Painters* (Museum of Modern Art, 1939). Unlike in Europe, where certain genres of folk art, like outsider art, were considered the expression of otherness and appreciated for their exoticism, in the United States popular art was tied to ideas of national character and a culture of individualism and nonconformity.[1] Alfred H. Barr Jr., the first director of the Museum of Modern Art, went so far as to identify three currents of modern art: the abstract, conceptual tendency represented by Cubism, the art of the unconscious expressed in Surrealism, and popular art produced by untrained and naïve artists, which grew indifferent to and independent of the academies.[2] Nevertheless, subsequent museum directors narrowed his expansive view, focusing their exhibitions on formalist, referential artists and movements. In 1953 the Museum of International Folk Art, the largest museum of its kind, was founded in Santa Fe; it extended and projected the identification of innate, raw, untutored aesthetic expression with distinctive national character traits onto a global survey exhibition.

In Canada the connection between folk art and community identity was encouraged by the Toronto-based Community Folk Art Council, established in 1963. Nationally, however, it was the Canadian Museum of Civilization (renamed in 2013 the Canadian Museum of History) rather than art galleries that led the promotion of popular art as expressions of the diverse multicultural mosaic that comprised the nation's population. Important exhibitions included *Folk Art in Canada: Land and People* (1992–95), *Just for Nice* (German Canadian folk art, 1993–94) and *Les Paradis du Monde: Quebec Folk Art* (1995–96). The Canadian Museum of History remains active in promoting its extensive collections by curating travelling exhibitions like *Wind Work, Wind Play: Weathervanes and Whirligigs* (2013).

The foundation of the Museu de Arte Popular (Museum of Popular Art) in Portugal in 1948, and the exhibitions that prefigured it, coincided with an earlier and wider renewal of interest in popular or folk art across Europe and North America both before and after the Second World War. In many cases this renewed interest was provoked by profound crises of ethnic identity and nationalist sentiment that invented a wholesome idea of nations as idealized communities.[3] The 1951 Festival of Britain coincided with the important exhibition *Black Eyes and Lemonade*, curated by Barbara Jones at London's Whitechapel Gallery, and various regional attempts to resuscitate folk art.[4] *Black Eyes and Lemonade* focused on everyday, as well as some extraordinary singular, British objects arranged by home, life-cycle celebrations, self-images, commerce and industry.

The relationship between folk art exhibitions, idealization and romanticism is close in many parts of the world. Similarly, the mobilization of this trinity in relationship to national crises and identity politics, although articulated differently, occurred historically under political and governmental regimes as diverse as those of post-revolutionary Mexico, 1920s–1930s Germany, 1930s–1950s Britain, the United States of the Great Depression era and the world-weary Portugal of the 1930s to 1950s.

At its outset the present research and exhibition pondered the question of the meaning of popular art, an awkward and orphaned category disowned at times by mainstream anglophone art history and anthropology. The sociologist Howard Becker, preferring the term "folk" over "popular," defined folk art as always being external to professional art worlds. "Folk art ... is art done by people who do what they do because it is one of the things members of their community, or at least most members of a particular age and sex, ordinarily do."[5] Community rather than individual is important in Becker's definition and affects the constraints and opportunities expressed in the works. Arthur Danto drew attention to the compounds formed from the prefix "folk": folklore, folk saying, folk wisdom, folk medicine, folk tale, which like folk art attest to an elaborate category of practice associated with traditional communities and an intimate connection to the environment.[6] Kenny reiterates Becker's position, affirming that "folk art ... is rooted in the idea of community, in the sense of being produced for and often by a group,"[7] while going on to note that such artists often subsume their authorship under community identity.[8] McMillan, using the same term, observes that folk art in Britain was often practised by working-class artisans and used its own distinct materials like bone, wood, straw, wool and broken crockery as opposed to the more durable materials like marble, stone and bronze favoured by the academy.[9] "Many of these works," McMillan feels, "represent a kind of condensation: a thing boiled down to its essence. The sense of time, the sheer labour involved, along with the at times intimate, miniaturized scale, suggest an interior (or internalized) work."[10] His co-curator Ruth Kenny emphasizes the use of found materials, idiosyncratic imagination and varying degrees of technical and aesthetic accomplishment,[11] while Charles Russell, like Barr and Danto, emphasizes that the artists were self-taught and their modes of expression were unconnected and innocent of the self-consciousness underlying academic art practices of their day.[12] For the Brazilian anthropologist Edison Carneiro, "Folklore is the culture of the popular become normative through tradition."[13] Many of these characteristics are also applicable to Portuguese popular art, although artists have more often served in apprenticeships or participated in training and are attentive to historical antecedents.

Interpretive frameworks, Kenny notes, have been sharply drawn between discussions of folk and professional artistic practices. Despite Danto warning of the parochialism that could result from all creative objects being categorized as art, canonical art schools and styles have mostly been discussed within a developed body of academic theory, while folk art is often described in relation to emotional expressions and historically transcendental, essentialized practices that are often pitched against high culture.[14] Nowhere is this clearer than in the common incorporation into the folk art category, both in Europe and the Americas, of outsider art produced by "creative individuals whose psychological or sociological conditions placed them on the margins of socially expected behavior."[15] Kenny emphasizes the difference between these, noting outsider art is indivisible into movements and periods, celebrates the raw visions of its makers, ignores everyday reality and seeks no audience or social consecration. Folk art, on the other hand, as it is in Portugal, "is rooted in the idea of community."[16]

The *British Folk Art* exhibition attempted to subvert the distinctive discourses that separate and distinguish folk from fine arts by examining folk art's formal compositions such as figuration and abstraction, which inadvertently pull it inside art historical discourses. *Heaven, Hell and Somewhere In Between: Portuguese Popular Art* attempts to do the opposite by examining how the category of "folk art" has been created, reproduced, hybridized and re-created as a means of inventing and signifying different evocations of the notion of community and nation within a specific territory. Folk art is here referred to as "popular art" to avoid the rural character, ahistoricism and essentialism usually ascribed it. Popular art, we shall argue, is an invented category produced through a cultural synthesis, which inevitably hides the often singular relations that connect creative individuals to socially, politically and academically sanctioned discourses. Rather than focusing on popular art by adopting an introspective and formalist or technologically centred analysis, this approach focuses outwards to enunciate the dense layers of associations and affects in which Portuguese popular art has been and is implicated.

Popular art in this book is therefore the starting point to uncover the changing and sometimes paradoxical everyday aesthetics of Portuguese life. Aesthetics is usually applied to isolated objects that have been removed from social life and institutionalized in museums, galleries and private collections. Popular art, even in the context of this more limited institutionalization, nevertheless conveys a general aesthetic affect, like those of Santa Fe's Museum of International Folk Art or Lisbon's Museu de Arte Popular, which often derives from assemblages and juxtapositions rather than from individual pieces themselves. The wider locations of popular art, in communities, in homes, in markets, in churches, in schools, on buildings and in the street—as part of public assemblages—create an everyday aesthetic capable of evoking different sentiments, memories and significations. Such an aesthetic creates deep experiences of social space capable of haunting us profoundly and helps distinguish society's "deep spaces" from those that are shallower or indifferently coded and less appreciated.

Nineteenth- and twentieth-century Portuguese imaginative culture has largely been shaped by three grand, core preoccupations endemic in its rich, hybridized roots: the struggle between official and popular religion, uncertainty around national identity and the pull between urban and rural cultures. The first of these conundrums involves the mediation and reconciliation of pre-Christian and Christian beliefs and practices, which at an institutional level is synonymous with the long struggle between popular and institutionalized religion. According to historical texts, this conflict became most attenuated between the third and fifth centuries but continued throughout the Middle Ages, the Renaissance and the Enlightenment and showed little sign of abatement until the nineteenth-century Republican period, when a secular state not only curbed the authority of the Church but also sought to combat superstition and insalubrious practices. After 1926 the Estado Novo, or "New State," combined secular and ecclesiastical authority to combat popular religion. Finally, with the advent of a liberal democracy in 1974, the growth of urbanization, modernization and consumer values began to break the authority of both organized and popular religion and their monopoly over taste and cultural expressions.

Since the 1960s the clash between vernacular and institutional religion has progressively lost much of its doctrinal relevance, though popular religious beliefs and values continue to exert a strong imprint on the creation and interpretation of popular images. In the first in-depth ethnographic field study of a Portuguese rural community, namely Vilarinho da Furna, and a later study of the village of Rio de Onor,[17] Jorge Dias, the founder of modern Portuguese anthropology, insisted on the influence of pre-Roman forms of social organization on the pastoral economy of the 1940s. His first work included a memorable description of how the community's leaders legitimized their positions by invoking a distant ancestral authority.[18] Even though the direct correlation between the head, the *juiz* or *zelador*, and his six-man council with saintly authority was no longer recognized at the time of Dias's fieldwork, the mechanism and belief were still remembered and were sufficient to legitimate the local government.[19] In a similar way, while the origins, significance or context of popular artistic themes may have been forgotten, forms and subjects persist and are transmitted through memory, which actively borrows and combines with the free-floating images and texts drawn from magazines, films, libraries and the Internet, to continually reproduce, reinvent and reconfigure ideas, age-old themes and montages.

Vernacular religion was an integral part of Portuguese rural life and coloured all its facets, including popular art, which was mobilized to define a majority social group, identified as the "other Portugal" up until the 1960s. Although, as a result of emigration, urbanization and a decline in agriculture, rural culture no longer possesses the rigid clarity, uniqueness or authority it once held in the past, it continues to be remembered, idealized and re-elaborated to support and uphold values, forms and styles of representation that supposedly have their roots in history.

Until the 1970s, the gulf between popular and institutional religion strongly asserted itself in the division between rural and urban society. More recently, religious differences have become attenuated in discussions about the proliferation of sanctuaries and cults devoted to Nossa Senhora, "Our Lady" or the Virgin Mary, in preference to other Catholic saints and images. Divine apparitions of Nossa Senhora have been recorded at Nazaré, Póvoa, Cós, Ortiga and Porches and more recently at Barral (1917), Vila Chão (1945), Ladeira (1962) and, most famous of all, Fátima (1917). Some writers, adhering to folkloric interpretations, have suggested that these cults may have grown from Roman goddesses, such as Diana. Others have proposed they may be older still and originated in the successive transformations and splintering of a mother goddess complex that had its origin in the ancient Near East 35,000 years ago.[20]

Interpretations like these, not surprisingly, are strongly rejected by orthodox Christianity, whose texts and narratives continue to uphold the purity of established doctrine.[21] Nevertheless, the increasing popularity of the Virgin Mary and her success in replacing older saintly cults cause concern within the Church, even though, in the case of the Fátima cult, the Church wields overwhelming authority over its liturgical organization. So strong are the differences on the authority of the Virgin Mary that some have argued that institutional recognition and proliferation of Marian cults form part of a clandestine strategy to convert Christianity into a matriarchal religion. Extremist proponents of this position even argue that the subversion of Catholicism prefigures the advent of the Antichrist and the inevitable Apocalypse. The persuasive power of text and image and their interconnective possibilities are so extensive that they can be manipulated to justify positions regardless of rationality or logical coherence.

The network of chapels and churches and the pilgrimages or *romarias* that connected them formed the basis of popular religion and rural society, which until the 1970s structured the world view and economic possibilities of Portugal's artisans and popular artists. The memory of popular religious practices and the attempt to reconcile this past world to present conditions influence a large part of contemporary popular art. Furthermore, in many texts the close relation between institutional religion and politics continues to reproduce a latent messianism—the belief in the second coming of a Messiah and the advent of a better age—that still haunts Portuguese thought as expressed in music, literature, popular culture and political rhetoric. It is even heard in the conversations of old men huddled in the shade provided by rural stores while surreptitiously sharing a glass of wine or port.

Portugal's second core semantic conundrum stems from the contradictions between its past as a powerful global power and its current position as a small though significant state within the European Union. The choice between identifying itself with a specific transcontinental idea of civilization based on its relations with its former overseas empire and its recent incorporation as an expression of a common European civilization and history has only slowly begun to be reconciled. Portugal's hesitation between these two identities came to a head between 1933 and 1968 during the dictatorship of António de Oliveira Salazar (1889–1970), when in its later years it continued to strongly assert imperial prerogatives over its African colonies at a time when other European powers were relinquishing their colonial territories. "Europe was the last continent where we had not landed," wrote Agostinho da Silva.[22] The reluctance to sacrifice one identity for another was echoed again between 1988 and 2002 through the exhibitions sponsored by the National Commission for the Commemoration of the Portuguese Discoveries, which sometimes reproduced colonially inflected ideological fragments to legitimate and attenuate new discourses that re-situated national identity within an incipient Europeanization.[23] This indeterminacy between two histories and two identities also impacts religious contradictions, since the older popular religiosity is widely regarded as part of a common European heritage derived from Celtic and Roman periods while Portugal's imperial expansion, which began in the fifteenth century, was encouraged by more cosmopolitan urban elite cultures. The differences between these rural and urban cultures constitute a third conundrum that has heavily marked Portugal's history. These three core conundrums—the conflict between popular and institutional religion and the rural and urban cultures they represent, and the contradictions between a European or a transcultural and transnational identity—have held powerful sway over the aesthetic imagination and intellectual foci of the many diverse descriptive practices and visualizations that reoccur throughout this album.

Finally, Portugal's historical success in overseas trade and its uncompromising messianic Christianity redirected it, just two centuries after it had won independence from Arab control in 1143, away from its European neighbours towards the trading partners that its increasing number of sea routes had opened. Consistent with this interpretation, the country remained outwardly focused for nearly half a millennium within an evolving culture of exploration, uncertainty and expectation that had long mixed fantasy and reality with art and science. The maps, armoury spheres and navigational instruments, which opened the possibility of exploration, were fabricated not by scientists but by astrologers and artists. Portugal's drive to commercial success was combined with its spiritual search for the centre of the world and the mythical kingdom presided over by a great imagined Catholic monarch, Prester John. The peculiar ways of perceiving the world that originated from these experiences are well attested to by the Portuguese writer José Saramago, who advises:

> The traveler [to Portugal] wishes he could have twenty senses, but would still not find them enough, so contents himself with the five he was born with to hear what he sees, see what he hears, to smell what he feels with his fingertips, and taste on his tongue the salt which at this very moment he can hear and see on the waves sweeping in from afar.[24]

If Portugal's most heroized literary figure, Luís de Camões, is the chronicler of this more expansive view derived from the sea, Saramago is the narrator of the land that demands similar extraordinary senses. Fernando Dacosta agrees with the need for a revision of our sensory registers: "We have always been a people of the sound and the echo—for whom hearing predominates over seeing."[25]

It was only with the fall of the Salazar dictatorship in 1974, which brought the country's long-drawn-out colonial wars to an end, and incorporation into the European Economic Community in 1986 that Portugal began to draw itself back into the continent of which it had always been geographically a part. By then it had become so ruined by poverty that returning migrants, who sought refuge from its wars in Africa, recounted to me in the 1990s their shock and disbelief at the conditions they encountered on their return.

Between 1986 and 2010 Portugal again prospered with a new geopolitical repositioning that united its destiny with that of the European Community. The country underwent profound infrastructural and political changes along with a sustained historical and ethnographic revisionism that sought to change its official collective historical narrative. Nevertheless, Portugal's nostalgia for the sea retains strong political interest. In a recent publication, *Portugal e o mar* (2011), Tiago Pitta e Cunha, a senior diplomat and government advisor, writes that many Portuguese associate the sea with history; they disregard its present or future economic development and connect it with *saudade*, the romantic longing and nostalgia for the past. "We have substituted the idea that we inhabit the land where the sea begins for the idea of the land where Europe ends."[26] He notes such an attitude limits the country's economic and political options, obscures the sea's importance as "the avenue to the world," and ignores the ocean's resource value that the country could exploit in concert with other European nations. Portugal, with one eye to the sea and the other on Europe, deep in manufactured nostalgia and bittersweet memories and divided between a burgeoning subaltern class that includes a diminishing number of rural inhabitants, an industrial working class, a growing deprived and unemployed population and a small privileged elite, is unique among European nations. These irreconcilable conditions, which effect the absence of coordinated planning policies and which have weakened its political will, have also led to the increasing ruin and destruction of Portugal's architectural patrimony, as hauntingly portrayed in works such as the photographs of Gastão Britoe Silva.[27] The Lusitanian imagination is multifaceted and riddled with paradox and contradiction, as are the politics, art and exhibitions that will be discussed later. Portugal's landscapes and histories create their own aesthetics, which, like ghosts, haunt its emerging future.

Stories

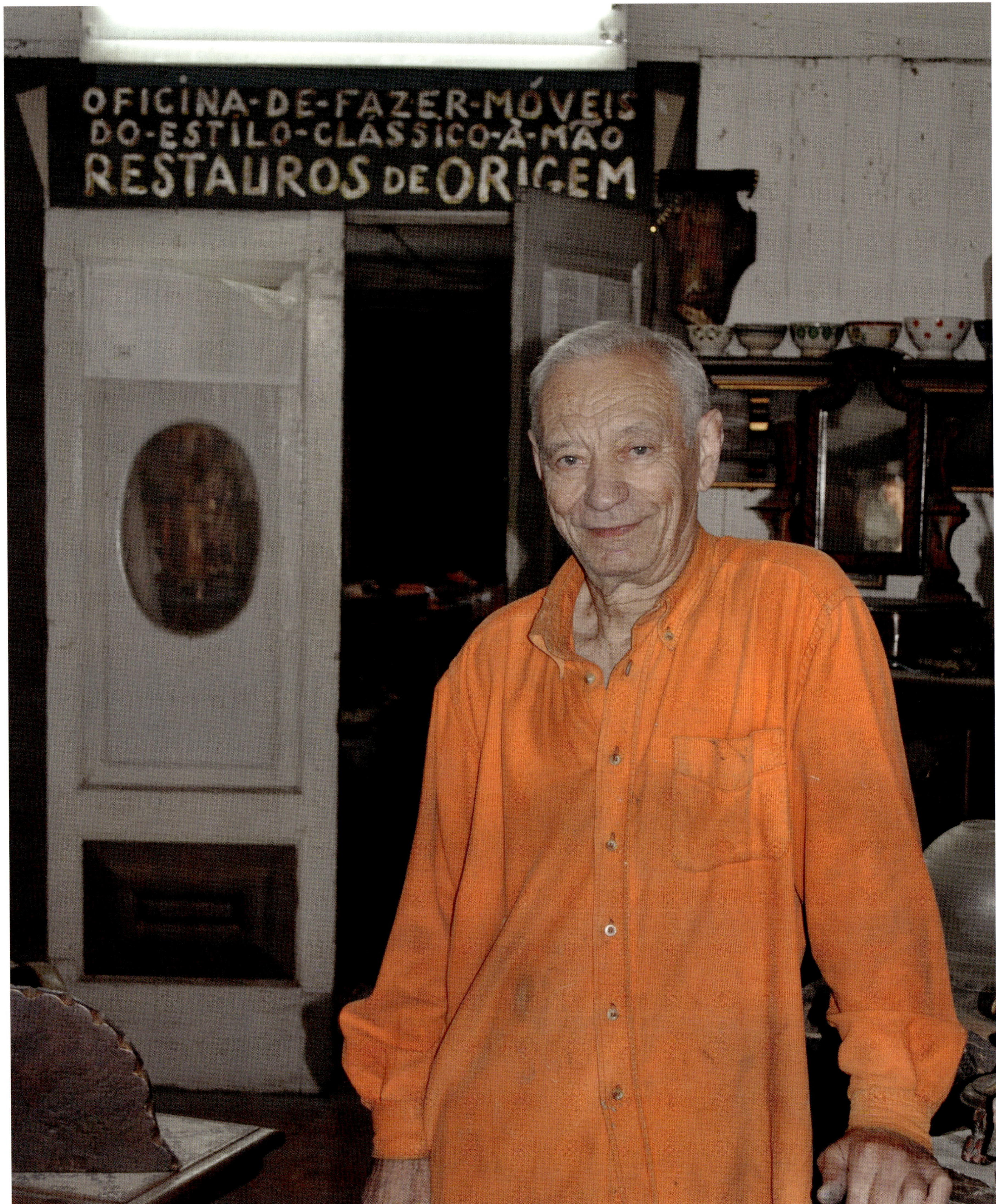
OFICINA-DE-FAZER-MÓVEIS
DO-ESTILO-CLÁSSICO-À-MÃO
RESTAUROS DE ORIGEM

1 The Kingdom of the Marvellous

God wills it, man dreams it,
[the work] is born.

Fernando Pessoa, "O Infante"[28]

IN A COUNTRY full of shrines and miracles, heavy with its otherworldly preoccupations and divine, and nowadays usually less than divine, machinations, and once described by the writer Miguel Torga as the Kingdom of the Marvellous,[29] there is a special place of dreams, a seldom-disturbed refuge, that has escaped all transformation by the external market for cultural goods and experiences. Hemmed in between the great baroque church of Santa Cruz and the small oratory chapel of Our Lady of the Tower, chiselled from one of the remaining gates of the medieval city of Braga, the Rua do Anjo winds its way up a gentle hill. Once busy with cabinetmakers and antiquarians, most of its shops are now closed, and except for a few establishments selling cheap factory-made furniture and a nondescript bar, the only clatter comes from the busy traffic that imperils children and other passersby alike. On a bend of this short, narrow street of three-storied buildings stands, at number 23a, the premises of David Silva Gomes, an extraordinary cabinetmaker and an unsurpassed bricoleur of all sorts of material contraptions.

Gomes's shop is surrounded by grand buildings that express and recollect acts of gratitude and miraculous occurrences drenched in fantastic stories. At the end of the street stands the impressive facade of the seventeenth-century Church of Santa Cruz and the grand hospital of São Marcos, founded in 1508 and topped by a balustrade supporting twelve giant figures of the apostles. The small oratory of Nossa Senhora da Torre, near the top of this short thoroughfare, was constructed between 1756 and 1759 to thank the Virgin for protecting the city from the Great Earthquake of 1755. Next to it the seminary church contains four magnificent side chapels with superb polychromatic sculptures of heroic size of the four evangelists. One chapel contains a relief sculpture of the Tree of Jesse, named after the father of King David, which traces the bloodline of Christ through its luxuriant stone foliage. São Jorge, so Saramago[30] tells us, regularly haunted Braga's streets until his horse tripped on its modern tramlines. It was here in Braga that the 1926 military coup that eventually brought the dictator Salazar to power was planned.

The first time I stumbled upon Gomes's shop, in April or May 2009, it appeared suddenly and unexpectedly like an apparition. Walking past its closed narrow green metal door, I obliquely glimpsed through its small square window a dark

facing
David Gomes in front of the doors leading to his workshop at 23a Rua do Anjo, 2011.

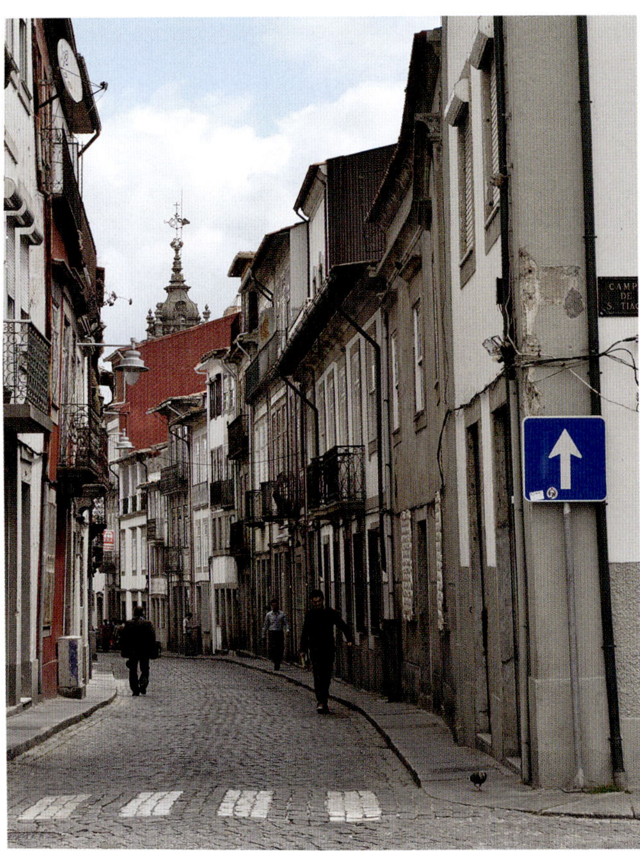

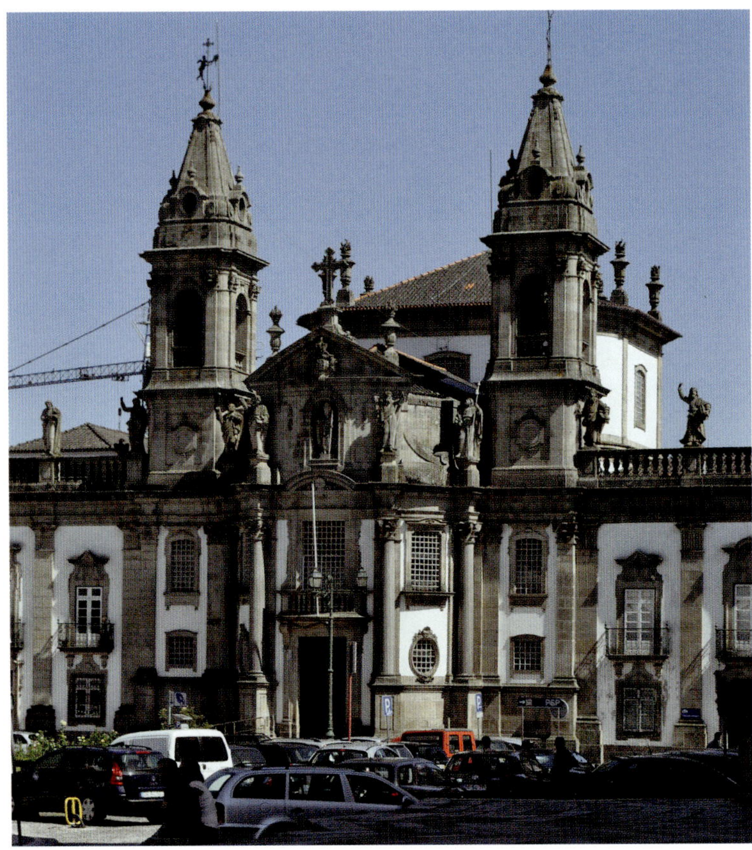

unlit interior, where I saw the ghostly outlines of objects obscured behind three fabulously painted and decorated baroque crosses that stood tightly huddled together, filling the little window. The glass was dirty and smudged and the objects behind it were cluttered and cobwebbed, as if they had remained undisturbed for centuries. Not quite believing in apparitions, I continued to walk down the hill, trying to contain my excitement until, five or six buildings later, I was unable to stop myself from turning around and retracing my steps back to number 23a.

I peered again into the dark window and, exhilarated by its contents, gently pushed the door open and entered. I wandered around that timeless dark interior as if in a dream. The shop was full of wondrous and improbable objects that lay jumbled in a sea of shadows. It was, it seemed, deserted, but I dallied for longer than I usually would in reeling euphoria and amazement. I called, perhaps too softly, yet nobody appeared, and after some taciturn minutes I left the shop to continue my exploration of the city. Less than a few minutes passed before I was magnetically drawn back to those gloomy magical premises again, determined this time to find or wait for the return of the shop's owner. At the back of the shop were two splintered doors with windows that looked into a large workshop even darker than the rest of the premises. I hesitatingly opened the door and quickly apologized for my intrusion, and out stepped David Gomes.

The man immediately began addressing me, leaving me in no doubt that he had already seen me repeatedly enter his premises and was curious as to what I was searching for. Without respite in his conversation, he said he thought I had come to steal his artifacts and creations, and if such was my intent I should not hesitate to carry them all away. He asked rhetorically why I hadn't already done so, insisting that nothing was of any use to him anymore, since nobody bought the things he made. So began my first meeting with David Gomes. He was born on 8 September 1936 in São Martinho do Dume, the son of José Vieira Gomes (1906–95) and Luísa da Silva Taveira (1910–84). He attended school in Dume and still lives in the village close to the church, and for most of their working lives he and his father occupied the same workshop on the Rua do Anjo.

With its dusty benedictions and cluttered stands and tables, 23a Rua do Anjo brimmed with enchantment. On the floor, on tables, on chairs and in cabinets stood clusters and piles of tools, books, decorative objects and boxes. Near the shop door a wrought-iron clothes iron that had long outlived its original function was placed with such precision and purpose that it appeared as an object of pure form. The place reminded me of the overpowering evocation of broken antiquity exhaled in Portugal by such places as Beja's Rainha Dona Leonor Museum, which occupies the beautiful former convent of Nossa Senhora da Conceição, or Aveiro's Santa Joana Museum in the fifteenth-century ex-convent of Jesus, both of which take their few visitors into a forgotten and much-faded world.

On the rung of a ladder sat three different-sized brass blowtorches of the kind my father had used when I was a boy. Here they clamoured to be enigmas, appraised as menacing, as their wide cut-out nozzles from which flame once roared clearly demonstrated. I recalled the noise of the pumping action necessary to build up pressure inside the vessel, and the wind-like roar of the flame came back to me, as mysterious now as it had been when I was a child. Hung from a wall to the right of the entrance was a small wooden plaque on which a neat row of forks was arranged over large letters that spelled "Portugal." Under them, small painted letters read "Forks for eating, 14th century." Slightly to its side was a giant pair of scissors and between and around it stood other objects, some surmounted by startlingly luminous saintly figures. On the walls hung mirrors, paintings and three dusty baseball caps painted green and decorated with pasted-on cut-outs of churches and clocks that seemingly warned that this might be a place out of time—suspended in a long, drawn-out pause that had been intoned for more than half a century.

Inexplicably scattered between the piles, paintings, mirrors, frames, decorative lamps, shelves and wall hangings were half a dozen small plaques carved with the insignia and names of North American soccer and hockey teams. Inexplicable, that was, until one of my later visits with my family and my colleague Eduardo Tomé, when Gomes confessed to being a staunch soccer supporter who, when not in his shop, liked to watch the game on television at home. He had a brother who, long ago, had emigrated to Montreal but who had once worked with him in their father's workshop at the back of the shop. His brother still visited Braga regularly, and I got the impression that these plaques inspired by a distant world expressed something of the loss he may have felt for his absent sibling.

On another visit I noticed a number of tall, spindly, brightly painted lamps that stood lengthwise on top of dusty furniture and piles of books and papers. They had elaborately carved and fanciful circular columns divided by blocks, with deep striations encircled by open petals or leaves reminiscent of the stems of exotic plants. These lamps were embellished with a combination of faded red, green and yellow oleaginous paints; some were speckled or had areas of gold, making them look like tropical palms that had surrendered their original function to Gomes's exuberant designs. At that moment it became clear to me that not only did David Gomes invent or reassemble pieces using everyday material culture and paint to generate new presences or phenomena, but his intention was to transform the space around his creations. His practices shifted not only the pieces he made but the space they inhabited,

facing, left
The winding Rua do Anjo leading to David Gomes's shop in Braga.

facing, right
The baroque church and hospital of São Marcos built in the sixteenth and eighteenth centuries on the corner of Rua do Anjo, Braga.

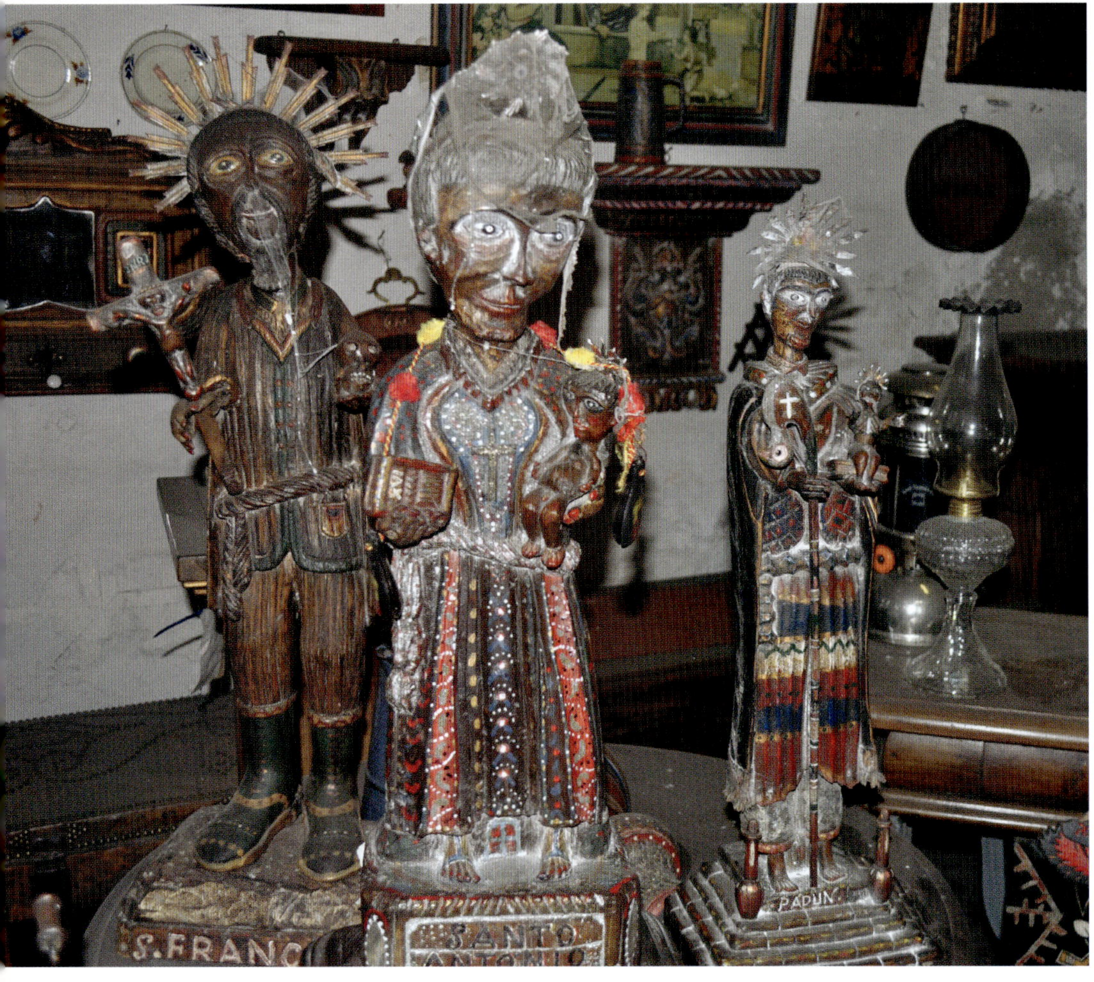

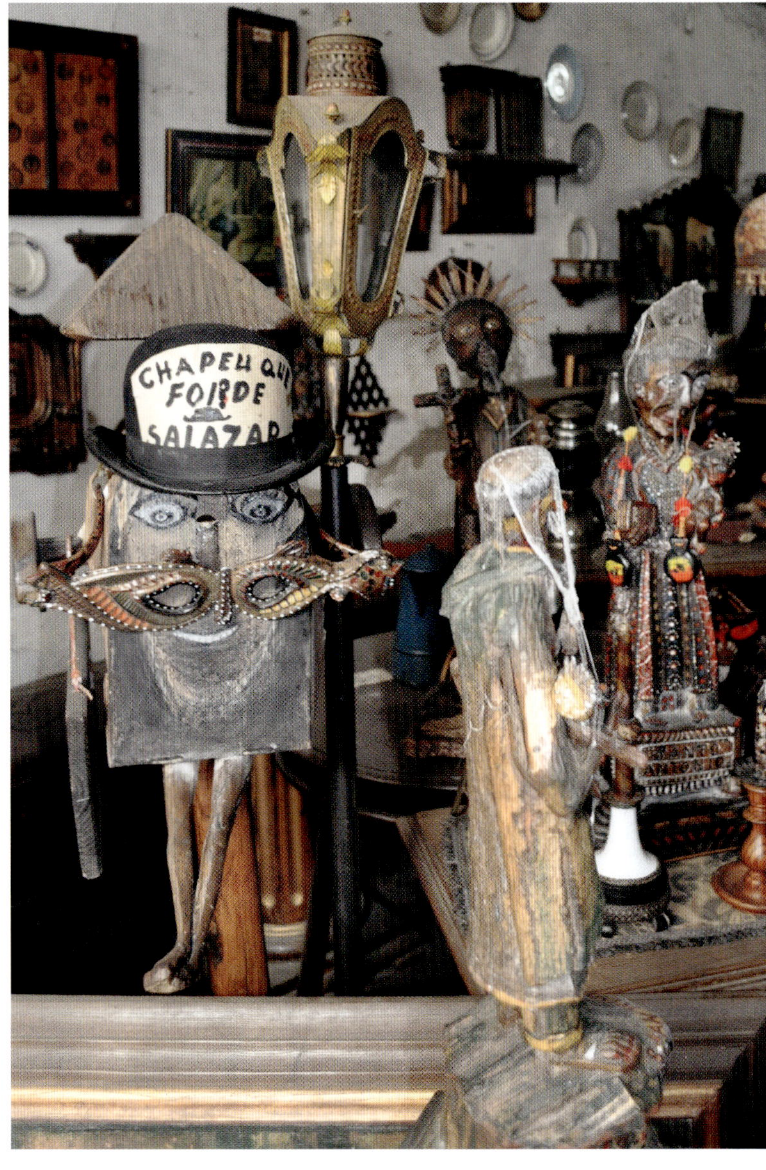

above left
Interior view of David Gomes's former shop located at 23a Rua do Anjo, Braga, showing his sculptures of São Francisco, c. 2005; Santo António, c. 2000; and Santo António de Padua, c. 2003; photo taken 2011.

above right
David Gomes's *Salazar's Hat* surmounting a mask of the dictator, c. 2003, surrounded by saints and other modified artifacts inside Gomes's former shop.

facing, left
Interior view of David Gomes's former shop, 2011.

facing, right
Interior view of David Gomes's former shop. Two of the three massive crucifixes acquired by MOA can be seen in the window at the back of the picture.

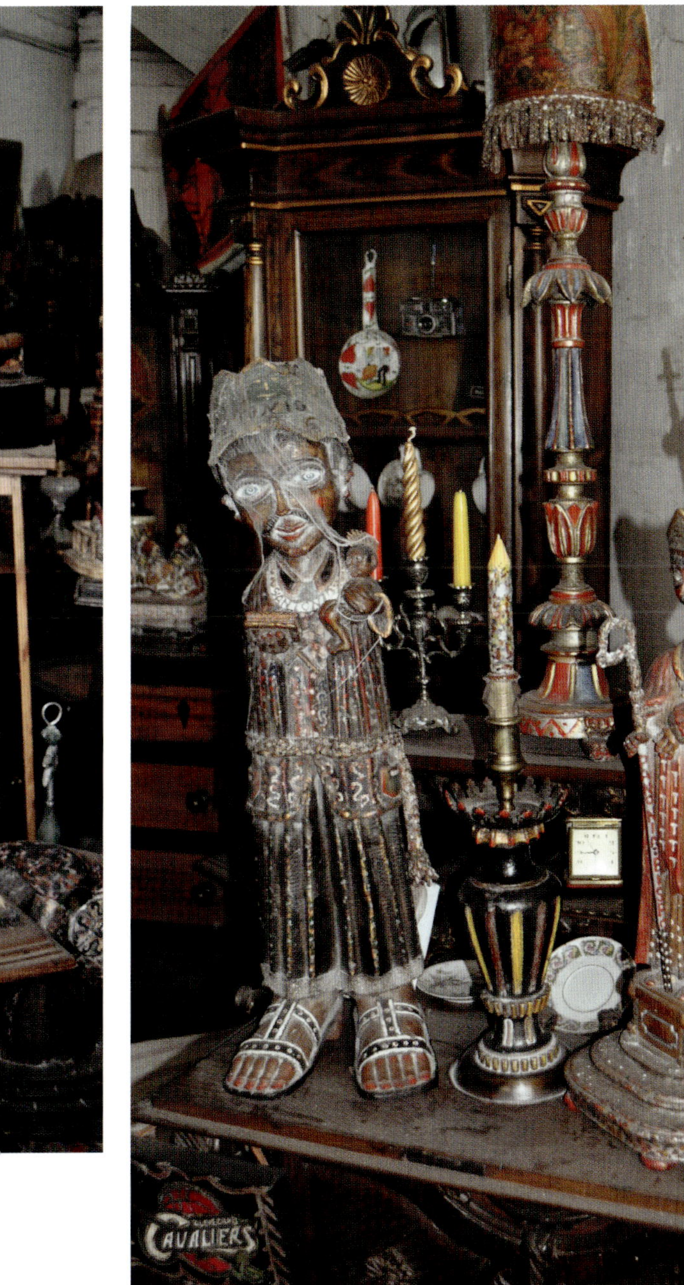
ALMANAQUE
SANTO ANTÓNIO
CAVALIERS

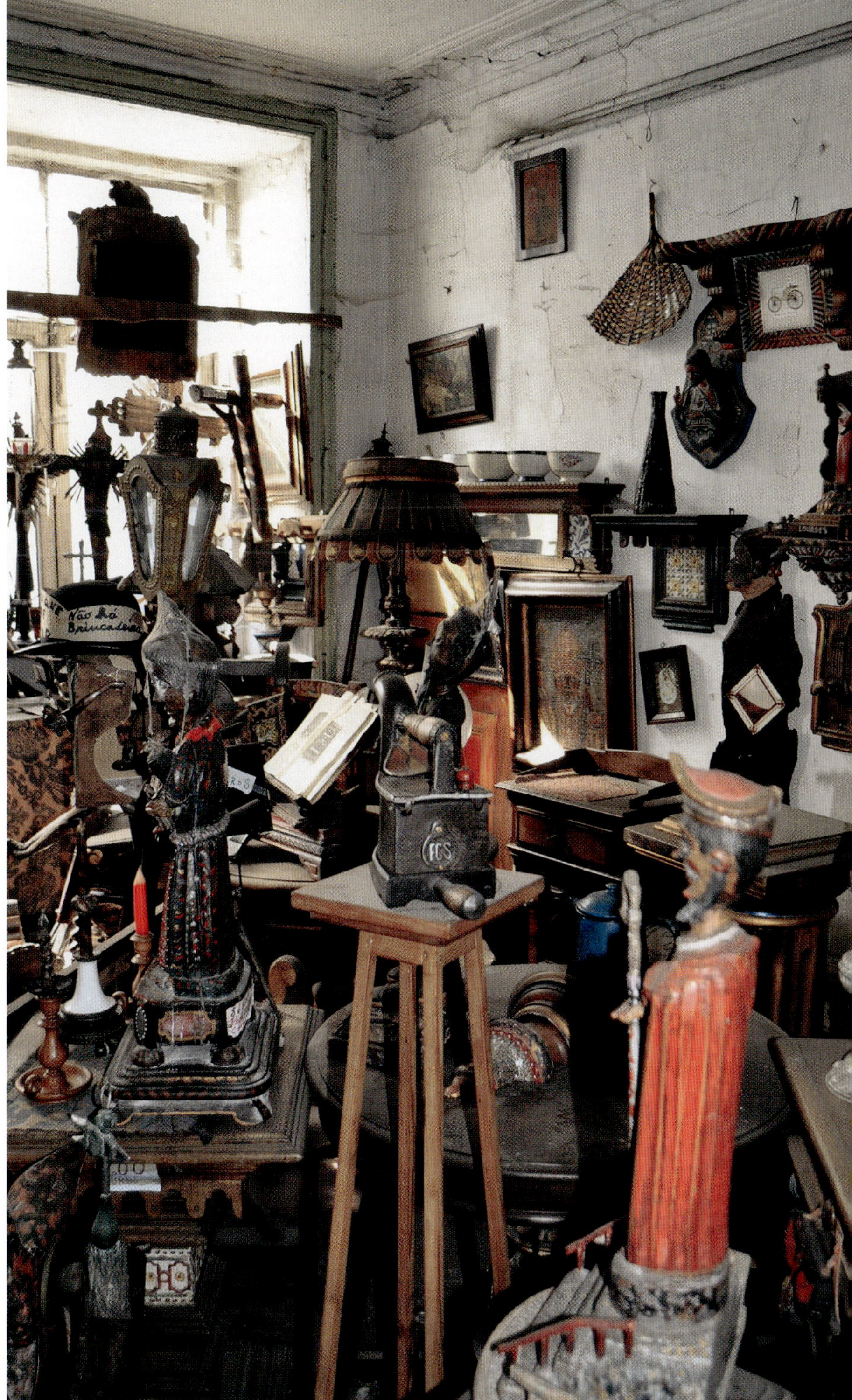

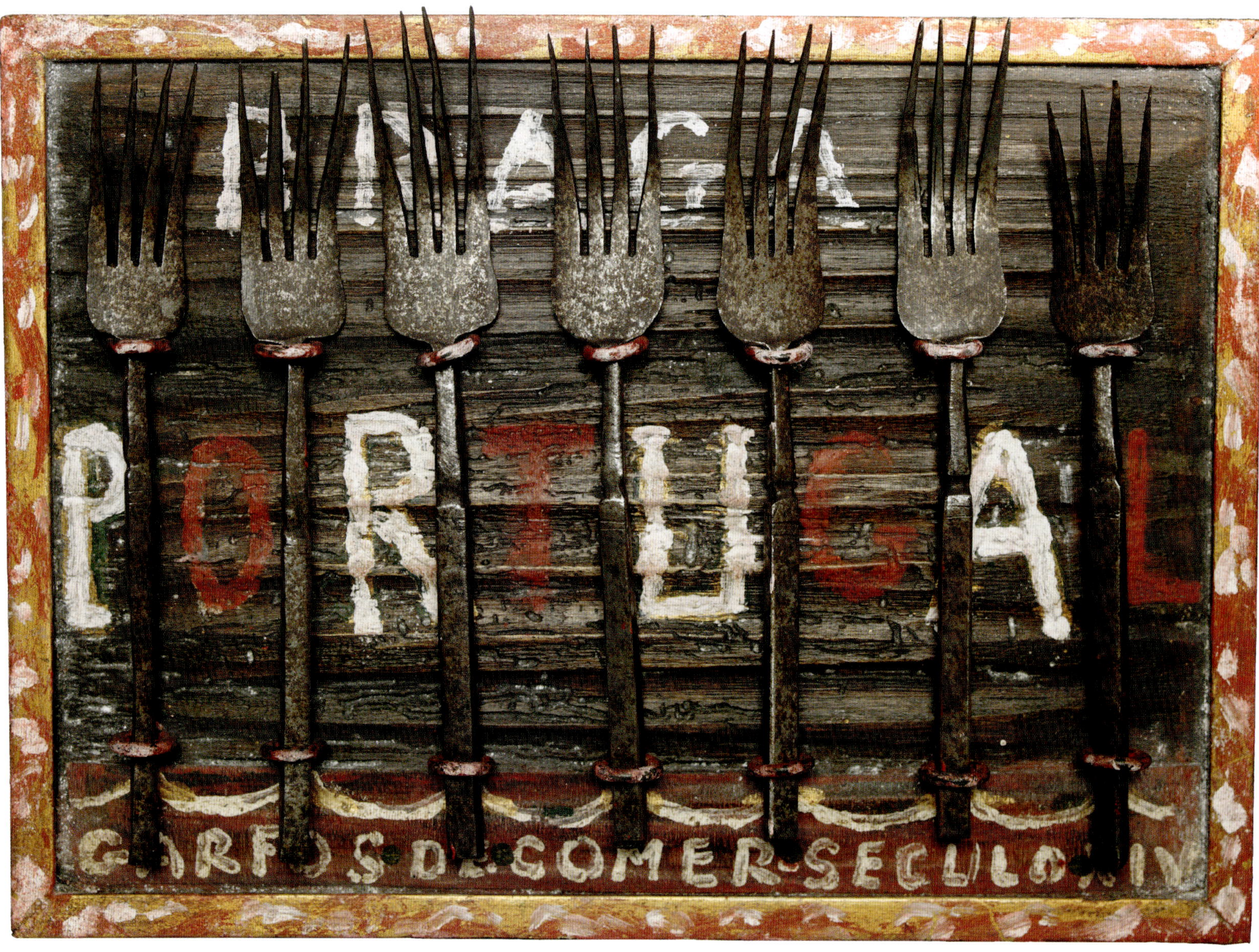

above
DAVID GOMES
Portugal, c. 2009
Private Collection

facing
DAVID GOMES
Rotating display cabinet for Escudos (Portugal's former coinage), n.d.
Private Collection

from prosaic chronological time into a metaphysical suspension where they are left to await the return of an age that will probably never be more than imminent. His pieces are neither copies nor commissions but made from his memories and imaginings of things he has seen or read. His mind mediates experience, he says, to produce something new and unique that can never be duplicated. Only when things he makes conform to the idea he sees in his mind is he satisfied, and only at this point, when the idea is perfected materially, does he feel able to part with a piece.

What could be more banal than the plastic insignia of a hockey or soccer team? Yet once carefully and patiently carved in wood, painted and reduced from an often large format to a twenty-by-fifteen-centimetre plaque, it readily commands attention as a work of intellect; human hands frame the game in a new light. His plaques return a human presence, for they bear the imprint of his carefully modulated actions, an interpretive subjectivity and will that restore the relationship between the work and its producer and owner and endow it with a deeper, honest significance. David Gomes's soccer plaques remind me of fetishes, another peculiarly Portuguese idea; he may hope that when stroked and activated, the plaques will spur the teams they consecrate on to success. It would have been wonderful to see the large plaque Gomes described that he made with his own team's insignia emblazoned on it and that hangs in his home.

On some of my visits in 2010 and 2011 I was struck by two shrines assembled from wood, string, ceramic and paper. The smaller of the shrines, around thirty-eight centimetres high, at first appeared unusual but unremarkable. The piece is composed of a stepped, semicircular base surrounded by a string barrier. From the base rises a wooden tablet, bevelled on both sides and slightly bent down the centre like the spine of an open, upright book. Stuck onto the tablet is a copy of an Indian miniature painting of four turbaned horsemen being welcomed outside the walls of a castle. Gomes has varnished the work to help return it to the age of the original, but a closer look reveals that he has also painted over the horsemen's eyes, making them blind. The device is painted in the same controlled palette he uses in all his work, giving it a texture and colour that appear older than its real age and make it resonate with the past.

However, none of the techniques, styles or presentations of Gomes's work are intended to deceive but to express the ambiguity he feels about the indeterminate nature of time, value and the world. In his conversations with Eduardo Tomé he has spoken of his absolute commitment to truth and perfection. He makes only pieces that are imbued with a truth that conforms accurately to the model in his mind. Talking to Tomé about his different renditions of the face of Christ, he insists on the absolute inability to depict the face as it was and locates the truth of the work in its conformity to the image of it in his mind, which changes with each piece: "I always make one piece after another piece after another piece and they are totally different. Who takes a piece of mine from here, takes a [unique] piece. There will never be another piece like it."[31]

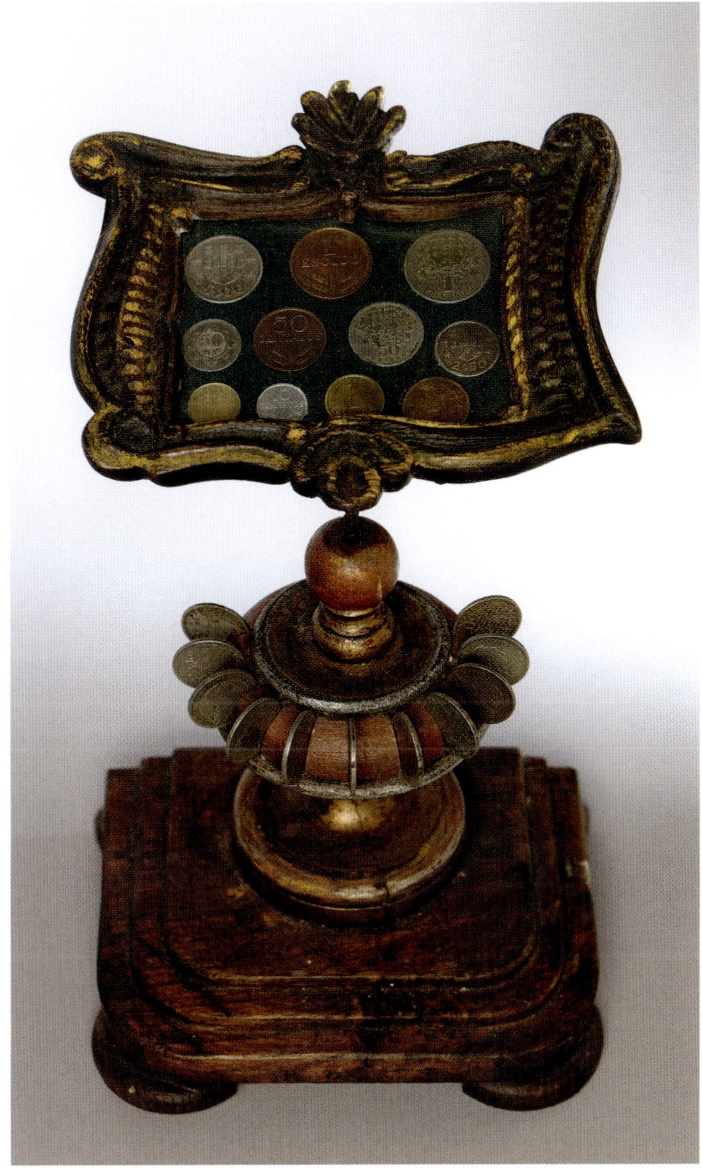

A different shrine was made from a large, conventional glass-fronted, dark-varnished cabinet of the type constructed in Portugal to contain the image of a household saint. Gomes had installed two small shelves, one on either side, at slightly different heights on which he had placed two identical "oriental" pitchers. Both were decorated with Chinese court scenes and with handles representing tigers but had been repainted in dark brown and deep green, typical Portuguese colours. This intervention makes explicit the orientalist imagination behind the shrine's constituent parts and ultimately recasts and re-exoticizes it as an abhorrent, impure image that nevertheless reminds us that Portugal is not just a sliver of land adjoining

facing, left
DAVID GOMES
Christ on the Cross, C. 2005
Private Collection

facing, right
DAVID GOMES
Christ on the Cross, C. 2002

the Atlantic Ocean and Mediterranean Sea but was once the centre of a spiritual and cultural universe that encompassed parts of China, Japan and India.

These two shrines surreptitiously convey strong Asian and Middle Eastern influences, and every time I stopped to look closely at the blinded knights of his Indian miniature, I could not help wonder whether Gomes wants us to recall Portugal's traumatic defeat at the Battle of Alcácer Quibir (1578), which resulted in the loss of the country's messianic king, Dom Sebastião, along with most of its nobility. The piece evokes for me Portugal's immense and infinite longing for redemption and rebirth. If history treated the country sometimes harshly, Gomes's work strongly intimates that even history can be suspended and substituted by a metaphysical *longue durée* in which the nation can rejoin its religious reverie to Dom Sebastião's ageless promise. The larger enclosed shrine elicits this memory of greater Portugal, a lost empire whose greatest chronicler, Luís de Camões, died and was buried in Macau, far from the land of his birth and where the great twentieth-century orientalist and passionate collector Camilo Pessanha (1867–1926) also rests. Along with the influential twentieth-century poet Fernando Pessoa, these writers combined in a literary union with the dreaming king that sometimes seems to embrace David Gomes himself in a bittersweet longing or *saudade* that runs deep through the nation's history. Therefore, it was not entirely surprising when, on my visit in July 2011, Gomes brought out of a glass-fronted cabinet of books an old miniature edition of Camões's *Os Lusíadas* (The Lusiads). The small book was beautifully bound in brown leather over which Gomes had painted his own design.

Not only does Gomes return his creations to distant times, but he also composes sets of objects that he assembles in extravagant miniature cabinets, shrines, frames and armatures. Portuguese coins that were replaced by the euro in 2002 are displayed under a tilted glass cover attached to a rotatable spindle supported by an elaborately stepped wooden stand; in other assemblages, forks are carefully suspended and aligned on a wooden plaque and a set of postal stamps are mounted in a winged baroque gilt frame. These works disclose Gomes's interest in sets, orders and sequences. His religious figures and two big wooden airplanes can be interpreted as sets themselves, which he intersperses with other curiosities. But unlike a museum curator, David Gomes insists that all his pieces have the same value; he loves each one and would miss and long for them all equally if any were removed. This museological preoccupation and propensity has turned the site of his trade into a house of images that testify to the unique interplay between his own values and inspirations and the material expressions they give birth to. In this antique world, values and meanings are turned upside down and the shop becomes a store of enchanted and invaluable objects, displayed within a dusty and cobwebbed interior as functionless testaments to the truth and authenticity of Gomes as the sovereign inventor of his own world. But he does not retreat into his refuge—he consistently and mischievously plays with the permutations between this world created by his free imagination and the world of commodity values and hypocritical superficiality that lies outside his green doors. A large sign painted in red letters in his shop reads "The best work and the highest prices," as if to answer two of his customers' most frequently asked questions.

The double doors at the back of the shop open into the old family workshop. Gomes's workshop is more spacious and orderly than his shop. Dominating the space in the centre are three intricately made and decorated single beds with

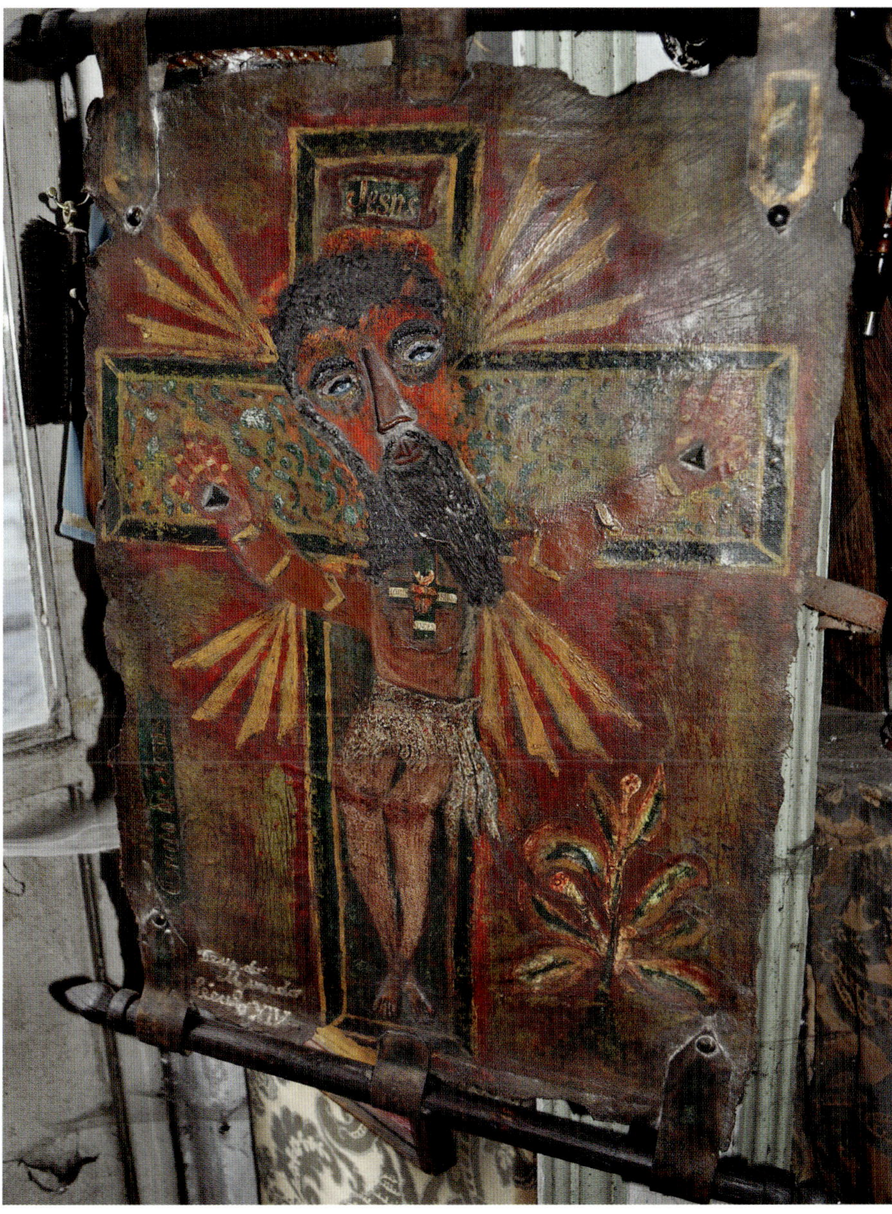

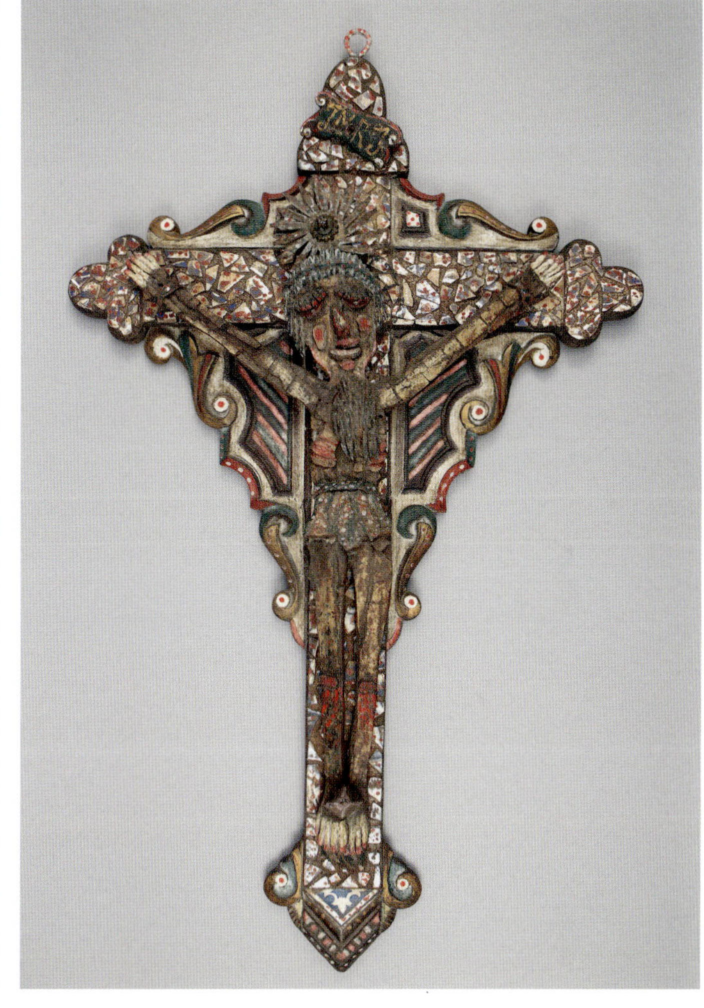

Manueline-style neo-Gothic spindles. Workbenches and tables run along the left side of the room, some cluttered with papers and long rolls of drawings and blueprints inherited from his father that stand upright, damp and decaying, in drawers and boxes.

When Nicky Levell and I have asked David Gomes why he makes or illustrates the subjects he does, he denies conscious reason: "because I did"; "it was what came to my mind"; "for no reason"; "who knows!" But his creativity, as he has confirmed in conversation with Eduardo Tomé, stems from an immense and rare freedom. Gomes watched the decline of cabinetmaking with sad resignation. He is proud that his father was the first cabinetmaker on Rua do Anjo and that his family worked continuously in the premises for well over sixty years. He shows us a ledger each time we visit him neatly detailing commissions and sales of furniture going back over a century and including works for council chambers, libraries, courts, police stations, local government, prestigious families and high-ranking individuals, like the former civic governors of Porto and Viana do Castelo. He recalls fondly how his father, José Vieira Gomes, took him when he was seven or eight during summer vacations to visit museums in Póvoa de Varzim to see and study old furniture; he guards the original scale drawings

facing
DAVID GOMES
Christ on the Cross, C. 2001

and plans they drew to make the fine, intricate furniture for which they were renowned. When at the age of nineteen he was enrolled for national service for eighteen months, he was stationed in his home city. He saw no exotic lands and took part in no military action, but continued to exercise his trade as a carpenter for the army. Later with his wife, Maria do Sameiro da Silva Barbosa, he took excursions to visit the palaces of Sintra, Vila Viçosa, Évora, Brejoéira (Monçao) and Valença, each time paying attention to the historic furniture displayed there.

Gomes's apprenticeship taught him among other things to make intricate, spindled headboards and the techniques for making joints inside cabinet drawers, which many times he showed us. He bemoaned how these techniques have been forgotten and constantly insisted on the superiority of the patiently trained hand over mechanized production methods. Modern furniture he dismisses as junk. "Cabinetmakers don't exist now, only the men that work in factories. In the time it takes me to make a drawer, a factory can easily make a hundred. But it can never make ones like I could make."[32] He laments that people no longer either have the money—or the "lifestyles" or connoisseurship—to appreciate or buy his kind of furniture, but he is also aware that his own crisis is bound up with that of the whole of the Rua do Anjo, a crisis that has reduced the number of businesses to less than half and left the survivors with hardly any customers. David Gomes is uncompromising—he has been called a perfectionist in newspaper reports—and staunchly refuses to abandon his standards and skills and make "rubbish" for those unable to recognize quality.

Placed open on a book support in the shop is his father's copy of *Mobiliário Artístico Português* (Portuguese Artistic Furniture; 1935) by Alfredo Guimarães, which once guided his family's business. On my fourth visit, in July 2011, he told me that many people had wanted to buy this book but he was ready to donate it to the UBC Museum of Anthropology (MOA) to complement the collection of his work we were buying from him. Regretfully I declined, believing it was too important in supporting and preserving his memories—before I realized how everything in the shop was so intimately connected and part of the identity he had constructed for himself. This book documents and illustrates Manueline furniture design, a style unique to Portugal during the peak of its power in the sixteenth century that inspired so much of the work Gomes loved to make or repair for his clients. Business had already begun to decline in the 1960s, and his customers became fewer each year. He joked that he received just one thousand escudos (about ten euros) a year in sales, and in local newspaper articles in 2007, 2008 and 2009 that criticized the demise of the Rua do Anjo, he repeated his complaints about the terminal decline of his trade. "People have changed. Now they don't have time. They enter their homes and only give it a [quick] clean to get rid of dust. It's very difficult to clean this type of furniture. There are few people that prefer this type of furniture. Most of my clients are now over sixty."[33]

THE CARNATION REVOLUTION

Forty years ago Gomes abandoned cabinetmaking in favour of inventing his own free forms of expression, including the pieces that we have collected for MOA since 2010. He is absolutely clear about the date he began to make his inventions—the day of the Carnation Revolution, 25 April 1974. The revolution played a major role in his thought and the development of his art, opening up his creativity in ways he had never imagined. "The revolution brought liberty to the country and personal freedom to me to do whatever I wanted,"

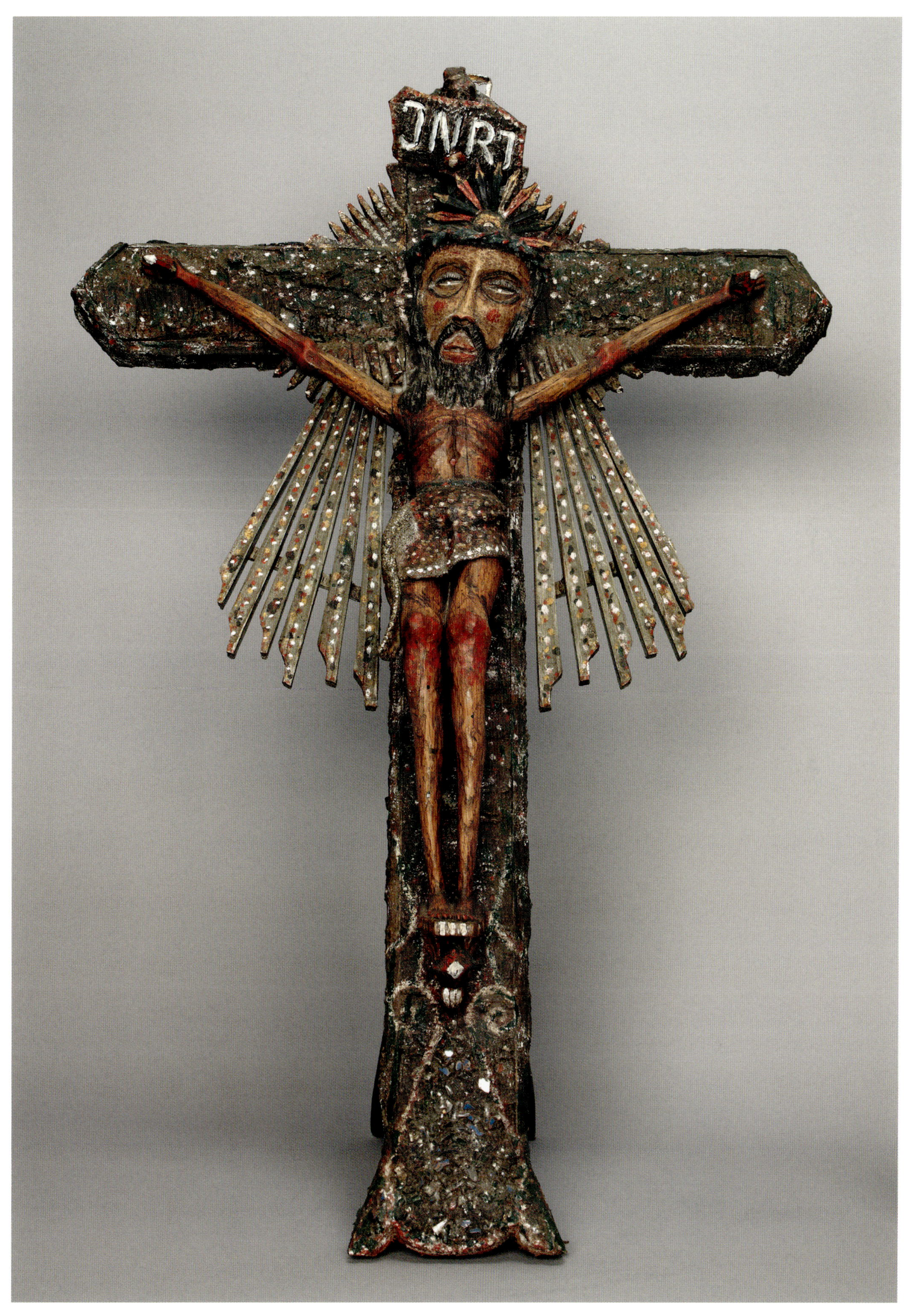

he explained in 2012. "Whatever comes to mind, I do, but I do it truthfully and on my terms." Since there were few people who would buy his objects or understood their value, Gomes decided he would make whatever it was he wanted for himself. "I never pay any attention to clients," he declared. "At times I am here at the door and I leave them over there. I am not here anymore to make money; I'm here because I like to be, I like to make whatever I like, I'm a free man."[34]

The myth-soaked history of Braga suffuses Gomes's shop, making it hard sometimes to separate fact from fiction. A work's age, provenance and price might be constantly adjusted as it is modified and as additional time is spent on its perfection. The journalistic accounts of his shop repeatedly confuse the age of his objects and the variable prices he ascribes to them. Gomes holds strong convictions on two particular pieces: *Salazar's Hat* and a child's bicycle.

Salazar's Hat seems to exercise endless curiosity among the shop's few visitors and the journalists who have interviewed Gomes. Once, when asked its price, Gomes jokingly set its value at one thousand escudos for each year the dictator had ruled the country;[35] a newspaper article published in 2009 was titled "*Salazar's Hat* (still) on sale." At other times Gomes claims he simply wants to be free of the burden of all the objects that surround him, but his severe words hide a deep and abiding bond between himself and the things he has created and his desire to keep the corpus of his work intact. "I like to look at these pieces... more than to have a bag of money";[36] his pieces are always with him, money disappears, he told Eduardo Tomé. Money and his works will always be incommensurable, perhaps because he considers the works to be so much part of himself. Money could never buy the time, revelation or conviction that go into perfecting his works. Perhaps paradoxically, he has insisted that he has never wanted a successor: "For what? To endure the same fate as myself?" he once retorted.[37]

Resting at the entrance to the shop is the second object Gomes reveres, a child's bicycle that once belonged to Alves Barbosa, a former Portuguese cycling champion; Gomes claims a friend rescued it after it had been discarded many years earlier.

Gomes repeats the provenances of these two objects and describes the circumstances in which they came into his possession on many of our visits and has even produced photographs of Salazar wearing a similar hat to the one Gomes guards in his shop. Gomes recounts how each time Salazar visited Braga, he would stay at the home of Dona Maria da Cunha Matos, a powerful matriarch who owned two estates in the area. Gomes's father often repaired furniture for Dona Maria, and it was on one occasion after they had transported a cupboard that stood in Salazar's customary bedroom to the workshop that inside he found the hat.

In 2010 the dust of the shop began to be disturbed when, after negotiating a sale with Gomes, I purchased the three large crosses that had stood in his window. Their place was taken by a handwritten note saying "the three great crucifixes have been bought by a museum for an exhibition in Canada." In July 2011 we agreed to buy several more of his pieces, including Salazar's famed hat.

Salazar's Hat somehow crossed a mysterious boundary once MOA had agreed to buy it. Originally the importance of the piece was in the story and the provenance of it, but little by little Gomes began making the hat into a larger humorous composition, which he insisted he never intended as being critical of the ex-dictator. When I first saw the piece in 2009, it was nothing more than a hat with a brim surrounded by a yellowing paper band that proclaimed its once nefarious owner. In June 2011 it had started to gain a surreal quality after Gomes had perched it on top of a cardboard mask on which was balanced a pair of painted wooden glasses. From the mask's chin he had attached a pair of diminutive outstretched legs. By July the cardboard mask had been replaced by one Gomes had made from wood and the legs had been moved so they stood upright, supporting the mask and hat.

David Gomes told us in June 2011 that the museum project had changed his life, and despite the taunts of his friends who came to sit and talk with him some afternoons, he had decided to keep his shop open. He reminded his friends of the exhibition in Canada and our promise to continue to return and work on the project.[38] Despite the work he did transforming *Salazar's Hat*, he had hinted in a 2008 newspaper article that his work might soon be coming to an end. "My life and my work," he reported, then seventy-two years of age, "is that of a craftsman. The truth is, when our hands no longer know how to make the work, that is where the problem is. The enjoyment I had was exactly doing this. It pains me not to continue doing more, but... I am not able."[39]

Gomes accepts the decline of his trade, and it would have been unthinkable to imagine he would ever vulgarly promote either himself or his considerable craftsmanship. Confident in their ability, it was by reputation that customers once commissioned him and his father to make furniture for them. David Gomes no longer wants to sell the things he makes and insists he has no use for money. At the same time it seems he cannot free himself from his premises at 23a Rua do Anjo, which anchor him to a sixty-year history of being a master craftsman and the world he created for himself. Neither is he oblivious to the modern world; although he disdains its mediocrity, tastelessness and cheap materialism, he enjoys sport on television and radio, particularly matches with his home team, Sporting Clube de Braga, and drives a car. I remember in October 2011, how at the end of the day he took off his bright orange work shirt, his trousers and shoes and changed into a set of clean, well-ironed clothes that would render him invisible in any crowd of men his own age. He left the Rua do Anjo for his house in São Martinho do Dume, where he was born and where he lived with his wife, who had previously worked for Banco Nacional Ultramarino and with whom he had had two daughters, Maria Luisa and Rosa.

David Gomes has been swept into the twenty-first century, dragging the shop and the selfhood it preserves with all its visually clanking contents with him. More than an extraordinary cabinetmaker, he is also a fine sculptor; the three Christs I first bought from him may rank among his finest figurative works. He seldom diverges from his well-tested palette of colours, and, like all the popular artists we will encounter in this album, he has his own distinctive style, in this case characterized by the painterly use of spotting and his renditions of hands and feet, which are usually disproportionate to the figure's body.

He had encrypted into his shop and his creations six decades of experience, during which he developed a powerful and efficacious hybrid style that substituted a historically constituted world for one based on archetypes: Christ and the saints, Salazar and the cyclist Alves Barbosa. David Gomes has nestled his thoughts and identity, with wit and humour, in his art and the spaces he has created around him.

IN 2012 I received an unexpected email from David Gomes's son-in-law telling me his wife's father had sold his shop but had kept a few things

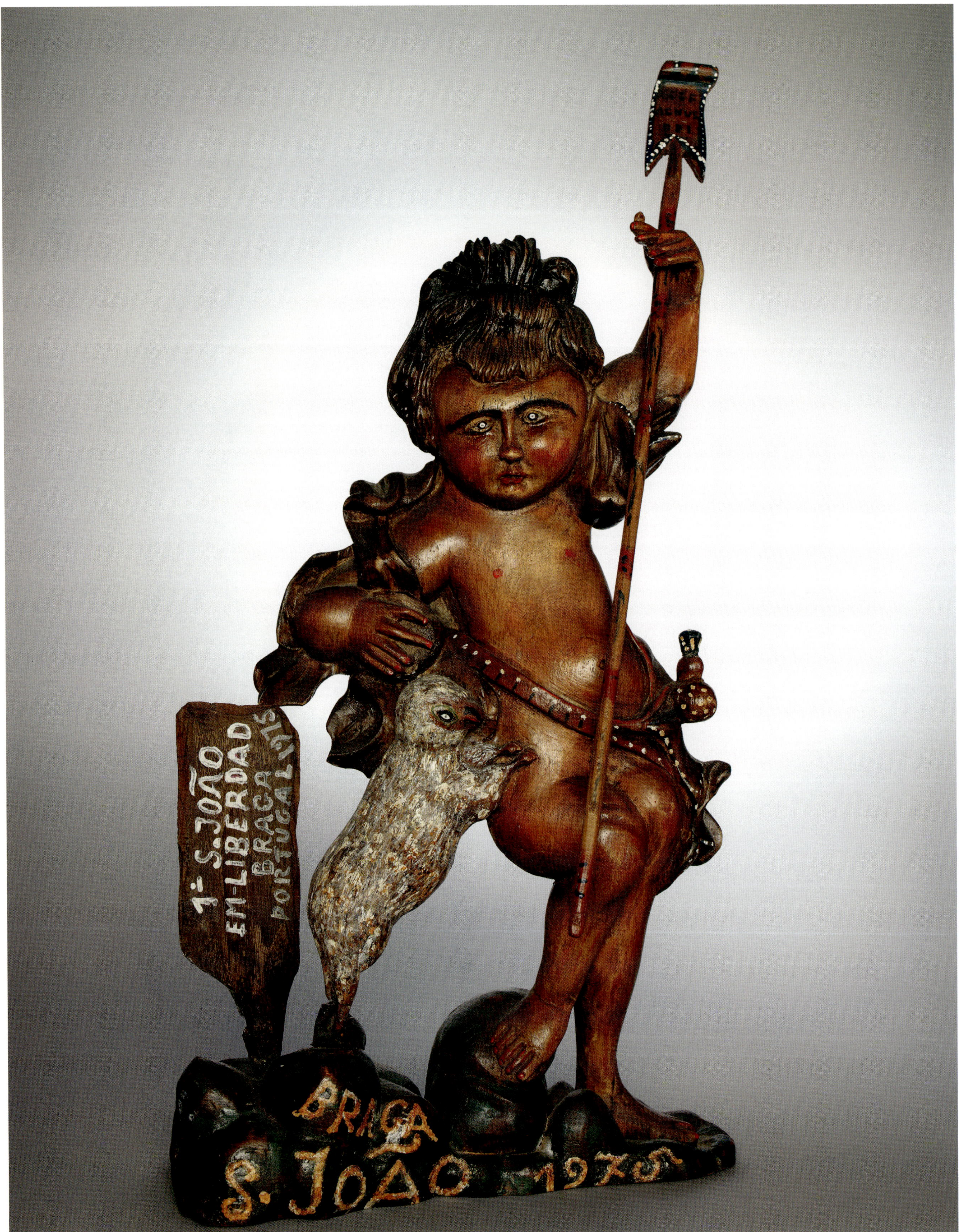

1º S. JOÃO
EM-LIBERDAD
BRAGA
PORTUGAL 1975
BRAGA
S. JOÃO 1975

facing
SCULPTOR UNKNOWN; PAINTING AND DECORATION BY DAVID GOMES
The First São João, 1975 (sculpture), c. 1997 (painting and decoration)
Private Collection

for me. When I returned to Portugal in August 2013 the shop stood empty, bereft of the ghosts and melancholia that had clung to it. The material expression of David Gomes's influences and his personal encounters with the saints and historical figures that helped shape Portugal had been finally renounced the year before, when the windows and doors of 23a Rua do Anjo were at last shuttered and locked. An antique dealer from Chaves in the north had bought everything in the shop, except for three pieces, and carried it away.

At the end of the summer, I visited Gomes and his wife, Maria do Sameiro da Silva Barbosa, again in Dume and saw for the first time *The First Liberated São João, Braga, Portugal* 1975. Until then I had had no idea of this piece's significance. Although this jovial, cheekily animated sculpture had been carved by a friend in 1975, it was then painted, lettered and modified by Gomes in 1997. This was one of his first works as an artist and proclaimed both Portugal's newfound liberty and the beginning of Gomes's extraordinary calling as a sculptor.

Many contradictions about David Gomes remain unresolved. In 2013 in Dume he told me that, although he was a Christian, he had no idea whether God existed or whether there was an afterlife. When I asked him this question, he replied by giving me copies of two books: *Ainda Devemos Batizar as Crianças?* (Should We Baptize Children?) by Domenico Grasso (1979) and *O Tema da Morte* (The Fear of Death) by Urbano Tavares Rodrigues (1958).

Every year on my return to Portugal in the summer, I telephone David Gomes. The line sometimes cuts out or crackles so we can barely hear each other and we frequently misunderstand each other's words, but somehow we still arrange to meet in Dume—the place where São Martinho in AD 572 held the Church council that ended the schism between Priscillianism and orthodox Christianity. Talking to David Gomes and looking at the work of other popular artists, I doubt whether São Martinho's purification of the faith was ever widely supported—or among others even known—and Gomes sculpted the only popular image of this saint, the patron of the village where he has lived all his life, that I have ever seen. The clutter of Gomes's shop was the clutter of history, which tirelessly and with infinite creativity and blind imagination assembles and reassembles and reinvents in different forms and idioms over and over again our understanding of ourselves within the world and our sense of the present and the past. His jumble of works representing past ages, regardless of their originality, edition or age, are fragments of Lusitania: the baroque concerto of the arts; the inspirations of freedom and independence; the imaginative worlds of saints and crucified demigods; the evocations of battles and the stories of fallen empires and a dictator. In his work he invents new idioms and object poems that preserve and transmit the hidden truths and heartfelt realities, which he protects from the present's galloping history. His shop was a veritable museum of Lusitania in which storage spaces, exhibition galleries and workshops intermingled—places where things were taken apart, reassembled, classified and reclassified and new things were invented by a man whom the philosopher and poet Teixeira de Pascoaes might have described as a truly Lusitanian soul.

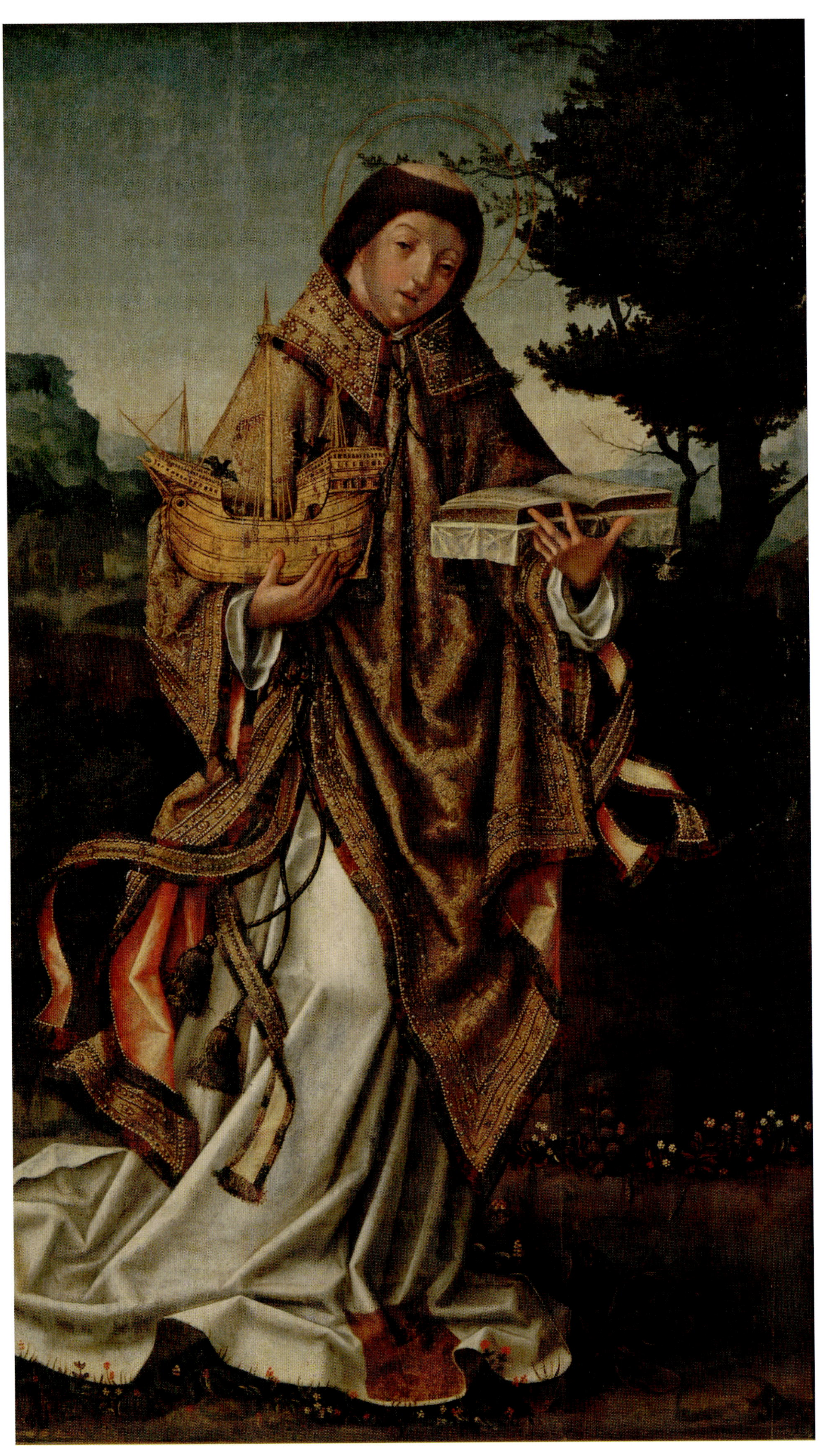

2 Imagining Portugal

Four Views of a European Romance

Nothing is in a straight line, not even time, which mixes centuries and cultures, races, creeds, rites.

Teolinda Gersão[40]

LIGHT AND SPECTRES: A LISBON OVERTURE

Gersão's description of the factually symmetrical but difficult-to-follow grid that organizes the street system on the undulating hillside of Lisbon's Bairro Alto provides an apt metaphor for Portuguese history and culture generally. Portugal has been conjured in European narratives, poetry, music, pictures and films as a republic of fables, a nation nestled in legends, dreams, marvels, even miracles, where the fantastic, no matter how improbable, has become metamorphosized into reality. No wonder, for Michel Déon,[41] that Portugal represents one of Europe's lost paradises. The Phoenicians named Lisbon Ubis Ubbo (gentle bay); the Romans, Olissipo, a name that some interpret as *aqua boa* (good water). The River Tagus and the play and shimmer of light and colour have provided the city's character and extraordinary attributes most remarked on by travellers since the late nineteenth century. It was along the Tagus that in the twelfth century two ravens miraculously guided the boat containing the mortal remains of the fourth-century martyr São Vicente after his resting place in Valencia was threatened with desecration—the same waterway on which Alain Tanner filmed the beautiful, strangely melancholic opening scenes of *In the White City* eight centuries later.[42]

According to legend it was Ulysses, the archetypal hero-adventurer, who founded Lisbon,[43] and it was there that the sea nymph Calypso fell in love with him. After Jupiter ordered that Calypso free her unhappy captive, who yearned to return to his native Ithaca, she transformed herself into a serpent whose coils, according to one version of the myth, formed the seven hills on which the city was built. Perhaps the story foretells the exotic and strangely melancholic character that infuses Lisbon, a character that has been eulogized by many of its most ardent lovers, biographers and fado musicians and that lies at the heart of the bittersweet nostalgia the Portuguese call *saudade*.

More sober archaeological chronologies date the foundation of the city as a Phoenician trading port to around 1200 BC. Travel writers of the last century repeatedly attributed similar romantic classical appellations to other parts of Portugal. Chronicles recall how Roman legions believed they had found the Hesperidean Gardens or the Elysian Fields and the waters of Lethe (the river of forgetfulness) on first encountering the northern Minho region, and references to Portugal's likeness to an imagined

facing
VICENTE GIL AND MANUEL VICENTE
São Vicente, C. 1516
Museu Nacional de Arte Antiga

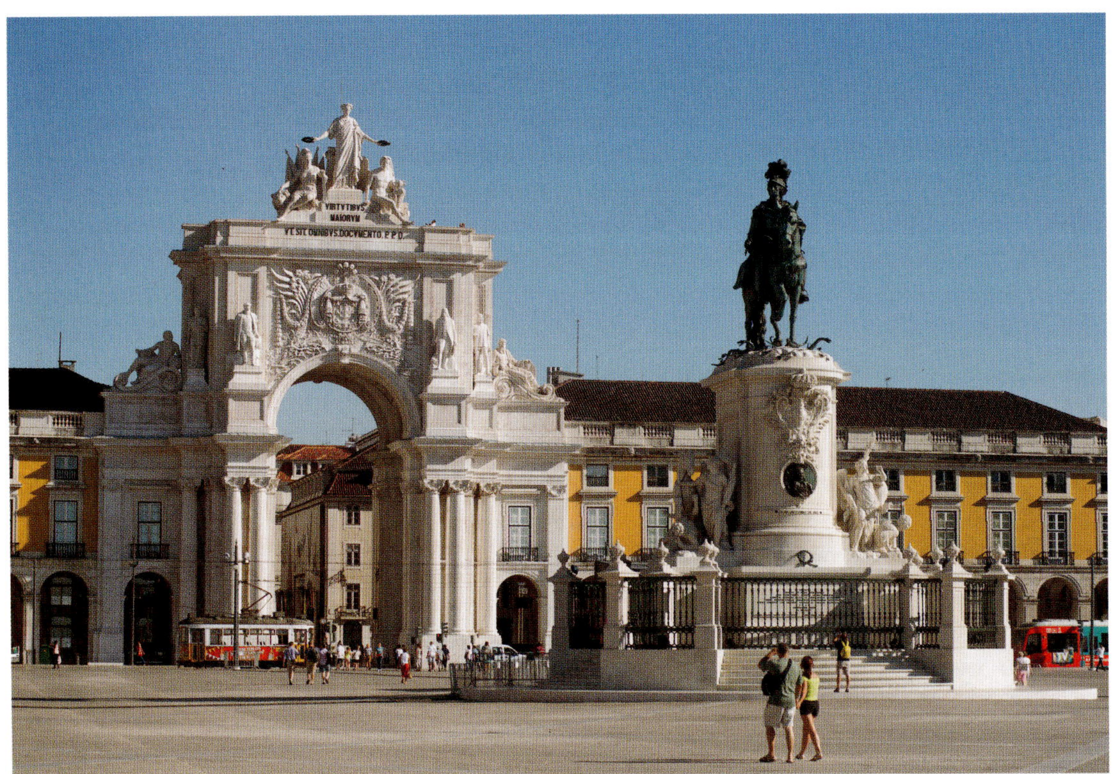

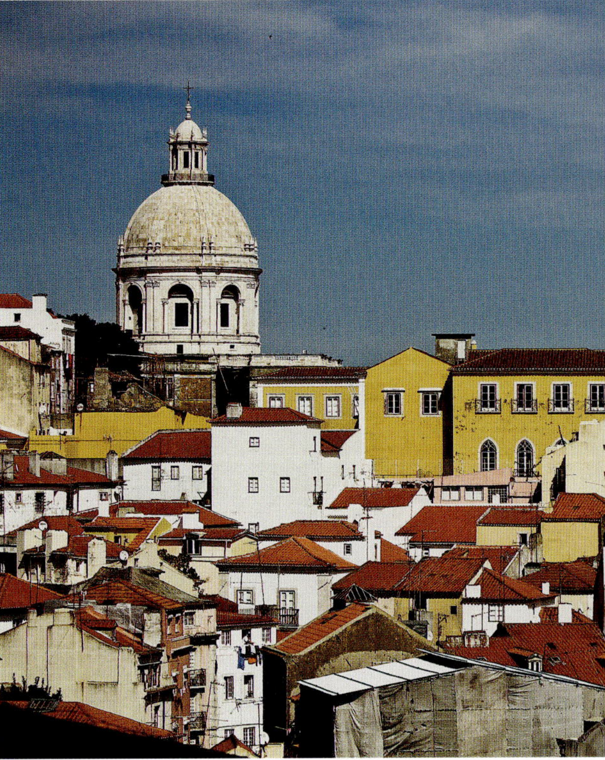

Arcadia are plentiful.[44] These designations have been often repeated by foreign mid-twentieth-century writers like Sacheverell Sitwell, who made frequent use of Arcadia to describe the landscapes of the mainland and invoked Hesperia in his descriptions of the island province of Madeira.[45]

Lisbon was not, however, always described in such romantic terms. Until the latter half of the nineteenth century it was the dirt and poverty that most visitors to the city remarked upon. In *The Journal of a Voyage to Lisbon* (1755), Henry Fielding, travelling the year before the Great Earthquake destroyed most of the city's buildings, described the place as "the nastiest city in the world,"[46] and Robert Southey, when asked for an account of the city in 1795, replied that "it is not pleasant to reiterate terms of abuse, and continually present to my mind objects of filth and deformity."[47] Byron, travelling in 1809 during a period of heightened political uncertainty, famously asserted Lisbon to contain "little but filthy streets and more filthy inhabitants," a statement that Rose Macaulay described as a "malevolent contemptuous sneer"[48] and that Dorothy Quillinan, Wordsworth's daughter, composed a diary of her own to refute.[49] Alfred Lord Tennyson visited the city in the summer of 1859 with his fellow poet F.T. Palgrave but left soon after, disappointed after being bothered by the heat and mosquitos.

However, if Lisbon provoked distaste from these Romantic visitors, the castles and rustic palaces of nearby Sintra, for Southey and Byron at least, attracted only their praise, though Tennyson and Palgrave remained disappointed by the lack of untouched solitude they had expected to find there. Little seemed to have changed in the condition of Lisbon's poor when, in the middle of the twentieth century, Simone de Beauvoir, in the third volume of her autobiography, *Force of Circumstance* (1963), highlighted again the hunger, poverty and ignorance that she thought the dictatorship, the Estado Novo (1933–74), seemed to have deliberately encouraged, while Saint-Exupéry emphasized the decadence of the European rich as they lost or gained fortunes at the Casino Estoril just outside the city. To be fair, however, Byron and Fielding had both acknowledged that the view of Lisbon from the Tagus was beautiful, and de Beauvoir had Henri, one of her characters in *The Mandarins* (1954), admit the same: "It was beautiful, that capital, with its quiet heart, its unruly hills, its houses with pastel-coloured icing, its huge white ships."[50]

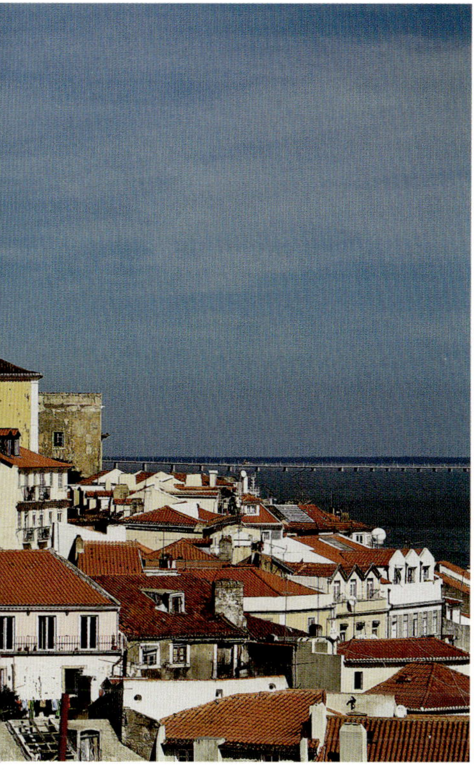

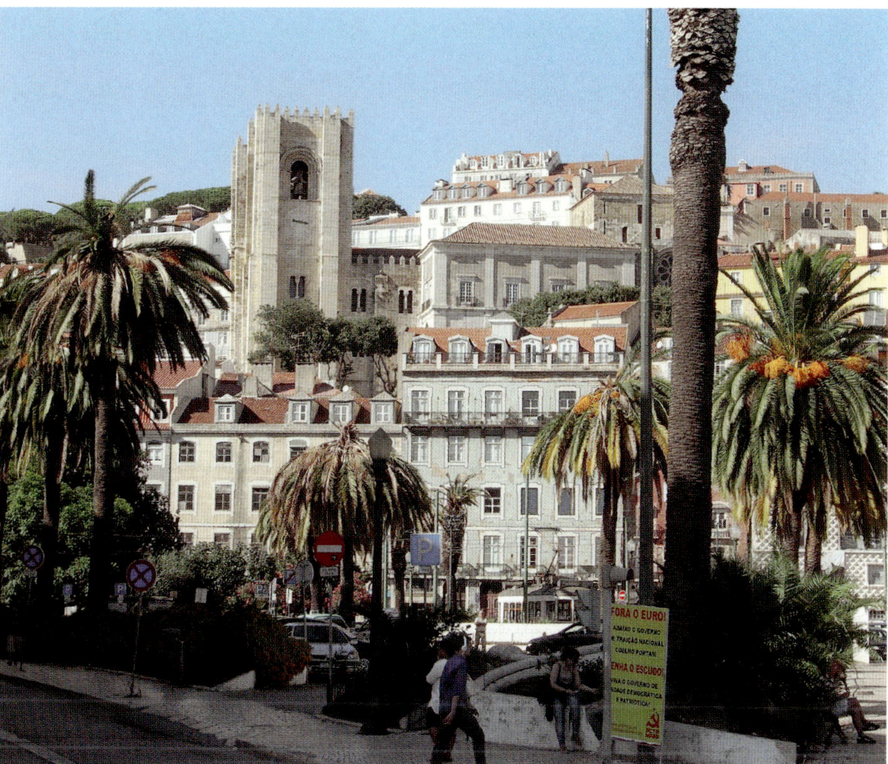

facing, left
The Praça do Comércio, built after the devastating 1755 earthquake and designed as the heart of Lisbon, looks out towards the River Tagus.

middle
The Alfama district, with the seventeenth-century church of Santa Engrácia overlooking the River Tagus and dominating one of Lisbon's seven hills.

above
The towers of Lisbon's twelfth-century cathedral from the Terreiro do Paço.

Positive views of the city and country gradually formed in the nineteenth century. Hans Christian Andersen (1805–75) visited Portugal in 1866 and praised the landscape, the capital and its inhabitants. The historian of religions Mircea Eliade was press secretary to the Romanian embassy in Lisbon from 1941 to 1945 and expressed his appreciation of the proportions and view of the Praça do Comércio in spring and the collections of the Museu Nacional de Arte Antiga, as well as the landscape around Buçaco and Luso and the monuments of Viseu.[51] The writers Stefan Zweig (1881–1942) and Ernst Jünger (1895–1998) both passed through the city, in the 1940s and 1960s on their journeys to Brazil and Angola, respectively. For Zweig, Lisbon was an "agreeable deception,"[52] its wide streets a contrast with its poorer quarters, though both displayed surprising colours; while for Jünger it was again the Praça do Comércio, one of the most beautiful plazas in the world, and the city's museums that caught his attention and enthusiasm. Zweig noted "the splendour in misery and the misery within splendour" that was such a contrast in the cities of the Mediterranean, only more accentuated in this city of the Atlantic.[53] South African poet Roy Campbell adopted Portugal as his home after fighting in the Spanish Civil War and the Second World War. His enthusiasm for the city led him to describe it as "vast and floral" and "the eighth wonder of the world."[54]

Ann Bridge and Susan Lowndes, in *The Selective Traveller in Portugal* (1949), continued this positive re-evaluation of Lisbon:

> Lisbon is a town with few buildings of real architectural note, though taken as a whole, it must be one of the most beautiful capital cities in the world. Built on a series of hills with deep valleys running down to the broad Tagus, the colour-washed houses attached like limpets to almost perpendicular cliffs, the unforgettable views from the many belvederes which have been opened up on every eminence, give perpetual delight to the visitor or the fortunate resident.[55]

Sacheverell Sitwell visited Portugal no fewer than five times before writing his 1954 work, simply entitled *Portugal and Madeira*, in which he described Lisbon as "the loveliest of all water towns."[56] What made the city unique for him was the quality of light: "What is rare and inimitable,

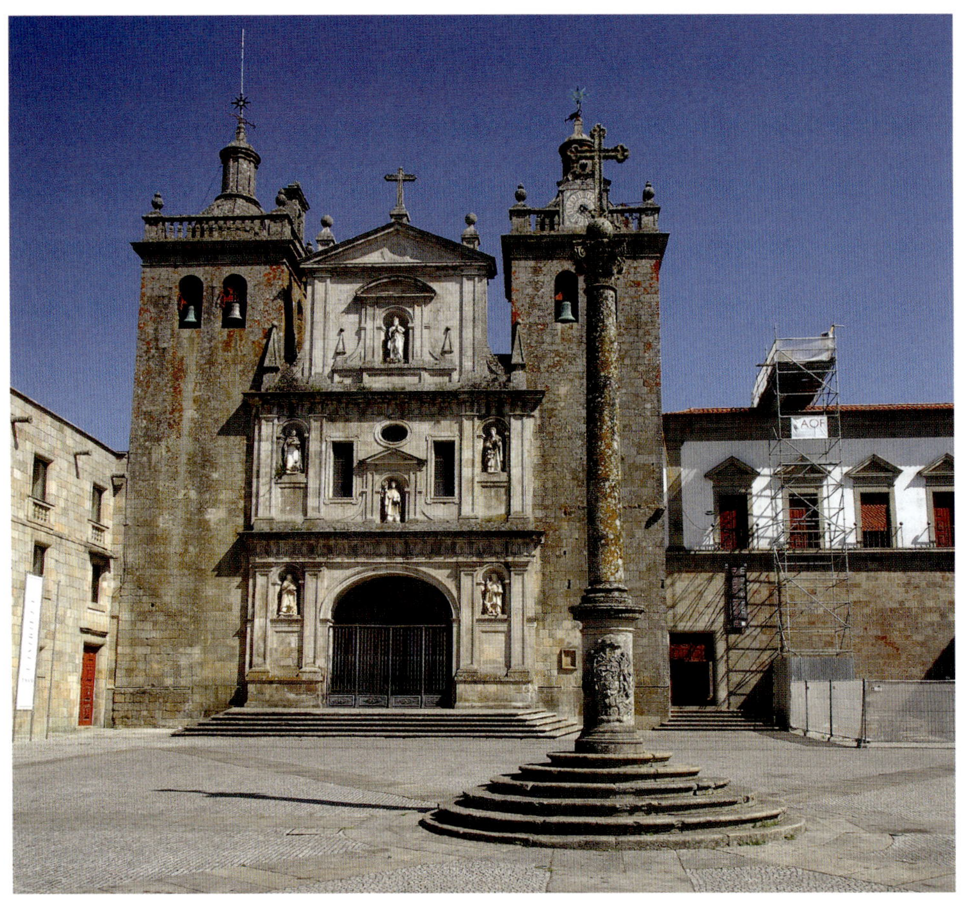

here, is the sunlight. You can walk down to the Tagus at the far end of the square [Praça do Comércio] and not be able to look at the far bank in detail because of the glare and quiver of the heat."[57] It was, however, the great Portuguese novelist, poet and essayist Fernando Pessoa (1888–1935) who more insistently drew attention to the effects of the quality of light on the perception of the city. In *The Book of Disquiet*, Pessoa wrote: "Nothing nature or the country can give me compares with the jagged majesty of the tranquil moonlit city as seen from Graça or São Pedro de Alcântara. There are no flowers for me like the variegated coloring of Lisbon on a sunny day."[58] And elsewhere, in his essay "What a Tourist Should See," Pessoa noted:

> For the traveller who comes in from the sea, Lisbon, even from afar, rises like a fair vision in a dream, clear-cut against a bright blue sky which the sun gladdens with its gold. And the domes, the monuments, the old castles jut up above the mass of houses, like far-off heralds of the delightful seat, of this blessed region.[59]

Portugal's José Saramago, in *The Year of the Death of Ricardo Reis*,[60] focused on the rain. After describing his initial glimpses of the outlines of Lisbon's buildings, recounted his protaganist's moment of self-doubt in the city's appearance, hesitating and asking whether it "is simply an illusion, a chimera, a mirage created by the shifting curtain of the waters that descend from the leaden sky."[61] What attracted Swiss writer Pascal Mercier in his acclaimed book *Night Train to Lisbon* was the play of the sky and moving clouds reflected on the water: "On the Tagus the clouds were reflected. They shared the sun-glittering surfaces, slid over them, swallowed the light and let it pierce through the shadow in another place."[62] Both visitors and inhabitants have remarked on the city's ephemeral character. Writing in the early 1930s, the British diplomat and folklorist Rodney Gallop recollected:

> One pale, clear winter's dawn, when a low mist lay over the misty water and there floated above it, earthbound no longer, the three hills of St George, Bairro Alto and Estrela, opalescent and ethereal as a mirage. Through the mist the dark sails of anchored barges could be dimly discerned, hung out to dry in the windless calm. Lisbon that morning had the dreamlike quality of a Turner.[63]

The Italian writer Antonio Tabucchi situated his novel *Requiem* (1991) in Lisbon, the city where,

facing
The twelfth-century Viseu Cathedral next to the later episcopal palace, now the Museu Grão Vasco, named after the Portuguese Primitivist master Vasco Fernandes (C. 1475–1542).

as in Saramago's work, his hero journeys "to dream and mingle with the living and the dead on equal terms."[64] When the streams of sunlight end at night, the city assumes a stillness "as if caught in a spell." The German writer Reinhold Schneider's (1903–58) meditations on the monuments and tombs of some of Portugal's most revered historical figures—Vasco da Gama, Luís de Camões and the doomed king Dom Sebastião—induced a feeling of melancholia that led him to confess, "I love the apocalyptic atmosphere of European history. It is for this deep reason that I love Lisbon."[65]

It is European film, however, that has been most effective in fixing the narrative focus on light. Alain Tanner's *In the White City* (1983) captures the attenuated contrast between the whiteness of the city bathed in bright sunshine with the dark interior spaces of its decaying buildings. In his documentary film *Táxi Lisboa* (1996), Wolf Gaudlitz repeatedly calls attention to the bright white roads and sidewalks made from small hammered pieces of stone *calçadas* that pave large parts of the city and gently reflect the sun. The quality of this shimmering light—what Pascal Mercier describes as "bewitching light"[66] whose luminosity consumes all past shadows and leaves only the option of uncertain futures—gives Lisbon a spectral existence. Tanner in *In the White City* and his subsequent film version of Tabucchi's *Requiem* (1999), Cees Nooteboom in *The Following Story* (1991), Wim Wenders in *Der Stand der Dinge* (1982) and *Lisbon Story* (1994), Mercier in *Night Train to Lisbon* and José Saramago in *The Year of the Death of Ricardo Reis* (1984)—all situate their protagonists, often including thinly veiled evocations of Fernando Pessoa, as captives of an enchanted dream with shifting time sequences that question the normal sensual foundations of reality and offer alternative ways of living in the world.

"Sometimes I dream that Lisbon doesn't exist and will only be a legend that one can recount, not to those who live here, but to those who come here visiting," writes João de Melo.[67] There is a hint that perhaps the city still lingers under Calypso's antique enchantment and its melancholia is a suffusion of her unrequited love for Ulysses, who has somehow become transubstantiated into the Tagus, leaving the city and river in an unbreakable clasp. Erich Maria Remarque, in *The Night in Lisbon*, comes closest to identifying the city and the Calypso myth: "By day Lisbon has a naïve theatrical quality that enchants and captivates, but by night it is a fairy-tale city, descending over lighted terraces to the sea, like a woman in festive garments going down to meet her dark lover."[68]

Spectral Lisbon exists. The city's double lies under the cobblestones of the Baixa, where the passageways and chambers of the forgotten settlement of Olissipo and later constructions—part of which were last thrust to the surface during the calamitous 1755 earthquake—were reburied by the Marquis of Pombal, who was entrusted with the city's rebuilding. These damp, cold, monumental doubles—dark underground sanctuaries, often of Roman or Arabic origin, that occupy huge unseen chasms, still buried under mud, sand and later constructions—are found in other Portuguese cities, too. They spread like rhizomes everywhere—under the Machado de Castro Museum and below the foundations of many of the older buildings of the University of Coimbra, or, as in Évora, subsisting among the tangled remains of later structures. Inconveniently everywhere, they pierce or jag out of the earth that tries to bury their memory.[69] Lisbon shares with Portugal a long-cast metaphysical and mythopoetic shadow that retains its near stillness: the complex Lusitanian metaphysic attempting to embrace

facing
Map of continental Portugal showing the place names referred to in this book.

and calmly preserve her myths from the virulence, conflict and rupture of twentieth-century modernity and insist on its freedom to inscribe and tell different stories than those propagated by the Internet and commodity fetishism of our time.

METROPOLITAN HISTORIES AND POPULAR MYTHS

Many of the historical and contemporary writers, poets and film directors who have shaped a Lisboan and, by default, Portuguese metaphysic were and remain urbanites. As the romance of Portugal was mainly constructed within urban cultures, so too were the myths and ideologies that masked national and governmental projects. The modern concept of the nation and the narratives that, since the fifteenth century, give it a historical genealogy and identity were repeatedly revised and perfected in urban centres like Lisbon and Coimbra. The culture of these cities established the shape of the society that emerged from them and that tainted all aspects of national life. These romantic and fanciful narratives also synthesized history and subjectivism, which helps explain why history was so slow to gain autonomy as an independent objective discourse in Portugal.

In the fifteenth and sixteenth centuries, Fernão Lopes de Castanheda, João de Barros, Damião de Góis, Diogo do Couto and Luís de Camões mixed literary genres, including poetry, verse and chronicles, producing a rich genealogical literature that mingled fact, allegory and fiction. In the nineteenth century Camilo Castelo Branco, Eça de Queirós and Almeida Garrett, novelists and playwright respectively, often based their short stories or plays on country legends and compiled collections of folk stories and popular literature. This blurring of genres was continued in the late nineteenth and early twentieth centuries by historian Alexandre Herculano (1810–77) and by various writers, including Fernando Pessoa in *Mensagem* (1934) and, more recently, Agustina Bessa Luís in *O Mosteiro* (The Monastery, 1995) and José Saramago in *Baltasar and Blimunda* (1987). The structures and themes of poetry and rural literature were considered by both folklorists and romantics to embody the national essence or soul, thereby creating a portal between history and ethnography in which history could focus on the survival of the past in the present and ethnography on the comparative study of the present and the past.

Portugal's early history was synthesized in the nineteenth century by Herculano and has been revised with similar encyclopedic compulsiveness and fervour periodically ever since. At the same time, the nation's cultural geography was surveyed and described by early folklorists and ethnographers, including José Leite de Vasconcellos, Adolfo Coelho, Teófilo Braga, Consiglieri Pedroso and Rocha Peixoto.[70] Some of the central themes that have structured Portuguese history over the past two centuries can be traced to Herculano's idealization of the grandeur and splendour of the Portuguese Middle Ages, including his description of the country's political decentralization, liberty, rural values, heroic spirit and unique system of municipal government, as well as the reasons for its eventual decline into decadence.

It was a remarkable achievement that, in the nineteenth century, a small country with a population of no more than 3 to 5 million was able to produce five, albeit short-lived, ethnographic journals: *Revista d' Etnografia e de Glottologia* (1880), *A Revista do Minho* (1885), *Revista Lusitana* (1887–89), *Portugália* (1888–89) and *A Tradição* (1899–1904). The voluminous work of their contributors—who collected and compiled ethnographic descriptions from literary sources, correspondence and fieldwork—stimulated the emergence of a collective consciousness of the nation's character. Portugal was envisaged as a vastly rural, picturesque and isolated land, with heterogeneous, deeply religious and practical, if impoverished, peoples.[71] History and ethnography came together to delineate more strongly than ever before a grandiose national past tempered by a decadent and impoverished present.[72] The details, textures and nuances within this picture were gradually added, beginning with the Geographical Society of Lisbon's 1880 "scientific excursion" to the Serra da Estrela in the north and the ethnographic fieldwork carried out by Jorge Dias (1907–73) at Vilarinho da Furna in the 1940s and in the following decade at Rio de Onor. Dias's crisp, precisely written texts, illustrated by clear, meticulous pencil drawings, are rightly acknowledged as masterpieces that mark the foundation of modern field-based Portuguese ethnography. By bringing together such national writers and literary scholars as Camões (1524–80), Gil Vicente (1465–c. 1536), Eça de Queirós (1845–1900) and Camilo Castelo Branco (1825–90) and artists including Columbano Bordalo Pinheiro (1857–1929), Amadeo de Souza-Cardoso (1887–1918) and António Soares dos Reis (1847–89), rural Romanticism and popular culture were born and imbibed with a new spiritual identity that quickly became synonymous with that of the nation as a whole.[73]

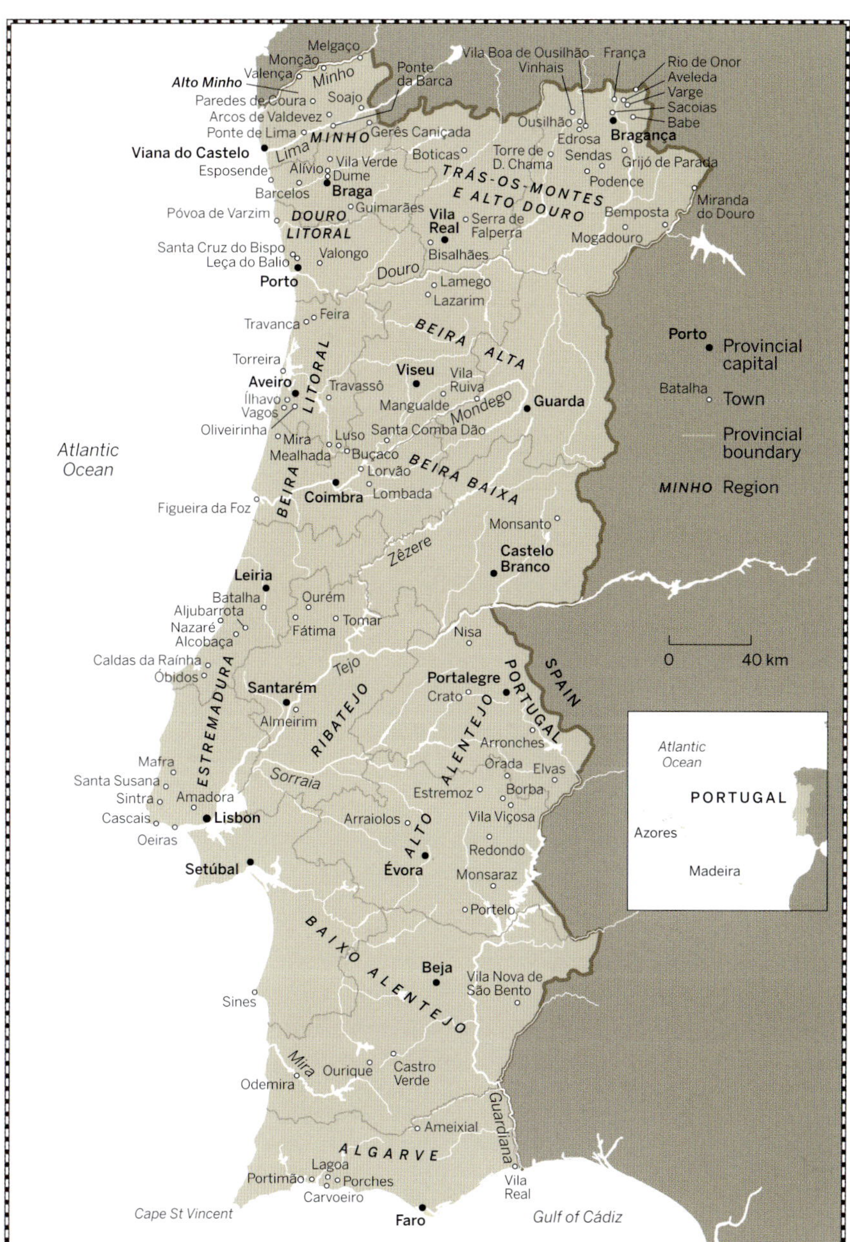

THE VACILLATIONS OF PORTUGUESE HISTORY

Portuguese history was before 1974 written and taught as a series of cycles marked by grandeur, heroism and tragedy. The archaic region of Lusitania, situated between the rivers Douro and Tagus, developed and prospered under successive waves of external conquest and subsequent independence. Although the Romans had conquered most of the southern and eastern part of the Iberian Peninsula by 216 BC, it was not until 139 BC that Lusitania and the western region finally fell. The new province of Hispania that gradually emerged from Roman rule brought four hundred years of prosperity until it fell prey to Germanic tribes that assailed the Roman Empire in the fifth century. Germanic domination, in turn, gave way to Muslim control, which, by AD 711, had absorbed most of the Peninsula into a province of the Caliphate of Damascus. From 756 until 1139 the Peninsula formed the independent, multicultural Muslim kingdom of Al Andalus. Christianity,

facing
World map (Peters projection) showing the extent of Portugal's far-flung imperial holdings at different periods of its history.

Judaism and Islam coexisted peacefully during most of this long period, though the Church was isolated from the rest of Christendom and its followers were more open to heresy in their interpretation and practice of their beliefs.

The reconquest of Lusitania, begun by Afonso Henriques, Portugal's first king (reign 1139–85), with the help of seafaring crusaders, eventually fixed and consolidated a new national frontier in 1297 that divided Portugal from the rest of the Peninsula some two hundred years before the consolidation of Castile. The boundaries today, it is usually emphasized, remain much as they did more than seven centuries ago, making Portugal one of the most politically stable geographical territories in Europe.

After the nation's territorial consolidation, Portugal took its fight against Islam and the propagation of its fervent Christianity to North Africa, defeating first the city of Ceuta in 1415, followed by Alcácer-Ceguer in 1458, Arzila and Tangier in 1471, Santa Cruz do Cabo de Guer in 1505 and Azamor in 1513. For most of the fifteenth century Portugal also explored more southern latitudes by sea, constructing forts and settlements along the western coast of Africa until, in 1488, Bartolomeu Dias rounded the Cape of Good Hope. Dias's survey voyage opened a route to the Indian Ocean, allowing Vasco da Gama to begin exploring East Africa and India, a move that ended the Arabs' commercial monopoly over the lucrative spice trade and their economic influence over Europe.

As more fleets sailed to the east, the Portuguese established more bases in quick succession, in Cochin (1502), Ormuz (1507), Goa (1510), the Maldives (1510), Malacca (1511), Chaúl (1516), Baçaim (1533), Macau (1557) and Pegú (1613). Florida was discovered in 1499 and Brazil the year after. At the same time, embassies were sent to most of the principal Asian powers, and Portuguese adventurers and merchants travelled as far as Sumatra, Java, Mindanau, Japan, Korea, China and Tibet. They took overland routes into the interior of Mali, Benin, Congo and Angola and may have been the first Europeans to visit Australia, 250 years before Cook.[74] It was a Portuguese captain, Fernão de Magalhães (Ferdinand Magellan), sailing under the Spanish flag, who in 1500 first circumnavigated the world. In just over a century, through military determination, diplomacy, trade and missionary zeal, Portugal revealed to an insular Europe the existence of nearly two-thirds of the world's surface.

During its Golden Age, rare and valuable goods including fine porcelain, ivory, tropical produce, spices and curiosities flooded into Lisbon, making it the most exotic emporium in Europe, a rival even to Venice. Competition inevitably led to hostility, and in 1506 Portugal defeated the combined navies of Venice and Egypt, giving it undisputed dominion of the sea. Nowhere was the pageant of Portugal better immortalized or more effectively expressed than in the spectacularly dressed envoys that King Manuel I sent to Pope Leo X in 1505 to request ecclesiastical favours, implore trade concessions and achieve legitimation of Portugal's burgeoning overseas empire. The gifts the Portuguese monarch bestowed on the pope included some of the rarest, finest and most valuable objects and specimens Europe had ever seen, including a live elephant, which made a spectacle that was still being recalled a century later.[75]

The triumphs of Portuguese history were punctured by a number of spectacular disasters that have likewise made indelible marks upon the national culture. The greatest calamity struck in Morocco in 1578 when a fleet of five hundred ships and eighteen thousand retainers, led by the

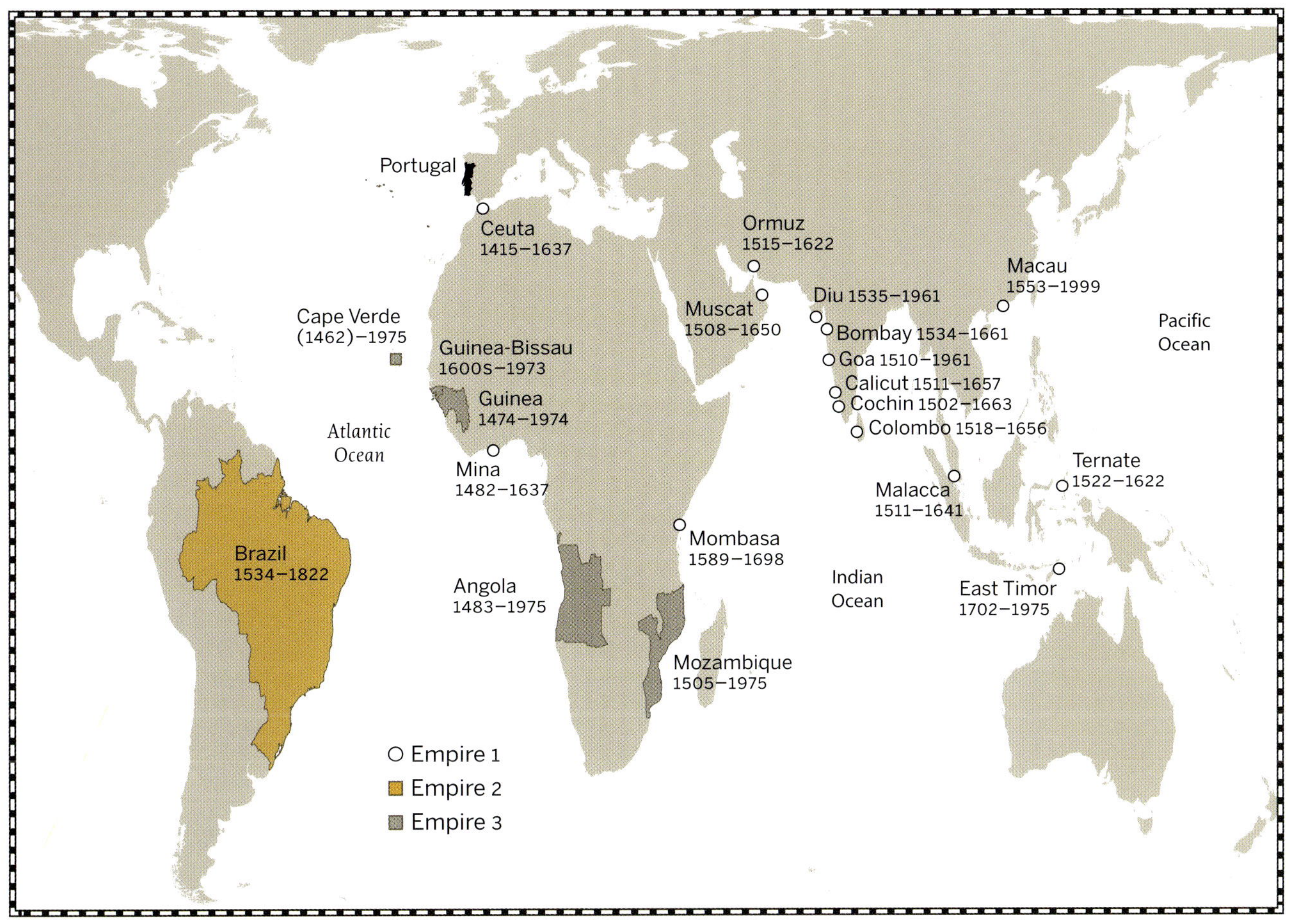

reckless and impulsive King Sebastião (reign 1557–78), were defeated and killed along with nearly all the Portuguese nobility. King Sebastião's defeat in the Battle of Alcácer Quibir marked the nation's final military adventure in Morocco and signalled the end of the Avis Dynasty and the beginning of a sixty-year union with Spain, a sorrowful, much-bemoaned development that slowly depleted Portugal's economy.

A second overseas disaster occurred in Japan. Colonization and missionary campaigns in Asia, which began in the sixteenth century, accelerated the martyrdom and sometimes beatification of a new generation of saints and converts. In Japan the Portuguese were expelled thirty-eight years after St. Francis Xavier first visited Nagasaki in 1549. Nearly forty thousand Christian converts were massacred along with many of the Portuguese priests who led them. The ranks of Portuguese martyrs and saints swelled over the next three decades as priests operating clandestinely in Japan met sorrowful fates.

At home the country's most dramatic physical disaster was undoubtedly the devastating earthquake and the ensuing tsunami and fires that destroyed much of Lisbon on All Saints' Day, 1 November 1755. The disaster destroyed an estimated thirty-three palaces along with the collections of antiquities, numismatics, natural history and "ethnographic curiosities" they housed.[76] According to some estimates, it killed forty thousand people and destroyed more than half the city, leaving the Crown and government to carry out their duties from a tented city and traumatizing King José I (reign 1750–77) so much, it was written, that he was unable to live in a stone building for the remainder of his life.

The tremor was felt throughout a large part of southern Europe, including Spain, France, Switzerland and Italy, and was discussed and debated throughout the continent. Immanuel Kant wrote three pamphlets in 1756 on it;[77] Voltaire in *Candide* (1759) used the disaster to dispute the magnanimity of God. Rousseau wrote to Voltaire

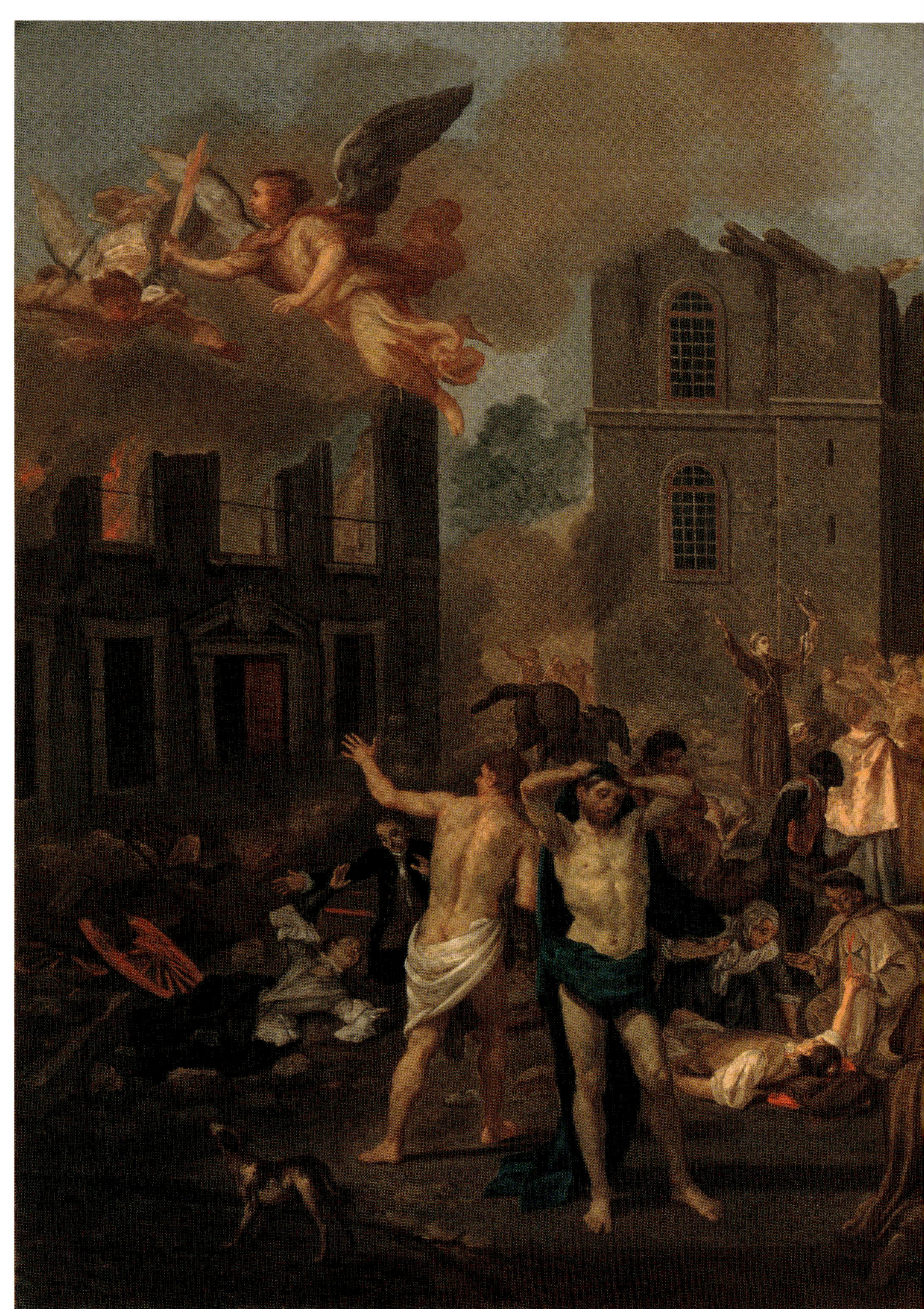

JOÃO GLAMA STRÖBERLE
The Lisbon Earthquake of 1755, eighteenth century
Museu Nacional de Arte Antiga

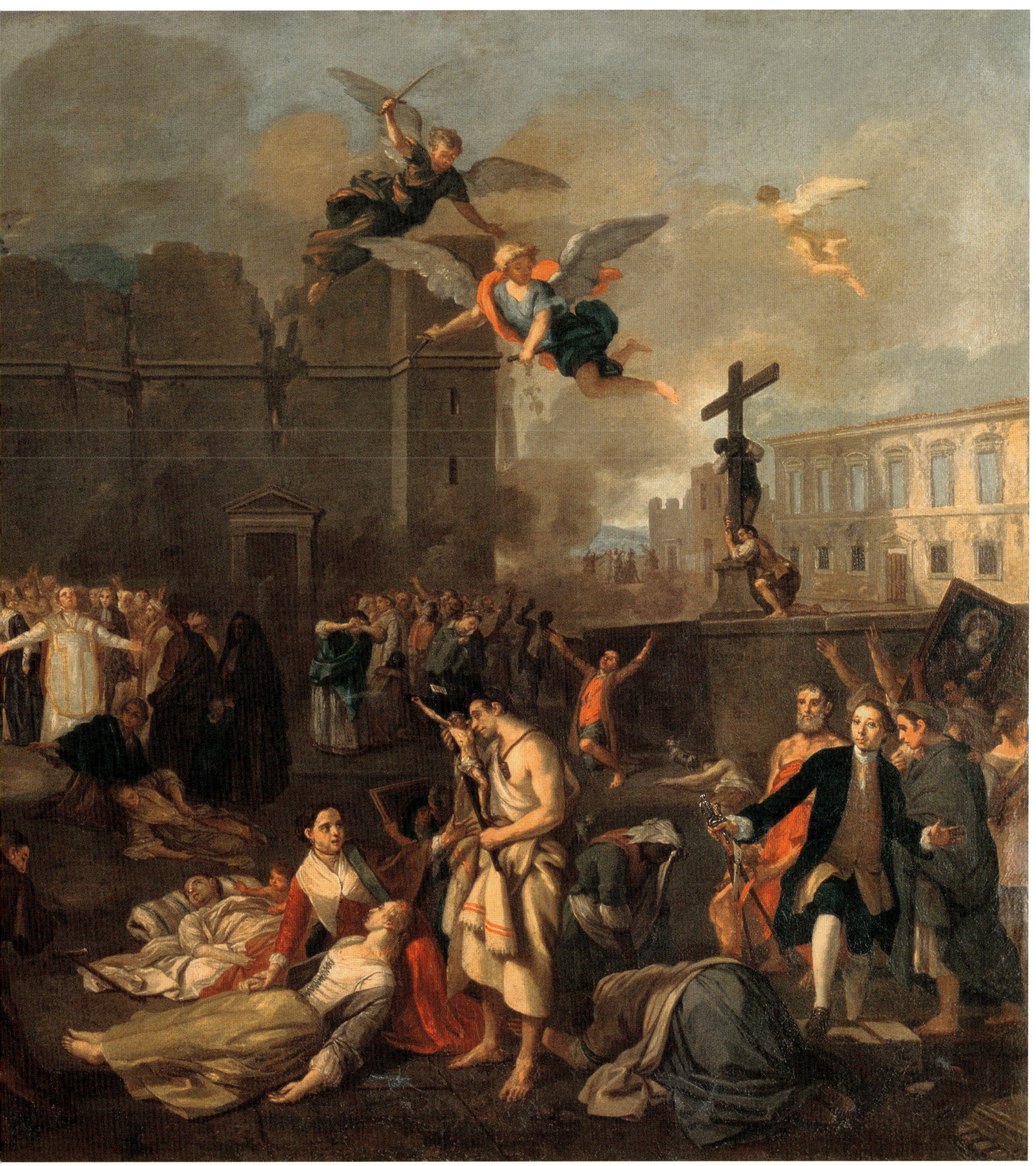

facing
Sculpture of the five chained Martyrs of Morocco in the twelfth-century Santa Cruz Monastery, Coimbra.

arguing that the disaster provided a dramatic and fear-inspiring warning against the increasing growth of cities and for the first time implicitly acknowledged the distinction between natural and man-made disasters. Others were not so kind, suggesting such a violent force must be God's punishment for the Portuguese's ruthlessness in commerce and their theologically and morally unjustifiable trade in slaves. João Glama Ströberle's painting *The Lisbon Earthquake of 1755* (eighteenth century), for example, depicted angels, some brandishing swords, flying through the air, unconcerned by the destruction and suffering of the city below.

Although many ascribed the catastrophe to divine displeasure, the ruins of this localized apocalypse gave rise to an enlightened architectural plan through which a new city was built under the supervision of the Marquis of Pombal (1699–1782). The harmony of the new city led travel writers Bridge and Lowndes to eulogize the debt architecture owed to earthquakes for creating the opportunities to construct "some of the finest municipal architecture in Europe."[78]

The past in Portugal is seldom erased or forgotten. Its performance or written testimony is replayed and retold every year through church and school services, processions, pilgrimages and visits that indelibly anchor it to the present. The Martyrs of Morocco, India and Japan survive in local popular memory through the religious cults that were developed around them. São João de Brito (1647–93), decapitated in India; São Gonçalo Garcia (d. 1597), one of the twenty-three martyrs of Japan, crucified in Nagasaki; and São Francisco Xavier (1506–52), who died of sickness in China—all are remembered during their saint's day festivals and, in the case of the last, sometimes portrayed in church paintings.[79] Every year in Travassô, near Águeda, on 15 and 16 January, a tableau depicting the beheading of five of the Martyrs of Morocco, executed in 1220, is still carried through the streets in their memory prior to Mass.[80] "Sebastianism," the belief based on the denial of the ill-fated king's death at the fateful Battle of Alcácer Quibir and the conviction that one day he will return to proclaim and preside over a new Golden Age, is even sometimes disparagingly reworked to mock politicians who do nothing as if they were waiting for the young king to return and solve the country's problems. Belief in Sebastião's return, particularly during times of strife and instability, was enshrined in poetry and spread as far as Brazil,[81] and Fernando Pessoa, in the most messianic of modern European poetical works, *Mensagem* (1934), dedicated a section to the mythologized, mysticized king and the great spiritual empire his return was expected to inaugurate.

Portugal's contribution to Renaissance science and arts is noteworthy, though surprisingly it is often overlooked and, until recently, infrequently celebrated. In the fifteenth and sixteenth centuries the nation was at the forefront of scientific developments that, in less than sixty years, helped create the greatest changes to European knowledge of terrestrial geography the continent had ever experienced. Printing presses made Lisbon into a publishing centre for Latin, Hebrew and Portuguese texts by the last quarter of the fifteenth century. At the same time, manuscript illumination and the production of handwritten books of great originality and flamboyance flourished.[82] Scholars studied classical medicine as well as the newly discovered drugs, techniques and theories that stemmed from the Orient and Brazil,[83] and developments in cartography and the invention and production of scientific instruments were nothing

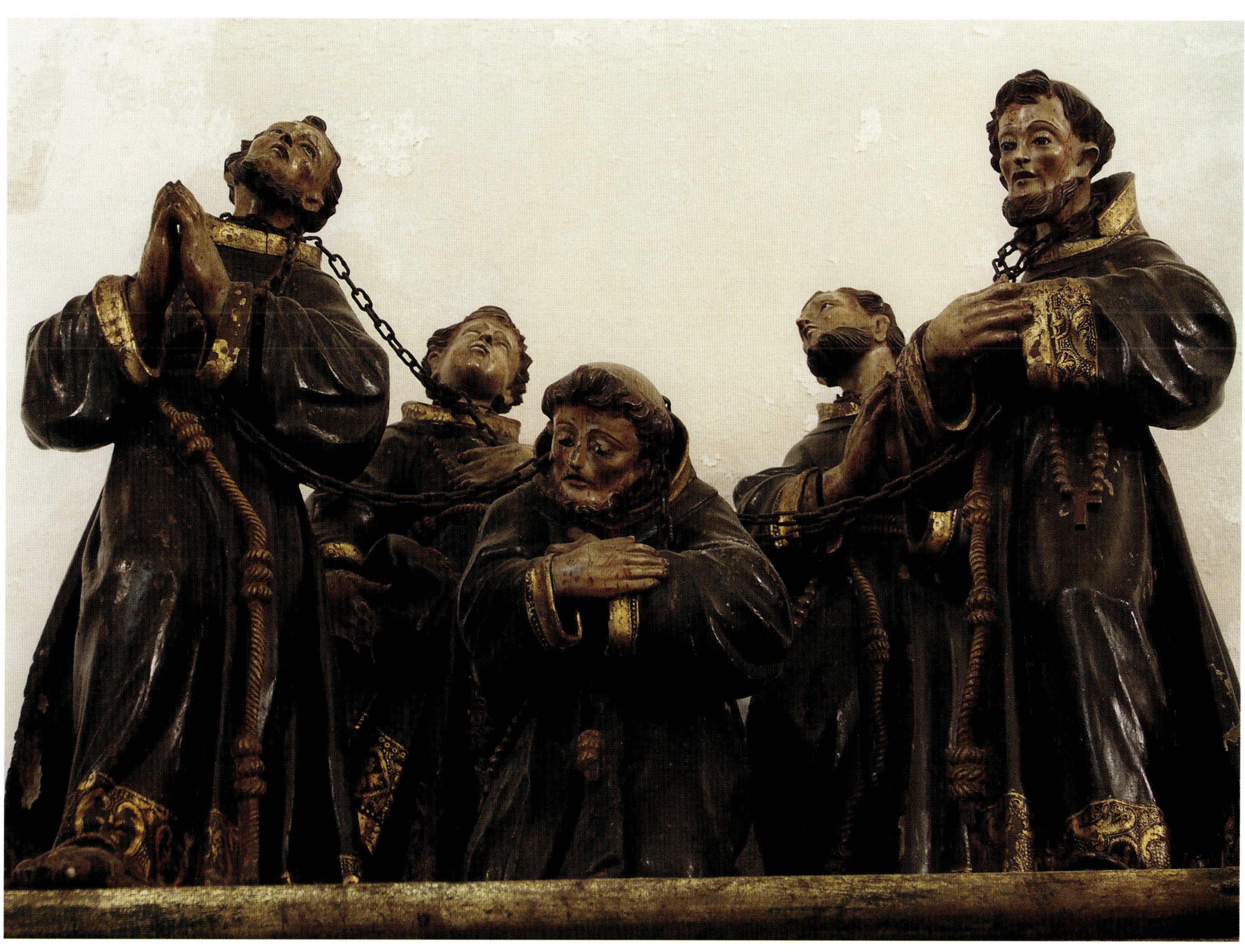

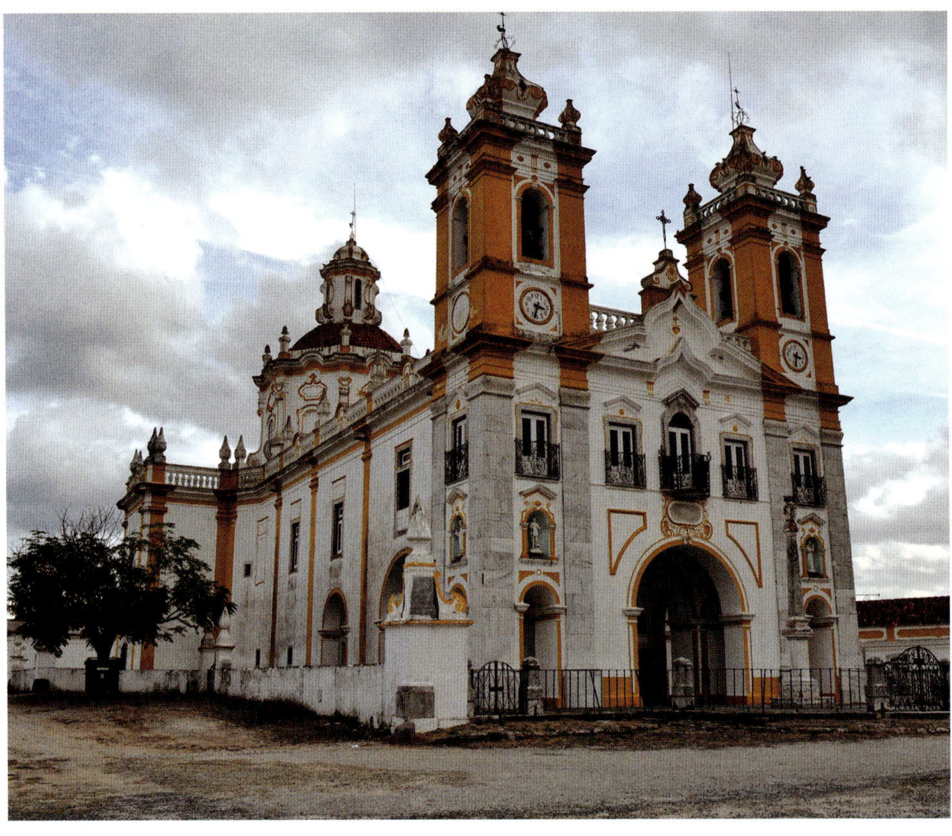

above
The pilgrimage church of Nossa Senhora de Aires in Viana do Alentejo was built in the eighteenth century.

facing
The passageway behind the central altar and adjacent rooms of the eighteenth-century church of Nossa Senhora de Aires in Viana do Alentejo are covered in photographs imploring the protection of the miraculous image of Nossa Senhora.

less than revolutionary. "The profusion of charts, tables, maps and globes that stemmed" from the hybrid knowledges compiled, synthesized and applied to precision navigational instruments was "unparalleled" and "the practical bedrock for all subsequent printed cartography over much of the globe for the next 200 years."[84] The Spanish annexation of Portugal in 1580, however, had a negative effect on the country's intellectual and creative ferment, encouraging scholars to gravitate towards the Spanish court.[85]

The Portuguese Primitivist School (1450–1550), including the painters Nuno Gonçalves, Vicente Gil and Francisco Henriques, increased the prestige of Portuguese art so enormously that Eliade and others have argued they created a unique canon, independent of the Mediterranean Renaissance, which established the realist tradition.[86] Outside this movement was the extraordinary work of Francisco de Holanda (1517–85), who created a metaphysical style of painting best represented in his works depicting the Creation. In literature, the rediscovery and translation of classical texts provided new models and idioms that Portuguese writers adopted to describe and allegorize Portugal's overseas adventures. Luís de Camões (1524–80), feted as the nation's greatest writer, immortalized the country's exploits in *Os Lusíadas* (1572), a heroic allegory in which Jupiter, Neptune, Mars, Bacchus and Venus all conspire to help or hinder the nation's destiny.

Camões's epic represented a cycle of almost mythical quests comparable to Homer's *Odyssey* and the deeds of Ulysses, which, for many generations of nineteenth- and twentieth-century schoolchildren, provided the thread that connected the nation with antiquity and the birth of modern European civilization. The reiteration of these historical antecedents also created the idea—an idea that, in the twentieth century, the authoritarian Estado Novo was only too keen to promote—that the Portuguese were God's elected people and that Christendom's saints and the Virgin, militarily and politically, had always supported their bellicose struggles.[87] Troops on leave in Portugal during the long-drawn-out colonial wars that began in 1961 in Angola before spreading to Mozambique and Guinea-Bissau paid homage in large numbers at the Marian shrines for solace and protection. Even today parts of the church of Nossa Senhora de Aires in Viana do Alentejo, still a popular pilgrimage centre, remain covered in ex-votos and photographs of those who entrusted Our Lady with their well-being or who have received miraculous intercessions from her renowned image.

In 1640 Portugal freed itself from its unhappy sixty-year union with Spain and proclaimed the restoration of its independence. This was the first of many historical restorations yearned for by the nation and later expressed in Pessoa's poetry. For many historians and politicians, the eighteenth century, the age of João V, when the wealth that had been severed after the loss of Portugal's Asian footholds was replaced by increased exploitation of Brazil, constituted a second restoration. Towards the end of the eighteenth century, the rebirth of Lisbon after the devastating earthquake, along with the promotion of science and the reforms introduced by Pombal to the country's finances and educational system, encouraged a belief in another restoration and a third cycle of revindication. The return of King João VI and the Portuguese aristocracy in 1821, after his court had fled Portugal in 1807 ahead of Napoleon's invasion, was celebrated as a fourth restoration. This again turned out to be overly optimistic; just as Portugal's Renaissance achievements had been shortened by the Spanish annexation, the Portuguese Enlightenment was itself curtailed by Napoleon's invasion and subsequent looting of the country's museums, libraries and private collections.

More recently, new restorations were promised by the military dictatorship after the coup of 1926, again by the opposition parties following the dictatorship's downfall in 1974, and by the current governing coalition since the 2011 debt crisis. Initial elation at the fall of the dictatorship was accompanied by a brief reoccurrence of Sebastian millenarianism,[88] perhaps to be expected given the widely accepted interpretation of Sebastianism by Costa Lobo,[89] who argues that the mystical cult around the young king's return emerged from the abyss between reality and desire and Portugal's yearning for independence from Spanish rule and consequent appetite for liberty. Finally, in 1980, as the year of Portugal's entry into the European

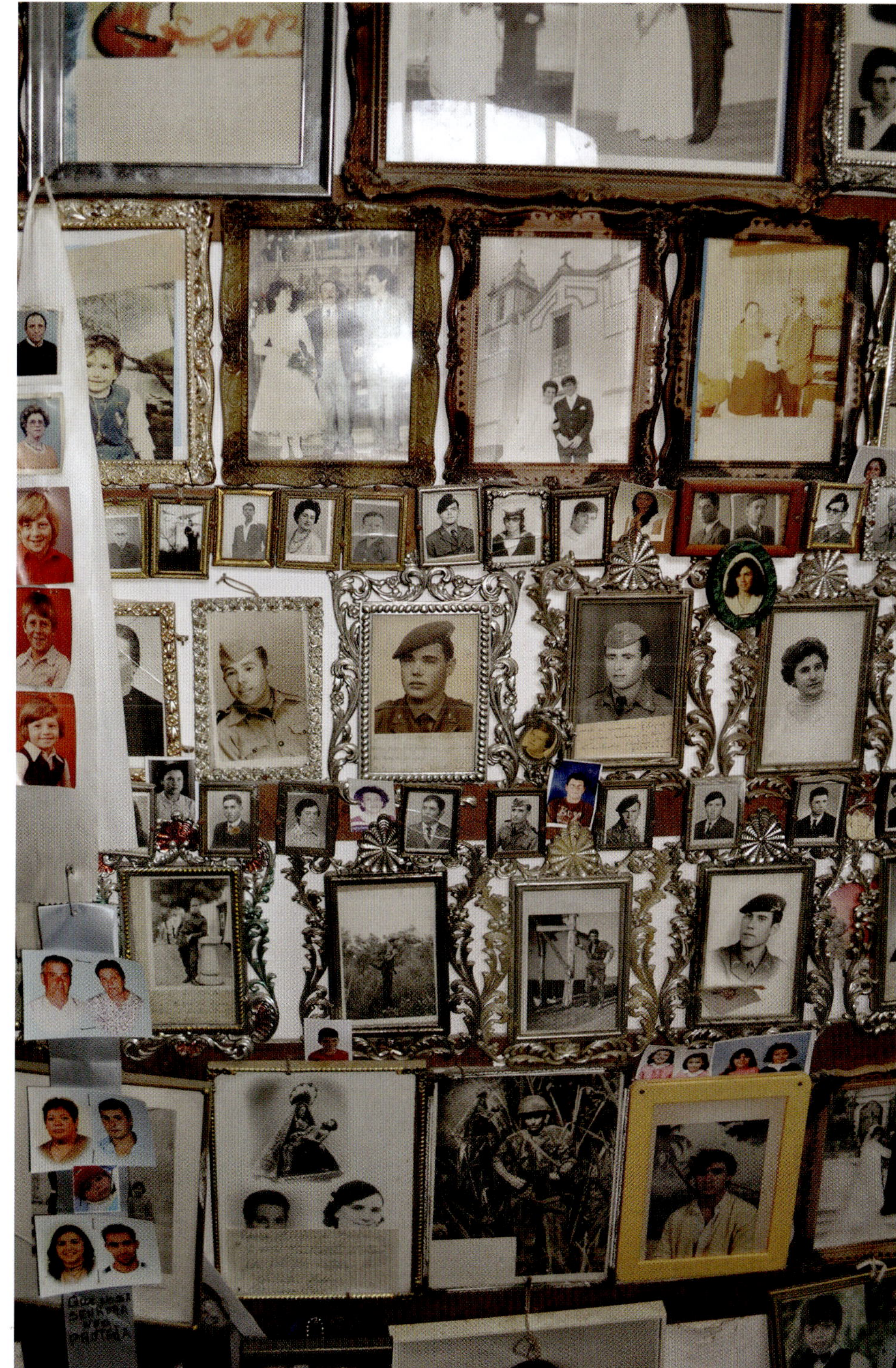

Economic Community approached, the rhetoric of restoration rose again. Despite a shared belief in the necessity of a sustainable restoration, modern Portugal has never achieved the prosperity it has yearned for, or, more importantly, the fairer distribution of wealth much of the population has for so long ached to attain. Portugal is a country of stark

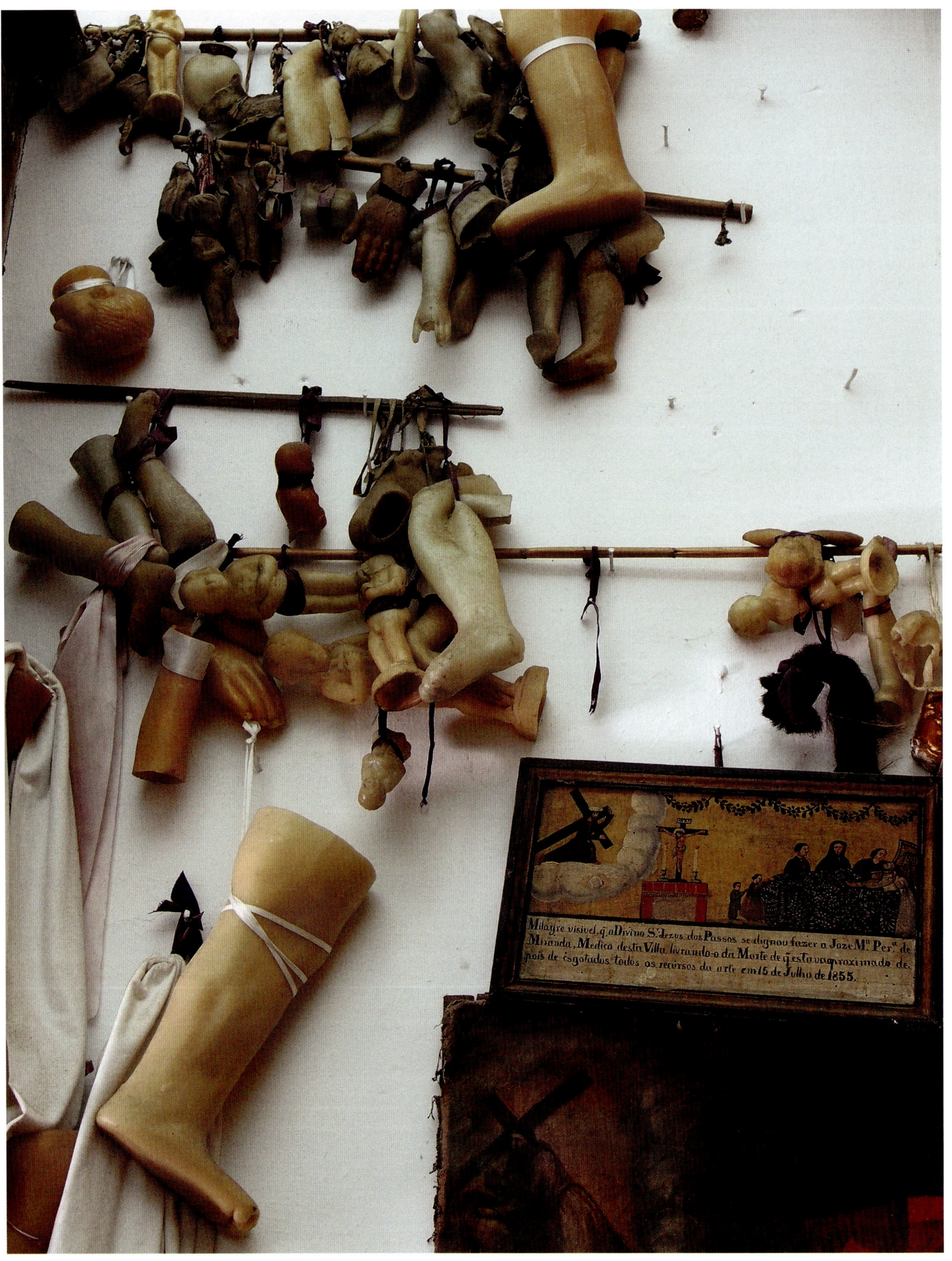
Milagre visivel, q̃. o Divino S.r Jezus dos Passos se dignou fazer a Joze M.a Per.a de
Miranda, Medico desta Villa livrando-o da Morte de q̃ estava aproximado de-
pois de esgotados todos os recursos da arte em 15 de Julho de 1855.

facing
Wax offerings of limbs and figures are suspended next to devotional paintings in the seventeenth-century church of Nossa Senhora dos Remédios in Castro Verde.

contrasts and inequalities, its history imbued with eternal returns, anticipation and longing mixed with commiseration and a too graciously accepted poverty. Portuguese history has been narrated as both glorious and tragic, or, in Pessoa's words, as a tarnished splendour wrapped in grief: "All is uncertain and dying. All is scattered, nothing is whole. O Portugal, today you are fog."[90]

URBAN AND RURAL CULTURES

The achievements and benefits of the Renaissance were not, as many histories overlook, equally shared by all of Portugal's population. The same could be said of the Enlightenment, which focused not only on a new knowledge paradigm but on more pragmatic political models. Both periods had their strongest impact on the life of the cities and the commerce and exploration on which these depended. Portugal's rural population created and experienced a very different world with its own history and localized identities. Documents testify that superstition was widespread in the countryside and among the uneducated urban populations. Pedroso estimated that there still exist around eighty thousand manuscripts from the sixteenth to eighteenth centuries in the national archives alone[91] that deal with the unorthodox religious beliefs and practices brought before the Inquisition and civic and ecclesiastical legislators. These sources reveal the coexistence of a wide range of beliefs and practices that, until the late twentieth century, continued to be documented by ethnographers in isolated rural areas. The *Constituições*[92] (Proclamations) of the archbishopric of Évora (1534) provided a long list of practices prohibited by the Church, including the use of sacred artifacts outside of church ceremonies, invocation of the Devil, divination and the making of figures and images or the use of skulls in divination, the use of human body parts, curing ceremonies and ceremonies designed to cause affliction, and the use of prayers and other religious formulas not approved by the Church.

By the end of the seventeenth century the Church felt it necessary to continuously repeat its warning against these practices, suggesting that they remained widespread. In the Constituições of the archbishopric of Braga (1693), divination, the casting of spells, the use of magic to find treasure or reveal past events and the invocation of evil spirits were again prohibited and made punishable by excommunication. The blurring of the borders between Christianity and demonic beliefs caused particular consternation; the use of sacred objects, including saintly images stolen from churches and kept in houses, and the mixing of scripture and excerpts from the Mass with satanic words and ceremonies constructed by the Devil likewise vexed ecclesiastical authorities.[93] Prayers to the moon and stars, non-church-based ceremonies to the saints and division of days between those thought propitious and those thought malevolent, as well as the other beliefs already noted, were outlawed by the Constituições of the bishopric of Porto in 1687.[94]

The situation was the same in the south of the country. The Constituições of the bishopric of Algarve in 1673 threatened excommunication of those found to have used enchantments, divinations or charms to cause or cure illness, heal wounds or control storms or the elements. People were also prohibited from blessing cattle or other animals or using magic to rid plants or crops of diseases.[95] Church legislation was aimed at preventing similar practices in bishoprics throughout the country. This legislation clearly suggests that a common stratum of indigenous beliefs and practices had created a specifically Portuguese hybridized Christianity

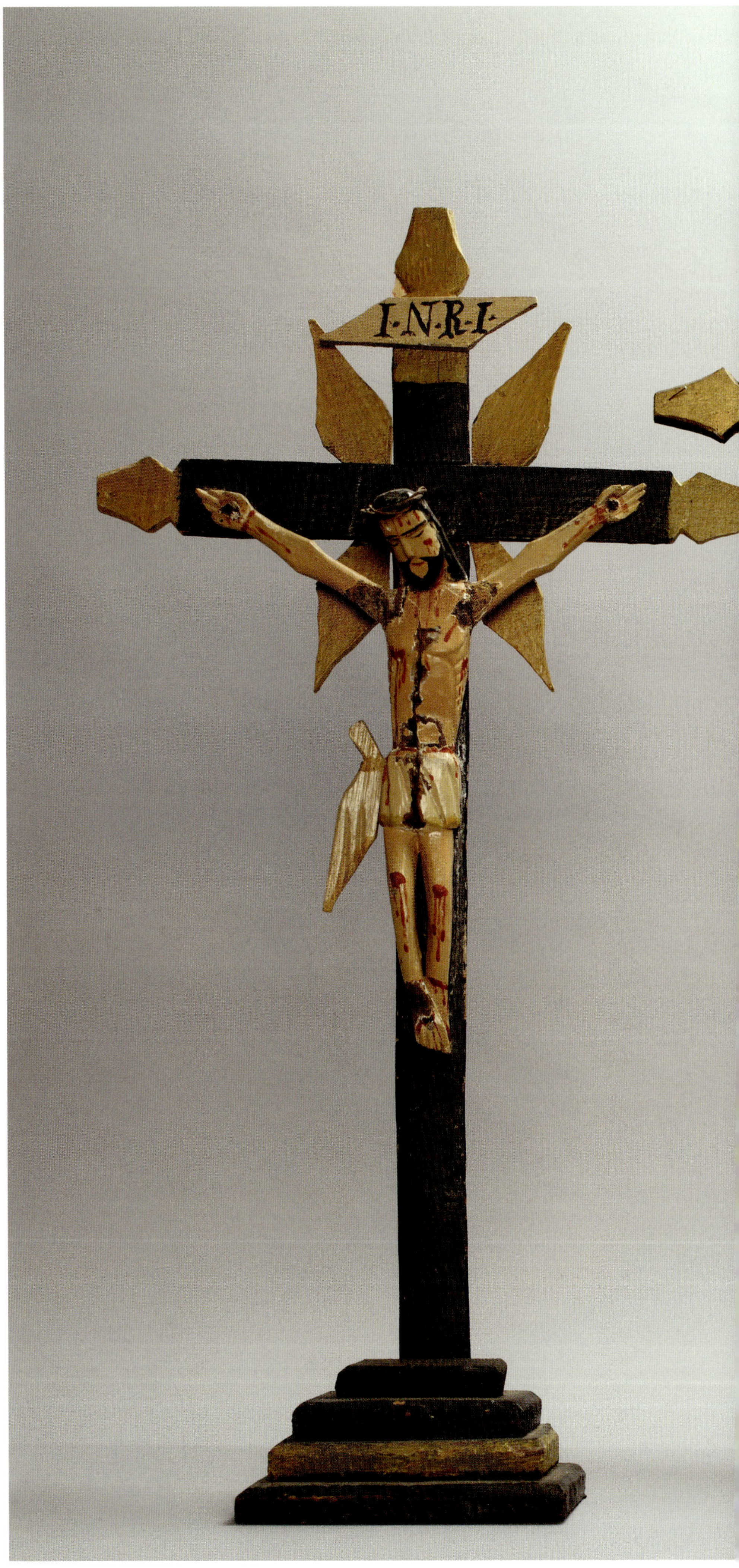

facing
Three popular images of Christ's crucifixion, made in the nineteenth or early twentieth century. During this period there was a popular cult in the Serra de São Mamede, near the Spanish border, that centred on the image of the crucified Christ.

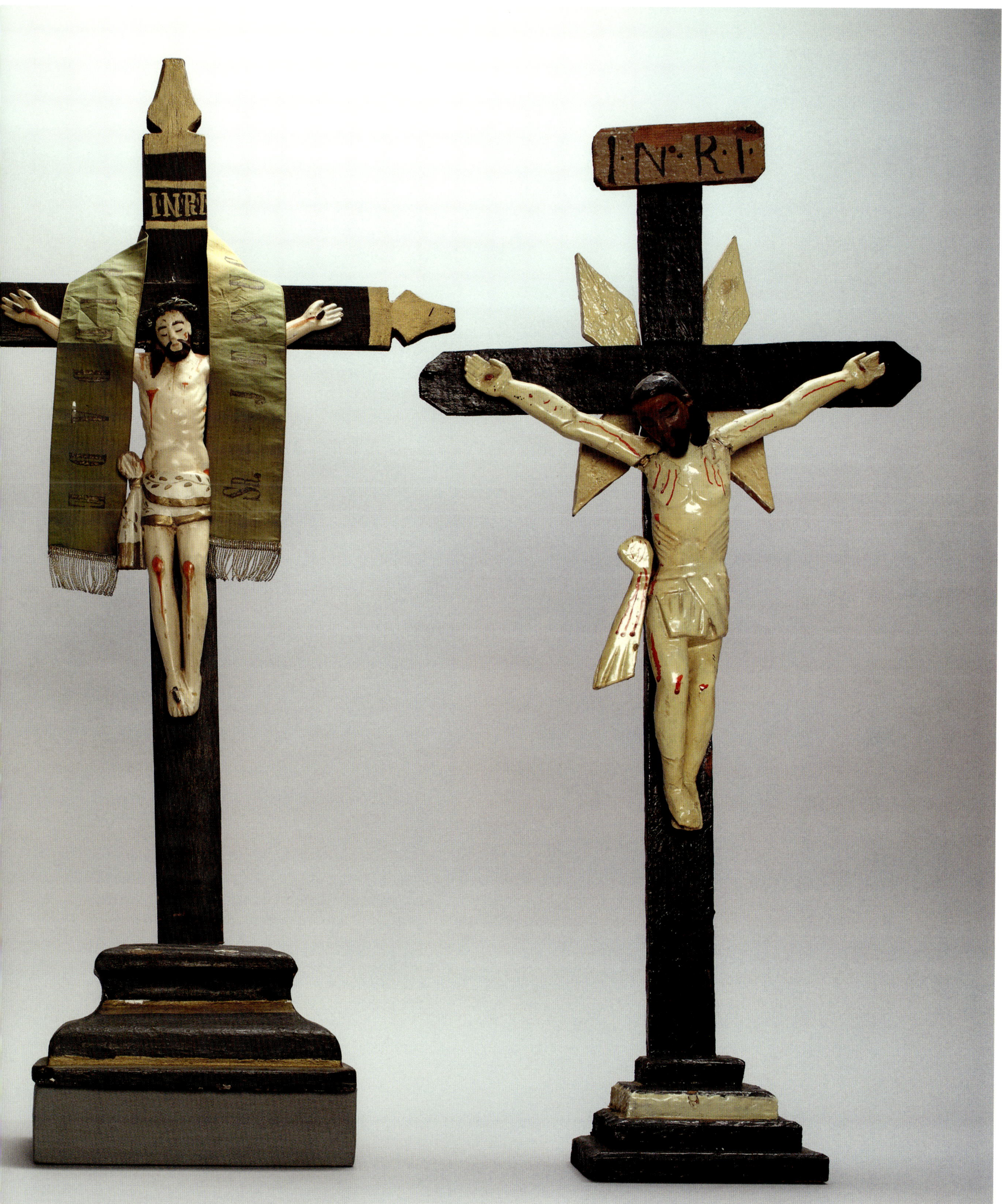
INRI
I·N·R·I

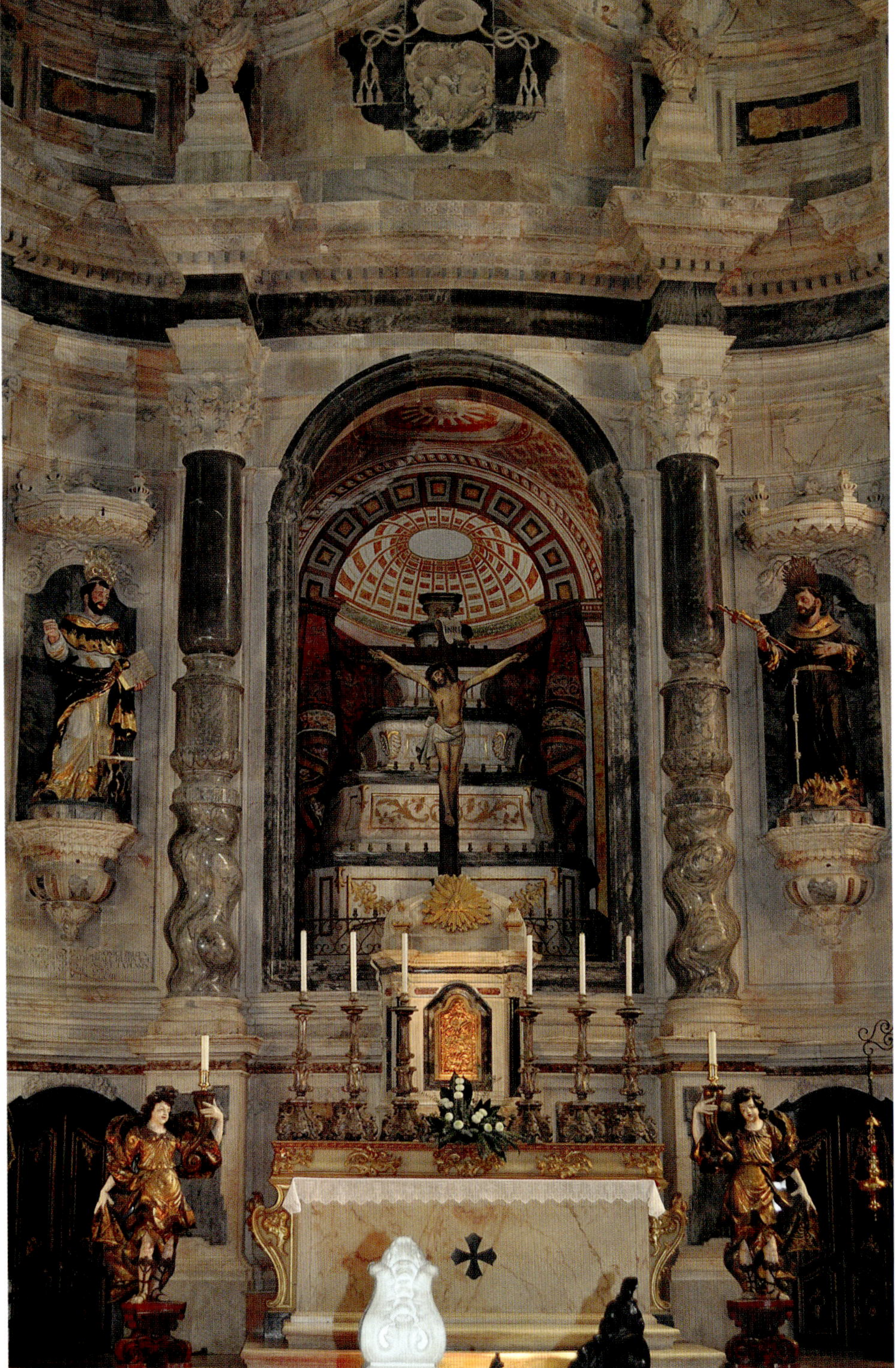

above
The magnificent altar of the fifteenth- to sixteenth-century church of São Francisco in Évora.

that persisted well into the eighteenth century. The bishopric of Viseu, in 1681, distinguished five categories of superstitions that could describe the situation in the country as a whole: idolatry (the worship of false gods), magic, divination, witchcraft and "frivolity."

Although polarized, these two worlds—the urban world of ecclesiastics, merchants, scholars, administrators and rulers and the rural and marginalized world of subsistence farmers, shepherds, journeymen and artisans—were interlinked. The Church attempted to purify religious beliefs in vain and would have to wait until the early twentieth century, when its campaigns had become infinitely more strategic and militant, before it began to erode the popular religion that was the backbone of rural society. This erosion had already started in the Republican period; by 1926, despite state hostility, mainstream Catholic publications had already distinguished between the old "dazzling" fairs and pilgrimages with their bands and fireworks—"celebrations that are more for the devils, for the passions, for the world, than for God and the saints"[96]—and the solemn observances devoted solely to an ecclesiastically institutionalized Holy Family.

After the 1926 military coup, Gomes da Costa, the government's provisional leader, promised to restore judicial recognition to Church organizations and reform the laws pertaining to the ownership of ecclesiastical properties. This law returned authority over independent brotherhoods—many of which had their headquarters at a shrine, which organized specific saintly cults—to the Church. The regime also gave priests authority within their parishes to help tighten centralized control over the rural parts of the country. With such powers the Church was able to use the National Republican Guard (GNR) to break up religious gatherings they disapproved of.[97] Emboldened by the new support of the dictatorship, the Church embarked on an open struggle to re-Christianize popular religious practices, particularly nocturnal ceremonies. It prohibited dancing, musical bands, fireworks and auctions near or around churches; regulated processions, faith organizations and the use of Church artifacts; and demanded fixed or percentage-based shares of all revenue from brotherhoods and celebrations for the dioceses.[98] The assault of the institutional Church on Portugal's rural world had begun.

In 1927 the archbishop of Braga explained:

> Human authority has two arms, and with these two arms we can work effectively to be good operators, good agents of national resurgence. Without one of these arms Portugal is a mutilated body, with it, that which was great will again be [great]. The Church is the arm that sustains the cross; authority is the arm that sustains the sword.[99]

Even in 1924 a religious brochure, *The Boletim de Fátima*, spoke of a "radiant and beautiful aurora" that connected Aljubarrota, Ourique and Fátima, three celebrated sites of divine apparitions given great political significance in Portuguese historiography. After 1926 the Boletim campaigned that the feast day of "the purest and most beautiful incarnation of the hero of Portugal, D. Nuno Álvares Pereira"—canonized as Santo Nuno de Santa Maria, the hero of Aljubarrota, the decisive battle that freed Portugal from Spain in 1385—should be made into a national holiday.

One of these strategies, predating the 1926 military coup but fortified after its success, consisted of manipulating the importance and organization of the shrine of Nossa Senhora de Fátima to provide an alternative model to the unregulated *romarias*, pilgrimages associated with a plethora of local saints and virgins.[100] Pilgrimage was one characteristic shared between popular and institutional religion, and in the case of Fátima it was channelled and regulated from the beginning, providing a model that was copied elsewhere. Civic and religious symbols were manipulated to knit together state and Church in a consecrated and privileged symbiotic constellation that endured for nearly half a century.

Although the fight by the institutionalized Church against popular religious expressions was largely successful, *romarias*, although attracting many fewer participants than before, are still organized and continue to voice hybrid Catholic beliefs. By the end of the 1970s anthropologist Pierre Sanchis had identified 216 remaining ones, of which 99 were devoted to the cult of Nossa Senhora, 83 to that of a saint and 20 to Christ.[101] Desanctified practices continued. Next to the hermitage of São Brás, in Santa Cruz do Bispo (Matosinhos), stands a sixteenth-century stone figure that, according to the anthropologist Veiga de Oliveira, on the occasion of the *romaria* was still embraced and bathed in wine by girls about to be married.[102] Baths of wine were also given in São Paio da Torreira, near Aveiro, until the twentieth century,[103] while devotees took baths in sacred streams, rivers or the sea as part of the *romarias* dedicated to São João (Porto and Braga, 23–24 June), São Pedro (Lisbon, 28 June) and São Bartolomeu (Esposende, 24 August). During the *romarias* to the sites associated with São Marcos (Castelo Branco, 4 April), São Mamede (Valongo, 17 August) and São Silvestre (31 December), rituals were performed to bless cattle and other farm animals, while the *romarias* to the Salvador do Mundo in both Viveiros and Boticas were made to ensure the health and fertility of cattle.[104]

The fertility and re-fertilization rituals included in *romarias* and celebrations such as those on the feast day of São João (24 June, which corresponds to the summer solstice), the feast day of Santo Estêvão (26 December, the winter solstice) and Carnival (which inaugurates the spring equinox) have been often interpreted as continuations of hybridized Christian practices and beliefs and their rearticulation into more or less coherent Catholic Indo-European religious matrices. However, anthropologists like Sanchis, Oliveira, Santo and Pereira, writing in the 1980s—and

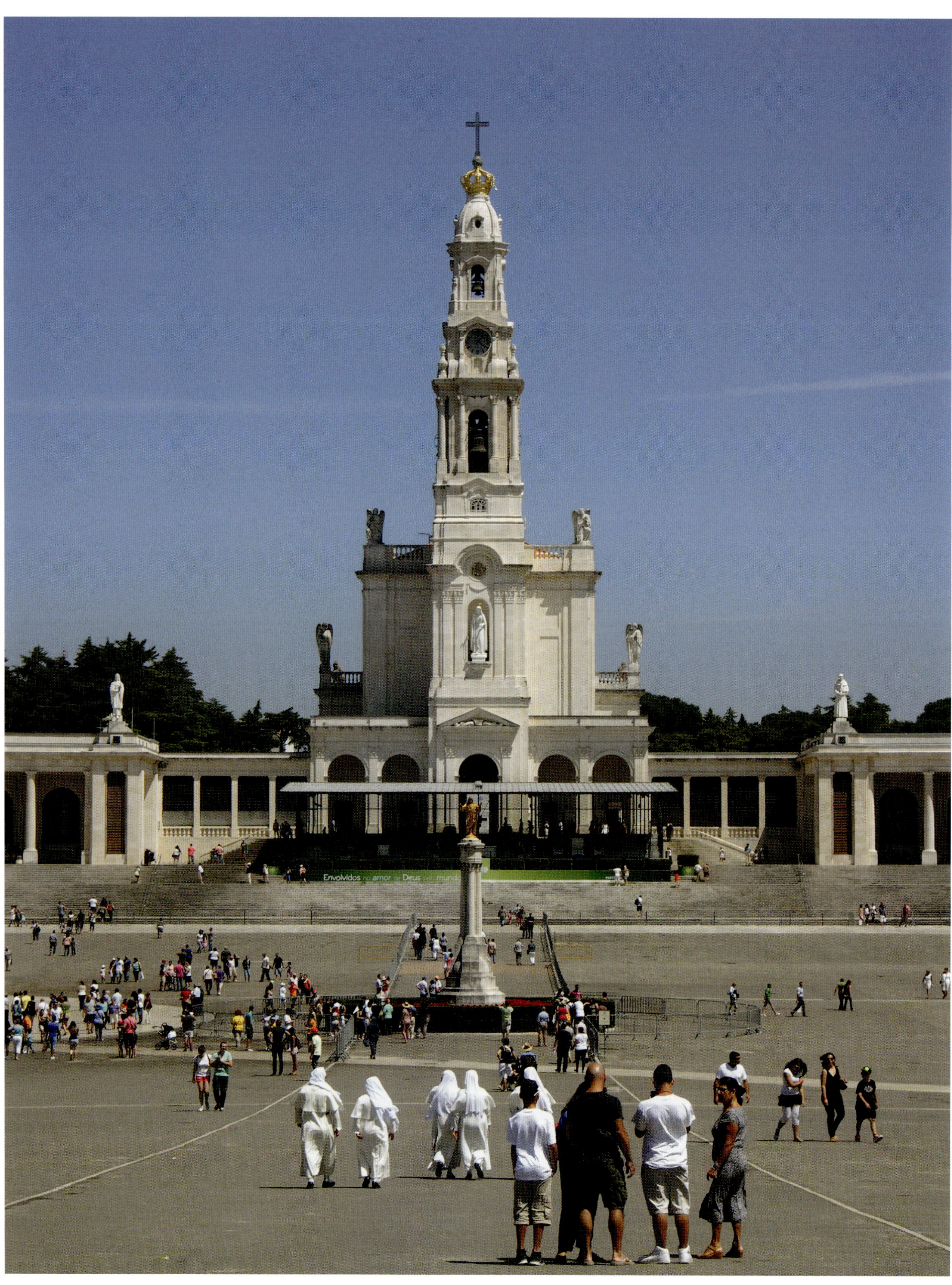
Envolvidos no amor de Deus

facing
The twentieth-century church of Nossa Senhora de Fátima, one of the major pilgrimage centres of the Christian world.

contemporary popular writers (Tiza, Morais, Maciel, Lopes, Barros and Costa) today—uncritically reproduce the folkloric literature compiled in the late nineteenth and twentieth centuries that assented cultural continuities. As has been amply documented, rural society even in the 1960s was sharply in decline;[105] emigration, a move from the countryside to the cities and the African independence wars had dislocated a generation of rural inhabitants, and the industrial reorganization of the economy was beginning to marginalize rural areas. Between 1963 and 1978 in the rural province of Minho, for example, revenue sent from emigrants was the second-most important financial activity after agriculture. Farms were barely sustainable and had an average land plot of just 0.5 hectares; 90 percent were smaller than 4 hectares and some communities had 33 to 37 percent of their menfolk working abroad.[106] Such wholesale social transformations eroded popular religion and its cultural expressions.[107]

Much of Portuguese ethnography in the late nineteenth and mid-twentieth centuries was focused on collecting and describing exotic cultural traits, which it explained as pre-Christian survivals instead of integrated aspects of a rural Portuguese religious milieu. Many writers were satisfied to draw parallels between Christian ceremonies and older rituals such as the cult of the dead,[108] Saturnalia, Bacchanalia[109] or the Florália[110] of ancient Rome and Greece, while others identified remnant beliefs and ceremonies dating from the Middle Ages.[111]

The Constituições studied by Pedroso, according to some of this older literature, demonstrated the continued existence of hybrid Christian beliefs well into the eighteenth century. Many of these practices were successfully repressed in the nineteenth century, but remnant traits continued to be a defining element in popular religion, they argued, until the late twentieth century. Theologians and later positivist philosophers tried to separate so-called superstitions like these and classify them as distinct from Christianity in an attempt to purify and rationalize orthodox dogma and reinforce the authority of the Church over popular interpretations and beliefs. By the 1940s the masquerades that are still part of Carnival in the villages of Lazarim or Mira in central Portugal, for example, received such strong ecclesiastical disapproval that they were prohibited for twenty years. Adão de Castro Almeida, a former mask maker in Lazarim, recalled in 2010 being forced to take refuge to avoid persecution. In Mira, too, João Pinho recounted how the Church and Estado Novo banned Carnival masquerades during the same period, and in Ousilhão, João Manuel Esteves told us that masqueraders or people wearing Carnival costumes were refused Christian burial. In Podence by the 1970s, when the anthropologist Benjamin Pereira and the film director Noémia Delgado made their influential catalogues and film *Máscaras*, one of the most renowned of these masquerades had almost become extinct until the film and the end of the dictatorship helped revive it.[112]

Two distinct but not entirely independent sources of cultural knowledge and practices have been woven into Portuguese history over the past five hundred years: the rationalist urban spirit that matured after the Enlightenment and a rural, popular stream of hybrid Catholic Indo-European beliefs that some researchers have attempted to trace to an even earlier time before Roman colonization. The interpretation of the relationship between these two worlds, or the focus on one to the exclusion of the other, has exerted a powerful influence on the construction of different notions of Portuguese identity.

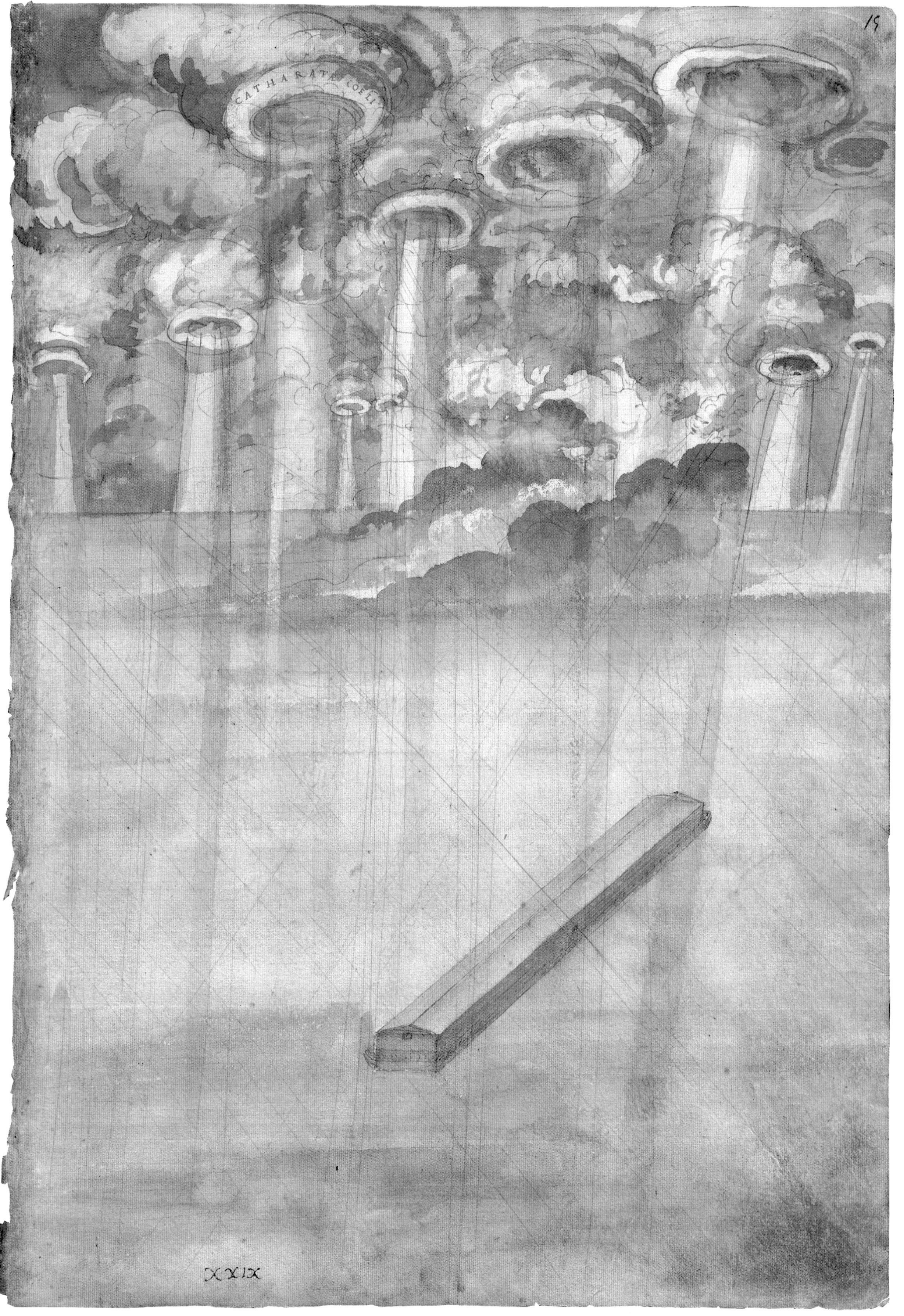
15
CATHARATE COELI
XXIX

3 Ploughing the Sea

Portuguese Longing and Identity

Language is a lookout for the universe. My language breathes the murmur of the sea, as other languages breathe the whisper of the forest, or the silence of the desert. That is why the sound of the sea has been our restlessness.

Vergílio Ferreira[113]

EARLY PORTUGUESE ATTITUDES towards the ocean were deeply ambiguous, and those in the agricultural north of the country were different from those in the south and centre, which had long benefited from Mediterranean trading networks. The Church's strong reverence for São Isidoro's (c. 560–636) *Etymologiae* (c. 600), a twenty-volume encyclopedia compiled from extracts by classical writers, expressed trepidation towards the ocean, in part because God had forbidden human passage to the unknown realms to which it might lead. Nevertheless, the memory of the importance of the sea for the Phoenicians and Romans, who had crossed it to extend their empires and attain enrichment and adventure, continued to exert a strong fascination.[114] The tension between these conflicting attitudes towards the sea expressed a facet of the persistent ambiguity between classical and Christian thought, popular religion and theological doctrine, coastal and inland communities and the north and south of the country, an ambiguity that maintained its hold throughout the Middle Ages.

In the thirteenth century the Italian city state of Genoa, part of a flourishing Mediterranean trading network, helped Portugal construct its first navy, and the two powers shared a number of joint maritime expeditions. Never underestimating the difference between the mild Mediterranean and the storm-ridden Atlantic, the Portuguese began to turn their gaze away from Europe to face the ocean. The Atlantic was conceptualized differently from the calm Mediterranean or the Red Sea and was associated with barrenness and death rather than life.[115] After Portugal had discovered sea routes across the Atlantic and Indian Oceans in the fifteenth and sixteenth centuries, it increasingly identified itself as a seaborne civilization, its economy ever more dependent on long-distance trade and its imagination dominated by apostolic zeal. So important was the sea to Portugal that between 1490 and 1520, a whole architecture emerged from seafaring traditions. Although short-lived, the Manueline style imprinted its unique and spectacular form of High Gothic, defining an

facing
FRANCISCO DE HOLANDA
De Aetatibus Mundi Imagines. The Flood (Diluvio), 1573

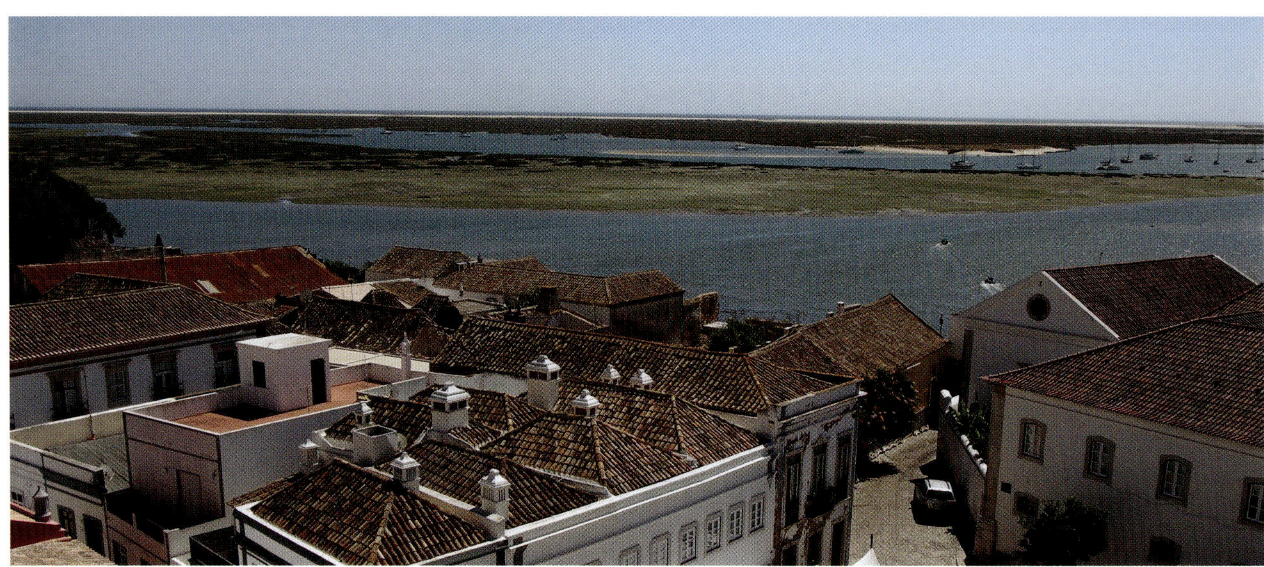

this page
The Ria Formosa wetlands and Largo da Sé from the tower of Faro's thirteenth-century cathedral.

facing, left
The sixteenth-century spherical fountain in Évora, Portas de Moura, which evokes the source of terrestrial waters in Paradise.

facing, right
Nineteenth-century sculpture of Saturn rising above the water at the Lago de Gadanha in the centre of Estremoz. An inscription on the pedestal reads "Time passes quickly."

era drenched in the intoxication of the sea. By 1525 King João III had grandly styled himself "Lord of Guinea and the Conquest, Navigation and Commerce of Ethiopia, Arabia, Persia and India."

In the early twentieth century the Portuguese state sought to deepen public awareness of the nation's historical achievements and maritime traditions and foment discussion on their implications for the country's identity. The Republican government (1910–26) developed this process begun earlier by the constitutional monarchies by creating a hagiography of national heroes, including navigators, poets, politicians and visionaries, organizing secular cults around their commemorations and incorporating them into standard educational curricula. This process was consolidated under the dictatorship (1926–74), with some important additions: a folkloricization of the importance of the sea to Portugal, an idealization of maritime history and seafaring communities and a major financial commitment to reanimating the long-distance fishing industry and affirming the importance of sea lanes for the territorial integrity of Portugal's far-flung empire. With the fall of the Estado Novo in 1974, the independence of all of Portugal's African colonies by 1975 and its integration into Europe in 1986, ambiguity rose again surrounding the essence of Portuguese national identity.

MYTHOLOGIES OF WATER

In the Old Testament book of Genesis, water is described as a primordial substance that existed before the creation of the world and will continue to exist after its destruction. According to Genesis, before the world existed "the Spirit of God moved upon the face of the waters,"[116] intimating that the sea was the very medium of creation and life itself. In the same account the sea creatures and birds are created on the fourth day of Creation, before those of the land. "And God said, Let the waters bring forth abundantly the moving creatures that have life, and fowl that may fly above the earth in the open firmament of heaven."[117]

God parted the waters between Heaven and Earth before creating Eden and a river, which

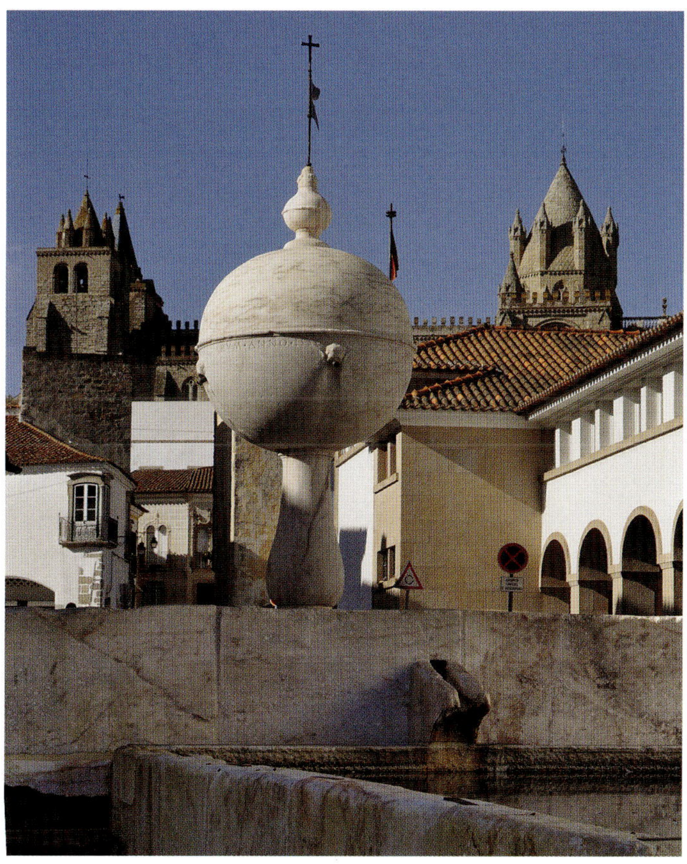

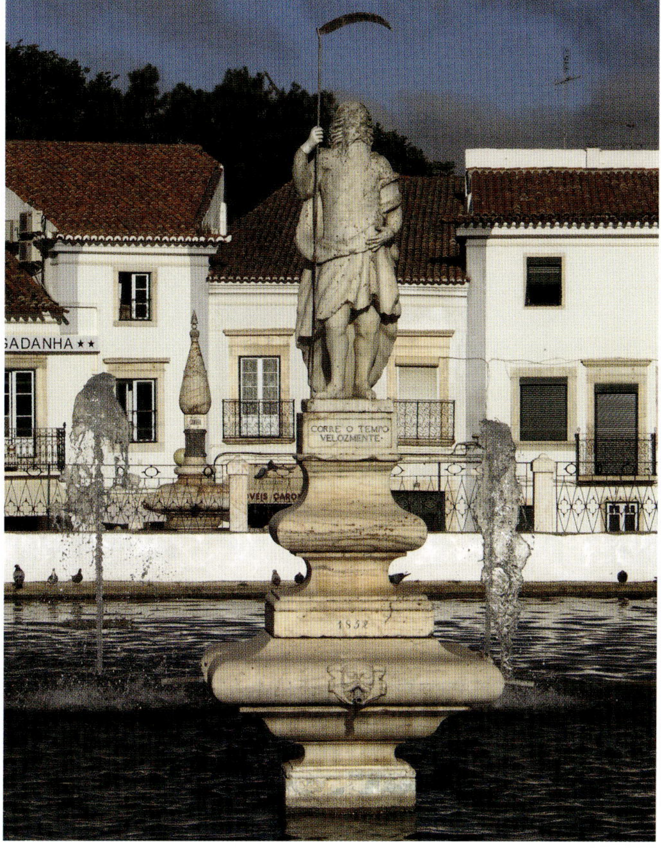

watered the garden before dividing into four other rivers that surrounded the different lands.[118] Based on this account, early theologians believed terrestrial water originated from the place of Creation. In the centre of the Biblical Garden of Paradise, by the Tree of Life, was the great fountain from which flowed the four rivers that divided the world before they emptied into the formless chaos that surrounded it. The springs that bubbled up from the earth were believed to be connected to the fountain and were likewise endowed with properties associated with immortality, wisdom and curative and restorative powers.[119] Water has always been at the centre of settlements, not only theologically through baptism, which attaches newborns to the community of God and safeguards them against *Diabo* (the Devil), but also socially, as people often settled around springs or rivers and built fountains in town centres close to chapels and churches.

Among its miraculous characteristics, water is indispensable in Portuguese life for baptism, blessing and curative ceremonies. Terrestrial water in Christian belief nourishes both the spirit and the physical body and has cleansing properties. For São Isidoro, water, along with fire, was essential to life. In northern Portugal, freshwater springs were thought of as living beings, and the invigorating qualities of a mother's milk were compared

facing
JORGE COLAÇO
The Boat to Hell, 1907
Palace Hotel, Buçaco

with the benedictions provided by these sacralized waterways. It has even been said that to bathe in holy water was like passing through the body of the primordial mother.[120]

The diversity of water spirits and sea creatures attests to the wide variety of properties and associations attached to water and to its central role in all societies. Early Christian texts like those of São Isidoro mixed scriptural authority with classical learning. The Greeks and Arabs referred to the Atlantic Ocean as the dark sea that began on the shore of Cape St. Vincent in southwest Portugal and, according to the ancient Greek geographer Strabo (64–21 BC), extended to the mouth of Hades at the world's end. This was a sombre, dangerous place, full of bad omens and distinct from the seas at the centre of the known world. The Romans and Greeks anthropomorphized it as Oceanus, the son of Uranus (Heaven) and Gaia (Underworld), a deep and vast void that encircled the world and from which all the creatures that inhabited its depths had emerged. Greek mythology populated the ocean with diverse supernatural beings. Oceanus and Tethys, both his sister and wife, belonged to a race of titans that had been deposed by Jupiter and his brother Neptune, who had then become god of the sea. Neptune held power over storms and crossed the waves in a chariot pulled by horses with golden manes and bronze hooves. In a third-century Roman mosaic in Faro, southern Portugal, Neptune has a strong bearded face, twin crab claws attached to his forehead and the four winds blowing from his hair. At Conímbriga, another third-century Portuguese Roman site, a triton, half man and half fish with hooved legs, is represented on a mosaic pavement. Nereus, the son-in-law of Oceanus, propagated his own playful offspring, the Nereids, who had magical powers and whose beauty captivated even Jupiter and Neptune. Along with other magical beings, Dryads, Oreads and Naiads, the Nereids lived in caverns and grottos and sanctified springs, streams and lakes that nourished the earth and sea. The gods gave authority over the forces of all these supernatural aquatic creatures to Leucothea and Portunus, once a mortal woman and her son, who safeguarded seafarers and watched over ports.

This complex amalgam of Christian theology and classical thought mediated an extensive discursive world in which acute fear of the ocean was intimately bound to the moral geography of Creation, Apocalypse and personal redemption. Medieval Christian cosmology was a European construction that was systematized, recorded, copied and disseminated in monasteries throughout the continent. In Portugal the monastic centres of São Mamede in Lorvão, Santa Cruz in Coimbra and Santa Maria in Alcobaça were the most important manuscript repositories that originally included various *mapas mundis*, including the ones that form part of the 1189 *Lorvão Apocalypse* and São Isidoro's *Etymologiae*. These early maps visualized the world as a roughly round land mass surrounded by an ocean, not dissimilar from the ideas propagated by the Greeks and Romans. Land was divided into three regions that corresponded to the three races engendered by the sons of Noah—Shem, Ham and Japeth, who, according to Biblical sources, were the ancestors of the peoples of the Orient, Africa (Ethiopia) and Europe, respectively. These three domains were divided by watery expanses, and only Christian Europe was illustrated as possessing order, harmony and a bountiful and benign nature, including social divisions based on the hierarchy of angels.

The ocean surrounding these land masses maintained its primordial, pre-Creation chaos, filled with deformed monsters, raging storms and

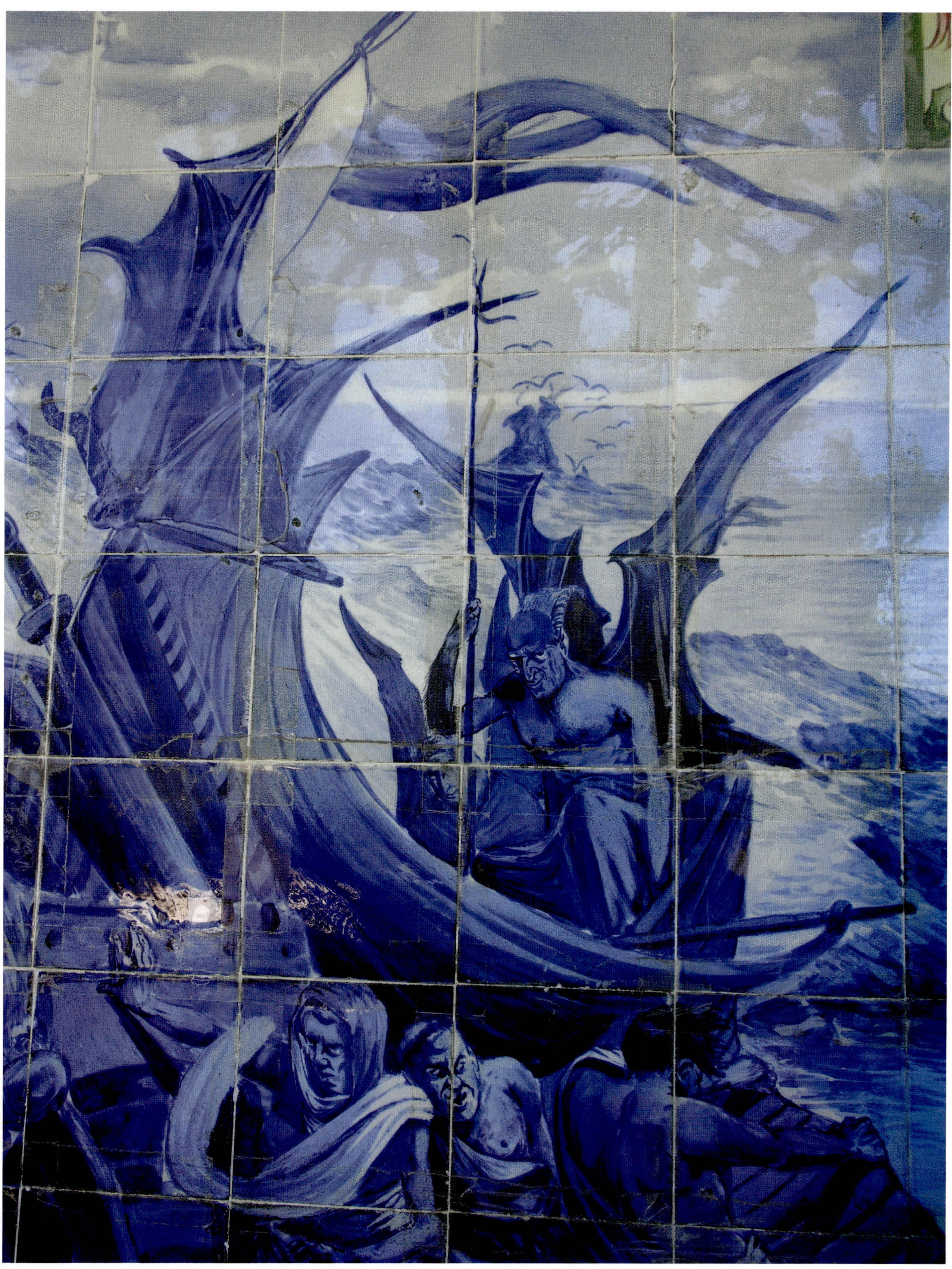

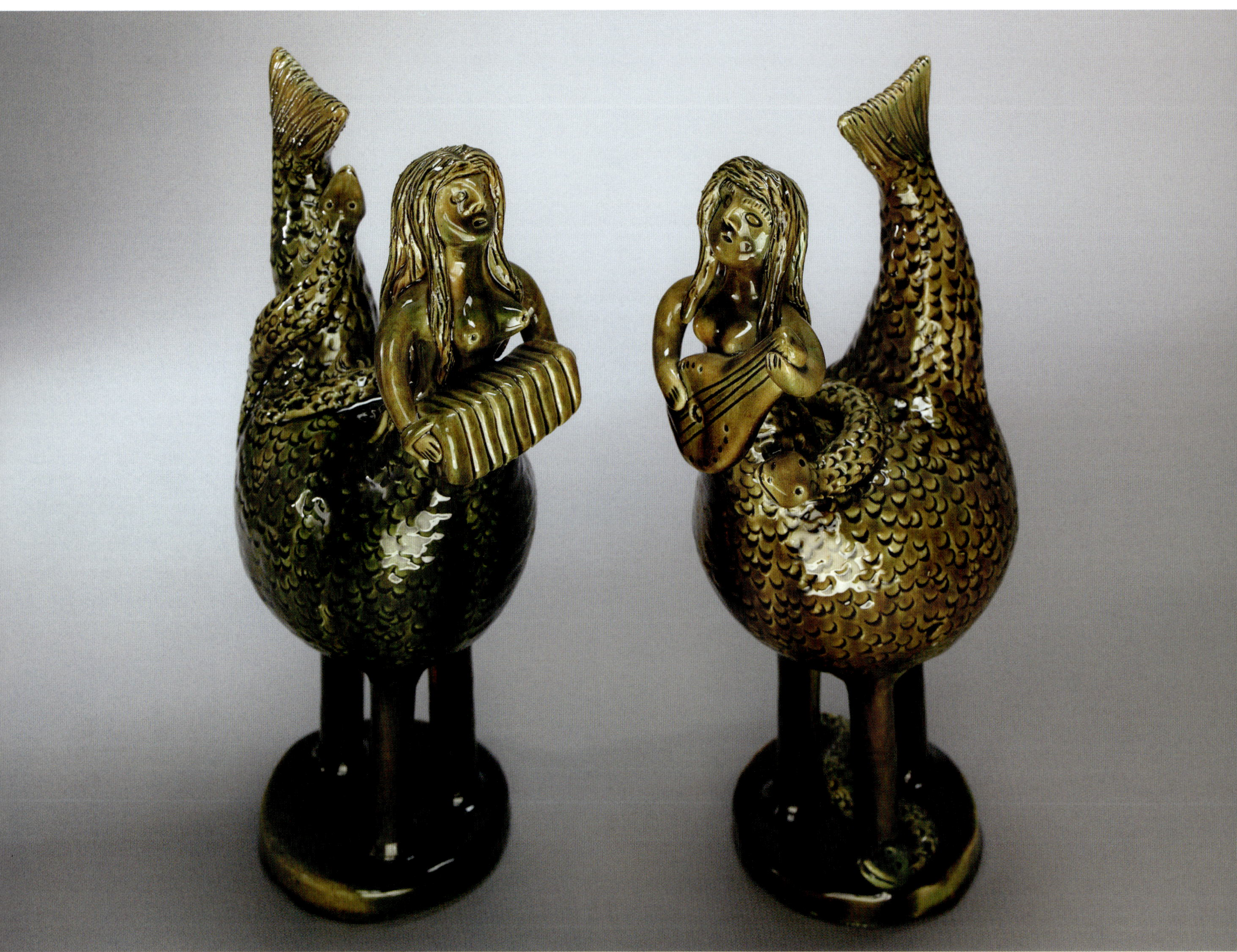

facing
ANTÓNIO RAMALHO
Two sirens playing guitar and accordion recall the rich classical and medieval bestiary of mythical sea creatures.

furious winds, which were believed to render it unnavigable by mortal seafarers. Sea monsters were said to increase in size and assume ever more horrific appearances as one sailed away from the known African coast towards India and the East. The seas of the world, for São Isidoro and classical literature alike, were like the sun, moon, sky and air, in constant motion. In Roman times, according to the chronicler Titus Livius (59 BC–AD 17), the River Lima in northern Portugal was called Flumen Oblivionis, the River Lethe in Hades, whose waters brought forgetfulness. Beliefs like these might have encouraged early medieval concepts of the sea to adapt some of its hellish attributes. Until relatively recently, there was a belief that Portugal's northern mountains were connected to the sea by subterranean rivers—"the arms of the sea."[121] Hieronymus Bosch's *Temptation of Saint Anthony* (1495) depicts hellish visions of fetid water, fish and monstrous sea creatures that suggest the two places could be similarly envisaged. In twentieth-century Portugal, popular beliefs still held that the dead made water become stagnant.[122] No wonder Gil Vicente staged the judgment of the soul on a featureless shore by the dark ocean in his *Boat Plays*, written between 1516 and 1519, or that Jorge Colaço painted the same scene in all its gloom and forlornness on ceramic friezes, *azulejos*, on the exterior of the Palace Hotel in Buçaco in 1907. The undifferentiated and formless nature of the ocean is the closest approximation to the imagination of the void, a dark, inchoate infinitude that swallows all.

The three land masses existed in a distinct temporal order of their own. While Europe constituted the world after humankind's fall and exile, Asia was believed to have been the original Paradise. One of the Church's concerns with navigation was that seafarers risked incurring the wrath of God for attempting to re-enter Paradise ahead of the appointed time of judgment. This was refuted by a different interpretation that argued that God's favour towards such endeavours was an indication that the Apocalypse, and with it the restoration of Paradise, was imminent. Exploration and the Discoveries, therefore, were closely associated with apocalyptic thought in which the mortal world would be destroyed to give rise to the Paradise of a Thousand Years.

References to supernatural water spirits in nineteenth-century Portuguese popular thought and literature may have been derived from some of these more ancient sources or conceived of independently. Coelho[123] and Vasconcellos[124] give extensive lists of streams, creeks, rivers and wells associated with one or more stories related to the Moorish enchantresses who were believed to inhabit them. These enchantresses were ambiguous creatures that could be either treacherous or generous, as João Manuel Esteves, the mask maker, recounted to me in Ousilhão in 2011.[125] However, despite rich mythological and theological antecedents, few descriptions of popular nineteenth-century maritime lore have been recorded.

The superstitious sixteenth-century attitudes towards the oceans soon gave way to navigational science, but given the continued denunciations made in the 1534 Constituições of Évora and the 1639 Constituições of Lamego, popular beliefs on the importance of water in divination, curative practices, blessing animals and other magical incantations appear to have continued unabated. The nineteenth-century folklorist Leite Vasconcellos gave plentiful examples of beliefs from all over Portugal on the curative qualities of water, the most efficacious of which appear to have coincided with the night of São João (24 June).[126]

Vasconcellos was fascinated by remnant beliefs in mermaids (beings that are half girl and half fish) and harpies (half girl and half bird). In the provinces of Minho, Beira Alta, Trás-os-Montes and Galicia he collected stories about mermaids that enabled him to supposedly trace them back to Syria and Nineveh, where such creatures were born from seafoam and were said to attract unwary sailors with their beautiful songs.[127] Only later did these creatures take on ambiguous qualities, sometimes causing shipwrecks and death while at other times guiding lost ships to safety and nursing the sick back to health. In both their physical description and their moral ambiguities, mermaids bear a close relation to the Moorish enchantresses of inland mythology. This possible contiguity might have arisen far earlier, and although visual representations are rare, the twelfth- and thirteenth-century monastery of Travanca, in Amarante, contains two stone sculptures of sirens holding fish. The historian José Mattoso interprets these images as once possessing either a protective or exorcistic purpose while also symbolizing the bountiful fish harvests to be found there.[128]

Although the oceans were, in the fifteenth and sixteenth centuries, partly domesticated by the invention and application of new scientific instruments, long sea voyages were still seen as perilous undertakings. Such fears were abated by rituals designed to sanctify the waters and the vessels that sailed on them. Rivers, streams and fountains that saints had used for bathing were thought to have miraculous qualities,[129] and the seas in the middle of the world were considered to have been partly sanctified by having come into contact with saintly bodies.[130] So efficacious were such contagions that the seaborne arrival of São Vicente in Lisbon was sufficient in itself to consecrate Portugal as a Christian kingdom. Throughout the fifteenth and sixteenth centuries the Royal House of Avis provided impetus for Portugal's maritime expansion and granted São Vicente special devotion, identifying him as the protector of maritime voyages and consecrating the magnificent church of São Vicente de Fora in Lisbon's Alfama district in his honour.

Between 1490 and 1520 the sea was consecrated to Heaven through its symbolic incorporation into a religious architecture known as the Manueline style, which combined fantasy and eloquence and brought the ocean's enormity into the spaces of Portugal's cities and towns. The style features knotted ropes, anchors, armorial spheres and heraldic insignia all carved in stone in a complex symbolic language representing the domestication of the oceans. The ropes and anchors bind heraldic insignia and the prowess of their owners and, in visual terms, convey their mastership over harnessing the void itself. At the Church of Jesus in Setúbal, a vaulted roof is supported by six columns sculpted as vertical twisted rope that seems to hang from the arches.

The Manueline style especially excited twentieth-century travel writers. David Evans described the famous window at Tomar's Convent of Christ as "flanked by two coral encrusted masts woven with seaweed, writhing with octopus tendrils and bobbing with cork-buoyed ropes."[131] Sacheverell Sitwell, on seeing the chapter house of the same convent, wrote half in awe and disbelief: "It appears to emerge there above that Paladian cloister as though coming up, dripping from the sea,"[132] and José Saramago compared the vault over the transept at the monastery of Santa Maria to the hull of a giant ship turned upside down.[133]

São Vicente was not the sole saint in Portugal to be recognized as the protector of seamen; Nossa Senhora, Santa Catarina, Santa Bárbara, São Pedro and Santo António were all believed to safeguard seafarers and fishermen. In the fishing port of Aveiro and elsewhere, the Galician saint São Gonçalo, sometimes identified with São Telmo, mentioned in *Os Lusíadas* (canto 5, v. 18) for the "fire" he sends to warn endangered ships of disasters, is also considered a powerful protector from seaborne danger. Seafarers could also gain protection, more surprisingly, from "witches," who dressed in white and could sometimes be seen dancing on the waves.[134] Others noted that in the Algarve, fishermen sometimes took witches to sea to divine where they should best drop their nets. Rose Macaulay, in her travelogue *Fabled Shore*,[135] recounted that even in the 1940s, an image of Santa Catarina guarded in the chapel at the mouth of the estuary in Portimão was carried to the sea in an annual procession "to bless the fishing." While people probably lost little of the fear associated with the ocean, popular religion at least invented ritual practices and holy weapons that seafarers and adventurers used to protect their long passages. As José Mattoso argues, popular religion did more than ecclesiastic doctrine to help the Portuguese overcome their Biblical fears.[136]

LUÍS DE CAMÕES AND THE INVENTION OF MARITIME ADVENTURISM

The nineteenth- and twentieth-century positivist philosopher and folklorist Teófilo Braga, noting the strong connection between literature and seamanship, insisted that Portugal's historical consciousness had been born out of its maritime adventures. Writing in 1911, he opined that Camões had "translated the Portuguese sensibility into the most profound revelation characteristic of the Lusitanian ethos."[137] This view that linked the seafaring tradition to a distinct literature and language whose style and subject encapsulated the nation's spirit has become the cornerstone of a cultural politics energetically pursued by successive Republican, totalitarian and democratic states.[138] It has been widely disseminated through education, tourist promotion and cultural patronage, as well as through the construction of monuments and the sponsorship of public commemorations, spectacles and related ceremonies, confirming Pessoa's wry dictum that "the imperialism of grammarians runs deeper and endures longer than that of generals."[139]

Much later and under widely different political circumstances, the influential Portuguese anthropologist Jorge Dias affirmed Braga's argument on the vital link between the sea and national identity: "The attractive force of the Atlantic, the great sea inhabited by tempests and mysteries, was the Nation's soul and it was with that the history of Portugal was written."[140] This view has become widely accepted and can be found in the humanities and social sciences and in a wide range of literary genres, philosophical schools and historical interpretations. Fernando Pessoa unequivocally declared, "My motherland is the Portuguese language,"[141] and, more recently, Fernando Dacosta claimed: "We are a people from the shadows, and not from the radiant light; we are more akin to the moon and the ocean, than to the sun and the solid earth."[142] Elsewhere, quoting João de Castro Osório, Dacosta insisted, less ambiguously, that "Portugal became a nation when she first set out to sail the high seas and began to write about it."[143]

In the sixteenth century Portuguese became a fully developed national language that distinguished itself from Galician and began its separate evolution. It adopted prose over poetry and, by applying strict rules of composition and a more rigorous narrative style, developed the chronicle as a literary genre. Many of the caravels leaving Portugal on their voyages carried chroniclers whose works,

facing
JORGE COLAÇO
Triton Carrying Venus, 1907
Palace Hotel, Buçaco

when they survived, sometimes became complexly entangled with those of other chroniclers. The journal of Álvaro Velho, who accompanied da Gama's ship, was freely used by Camões, as were the accounts penned by the anonymous writers of various popular pamphlets describing maritime disasters that were eventually compiled in the eighteenth century under the title *História Trágico-Marítima*. There also began to emerge in the sixteenth century a literary genre that combined romance with ethnographic or historical description, myth and fact. In its earliest florescence this movement included the works of Fernão Lopes, João de Barros, Damião de Góis and Diogo do Couto. Luís de Camões's (1524–80) *Os Lusíadas* (The Lusiads), which combined mythical and factual strains and narratives with a strong national fervour, attracted wide popular and political appeal and in the nineteenth century became consecrated as a national epic. Written in verse, *Os Lusíadas* created the matrix that conflated Portuguese history and literature into a powerfully persuasive literary genre that, for almost half a millennium, tied national identity to the country's maritime adventures.

Camões began his work unapologetically by proclaiming: "Arms are my theme, and those matchless heroes / Who from Portugal's far western shores / By oceans where none had ventured / Voyaged to Taprobana and beyond, / Enduring hazards and assaults / Such as drew on more than human prowess / Among far distant peoples, to proclaim / A New Age and win undying fame."[144] He goes on to not only describe Vasco da Gama's epic voyage and adventures to discover a transoceanic route to the East but also, through clever literary techniques, retell the nation's foundation narrative and look seventy years into the future to foretell the effects da Gama's exploits would have on Portugal.

The country's foundation narratives are encapsulated in da Gama's descriptions of the Portuguese's deeds to the Sultan of Malindi[145] and through the exposition of paintings da Gama gives his loyal Hindu friend Catual.[146] The future prizes resulting from da Gama's newly found sea route are foretold by an admiring muse who uses her powers of prophecy to reveal them to him and his crew during their temporary respite on the Island of Love during their return journey.[147]

Camões interweaves three separate and distinct sets of immortals and supernatural-like creatures that intervene in the progress and setbacks of the expedition. First is the Christian God, who testifies to Portuguese valour and recalls the millenarian responsibility entrusted them:[148] "You Portuguese, as few as you are valiant, / Make light of your slender forces; / Through martyrdom, in its manifold forms, / You spread the message of eternal life; / Heaven has made it your destiny / To do many and mighty deeds / For Christendom, despite being few and weak, / For this, O Christ, do you exalt the meek!"[149] Second are the Olympian mortals who, hidden from mortal sight, argued and wove the tapestry of their adventures. Jupiter, Mars and Venus acknowledge da Gama's qualities and help him and his crew on their voyage, while Bacchus, cast as India's ruler, fearful of losing his kingdom and jealous of mortal courage, conspires to destroy their aspirations. The third supernatural is the anthropomorphized fury of the storm, Adamastor, who threatens to destroy the caravels as they attempt to round the Cape of Good Hope. There are no strange hybrid creatures, sea monsters or mystical fatalism in *Os Lusíadas*, except those derived directly from classical mythology, which are clearly separated from the chronicle itself. The distinctions Camões makes between these different categories of creatures and

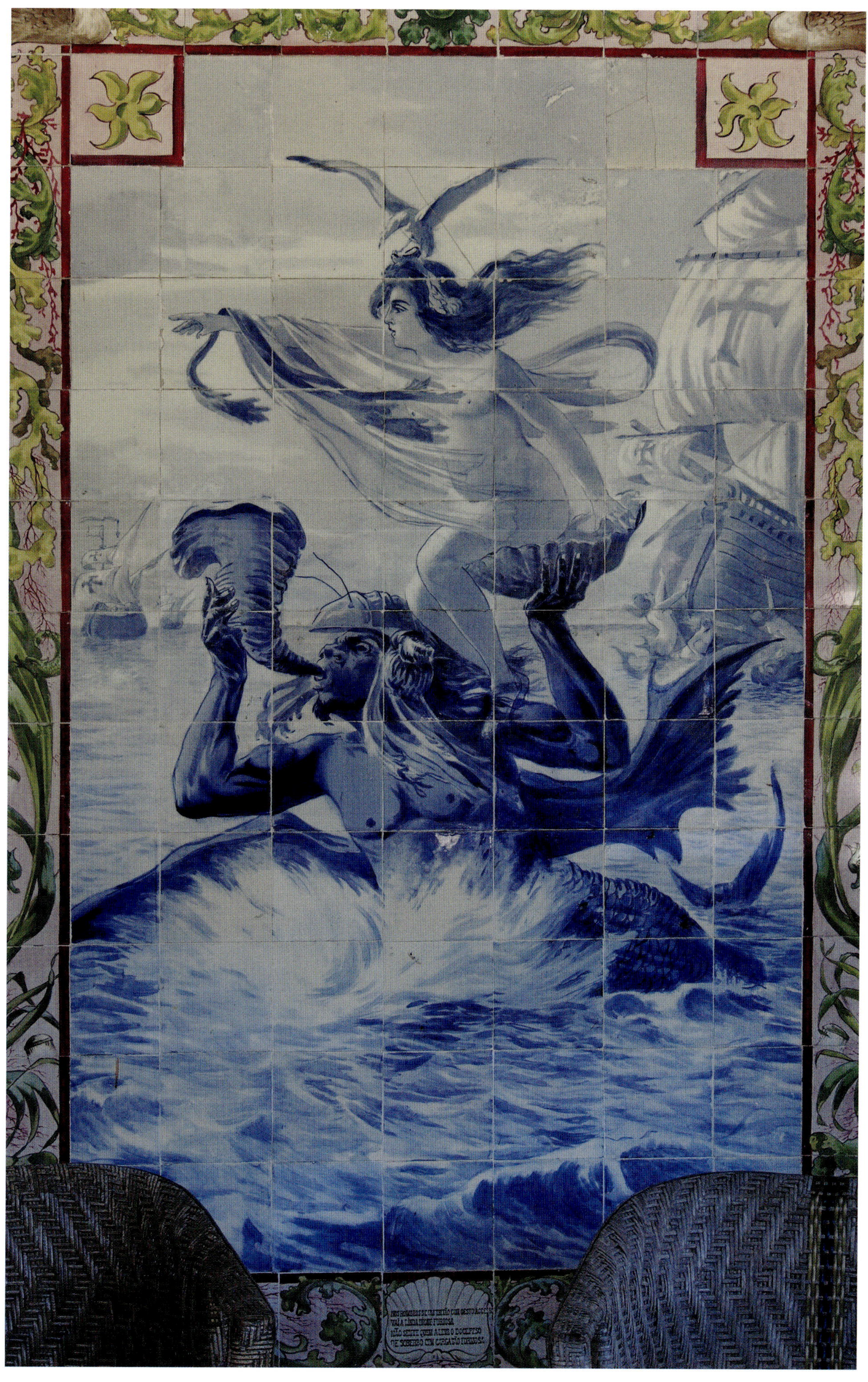

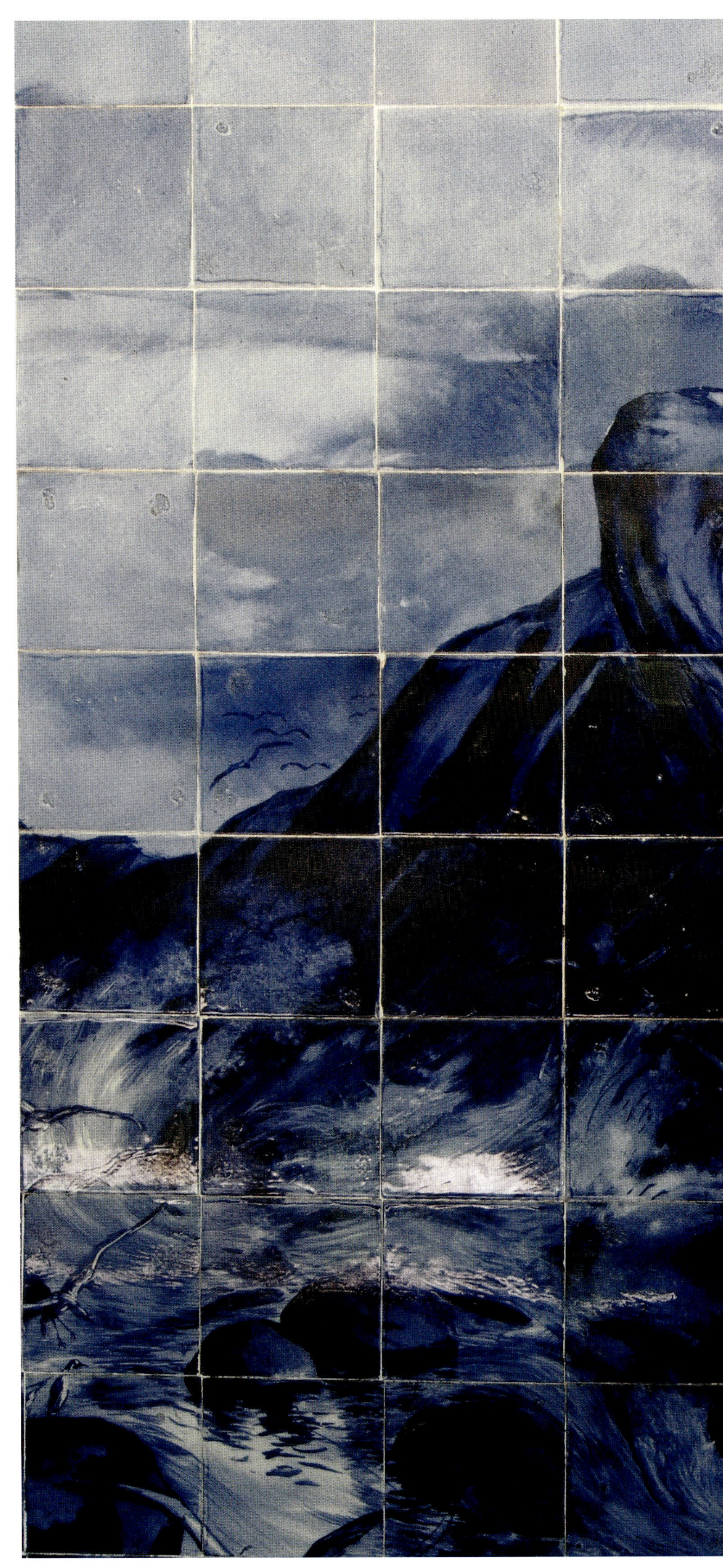

JORGE COLAÇO
Adamastor, 1907
Palace Hotel, Buçaco

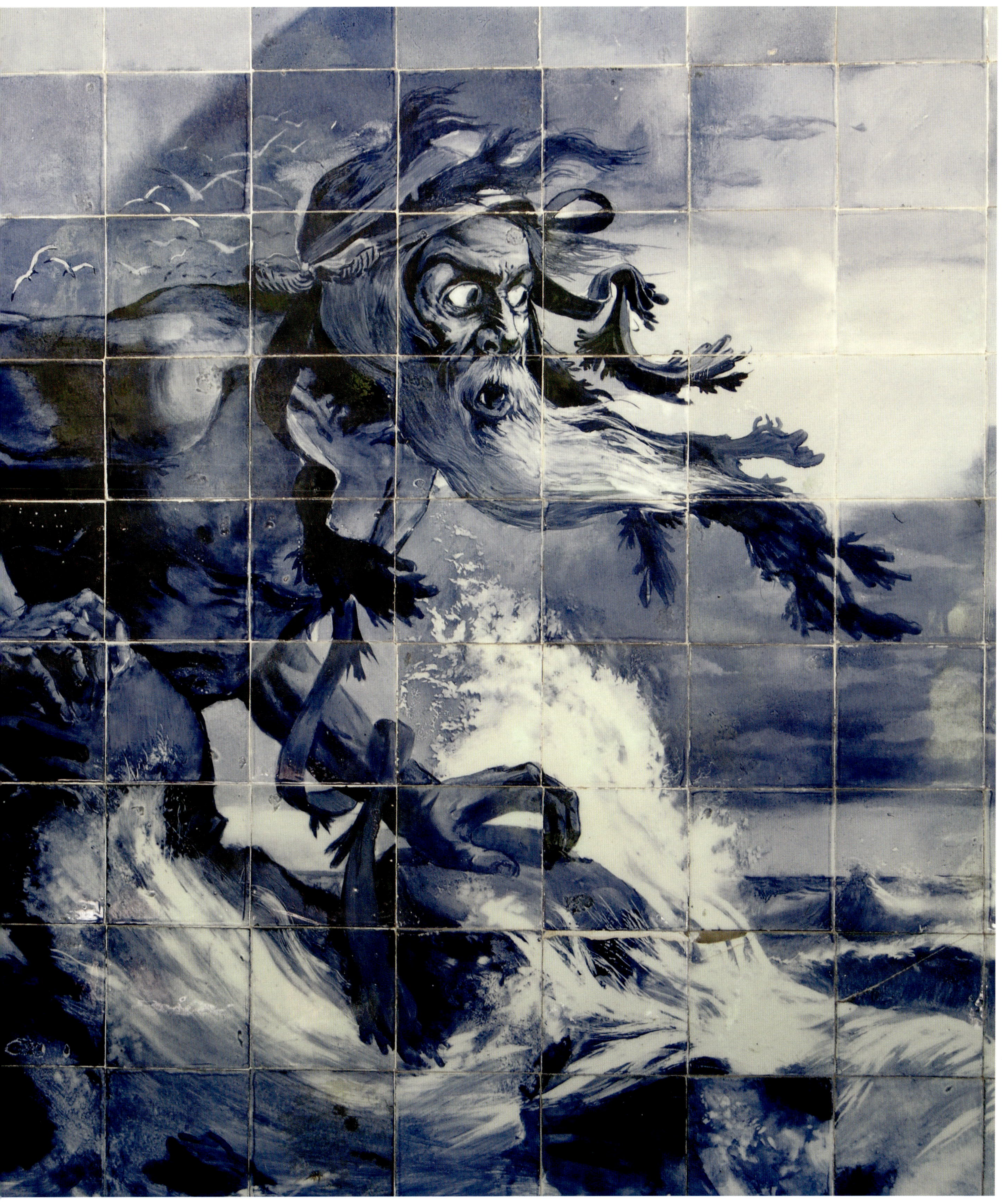

his acknowledgement of the difference between the allegorical Olympians and the Christian reality upheld by the Portuguese define the modern nature of his work, which coincides with the beginning of a new urban mentality that contributed to the development of European cosmopolitanism. Mircea Eliade was clear about Camões's intellectual contribution, which "introduced into the European mental universe and validated aesthetically a whole exotic oceanography and biology."[150]

The text of *Os Lusíadas* is almost equally divided between narrating da Gama's feat of seamanship and iterating Portuguese history, arms and moral integrity.[151] Da Gama's journey is divided into two phases, the first of which covers his voyage from Portugal down the west coast of Africa to the Cape of Good Hope—that is to say, the charted sea route. At the point when he enters the tip of Africa and passes the gateway to the unknown world, marked by the menacing and stormy fury of Adamastor, the second phase of the adventure begins. The epic revolves on this pivot between the navigation of the Atlantic's charted waters and the adventurer's descent into the unknown seas of the East. Only by completing this passage was a malign and prodigious nature domesticated, European ignorance dispelled, riches and fame obtained and the divinely sanctioned apostolic mission re-energized.

Da Gama himself occupies the centre of Camões's epic, his greatness and talent repeatedly compared to those of Ulysses in Homer's eighth-century BC epic *The Odyssey*. Camões challenges Homer as a writer of fables. Whereas Homer staged *The Odyssey* within the domesticated confines of the Mediterranean Sea, Camões chronicles the Portuguese's real confrontation with a much more dangerous, tempestuous ocean at the world's end: "Boast no more about the subtle Greeks / Or the long Odyssey of Trojan Aeneas; / Enough of the Oriental conquests / Of great Alexander and of Trajan; / I sing of the famous Portuguese / To whom both Mars and Neptune bowed. / Abandon all the ancient Muse revered, / A loftier code of honour has appeared."[152] Portugal, in Camões's work, is no longer preoccupied with theological decadence or ancient divinities. Instead it asserts its modern superiority over their previously uncritical adoration and mythological stature. This is the world of the Renaissance at its most accomplished.

The affinity between *The Odyssey* and *Os Lusíadas* runs deeper than Camões suspected. Ulysses was modelled on another of Homer's heroes, Achilles, whose adventures were described in *The Iliad*. Achilles, it has been argued, was the first Western heroic character to combine valour, strength and determination with wisdom to triumph over overwhelming adversity,[153] much like Camões's own heroes. All three epics of heroism describe rites of passage: the voyagers leave their safe, everyday European worlds and enter a period of separation and estrangement, which in *Os Lusíadas* is marked by the furious intervention of Adamastor and continues until the travellers return to their society of origin. Nothing, however, is the same after da Gama's return. Not only has the explorer undergone an apotheosis to become a hero and an immortal, but the geographical and ethnographic knowledge of the Orient he has brought back has radically changed Europe's cosmology, its economic future and its cultural identity, which could no longer be fashioned from a diminished classical Greek and Roman alterity but now needed to be reconstructed anew in opposition to a more startling revelation of an Oriental Other.

Fernando Dacosta has reminded us that Portuguese maritime adventurism has another, less discussed melancholic aspect to it drawn from the trauma of departure, separation and longing that long periods of absence inevitably entail.[154] There are places in Lisbon impregnated with sorrow and other sites that paradoxically exude both joy and disappointment. The fleets and caravels departed Lisbon from Belém, at a place since named the Beach of Tears. There, for generations, families and friends gathered to share their anguish and utter their farewells to those departing, while the neighbourhood of Santa Catarina, high above the Tagus, provided a lookout point where family and friends afflicted by loss or longing would gather in the hope of sighting the returning ships carrying their loved ones. The *História Trágico-Marítima, Os Lusíadas* and other fifteenth- and sixteenth-century chronicles also mentioned this sea-induced malaise that brought terror, sickness, privation and insecurity and gave rise to masses of tortured memories that were never mentioned in the public ceremonies dedicated to maritime heroism.[155] "In gloom I sail in agony," Álvaro Brito wrote, "of all that lies untold. I am about to round the stormy seas of misery."[156]

These traumas were not only the stigmata borne by seafarers but shared by those they left behind, who never knew whether they would see their loved ones ever again. "Their tears," Maria Luísa Guerra movingly writes,

> were the mirror of the tears of all the mothers, of all the fathers, of all the sons, of all the wives, of all the girlfriends, of neighbours, friends and relatives that year after year came to say goodbye, with the same sorrowful heart. A whole people, afflicted and stupefied, looking at the ships as if they departed for another world, was an experience that shaped souls.[157]

For Guerra it was these experiences of a seafaring nation—the absence of security or foreknowledge, the anguish mixed with anticipation, the feelings of abandonment, the fear of solitude and death and the forsaking of love and familial affinity—that fashioned Portugal into a melancholic nation.[158] "They navigated between two infinites; the silence of the stars and the melody of the waters, with neither the outline of hills or tree trunks. Only the distance, each time greater and more transparent. Only the same faceless water."[159]

While maritime heroism found its expression in literature, the tragedy and distress caused by the sea gave rise to a different expression in music; its unique dirges were based on themes of unrequited love, pain, separation, crimes of passion, jealousy, poverty, sadness and fatalism, but also luck and hope. Fado music took root in the first half of the nineteenth century in Lisbon's poorer Alfama and Mouraria neighbourhoods, mainly inhabited by fishermen and their merchant wives who sold their catches,[160] areas with complex histories and varied popular cultures.[161] The early twentieth-century sociologist Oliveira Martins emphasized fado's strong attachment to the sea:

> The moaning tones of the sound of the guitar can be heard throughout the whole of the west coast; these monotonous songs like the sound of the sea, sad like the life of sailors, unfurling with the night over the Mondego, over the Tagus and over the Sado, translating unconscious memories of some ancient race that have lingered on our coast, giving us a vague hope of a future world to discover and lost lands to conquer.[162]

Teixeira de Pascoaes described the *saudade* or "longing" that this music expresses as the most unique and distinguishing feature of the Portuguese spirit,[163] while for Guerra, fado is the most audible expression of the distress and misery of

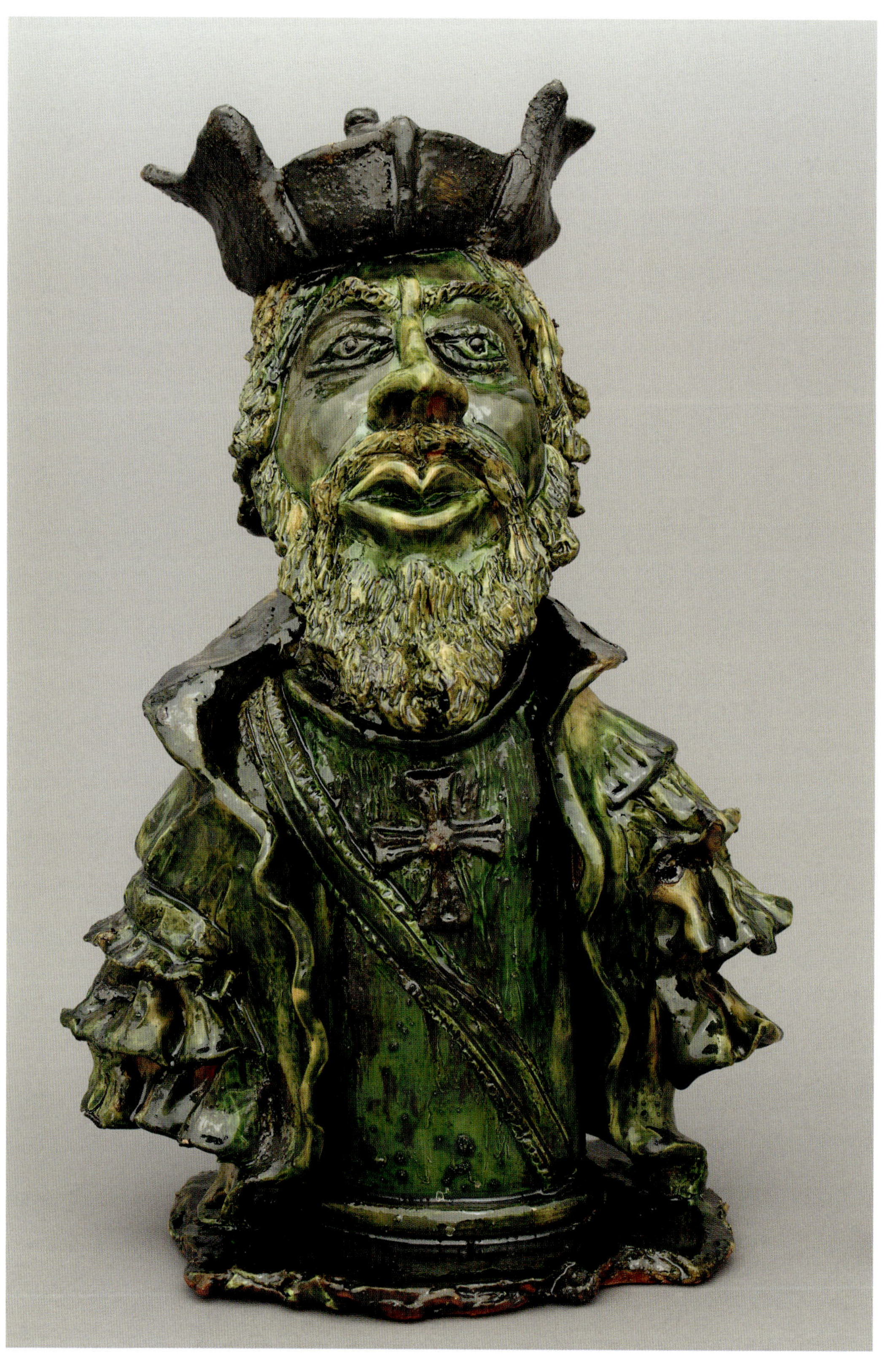

above
LAURINDA PIAS
Vasco da Gama, 2012

facing, left
LAURINDA PIAS
Luís de Camões, 2012

facing, right
LAURINDA PIAS
Infante Don Henrique de Avis (Prince Henry the Navigator), 2012

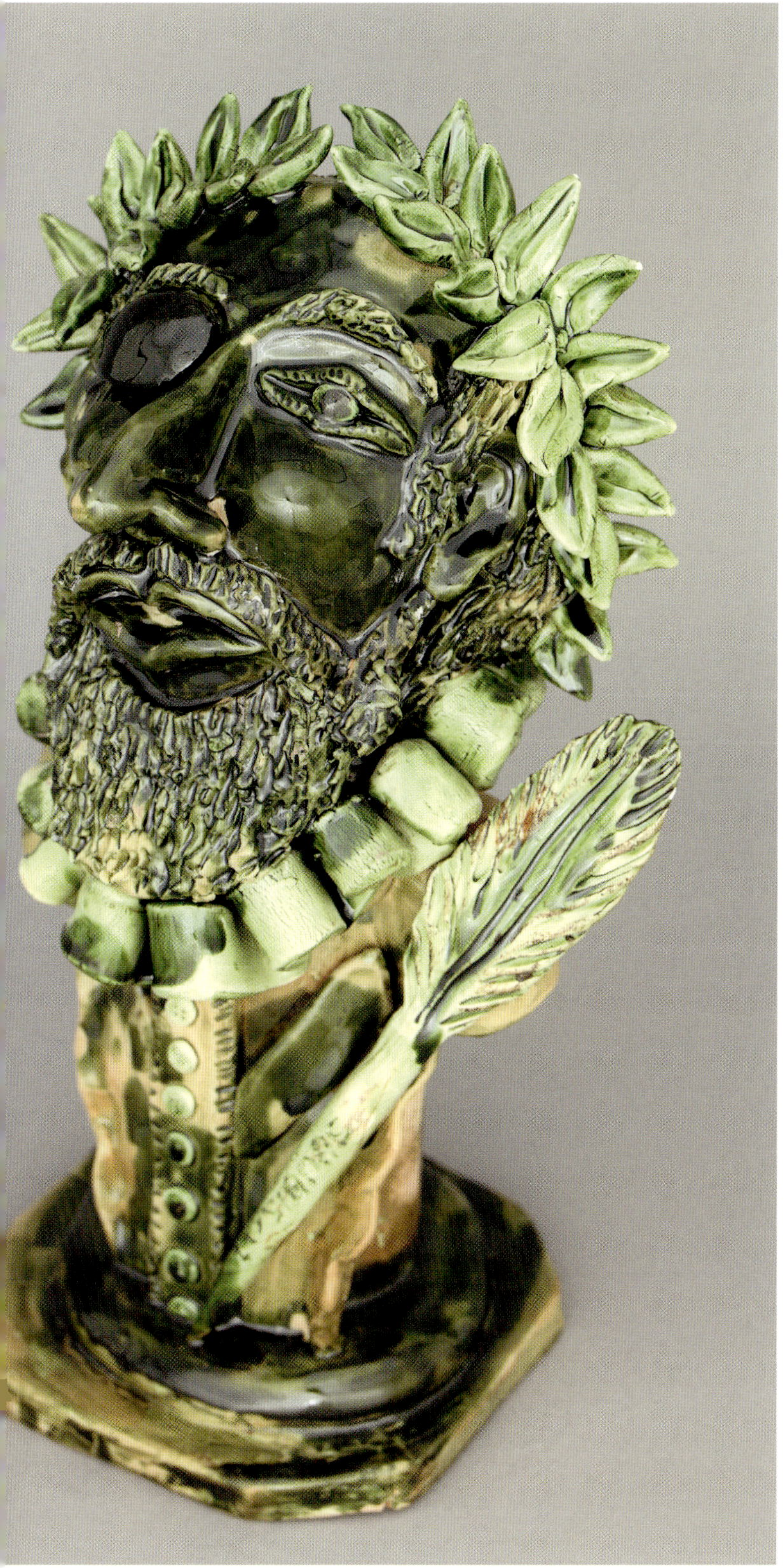

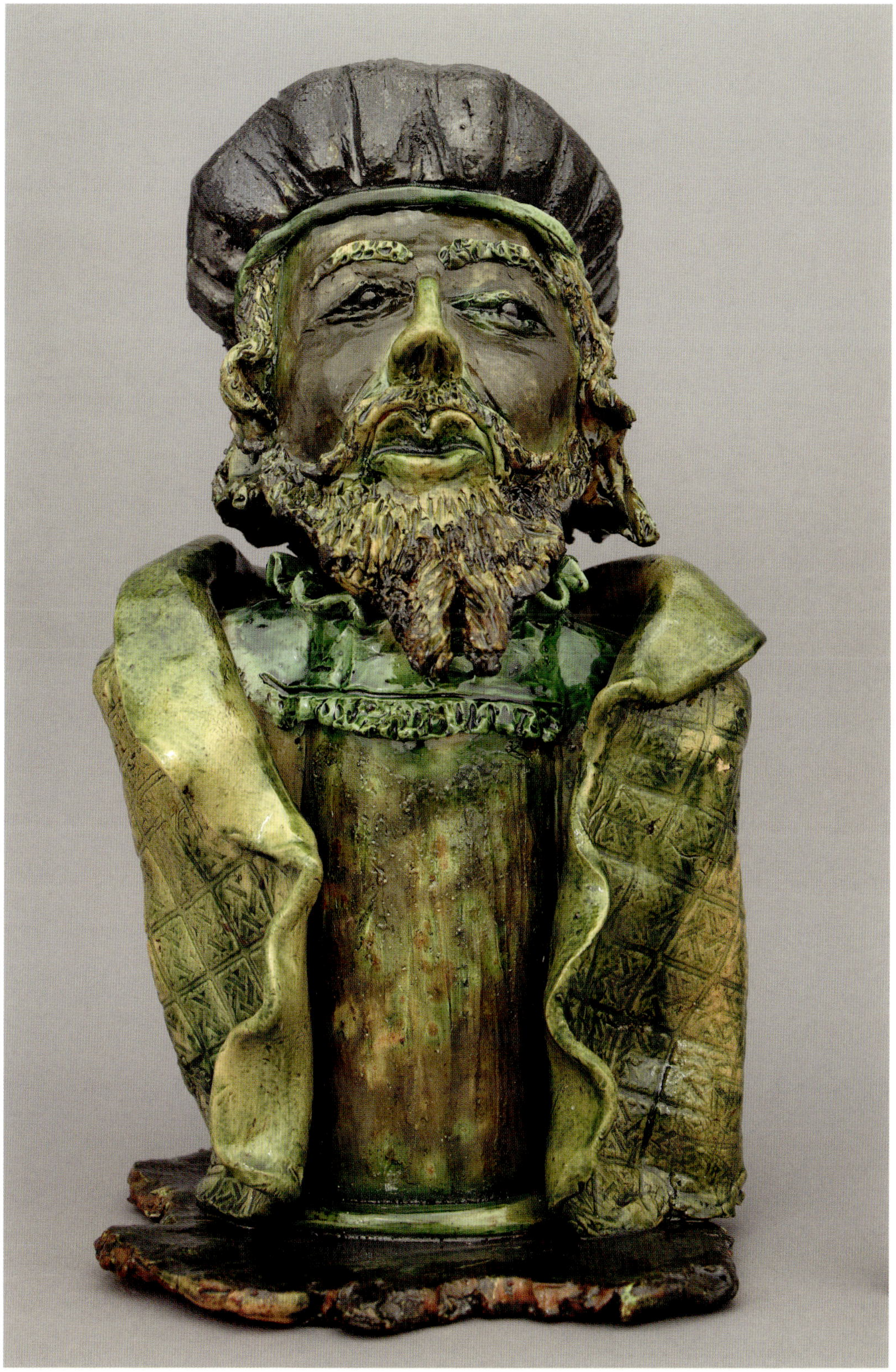

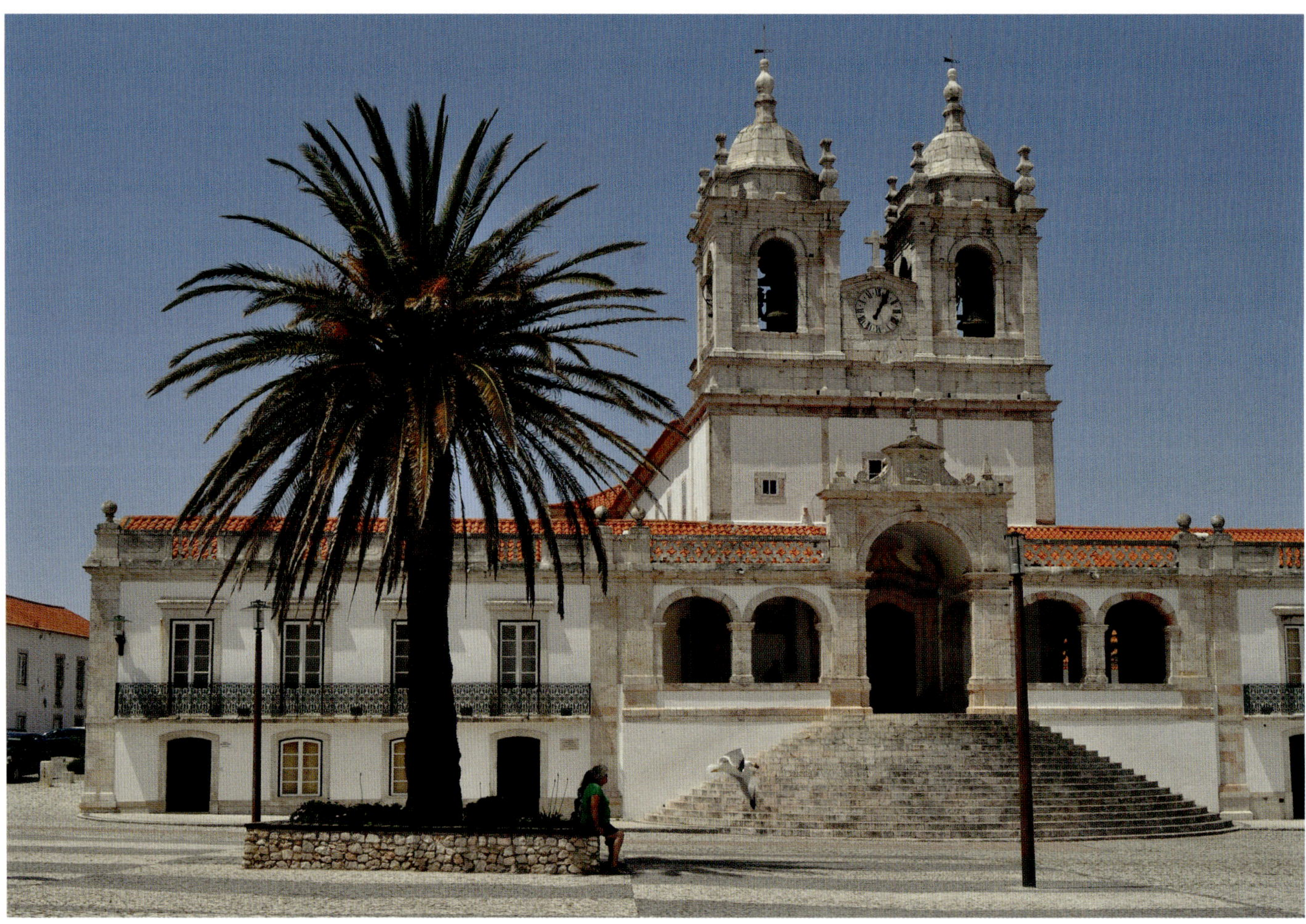

above
The sixteenth-century pilgrimage church of Nossa Senhora da Nazaré was a place of intense devotion focused on ensuring divine protection of the lives of Nazaré's fishermen on the stormy Atlantic waters.

facing
Registo of Nossa Senhora da Nazaré, c. 2010.

generations of Portuguese seafarers. Both authors, regardless of whether they regard the music as primarily associated with heroism or trauma, agree that fado became the most poignant expression of the nation's soul.[164]

Camões's account of the discovery of the maritime route to India had, by the nineteenth century, made him one of Portugal's most lauded historical heroes, his tomb resting alongside that of Vasco da Gama in the Jerónimos Monastery close to the Beach of Tears. So esteemed had he become that the unveiling of the first monument in his honour, in Lisbon in 1867, was solemnly presided over by King D. Luís. His nineteenth-century adulation was evident in the age's second wave of Romantic literature on sea voyages by such authors as Francisco Bordalo, João Carvalho Viana, Pedro Celestíno, José Augustinho and Augusto Branco, which his work inspired. Camões's standing is also attested to in the many busts made of him by respected sculptors.[165]

In 1880, the tricentenary of Camões's death, he was feted with conferences, public lectures, exhibitions, musical commissions and new editions of his works.[166] The Geographical Society of Lisbon organized conferences and lectures that acknowledged the nation's spirit that his work embodied,[167] and in the following year António Gonçalves (1848–1932) was commissioned to make a monument to the author for the city of Coimbra. At a conference in honour of Camões at the University of Coimbra in 1924, Mendes dos Remédios described him as a "symbol of patriotism and Christian belief";[168] the president of the Lisbon Municipal Council proclaimed him the "greatest exponent of the Portuguese race" and *Os Lusíadas* the "repository of its traditions."[169] *Os Lusíadas* continued to be revered and celebrated for its authentic revelation of the national spirit throughout the period of the Estado Novo. It was so highly endorsed that in 1960, Salazar's minister of education, Francisco de Paula Leite Pinto, referred to it as Portugal's “sacred book of patriotism.”[170] Episodes were illustrated in *azulejos*, painted ceramic friezes, by Jorge Colaço and João Vaz at the Palace Hotel in Buçaco and in the hallway of the Central Library, the location of the former Vasco da Gama Institute, in Panjin, Goa. Camões's birthday, 10 June, was one of Portugal's first national holidays and was later reserved by the military for the awarding of decorations and medals for combatants in the colonial wars.[171] Luís de Camões was transformed into one of the most potent symbols of imperial Portugal.

THE MARITIME TRADITION AND THE ESTADO NOVO

In his 1995 article on the heroes of the Estado Novo, Arlindo Caldeira focuses on the shifts, between the Republican period and the dictatorship, in the hagiography and celebration of the nation's heroes. After the 1926 military coup, official ceremonies marking religious events and deeds of the Portuguese monarchy were introduced into the national calendar, while figures previously given importance under the former Republican regime, such as Gomes Freire de Andrade, the founder of Portuguese liberalism, and Egas Moniz, an advisor to Portugal's first king, Afonso Henriques, disappeared from school textbooks. Even the importance of the Marquis of Pombal was understated by the dictatorship, perhaps because of his involvement with the secularization of the state and the expulsion of the Jesuits, while the achievements of João III (reign 1521–57), particularly his institutionalization of religion and government, were given greater attention.

The heroes of the dictatorship were men of action like Camões and da Gama, but also those who combined great deeds with an ascetic, mystical and solitary love of the nation and service to God, like the Infante D. Henrique and Nuno Álvares

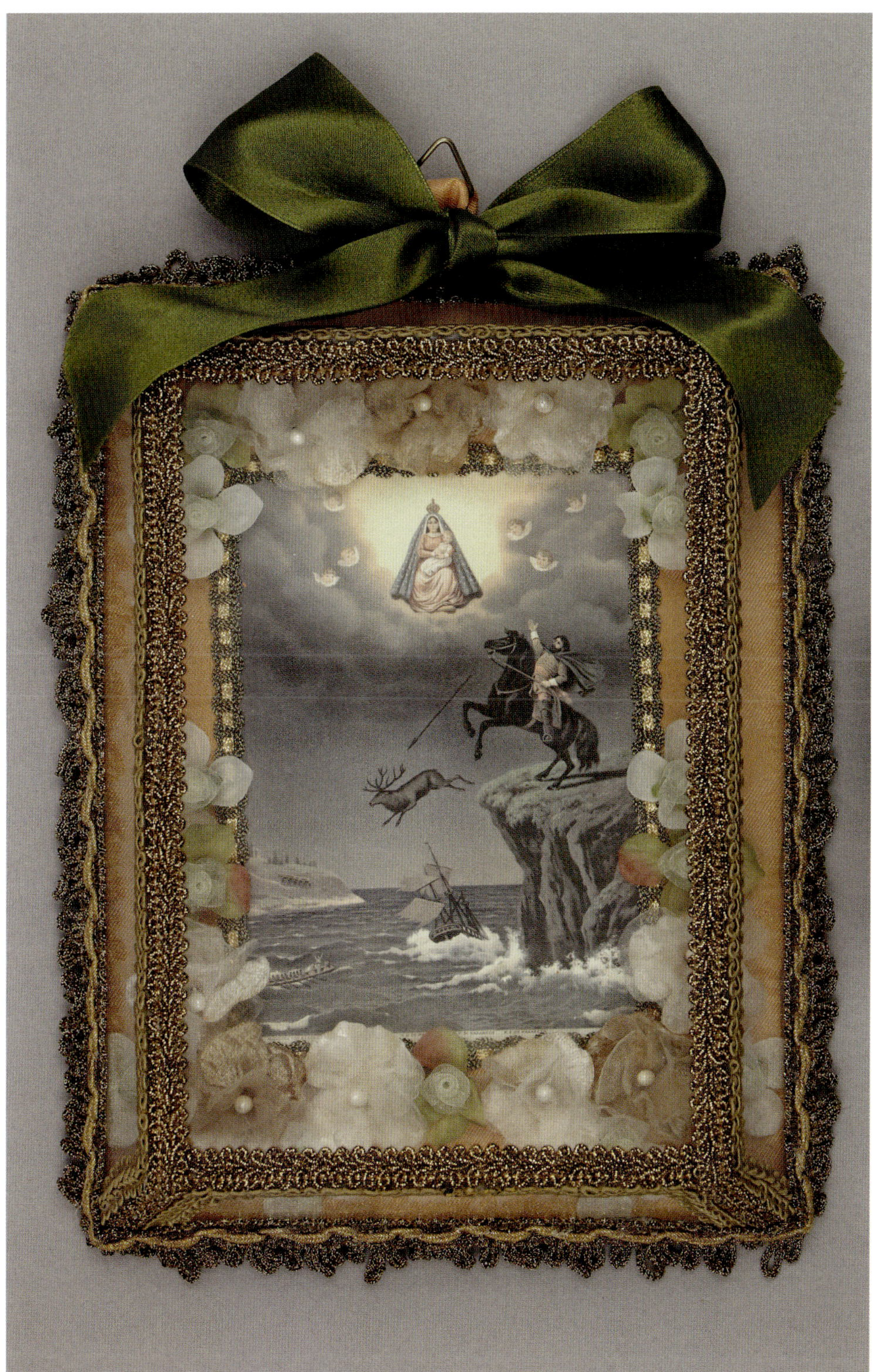

Pereira, the Santo Condestável. These idealized heroes may have personified Salazar's own feelings and values.[172]

The Portuguese seafaring tradition was more important to the dictatorship than it had been for the Republic. It provided a means of plotting the

facing
Fishing boats on the canals in Aveiro, now used to give tourist cruises, were designed with supposedly Phoenician-style heads. The paintings and cartoons decorating them are more recent innovations.

course of the national spirit from the fifteenth and sixteenth centuries to the present. Portuguese fishing communities had always appeared different from others elsewhere and had created a culture of their own based on language, popular religious devotion, communal organization, independence and, until quite recently in some areas, dress. In Póvoa, for example, fishing men and women were divided into companies, each responsible for their own boats and nets, that shared knowledge and information about changes in the sandbars and banks and the movements of the sardine shoals. Captains and crews discussed their daily work together, communities had internal processes for settling disputes and companies had their own cooperative credit unions to provide their members with partial security outside the fishing season (October–March). The profits from these corporate ventures, much admired by the Estado Novo, were shared. These were insular communities with deep religious roots in which womenfolk were accustomed to spending long nightly vigils praying for their menfolk at sea and sometimes cursing their divine protectors and protectoresses when they failed to look after them. The deeply felt pleas for protection from the waves are evident in the varied and plentiful offerings beseeching saints and miraculous virgins that were displayed in the many coastal churches. Ex-votos and model boats hung from church walls and niches, such as at Caminha (Chapel of the Almshouse)[173] and in Setúbal in the Chapel of the Senhor de Bomfin, which sixty years ago was described as "full of votive paintings of naïve nature and . . . hung with enough internal organs and limbs of wax to fill the most dreariest and most horrible of anatomical museums."[174] The discrete character of these communities whose inhabitants were supposedly descended from the Phoenician trading centres of Tyre and Sidon was celebrated and folklorized by painters and writers, particularly travel writers, for their exotic origins.[175]

In some places, like Póvoa, ex-votos had already been transferred to museums by the mid-1960s, while today, despite careful searches, the churches in ports like Figueira da Foz, Nazaré and Mira are bare of such devotions. Model boats are still made in Nazaré, but the poetry of the age-old ships hanging from church rafters has perhaps best been retained in the boats carved from walnut by João de Deus Ortega, an artist with strong Christian faith, in the village of Sendas. His works convey easily identifiable Lusitanian themes and imagery: Jesus and the apostles in a boat inscribed "*Vamos á Pesca*" ("We're going to fish"); Afonso Henriques on horseback; or the 1960s folk music group Trio Odemira, as well as other Portuguese musicians.

Although Portuguese local sardine fisheries survived into the twentieth century, the long-distance Cod Fleets moored at Aveiro, Viana da Foz, Lima and Porto were in an acute long-term decline from the sixteenth century onwards, due to the greater profitability of trade and commerce along the newly opened sea lanes to India and Brazil.[176] An attempt was not made to revive the fleets until the early nineteenth century, but it was short-lived because of changes in duty and taxation; by the end of the First World War only eleven such vessels remained.

From 1934 the state energetically intervened in the fisheries, both to rebuild the long-distance fleet and to help lift communities out of the poverty that government indifference had fostered. The state's strategy was to conflate local conditions with national priorities so that local assistance would benefit the nation as a whole. Such a strategy, like that enacted in rural areas, enabled the Estado Novo to deviously politicize fishing

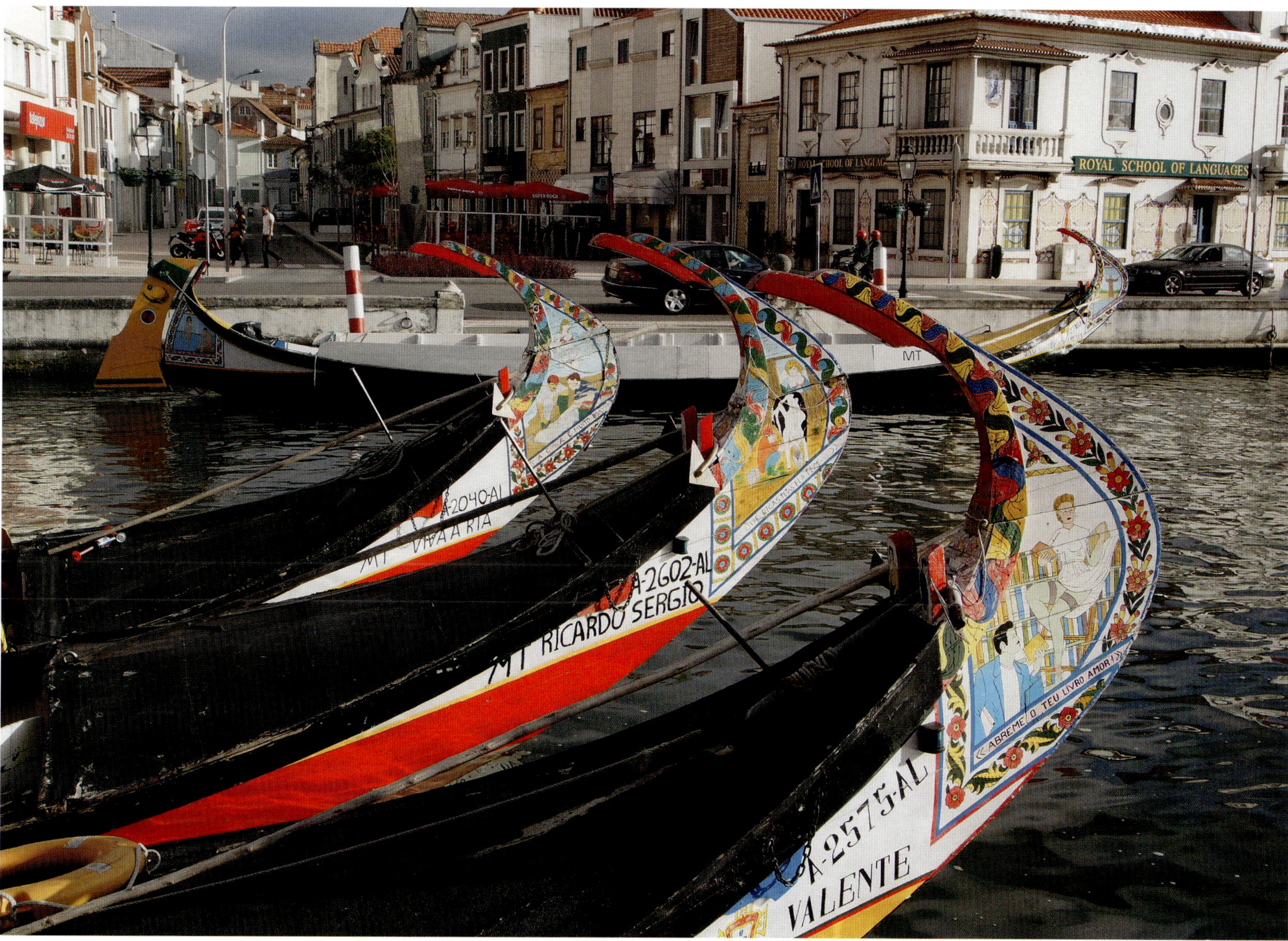

communities while appropriating their cultural symbols and values to cloak its own politics.[177] The government policy constructed new, more sanitary neighbourhoods using vernacular architectural styles and provided basic education, including lessons on religion and morality, in Casas dos Pescadores (Houses of the Fishermen) and applied fishing skills in Escolas de Pesca (Fishing Schools). These organizations were operated under the guidance of captains of ports or their delegates. In addition to their primary didactic purposes, like their rural counterparts, they sometimes included libraries, cinemas and sporting facilities.

The Campanha do Bacalhau (Cod Campaign) was at the centre of the state-sponsored revival that strove to replace imported with domestically caught cod. The Campanha expanded and modernized the fleet, providing better crew conditions and, between 1934 and 1967, doubling the number of its vessels.[178] The life of the cod fishermen was so gruelling and perilous—voyages in the frozen waters of the North Atlantic lasted up to six months—that during Portugal's wars in Africa, the government recruited crewmen as an alternative to military service.[179] Ideologically, Salazar attempted to recapture the bravery and determination of the sea voyages of the sixteenth century through his new White Fleet, whose adventures were narrated and disseminated in films, magazines and newspapers that proudly announced Portugal's

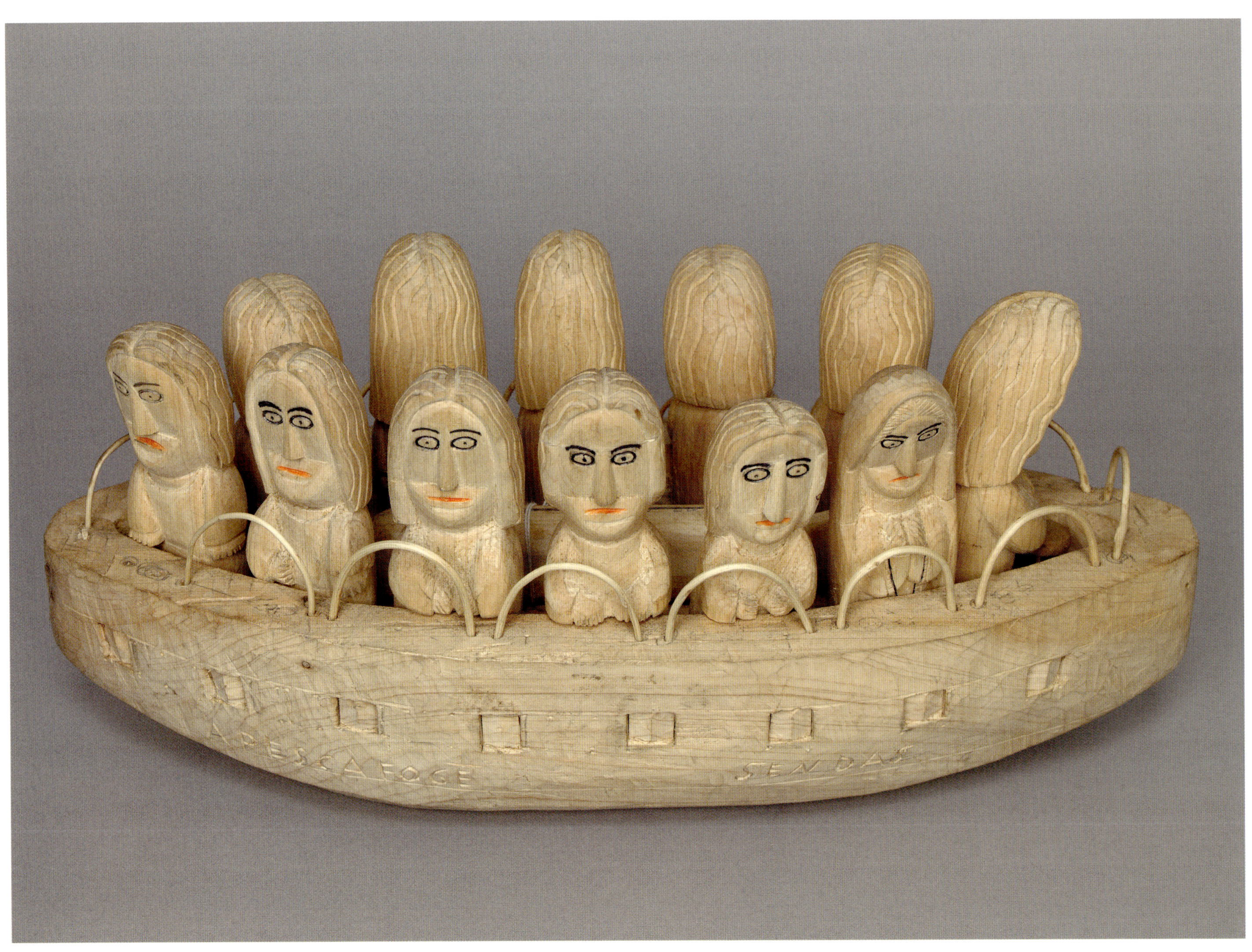
A PESCA FOGE

"return to the sea." The fleet's annual departure was marked by a benediction attended by Church and state dignitaries at which the vessels and their crews were blessed before they left Belém. Seafarers were feted through exhibitions, folkloric dances and cultural events organized by the Casas dos Pescadores and through populist ceremonies staged at the opening of new facilities, which were encouraged by the Estado Novo.[180] The drama of seafaring was reanimated by documentary film, photography, music, literature and major artistic commissions, including the murals by Domingos Rebelo (1891–1975) in the National Assembly, the Ministry of Education and the Central Council of the Casas dos Pescadores.

The White Fleet and the ceremonies attached to it disappeared with the fall of the Estado Novo in 1974; the collapse of the dictatorship also led to Portugal's withdrawal from Africa, which for some symbolized the end of the country's maritime ambitions.[181] In the place of maritime adventurism, the European Union and Portuguese municipal councils contributed to the construction of museums to preserve the memory of the different seafaring traditions. In central Portugal, towns such as Figueira da Foz, Nazaré, Mira, Póvoa, Ílhavo and Aveiro have benefited from the urban regeneration stimulated by this recent museumification. The Ílhavo Maritime Museum tells the story of the town's relationship to the Cod Fleet; Aveiro's fish market has spurred the development of restaurants, bars and tourism; and the old fish market at the Cais do Sodré in Lisbon has been refitted as a flower and antique market while the former cod storage building nearby has been transformed into the Museum of the Orient.

Crises provoked in the national identity that the Estado Novo attempted to construct have returned Portugal to the ambiguity it faced in the past. Change and insecurity have aroused a variety of responses, some of which have attempted to rework the strong mystical and messianic threads of the country's history into a new distillation that too often ignores sociological and economic factors.[182] Dacosta substitutes the essentialization of Lusitanian identity pursued for so long with the idea of racial miscegenation that seafaring adventurism brought about: "We are of African breed—we have the body and soul of Africa; even if we are fair-skinned, blue-eyed people, even if our culture is Anglo-American, we are mestizos." And later: "We are a patchwork of peoples . . . We are Lusitans and Jews and Arabs and Visigoths and Africans, and we unashamedly rejoice in being so."[183]

Dacosta insists that *saudade* remains at the heart of Portuguese identity, but he believes that it is not a longing for the past but, as it is for Pessoa, a resurgent messianism; the yearning for "the utopia, the dream we had in the past and which has not yet been fulfilled."[184] Mattoso, Daveau and Belo, in *Portugal: O Sabor da Terra* (Portugal: The Flavour of the Earth), suggest an alternative approach to Portuguese identity based on the strong topographic and aquatic diversity, geographical regionalism and local history that inform the uses, exploration and possession of the lands.[185] For these authors it is an understanding of the modalities between communities and the land and the shared sensory experiences and narratives of local history and culture that have given rise to a particular Portuguese "way of being." To grasp this way of being one cannot limit one's gaze to the land and history of Portugal alone, but must also contemplate the foreign shores on which Portuguese fleets have docked and the seas whose winds have conveyed them far and wide and brought other cultures and ways of knowing that have also long become part of Portuguese identity.

facing
JOÃO DE DEUS ORTEGA
Boat with the Twelve Apostles, C. 2005

Things

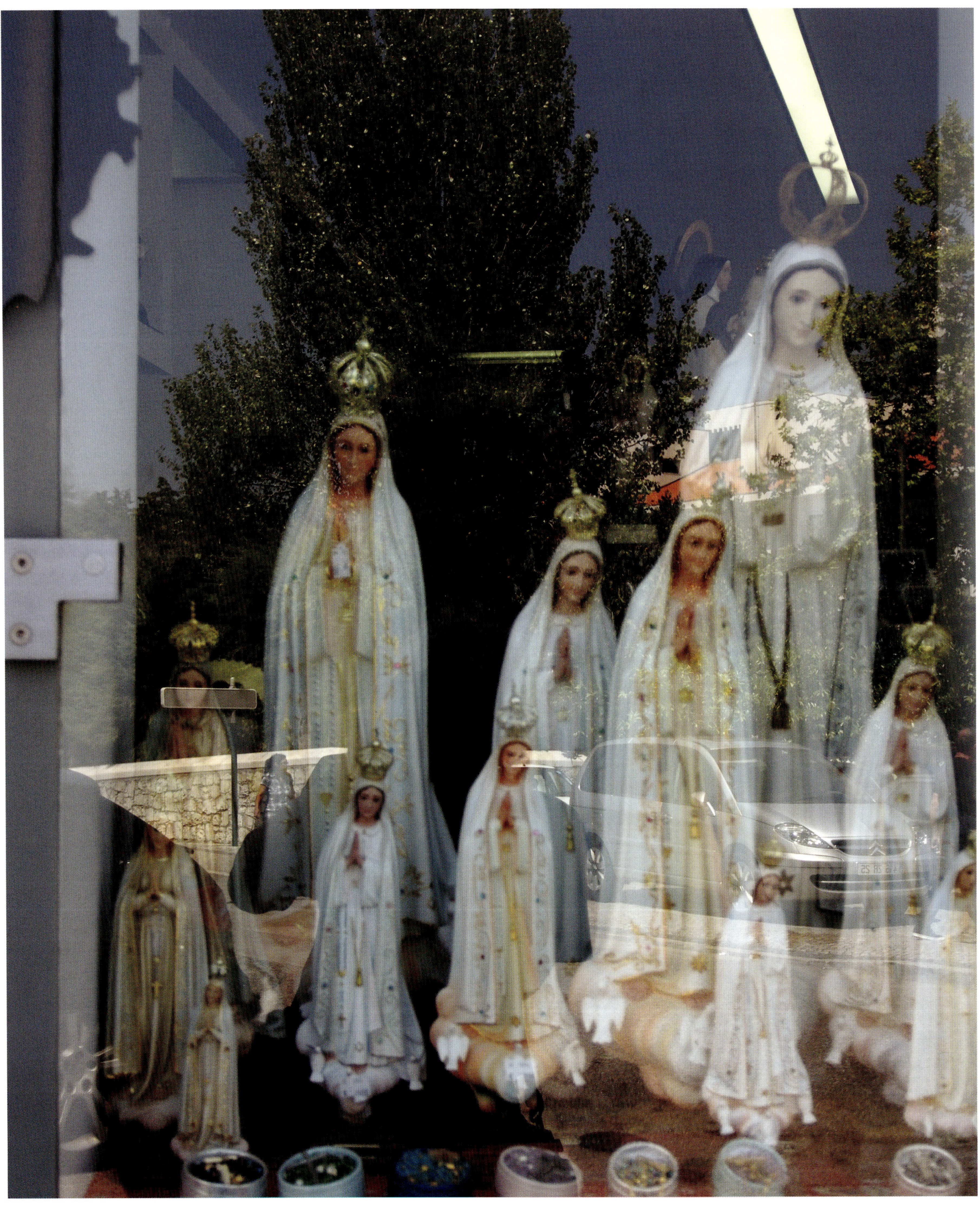

4 Religion, Politics and the Invention of Popular Art

All humanity lives a more or less double life; a real life and an imaginary life; one that is imposed by necessity and the other which is formed by their ideals.

A. de Sousa Silva Costa Lobo[186]

A PANTHEON OF SAINTS

Local saints that may have had their origins in the religions of Rome and Athens, or even in their supposed Ibero-Celtic antecedents, are still revered in different regions of Portugal. São Martinho (along with São Vicente), the patron saint of vintners and drinkers, shares the same feast day as that reserved in antiquity for the Roman god Bacchus, while São Jorge, the nation's patron saint, is said to represent a peculiarly Christian transfiguration of Jupiter or Zeus. Some writers argue that many of the most popular and deeply rooted versions of the cult of the Virgin Mary have even earlier origins, in a pre-Roman earth-mother deity.[187] What is clear is that as far back as the eleventh century, as illustrated in the *Cantigas de Santa Maria*, where the Virgin is shown interceding to increase the catch of fishermen, saints, like pre-Christian deities, were approached pragmatically to intervene in the world on behalf of humanity.

The historical roots behind these conjectured transformations are, despite the impressive literature, intricate and difficult to ratify. The Roman conquest that began in 216 BC in the south of the Iberian Peninsula and moved slowly northwards took more than two hundred years to complete. The Romans found it easier to impose their beliefs and ways of life in the plains and gentle undulating hills of the south than in the mountainous central and northern parts of present-day Portugal. Ibero-Celtic religious traditions maintained themselves longer in the north and only slowly melded with those from Rome. So when Christianity arrived several centuries later it confronted a more complex and resistant mix of Roman and Ibero-Celtic thought and religious practices in the north than in the south that resulted in different processes and patterns of syncretization.[188]

Religious syncretism was further complicated by the fourth- to sixth-century schism between Priscillianism and orthodox Christianity, which was strongly felt on the Peninsula. Of Egyptian origin, Priscillianism was based on a dualistic belief in the existence of two kingdoms—one of light and the other of darkness. Human souls were intended to vanquish the Kingdom of Darkness, but as they fell in battle, they became imprisoned

facing
Imported resin figures of Nossa Senhora de Fátima reflected in the window of one of the town's many religious souvenir shops, Fátima.

facing
Registo of Santo António, c. 2010.

on earth in bodily material forms. Severed from God, people were constituted from both kingdoms—from the Kingdom of Light by the Twelve Patriarchs or Heavenly Spirits that represented different human powers, and from the Kingdom of Darkness by the twelve signs of the zodiac, representing material manifestations associated with Hell. Salvation, according to Priscillianism, could be attained only by freeing the soul from its material body, but since the Twelve Patriarchs had failed to liberate the soul, only the teaching and sacrifice of Christ could free it from its material bond. A Church synod convened in Saragossa in AD 380 attempted to resolve the schism within the Church, but the Priscillian leaders refused to attend and were excommunicated. Later, after protracted political wrangling, the heretic leaders were finally captured and executed, although they were subsequently beatified as saints and martyrs. Repression only attracted more followers to Priscillianism. In AD 563 and AD 572, two subsequent councils convened in the northern city of Braga and attempted to curtail "pagan" influence. São Martinho is credited with finally healing the schism by pardoning Priscillian and his followers and formally expunging their doctrine.

Priscillianism, with its mystical qualities, easily absorbed spiritual influences from other religious traditions—including the Peninsula's pre-Christian heritage—and was more sympathetic to their coexistence than the orthodox Church. The decrees issued by two councils of Braga reformed orthodox Christianity while condemning Priscillianism and leaving it no option, if it was to survive, but to adapt itself within the orthodox Church. The authority and jurisdictions of more than a few minor Roman patron deities, it is often argued, remained vigorous for a much longer period of history through their reinscription in Christianity as martyrs and saints.

In contemporary Portugal one occasionally unexpectedly encounters statues devoted to Roman gods, many erected in the nineteenth century as part of classical revivalism. In Estremoz a statue dedicated to Saturn faces the convent church of São Francisco, while Arronches has a statue of Neptune facing the church of Nossa Senhora da Assunção. Through the engraved script around its portico, the latter church seems to retort back to the pagan Neptune with the reminder that "*Paraíso para sempre. Inferno para sempre*" (Heaven is Forever. Hell is Forever). Not surprisingly for a maritime nation, Neptune is well represented in public sculpture, and bronzes of the god adorn the gardens of the Queluz National Palace, the Quinta do Carmo in Estremoz, the garden of the Marquis of Pombal in Oeiras and the water gardens that run down the Paseo dos Restauradores in Lisbon. These are not evidence of pagan continuities but of the allegorical reinscription of historical gods and heroes into new nineteenth-century public and private spaces.

For centuries Christian saints have conflated unlikely associations and liaisons that continue to be acknowledged in Portugal: Santa Dymphna shares her duties as patron of the family and harmony with her responsibilities for insanity, nerves and runaways; Santo António, patron of the poor, also cares for amputees, gravediggers and lost articles (usually lost through the intervention of Diabo, the Devil);[189] and São Francisco de Assis, patron of animals and birds, also helps control fire, regulates merchants and brings solace to those who must endure solitary death. The patron of dogs is São Roque, who also holds power over plagues and pestilence. Neither should it be forgotten that mad dogs have a saint all of their own, Santa Quitéria. São Sebastião, who is patron not only of athletes but also of undertakers, provides one of the most bizarre parallels of all.

Santa Luzia was martyred in the fourth century, when her eyes were gouged out; she is now the patron saint of opticians and her image is still found in some of their waiting rooms. Before her, in the second century, Santa Apolónia had her teeth torn out of her gums; she is now patroness of dentists, and her name, if not her historical or religious significance, is preserved today in the name of Lisbon's main train terminus. Gallop, in 1936, listed a whole hagiography of saints that he found still had acknowledged connections to a person's health and well-being in Portugal:

> Sight is protected by Santa Luzia and S. Longuinhos, the hearing by S. Ovídio, the skin by S. Bento, the bladder by S. Vicente, and the throat by S. Blas. S. Amaro cures lameness, S. Sebastião the plague and St Paio fever. The head, together with all mental disease and weakness, is the special province of St John the Baptist, perhaps because he lost his own.[190]

Santa Rufina, a third-century Roman martyr, is the patron saint of potters and pottery merchants. She and her sister, Justina, so the legend tells, supported themselves and their poor compatriots by making and selling fine pottery in their home city of Seville. After the sisters refused to allow their wares to be used in a Roman religious ceremony, they were attacked by an angry crowd, who destroyed their pottery. This provoked the sisters in turn to destroy what for them was a pagan image of Venus. For repeatedly refusing to renounce Christianity, they were imprisoned, tortured, made to walk barefoot in the mountains and finally re-imprisoned and denied food or water. Justina died first, and her body was cast into a well. Rufina, still adamant in her faith, was fed to the lions. Surviving even this ordeal, she was

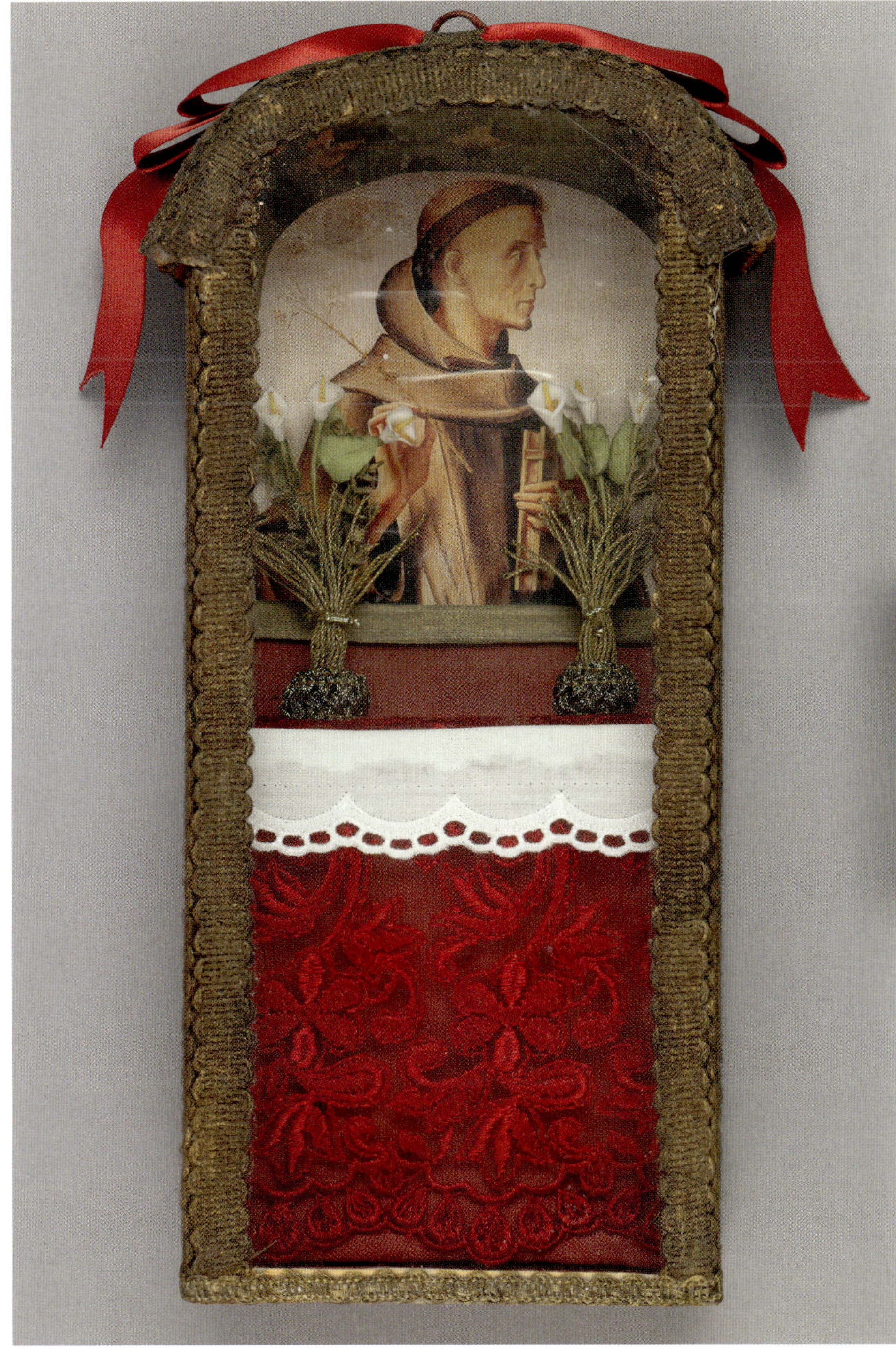

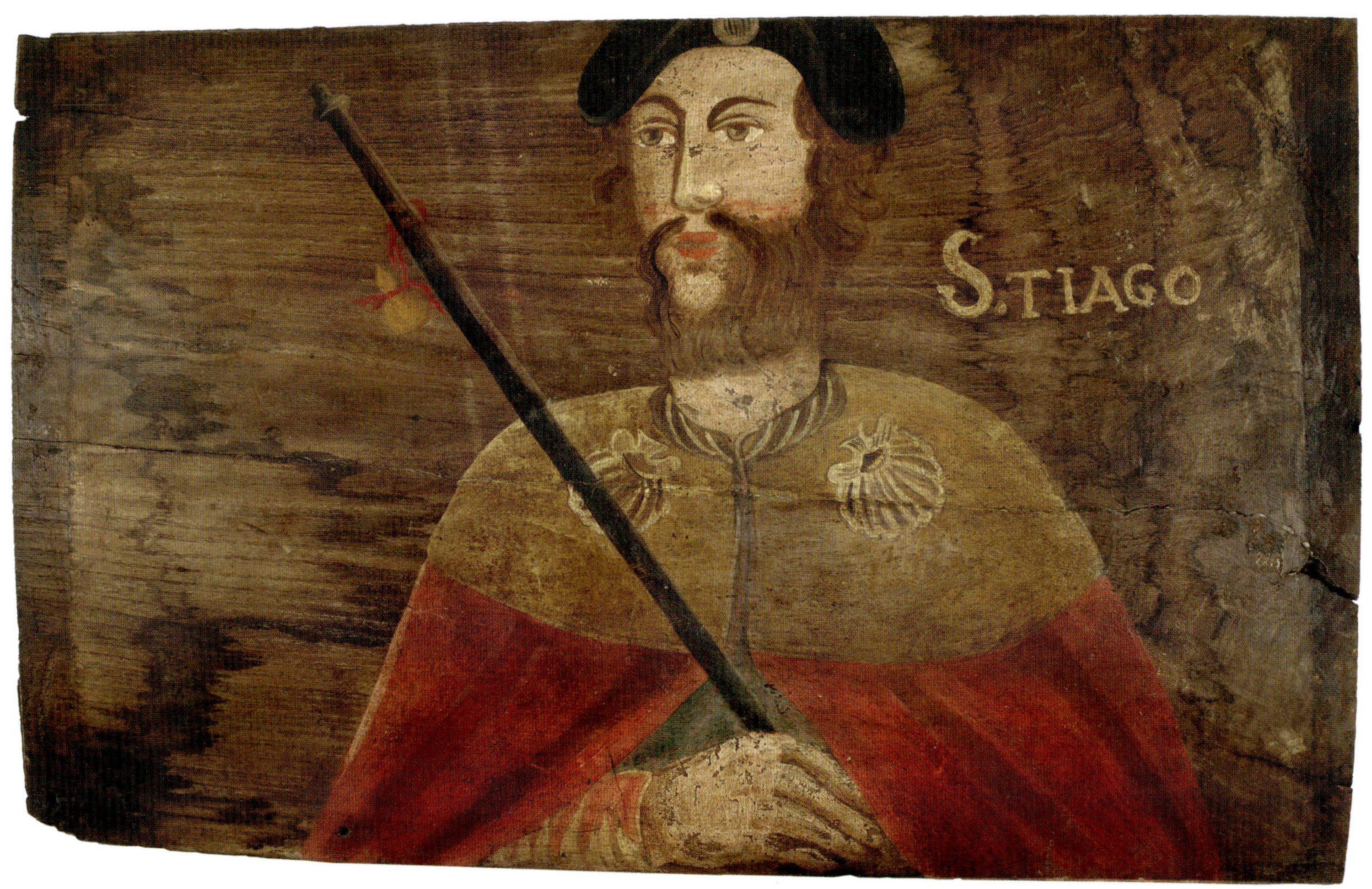
S.TIAGO

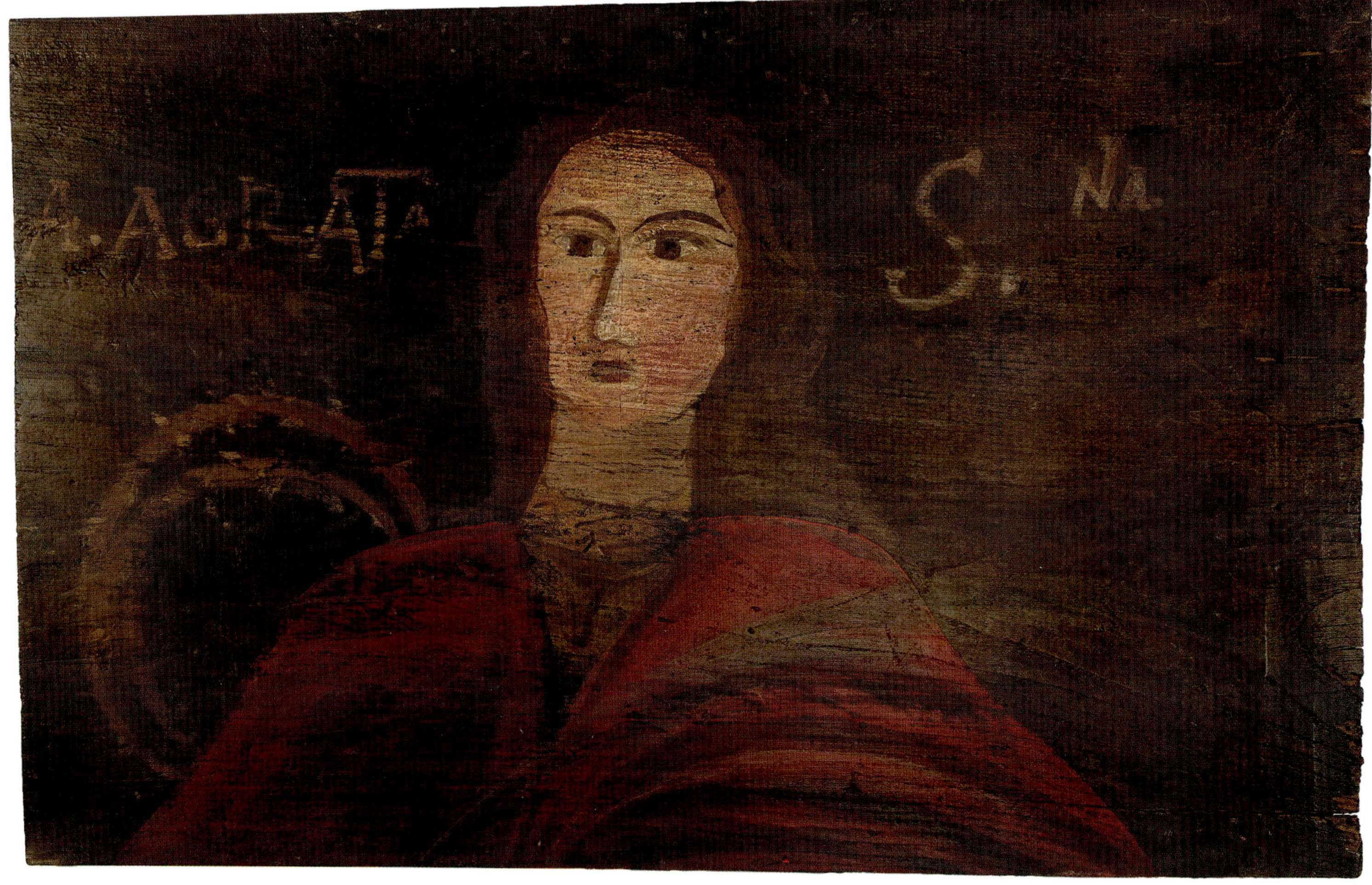
A.AGRATA
S. NA

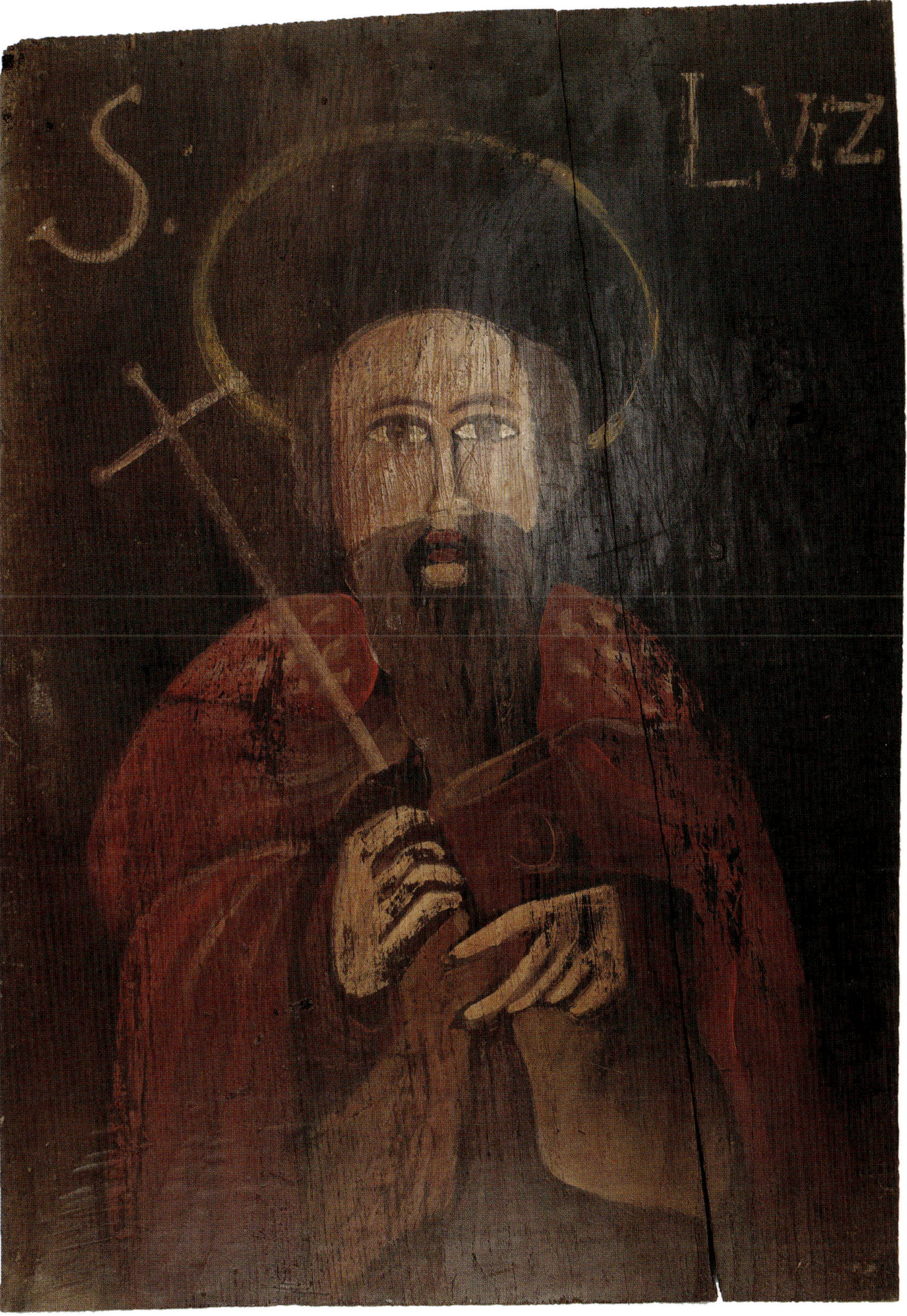

facing, top
ARTIST UNKNOWN
Santiago, nineteenth century

facing, bottom
ARTIST UNKNOWN
Santa Agatha, nineteenth century

above
ARTIST UNKNOWN
São Luís, nineteenth century

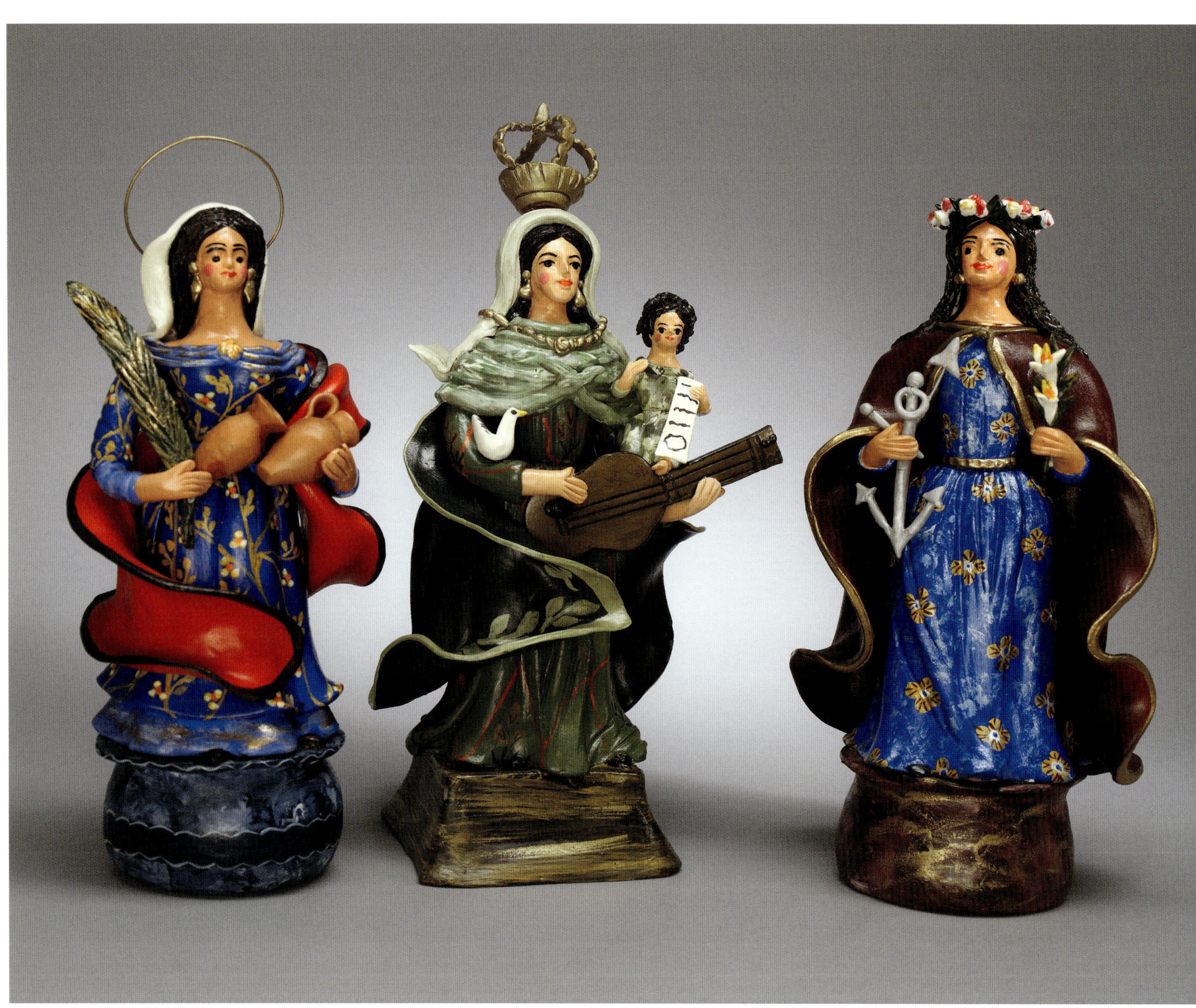

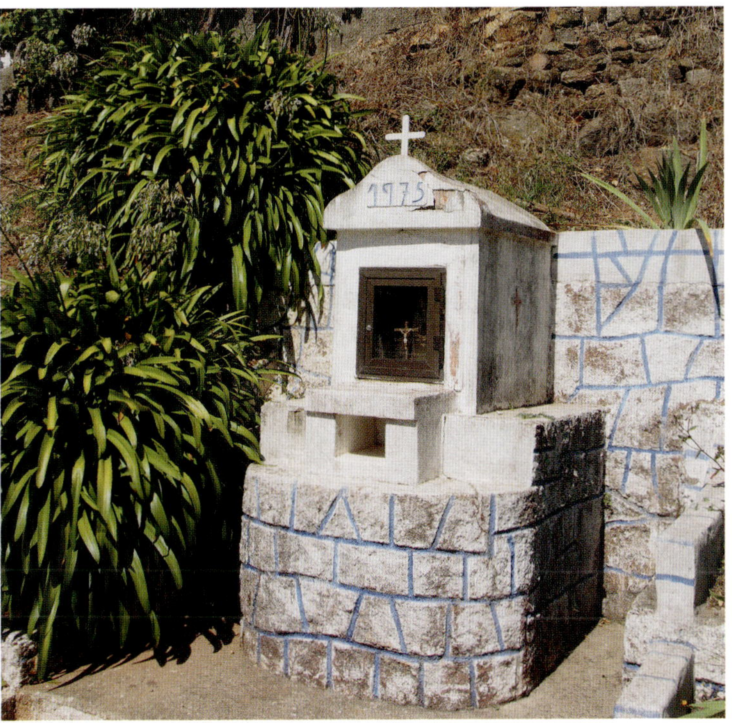

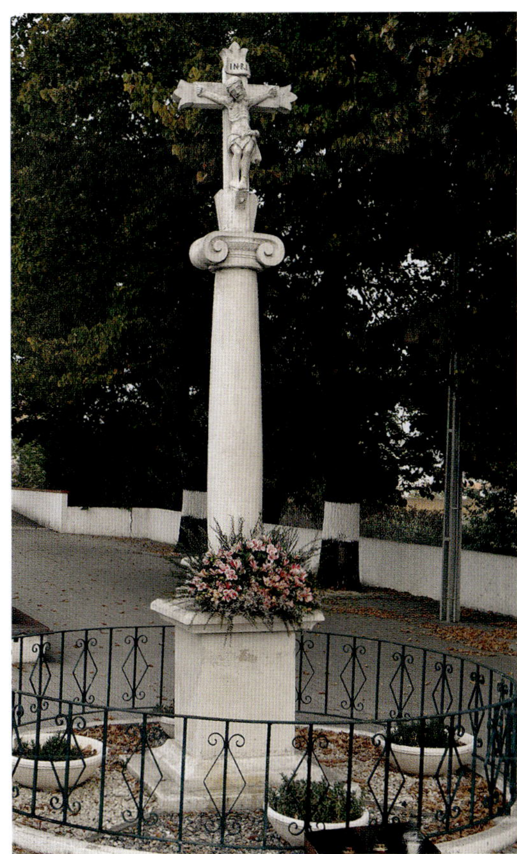

facing
PERPÉTUA MATILDE FONSECA SOUSA AND MARIA INÁCIA FONSECA MATEUS
Santa Rufina, Santa Cecilia, Santa Filomena, 2011
Respectively, the patroness of potters, the patroness of musicians, and the patroness of babies, children and lost causes.

left
Roadside shrine containing a small image of Christ on the cross in Buçaco.

right
Elaborate roadside shrine at Avelãs de Caminho.

finally strangled or, according to some accounts, beheaded and her body burned. On the Calçada Conde Penafiel in the centre of Lisbon is a ceramic workshop specializing in the fine reproduction of historical wares that still bear the saint's name, but elsewhere in the new economy of mass-produced tourist wares their patroness has been all but forgotten, even by potters themselves.

Saints and divine patronage abound in Portugal. The country has between five and nineteen distinctive Santa Combas, each with their special jurisdiction related to a town or region. Lima, Dão, Sines, Lamego, Coimbra—each has its own unique, but largely forgotten, Santa Comba along with a special story about her and, somewhere, a chapel or image devoted to her. Santa Comba de Coimbra is said to have escaped persecution for refusing sexual invitations by taking refuge in a forest that her pursuers then set ablaze. The flames refused to burn the saint's body, so her enemies tied her against the trunk of a leafy tree where she was shot with arrows.[191] In the Cathedral Sé Nova in Coimbra is a dark, lightless side chapel dedicated to Santa Comba; a carved image there shows her with long braided red hair, tied to the tree where she died, looking not unlike a female version of Christ on the cross.

Américo Cortez Pinto collected some of the devotional stories connected to national saints in an illustrated book, *Santos de Portugal*, published in 1956. Other miraculous stories and saintly characteristics can be found on the shelves of Catholic bookstores or seen illustrated on painted tiles and wooden ceilings in the country's churches, monasteries and convents. (In rural villages and towns the presence of a saint, through his or her relics or effigy, symbolized the community, encapsulated its history and identity and focused its energy.[192]) Saintly images or crosses decorate roadside shrines and the walls of houses; saints' names are given to towns, neighbourhoods, roads and streets; and their relics, still accredited supernatural powers, are dispersed throughout the country in richly worked gold and silver reliquaries or preserved in the cavities of wooden busts supporting their sculpted likenesses, such as those in the cathedrals of Faro, Viseu and Coimbra or the Museu do Abade de Baçal in Bragança.

facing, left
Procession saints carried in boats decorated with elaborate floral displays during the Festival of São Bartolomeu in Esposende, 2014.

facing, right
Procession of giants and big heads during the Festival of São João in Braga, 2011.

Reliquary busts were made until the eighteenth century, usually in wood, but in Coimbra in faience too. The saints, Virgin Mary and Christ are thought to intervene between humanity and a God whom, it is often reported, mortals find to be too far removed or intimidating.[193] Sanchis recorded an agricultural labourer in Alentejo musing, "We don't know whether God exists, but we cannot deny that this saint (Nossa Senhora d'Aires) has worked many miracles."[194] In recent years, as in other parts of Christendom, ancient saints have been given new responsibilities; though not perhaps widely acknowledged by all their adorers, Santa Clara looks after television and Santa Isidora ensures the smooth functioning of computers and the Internet.

PORTUGUESE POPULAR RELIGION

The saints of popular religion are linked together by the celebration of saint's day festivals and fairs and the annual *romarias* (pilgrimages) made to their sanctuaries. The focus of each *romaria* is a particular saint who is attributed special powers over a specific jurisdiction of great importance to his or her followers. *Romarias*, though significantly fewer and less popular than in the twentieth century, have both religious and secular aspects, including the celebration of Mass, sermons, ritual practices and processions.[195] They sometimes include markets, auctions, food and drink stalls and fairground rides, and provide a regional meeting place for the exchange of news and ideas; the encouragement of business transactions, particularly related to animal and produce sales; the enjoyment of drink, music and dance; and the display of wealth through dress and jewellery.[196] They also in the past included itinerant puppeteers, theatrical performances, games, circus performers and even exhibitions of waxworks and curiosities. In August 2014 the Fair of São Mateus in Viseu included a large area devoted to fairground rides, concert stages and stalls selling everything from Lego to ex-military uniforms and wood-burning stoves as well as more traditional handmade pottery and hardware. That same year, the saint's day ceremony for São Bartolomeu in Esposende had more eateries than goods sellers. Dias noted that even in the 1940s many *romarias* were losing their religious significance and becoming venues for secular entertainment.[197] Another anthropologist, Pierre Sanchis, stressed that by the late 1970s, it would have been wrong to consider them as purely religious or spiritual events. The *romaria* is a total social situation—life, party, "lived dream"—that constitutes a break in everyday life and even a different universe.[198] It is a place, he argued, where social relations are intensified and social rules relaxed, with light or no work. A *romaria* possesses a lyrical, incandescent quality.[199]

The essence of Portuguese traditional rural society was based on *romarias*.[200] According to Ernesto Veiga de Oliveira, family structure, social ancestry, economic and material concerns and tastes, simple technology, professional activities, spirituality, and folk art and entertainment were all influenced by rich, interconnected, popular religious traditions.[201] For Sanchis it was the reciprocal presentation of gifts, vows and promises between the worlds of people and rural saints that constituted community.[202] These urgent requests and vows could not be revealed to any other than the saint, Virgin or Christ figure, in fear that they might be rendered ineffective or null.[203] A vow is "what enables, a man, who is a creature destined for death ('like a dog'), to transcend the limits of his earthly life and to communicate with the cosmic mystery which surrounds and awaits him."[204] Connections and passages between worlds depend on vows; without them death brings only the void.

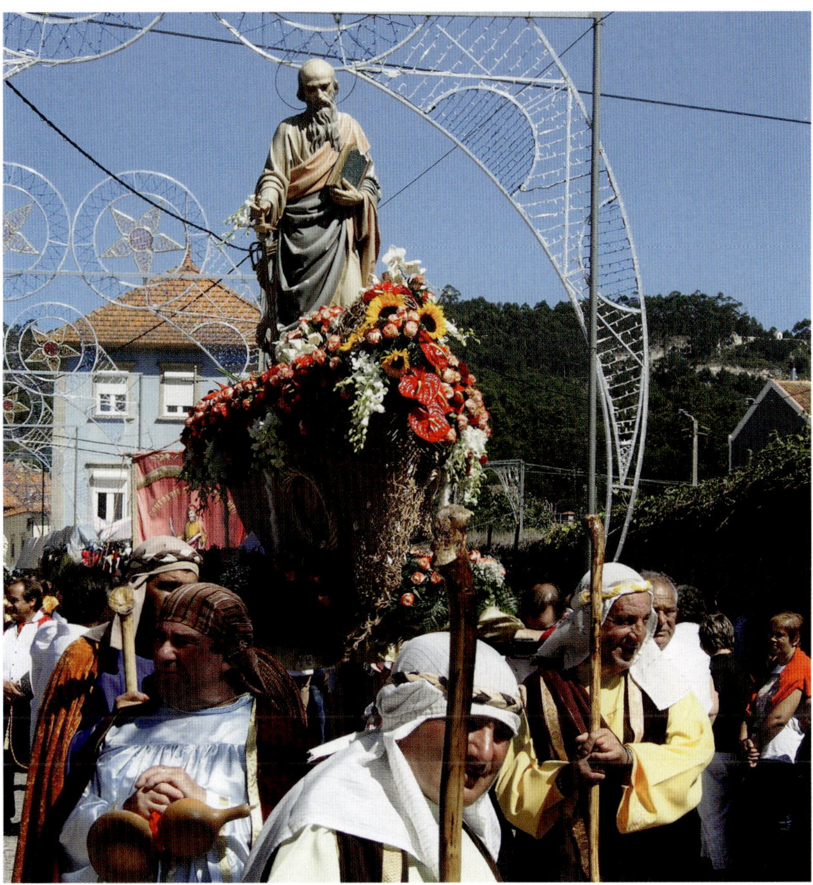

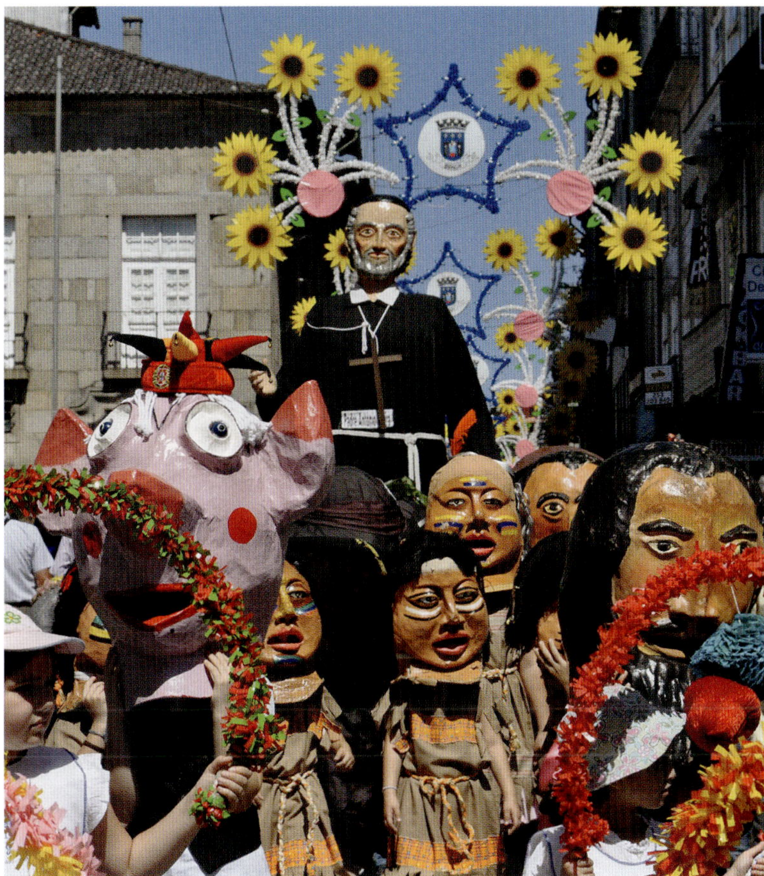

In Alentejo the anthropologist José Cutileiro found that relations between individuals and saints were highly personal and were based on familiarity and personal preference rather than in accordance with ascribed powers and jurisdictions. Furthermore, families might have a special relation with more than one saint.[205] In the past, at specific times during the *romaria*, the organizing committee collected money in exchange for images of the saint, called *registos*. The size and elaborateness of these images were directly related to the amount of the gift. Small *registos* were attached to the hats of pilgrims, while larger ones were used in the home as a "protective presence."[206] As in the past, pilgrims who take part in *romarias* visit sanctuaries to make requests and vows and later return to renew their pledges or give thanks for their supplications being answered.[207] When a saint intervenes on one's behalf, promises must be acknowledged and reciprocated through devotional rituals: a visit to the shrine carrying the statue of the saint in a procession or *de joelhos*; a pilgrimage undertaken on one's knees; or offerings in the form of money, gold, *tranças* (locks of hair), ex-votos made of wax or, more rarely, paintings depicting the miraculous event.[208]

Sanchis, based on his observations in the north of the country, noted the importance of promising gold to saints; the amounts involved were large, often in the form of jewellery that had been accumulated over generations and that usually constituted the only riches a family had.[209] In contrast, Cutileiro, who worked in southern Portugal, found that offerings made to saints in the poorer region of Alentejo were of much lower material value.[210] Failure to repay obligations to holy figures could result in the loss of luck, ill health or even death. In both areas saintly cults were normally organized by a brotherhood or commission (*mordomia* or *confraria*) constituted according to established rules to ensure the maintenance of the sanctuary, decorations and the organization of the celebration.[211]

Romarias have been divided into those centred on a saint in a village or town church and those focused on a regional shrine, usually in a rural setting.[212] Most *romarias* take place in the summer, so chapels and shrines located in the country allow the devout to camp in the fields, woods or beaches surrounding them. It has repeatedly been noted that these sanctuaries are often in places associated with pre-Christian cults.[213] One extensive cycle of *romarias* is located around Leiria, Nazaré and Fátima and dedicated to various manifestations of the Virgin Mary. Others are found in the north of the country: in Chaves dedicated to São Bartolomeu for exorcism or in Viana do Castelo sanctified to Santa Luzia. Wright and Swift noted that the five largest *romarias* in the mid-1960s were those dedicated to São Torcato at Guimarães, São Bento da Porta Aberta in Gerês, Senhora da Peneda at Soajo, Santa Marta in the Serra da Falperra and Nossa Senhora de Agonia at Viana do Castelo.[214]

Popular religion, for the anthropologist Santo, was never completely isolated but always linked to institutionalized religion, with which it shares common points of articulation that condition its relative autonomy and operation.[215] The followers of popular religion, he noted, are not limited to impoverished groups and classes but constitute the social majority, linked to specific types of culture based on close neighbourhoods and the collective transmission of social memories. Popular religion is neither formal nor reproduced through teaching but is spontaneous and collectively created. In Vilarinho da Furna,[216] practitioners viewed popular and Church-based aspects of religion, despite conflicts and contradictions, as compatible and essentially linked.[217] Popular religion for Sanchis, however, exists only because an official religion declares some practices to be unacceptable. Because of this attitude, there exist "two mentalities, two visions of the world, two cultural and religious universes."[218] By the 1970s this traditional world of popular religion had lost its coherent and integrative character and functions. Changes in agricultural production, land ownership, credit and emigration fundamentally altered the character of rural society.[219] Because of these changes, in the past forty years the idea of Portuguese popular religion and culture has needed to be rethought to incorporate urban as well as rural expressions and consider the effects of the Internet, tourism, commodification, sponsorship, diverse audiences and new controls on performances.[220]

The diversity, ambiguity and multivalent meaning inherent to Portuguese saintly characters have historically enabled their manipulation by different communities of devotees and between congregations and Church authorities. The same saint can have different jurisdictions and significances for different followers and can be approached in many ways, from formal and hierarchical to familiar and egalitarian. A saint may even elicit divergent ritual practices and attitudes, such as having one significance for institutionalized religion but quite different ones for their adherents, and can provide a medium through which antagonism or opposition between groups and classes can be expressed and targeted.[221] For example, Santa Comba, according to one source, was originally a witch until she was visited by Christ, who warned her to relinquish her beliefs and convert to Christianity. Once the saint had been incorporated into Christianity, her popular followers attributed her powers, not recognized by the institutional Church, to intercede in matters involving witchcraft.

Consistent failure to acknowledge the essential articulations between popular and institutional religions has had serious historical implications for understanding popular culture and art. The anthropologists Pina-Cabral and Feijó have argued that the animosity between politics and religion during Portugal's early Republican period originated from successive governments wanting to cut the superstitious elements from core Roman Catholic beliefs in order to purify religion as part of a program of rational enlightenment.[222] Nevertheless, in at least one community in Alentejo, viewed by anthropologists over a fifty-year period, whether the Church had or did not have a resident priest made no marked difference on the support given to organized religion. Belief in popular forms of Christianity involving personal relations between believers and saints continued to be strong, which made organized religion almost superfluous to some areas of religious life.[223]

Many of the saints, and the local stories told of their more senior heavenly compatriots, subsist at the margins between often fading local cults and globalized Church authority. Although popular and institutionalized interpretations and ritual prescriptions sometimes clashed, there was often mutual agreement around the symbiotic relationship between the Church and local communities. Ritualization of some aspects of popular religion could have been achieved only with the cooperation of the Church.[224] Therefore, political persecution of the Church affected the organization of popular religion as much as armed conflict, which disrupted its ceremonial organization and expressions.

The decline in institutional religion began in the eighteenth century with the rise of anticlericalism and the introduction of laws limiting Church authority and continued until 1926 and the rise of the Estado Novo. The first limitations on Church power were introduced in 1757, when the Marquis of Pombal, leader of the reformist government of José I, expelled the Jesuits, created a state educational system and severed formal relations with Rome. Although some of these decrees were appealed, anticlericalism continued, leading to the expulsion of various religious orders in 1821 and the confiscation of their property. Napoleon's military intervention from 1807 to 1814 destroyed much of Portugal's and Spain's administrative and economic infrastructure, but the civil war between liberals and absolutists that followed and continued until mid-century created even greater damage, disrupting internal trade, creating a crisis for artisans and further dislocating religious practices.

EMPIRE, POPULAR CULTURE AND THE ESTADO NOVO, 1933–74

Readers of Cortez Pinto's short book *Santos de Portugal* (Saints of Portugal), published in 1956 to promote mass adult education, will be surprised to come upon a preface by the founder of the Estado Novo, António de Oliveira Salazar, who held dictatorial authority from 1932 to 1968. "Portugal," Salazar wrote,

> was born in the shadow of the Church and from the beginning Catholic religion was the formative element of the nation's soul and formed the predominant character of the Portuguese people. In their travels across the world—to discover, to trade, to spread the faith—they have without hesitation assumed that Portugal would always be Catholic. To adhere to the principles of just one religion and the dictates of only one morality, what we might call the Catholic uniformity of the country, was throughout the centuries, one of the most powerful factors in the unity and cohesion of the Portuguese Nation.[225]

This religious commitment and its spiritual implications strongly influenced and sustained the philosophy of the Estado Novo, which was organized as a rational, technocratic, corporative structure that encompassed and attempted to balance conservative economic, social and religious interest groups by subordinating them to a distinctive spiritualist and anti-individualist philosophy. The 1933 constitution declared Portugal to be a corporative nation—a "unitary and corporate republic founded on the equality of its citizens... and the participation of all the constituent forces of the Nation in its administrative life." By organizing workers and owners together in the same corporation, the Estado Novo strove to minimize conflicts and create a harmonious order bereft of class conflict and egoistic individualism. From the 1930s onward, by monopolizing and coordinating all channels for propaganda—including primary and secondary education, unions, museums, the Casas do Povo (Houses of the People, or community centres) and Casas dos Pescadores (Houses of the Fishermen), sports and recreation clubs, youth movements and women's associations—the dictatorship sought a total grasp over society, to forge the birth of a "new man" and "reportuguese the Portuguese."[226] The paramount function of the state was to provide leadership based on Catholic morality, faith in God and the greater glory of the nation.[227] The assertion that the Estado Novo was bereft of any defining ideological vision and content, more disposed to encouraging apathy and the proclamation of "Fado, Fátima and Football,"[228] obfuscates its reoccurrent contradictions, notably a reassertion of some of the ideological threads that had long been part of Portuguese history.

The Estado Novo included both continental Portugal and its overseas colonies in its political and economic system.[229] The nation-state's historical mission complemented the then-current imperial system by reserving the right to civilize and improve the morals of Portugal's colonized subjects as well as renovating the cultural values and aspirations of its metropolitan citizenship. The state legitimated its exercise of power by claiming to model itself on what it defined as the "natural constitution of society," composed of the mutual rights and obligations between the family, parishes, municipal authorities and corporations, firmly mediated through universal Christian values. The Salazarian trinity—"God, Country, Family," in that hierarchical order—was easily transposed to acclaim the correspondence between Christ, Salazar and each family's patriarchal head.

The Church, through the state's planned re-Catholization of the country, played a key role in legitimating and furthering state ideology. The religious orders previously expelled from the country were invited to return, and former anticlerical policies were abolished.[230] The Church reasserted its former conservative role and authority through the teaching of religion and morals in schools—subsidized after 1940 by the state—as well as by the support it gave the family, its refusal to sanction divorce and its active missionary campaigns. The family was substituted for the individual as the cornerstone of both state and Church ideology. The social family unit was an expression of the Holy Family. As a fundamental element of the natural constitution of society, the family was also heralded as the source for the conservation and dissemination of the race, and as a primary base of education, discipline and social harmony. The participation of male family heads at parish meetings fulfilled a fundamental integrative function. The Estado Novo, professing deep disregard for the institutionalization of political differences, was fused to social and cultural organizations to generate and reproduce the appearance of a unitary, consensual society in which ruled and rulers were indivisible.

At its core, Salazar's Estado Novo espoused a redemptive, millenarian ideology that launched a new project of national and imperial restoration through the reaffirmation of the values and beliefs of an idealized and selective past.[231] The turbulent years of the First Republic (1910–26) that had preceded the military's and Salazar's usurpation of government were repeatedly referred to as a period of "dissolution," "ruin," "anarchy" and "national disorder" responsible for the empire's decadence. The Estado Novo claimed to represent a new model of society that would reawaken religious values and popular support and build a new patriotic consensus between political factions based on the historical responsibilities to its empire.[232] This would be not a militant society but a monastic idyll of modest houses, rustic farming, frugality, modesty, virtue and obedience to Christ, all necessary for a life of rural peace and harmony and a cure against republicanism, bolshevikism, fascism and capitalism that the Estado Novo saw as assailing Europe.[233]

Restoration had both past–present and present–future orientations. It was understood as a revalorization of the historical achievements of the nation's past and a reaffirmation of the divine election of Portugal in propagating Christianity. In addition, it provided the rationale for a nervously planned modernization of the country that was intended to raise it again to greatness. The combination of these two projects generated contradictions, particularly during the early period of the dictatorship (1926–40), when agrarian interests and rural ideals of national identity clashed with a new ethos of industrialization. Industrial development was accelerated by the Second World War but at the same time restrained through the growth of government bureaucracy and state intervention. Only after the war, from 1945 to 1960, was the economic sector reformed to encourage the development of new industries, restructure existing production and protect the country's internal market. This modernization was combined with literacy campaigns, an expansion of higher education and improvements to the country's infrastructure.[234] Better sanitation, the encouragement of sport[235] and attempts to improve living standards were part of this program.

The historian Medina has argued that modernization was, however, never seriously pursued as an alternative to the rural idyll that was at the core of the state's world view.[236] Joana Damasceno, in contrast, draws attention to the connections between key aspects of the modernization program—better roads, sanitation and a network of inns (*pousadas*)—and the state policy to encourage tourism.[237] The fulfillment of these aspirations, whether ideological or practical, was modulated through the state's overarching vision and determination to re-secure the nation's grandeur as an idealized model of medieval European society. This romanticized historical period coincided with Portugal's own apogee of political, geographic, commercial and religious dominance.

Article Nine of the government's ten-point plan, promulgated a year after the 1933 ratification of the new constitution and intended to consolidate the regime's legitimacy, made the vision explicit: "The Estado Novo will restore Portugal to its historical grandeur, in its plenitude to spread its universalist civilization to its vast Empire. It will return Portugal to be one of the major spiritual powers of the world."[238] In this view, nothing was accidental or arbitrary about the history of the nation, which had a prefigured (divine) destiny revealed through its heroes and martyrs. The nation's spirit was continuous, evolutionary and organic and was transmitted through the generations by the souls of its people. These essentialized national values were embedded in myths that had already begun to be intellectually synthesized in the nineteenth century.[239] On a visit to Portugal in 1935, the philosopher Unamuno defined the philosophy of the dictatorship as "bellicose scholasticism with a drop of ecclesiasticism."[240]

The past was essentialized and used to guide the development of the future, through recourse to what the Estado Novo referred to as the "spirit." The head of the Secretariat of National Propaganda, António Ferro (1895–1956), explained "the spirit is also substance, a precious substance, the prime substance of the souls of men and the souls of the communities."[241] The spirit defined the essential "Portugueseness" of the nation and empire. Ferro saw his duty as Salazar's propaganda chief to defend Portuguese culture and create, somewhat paradoxically, "a Portugal with an ancient soul and a new sensibility."[242]

The Estado Novo gave "spirit" material incarnation by reinventing folklore, reconstructing and conserving historical monuments and supporting and valorizing popular art, particularly the work of rural artisans.[243] The restoration of historical sites and monuments and ambitious exhibitions to concretize a new mentality guided the creation of new symbolic spaces underwritten by the values associated with an idea of Lusitania that originated from the village,[244] the country, the African colonies and the seaborne adventurers. As Joana Damasceno aptly summarizes: "Tradition was part of Portugal's continuity and ethnography was its best expression."[245] In fact, although it was not published until 1948, Jorge Dias's rich ethnographic description of the social and political organization of the rural community of Vilarinho bore close resemblance to the corporate structure idealized by the Estado Novo. The philosophy of spirit was a strategy of cultural totalization in which landscape, monuments, folk art, civic ceremonies and artistic productions came together in a synthesis that elided all contradiction.[246] This approach reduced ethnography to a tool to fulfill the state's preconceptions of its nature, identity and destiny[247] and enabled the historical and ethnographic synthesis of the spirit to be seen, aided and actively propagated to achieve the nation's longed-for apotheosis.

The essentialization of Lusitanian history as spiritual revelation was reproduced by foreign travel writers, some of whom were impressed by Salazar's values. Wright and Swift, the authors of three popular travel guides to Portugal, described the mountainous landscape of the north using epic transcendentalist idioms similar to those that had been reiterated countless times before them, as "monstruous, turbulent rock formations" that had been visited by pilgrimages since prehistory and re-consecrated since the Middle Ages by Christians.[248] This millenarian history was reproduced at the village of Bisalhães, where Wright and Swift saw "an unbroken tradition" in pottery decoration[249] that connected souvenir shop ceramics to ancient votive offerings.[250] Two other travel writers, Bridge and Lowndes, also affirmed, though less poetically or enthusiastically, the "inevitable and intimate connection between both the historic past and these [current] manners and customs."[251] Such modest observations might go unremarked except that the government propaganda chief, António Ferro, assisted Bridge and Lowndes with their work.

Government support did not unduly influence the production of popular art, which received its stimulus from the growing network of Casas do Povo, which were furnished with regional furniture styles and sometimes displayed small local ethnographic collections.[252] In fact, popular art—despite the ideological support given it—declined economically during the Estado Novo period. Júlia Ramalho (1946–), a potter from Barcelos, explained to me in 2010 and 2011 that neither of her parents had become potters for economic reasons. Zé Augusto (José Augusto Ferreira dos Santos, 1930–2012), an Aveiro-based artist, recalled in 2011 that for him and his family the period had been very bleak, with food shortages so acute they sometimes had nothing to eat for days. He painted a series of harrowing canvases of these years, showing vulnerable emaciated figures bent over each other in protective positions.

An appreciation of the ideological foundations of the Estado Novo is essential to understanding the re-emergent discourse and the uses to which popular art was put during much of the twentieth century. By dismissing and eliding the period between the late eighteenth century and the 1926 coup, the Estado Novo constructed a telescoped concept of history that linked it directly to the Golden Age and reaffirmed the idea of historical predestination that continues to haunt Portuguese thought to the present day. So ambitious was the state's manipulation of chronology and Lusitanian identity that at the opening of the 1940 *Exhibition of the Portuguese World* in Lisbon, the deputy mayor made a grandiose claim: he compared the apparition of Christ at the Battle of Ourique, credited with assisting Portugal's first king, Afonso Henriques, in his victory against the Moors, to the visitation of Nossa Senhora at Fátima that affirmed Salazar, the country's one-hundredth prime minister, as a divinely favoured leader.[253] In the ideology of the Estado Novo, spirit took precedence over historical chronology, continuity over struggle or dissension, and unity over class, gender and racial divisions. From 1930 to 1950 this timeless essentialization of the nation was given one of its most important manifestations through folklore and popular art.

ARTISANS INTO ARTISTS

The Estado Novo continued the practice begun in the Republican period of exhibiting popular art in national and international exhibitions.[254] Governmental and commercial sponsorship of popular art began in 1931 when small exhibits of figurative pottery were shown at national and later international exhibitions and conferences. The popular art encouraged by the Estado Novo mainly comprised miniature pieces, excessively decorated and intended for external rather than community consumption.[255] Nevertheless, by the early 1940s the pottery centre of Barcelos was producing large quantities of whistles, bells, doves, hens and roosters as well as some figurative pieces (bandsmen, couples), using moulds to satisfy growing demand.[256] Adopting miniaturization, models and copies, craftsmen attempted to represent rural life in all its plenitude and diversity. Dolls dressed in regional costumes, carts and oxen, dovecotes, animals, neatly uniformed bandsmen, processions—all were exuberantly rendered in clay, while elsewhere elaborately decorated ex-votos or *registos* were displayed as expressions of the country's religious sentiments. These works had a long tradition and were not engineered directly by the Estado Novo. They created a somewhat infantilized, idyllic and harmonious image of rural life completely divorced from its persistent poverty, illiteracy and exploitative relations.[257]

The rural ideals of the Estado Novo were intoned in popular songs and visualized in propaganda. Ferro was a strong advocate for a national film industry, particularly after the success of the comedy *A Canção de Lisboa* (The Song of Lisbon;

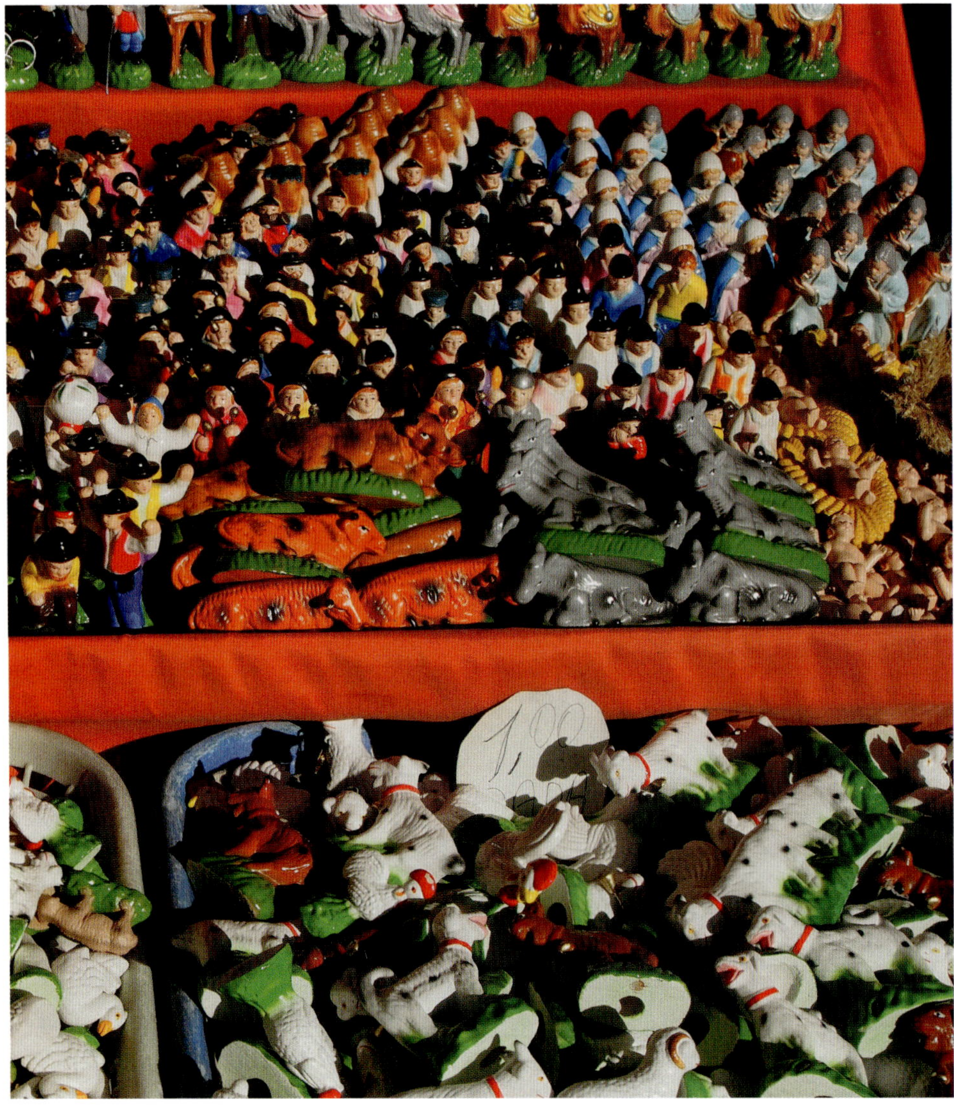

above
Moulded ceramic whistles and figures for sale at the Fair of São Mateus in Viseu, 2014.

facing
MARIA HELENA PEDRO DA SILVA
Ceramic figures of bandsmen, Barcelos, 2010.

1933), but his ambition remained limited by financial resources. "A Casa Portuguesa" (The Portuguese House), sung by the famed fado singer Amália Rodrigues in the 1950s, embodied the regime's strongly held rural ideals. Graphic illustration, including highly innovative designs by Stuart Carvalhais, Almada Negreiros, Jorge Barradas, Martins Barata and Paulo Ferreira, also provided an often-impressive means to disseminate state ideology. Especially notable is the set of seven lithographs by Martins Barata printed in 1938 to celebrate the tenth anniversary of Salazar's economic reforms, which were distributed to all the country's primary schools under the title *A Lição de Salazar* (Salazar's Lesson).[258]

Among this set was one entitled *Deus, Pátria, Família. A Trilogia da Educão Nacional* (God, Country, Family. The Trilogy of National Education) showing the idealized interior of a rural dwelling. The room is clean, lit by brilliant sunlight that pours through the open door and window, through which can be seen a distant castle with the national flag. The house has a wood-beam ceiling and tiled floor. Ubiquitous decorative and utilitarian wares include rustic ceramic bowls, plates, water jugs and storage jars; artisan-made furniture; a glass and metal lamp; a domestic altar with a large cross flanked by pottery candle holders and stylized paper flower arrangements; basketwork and white tablecloths. The scene, which is centred on the return of an agricultural labourer to a welcoming family, expresses the rural idyll and embodies the folk values intrinsic to the Estado Novo, which Salazar reputedly also observed in his private life. His home, considered a modest rural house in Santa Comba Dão near Coimbra, was the source of frequent references that reiterated its rural appeal, unsophisticated furnishings and modest size and gardens.[259]

The room portrayed in this mass-distributed lithograph, constructed and furnished with natural materials, is clean, simple and sustainable, yet lacks electricity, modern appliances or factory-made goods.[260] The lithograph illustrates the ideal place of popular "art" in the ideology of the Estado Novo. As with most rural dwellings used by agricultural workers, the kitchen was the main family room and a repository for most material possessions and decorations, with the fireplace reserved for the most treasured pieces.[261] The illustration seems to visualize Vasconcellos's description of nineteenth-century traditional rural Alentejo houses.[262] In *Portuguese Ethnography*, Vasconcellos argued,

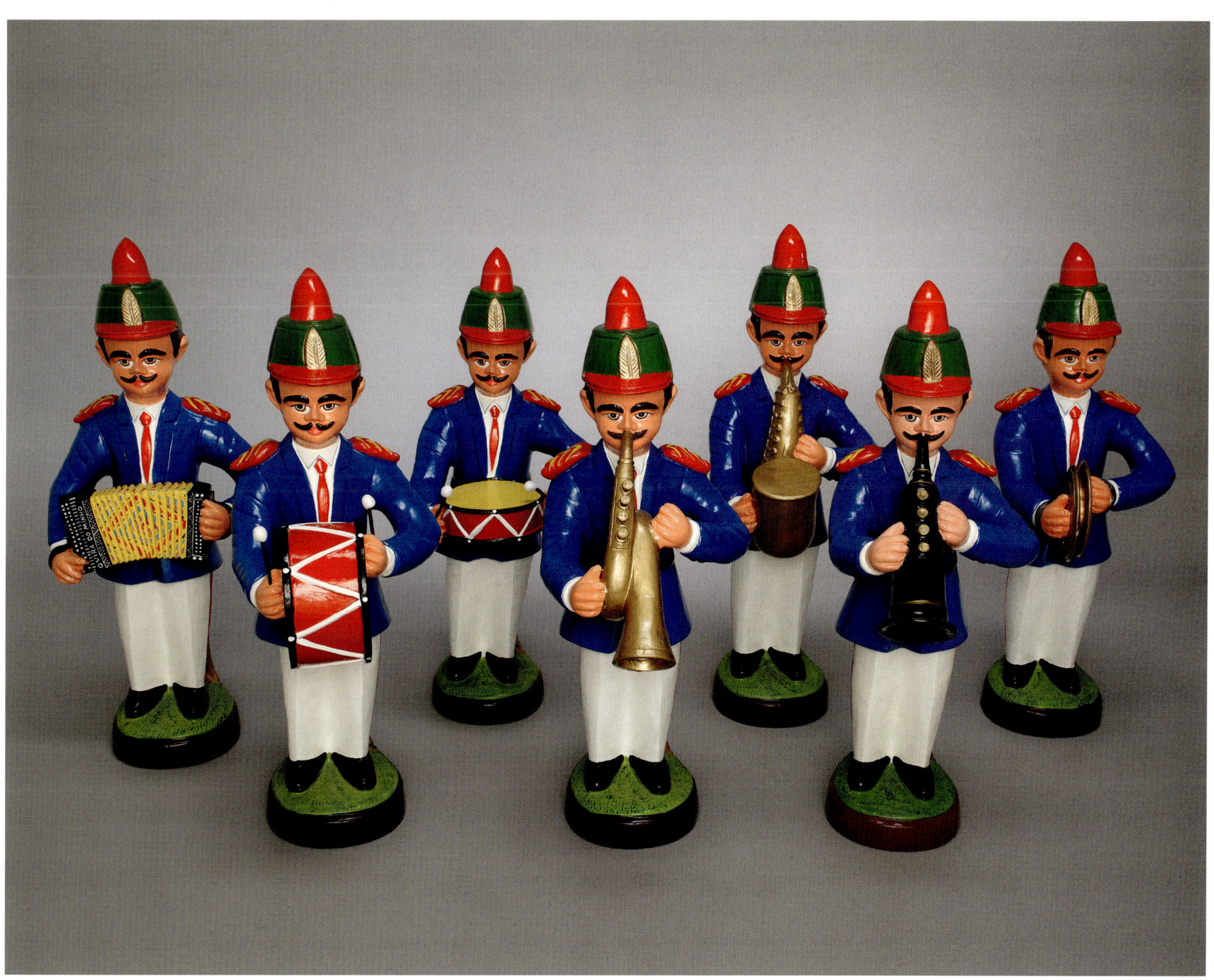

facing, top
Blackware ceramic pitchers, Molelos, Viseu, c. 1920–2011.

facing, bottom left
Ceramic pitchers, Barcelos, c. 1930.

facing, bottom right
Pottery stalls at the Fair of São Mateus in Viseu in 2014 sold a variety of brown and black earthenware.

> houses in Alentejo are remarkable in three ways: the way they are designed (for comfort); their cleanliness and their artistic layout. They are supplied with everything that is practical: everything is clean, objects for everyday use are artistically laid out in a symmetrical fashion; the shelf with the pots on it leans against the wall next to the bottle rack where everything is arranged according to size. Bowls are displayed in a line, lemons are placed in them, the least ripe together and the most ripe in the centre for easy access.[263]

The utilitarian vision expressed by the *Deus, Pátria, Família* (God, Country, Family) lithograph was reaffirmed in a number of international exhibitions, such as the 1940 *Exhibition of the Portuguese World* in Lisbon, which reinforced the value of hand-produced goods. Most of the pottery displayed in international and national exhibitions came from the five main pottery centres in the country: Barcelos, Coimbra, Caldas da Rainha, Mafra and Estremoz. Originally all had produced mainly utilitarian wares, some decorated like those of Caldas da Rainha and Coimbra, but by the late nineteenth century all had begun to produce at least some figurative pieces.

POTTERY CENTRES IN PORTUGAL

Barcelos and Estremoz figurative traditions have long existed, though the accuracy of the much-quoted reference to sixteenth-century figurative wares from Barcelos, made by Fr. Bartolomeu dos Mártires (founder of the convent of Santa Cruz in Viana do Castelo), has recently been disputed.[264] This dates the earliest confirmable description of Barcelos figurative wares to José Augusto Vieira's work O *Minho Pitoresco* (1886). Vieira wrote: "The dolls (*bonecos*) of Prado, of archaic inspiration and barbarous vagueness that at times borders on delirium, can tell complicated fantasies, a genre of story about witches narrated in fables of clay."[265]

H.N. Shore mentioned figurative works in his 1898 book *Three Pleasant Springs in Portugal*. At the Matosinhos Fair he encountered hundreds of utilitarian and figurative pieces, "strange," "crude" and "barbarous looking" images of birds, animals, reptiles, insects, ox carts and agricultural and domestic implements, coarsely glazed and painted red, yellow and brown. "The most singular aspect of this collection," Shore noted, "was that every piece possessed a whistle."[266] Two years later, in 1900, the antiquarian Rocha Peixoto published the first scholarly work on Barcelos pottery, *As Olarias de Prado*, in which he confirmed the provenance of such pieces.[267] Peixoto described the modelling and moulding techniques, the use of the wares by children as toys and their inspiration derived from common themes and local flora and fauna.[268]

A 1909 newspaper article in *A Ilustração Popular* reiterated previous references to the primitive, crude and ugly qualities of the Barcelos clay models, referring to them as "monstrous figures and fetishes speckled with inconceivable colors."[269] Despite these early derogative accounts, by 1940 Secretary of National Propaganda Ferro was objecting to the application of new decorative techniques and urging pottery makers to preserve their works' rustic appeal and promote them as a quintessential expression of Lusitanian identity.[270]

To begin with, only women in Barcelos made decorative pottery, shaping the fanciful designs to make whistles, while men dedicated themselves exclusively to producing economically important utilitarian wares such as jugs, plates, cups, bowls, casserole dishes and storage containers. Figurative pieces were unglazed and were fired only when space remained in the kiln after it had been filled

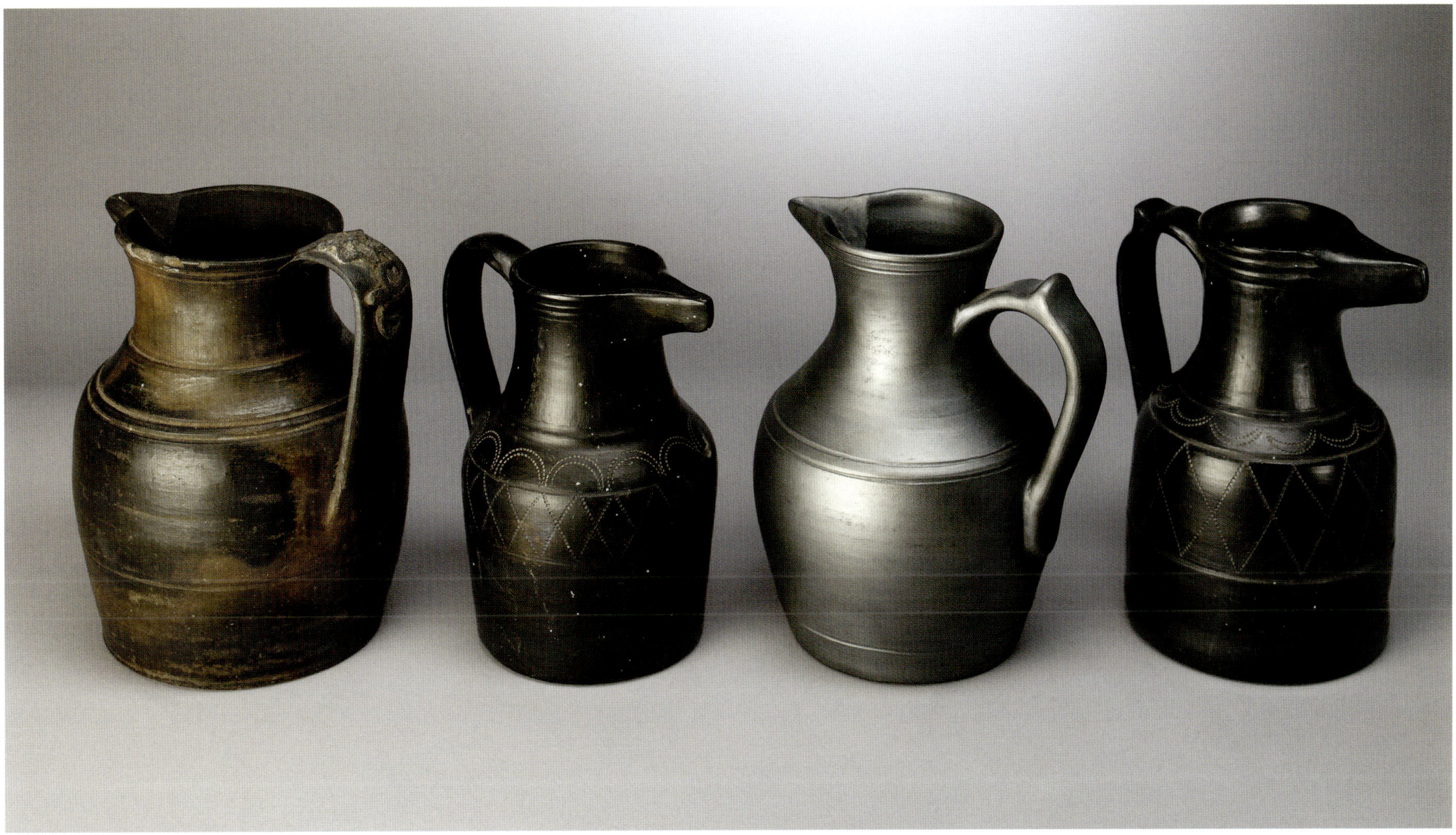

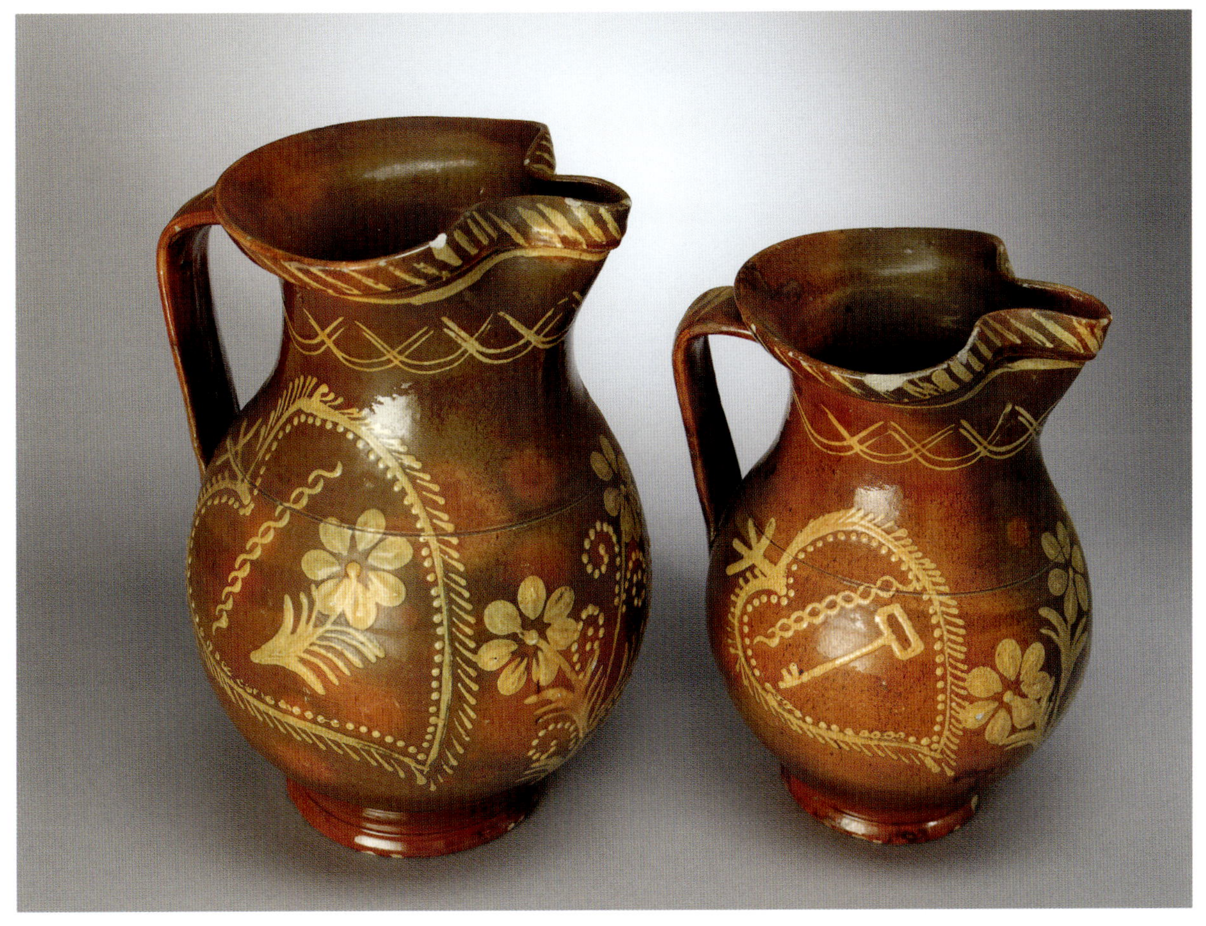

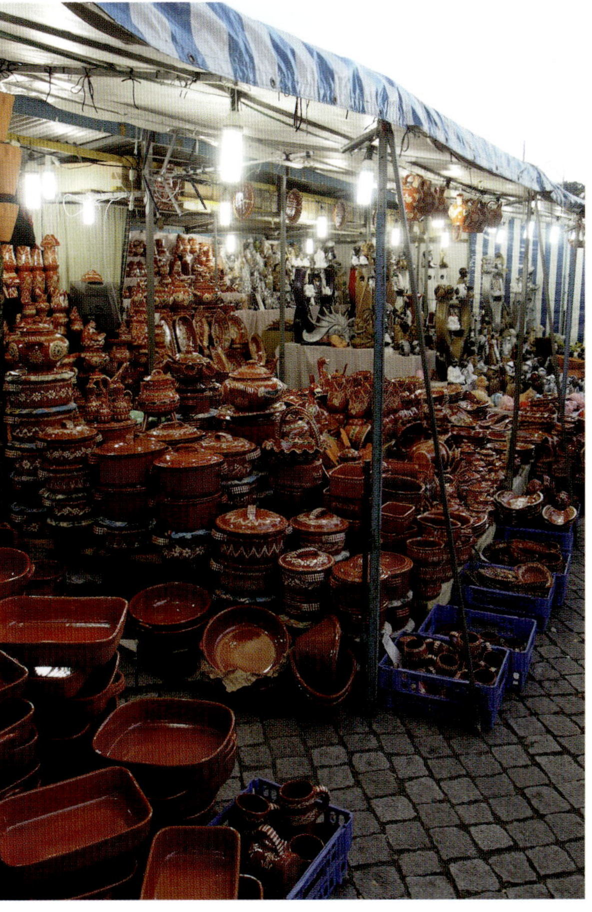

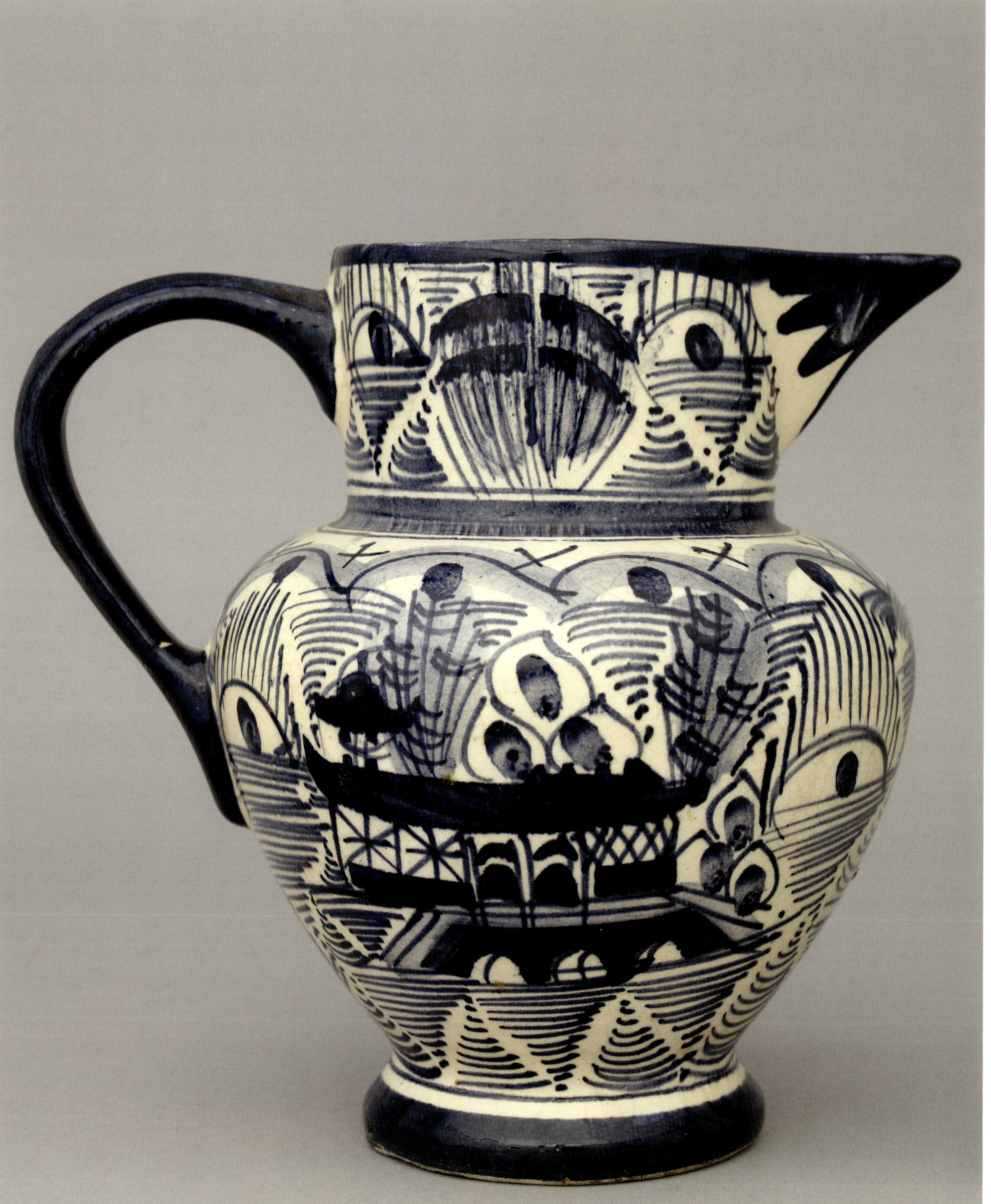

facing
Ceramic pitcher, Coimbra, c. 1950.

with practical wares.[271] Both were sold uniquely at country fairs, to be used by children and adults alike. Whistles grew more elaborate and inventive in form, until by the end of the nineteenth century their production assumed an economic importance of its own.[272]

Pottery workshops in Estremoz, though no longer as numerous as others in the Alentejo region such as Crato, Nisa, Portalegre and Redondo, were established as early as the thirteenth century. Royal decrees of 1258 and 1512 reminded potters of the tribute they were obliged to pay. Estremoz pottery became famous for its quality in the fifteenth to seventeenth centuries and, because of local demand, continued to flourish well into the nineteenth century.[273] The school of arts and crafts was established in the town in 1924, offering courses in stonemasonry and pottery to help maintain local industries. The school cooperated with the museum, which has a collection of eighteenth- and nineteenth-century figurative works, to re-establish local figurative production. It developed particularly close relationships with Tiana das Peles, a senior potter, and Mariano da Conceição, an artisan from a line of potters who worked to re-establish the figurative tradition until his premature death. Banha da Conceição and his sister Sabina Augusta da Conceição resumed Mariano's work and were later joined by their other sisters Maria Inácia Fonseca Mateus and Perpétua Matilde Fonseca. The collections of the municipal museum also converted Afonso Ginja from working as a stonemason to become a potter. He now works with his brother Arlindo in a shared workshop that was established in the museum in 1979. The only existing non-figurative workshop in Estremoz is the Olaria Regional, founded by José Ourelo in the 1940s.[274] After Ourelo's death in 1983, Mário Lagartinho took over the workshop, but had to halt production in 2014 because of ill health.

Coimbra has been an important ceramic centre since at least the sixteenth century, producing simple decorative faience for domestic consumption. From the eighteenth century, the university town increased production substantially, which, together with the introduction of new materials and greater division of labour, gave it competitive advantages over those centres producing rustic wares.[275] The style of the work—floral and botanical motifs, crude figures and armorial devices using a mainly blue palette—became standardized and aimed at a more refined market than those of Barcelos or Estremoz. Figures of saints, including reliquary busts, were produced beginning in the eighteenth century,[276] many destined for family altars along with related religious objects, such as fonts for holding holy water. By the nineteenth century ceramic production in Coimbra was divided between faience and earthenware factories, and different qualities of pottery were produced to accommodate growing differentiation in the market. At this time the orientalist motifs that distinguished Coimbra ceramics from those found elsewhere in Portugal were introduced. By the 1960s Coimbra had lost the utilitarian market and refocused production on decorative wares. At the same time, decoration became highly influenced by earlier designs, which have become increasingly directed and are now largely limited to the tourist and collectors' markets.

In other parts of Portugal, such as the region around Caldas da Rainha, where makers also seemed to be mainly men, figurative forms had already been incorporated into utilitarian wares. Caldas da Rainha is also a long-established pottery centre whose wares are mentioned in historical documents from the twelfth, fourteenth

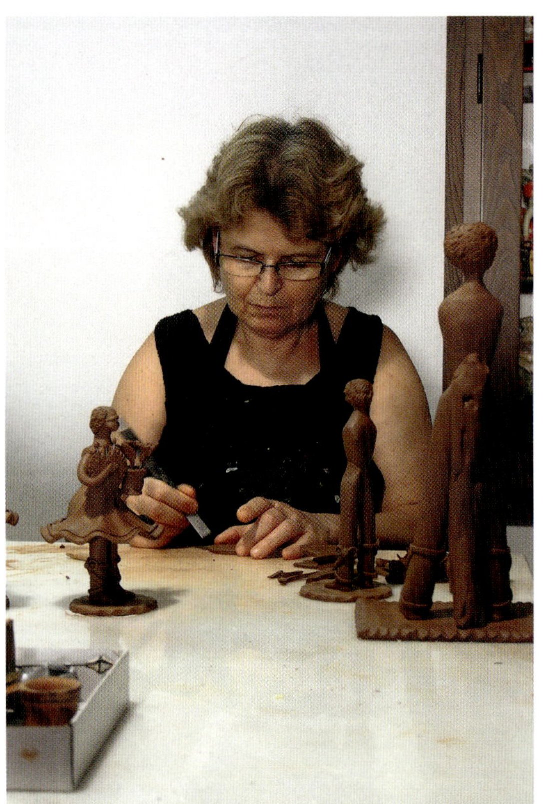

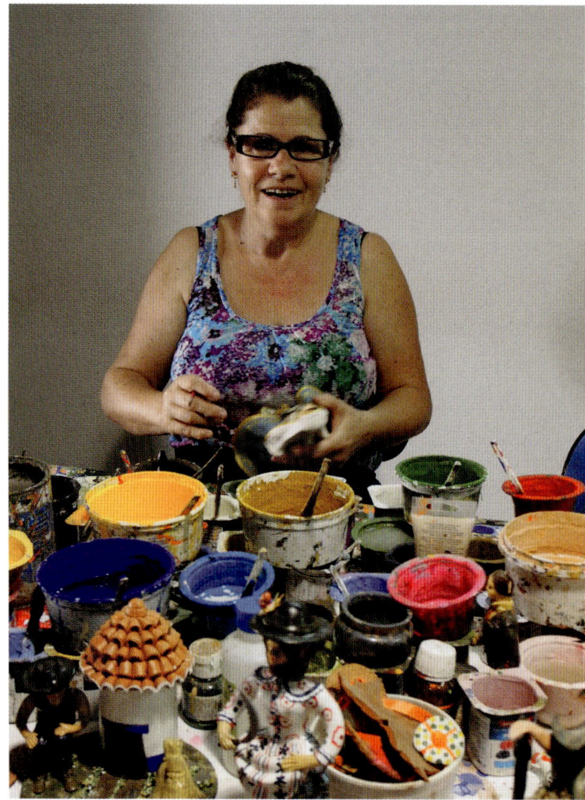

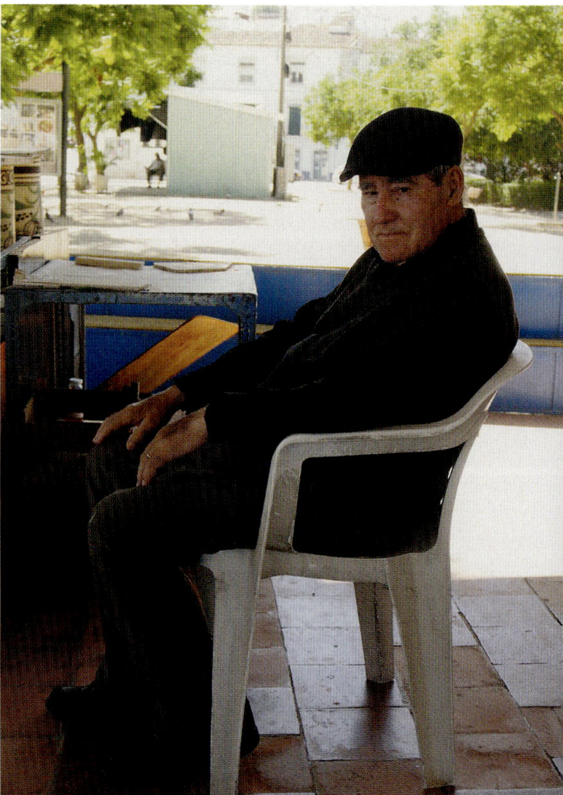

top left
Ceramic artist Maria Inácia Fonseca Mateus, 2011.

top centre
Ceramic artist Perpétua Matilde Fonseca Sousa, 2011.

top right
The owner of the last domestic pottery workshop in Estremoz, Mário Lagartinho, 2014.

facing, left
Ceramic artist Afonso Ginja, 2011.

facing, right
AFONSO GINJA
Figures representing spring and "love is blind," 2012.

and fifteenth centuries. In a manuscript from 1195 reproduced by Alexandre Herculano in his *Portugaliae Monumenta Historica*, the regional town of Leiria is mentioned as a pottery centre, and references to the distinctive green, white and yellow clays of the area begin to appear after the fourteenth century.[277] The first kilns in the region were dated by Avelino Belo to 1488. By 1656 manuscript sources attest to the quantity and quality of wares produced in Caldas.[278]

The town of Caldas da Rainha took on a new significance with the establishment of Rafael Pinheiro's Fábrica de Faianças (faience factory) in 1884. Pinheiro introduced elaborate decorative works reviving Renaissance and baroque styles. After Rafael's death and the factory's temporary closure, his son Manuel Gustavo re-established the works in 1908. He adopted a contemporary style intended to convey unique Portuguese decorative themes based, in part, on the flora and fauna of the area and the nearby sea.

Emerging at the time of the liberal reforms and the advent of modernity, the Caldas workshops created new domestic markets among those sectors experiencing embourgeoisement and provided a material culture that could be used and displayed to express new values. During the same period—the late nineteenth century—the Coimbra and Caldas workshops reduced the market share for traditional pottery and contributed to its decline. The Barcelos pottery partially survived through the ideological and financial support for utilitarian crafts it received in the 1930s from the Estado Novo[279] and the growing popularity of rustic figurative work during that period; from 1938 to 1966 there were an estimated 549 potters in Barcelos.[280] Wares from Barcelos and Estremoz were considered "pure," "typical" and more genuinely Portuguese than those from elsewhere.

In the late twentieth century Caldas began producing the popular *malandrices*, phallus-shaped pottery whose production grew up beside the established ceramics factories and workshops, which disdained them. Usually *malandrices* were made on the side—in makeshift sheds next to the homes of artisans employed by the established companies—and were sold at country fairs and football stadiums. Made from poor materials and rough moulds using crude production techniques,

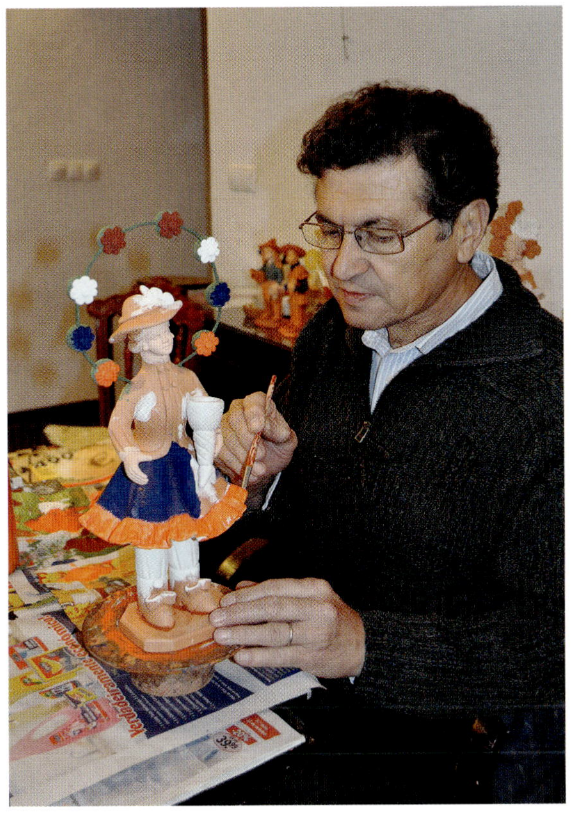

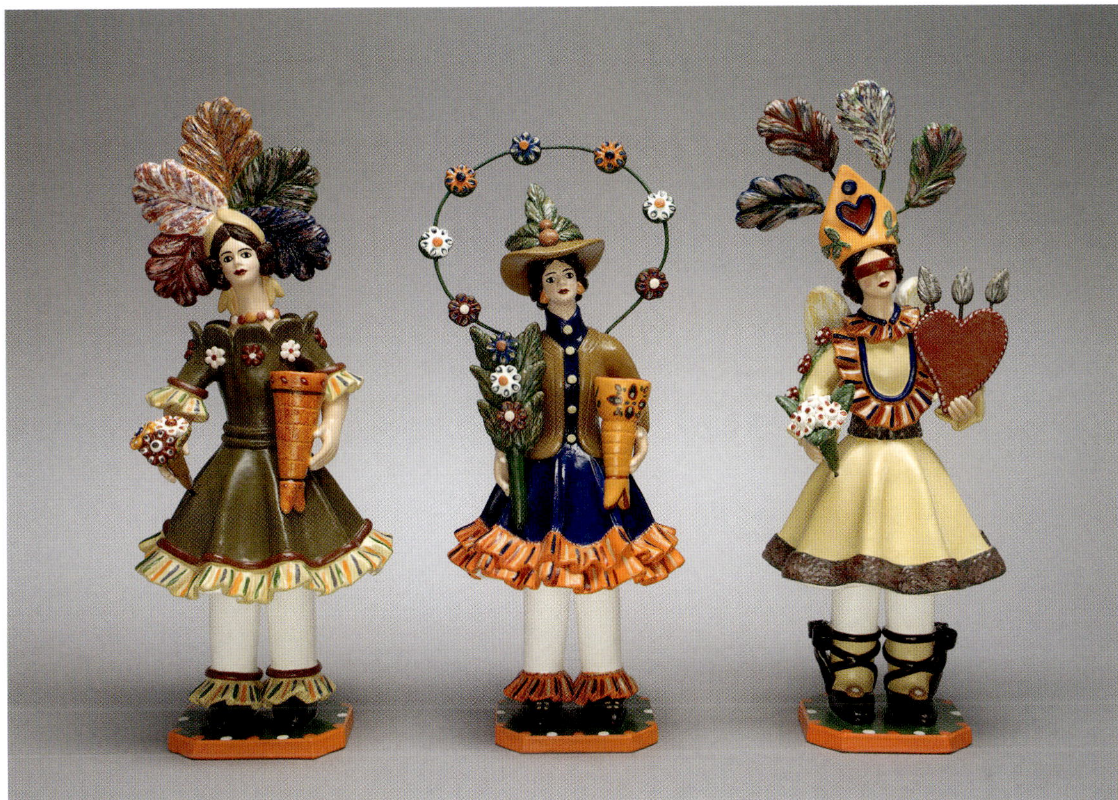

they were usually broken or disposed of after they were used in celebrations or as part of joking behaviour.[281] They are part of a tradition of disposable pottery articles that includes the old whistles of Barcelos and the piggy banks still found in stores and workshops up and down the country.

There was a second revitalization of pottery production during the 1960s and 1970s, when Patrick Swift worked to renew the almost lost tradition at Porches in the Algarve, Luís Soares re-stimulated the Cascais style and Afonso Ginja used the collections of his local museum to create high-quality reproductions and original works to reinvigorate Estremoz figurative pottery. These enthusiasts were later joined by Sérgio Amaral, who reintroduced black pottery production in Mangualde. This intervention to rescue traditional regional pottery styles coincided with a strong interest in collecting popular art in the wake of its gradual disappearance. In the 1960s and early 1970s increased interest among collectors also led to the foundation or growth of important regional and local museums. José Régio in Portalegre (1971), Júlio Reis Pereira in Estremoz (1975) and Joaquim Selles, whose collections founded the Museu de Olaria in Barcelos (1963), contributed enormously to preserving Portugal's rural heritage by supporting new and established museums that preserved and displayed their collections.[282]

In 1968 pottery production in the centre and north of the country remained vigorous. Wright and Swift described impressive commercial displays of pottery at Alcobaça,[283] which can still be seen today. They also commented on the plentiful whistles and figurative pieces in the fair at Óbidos[284] and the availability of black pottery at the fair in Viseu, which continues up to the present.[285] The state of the industry was not, however, as good in the south of the country, where, if not for Swift establishing a workshop of his own at Carvoeiro in the Algarve, Lagoa pottery would have disappeared.[286] Wright and Swift also documented the impoverished conditions in which some potters lived, countering the official romanticism around craft production. Writing of a potter's house in Bisalhães, Wright and Swift noted: "The path up to the door, and the surrounding ground, was black as soot. The jet-black clay was piled up like miniature slag heaps about the huddle of houses. Set into a mound of

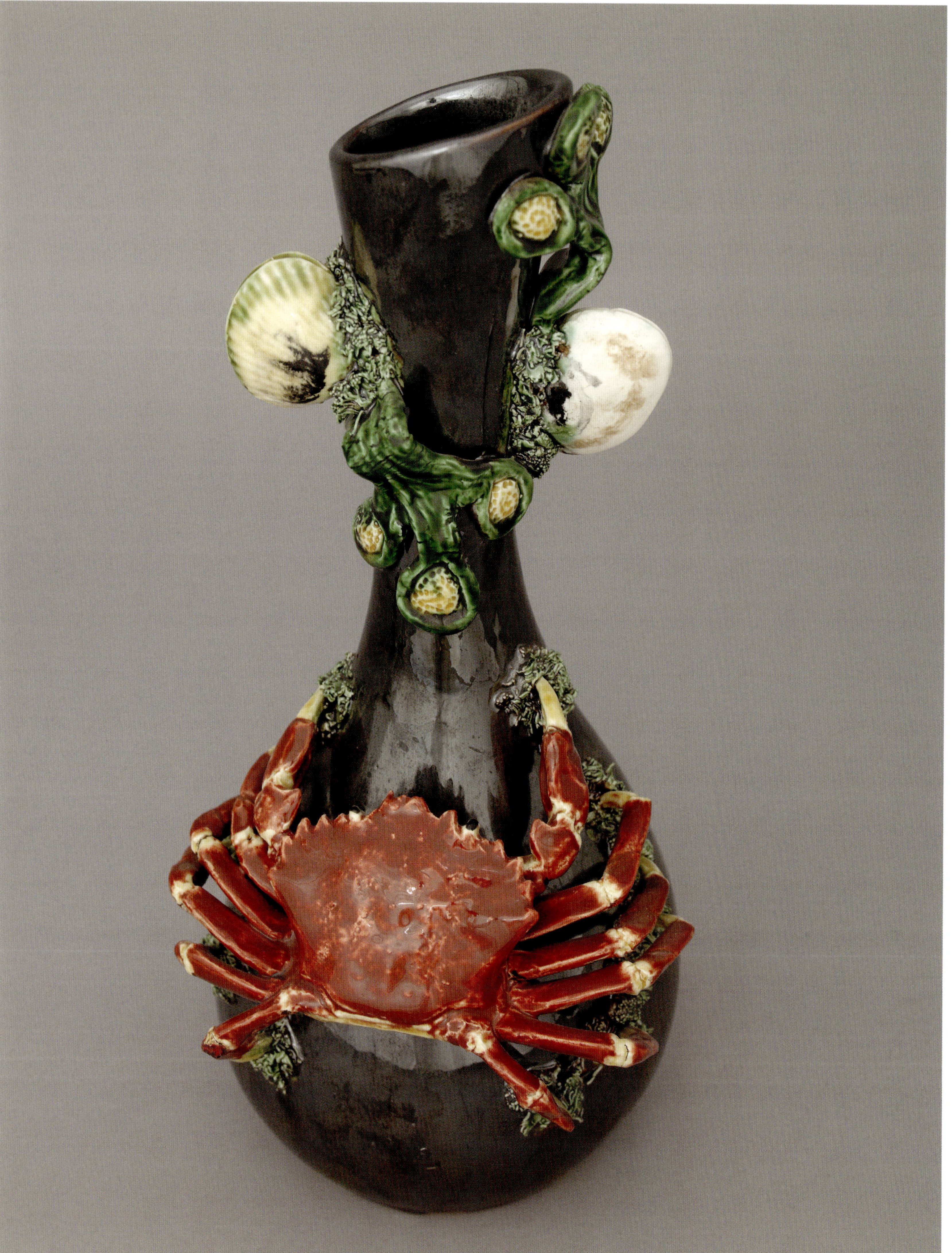

facing
Vase, Caldas da Rainha, c. 2009.

black clay and coal-like rubble at the side of the house was an oven."[287] The poverty was extreme and the potter, who is never named (although they note that he had trained other artisans who had travelled the world), was able to make no more than eight pots per day, insufficient to sustain even a modest lifestyle.[288] The impoverished conditions of popular artists were ignored and obscured by the idyllic images the Estado Novo created for outside consumption.[289]

Many artisans at this time sold their own work, but despite attending markets as far as Porto and Braga, their sales could not lift them out of poverty. In those days potters typically followed a cyclical lifestyle, with production centred on November to April and sales concentrated in the season of *romarias*, which unfolded from May to October.[290] This cycle continued to regulate the lives of potters and other artisans until the 1970s, when changes in lifestyle, consumption and the availability of alternative materials decreased both attendance and sales at country markets and *romarias*.

The 1970s also saw innovations in pottery production—wood-fired kilns were replaced by models using gas and electricity (though there still exist a wide variety of older, double-chambered kilns);[291] moulded works gave way to combined modelling and moulding techniques; and innovation in decoration promoted the revaluation of some works as art.[292] Only when new and specialist markets slowly emerged, including the burgeoning tourist market, was pottery revalued and the economic situation of potters improved.[293]

Sales venues, *romarias* and saint's day celebrations are being supplanted by craft fairs and artisan markets, which are now organized at international, national and municipal levels. Such fairs and markets also encourage sociability between potters and artisans generally and attract popular public support. But unique religious and cultural experiences, many strong and centuries old, have been lost to these secular events, as has the religious cohesion that helped knit communities together.[294]

Historically, economic marginalization, insecurity and the sharp seasonal division of their work contributed to the development of close supportive communities and a unique shared culture among potters.[295] The *romarias* provided the opportunity for potters from different regions to mix and compare their wares and promoted cross-fertilization and innovation of themes and designs. Frequently in rustic production, the whole family was involved in one stage or other of the process. Craft, and pottery in particular, was tied closely to religious thought and elicited a sensibility for a modest and elegant beauty. The ceramic historian Fernandes reminds us that

> God created men with his own hands, taking a piece of clay and fashioning us in His image and likeness. He held us in his hands, moulding us according to His will, modelled us and left us with the sensation that 'now, O Lord, thou art our Father, we are the clay and thou art our potter and we are all the work of thy hands.'[296] God did not have recourse to any other instrument to conceive us."[297]

The hard itinerant life of a potter, with its privations and poverty, could be compared to the life of Christ himself. As the potter Angelica Cruz muses: "I was born surrounded by clay, I grew surrounded by clay and I will die because of clay."[298]

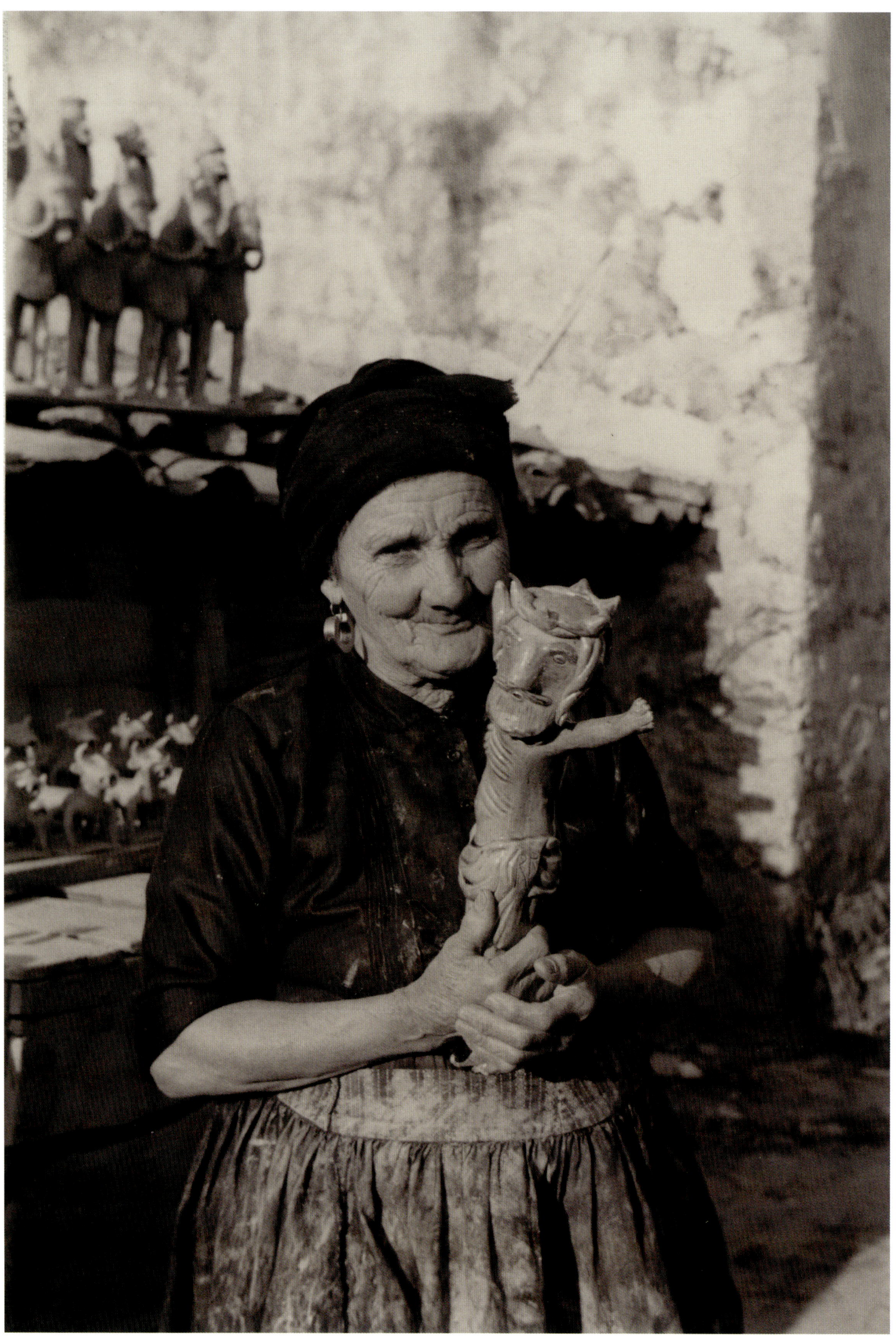

5 Saints and Their Makers

The Voices of Criticism

In order to invent heaven and hell a man would need to know nothing except the human body.

José Saramago[299]

FIGURATIVE POTTERY IN northern Portugal "was born from a tendentiously feminine world."[300] In the nineteenth and twentieth centuries women occupied a socially mute position in a country that, for much of the last century, the Estado Novo attempted to domesticate even more. Within this quiescence, maintained from 1926 by state-sponsored censorship, intimidation and fear, women suffered an additional, older muteness imposed by long-established asymmetrical gender relations.

Religion and politics under the Estado Novo were mainly patriarchal domains. Usually only men became members of the brotherhoods and commissions that cared for local saints and planned their ceremonial processions and feast days, and often men alone had the right to represent their families at parish meetings. A woman's property, upon marriage, usually passed to her husband. Propertyless, a woman was expected to assist her husband in agricultural work, tend the garden, devote herself to religion, be a good wife and mother and organize the home. According to one old woman in Minho, north of the village of Vila Ruiva in central Portugal, "Men and women have different *superioridades* [strengths]: men go out to work, women stay at home."[301] Nuno Porto, writing on Vila Ruiva in 1991, noted that the Estado Novo reinforced traditional family structure, confirming it as a privileged site of affection, sexuality and masculine authority, consecrating the roles of both a regenerated Church and the male as responsible for the fulfillment of a family's social and economic obligations.[302] During this period men mediated external relations with the family, while women's authority and space for interactions were confined largely to the home;[303] men were invested with the exercise of reason, while women were associated with the expression of sentiment. Since sentiment was subordinated to reason, the social power relations between men and women were neatly reiterated through supposedly different mentalities.[304] In Minho, this gender asymmetry that gave moral superiority to men was thought to have been instigated by God after Eve tempted Adam and brought death to humanity. From then on women were considered morally weak and temptresses, while men were more controlled.[305]

In the case of potters these gender-based mentalities were expressed through useful and valued products. Utilitarian works were always made by men, while fanciful dolls or *bonecos*, of no

facing
Ceramic artist Rosa Ramalho, 1968.

facing
Ceramic artist Júlia Ramalho holding one of her niche altars of Santo António, 2011.

practical value, were made by women.[306] These qualities were the basis of the familial economic unit and established an idealized harmony within the rural milieu.[307] José Cutileiro's work conducted twenty years earlier in the south-central region of Alentejo closely affirms Porto's and Pina-Cabral's descriptions of Vila Ruiva and the Minho villages of Couto and Paço. In the community where Cutileiro worked, men were expected to respect and understand the limits of their authority and not trespass into the female domain. In the domestic sphere women could, nevertheless, exercise considerable power and authority;[308] they determined dress and clothing, which publicly expressed the family's wealth; assumed responsibility for the family budget; and looked after the family, mediating conflicts when the husband worked away for any protracted time. Women also played an important role in decisions on emigration and intervened between this world and that of the saints to ensure the protection of the family and home.[309]

In much of the Portuguese countryside before the 1970s, a woman's obedience was valued over curiosity, domestic and economic obligations overwhelmed creativity, submission was favoured over independence and silence was preferred to dialogue. Nevertheless, these ideals were pragmatically applied, and in Minho there were overlaps in the division of agricultural work and in other economic and organizational activities as a result of male absence. This, however, only fortified men's authority, as the money they earned abroad was often invested locally in small land holdings, which the women worked.[310] When a man died his widow wore black to express her withdrawal from the world and her submission to the spectre of patriarchal memories and the anticipation of her own death and judgment. This stark division of roles was mediated through life-cycle and civic ceremonies, leaving only joking behaviour as a means to resolve tensions over gender and sexuality. The world of Portuguese women was an interior world—confined to house and mind—that in many places, few breached. Within this silent world, the potter Rosa Ramalho (1888–1977) was one of the few women who expressed her rich imaginative creativity.[311] There were notable women potters before her, including the well-known Maria dos Cacos, who made and sold figurative work in the Caldas area from 1820 to 1853,[312] but it was Rosa Ramalho who best revealed the rich creativity, the restless play of thought and images and the uniqueness of a female imagination expressed through the play of hands rather than the syllables of the voice.

ROSA RAMALHO AND THE BEGINNING OF RELIGIOUS IMAGES

The prominent position that Rosa Ramalho attained among the popular artists of her time was extraordinary. Moreover, her reputation long continued to increase, as the list of posthumous exhibitions in which her work was included clearly attests. These include the 2001 exhibition *Os Artistas e a Cidade* (Porto 60/70: Artists and the City) at Museu Serralves, Porto, Portugal's premier museum of contemporary art, and *Mestres Artesãos do Século* (The Century's Master Artisans), organized by the Institute for Work and Professional Training; more recently, in 2007, the Museu de Olaria in Barcelos curated a major retrospective and published the most comprehensive catalogue to date of her work. Ramalho's creative corpus is all the more surprising because, while she had worked with clay as a young girl, she did not return to pottery until the age of sixty-eight, in 1955, after her husband's death and the loss of his mill, where she had worked. She did nearly all her work in the twenty-two years before her death in 1977. Maria E. Pereira de Costa, a

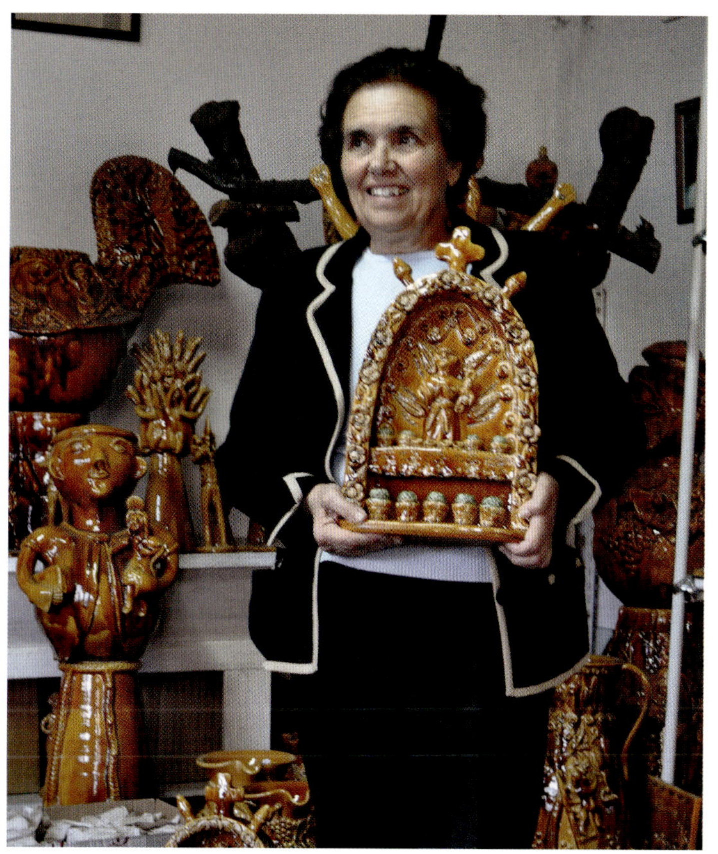

friend of hers, recalled in conversation with me in June 2011 that in the 1960s, the Barcelos municipality would purchase or commission works by Ramalho for official presentations and later as prizes for municipal and professional competitions, and she would deliver pieces personally to the mayor's office, where Pereira de Costa worked. Collectors sought out Ramalho's work from early on and the fame she quickly attained even attracted the interest of several German commercial ceramics companies.[313]

Historians of pottery like Rios, Ramos and Régo[314] and Fernandes[315] attribute the post-1950s positive revaluation of Barcelos pottery to Rosa Ramalho and her relationship with the artist and teacher António Quadros Ferreira. He lauded her work for its "archaic," "raw" and "brutal" expression, which, along with Picasso, he insisted, had been a major influence on him. From the outset, Ferreira became Rosa Ramalho's fervent advocate and a major collector of her work. He invited her to give classes at Porto's Escola Superior de Belas Artes and organized the first exhibition of her work, at the Cooperativa Árvore.[316] Ferreira met Ramalho in the 1950s at fairs at Paranhos, Carvalhos and Serra do Pilar, where she and other potters sold their work. During this period she began to sign her pieces "RR," a sign that she had moved beyond the anonymity of the artisan to the individual realm of artist.[317] Under Ferreira's mentorship, Rosa Ramalho's work came to be acknowledged, by state and public alike, as embodying the quintessential elements intrinsic to a distinctive Portuguese art and identity.

Ramalho was perhaps the major exponent of much of the corpus of forms that still frames the figurative work of Barcelos. She experimented in the creation of high-relief plaques whose subjects included Christ, the saints and the Last Supper, all finished in a vitreous lead glaze. Working with Rosa Barbosa Lopes and others in the 1960s, she also designed and executed the first small niche altars depicting figures such as the crucified Christ, disembodied angels suspended around a saint, or the Virgin. Her niche altars, a form that goes back to Roman times, are stylistically closely related to her plaques, but probably have a more direct connection to the altars commonly found in churches. Rosa's granddaughter, Júlia Ramalho, has also borrowed from the same genre and subject, but has recently begun to depict Santo António flanked by pots of green basil to ward off spells and evil spirits.[318] Júlia has further elaborated her grandmother's repertoire of images to include figurative sculptures and relief plaques, including a figure of Bacchus holding a suckling pig that is awarded in an annual gastronomy competition in Barcelos.

Given the Estado Novo's strong support of the Church and its strategic function in creating a forceful Christian morality and apostolic mission, the importance of religious themes in popular art is not surprising. However, large figures of Christ and the saints do not appear to have been made in

facing, left
ROSA RAMALHO
The Devil Playing the Guitar, C. 1950–60

facing, right
ROSA RAMALHO
São Pedro Holding the Key to Heaven, C. 1950–60

Barcelos before the 1950s and 1960s. Many of the saints moulded or fashioned in Barcelos are central to Portuguese popular and institutional religion, whereas representations of local or more obscure saints are rare. Surprisingly, however, the most popular religious figure in Portugal, the one for whom most *romarias* are still organized, the Virgin Mary or Nossa Senhora, is, with the exception of Laurinda Pias, seldom represented by these potters; this is stranger still given that the role of women within the traditional family and the nature of family love was modelled upon that of the Virgin and the Holy Family.[319]

Despite this one seeming paradox, the sociability and religious values transmitted through the *romarias* have nevertheless had a longer-lasting influence on popular art than institutionalized religion. Peixoto, in his 1900 publication, gave a long list of dispersed fairs in the late nineteenth century at which Barcelos pottery was sold and that provided mutual contact between popular art, religion and commerce. These fairs, many originating in the Middle Ages, took place in Coura, Monção, Melgaço, Pontes, Barca, Arcos de Valdevez, Lamego, Viseu, Porto, Oliveirinha (Aveiro) and Figueira, and others were held as far north as Galicia in Spain.[320] In Barcelos, as in the rest of northern Portugal, potters and their families had to spend May through October attending fairs and *romarias* in order to sell their wares. This part of the annual work cycle was hard, not only socially and financially—camping out sometimes in inclement weather, fear of robbers and everyday theft, paying for transport—but because the sheer number and quick succession of *romarias* required stamina and perseverance. Rios, Ramos and Régo, building on Peixoto's earlier work, list the annual *romarias* attended by many Barcelos potters in the twentieth century.[321] The season began with the Celebration of the Crosses in Barcelos at the beginning of May, followed by the celebrations of the Senhora da Hora, of the Senhor de Matosinhos and of São João, all within the Porto metropolitan area. Artisans then continued to the fairs of Fontainhas and São Pedro in Vila Real. In the middle of July they attended the Gualtarianas in Guimarães. In August it was the Senhora da Agonia in Viana do Castelo, then on to the Feira da Luz in Carnide, Lisbon. They set up stalls at the October fair in Vila Franca de Xira followed by the Fair of Piedade in Santarém, and finished in Tomar at the Fair de Santa Iria. They might add to this gruelling annual itinerary the Feira dos Santos in Vila Nova de Ourém or that of Nossa Senhora dos Remédios in Lamego in northern Portugal. So widespread was their pottery sold that Macedo Correia wrote in 1965 that "there is no fair or *romaria* without the pottery of Barcelos."[322] Catholicism and small-scale commerce, religion and folk art, performance and plastic expression, popular values and pottery styles—these many dichotomies were all intimately connected and represented the two sides of an artist's experience.

Rosa Ramalho may have been the first potter in Barcelos to model religious images. Her pottery depictions of the crucified Christ became iconic, and her figures of Santa Isabel la Raînha (Queen Santa Isabel) holding the bunch of roses that allude to the saint's miraculous ability also achieved wide popularity in paintings, prints, more formal sculptures and the Portuguese decorative tiles known as *azulejos*. Santa Isabel, known in English as Elizabeth of Portugal, is especially revered in Coimbra; most older women in the area are able to recount the stories of how she changed roses into bread and the help birds gave her to weave and spin. When Isabel's husband, Dom Dinis, the founder of the University of Coimbra, was unable to pay for the

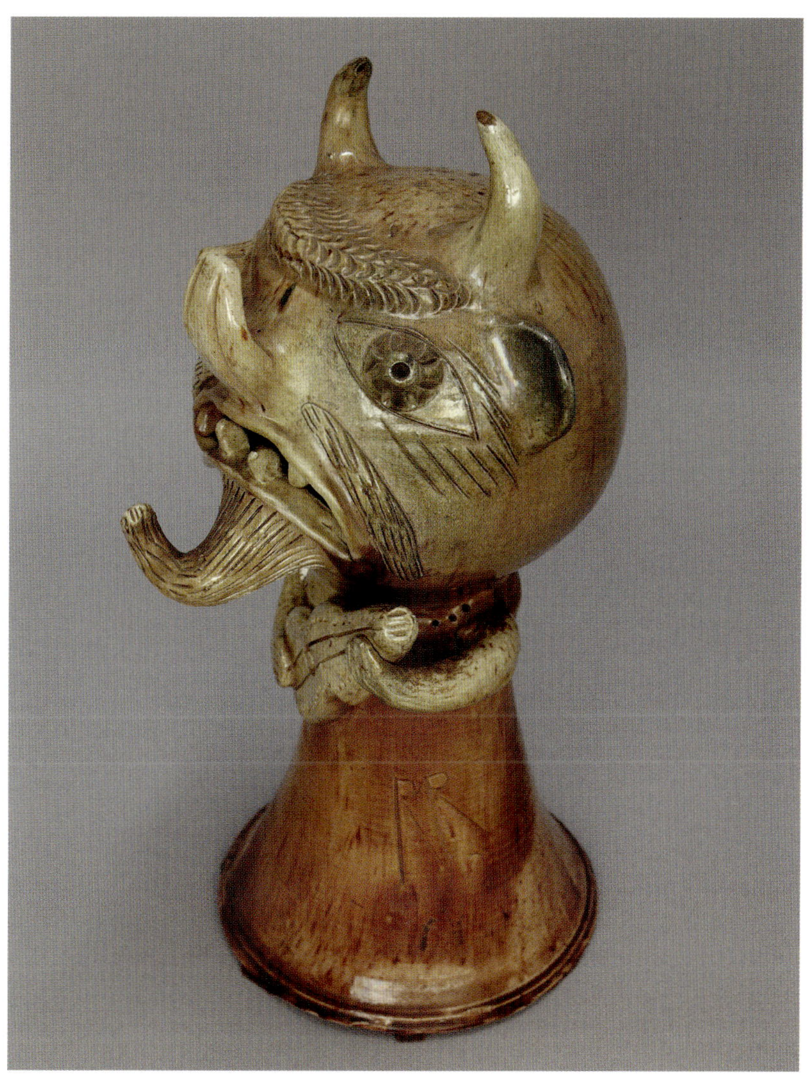

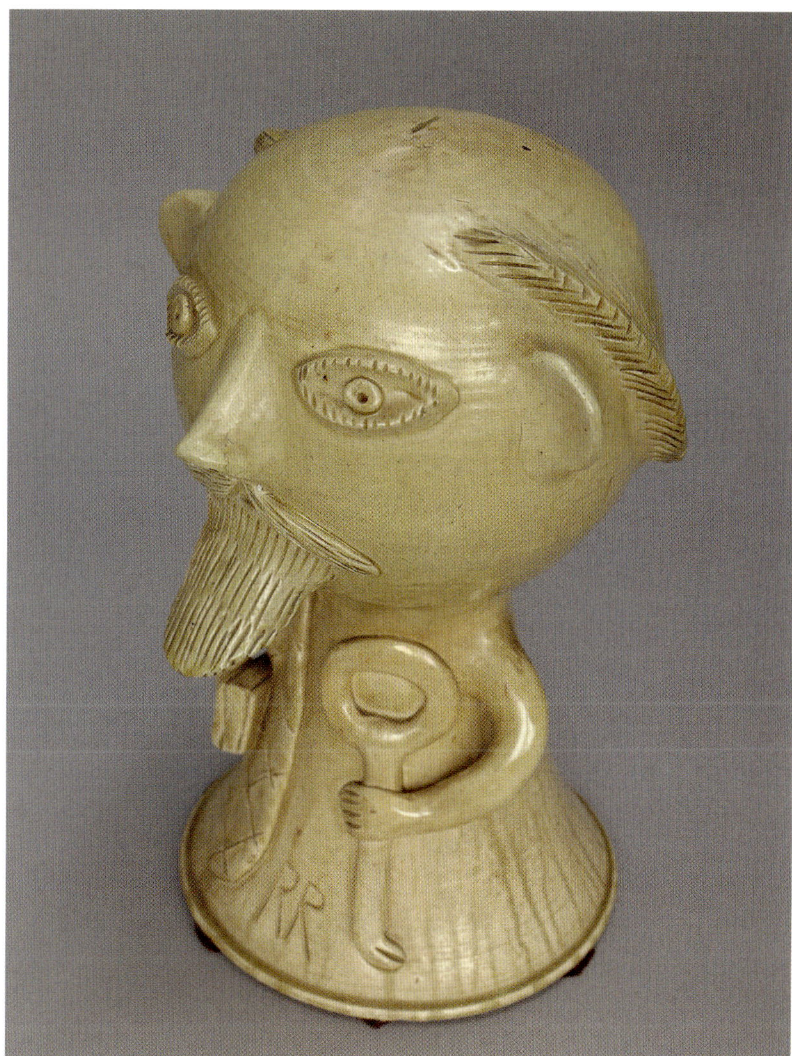

construction of the twenty-eight-metre-high turret of his castle at Estremoz, so the story goes, she presented his workers with roses, which by the following day had turned into gold.[323] The saint's cult is closely associated with the monastery of Santa Clara in Coimbra, where, after renouncing her royal title and position, Santa Isabel lived and where her body now lies.

Santo António is perhaps the most commonly modelled saint today, popular not only in Lisbon but throughout the country. Referred to as the saint of love and described as humble, charitable, tireless in his missionary activity, scholarly and helpful in finding lost objects, his life and purported miracles are the subjects of many stories and an abundant literature. Santo António's popularity has increased throughout the last century, greatly stimulating the market for his images. These have proliferated not only in number but also in style, ranging from brightly coloured, pop art–style moulded images to the naturalistic, clay-brown, rustic depictions made by the Caldas artist José Franco (1920–). Santo António is usually shown holding the infant Jesus, reminding his adorers of the miraculous apparition of the Christ child and the kiss he bestowed upon the saint.

Other saints commonly represented by potters include São Pedro and São João Baptista, who, together with Santo António, are referred to as the *santos populares* or "common people's saints." This triad is always depicted in the most intimate style of any religious figures, a reminder of the argument that the strength of popular religion stems from the belief that the saints are intermediaries between God and humanity. In Portuguese communities with scarce resources, one's lot in life

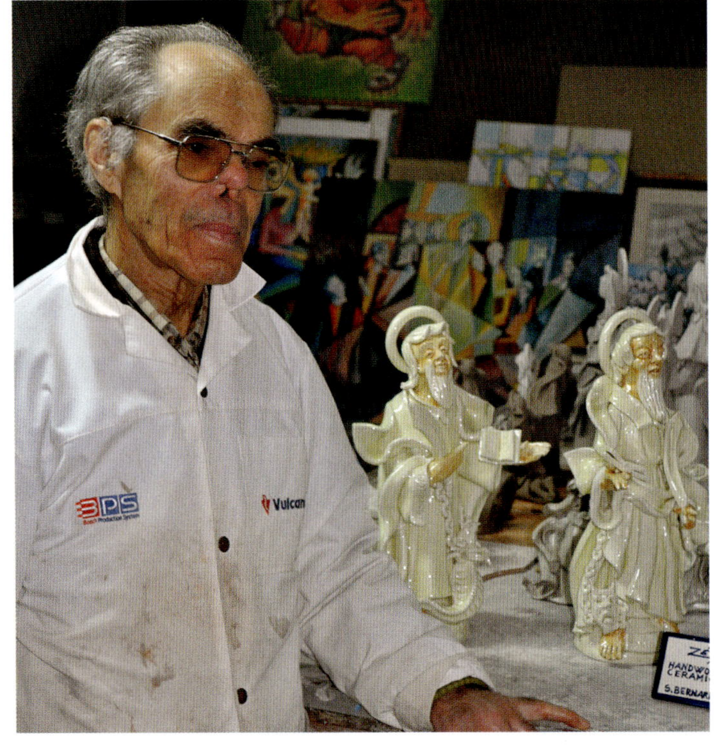

above
Artist José Augusto Ferreira dos Santos, 2011.

facing
JOSÉ AUGUSTO FERREIRA DOS SANTOS
The Three Popular Saints: São Pedro, São João Baptista and Santo António, c. 2010

was determined by luck, *sorte*, which constituted personal destiny sent by God. Luck determined personal fortune, the course of marriages, health, prestige and the outcome of dealings with authority and, when needed, could sometimes be manipulated through saintly intercession.

Nothing, according to Rodney Gallop, could be more different from Church doctrine than popular attitudes towards the three *santos populares*. Reaching back to nineteenth- and early twentieth-century folkloric traditions, Gallop wrote, "The three saints have been merged in the single conception of a jovial patron of revelry, a very jolly saint, heir to the mantle of Dionysius and Bacchus, with a good taste in wine and an eye for the girls."[324]

The festivals for these saints, on 13 June (Santo António), 24 June (São João) and 29 June (São Pedro), represent the culmination of the festive year and, with the festival of São João, the beginning of the summer solstice. The Day of São João is still referred to as the best day of the year because of the joviality, conviviality and good humour it continues to provoke in celebrations today. Zé Augusto, an Aveiro-based artist, perfectly captured the sympathetic characters of these saints, expressing through clay their humility, humanity and informality, qualities that together communicate the munificence of their divine jurisdiction. The three saints can be seen to invoke a symbolic expression of wholeness—São Pedro associated with the sky, through his guardianship of the door to Heaven; Santo António the sea, through his miraculous sermon to the fishes;[325] and São João the earth, through his wanderings and association with wilderness. Gallop, applying a genealogical argument typical of early folkloric studies, went so far as to suggest that together, the three saints might have once comprised a unitary pre-Christian deity or pagan trinity.[326]

CREATIVE WORK AS CRITICAL EVOCATION: ROSA AND JÚLIA RAMALHO

The popular cult of saints never neatly coincided with either ecclesiastic ideas of the proper relationship between believers and divinity or orthodox Christianity. The inflections and extension of Christianity that were attributed to successive and diverse waves of non-Christian influences still, it is commonly argued, bear exotic traits that can be detected in the styles and iconographies of popular art. Such apparent exoticisms are now more commonly derived from images or stories in the press, in magazines, on television, on the Internet or in radio broadcasts than from popular beliefs that had their origins in past *romarias*, "heresies" or pre-Christian religions. Stylistically, most if not all depictions of religious subjects in popular art express the affinity that is believed to exist between saintly personages and ordinary people.

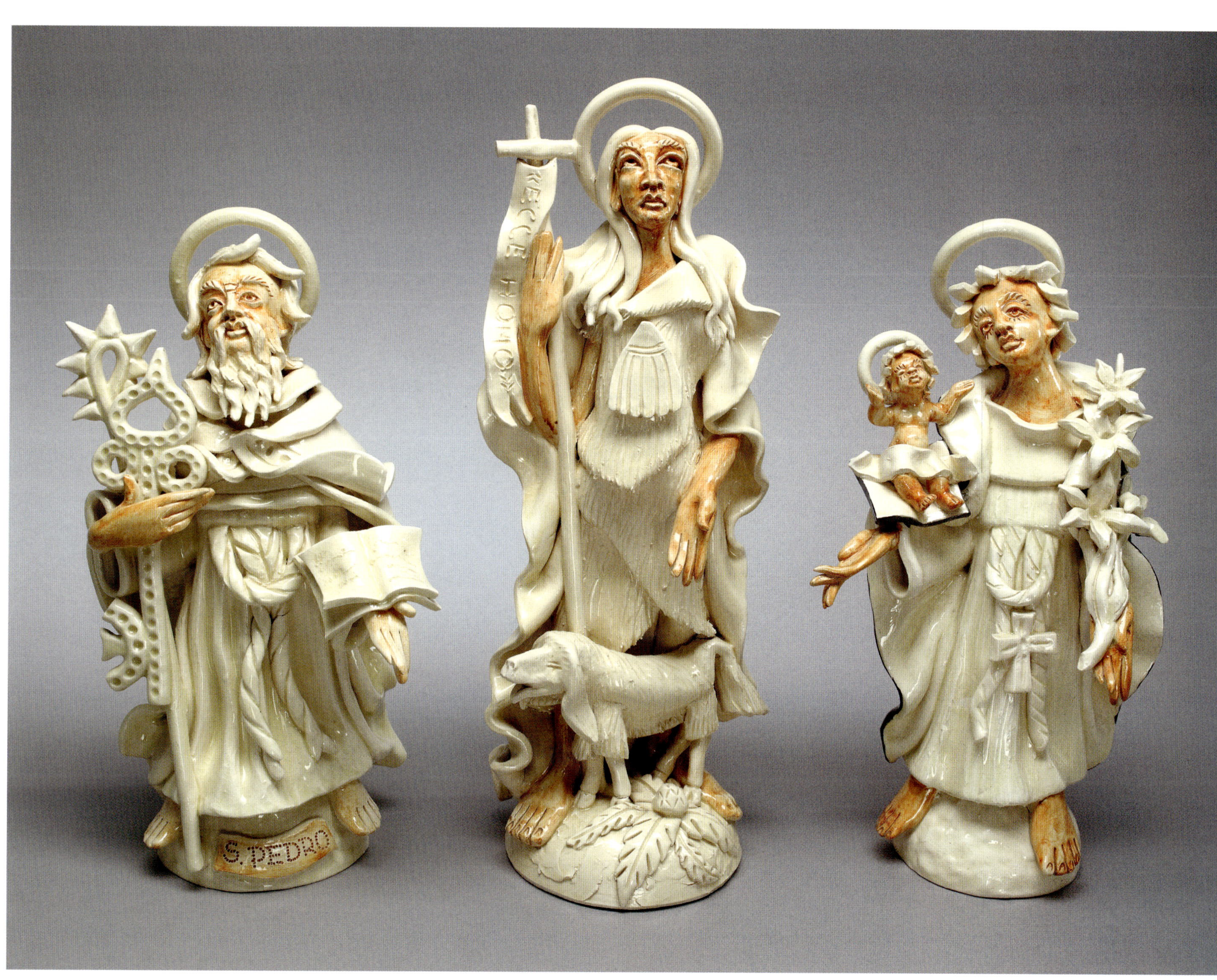
ECCE HOMO
S. PEDRO

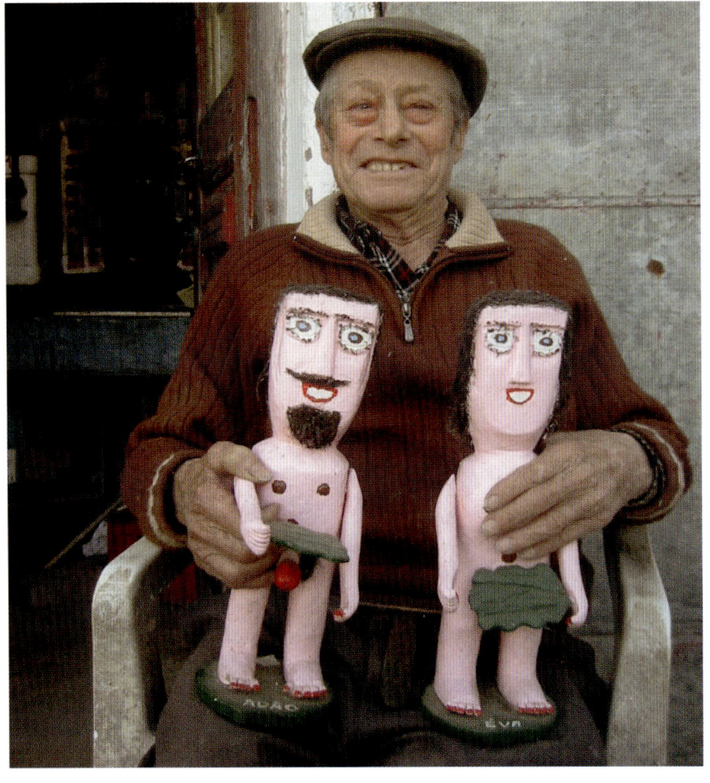

above
Artist Joaquim Paiva holding his sculptures of Adam and Eve, 2009.

facing
JOAQUIM PAIVA
The Holy Trinity, C. 2008

In his ethnography of Vilharinho, Dias commented on the ability of some villagers to master diverse arts and crafts. Describing one of his collaborators, António Francisco João, Dias noted that apart from being a shepherd and agricultural labourer, he was also an able "carpenter, iron worker, stone mason, cobbler, clog maker, tailor and sculptor . . . a man capable of faithfully copying images of saints he had seen in Braga or Porto."[327]

Unlike potters, woodcarvers often still practise additional jobs. Most popular artists do not copy official images but create their own interpretations of saintly characteristics that, like those of Zé Augusto, David Gomes or Joaquim Paiva (1930–2010), are far removed from images in churches and monasteries. Cutileiro noted that in Alentejo women often humanized the saints to whom they were closest.[328] Relations between the followers and divinities were characterized by familiarity rather than by awe and respect. Dias, writing more generally on rural Portugal, believed that village churches were valued not for the institution they represented but because they were inhabited and shared by good saints and mortals—characteristics clearly expressed in popular art.[329] All the barriers and conventions that, in institutionalized religion, separate the congregation from the presence of God, the Holy Family and the saints, have been dispensed with in these ceramic pieces so that in the domestic space there is a contiguity, similarity and familiarity between the divine and the everyday; between saints and humans; between the behaviour and values of supernatural and ordinary personages; and between the reign of Heaven and the temporal world.

Such common values might be compared to the spiritual revelation that linked divinity with the essence of Portuguese identity under the mentorship of the Estado Novo and later governments, but the argument is not completely persuasive. In contemporary popular art, the work of the spirit has been subverted; instead of being constituted between Church and state, it has been appropriated and transfigured by such artists as Rosa and Júlia Ramalho; Manuel, Francisco and Domingos Lima (Mistério); Júlia Côta; the Baraças and Zé Augusto.[330] The ceramic sculptures of these artists suggest that saints and ordinary people share common values of goodness, kindness and humility. This is a long way from the orthodox image of saints: transcendental, institutionally alienated beings separated from common experience by a fault line that values apostolic and millenarian ambitions over those of the hearth and everyday labour. This is art for this world and the present, not an imagined other world in some indeterminate future.

The plasticity and naïveté of expression become jocular and even irreverent in the late twentieth-century woodcarvings of Joaquim Maria Silva Paiva, whose sculptural style was

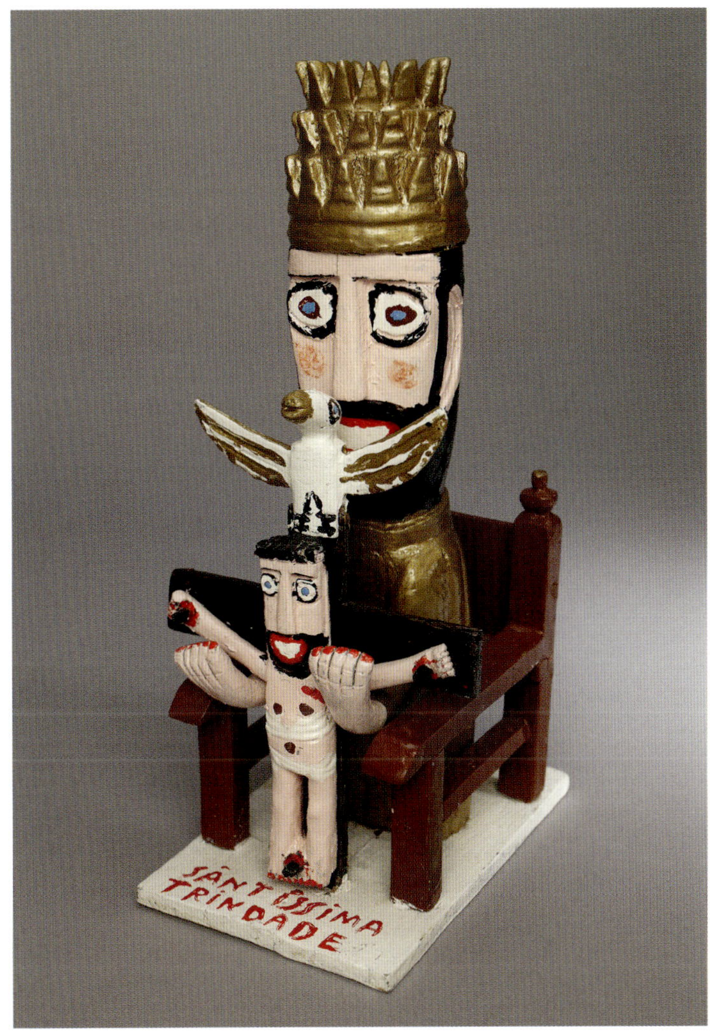

direct and repetitive and use of solid colour striking. Like so many other carvers and potters who make figurative work, Joaquim Paiva referred to his creations modestly as doll figures (*bonecos*) regardless of whether they represented saints or humans. The work of these artists provides plausible, irreverent responses to the established order. Now they employ agency rather than simply yield to market and governmental demands, as Vera Alves suggests occurred during the Estado Novo.[331]

One of the paradoxes of this rural world view is that the ambiguity and belligerence that sometimes characterize human behaviour were also imputed to saintly personages. Gallop noted that in the 1930s, images of saints were often treated like human beings. They were cajoled, honoured with prayer and given penitence, vows and votive offerings in exchange for benefits, but if they failed to comply with mortal requests they were sometimes treated with disrespect and even punished for their intransigence. Gallop listed a number of historical examples with punishments ranging from the image being turned to face the wall to it being physically chastised. From the early nineteenth century Gallop compiled accounts of Santo António, who, when having failed to bring hoped-for prosperity through a beneficial wedding, might, for example, "become liable to the grossest possible indignities," while sailors who had been unsuccessful in persuading the saint to send propitious winds might tie his image to a mast and flog it. In another story, the inhabitants of Castelo Branco were so enraged by Santo António for allowing the Spanish to plunder their town after he had promised to protect them, that they broke his images. Yet another figure of Santo António that had received special reverence but had not reciprocated in kind had its head broken off and replaced by the head of São Francisco. Similar rage could be meted out to Nossa Senhora da Nazaré. When storms broke that threatened or took fishermen's lives, she was sometimes publicly cursed. At the more northern fishing port of Póvoa de Varzim, people were reputed to even stone their saints and break their chapel windows if they lost men at sea.[332] These attitudes were still prevalent in rural areas in the 1960s[333] and can be interpreted as strategies of empowerment that provided communities with agency over their experiences of suffering and exploitation.

In popular art, Rosa Ramalho's formula for subversion in her pottery figures depended on altering the gaze and vocation of the onlooker rather than on the explicit critical content provided by the artist. Moral and ontological ambiguity was expressed in anthropomorphic and zoomorphic characters that deliberately blurred reality and imagination and created a labyrinth of mental mirrors that avoided the rules of censorship and

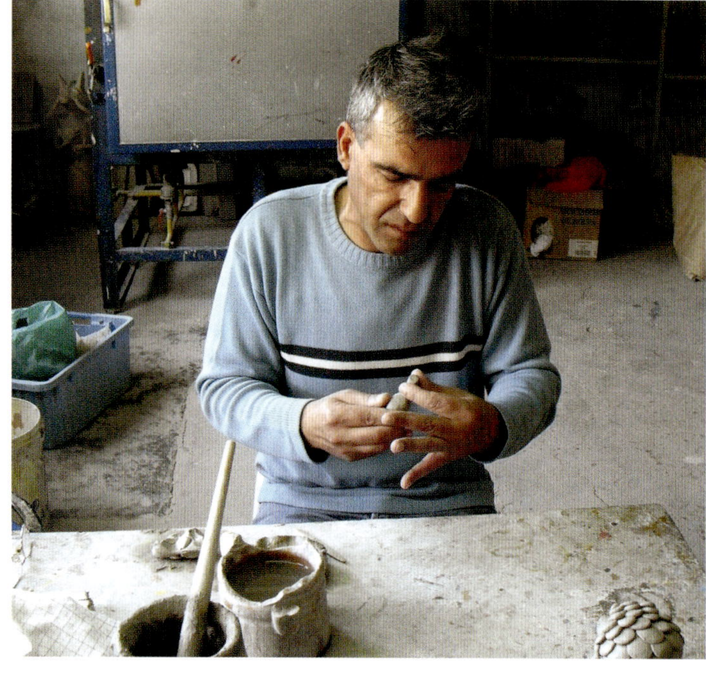

above
Ceramic artist António Ramalho, 2012.

facing
ANTÓNIO RAMALHO
Figurative works, 2008.

political reaction by effectively creating a space for free contemplation. Her dolls, *bonecos*, gained form and existence from the hardship amassed from a lifetime of endeavours, frustrations, joys, fancies and aspirations under the unremittingly patriarchal Estado Novo. Her sculptures emerged from her hands and intellect with unparalleled force and radical potential. For Rosa Ramalho, the work of art was a surrogate that opened a space for independent thought and expression, a medium through which to stimulate a person's departure from a determined to an indeterminate condition in which freedom of thought could again take root.

The dissent that Ramalho's work can still evoke questioned the values, ethics and actions of the patriarchal milieu that the Estado Novo and the Church upheld. Nevertheless, the power of her work, like that of her granddaughter Júlia's and great-grandson António's, is not limited to one milieu but capable of radical destabilization within other types of society, including twentieth- and twenty-first-century liberal democracies. For Ferreira, Ramalho's work provided dissonance that partly compensated for the isolation of Porto as an art centre ignored by the Estado Novo and closed to outside influences. Her work stimulated a fresh look at the "reality" within the city, allowing people to imagine a different Porto. Her *bonecos* generated an emancipatory stimulus against an orthodoxy that was so pervasive it left no space or material armatures for alternative possibilities.

For Ramalho, the contradiction she expressed in her work was between the popular world of religion and the institutional authority of the Church and its fixed iconography. Many of her works reference back to the world of the *romaria*, the world the Estado Novo attempted to colonize and use in its own expression of state ideology but that remained stubbornly resistant and outlived the state itself, only to succumb to secular liberal democracy. This world became visible through Rosa Ramalho's work, not as a viable alternative to modernity but as a contradiction between the rational and the "other" located at its very core, a defiant stand against the sedentary, ordered lifestyle expressed by the idyllic rural house popularized by *Deus, Pátria, Família* and the aesthetic preferences of Salazar and his government. Ramalho's work insinuated that there were alternatives to the world condoned by the Estado Novo. It could not define what these alternatives were but, by relativizing the essentialized appearance of existing conditions, it showed that they were possible. Her legacy, transmitted through her granddaughter Júlia and her great-grandson António, continues to play a similar subversive role today, not by articulating an alternative to our existential condition but by relativizing it and thereby opening a portal to other realities—a kind of alterity device.

These other realities, further developed in Júlia's and António's work, reference mythology and the past. The iconographic and stylistic rendering

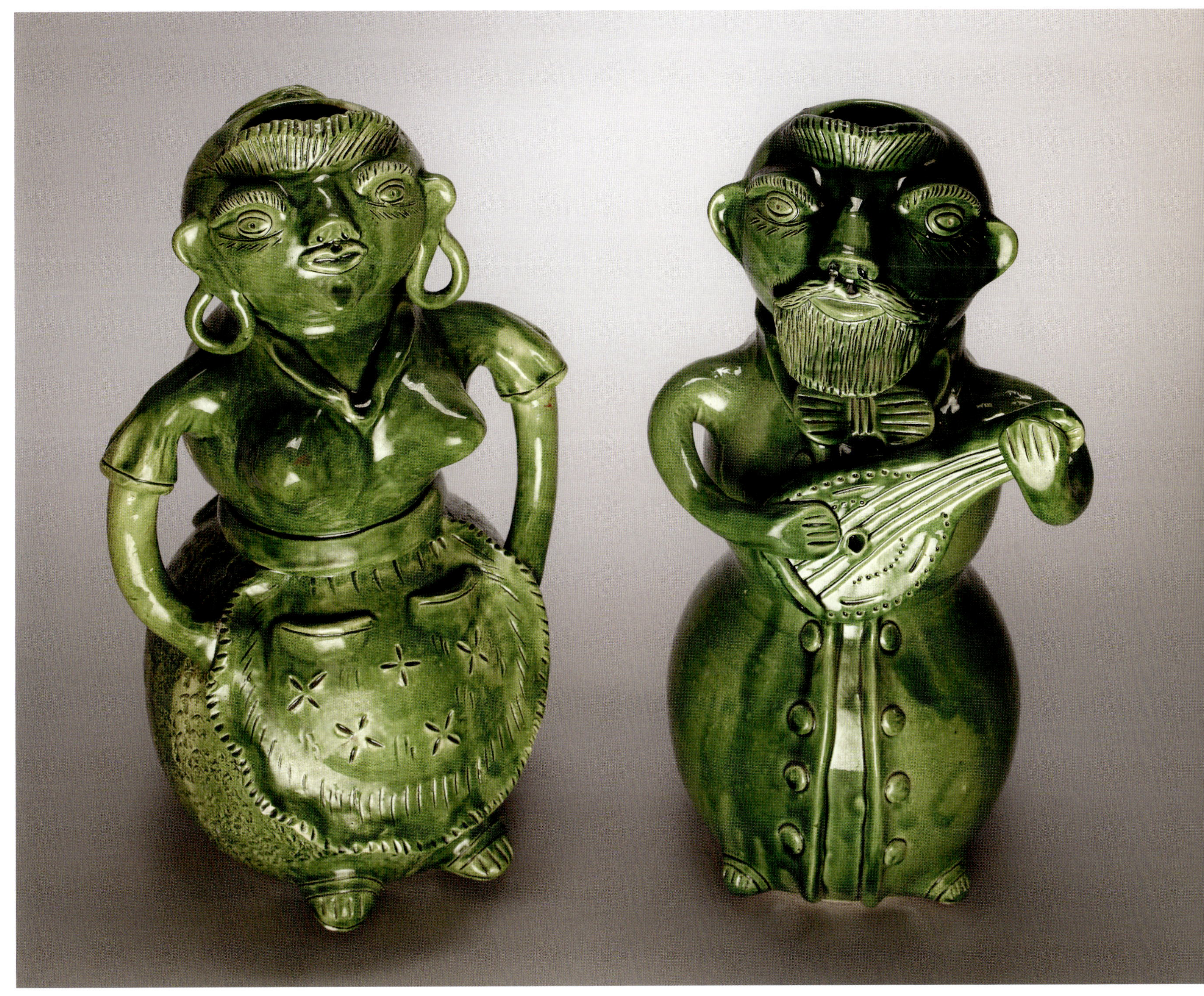

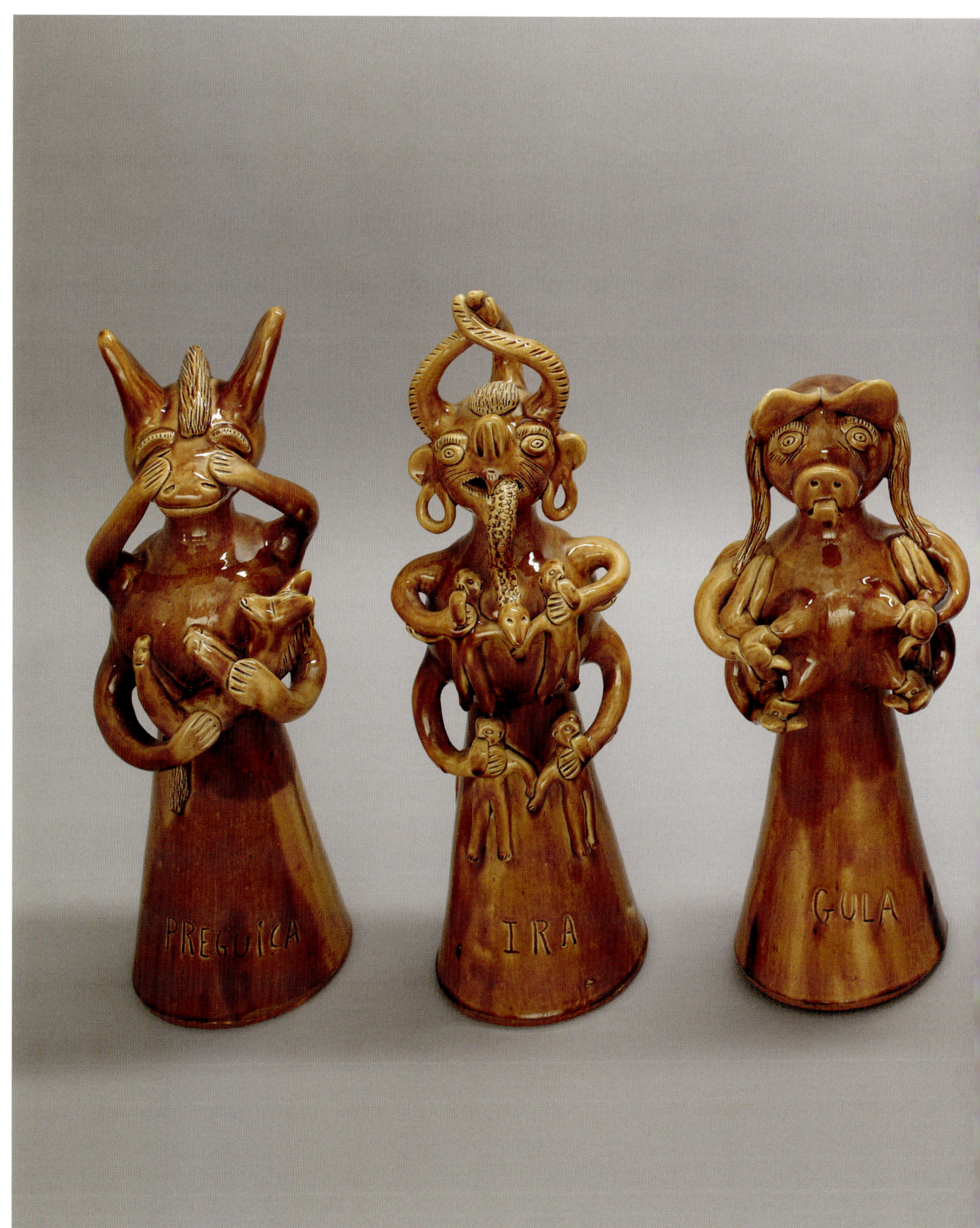

JÚLIA RAMALHO
Anthropomorphic caricatures representing the seven deadly sins, 2011.

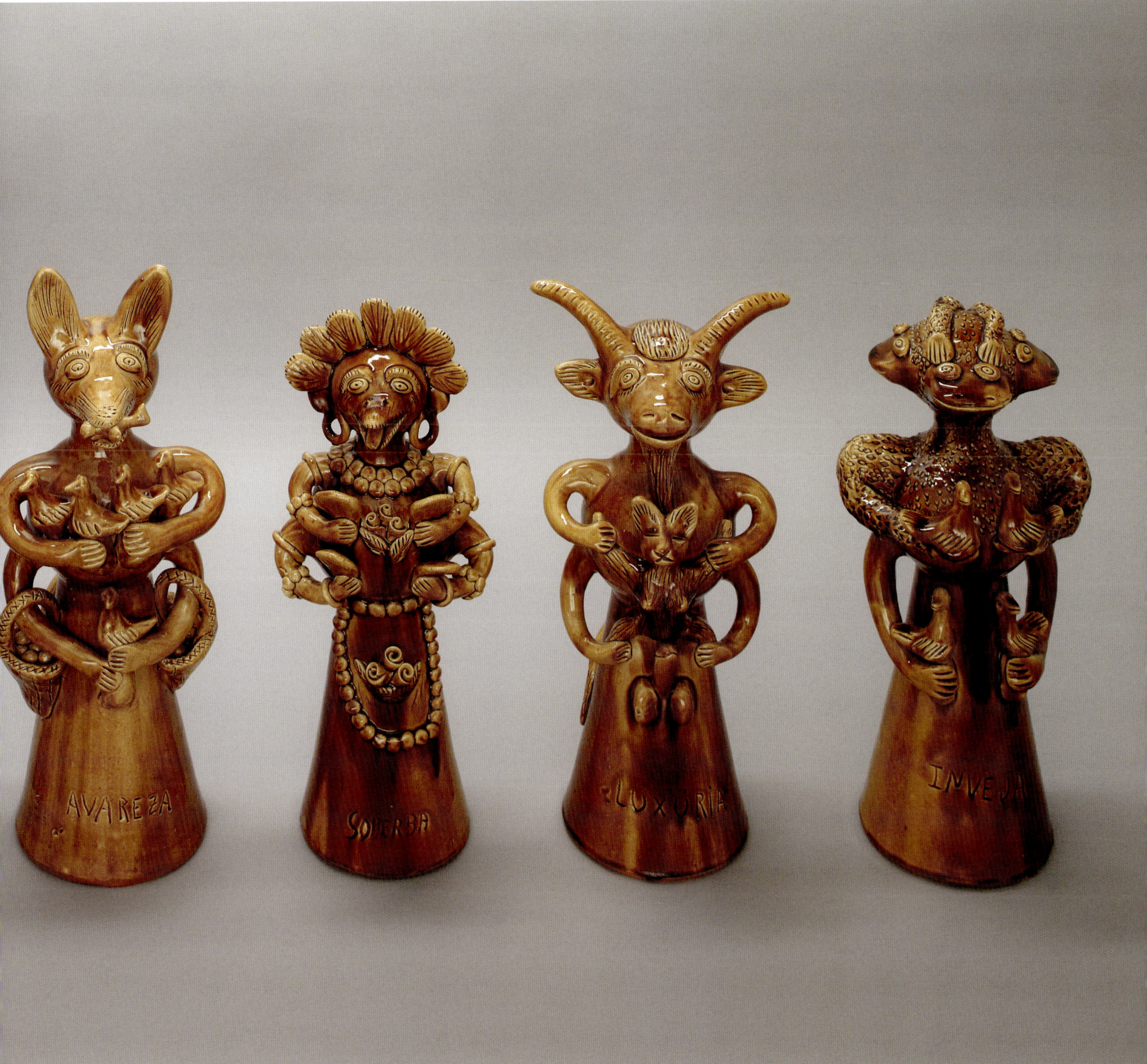
AVAREZA
SOBERBA
LUXÚRIA
INVEJA

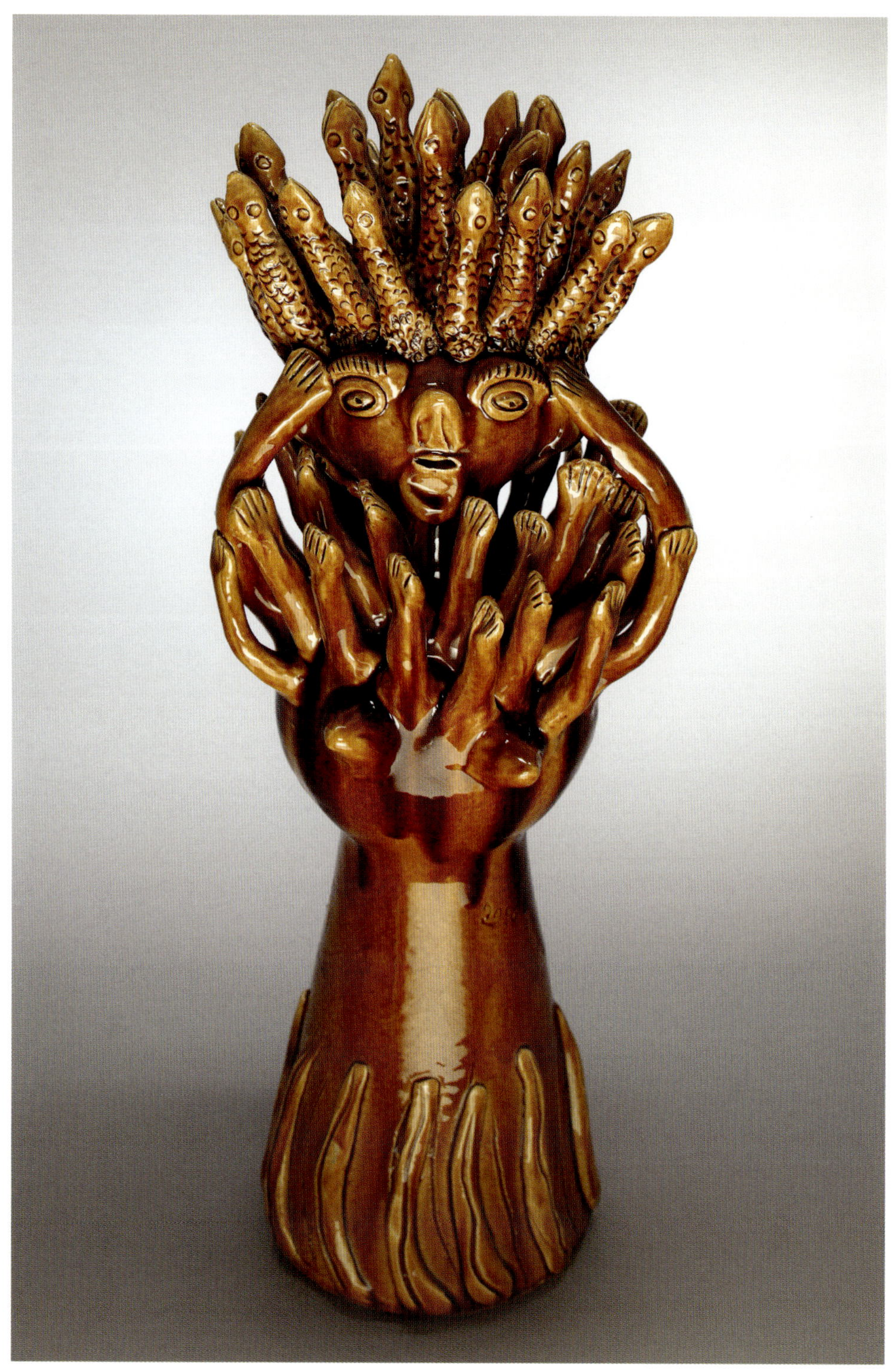

used by Júlia Ramalho in her three original sets of pottery figures representing the vices, the virtues and the zodiacal signs also depart from institutionalized Church expressions that would deny the anthropomorphization or zoomorphization of moral categories. The seven vices and the astrological signs are represented by womanhood and animals. The vices have human form but animal heads: goat (lust), three-headed frog (envy); woman (rage); fox (avarice); sow suckling a piglet (gluttony); peacock (pride); and donkey (sloth). In contrast, the virtues all have heads with female features. The most notable feature of the three sets of figures is the unexpectedly sharp division between good and evil. There is no ambiguity or interstitial space allowed for mixing categories.

Other Barcelos artists also combine animal and human attributes in their work. Manuel and Francisco Esteves Lima (Mistério) denied that the different animal heads attached to their works that comprise the *Three Wise Women* had any specific significance. The animal heads were, they told me emphatically, the product only of their father's imagination, though in later interviews with Eduardo Tomé they recalled that depictions of such creatures on church panels and in films like *The Lord of the Rings* made them wonder if their father, Domingos, might originally have thought of the heads as types of masks.[334] Despite this it is difficult to find any coherent source from which such image sets might be derived. In Renaissance Europe, builders' guilds incorporated references to the cardinal vices and virtues into their edifices, although in the case of the vices, there appeared to be little symbolic systemization. The Flemish master Pieter Bruegel the Elder (1525–69) represented the seven vices as monsters in a series of engravings,[335] but other references are rare. Renaissance scholars and master builders were aware that the Greeks and Romans believed that the boundaries between animals and humans could be transposed—Ovid's *Metamorphoses*, in which the gods change people into animals and plants, and *Aesop's Fables* are cases in point—but Christian Rome did not, it would seem, systematically use animals to symbolize sins. There are common

facing
JÚLIA RAMALHO
Medusa, C. 2008

non-systematic associations made between animals and moral categories that Júlia Ramalho and the Esteves Lima brothers may have been familiar with—the male goat to represent lust and the female goat to represent motherhood; the pig to represent greed; and the frog to symbolize envy[336]—but these are isolated examples. The fox, in Roman belief, was identified with fire devils and in Christianity his supposed deviousness associated him with the Devil. There was, however, according to George Ferguson, a more coherent systematization for representing the virtues that was used in Church symbolism across Europe.[337] None of these symbolic associations correspond to those employed by Júlia Ramalho. She reserves for herself a freer play of indeterminacy in these animal/human figures, using insinuations and deliberately ambiguous provocations to encourage the onlooker to think about the meaning of their double natures.

POPULAR ARTS AS SOCIAL COMMENTARY: RAFAEL AND MANUEL GUSTAVO BORDALO PINHEIRO

Such strategies of opening spaces of ambiguity are distinct from the explicit and conscious technique of representation pursued by the renowned Portuguese caricaturist and ceramicist Rafael Bordalo Pinheiro (1846–1905). From 1900 to 1907, Rafael, followed by his son, Manuel Gustavo (1867–1920), published *Paródia*, a biting satirical magazine that used illustration and print to comment on the social issues of the constitutional monarchy (1834–1910) and Republican periods (1910–26). Rafael Pinheiro's works were explicit and direct, as Portuguese society at the time was more open and grudgingly allowed such criticism; Rosa Ramalho had to endure much harsher conditions under the Estado Novo, which goes some way to explaining the relative nuance of her work. Pinheiro was also an educated male member of the urban elite who created a very different body of work than that of Rosa Ramalho, an uneducated woman among the rural poor, albeit one, unlike most others, who mixed with intellectuals, foreigners and even politicians.

Rafael Bordalo Pinheiro employed zoomorphic symbolism in his cartoons to lampoon the different categories of political and social organizations. O Grande Porca, the "Fat Pig," was politics; O Grande Cão, the "Fat Dog," was finances; A Galinha Choca, the "Rooster Hatch," referred to the economy; O Grande Papagaio, the "Big Parrot," stood for parliamentary rhetoric; and A Grande Toupeira, the "Fat Mole," symbolized sloth and lack of responsiveness. Manuel Gustavo, who followed his father as a caricaturist and ceramicist, added O Grande Caranguejo, the "Big Crab," its slow and clumsy movements representing progress, and O Grande Rato, the "Fat Rat," symbol of the bureaucracy that ravenously gnawed through government budgets.[338] A series of seven postcards, drawn by an unknown artist and published in Portugal during the late nineteenth or early twentieth century, caricatured seven politicians and personalities of the day (including the Portuguese everyman Zé Povinho; see below) as representations of the seven vices. Such overlays of mythological and religious symbolism and political satire provided a potent critique of the failures of the constitutional monarchy and Republican periods.

The most enduring of Rafael Bordalo Pinheiro's images is the figurative expression that became associated with the collective embodiment of the Portuguese "peoples," Zé Povinho. First modelled in 1890, Zé Povinho, the everyman of Portugal, quickly achieved popularity and infamy. The character, like others, had its origin in a

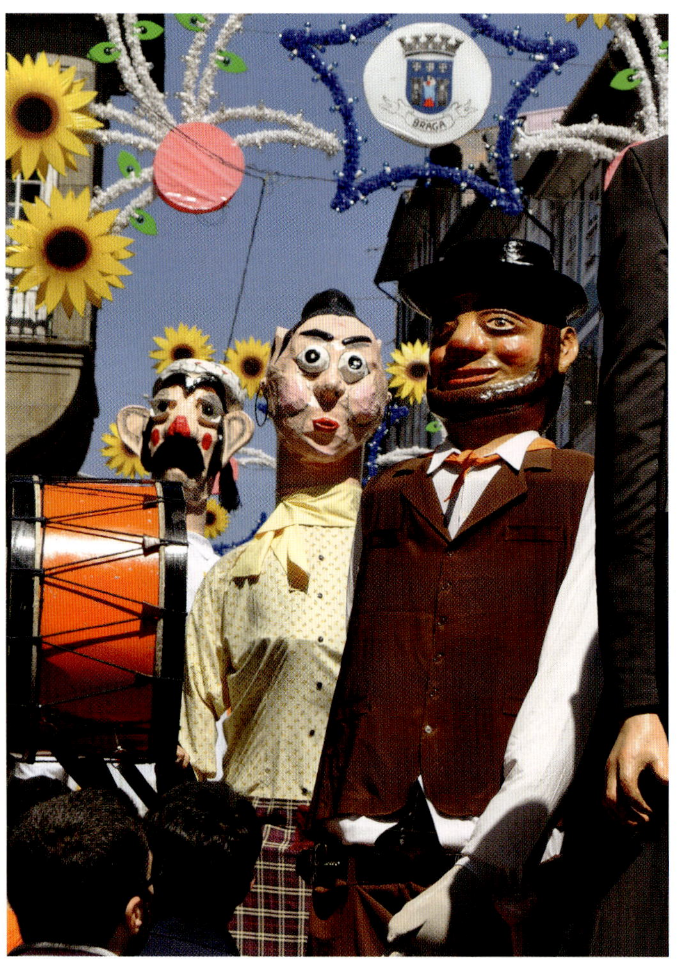

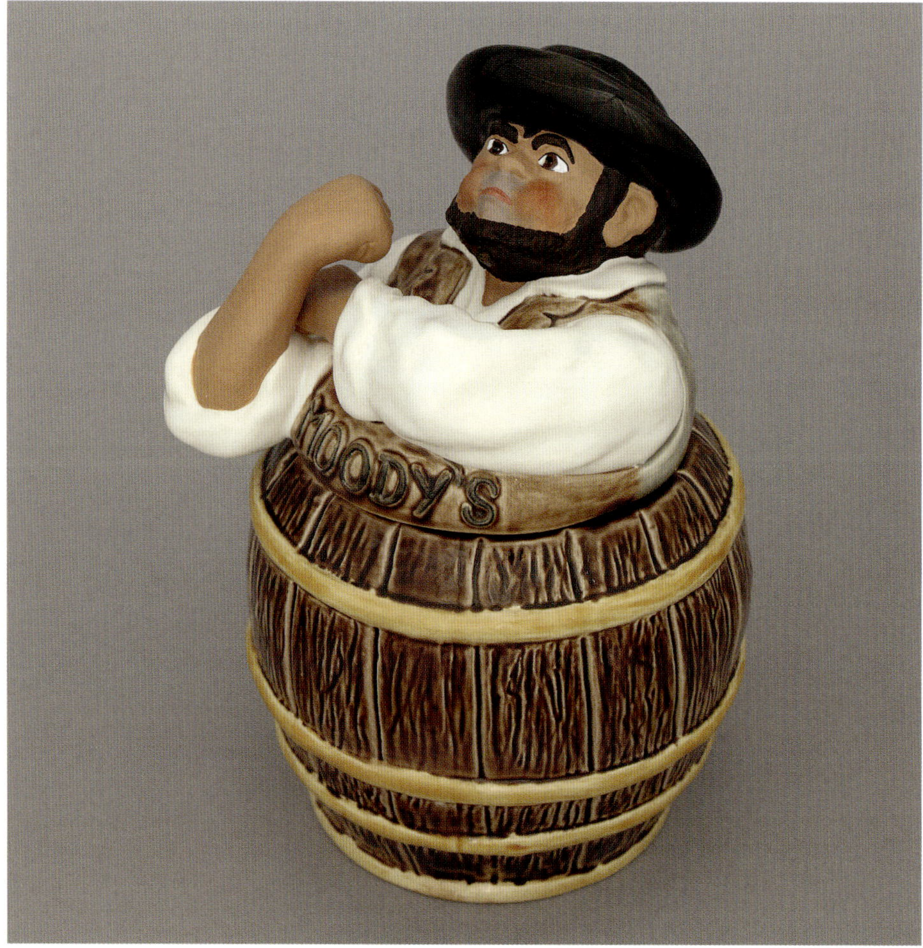

drawing Pinheiro made for the satirical magazine *A Lanterna Mágica* on the eve of the feast day of Santo António in 1875. After its first appearance he redrew or revised the image nearly six hundred times for different cartoons and publications.[339] The figure, with his "face like a dried raisin, ruddy complexion, doppled hat and scruffy brown suit," was supposedly modelled on one of Pinheiro's acquaintances, Luís de Oliveira Guimarães.[340] The pottery form also went through different versions. Zé Povinho exuded confidence, curiosity, strength, determination and practical intelligence and had an irreverent expression that provided a counter-image to the dandyism, superficiality and paternalism of the Republican period and the later totalitarianism of the Estado Novo. He is usually portrayed as helpful and, like the self-image of the people themselves, he retains an uncompromising contempt for the rich and powerful despite often being the victim of political and economic circumstances. The anthropologist João de Pina-Cabral refers to him as a "dim-witted looking man" but one endowed nevertheless with a natural intelligence.[341] The long-suffering Zé has been drawn escorted by Death, in disputation with a female figure representing France; on his donkey, accompanying Don Quixote towards an unknown European future; as a seated giant supporting a diminutive king; and as a sleeping Gulliver on whose body the whole nation stands. Sometimes he is shown slumped with his hands in his pockets, emerging from a barrel or giving a rude and dismissive signal with his right arm raised and his left hand squeezing his bulging right bicep (the *manguito*). Although not inherently lewd, Zé is direct and assertive.[342]

Zé Povinho remains a popular caricature. In July 2011 the Pinheiro factory brought out a limited edition[343] of the figure inscribed with, under the usual lettering, "*toma* [take this], Moody's,"[344] the name of the international credit rating agency that caused outrage in Portugal when it downgraded

facing, left
One of a number of giant figures of Zé Povinho paraded during the Festival of São João in Braga in 2011.

facing, right
Specially made in 2011 by the Bordalo Pinheiro factory, a figure of Zé Povinho gives a dismissive "up yours" to Moody's, the international credit rating agency that downgraded Portugal's economic status, triggering an increase in the interest on its national debt.

the country's credit rating, thereby pushing up the nation's already exorbitant debt. The achievement of Pinheiro in creating such an embodiment of the people is outstanding and provided a platform for explicit critical comment that other forms of print or popular art did not. Among the giants and big heads that took part in the Day of São João celebrations in Braga in 2011, Zé was ubiquitous, represented by two giant figures towering over and teasing the crowd alongside other caricatures, including politicians, religious figures, medieval kings and queens, and superheroes.

Zé Povinho was one of many caricatures Pinheiro created, including priests, politicians and others who had transgressed their public trust. Pinheiro, reflecting the mood of the country as a whole, was particularly incensed by the 1890 British ultimatum that Portugal withdraw her ambitions to annex the region that would become Zambia and Zimbabwe, territories that could have connected its colonies of Angola and Mozambique. Pinheiro's anger at Portugal's capitulation brought a new line of works, including toilet pots and spittoons in the shape and colours of a satirized John Bull. Vasco Lopes de Mendonça (1881–1963), Rafael Bordalo Pinheiro's nephew, continued the satirical tradition, parodying, among others, authoritarian leaders including Salazar, Carmona, Hitler and Mussolini.[345]

This disdain for authority figures is also evident in Barcelos pottery. The preponderant genre of non-utilitarian pots produced in the region is probably figurative groups. Painted in bright colours, these often depict aspects of a traditional life that have now almost disappeared—oxen pulling carts laden with people and wine barrels, the slaughter of a pig, baking, harvesting grapes or making wine, processions, *romarias*, village dances, musicians, even confessions. Interestingly, many of these tableaux first appeared in the first half of the twentieth century (Ana Baraça) and their themes and styles have often been repeated by successive generations of family members, as in the case of Domingos, Francisco and Manuel Lima (Mistério) or the Ramalho family. These are pottery works that essentialize and reproduce commonly held expressions of Portugueseness, but that also retain their implicit criticality. Potters in the region of Aveiro, such as Zé Augusto, substitute fishing and salt making in place of agriculture to reflect the traditional local economy. These works stand uneasily, destabilized between the old boundaries of the official world of the Estado Novo and the memory of its populist other. Joaquim Paiva once made similar figures out of wood, depicting bull rings and hunters, traditional sports and entertainments that express masculine identities.

New subjects have emerged among tableau makers that provide additional opportunities for critique and social commentary. Júlia Ramalho has made tableaux never dreamt of by her grandmother, including schoolteachers, priests, doctors and dentists, audiologists, cardiologists, psychiatrists, opticians and midwives assisting at births. These professional authority figures are seldom parodied or portrayed alone but are often depicted with someone else—the patient, the accused, the victim—whose passive body is being acted upon in one way or another. They stand over their conscious or sometimes anaesthetized patients or are separated from them by a desk or the panel of a confessional booth to symbolize the difference in status, authority and power. Books, as sources of professional authority, are ubiquitous in scenes modelled by the Baraça family, whose repertoire of polychromatic images is extensive. Vitor Gonçalves has modelled entire court scenes, but seems especially fond of surgical operations and dental work to illustrate these

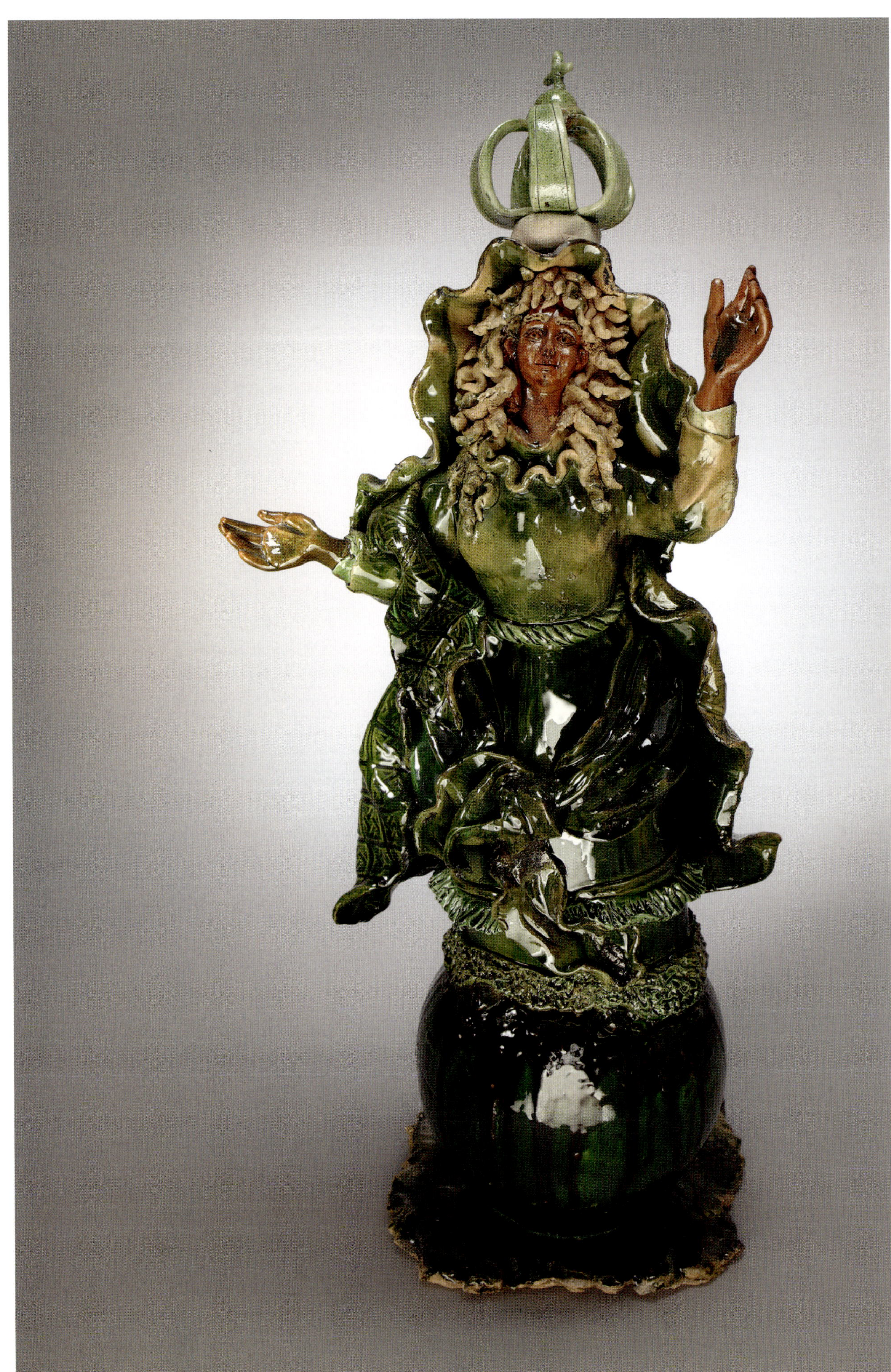

right
LAURINDA PIAS
Nossa Senhora, 2012

facing, top left
Ceramic artist Laurinda Pias, 2012.

facing, top right
Ceramic artists Maria Helena Pedro da Silva and Basílio Silva, 2011.

facing, bottom left
Ceramic artist Vitor Baraça, 2011.

facing, bottom right
Ceramic artist Manuel Esteves Lima (Mistério), 2011.

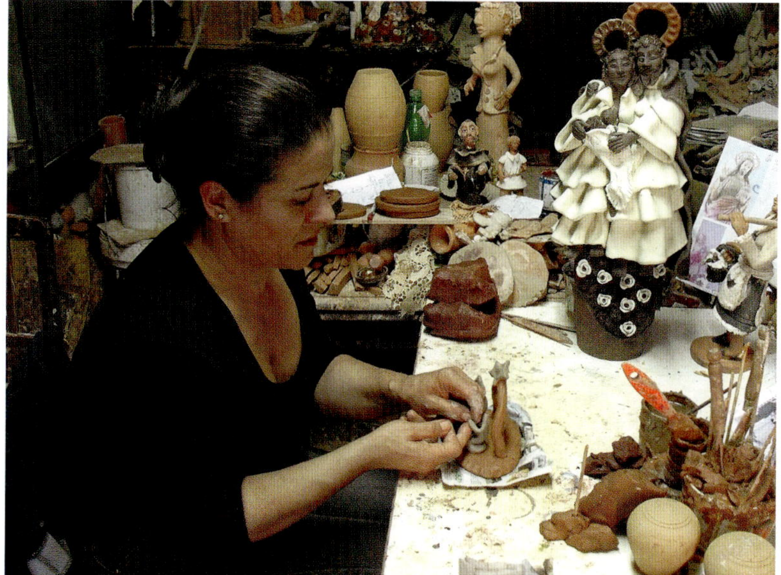

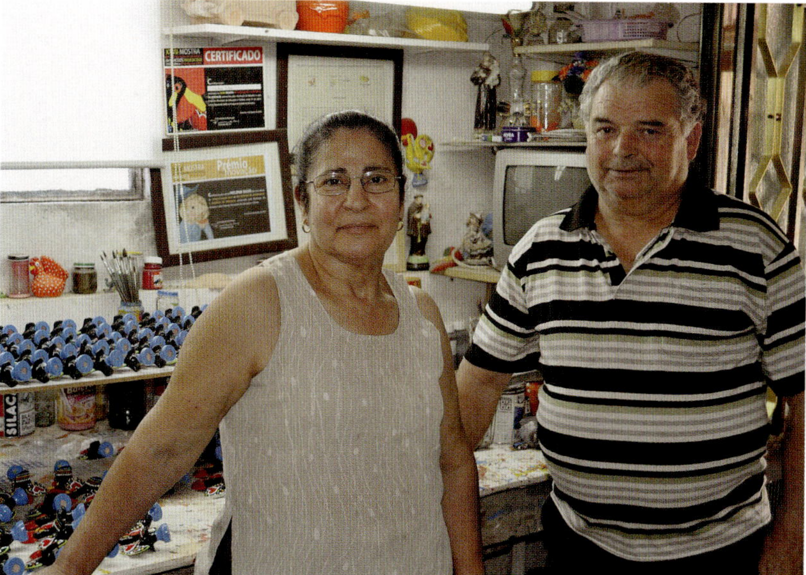

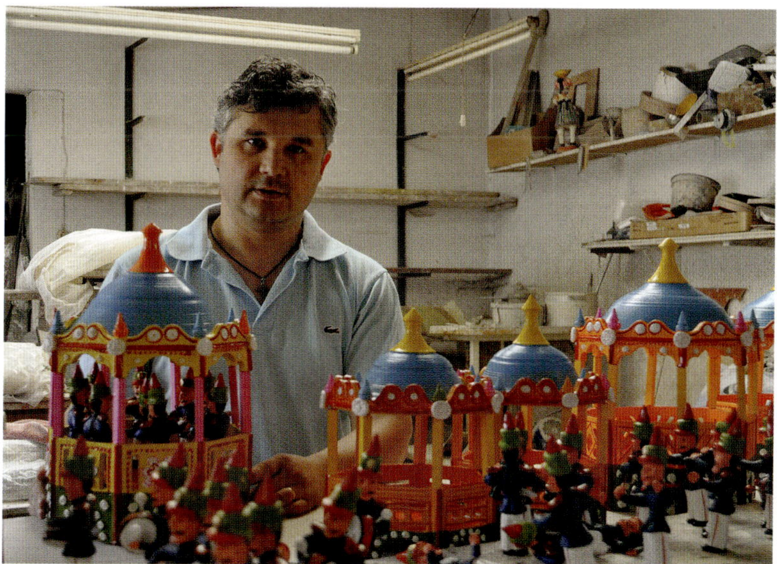

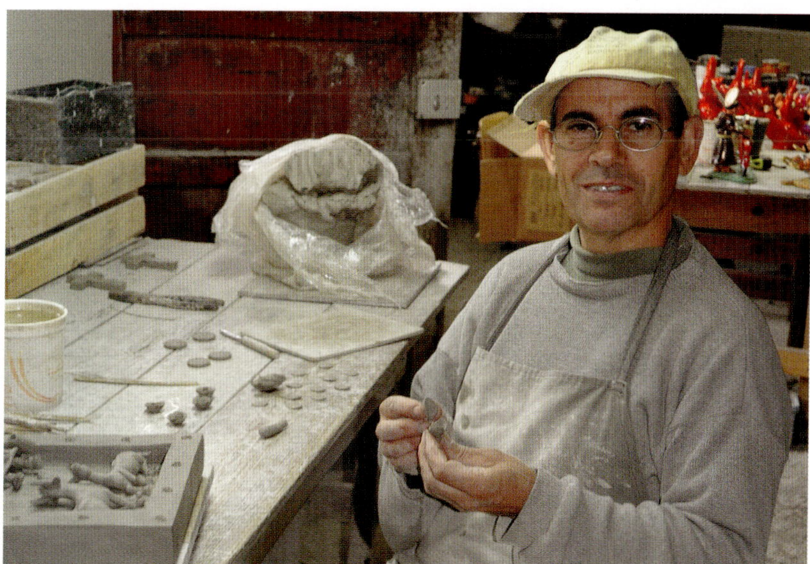

differential relations between clients and professionals. The professions remain well represented by the potters of Barcelos, even if their patron saints are now seldom acknowledged or modelled. This world, somewhere between Heaven and Hell, whether rural or urban, is expressed using the same intimacy and congeniality found in the representation of the saints. There is, however, a distinction between the interaction of people in the disappearing rural world of the past and their survivors, who have been subordinated to professional practitioners—representatives of the new technocratic classes that have replaced the saints in granting or denying the common people good health and fortune.

CONTEMPORARY POPULAR ARTS AND SOCIAL COMMENTARY: FRANCISCO AND MANUEL ESTEVES LIMA

Satirical works that can be mobilized to explicitly critique government and elites have become a recognized genre of popular art. In July 2011 I was able to buy from the Mistério studio a plaque that a government official had commissioned in 2009 but had not purchased after deciding it was "too political." The plaque, like more traditional ones depicting the crucifixion, is split into an upper Earth and a lower Hell. Perched on top is the figure of the then president of Portugal Aníbal Cavaco Silva, waving the national flag. The upper section of the plaque shows Zé Povinho, the Portuguese

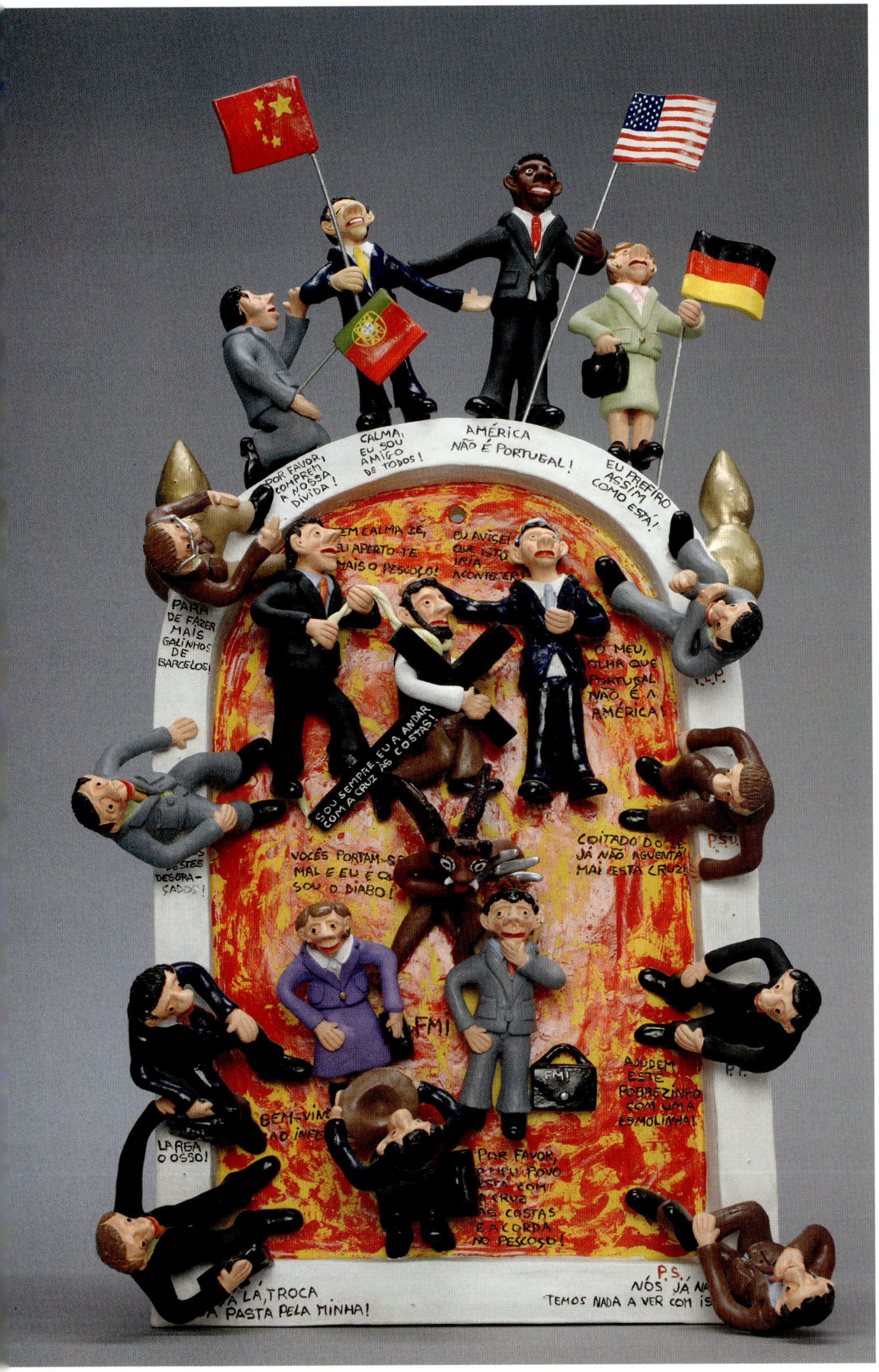

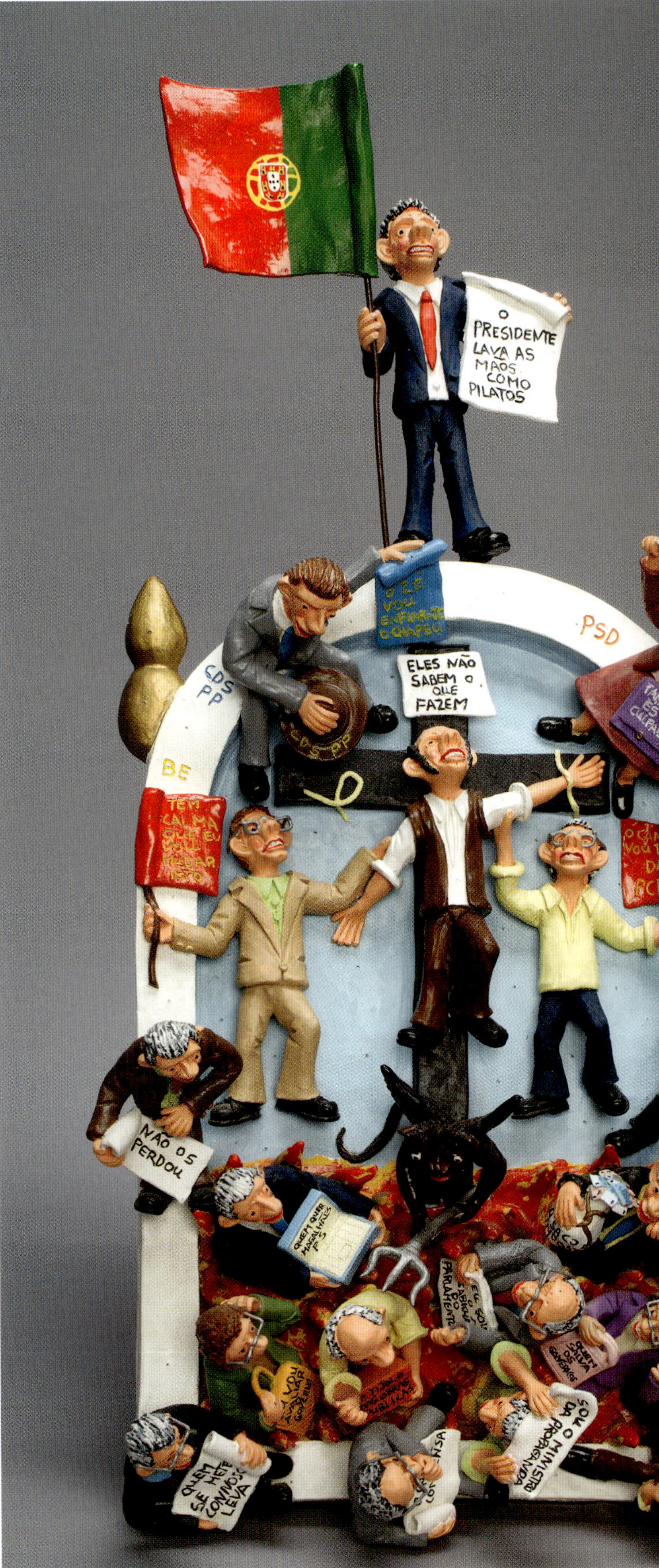
O PRESIDENTE LAVA AS MÃOS COMO PILATOS
PSD
ELES NÃO SABEM O QUE FAZEM
CDS PP
BE
NÃO OS PERDOU

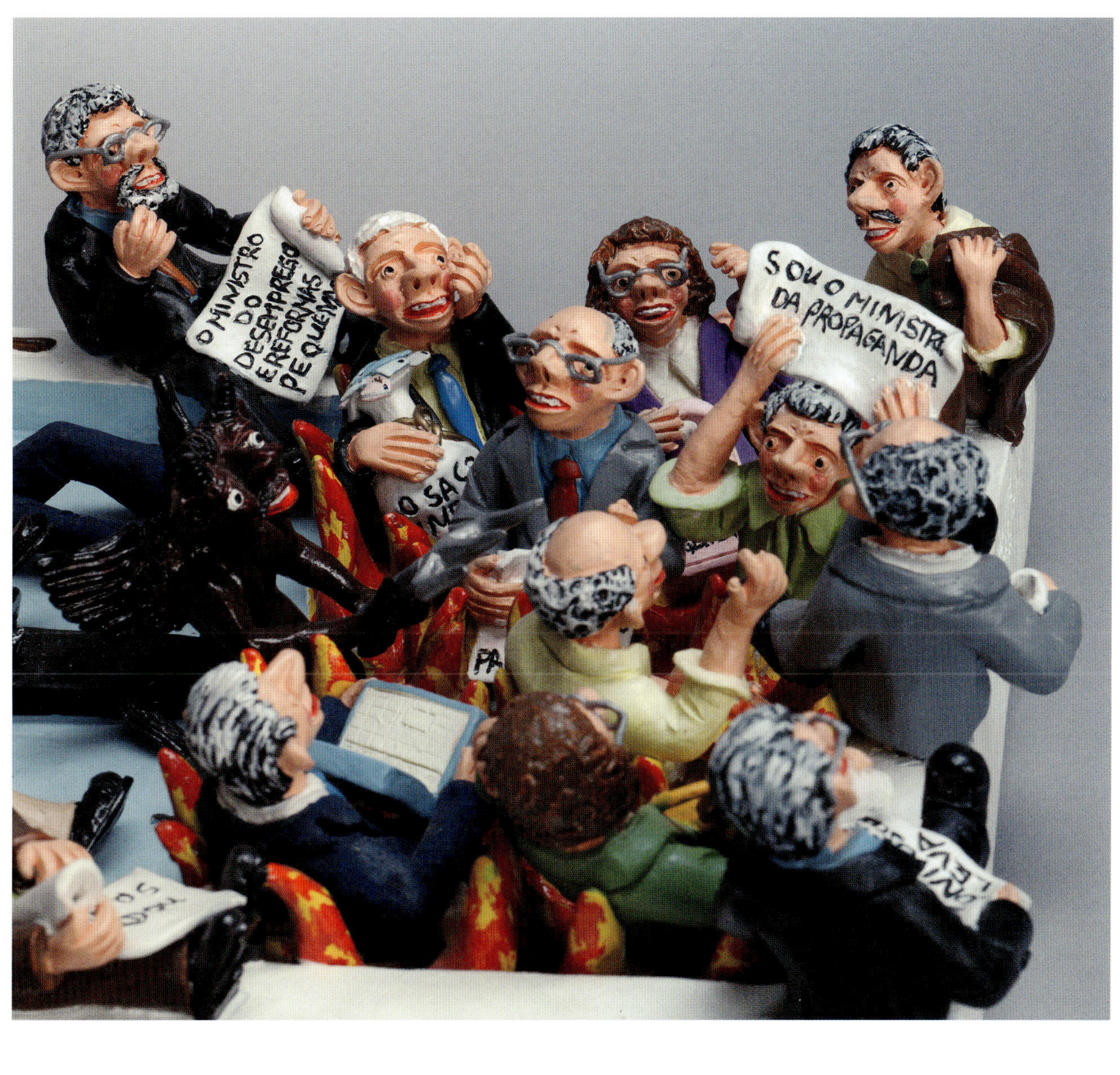

facing, left
FRANCISCO ESTEVES LIMA (MISTÉRIO)
Plaque, 2011
Inspired by the debt crisis and the humiliation of the Portuguese people, the plaque shows representatives of the International Monetary Fund and the European Central Bank burning in Hell.

middle
FRANCISCO ESTEVES LIMA (MISTÉRIO)
Plaque, 2009
The work shows the crucifixion of Zé Povinho, the embodiment of the Portuguese people, who are pulled in two directions by different factions of the left while the ministers of the incumbent socialist government burn in Hell.

above
FRANCISCO ESTEVES LIMA (MISTÉRIO)
Plaque (detail), 2009
The work shows former prime minister José Sócrates and his ministers being tormented by the devil.

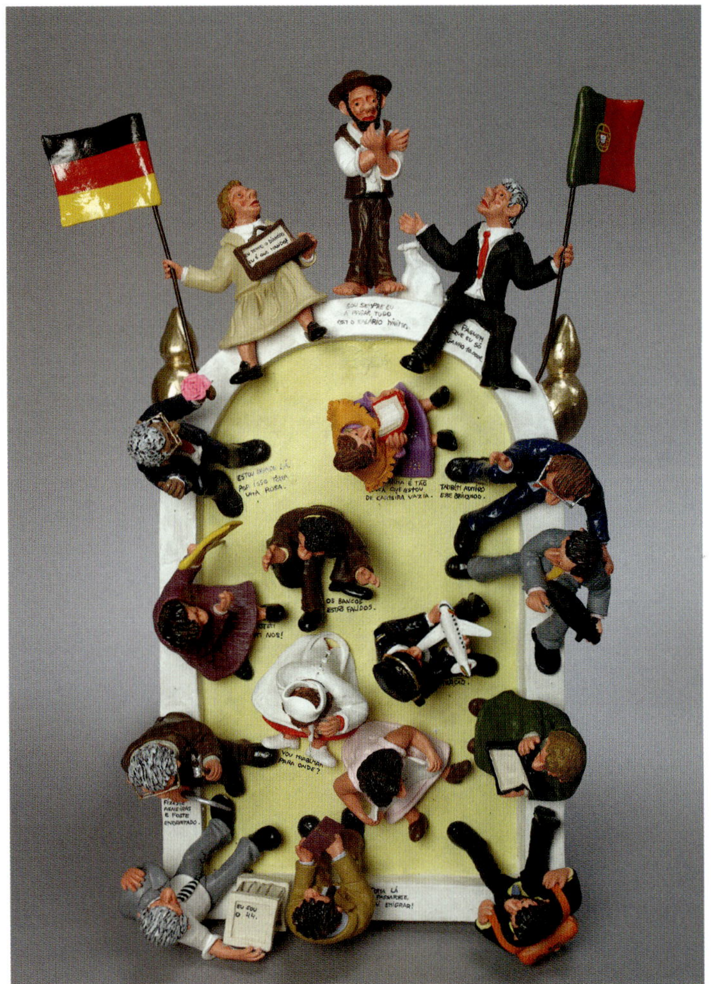

everyman, being tied to the cross, with his two arms being pulled in opposite directions by the leaders of the Left Bloc and the Communist Party. Below them in Hell, Diabo, the Devil, uses his pitchfork to ensure the then prime minister, José Sócrates, his ministers and one of his most ardent opponents, the right-wing politician Paulo Portas, the current deputy prime minister, remain in its hottest flames, while other ministers wave derogatory scrolls that refer to their blemished achievements.

A second plaque was commissioned in 2011 specifically for MOA. The Esteves Lima brothers chose to focus this work on Portugal's insolvency and the financial rescue plan and austerity measures imposed on the country. The plaque is surmounted this time by world leaders Barack Obama, Angela Merkel and Hu Jintao, each gripping the flag of their respective countries. A kneeling Portuguese president begs the three leaders to help Portugal. Inside the fires of Hell, it is Zé Povinho, the symbol of the Portuguese people, who is crushed, carrying his heavy cross of debt, while being encouraged and admonished by politicians. The Devil sits with representatives of the International Monetary Fund and the European Central Bank listening to a hapless prime minister, Pedro Passos Coelho, who kneels holding an open hat in which to receive a rescue package. Eight bankers and politicians from different parties sit on the sidelines with feet partly dangling into the flames.

A third plaque was commissioned in August 2014 following the insolvency of the Bank of Espírito Santo, outrage over the salaries of executives of the national airline, TAP, and the announcement of a new report that found that the stringent austerity measures imposed on the country were not working. These works represent popular histories of the plight of the Portuguese people under the austerity regime. By using historical symbols and religious iconography, they transform the particularities of Portugal's current series of crises and the suffering they entail into the archetypes of a de-historicized and reoccurrent national malaise.

The Esteves Lima brothers learned to work clay from their father, who was taught by an aunt who made toys and figurative wares. Their father, Domingos Gonçalves Lima, who first used the name Mistério, began learning his art at age twelve by helping prepare the clay and selling the finished pieces at market. Manuel began helping his father when he was seven and Francisco joined them at fifteen; the brothers were assisted by their mother, Virgínia Coelho Esteves, who until recently painted the figures. Both brothers drew a distinction between the crude figures made by their father's aunt and those of their father, which became more elaborate and diverse and included religious figures. The brothers share a workshop, and their repertoire, based on their father's work, has expanded to include saints, figurative groups and animals as well as special commissions. Manuel links social criticism with humour and has described how some clients can be absorbed by a piece when they recognize the subject it satirizes. The ability of work to trigger laughter provides a way of rejecting political and religious conventions. Animal-headed humans and both female and baby devils, first modelled by their father, follow on the same strategy that underlines the composition of the plaques discussed above, though both artists claim they prefer real to imaginary subjects.

Popular culture was reduced by the Estado Novo and the governments that followed it to political culture, which, despite attempts to reinstitutionalize it within discourses on heritage, is only now beginning to be appreciated for its independence and full critical and creative potential. During the time of the dictatorship, António Júlio de Castro Fernandes, then sub-secretary of corporations and social welfare, described it thus: "Strictly speaking popular culture is what the people themselves create. This is folklore. But in a more general sense we can see popular culture as the perfection of the mentality of the people."[346] Folklore, for the Estado Novo as for the governments that have succeeded it, is not what the people create but what the government imagined they created and the official strategies in which such creativity can be channelled to perfect it. *Romarias, ranchos folclóricos* (folk dance groups), gastronomy, village saint's day festivals, Lisbon's popular processions and state-sponsored rural ethnographic projects established the official version of popular culture, intrinsically linked to the idea of an "elected people" and an enduring "national spirit," that the Estado Novo portrayed as having been constructed from regional diversity.[347]

Since the fall of the dictatorship in 1974, despite global integration and their diminishing importance, rural and fishing communities have continued to be textualized and portrayed as the heart of Portuguese society and the embodiment of national culture—no longer as part of a messianic project of national renovation, but as the indispensable ingredient of an idea of patrimony that is irreconcilably determined and manipulated by a model of economic development heavily based on tourism. The research of anthropologists, folklorists, documentary filmmakers and photographers is transformed into promotional literature, criteria for competitions, exhibitions, television programs, blogs and guides for community-based preservation programs that circulate popular culture and art endlessly in spirals of innovation, reinvention and re-authentication. These continue to expand the folkloricization, objectification and revalidation of local arts and cultures according to regional, national and international tastes and values.[348]

Attempts to coerce uniformity and a singular identity have only exacerbated the national and international clamour for alterity and spectacle based on a deepening of the nation's supposed exoticism and desire to be a place under the sovereignty of Heaven, built and guided by divine and mythological personages and populated by the devotees of many great, as well as obscure, saintly cults. It is a place where saints are said to mix with humanity, though in reality, Heaven and Earth, Church and government, though perhaps in constant conversation, have created a country of simulacra in which the Lusitanian imagination becomes ever more shrill and diminished under the spell of international markets and the ever-expanding cycles of commoditization.

facing
MANUEL AND FRANCISCO ESTEVES LIMA (MISTÉRIO)
Austerity, (plaque), 2015
Zé Povinho complains, "I always have to pay for everything on my minimal salary," while Angela Merkel sits expectantly with an open case and Portuguese president Aníbal Cavaco Silva exclaims, "Pay them. I only earn 10.000 Euros." In the centre of the plaque an old woman looks at her empty wallet and a businessman exclaims, "The banks are crashing." A seated nurse asks Minister of Health Paulo Macedo, "Where am I going to work?" He replies by offering her a passport. A teacher sitting next to the nurse awaits the deliberations of Minister of Education Nuno Crato, who carries in his backpack wads of evaluation forms. The "commandant" of TAP (airline) offers Deputy Prime Minister Paulo Portas, shown playing with a submarine, an aircraft for privatization, while Finance Minister Maria Luis Albuquerque worries over her moneyless suitcase.

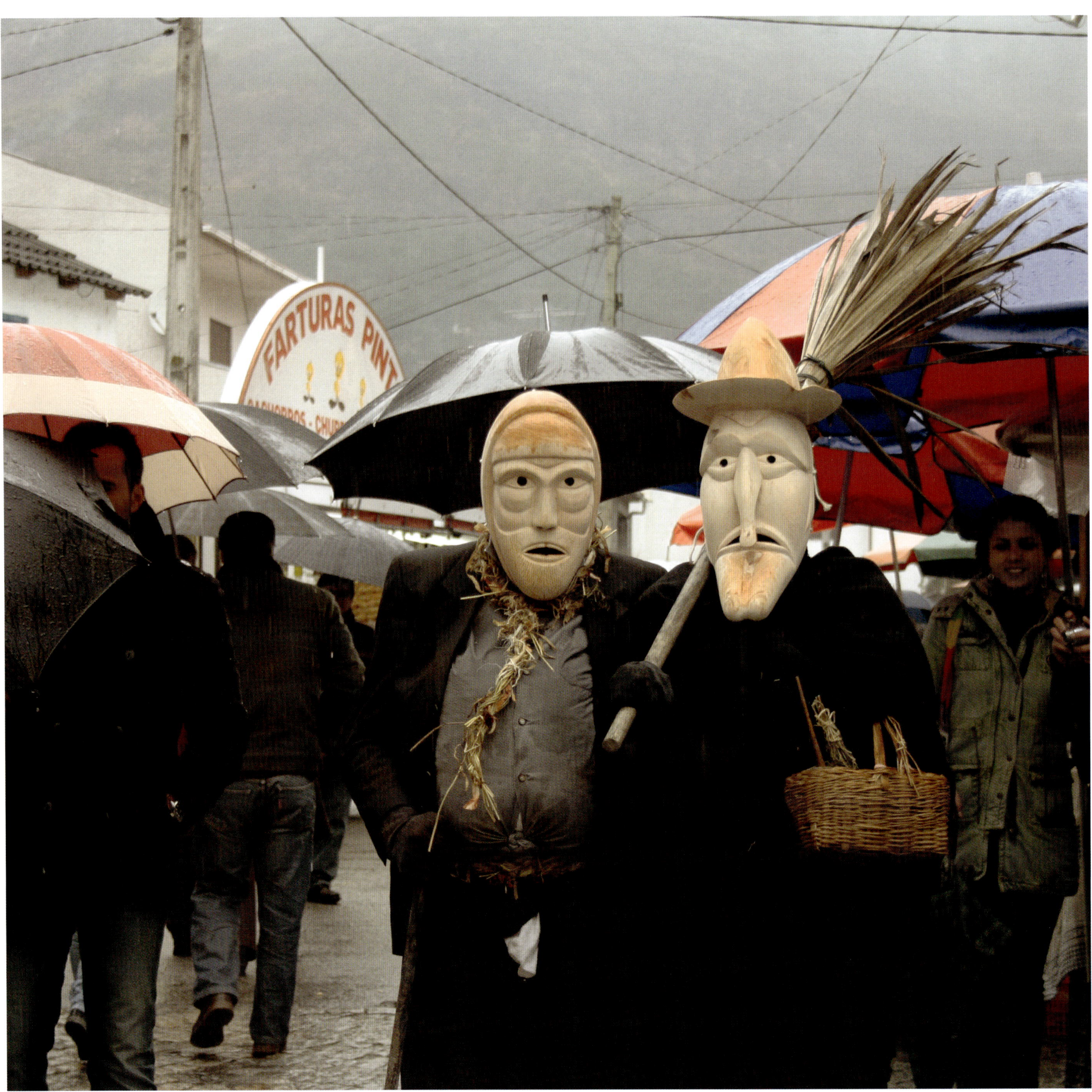
FARTURAS

6 A Portuguese Demonology

The Representation of Evil and Sin

In the regions secluded from civilization, numerous and sinister hordes of witches, werewolves [and] powerful sorcerers, who can injure men just with their evil stare, have made their refuge, and Moorish enchantresses [*mouras encantadas*], in springs and rocks, are still able to lure unsuspecting wayfarers.

Jorge Dias[349]

DIABO AND THE INCARNATION OF EVIL

Images of Diabo, the Devil, and his hellish compatriots, are few in Portuguese churches. In Monsaraz, in Alentejo, the cupola of the chapel of São João Baptista is decorated with mural paintings dating to 1622 that, although much damaged, show the seven-headed dragon of the Apocalypse. A more complete painting of the Beast of the Apocalypse, dating to the 1520s, has been preserved in the Casas Pintadas in Évora, where, surrounded by panther, lion, peacock, swan, griffin, dragon and lizard, it confronts the seven virtues assembled to defeat it. Near Portel, also in the Alentejo, the cupola of the chapel of São Farausto is also painted with a mural depicting a large winged beast standing at the back of a group of three figures representing São Bento, Santa Isabel la Raînha and São Luís. In the Viseu Cathedral (thirteenth–seventeenth century) in the province of Beira Alta, the backs, arms and undersides of the choir seats are carved with "faces and bodies of a surprising beauty: demons, chimeras, goats, dragons, fish and heads of the damned,"[350] many of which are now damaged or missing. But the most prominent representation of Diabo and the Beast of the Apocalypse is not in Portugal but in its former colony Macau, massively sculpted on the front facade of the former church of Nossa Senhora da Assunção (commonly known as São Paulo), consecrated in 1603.

Despite the paucity of historical images, Portuguese literature includes an extensive vocabulary and an impressive number of different names by which the Devil is known: "Diabo, Mafarrico, Porco-Sujo, Bicho Negro, Galhardo, Provinco, o da carapuça vermelha ('he of the scarlet cap'), Trasgo, Crespo, Manquito, Zangão, Farrapeiro" and so on.[351] Another name sometimes given to him was "Fear."[352] In contrast, his diabolical hordes bear such infamous names as Homem das Sete Dentaduras (Man of the Seven Teeth) and Secular das Nuvens (Secular of the Clouds).[353] In Minho it was believed the Devil could assume the forms

facing
A masked witch and an old woman at Carnival in Lazarim, 2010.

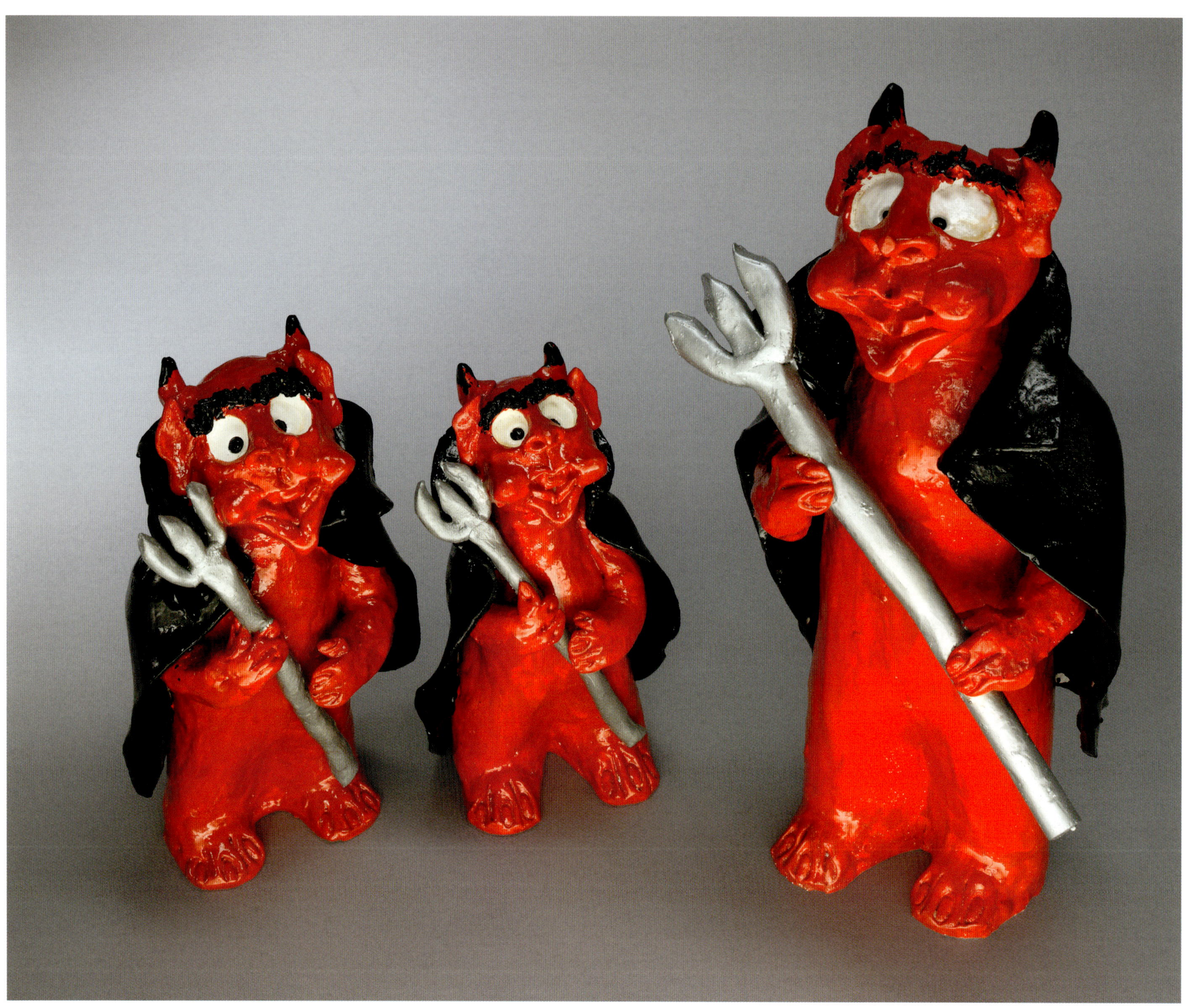

facing
NELSON OLIVEIRA
Three devil figures, Barcelos, 2011

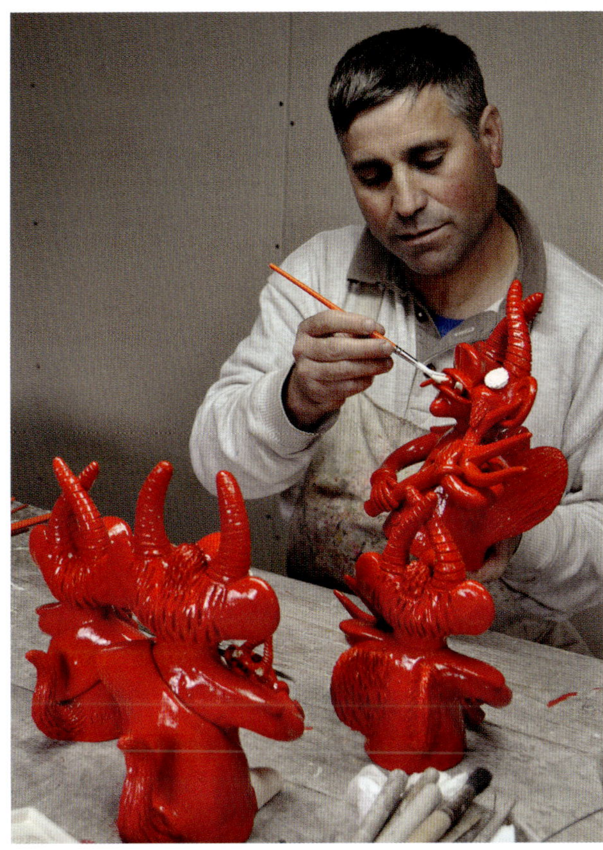

left
Ceramic artist Francisco Esteves Lima, Barcelos, 2011.

of animals like a wolf or a sow with her piglets.[354] When the Devil is represented in religious paintings, it is nearly always at the foot of the victorious São Miguel, the angel who helps free repented souls from Purgatory, or as a serpent that encircles the world on which stands the Nossa Senhora da Conceição. Small moulded images of São Bartolomeu, a powerful exorcist, also sometimes show him standing on the prostrated body of a dragon-like Diabo.

In the reports of the Inquisition, Diabo was conceptualized in many different forms. Sometimes he appeared as a beautiful woman with a long tail or took the appearance of a man dressed in white with a dark face and elongated fingers. In other descriptions he assumes the form of a cat by day who can transform himself into a small human figure at night.[355] Manuel and Francisco Esteves Lima have inherited the model of the Devil made famous by the pottery figures of their father, who intended it to be the ugliest form he could imagine. The family has included in their diabolical coterie pottery figures and busts of female and even baby devils being suckled by their devil mothers. Domingos Gonçalves Lima once explained, "I always make *diabos* and *diabas* [male devils and she-devils]. The *diabos* do not marry; they are opposite, they join together. They *largam* [leave each other] and the *diabas* give their children their breasts to suckle... The *diabos* [and] saints... are composites, they have a little of everything."[356] His son Manuel believes the devils he and his brother make represent people's bad sides, which is why they widen the traditional male identity of evil to include women and children. In legend, Diabo is accompanied sometimes by a consort, either his wife or mother.[357] Portuguese folklore also includes lesser *diabos*, called *diabretes*, that act like satyrs or poltergeists and delight in causing domestic mischief—turning off lights, breaking pots, throwing stones at the attic, imitating voices of different people—but are not thought to incarnate evil.[358] Manuel and Francisco Esteves Lima also fashion mischievous devils undertaking everyday activities—cycling or riding in carts, for example—that recall the *diabretes* and Manuel's identification of them with ordinary people.

The plurality of names given Diabo has been interpreted using the folkloric argument as indicative of the amalgamation of different supernatural creatures that may once have belonged to a pre-Christian form of religion. Following the lead of various Portuguese folklorists, like José Leite de Vasconcellos, Gallop suggested that Dianho, one of the names attributed to Diabo, may have been derived from Janus (Dianus) or Jana (Diana),[359] thus establishing a link between Roman and Christian religions. Gallop also recorded that a village near Sintra bearing the name of "Janas" has a circular church built on the foundations of an older temple; the church may have been consecrated to the goddess.[360] Pedroso, in the same interpretive vein, also believed that the popular concept of

Diabo in Portugal was probably conceived from an amalgamation of different pre-Christian and Biblical supernatural beings.[361] The art historian Robert Hughes was more explicit and believed Diabo not only is a transfiguration of the iconography of Pan or Dionysius, but shares with them underworld associations and pleasurable pursuits that Christianity recategorized as sins.[362] Christianity therefore polarized the concepts of good and evil, which some communities equated with the antagonistic but unequal pairing of the Devil and São Miguel. The seven-headed Beast of the Apocalypse represents all seven sins that, as depicted in the Casas Pintadas in Évora, are held in unsteady equilibrium by an equal number of virtues, which it was believed would one day triumph over them.

From the Middle Ages, the idea that there was a supreme god of evil that balanced the god of goodness became ingrained in popular religion. The god of evil and his horde possessed all the inverted characteristics and structural attributes of God. From this idea of inversions arose the idea of the mother of Diabo as the inverse of Mary, the mother of God. The Diaba of popular religion was attributed such horrendous and terrible appearance that, it was said, she even made the Devil himself tremble with fright.[363] In some parts of the country, folklorists recorded that the lascivious sexuality attributed to Diabo was closely associated with São Hilário. Gallop recorded a belief that no woman could enter Paradise without having lost her virginity. São Hilário, it was believed, could intercede by taking her virginity in return for a coin left in her coffin.[364]

Diabo is more powerful in popular thought than in orthodox interpretation, where he is a figure of temptation. In Biblical accounts of the Garden of Eden, Diabo was represented as a serpent, and in most medieval paintings he is shown as a kingly man, the beautiful fallen angel Lucifer, who assumed his grotesque form only after the tenth century.[365] In the twelfth-century *Lorvão Apocalypse* (a copy of an eighth-century work), Diabo is illustrated as a seven-headed serpent spitting fire and elsewhere as a horned dog with a five-horned serpent rising upwards from its neck and another horned head sticking out from its breast. In this latter depiction the beast has two hairy tails on his back and front and instead of paws has claws like those of a griffin. However, the popular version of Diabo envisages him not as a representation of absolute evil as in orthodox Christianity, but as a trickster. He can be flirted with, joked about and even fooled. He can at times be well mannered, generous and even modest,[366] somewhat like the Antichrist himself. In Gil Vicente's sixteenth-century *Boat Plays*,[367] the Devil is described as a fair and reasonable man who argues with his angelic counterpart about the final destination of the souls that meet them by the shores of the ocean.

Júlia Ramalho seldom depicts Diabo, but her grandmother Rosa did attempt to capture his image in clay. Rosa Ramalho caricatured Diabo with a large head, short, goat-like horns and a wide, gaping mouth with wide gaps between his few teeth. Her compositions overwhelmingly convey a sense of parody and humour. She never called him by name, but by the word *cabeçudo* (giant papier-mâché heads that are often paraded in the Peninsula). By rendering the icon of evil ridiculous, it is possible to socially weaken or make his source of power ineffective. Nevertheless, although her images might diminish Diabo's authority over human will, she still acknowledged his role as the gatekeeper of Hell. This role could be subverted only by attacking the basis of divine authority itself, and Rosa Ramalho was, like her granddaughter, devoutly Catholic. She seems to have therefore coupled her *diabos* with representations of São Pedro, whom she also referred to as a *cabeçudo*. São Pedro is depicted in similar style and size to Diabo—a large round head, with an affable expression of surprise, and a corpulent body. São Pedro holds the key to Heaven, just as Diabo guards the door to Hell. Both undertake similar, but inverted, responsibilities in sorting and housing the souls of the wicked from those of the devout.

The Portuguese Christian image of Hell, sometimes argued to have been borrowed from Greek and Roman antiquity in which Hades was believed to exist under the earth, was thought of as a place of bubbling lava, sulphurous stench, fetid heat and lava tuft caves,[368] with people being boiled in cauldrons and tortured by demons, much like the sixteenth-century anonymous Primitivist painting *Inferno* in Lisbon's Museu Nacional de Arte Antiga. Hell was likened to a cauldron in Portuguese popular religion, full of hot oil in which condemned souls were forced to live. Diabo resides in Hell, a great cavity in the earth that leads to the centre of the world that is always ablaze with fires. Disagreement existed as to where the entrance to Hell was located: it might have been Boca do Inferno in Cascais, Vale do Inferno near Coimbra or elsewhere in Portugal.[369] During the Middle Ages the entrance to Hell was depicted as the great jaw and mouth of the apocalyptic beast Leviathan, whose body was made of burning souls and suffering bodies.[370] Dias noted that in Vilarinho da Furna there was a shrine with niches that contained boards on which pictures had been painted of souls not in Hell but in Purgatory, to remind those who passed to offer them prayer;[371] a similar theme is depicted in the church of Podence and in the streets, including the Rua Direita, around the castle in Estremoz, where old street signs still depict burning souls. The subject was taken up again in paintings on tiles, such as the large composition on the building at the corner of Rua do Almoxarife in Coimbra. Most people die in a state of sin, often it was thought because they had outstanding debts or unfulfilled promises made to saints. They were dispatched to Purgatory, where, depending on the seriousness of their sin, they endured pain until being redeemed to enter Heaven. The souls in Purgatory required food and prayer. Roadside reminders of their perilous situation, such as those in Estremoz and Coimbra, also prompted the living to remember them through prayers, which could help shorten their suffering. Souls could be redeemed by São Miguel, but some in great pain could return to haunt the living.[372] In popular thought, souls were always considered good and worthy of prayer, but spirits were always bad.[373]

In his study of Vilarinho, Dias commented on how close and unthreatening the ancestors were still thought to be to the living. The obligation of those still alive to ensure regular Masses to ease the suffering of their dead family members or prevent their capture and entrapment in Purgatory was commonly acknowledged. During the visitation of Nossa Senhora in Fátima in 1917, the children who witnessed the apparitions were repeatedly told to pray earnestly for the suffering souls. Only prayer to Nossa Senhora could bring them relief.

In the millenarian interpretation of Portuguese history, the fate of the nation oscillates between repeated periods of glory and periods of decadence. Heavenly hosts, Christ, São Jorge, São Bento and Nossa Senhora, this school insisted, helped impart to Portugal fame and prestige beyond its size, but, like the ambiguity sometimes ascribed to Diabo, they might also allow disasters, like the Great Earthquake of 1755, if angered, ignored or

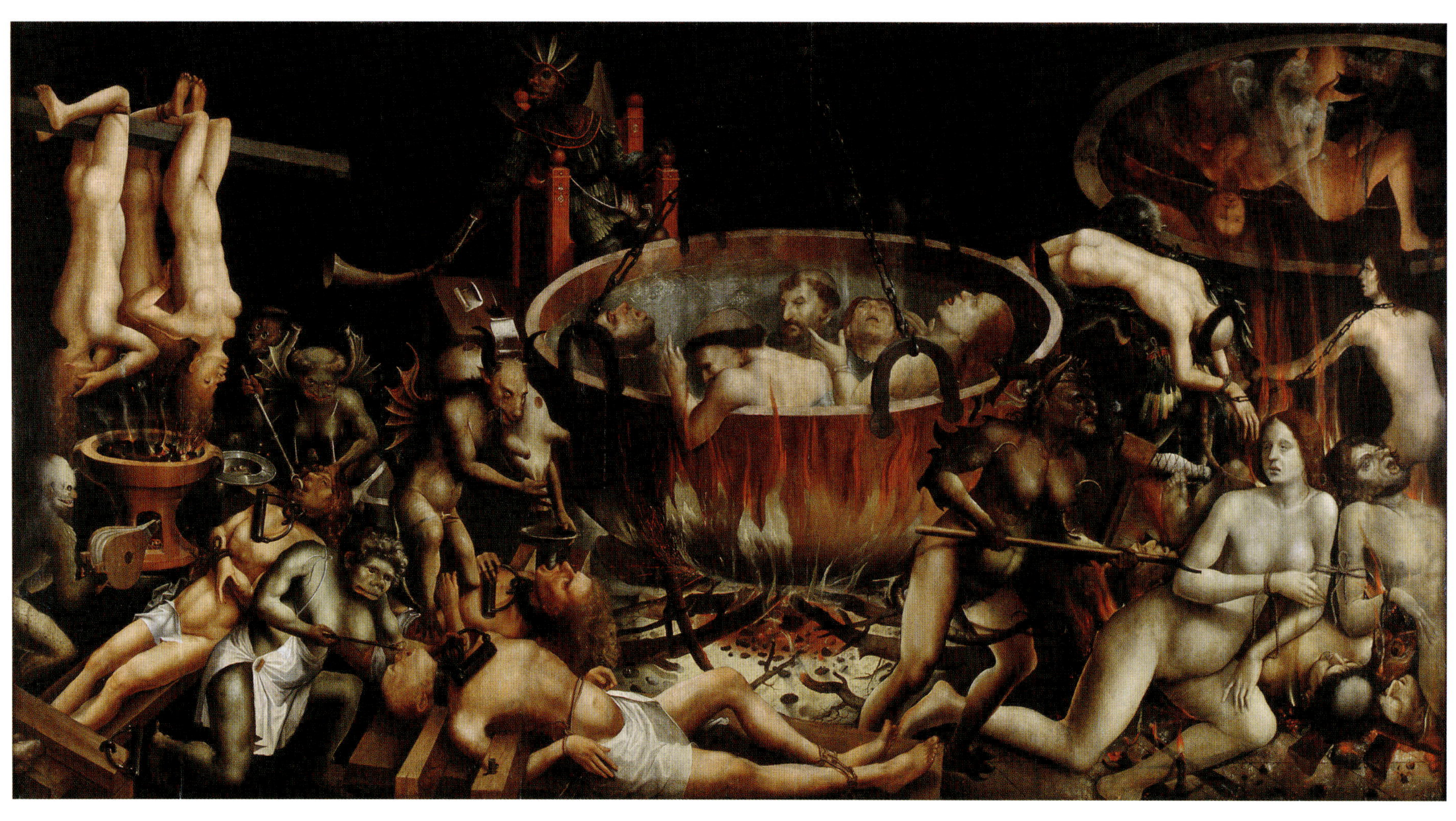

defamed. This idea of history as a series of alternations creates a binary structure to Portuguese thought that reiterates itself in diverse areas. Day and night were thought to correspond to the different jurisdictions of the courts of Heaven and Hell, while noon and midnight, as turning points of the day, were each associated with diabolical influences.[374] The division of the year into the solstices, whose alternations are marked by the feast days of São João and Santo Estêvão, although now largely secularized, are still acknowledged and widely celebrated. The relationship between people, God and the saints and between people, Diabo and his horde were sometimes conceptualized as binary inversions. To recover from sickness or increase luck, success or happiness, people would make a promise or vow to an image of a saint. If the wish was answered, they would comply with their promise in order to fulfill their reciprocal obligation. Repayment might take the form of a long pilgrimage, sometimes undertaken on one's knees, or offerings of ex-votos such as candles, first harvests, wax models of parts of the body affected by sickness[375] or, particularly in the case of sailors and fishermen, models of boats or paintings showing their rescue or escape from stormy weather.[376] Giant tropical snakes were even hung on the walls of the church in Alívio, Vila Verde, as offerings to the Senhora do Alívio.[377] Similarly, favours can be asked of Diabo, who also demands reciprocity. Failure to comply with vows made to any category of supernatural being, it was believed, could result in punishment and even premature death.

Dualism also structured traditional rural beliefs around weather and the relationship with the fall of adequate or excessive rain. Dias noted a belief common in much of Iberia that, although God was invoked to send rain, it was the *nuvens* (clouds) that needed to be propitiated to prevent too great a downpour, which might endanger crops.[378] Vasconcellos[379] and Pedroso[380] recorded the belief that every individual is accompanied through life by a light and dark shadow—a guardian angel on their right side and the Devil in disguise on their left—each competing to influence the actions and behaviour of their human companion. Furthermore, like the hierarchical court of Heaven, Diabo was attributed his own anarchic court, with powers and influences that are the inverse of those wielded by God. When taken together these characteristics suggest rural Portuguese traditional thought was structured by a strong binary division, which generated a complementary though inverted relationship between God and Diabo.

One rare account of a Church-based depiction of Diabo was described by Pierre Sanchis.[381] In 1809, the account told, there stood in the monastery in Amarante two black wooden images of male and female *diabos* that were described as "creative natural forces." Both were revered and regularly petitioned for (mainly sexual) favours and, like the local saints, were taken on procession as part of the *romaria* to celebrate the Body of God. During the Napoleonic invasion, the *diabos* were being taken in procession when drunken foreign soldiers assaulted them and burned them along with Church insignia. There was widespread condemnation from the people of the town, who asked the priest to arrange for copies to be made. This was done and promises and offerings continued to be made to them, especially on the feast day of São Bartolomeu. When in 1870 the bishop of Braga heard of these practices, he demanded the images be removed, leaving the priest to mediate between his congregation and ecclesiastical authority. The priest had first planned to cut off the sexual organs of the two figures, but

facing
ARTIST UNKNOWN
Hell, 1510–20
Museu Nacional
de Arte Antiga

then an English collector intervened to purchase them. This caused even greater consternation among the townspeople, and the *diabos* were finally repurchased by the municipality and placed at the entrance to the town.

The travel writers Wright and Swift then took up the story.[382] They believed that the copies of the two *diabos* may have been made by the sculptor António Ferreira, otherwise known as Ferreira dos Diabos, and are still preserved in the small town museum. The two *diabos* were originally installed in the sacristy but were condemned as being "obscene, offensive, and the subject of a cult," so they were sold to an Englishman, Alberto Sandeman of Porto, for three pounds each. They reappeared at the World's Fair in Paris in 1889 advertising their owner's port wine and were subsequently donated to the town's museum. What such images were doing in a Christian church might be explained by the travel writer Sacheverell Sitwell, who noted that "the organ in São Gonçalo at Amarante is upheld by a pair of tritons, and between them is a merman with two forked black tails."[383] The two original figures reported by Sanchis and Wright and Swift might therefore have been mythological creatures.

Although the cult is now long extinct, Sanchis noted that another sexualized cult around São Gonçalo, in the same town, had probably assumed its telluric and sexual associations in the nineteenth century.[384] São Gonçalo had special authority over prostitutes in some places, including Estremoz,[385] and his cult involved considerable phallic symbolism. Oliveira[386] and Wright and Swift[387] recorded that until the 1950s, on São Gonçalo's feast day it had been common for young men to give girls phallic-shaped sweetmeat, seemingly as part of a courting ceremony. They also noted that above the saint's tomb was inscribed the words: "Why do you not wed the young brides? What harm have they done you?"[388] The Church, in this instance, rid itself of what it perceived as images of evil but allowed the association and powers of the two diabolical images to be transferred to a Christian saint, while the representation of Diabo was limited to the form of a dragon, trampled and dominated by São Jorge.[389] São Gonçalo was also venerated in Bunheiro, near Aveiro, where he was closely associated with weddings at which equally licentious and obscene promises were made to him.[390] Pina-Cabral, after iterating the stories of São Gonçalo, suggested that the annual feast at which phallic-shaped bread was used to hit the head or backside of girls continued to be practised into the 1980s and served as a ritual of gender affirmation.[391] He also recorded that on the feast day of São Mateus (17–18 September) near Figueira da Foz, painted clay images of phalluses were offered to an image of Diabo found in a local church.[392] Oliveira recorded that similar scatological and obscene promises were also made during the *romaria* of São Mateus near Soure.[393]

In popular thought Diabo was associated with São Bartolomeu, who was believed to be efficacious in exorcising malevolent spirits. According to a thirteenth-century legend, Bartolomeu accompanied Christ from the time of His first miracle, turning water into wine, until His death and resurrection. On his subsequent return to the East, the saint encountered King Polímio, whose daughter had been possessed by Diabo. Bartolomeu exorcised the malignant spirit, prompting the king to destroy a pagan temple and convert to Christianity. However, the priests of the old religion conspired with Polímio's brother, Astíages, ruler of another region of Armenia, to invite the saint to purge his land of diabolical influences. When São Bartolomeu arrived, he was ambushed and flayed alive. Immediately, Astíages and his priests became possessed by Diabo and suffered terribly for thirty days, at the end of which they choked until asphyxiated. In accordance with his legend, images of the saint depict him dominating Diabo while holding the knife used to flay him. Epilepsy is widely thought to be one of the afflictions sent by Diabo, and the pilgrimage to the shrine of São Bartolomeu in Esposende is accompanied by ritual bathing in the sea to cure those afflicted.[394]

In the early twentieth century in Lisbon and Santarém, on the eve of São Bartolomeu's feast day (24 August), Diabo was believed to return to the earth.[395] Elsewhere, people believed Diabo and his minions, including the *mouras encantadas* (Moorish enchantresses), made themselves visible at midnight on the Day of São João (24 June).[396] On this day, folklorists recorded, the enchantresses changed their appearance from their usual snake-like form to become human.[397] Wright and Swift retold the story first written by the nineteenth-century Romantic writer Camilo Castelo Branco (1825–90), in his *Noites de Lamego*, of his experiences on the feast day of São Bartolomeu in Chaves, a village in northern Portugal he had visited to see the exorcism ceremonies. The village was believed to have suffered a particularly deleterious infestation of demons, which mainly took possession of young girls and forced them to make obscene gestures. According to Wright and Swift:

> When Castelo Branco arrived on the scene he found five cases of possession awaiting the ministrations of the saint, each victim firmly held by ten strong Barroso men. The sacred effigy—a heavy stone statue—was carried out and placed on the heads of the possessed, one after the other. Meanwhile the demons raved and ranted in rage. The priest in a furious voice berated the devils, insulting them and ordering them back into the depths of hell whence they had come to torment the innocent girls of Chaves. The girls, completely worn out by the struggle, finally collapsed exhausted into the arms of their mothers. Little by little they recovered and in the end, quite calm, went to the altar of the saint to give thanks. After which they made a round of the church on their knees. It was said that within a few weeks these girls would marry the man whom the Devil in his ranting declared they would.[398]

Related to Diabo are other sinister and not-so-sinister creatures that fall under his jurisdiction. Although the First Council of Braga of AD 561 refuted and condemned the belief that Diabo had created beings of his own, denied his mastership over natural phenomena including storms, thunder and lightning, and strongly rejected the idea that personal fate was dominated by astrological influences, such beliefs remained common in the Portuguese countryside well into the twentieth century. In Bragança, Diabo or another "visible demon" was incarnated in the "Secular das Nuvens."[399] According to Pedroso, these were golem-like creatures who walked the clouds, where they battled using lightning and thunder as their armaments. Their presence was seen in the darkest of clouds that passed directly before storms, and their battles were thought to foretell real wars and revolutions at home. They were believed to be human fabrications, made from killing a man slowly after he had been excommunicated and then emptying his body of all its flesh, entrails, blood and bones, which were carefully kept in a vat. After a year the Secular das Nuvens leaves the body to take flight in the air. Able to go to neither Heaven nor Hell they were damned to remain in the sky. Sometimes, it was noted, they could temporarily assume human form and appear on the earth during a storm.

Other strange supernatural creatures were also thought to exist elsewhere in Portugal. Mountains were the home of monsters.[400] Rocks, springs, mountain caves, ruined towns, castles and mines were all widely thought to house human-like nymphs, sprites, Nereids and other nature spirits; wells, it was recounted, may have an old woman at their bottom who waited to devour children.[401] In the province of Algarve, *jãs* or *jans*, benign small girls with long hair and extraordinary beauty, were thought to inhabit caves, fountains and rivers. Many of these were identified as *mouras encantadas*. Vasconcellos, writing in the nineteenth century, opined that there were few places in Portugal without stories of these enchantresses, and even today, stories are still told of them.[402]

In some traditions the enchantresses were said to have been left by the Moors when they retreated from Portugal in the twelfth century, while in others they were described as robed in white garments and related to the Roman cult of Diana or the Greek goddess Moira.[403] Sometimes the enchantresses were described as having snakes' tails and being related to mermaids: "To mortal eyes they are visible only on the night of São João, when they may be seen combing their hair like mermaids with golden combs, spinning or weaving with golden thread, or laying out figs in the dew, which turn to gold in the hands of any mortal who can seize them."[404]

Mouras encantadas were thought to have built great monuments in just one night, such as the cathedral in Viseu, the church of Leça do Balio and the convent of Vila da Feira.[405] They were also said to have the ability to transform coal into gold and vice versa and were guardians of ancient treasures.[406] They performed tests on those they encountered, asking their mortal acquaintances to choose between material gifts or end the enchantment that afflicted them (usually by a kiss).[407] The places inhabited by the enchantresses were, it was believed, sometimes marked by the construction of chapels dedicated to the Virgin, who occasionally inherited some of their attributes.[408] Despite the benevolence popular belief ascribed to these beings and the offerings and promises made to them, the institutional Church treated them either as illusions or as manifestations of creatures sent by Diabo. It is worth noting that Diabo is also in some parts of the country associated with water, wells and bridges spanning rivers,[409] suggesting his close relationship with the *mouras encantadas*.[410]

Other supernatural creatures included *olharapos* (one-eyed cannibal giants), *almanzonas* (amazons), *lobisomens* (werewolves), giants, dwarfs and ill-defined monsters like the Medo, Pesadelo, Trasgo, Tardo and others never depicted in popular or any other art. Illnesses, it was recorded, were sometimes envisaged as spirits or souls from another world that could enter the body, particularly at sunrise, noon or sunset, and could only be cured by exorcism and the use of amulets and mirrors to reflect them back into the bodies of those that had directed them.[411] Malign influences were particularly attracted to the living at transitional moments in life like birth, marriage and death, which encouraged a wide range of related beliefs and prescriptions to prevent them causing harm.[412] These included the intervention of the Moorish enchantresses, who were accredited with healing powers.[413] In Vilarinho, Dias found illnesses were never attributed to natural causes and were combatted with magical processes.[414] Writing some four decades later, Pina-Cabral noted that bone-setters, traditional midwives, doctors, pharmacists and saints might all be addressed to ensure afflictions are cured both practically and morally, agreeing that both scientific and magical practices were weighed equally.[415] Dias and Pina-Cabral noted that stories of witches and werewolves abounded in these northern villages, as elsewhere in Portugal.[416]

THE REPRESENTATION OF EVIL IN POPULAR ART

Both the Estado Novo and the Church upheld absolute values of good and evil in which the political good and national aspirations complemented religious grace and followed divine will and destiny. Such moral absolutism, which outlasted the political structure that supported it, exerted a pervasive influence on popular art by focusing it on the representations of good and evil as major themes. Artists do not usually mould or sculpt in clay or carve wooden images of saints connected with the Devil: São Jorge (Santo Dragão), São Miguel (with Diabo underfoot), São Bartolomeu, São Hilário or São Gonçalo. In Aveiro, where São Gonçalo is highly venerated, I found nineteenth-century representations of the saint in antique shops and works by the contemporary painter and ceramic artist José Ferreira dos Santos (Zé Augusto), who until his death in 2012 still fashioned saintly images; images of São Bartolomeu and São Hilário he made only on commission. Most representations of São Bartolomeu and São Hilário are now mass-produced in China by injecting resin into moulds and, along with the more popular and common saints, are exported to Portugal for sale.

More often than not, contemporary images of Diabo in popular culture represent him as a non-menacing, almost derisive character. Such figures are always painted in red and black, sometimes with other colours added. Their features range from mildly ferocious or menacing, like the busts and figures moulded by Domingos, Francisco and Manuel Esteves Lima and similar ones by Júlia Côta, to almost endearing creatures, like those by Nelson Oliveira, which depict Diabo and his family with infantile faces, plump cheeks, wide eyes and awkward chubby bodies. In contrast, Irene Salgueiro's *diabos* are distinguished by their androgynous appearance. Their heads are adorned with multiple horns and they have expressive, kindly, almost human faces, while their conical bodies are often depicted grasping guitars, sepulchres or baskets of fruit. Many of these works are best compared to the lesser *diabos*, the mischievous *diabretes* found in Gil Vicente's comedies, rather than the lord of evil. Diabo is, however, capable of transforming himself into different animal forms, including horses, donkeys, bulls, even mosquitos, but according to folklorists he can always be identified by his goat hooves, which he is unable to hide.[417] Not all the pottery figures described above include the core characteristics of Diabo found in Portuguese mythology, like horns surmounting a male figure of grotesque and horrific form with long hairy tail.[418] The affable, even endearing characteristics given their contemporary plastic representation by Oliveira and Salgueiro are far removed from Pedroso's summary of popular stereotypes of Diabo originally published between 1880 and 1882.

The universe of supernatural and marvellous creatures that constitute a large part of the Ramalhos's bestiary provides an interesting example of how this strongly polarized and oppositional dualism promulgated by state and ecclesiastical institutions was mediated through individual artistic creativity.

Júlia Ramalho has followed her grandmother's example of making *bichos bravos* (vicious pests) and *porcos espinhos* (spiney pigs), but has significantly increased this imaginative genre through

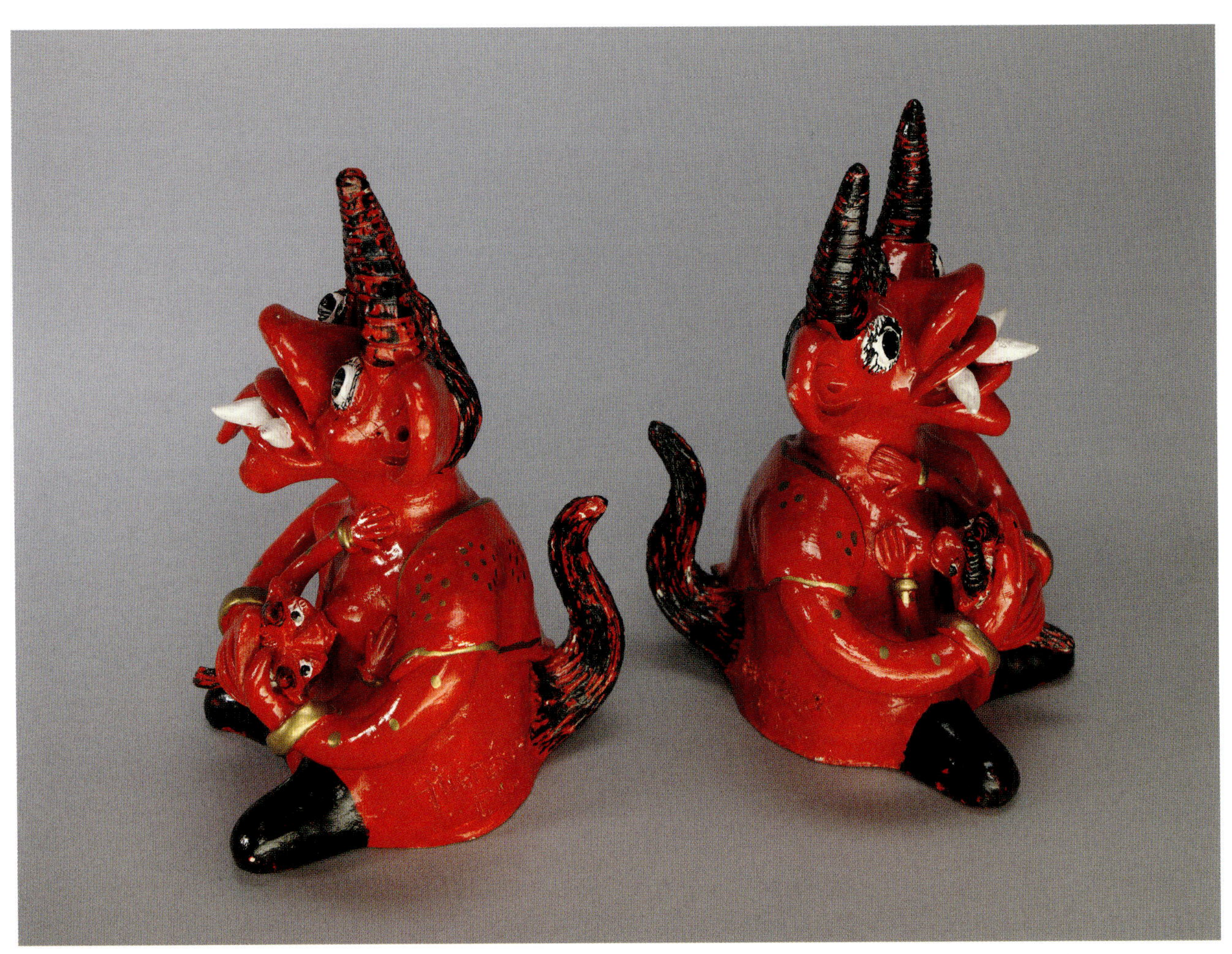

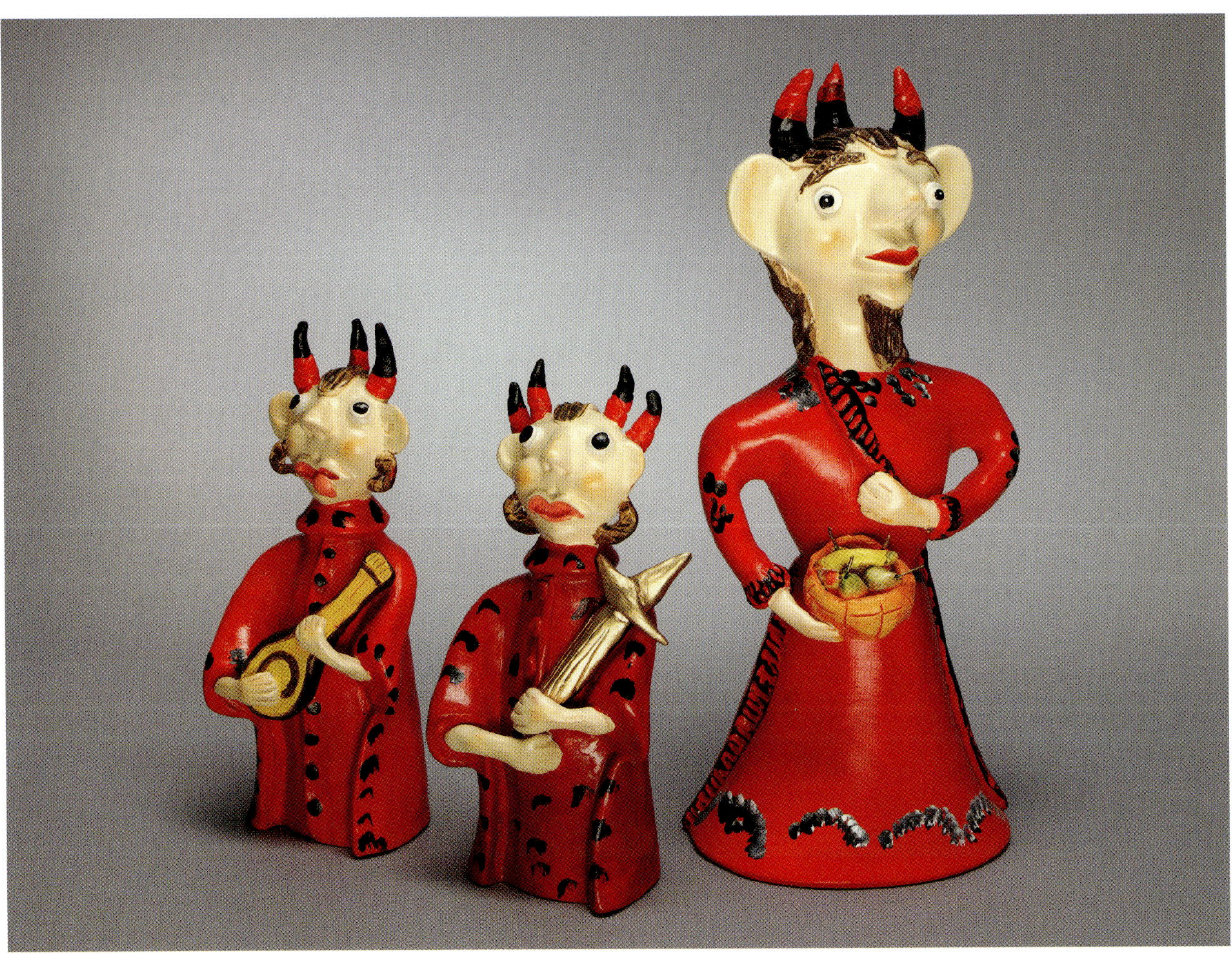

facing, top
FRANCISCO AND MANUEL ESTEVES LIMA
Devils Suckling Their Young, 2010

facing, bottom
IRENE SALGUEIRO
Devils, 2010

figurative representations of Medusa, the seven vices and mermaids. Mermaids, nymphs, sea gods and scaly, upright-standing sirens have further been added or elaborated over previous versions by António Ramalho, Júlia's son. The originality of these representations may have been influenced by two distinct sources: texts, including Biblical stories and the great epic poem of the Portuguese Discoveries, *Os Lusíadas*; and the experience of everyday rural life.

In 2009 I asked Luísa Cruz if she could ask Júlia Ramalho about the source of her inspiration for her unique and startling figures of Medusa. Júlia responded by saying that as a girl she had won a book at school, and among the images she remembered was one of Medusa with her head of snakes. Since then I have noticed that she also makes mermaids and occasionally plaques and figures that represent Neptune in a similar style to others that depict Diabo. In our first conversation, in June 2011, Júlia Ramalho and I discussed *Os Lusíadas*, Neptune and Adamastor and their depiction and significance in her work. The episode of *Os Lusíadas* in which Adamastor, the embodiment of the elemental power of the storm, lashed Vasco da Gama with torrential rainfall and tumultuous waves as he rounded the Cape of Good Hope en route to discovering the East is one of the work's best-known passages and familiar to most Portuguese schoolchildren. These episodes also informed her imagery of the demonic.

In fact, the mass reading of Camões's *Os Lusíadas* must have had a marked effect on generations of Portuguese children and adults as they lost themselves in da Gama's adventures and created a rich imaginary world of mermaids, sea monsters, omnipotent Jupiter, angry Neptune, beautiful but dangerous sirens and scheming demigods that confronted and either supported or opposed the Portuguese in their fulfillment of their myth-soaked destiny. António Ramalho's figure of Neptune wears a crown and has long, unkempt hair and beard, while his lower torso and feet are submerged in whelks and molluscs, recalling Camões's description of Titan.[419]

António has added to this iconography the characteristic four-armed anatomy developed by Júlia for many of her supernatural creatures and an extra eye in the centre of Neptune's forehead.

In its provocation of imaginative furor, even when intended solely as an allegory, *Os Lusíadas* rivals the Bible as a source of the marvellous. Together, the two texts offer the possibility of different hybrid or allegorical interpretive strategies, ranging from their complementary potential, in which image worlds can be elided together, to alternative iconographies that express different but related worlds. The dissemination of the Bible and *Os Lusíadas* to a mass population in the twentieth century provided a richer imaginative universe to inspire the work of popular artists than that available to their nineteenth-century forerunners.

The worlds constituted through the various interpretations of the Bible and *Os Lusíadas* provide an axis on which the contradictions and ambiguities between the idea of Portugal as the centre of a distinctive model of civilization and its existence as a European nation has been orchestrated. The world of much of the popular art discussed here has until recently ignored European-wide subjects or themes, even though these have played a major role in the modernization of the country. Instead it has preferred to develop itself creatively and imaginatively within a distinctive universe constituted by a fragmented Portuguese mythology loosely related to past conditions of existence. Much of Portuguese popular art of the twentieth century was an art of nostalgia—an idealization of a world that it can only imagine through family memories and the reproduction of subjects and themes begun by past generations and filtered through a specific literary and religious tradition. Such memories, however, seldom reach back more than a century and firmly place their inception in either the Republican era or the dictatorship. The representation of good and evil, far from being transcendent and eternal, belongs to a specific time and place.

An exception to this closed-off field of representation is provided by the work of the Ramalho family and Manuel and Francisco Esteves Lima. António Ramalho has continued the themes invented by his mother, but his figures of the Devil now include facial hair reminiscent of the tentacular beard of the character Davy Jones from Disney's *Pirates of the Caribbean*. He has also developed the sirens that may have had their origin in his great-grandmother Rosa Ramalho's *Galo mulheres* (Rooster Women) and *Galinha homem* (Chicken Men). António Ramalho's careful reworking has given the sirens scaly bodies, sometimes decorated by a snake, and tripods for legs and feet, and they play accordions and Portuguese guitars. He has also continued to make the *bichos bravos* invented by Rosa and continued by Júlia. These creations evoke a still ill-defined relation to the nineteenth- and twentieth-century universe of popular religion and mythology.

Quite distinct from these literary and religious inspirations is the world of hard experiences faced by Portuguese communities through much of the nineteenth and twentieth centuries. Pests, *bichos*, part of everyday rural living, come from the world of experience. In Portuguese, *bicho* has no precise meaning and can be used to describe anything with a potentially beastly nature or that creates discomfort, harm, illness, irritation or, as in the case of spiders, fear. *Bichos* are nuisances and irritations that occur in a great many forms and are endemic to country living. They include fleas, lice, ticks, worms, grubs, chigas, woodlice, wire worms, earwigs and parasites as well as leeches and snakes. Some are small, barely visible animals that bloat themselves by feeding on a host's blood, irritating the skin and causing rashes, sores and infections by provoking scratching. *Bichos* cause skin to flake under the hair and can cause sickness, grave irritation and even death in animals. They can be felt crawling on the skin but cannot be seen. Some have wings so small they easily slip through the gauze of mosquito nets and bite in the night. They include worms that burrow into wood, maggots that putrify fruit and ants that infest old properties and stone walls, run over your skin and congregate around food. Ticks begin with small bodies until, having attached themselves to domestic animals and sometimes children, they engorge themselves on their blood and become five or six times their original size. There are many variations on *bicho*, including *bicharoco*, a large worm or repulsive animal, and *bicheira*, a boil or wound infected by worms. *Bichento* means to be wormy; *bichanada* refers to lots of whispering and implies suspect conversations; and *bicho-careta* is a nobody. *Bicho* can also be used to mean "an ugly customer" or vermin. One of the designations of Diabo, according to Gallop, was *o Bicho Preto* or the Black Pest.[420] Like Diabo, *bichos* are everywhere and in the hot summers accompany you throughout the day and night.

Rosa Ramalho magnified this tiny world of *bichos* to create what earlier commentators described as those "primitive," "barbaric," "crudely formed," "inconceivably speckled and coloured little animals."[421] She re-scaled these pests to make their size correspond to the damage and discomfort they breed and, since their actions are blindly driven, she invested them with an understated demonic origin and nature. By visualizing and expressing animal species that molested the living world around them, the potter created potent symbols for expressing social, political, religious and gender-based forms of molestation. Once named and imaged, pests gain a materiality that can provide the focus for resistance against them.

Júlia Ramalho's Medusa figures raise different issues of representation to those of her and her grandmother's *bichos*. Júlia renders Medusa in two distinct forms: as an onion-like bulb, the figure of Medusa appearing to sprout directly out of the vegetable, the snakes straining upwards from her head, and a full-form figurative version more closely based on classical Greek mythology. In the onion figures Medusa is surrounded by high, outstretched hands, and the outside of the bulb is decorated by flame, locating the creature in Purgatory or Hell. Júlia uses a similar style in her depictions of Bacchus, though here the vegetative shape more resembles a gourd from which emerges a human-like head, a diminutive pair of feet and hands that hold goblets. Bacchus's gourd-like body gives him a rotund appearance and is decorated by vines carrying bunches of grapes and leaves sculptured in relief. More than the vices and virtues, the vegetative figures of Bacchus and Medusa express a hybrid and allegorical imagination and telluric interest. Manuel Gustavo Bordalo Pinheiro's representations of nature—snakes, lizards, frogs, crabs, fish, lobsters or fruit—used a romantic natural realist style, with an earthy palette like a still life that conveyed a sense of melancholia and even evoked a tinge of evil or menace; Rosa and Júlia Ramalho's animal images are never so gloomy, and neither are their pagan idols.

Júlia Ramalho treats the subject of good and evil, the Christian and the pagan, seriously, and we are left in no doubt about the outcome of unchecked evil. Her work depicting the seven vices surrounding and enclosing the space in which Christ is being crucified is almost the inverse of the sixteenth-century representation of the Beast of the Apocalypse surrounded and menaced by the animal symbols of the virtues, which was discussed at the beginning of this chapter. Júlia Ramalho opens a portal through which to consider the effect of vice and corruption in the contemporary world. Other artists, the Esteves Lima brothers and Côta, for example, disconnect evil from the representation of the Devil, leaving him an empty icon and relocating evil in humanity itself. Irene Salgueiro and Nelson Oliveira take this strategy much further still by infantilizing and domesticating Diabo as a witless buffoon.

PORTUGUESE MASKS

Diabo is commonly represented in masquerades performed during the saint's day celebrations that coincide with the autumn equinox and the winter solstice. In these contexts, Diabo's mask, costume and actions identify him as the lord or harbinger of evil with an iconography that coincides with scripture and the older mythology already described. In the Festa do Chocalheiro, celebrated on 26 December on the feast day of Santo Estêvão, in Bemposta, Mogadouro, in the northern province of Trás-os-Montes, Diabo, accompanied by two stewards, harasses and frightens villagers. He wears a mask (or *carocha*, as it is locally called) that is one of the most iconographically inspired depictions found in Portugal. His costume includes a dark one-piece suit with hood, tied at the waist with a belt in the form of a long snake on which three or four bells are tied. A tail made of horsehair is

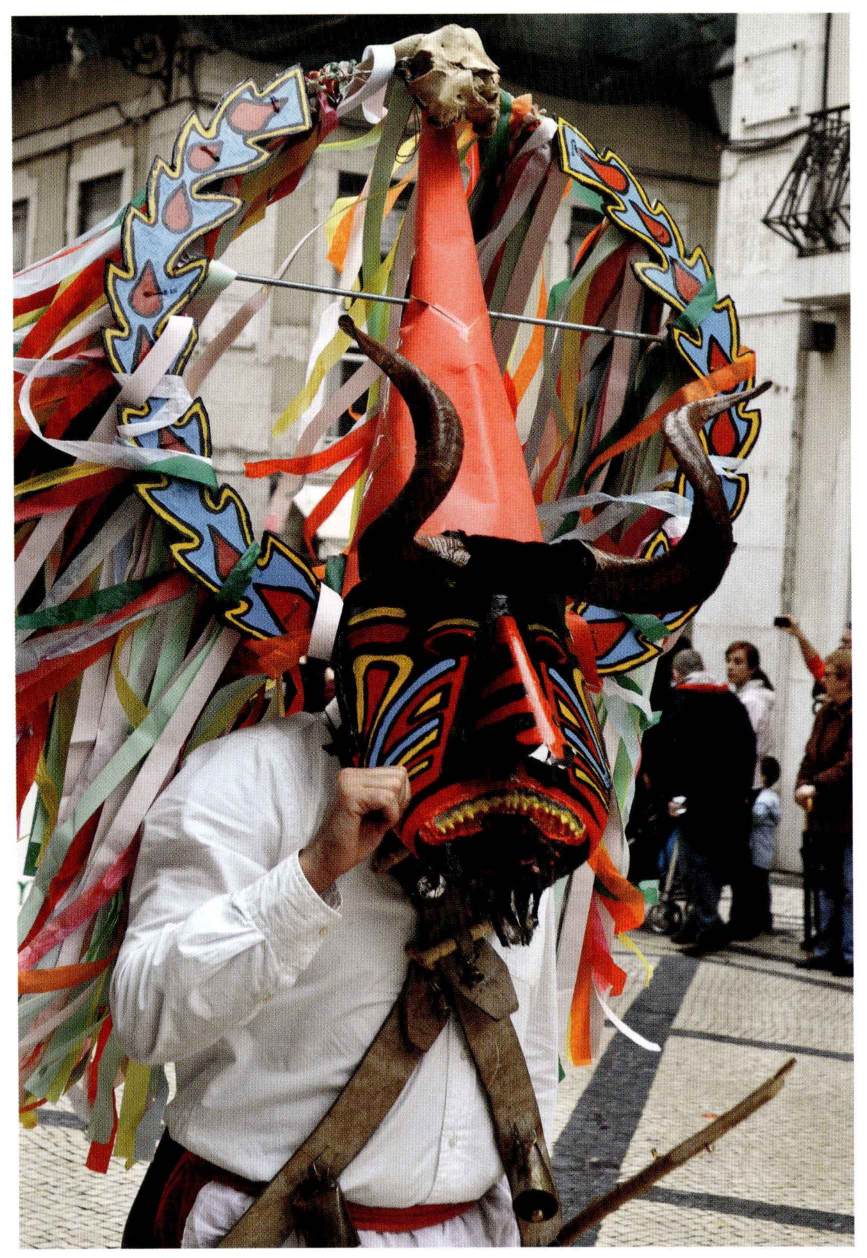

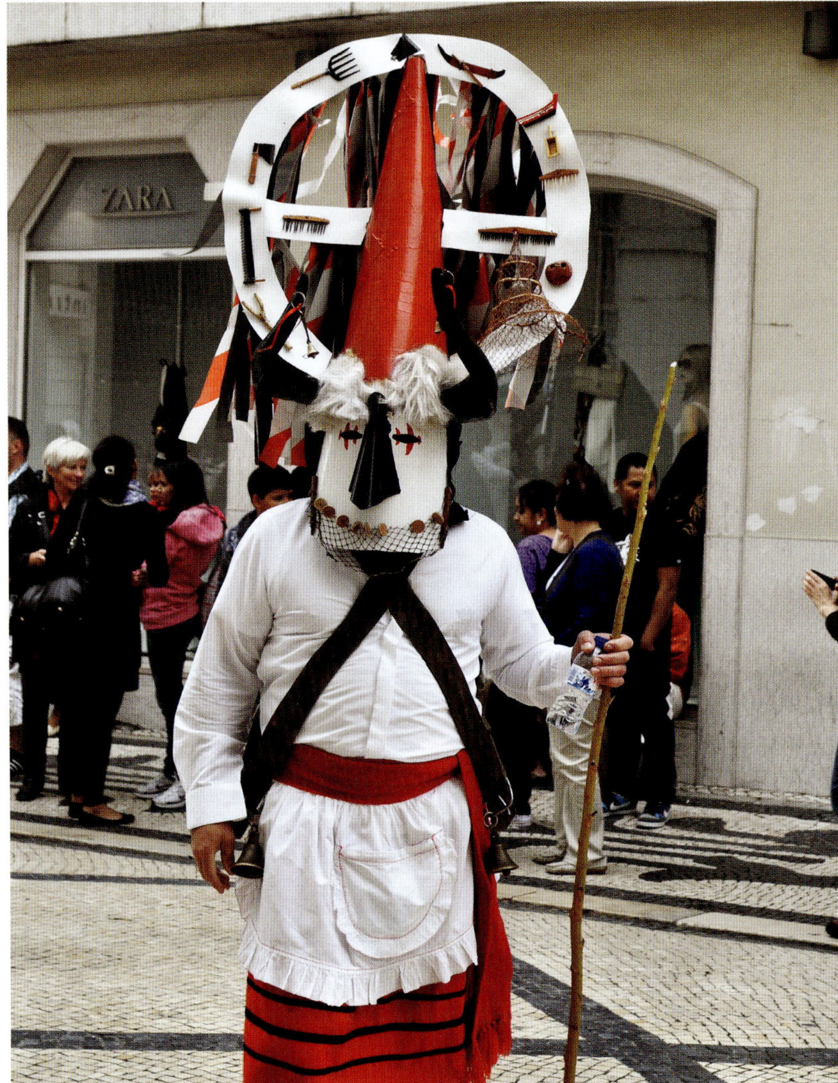

attached to the suit's back, and the back and front are crudely painted in yellow and white with a skull or the picture of a demonic figure. The cap is tucked under the wooden mask that covers the face. Tufts of horsehair stand upright between the mask's horns. On the forehead, between the two horns, is carved a serpent that slithers from an apple down the left side of the mask—an allusion to Diabo's association with original sin. The mask has wide eyes and a large nose outlined in red and white, a moustache and beard and an open mouth revealing irregularly placed and broken teeth and a red tongue that limply lolls downwards.

Other demonic masks and masquerades that make an appearance between 25 and 26 December are mostly limited to Trás-os-Montes, formerly the most isolated part of northern Portugal. They are no longer used only by boys to mark their coming-of-age ceremonies, known in different villages as the *festas dos rapazes* (boys' ceremonies) or *festas dos caretos* (mask ceremonies), but also used in performances which in many cases include girls, children and older men and are becoming spectacles and emblems of local and regional identity. Masks are made of wood or metal or less commonly hide, cardboard or plastic, and are worn with one of two types of suits used throughout the area at Christmas or for Carnival celebrations.

At the end of a dirt road in the small village of Ousilhão, near Vinhais, stands the small house of João Manuel Esteves (1938–2014) and his wife, Rosa Videira. In 2011 on a wet and cold day, they welcomed us with wine and biscuits. Esteves gave my son Marcel a xylophone he had made and

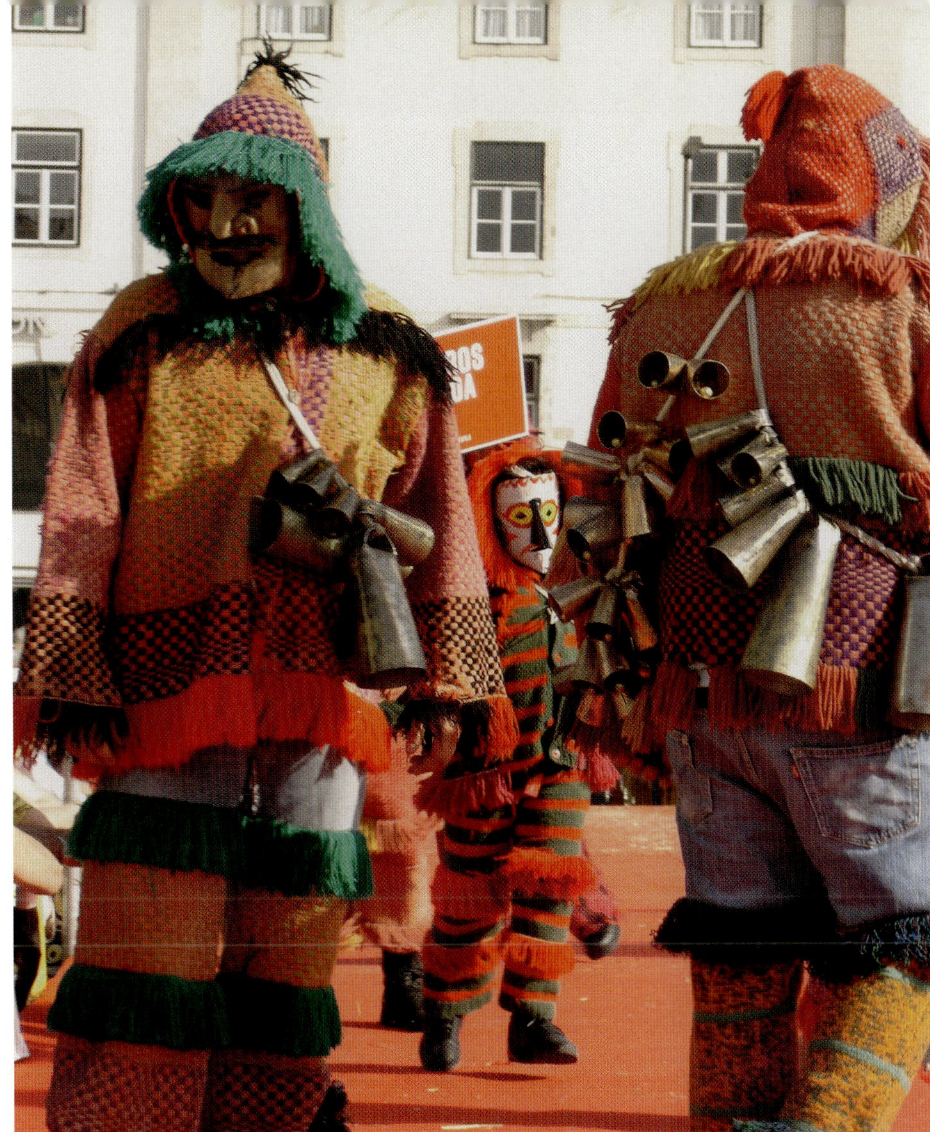

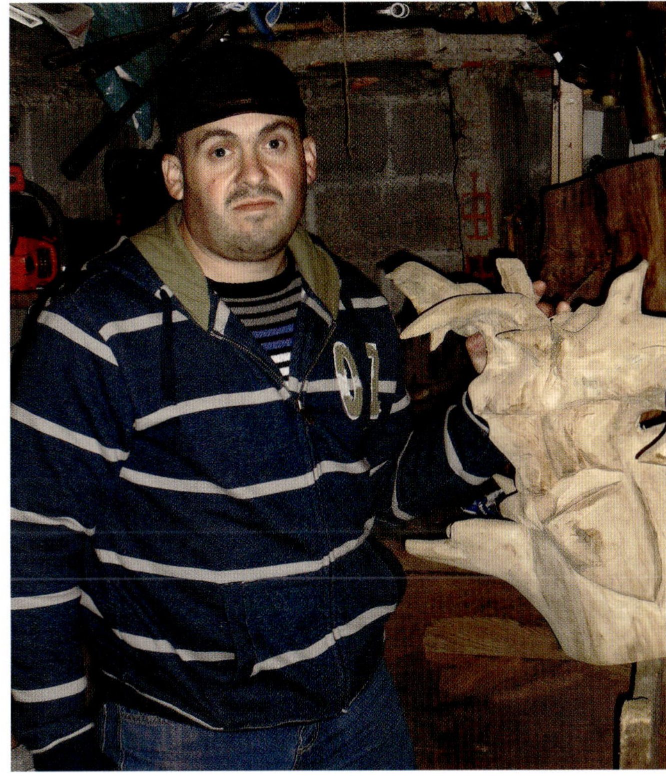

encouraged him to play. We all sat wrapped up in woolens and jackets, facing a long row of wine barrels. Esteves made in his spare time one of the most extensive repertoires of mask types in the area. He carved most of the masks from walnut and no longer painted them, his original practice, though he did mark the mouths, eyes, noses and moustaches by charring the surface. Esteves was the first carver in Ousilhão to make wooden masks, which have now supplanted older-style masks made from paper, cardboard and tin. In 2011 the village had three mask makers. Some of the masks they carve represent multifarious images of Diabo; some profile his characteristic traits—horns, moustache and beard—while others portray contorted, disfigured faces, or those of old people. Esteves sometimes substituted serpents for noses or carved a reptile on the cheeks. He also carved roosters or wolves on the top of masks and created works with not one face but two or three. Many of his masks were not grotesque at all but represented images of ordinary Portuguese men.

According to Sofia Maciel, who has researched the region's ceremonies,[422] these masks have no single meaning or function. During the festival for Santo Estêvão, maskers freely circulate, running, leaping, climbing and somersaulting through the hamlet and going from door to door collecting alms, cured sausages, bread and wine, which are later consumed at a community-wide feast. As elsewhere, the wild, ribald, drunken behaviour of masqueraders is fixated on "attacking" and frightening unwary girls and young children, but their disrespectful actions sometimes inadvertently provoke the ire of older men. Their antics also provoke laughter, particularly their satirical mimicry and descriptions of the old and politically powerful.

For Maciel, animal representations are symbols of fertility and represent the divisions of the land; they also provide metaphors for evil or sinful behaviour and evoke the lord of evil, or the master

facing, left
Carnival mask and costume from Mira at the Iberian Mask Festival, Lisbon, 2011.

facing, right
Carnival mask and costume from Mira at the Iberian Mask Festival, Lisbon, 2011.

above left
Caretos festooned with bells, Vila Boa, 2012.

above right
Mask maker António José Vale, Vila Boa, 2012.

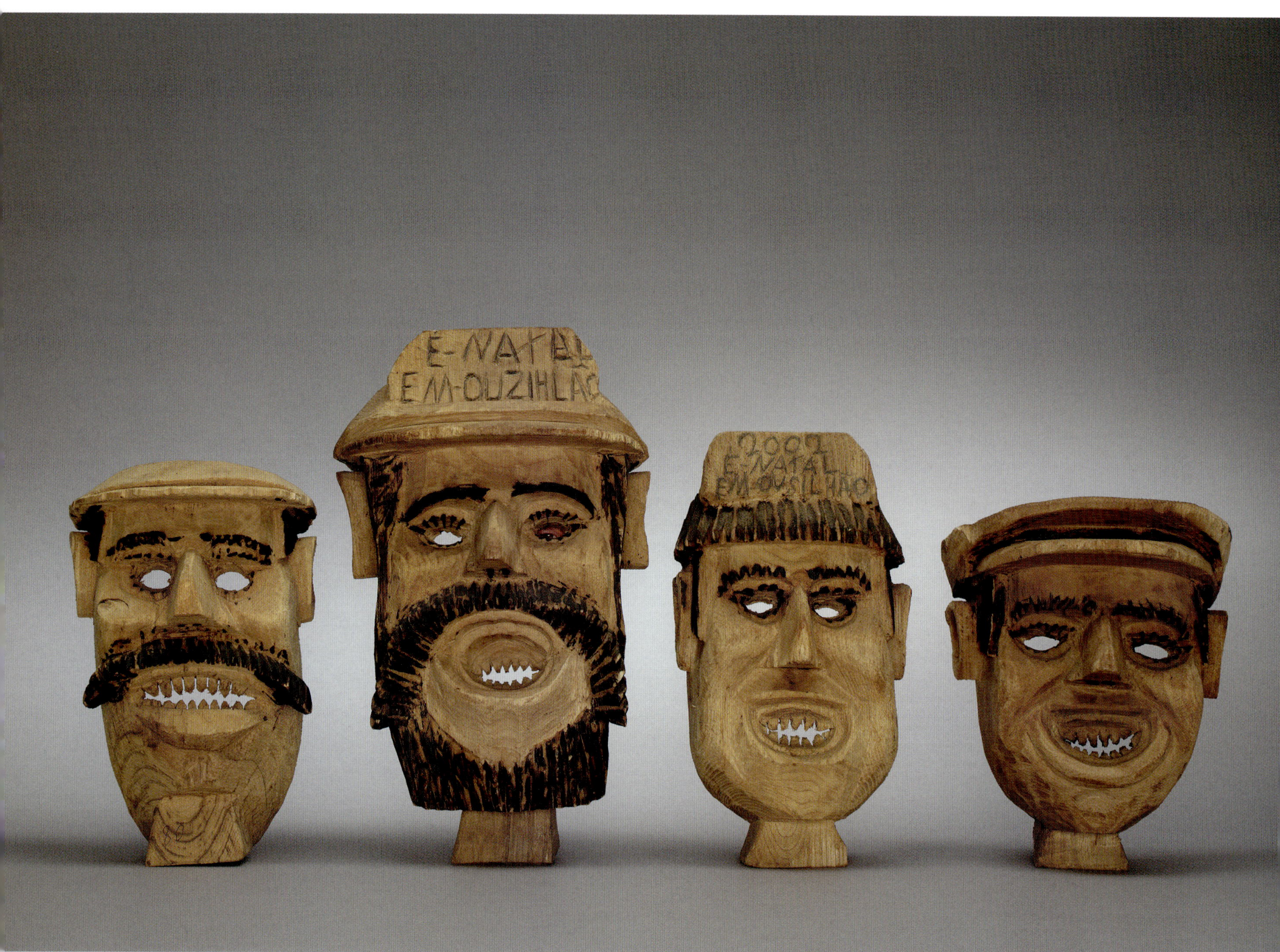

of nature, who, because his human-masked representatives collect alms during this ceremony in the name of the Christ child, has temporarily been domesticated to Christianity and incorporated to benefit humanity. Their wild appearance; thrilling, frightening and unpredictable behaviour; and the baleful and disharmonious clapper of bells that accompanies them collapse barriers between the social and the sacred, between Christian and pagan typologies—between classes and individuals—to suspend social conventions and threaten community security. To further provoke disgust and fear, some masqueraders pour eggs and ashes over their costumes and hang dead animals like lizards on their lapels and masks. Their behaviour incites the temporary emergence of an anti-structure, a period free of the constraints of time and place that suspends normal established relations, which are

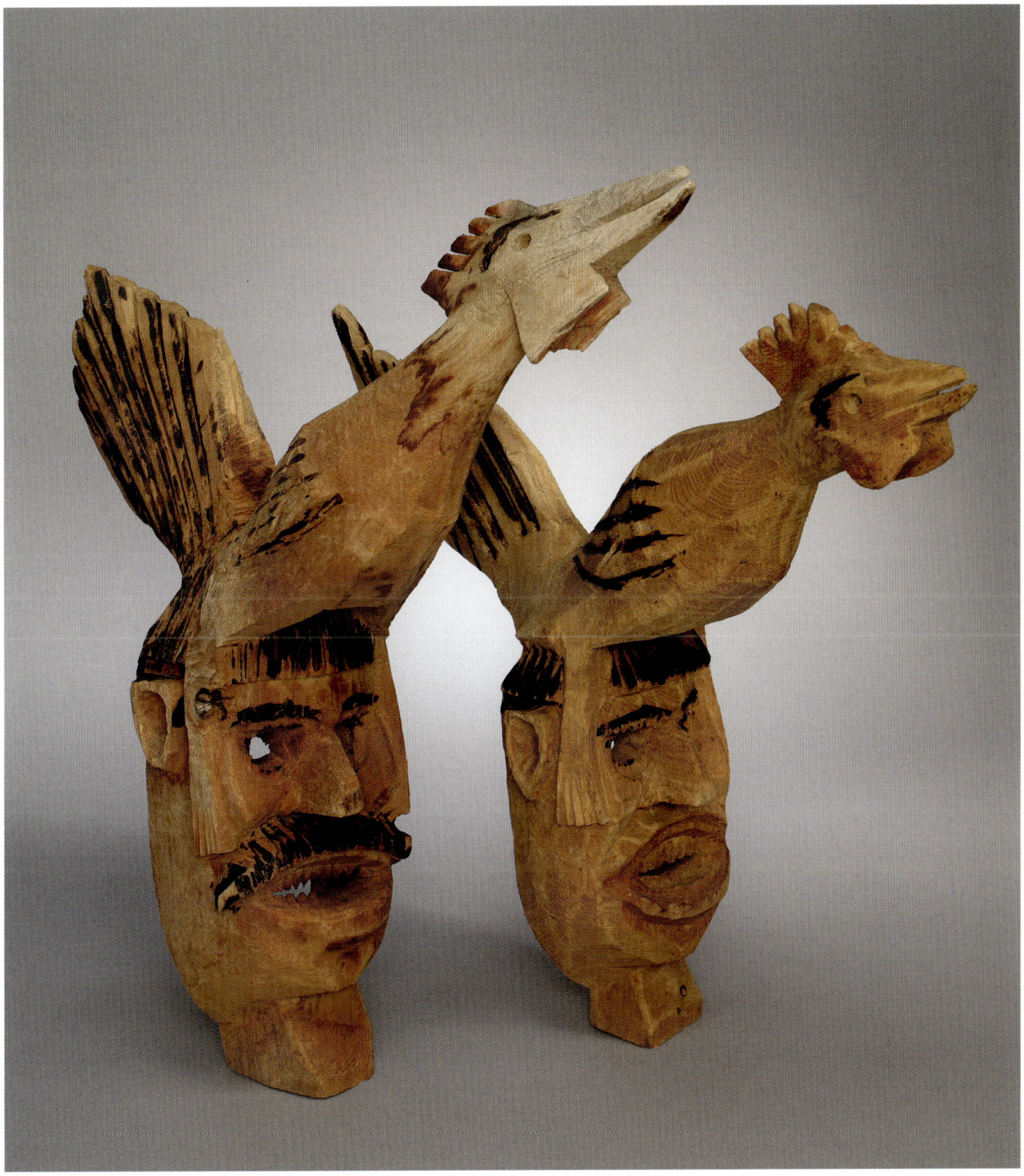

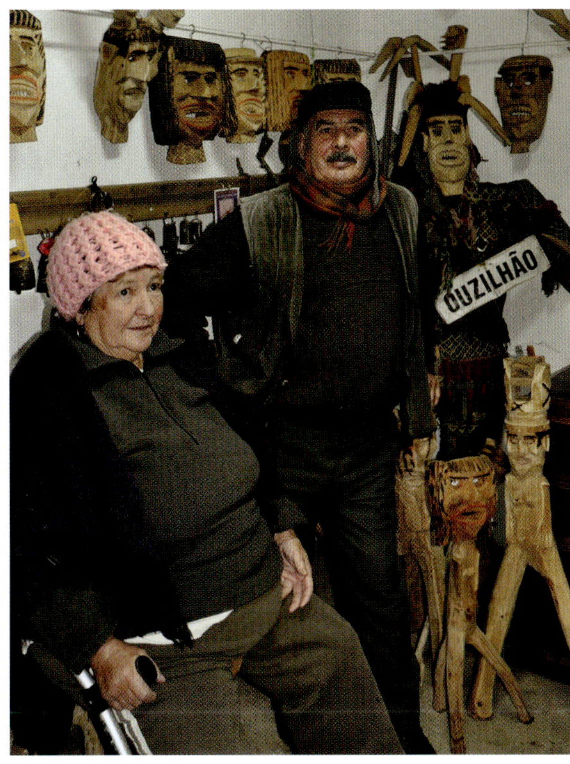

facing
JOÃO MANUEL ESTEVES
Christmas in Ousilhão, C. 2007

left
JOÃO MANUEL ESTEVES
Man/rooster masks, Ousilhão, C. 2009.

above
Master carver João Manuel Esteves and his wife, Rosa Videira, in their house in Ousilhão, 2011.

rendered insecure and unpredictable. João Manuel Esteves believed the inspiration behind the variety of the masks he made came from his dreams, stories, anxieties and experiences, but he also acknowledged that sometimes the form a carving took was implicit in the shape of the wood he used. He was both a farmer and a carver, strongly devoted to the celebration of the feast day of Santo Estêvão, a former masquerader and a man steeped in stories about Moorish enchantresses and the vicissitudes of a hard rural life. The masks he made aggrandize the saint's day, but he also felt there is something inexplicably bad in them that makes them more ambiguous than simple devices of concealment and mimicry. This ambiguous nature always persists in his masks regardless of whether they are being performed or sitting mutely in a museum.

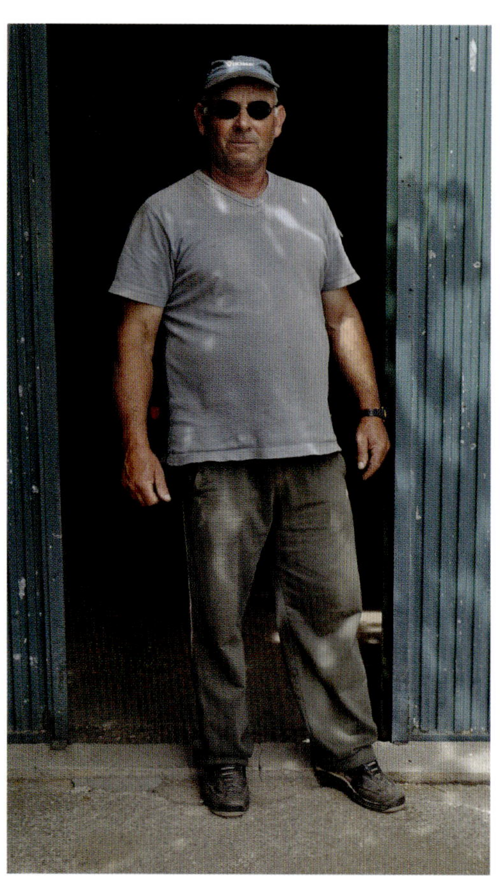

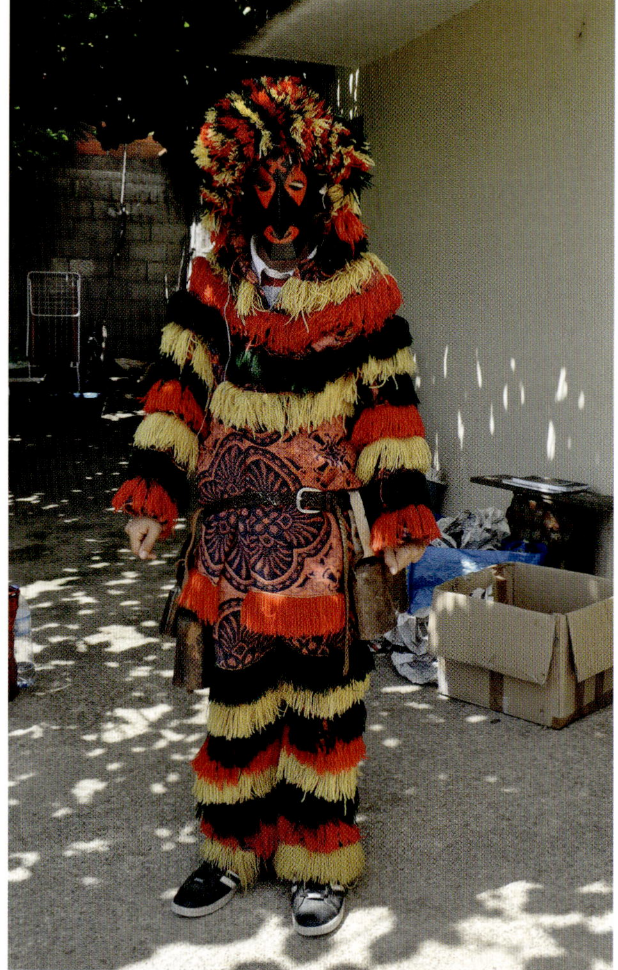

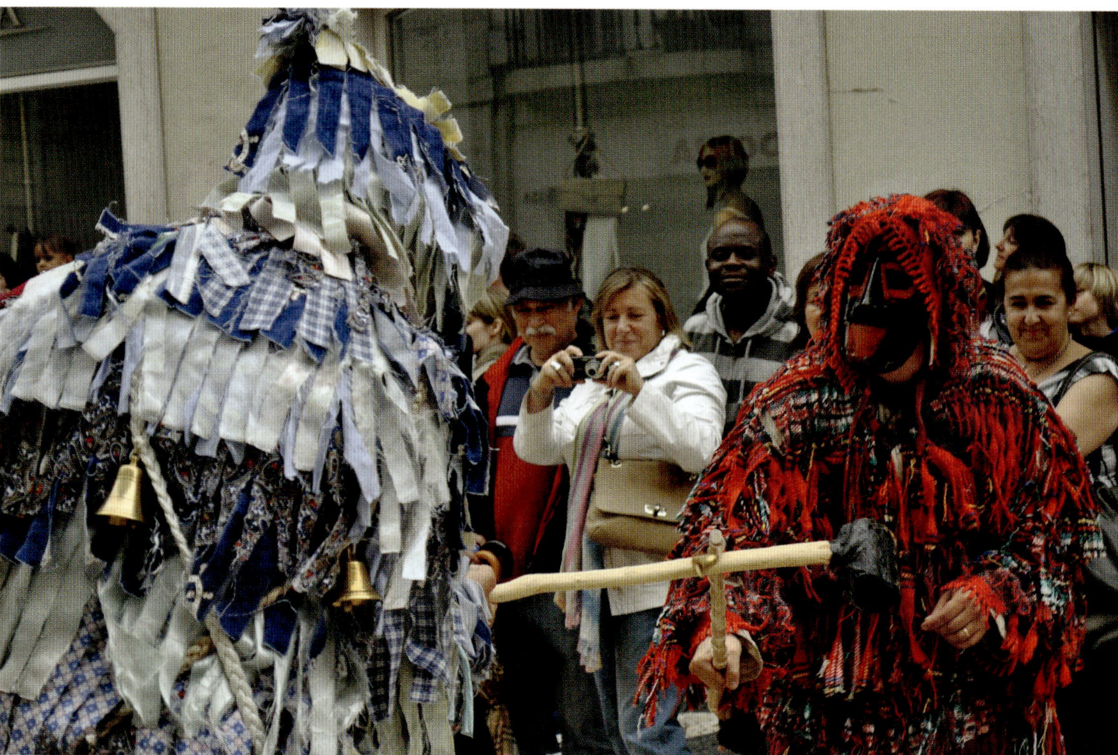

top left
Mask maker José Alves, Podence, 2011.

top right
Careto in characteristic Podence-style costume. This costume, once belonging to José Alves's son, was acquired by MOA in 2011.

bottom
Caretos in characteristic Aveleda-style costumes in combat, 2011.

facing
JOSÉ ALVES
Carnival masks, Podence, 2010–11.

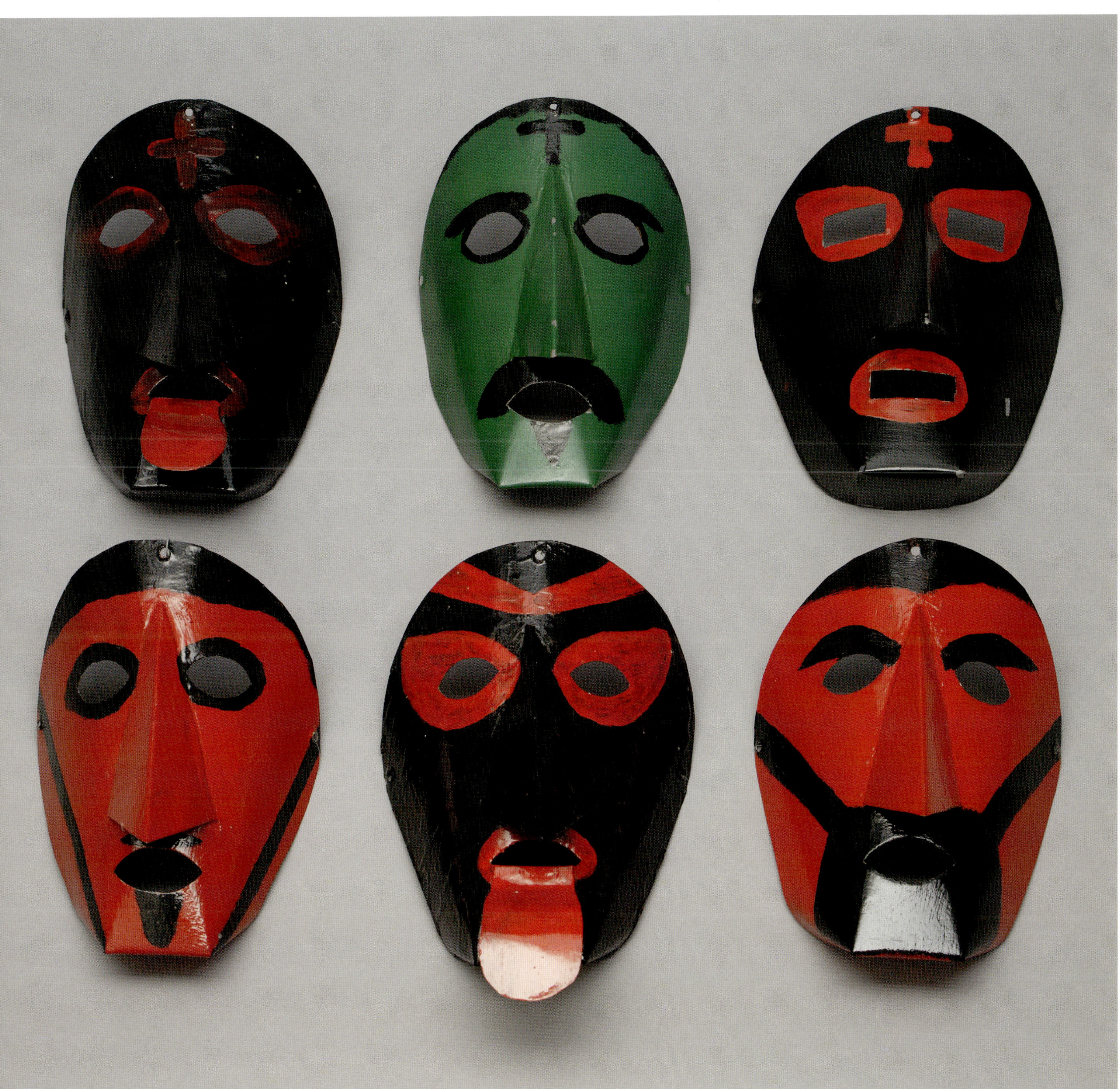

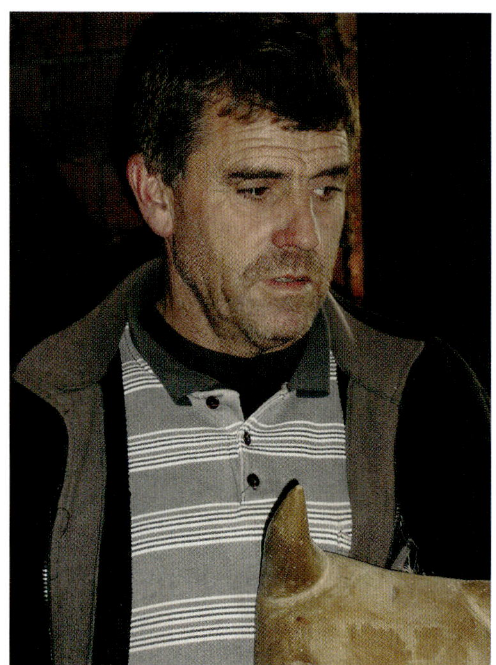

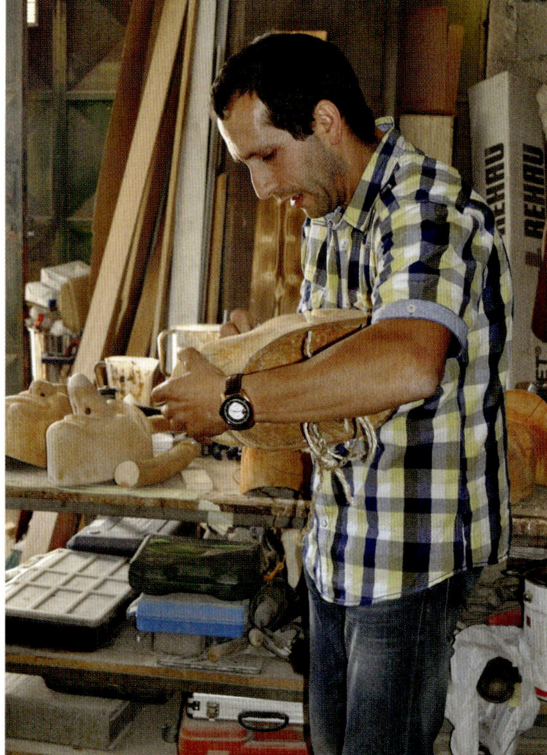

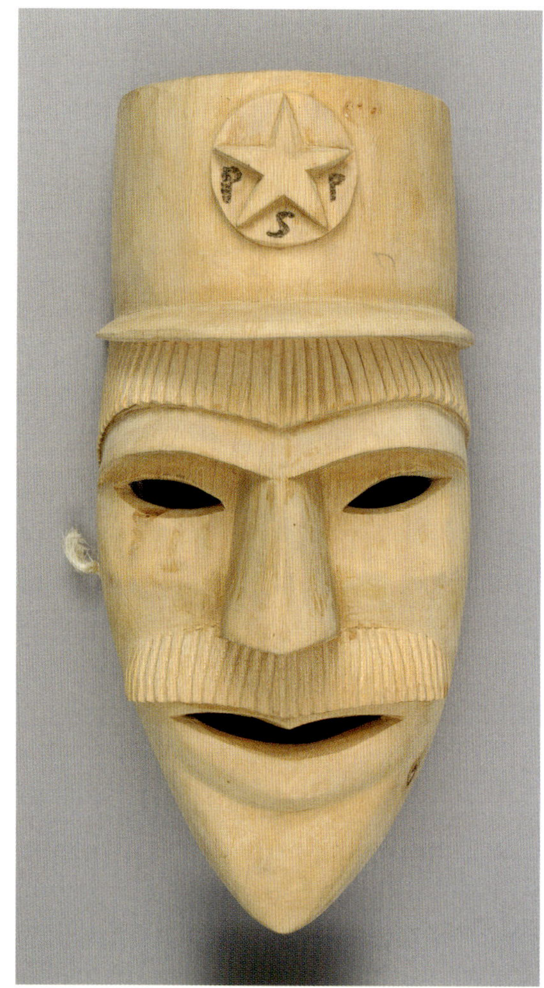

above
Mask maker Adão de Castro Almeida, Lazarim, 2012.

middle
Mask maker José António da Silva Costa, Lazarim, 2010.

right
ADÃO DE CASTRO ALMEIDA
Carnival mask representing a policeman, 2012.

facing
JOSÉ ANTÓNIO DA SILVA COSTA
Carnival masks representing, from top left, Pedro Passos Coelho (prime minister), Paulo Sacadura Cabral Portas (deputy prime minister), Carlos Castro (late gossip columnist), Luís Filipe Vieira (football club president), Jorge Nuno Pinto da Costa (football club president) and José Sócrates Carvalho Pinto de Sousa (former prime minister), 2011.

In Grijó de Parada, Torre da Dona Chama, Varge and Aveleda, four villages close to the city of Bragança, masks are usually made of metal and carry none of the sculptural innovation found in the wooden masks of Ousilhão. But because of their similar moral ambiguity, they function with a like purpose, regardless of whether they have elaborate or simple iconographies. In performances connected to the feast day of Santo Estêvão, Diabo inaugurates the period of anti-structure during which the social body and social-divine relations on which life and well-being depend are temporarily denuded and exposed through satire, indiscretion, revelry and ribald behaviour before it is quickly contained and commitment to social order is reconfirmed.

Diabo also appears in Carnival, which, unlike the feast day of Santo Estêvão, is marked by celebrations throughout the country in the weeks before the Catholic holiday of Lent. Carnival also reverses social relations and modes of behaviour, reiterating the identification of the demonic with anti-structure and reconvening the performance of some of the masks and costumes already described.

In Podence, another small village in Bragança district, masks are made by only one farmer/artist, José Alves, using zinc sheet painted red and black. Apart from their cut-out eyes and mouths, their jagged teeth and sometimes lolling tongues, and their sharply projecting noses, all their characteristics, including beards, moustaches, lips and eyebrows, are rendered in paint. Various shadings, patterns and the occasional cross are also painted on them. Alves describes them as representing demonic forces, witches, sorcerers and devils, but is unclear on any specific iconography and acknowledges they are used in both secular and religious performances. His own dedication is not to religion, he says, but to the festival in which the masks are used and in which he has participated all his life since it was

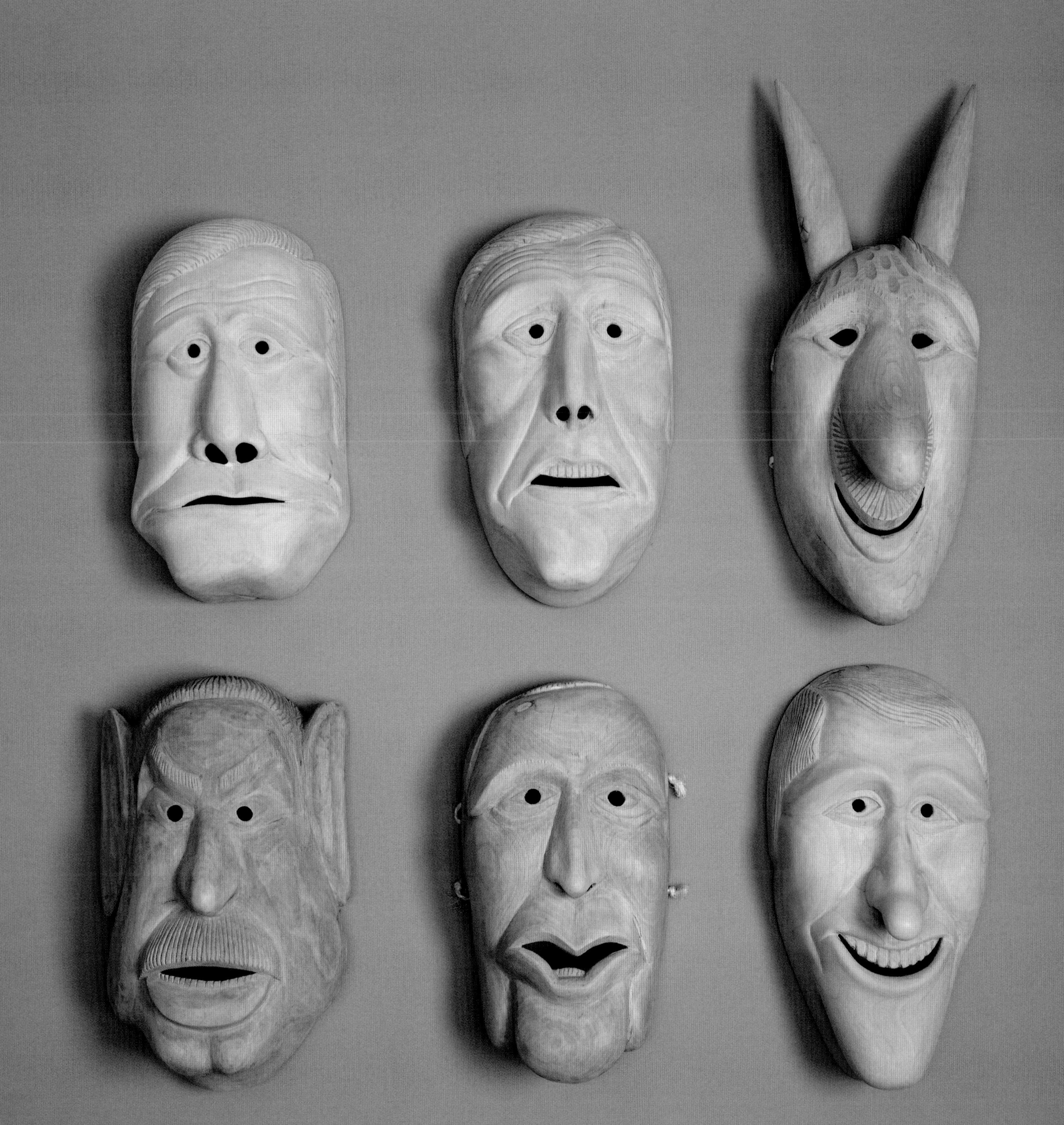

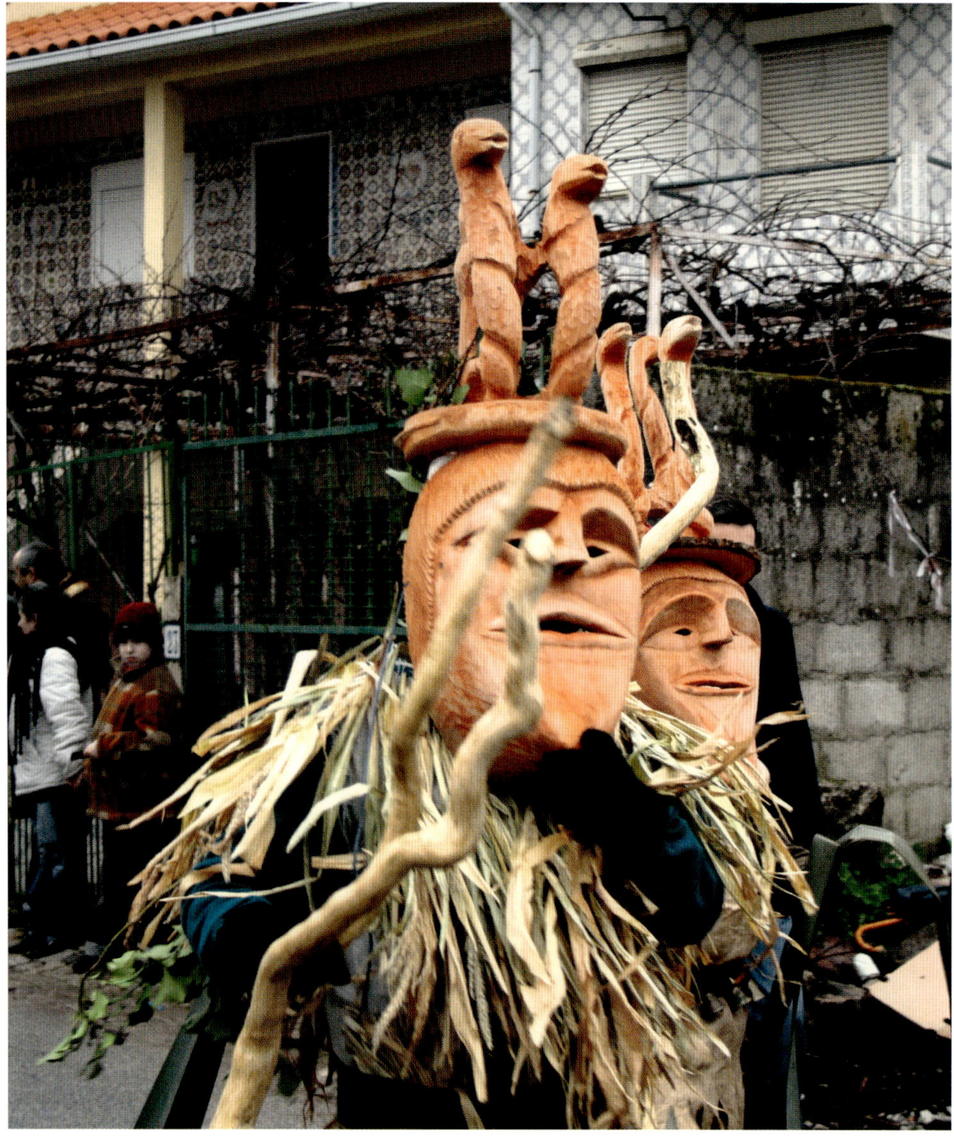

above and facing
Masked devil impersonators at Carnival in Lazarim, 2010. The masks above, carved by Carlos Cabral, are now in the MOA collection.

restarted in the 1970s.[423] More recently, Alves has innovated a more literal style to his masks by attaching folded metal horns to make them appear more diabolical, though because the horns do not allow the masks to be properly attached to the costumes and would be dangerous if fallen upon, they are intended only for tourists. Horned metallic masks are used elsewhere, such as Aveleda and Varge, but it is more usual for wooden masks to be horned than metallic ones. Despite this different iconography, the ethnographer Sebastião Pessanha writing half a century ago was clear that within the different districts of Bragança, the *careto*, the mask, always represents the Devil.[424]

In Podence, authentic masks are believed to prolong the lives of their users and cure illness. They are danced with an elaborate and expensive costume that is usually a prized heirloom and is passed from generation to generation; one in MOA's collection originally belonged to Alves's son. The number of sheep, goat or cowbells attached to the belt of the masquerade costume indicates the wealth of the dancer (twelve is rich, eight poor).[425]

The Carnival in Lazarim, in the northern region of the Douro, is both well known and documented. Like other religious celebrations in the area,[426] it has been incorporated within a national and global market of cultural production. It attracts tourists and other visitors and is supported through promotional literature, film and the Internet. One of the innovations this has given rise to is the establishment of a concourse and awards for best masks, held at the end of the Carnival period. While such concourses may stimulate mask making, they also generate rivalry and sometimes animosity between participants and promote the international commoditization of masks.

Until recently the small village had three extraordinary woodcarvers who made Carnival masks: Afonso Costa, the most senior mask maker, who now seldom works; Adão de Castro Almeida; and José António da Silva Costa, a young, self-taught mask maker who specializes in carving caricatures.[427] In addition to making masks, the last two have full-time jobs, one as a teacher and carpenter, the other as a school bus driver. Lazarim masks show remarkable variation in iconography and are very different from those of Ousilhão and Podence. The faces of national and local personalities are caricatured, as are the established repertoire of figures that appear in Carnival throughout the country: *diabos*, witches, sorcerers, kings, the elderly, policemen, Christ and Death. Unlike other mask makers, José António de Silva Costa focuses on caricatures of individuals who were recently in

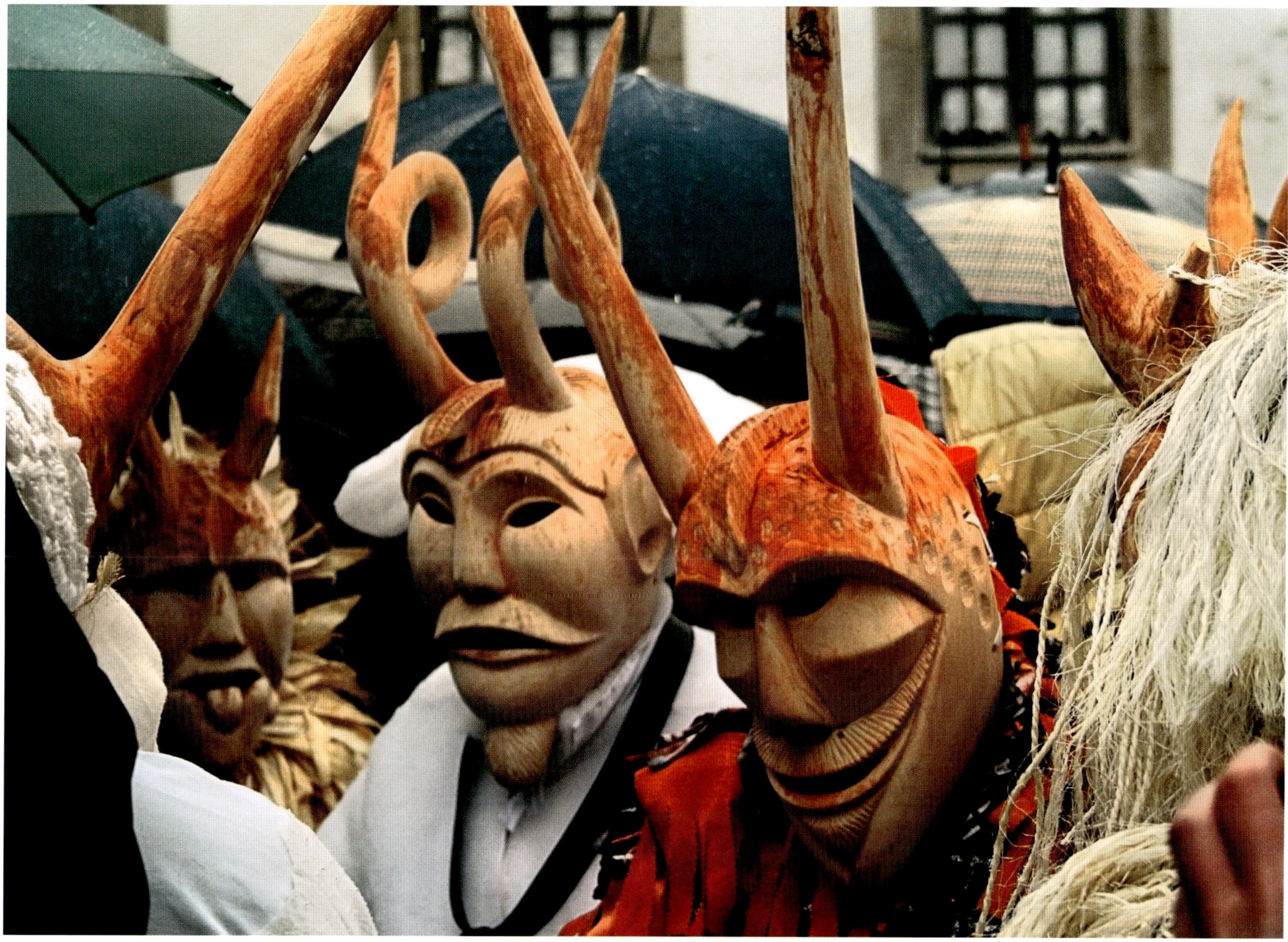

the news. In 2011 we were able to buy from him masks of the chairmen of two of Portugal's most famous football teams (Luís Filipe Vieira of Benfica and Jorge Nuno Pinto da Costa of F.C. Porto) and a caricature of Carlos Castro (with a long phallus in place of a nose), a notorious Portuguese gossip columnist who hit the international news after being castrated by his lover. MOA later commissioned additional masks representing politicians Pedro Passos Coelho, Paulo Portas and José Sócrates and the contemporary fado singer Mariza.

Close to Lazarim lives a fourth mask maker, Carlos Cabral, who has a unique style and an extensive repertoire that includes Egyptian pharaohs and devil masks with upright-standing serpents.

Beliefs and rituals have become largely secularized in Portugal, and performances are enacted to attract new market interests in rural areas. The invocation of rural pasts through pottery production or rustic supernatural ceremonies provides one strategy through which communities continue to craft and elicit recognition of their uniqueness and affirm an identity that distinguishes them from an increasingly homogeneous world. For some like Esteves, his masks connected him to the past and reflected a disappearing rural world that he sometimes saw, as John Berger puts it, between the frames of our ordinary visual order.[428]

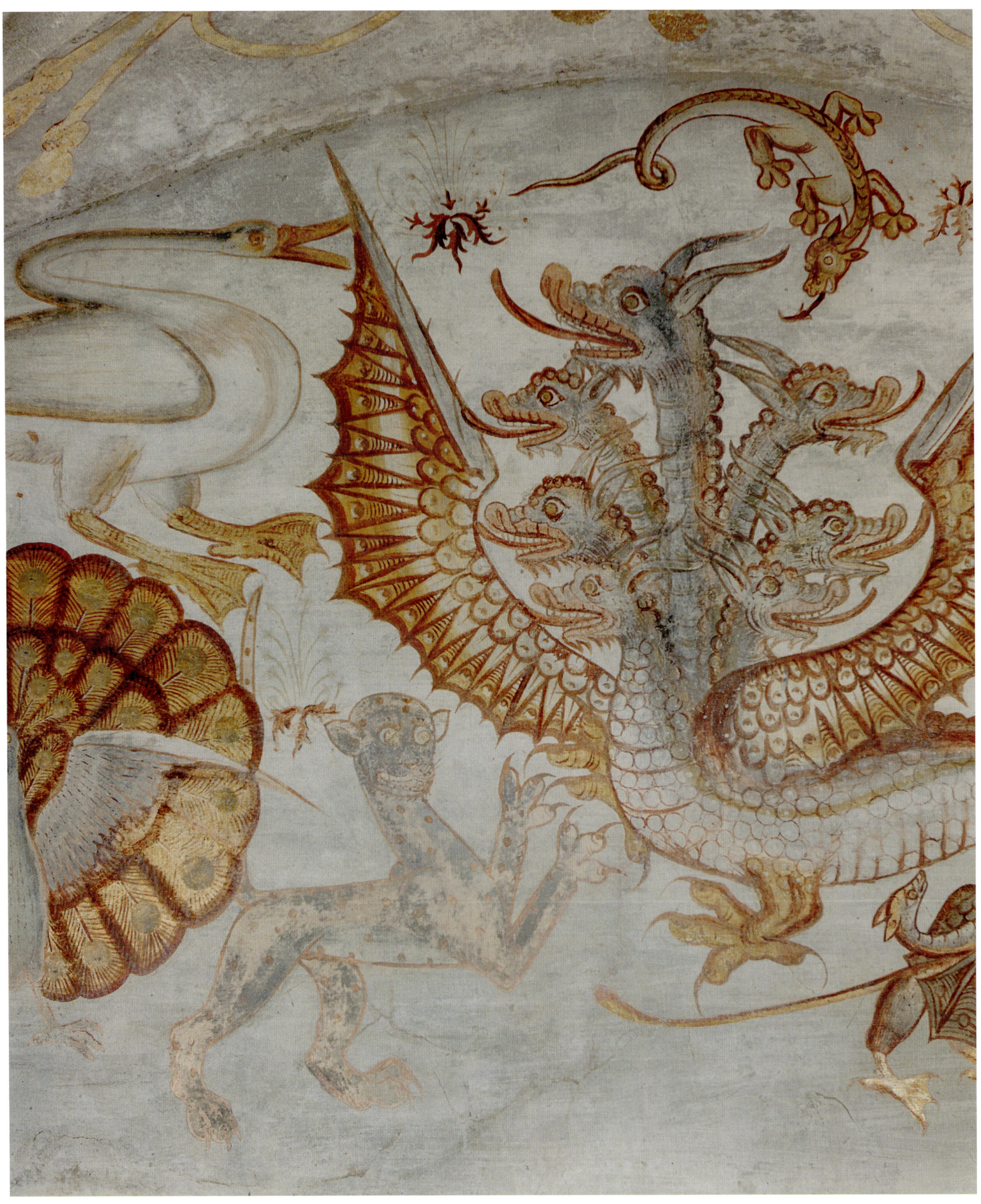

7 Creation and Apocalypse

Battlefields and Dystopias

Let the light fail it, let the sun be veiled and let the world show forth signs of the end; let monsters breed, let blood like rain descend and let the mother not know her own child.

Luís de Camões[429]

EVEN BEFORE THE Estado Novo, much of Portuguese history was an idealist construction in which empirical facts and events were subordinated to fervent theocratic or theological images of glory and redemption while being simultaneously haunted by a repressed demonology and the indeterminate threat of retribution and cataclysm. Ecclesiastical history and the popular beliefs of the Estado Novo incorporated human and supernatural protagonists who jointly navigated their course to a common destiny foreshadowed by prophecy. The course of these events was imagined to be cyclical or spiral rather than linear and emphasized alternations of fortune, each holding its own divine lesson, instead of a singular cumulative evolutionary process.

Portuguese history was inscribed as beginning with the seven days of Creation as described in Genesis and ending with the advent of the Apocalypse as foretold in the gospels. The cataclysmic beginning and end of the world, detailed and depicted by a long line of seers, prophets and artists, would prefigure a new creation ruled over by the good that would dissolve the distance between God's purity and the world's decadence. Between Creation and Apocalypse humanity was required to subordinate itself to what in the twentieth century the Estado Novo envisaged as the natural constitution of society based on established Christian values and mutual rights and obligations. The ossuary chapels in Faro Évora and Campo Maior, made or decorated from human bones, were built to encourage meditation on one's conduct while alive in the face of an inevitable death and its consequences for the life to come. The pact between Church and state required to achieve such a condition influenced many aspects of Portuguese thought and life and encouraged the continuity of a strong millenarian belief in the nation's redemption and future greatness. During periods of economic and political difficulty, however, the remnants of this fatalistic attitude also encouraged despair, alienation and expressions of dystopia—more recently reflected through graffiti and murals painted in urban areas.

HISTORY AND SANCTIFICATION

Portugal's intellectual heritage of mysticism, theology and theocracy has deep roots widely expressed in painting, decorative and graphic art,

facing
ARTIST UNKNOWN
Seven-Headed Beast of the Apocalypse, C. 1520
Casas Pintadas, Évora

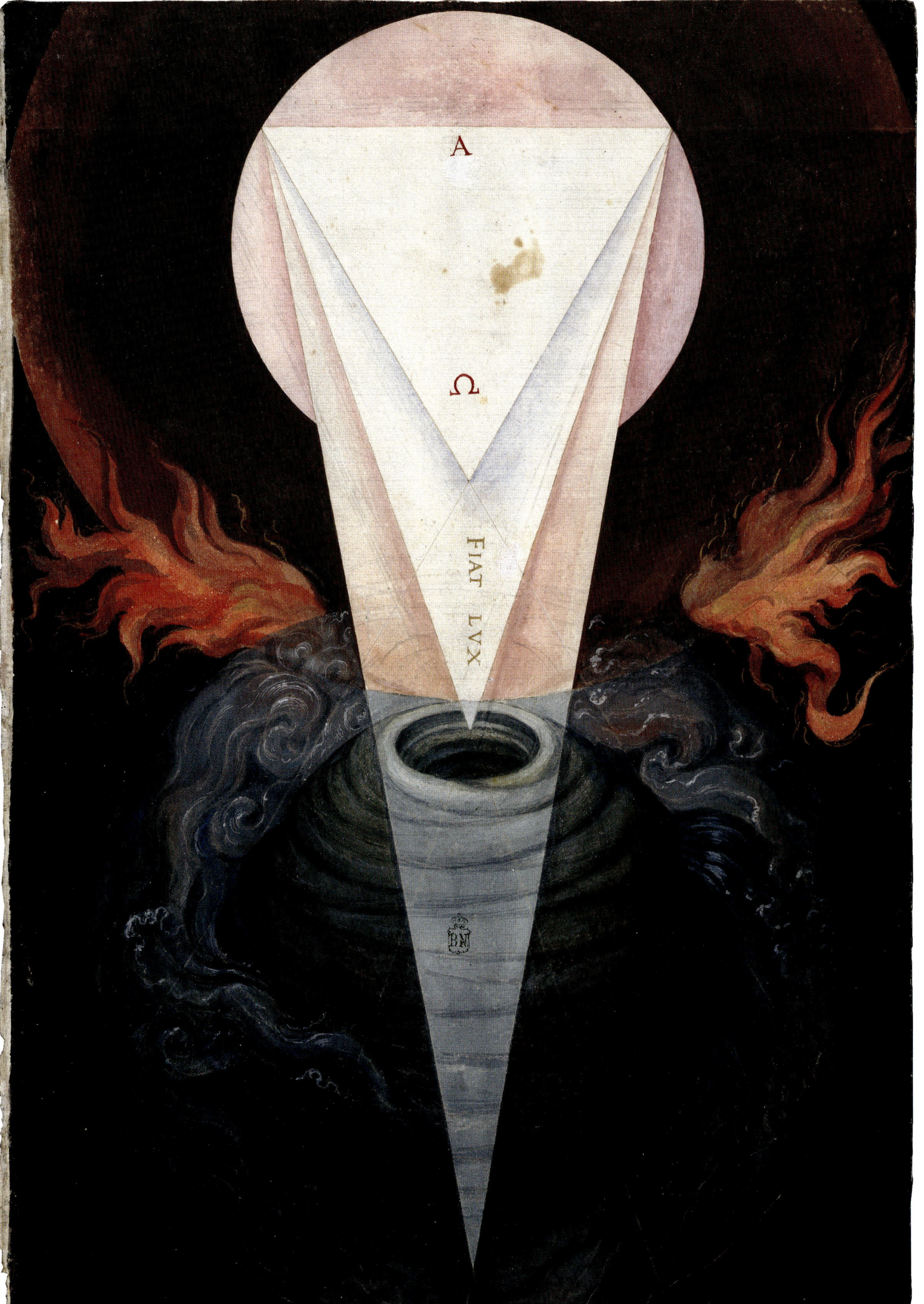
A
Ω
FIAT LVX

facing
FRANCISCO DE HOLANDA
First Day of Creation, De Aetatibus Mundi Imagines—Dies Unus, 1573

theatre, literature, garden design and the performance of spectacles and religious celebrations. The Portuguese Renaissance painter Francisco de Holanda (1517–85), believing that since Christ's crucifixion the world had fallen from a state of perfection into decadence, encouraged the study of the ancient world to better understand God's nature and worldly significance. During his two-year residence in Rome between 1538 and 1540 he completed the *Antiqualhas*, a set of drawings depicting the city's and country's ancient monuments that not only influenced Portuguese thought but also his later treatise, *Da Pintura Antiga* (1548). In this latter work he argued painting was the most noble and virtuous of all human activities and commended its study, along with architecture and arms, to provide insight into the perfection of divine design, prior to its decay and destitution. Copying older works, regardless of their distinguished pedigree, was not sufficient for Holanda and would only, he believed, accelerate art's decline. Holanda studied art's most perfect manifestation in ancient times, Creation itself, as a model for new works. Starting in 1551–55, though temporarily abandoning his ambition until 1573, Holanda worked on his *De Aetatibus Mundi Imagines*, an unrivalled attempt, except for Michelangelo's Sistine Chapel, to depict each of the seven days of Creation and the deluge God later sent to destroy it.

Holanda's work follows two radically different styles because of the censorship imposed on his early illustrations by the Inquisition, which King João III had invited into the country in 1536. The influence of neo-Platonism, synthesized from Plato's *Timaeus*, Hermes Trismegisto's *Poimandres* and Dionysius Areopagita's *Divine Names*, led Holanda in his earliest pictures to evoke God's creation through spherical, triangular and other volumetric abstractions, a style he abandoned in later illustrations in favour of the neo-baroque preferences of the counter-reformation.

No more startling depiction of history's beginning exists than the early illustrations of Holanda's *De Aetatibus*. These must surely have accomplished the artist's ambition to encourage meditation and spiritual improvement—despite their unavoidable inferiority to the divine model, which would always remain unknowable until God's final destruction of the world and the descent of the Kingdom of Heaven. Holanda's spatial images in his rendition of the first four days of Creation, for example, allude to the increasing temporal and existential distance between God and the world and encourage us to ponder how far the world had accelerated away from God's light even from the instant of its creation. Only once cleansed by the Great Flood might the world temporarily be redeemed. Holanda's illustrations combine the wonder of Creation with the insinuation of its inevitable destruction, producing an essentially fatalistic and melancholic world view. The mysticism, grandeur and existential solitude that haunted this idea inspired magnificent art, transformative scientific discoveries and exquisite gardens, but also contained the seeds of personal resignation and political apathy. It was for many in mid-twentieth-century Portugal difficult to think independently of Creation and cataclysm or of a national history completely free from supernatural intervention.

The ecclesiastical history, which preceded the secular history constructed by the constitutional monarchy and the short-lived Republic, portrayed Portugal as a singular nation under the protection and guidance of God. Since the twelfth century different supernatural agencies were claimed to have militarily aided the various Iberian campaigns to defeat Moorish rule and consolidate the new national borders. In the Battle of Saragossa (1118),

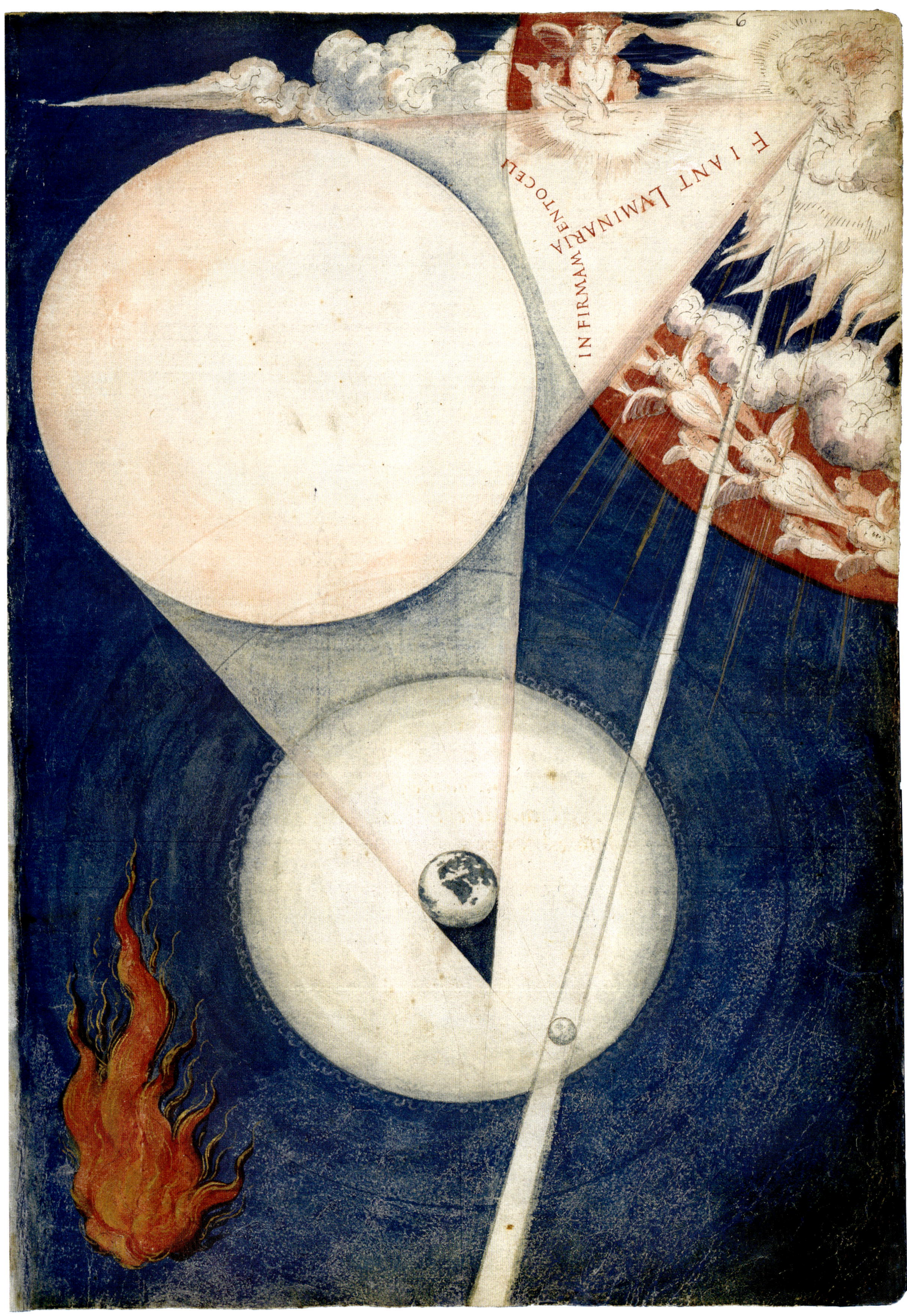
FIANT LVMINARIA
IN FIRMAMENTO CELI

facing
FRANCISCO DE HOLANDA
Fourth Day of Creation, De Aetatibus Mundi Imagines—Dies Unus, 1573

São Miguel told the Aragonese king Afonso I that his armies would suffer no further casualties in their independence struggle, while before the decisive Battle of Ourique (1139), a vision of Christ appeared on the cross and promised King Afonso Henriques victory and protection of the new Kingdom of Portugal. São Tiago was said to have intervened in the Conquest of Coimbra (1064) and in the struggles in Mau Vizinho and Vale da Batalha in the north of Portugal.[430] Combined Spanish and Portuguese forces received similar divine assurances at the Battle of Salado (1340). In the war of independence from Spain (1385), stories circulated of São Jorge descending from the skies on a white mount to help an apparently hopelessly outnumbered Portuguese army gain victory over Castile at the Battle of Aljubarrota; in gratitude the Portuguese built the great Gothic-style monastery of Santa Maria da Vitória (1388–1433) at Batalha. A large cross on the outskirts of Vila Nova de São Bento memorializes São Bento's intervention during the struggle for independence from Castile in the early seventeenth century and his later support for Portuguese smugglers avoiding tax on their imports from Spain. Reports of divine assistance continued to be repeated during Portuguese military campaigns in Africa, India, Malacca and Goa in the nineteenth and twentieth centuries.[431]

The memory of the miracle of Ourique is kept alive locally by a recent tiled plaque, in the town's school, commemorating the Portuguese victory over the Moors and, decorating a bench outside the town hall, a few poorly painted tiles showing the apparition. Little remains of the once formidable stronghold built by the Arab settlers in 711, since made into a garden and lookout point over the Alentejo plain, though a statue of the Portuguese victor now stands in its shadow. In the nearby town of Castro Verde, Christ's apparition and the Battle of Ourique are strikingly commemorated in both the eighteenth-century church of Nossa Senhora dos Remédios, through a series of allegorical paintings by Diogo Magina, and in the Basilica of Nossa Senhora da Conceição, in a more impressive blue and white tiled rendition of the event completed in 1730 that covers its interior walls.[432] This divine sanctification of the nation has been the subject of tiled paintings elsewhere in the country, including the church of São Vicente de Fora in Lisbon, an eighteenth-century piece in the medieval monastery of Alcobaça and a more recent 1922 work on blue and white tiles decorating the Pavilion Carlos Lopes facing Edward VII Park in the centre of Lisbon. Stories of supernatural intervention can also be found in literary works, the most eloquent of which are Fernando Pessoa's poetry and writing on the apotheosis of the slain King Sebastião.

The spiritual conversation between Portugal and Heaven lost none of its vigour in the modern era. In 1917 in the village of Fátima in central Portugal, three shepherd children reported witnessing an apparition of São Miguel, the angel of Portugal, warning them of the pending visitation of Nossa Senhora (Our Lady), who would appear the following year. Lucía, the eldest of the three children, reportedly saw the Virgin repeatedly before receiving other visitations in 1926 and 1927 from Christ. These visions of Nossa Senhora, the most acclaimed of the twentieth century, were accompanied by visions: one of a dull, burnt-out sun oscillating spasmodically in the sky and another revealing to the children alone the punishment of the impious in Hell, together with prophecies of terrible wars and suffering to come. In 1946 Lucía entered the Carmelite convent in Coimbra, where she remained until her death in 2005. She was beatified in 2008.

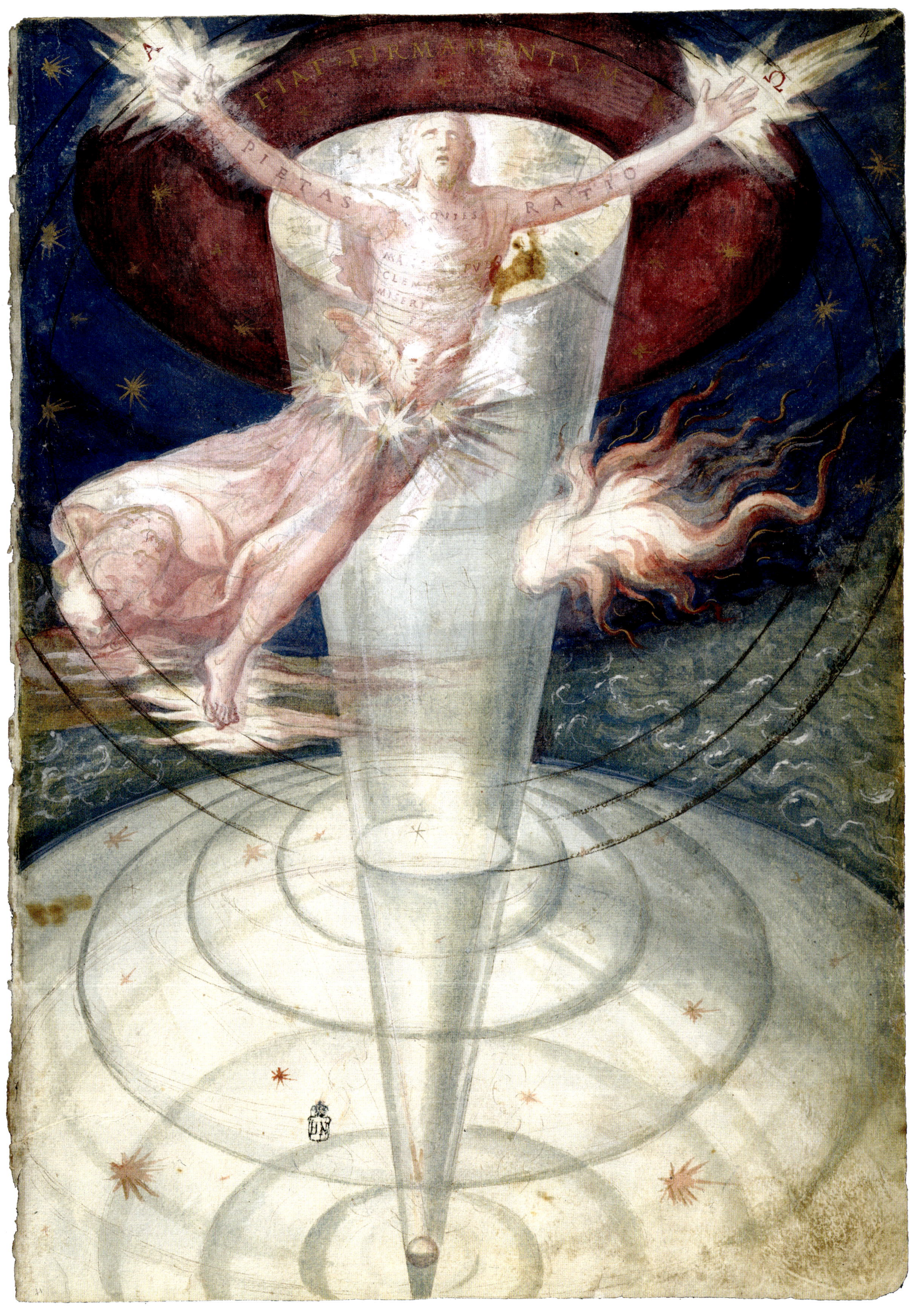
A
FIAT·FIRMAMENTVM
Ω
PIETAS
RATIO

facing
FRANCISCO DE HOLANDA
Second Day of Creation, De Aetatibus Mundi Imagines—Dies Unus, 1573

The apocalyptic warnings conveyed by Nossa Senhora, so it has been argued, were part of an ancient tradition used in the early Judeo-Christian world as a vehicle to induce nationalist fervour and universal significance. Ideologues of the Estado Novo manipulated the apparitions at Fátima to reinforce the idea of Portugal as an elected nation with a divinely sanctioned mandate and responsibility encapsulated in the state's programs of national renovation. The neo-baroque sanctuary at Fátima has since grown into one of the largest Christian holy sites in the world, attracting 4 million pilgrims annually, especially on 13 May and 13 October, the anniversaries of the first two apparitions.

THE ROOTS OF APOCRYPHAL AND MILLENERIAN THOUGHT

The philosopher Jacob Taubes wrote, "In apocalypticism history is not recorded in the form of a chronicle; rather, apocalypticism attempts to gain knowledge about the future from the past and the present. Not only is the future broadly sketched out, but the significant question is when is the end coming?"[433] The fear of impending catastrophe provoked towards the end of the fifteenth century by Vasco da Gama's discovery of a sea route to the East and Pedro Álvares Cabral's discovery of Brazil was rooted in one and a half millennia of speculative theology that had permeated Judeo-Christian Europe. The apocalyptical idea, derived from elements that predated both Judaism and Christianity, was initially disseminated through Old Testament accounts. In the book of Daniel, the prophet recounts a dream in which four beasts, symbolizing four successive world powers, appeared to him, followed by Christ, who, gloriously carried on clouds, ended all the earthly tyranny that the creatures symbolized. In the Old Testament books of Ezra and Baruch, Christ is described as a warrior king. Ezra refers to him as the Lion of Judah who kills the last of the beasts, the eagle representing Rome, bursting it into flames and then exterminating the hordes of unbelievers with his fiery breath. The book of Revelation, written by St. John, symbolizes the tyranny of Rome through a ten-horned monster.[434] Baruch instructs his readers that only when evil has reached its zenith will Christ return to pitilessly combat and defeat its leaders and armies before inaugurating a thousand-year rule free of pain, suffering, strife, untimely death and hunger.[435]

At the end of His reign the dead will be resurrected to face the Final Judgment, which would divide the souls condemned to Hell from those who would join the saints in a New Jerusalem that would descend from Heaven to become their home for eternity. In the *Lorvão Apocalypse* (1189), the celestial Jerusalem is illustrated as having twelve gateways arranged around three concentric circles, each flanked by one of the apostles. It is luminous, "having the brightness of God, and His light similar to a precious stone, as if a jasper, like to crystal. And the city does not need the sun or the moon that they shine in her; for the brightness of God has illuminated it and His lamp is the Lamb."[436] The concentric circles represent the vast space between God and the world, the circles of bodies, demons and the courses of stars that separate Him from humanity. The luminosity shown here is a pure brilliant light emblematic of a pure world without death, putrification, violence, lies, deceit and injustice, as opposed to the world made from light and darkness. "The realm of this world, in which life resides, is a demonic force as such. Apocalyptic times are demonized ages."[437] John Berger notes: "Most prophecies, when specific,

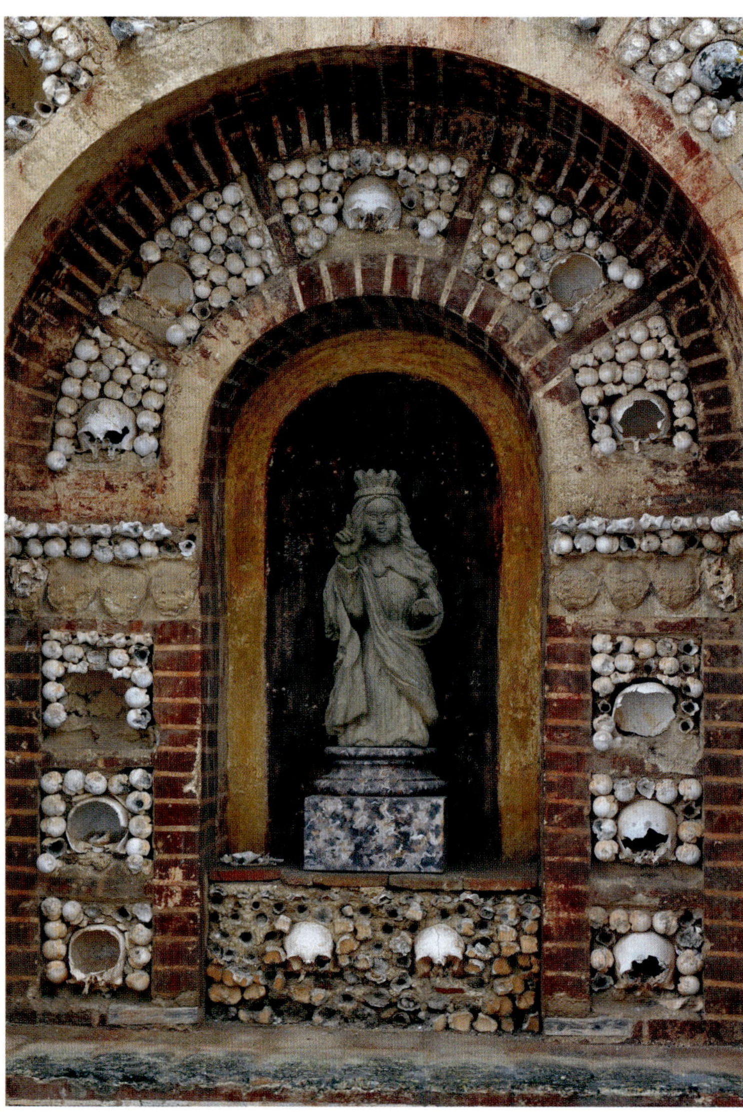

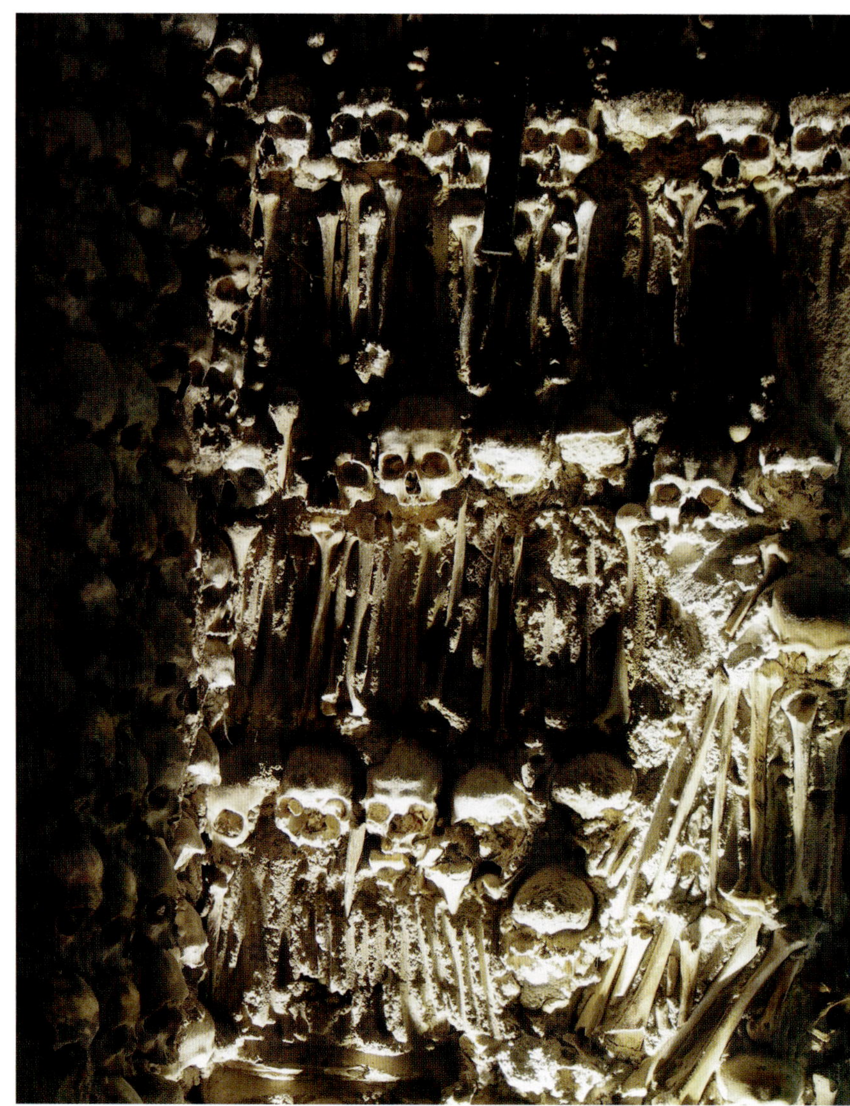

are bound to be bad, for, throughout history, there are always new terrors—even if a few disappear, yet there are no new happinesses—happiness is always the old one. It is the modes of struggle for this happiness which change."[438]

Biblical and related prophecies were compiled in the second century by Irenaeus (AD 130–202), one of the early Church fathers, in the final chapter of his monumental work *Adversus Heareses* or *Against Heresies* (AD 180). By AD 150, with the Apocalypse still not having arrived, the Church stripped all references to it, except for the account in the book of Revelation, of canonical authority. By the fourth century the Church had dismissed the prophecy entirely by reinterpreting the Apocalypse as an allegorical account of its victory over the factional struggles that had previously assailed it.

Despite the Church's denial of the scriptural authority of apocryphal literature, popular speculation on the fate of wrongdoers and the redemption of the good and faithful continued unabated. Encouraged by, among other sources, the *Sibylline Oracles*—compilations of Jewish prophetic sources from the second to sixth centuries—and literature that foretold the reunification of the western and eastern Roman empires under a powerful monarch who would mete out the baptism or hellish death of unbelievers, the beginning of a new plentiful age was eagerly anticipated. After his task was finished, so the prophecy held, the triumphant monarch would lay down his crown at Golgotha, the hill where Christ was crucified, and deliver Christendom into Christ's keeping. In some versions the conqueror is identified with a slumbering monarch,[439] clearly suggesting a link between the apocryphal tradition and the legends about Portugal's King Sebastião (1554–78).

The Golden Age thus inaugurated was identified with the millennium empire that eventually, it was believed, would collapse under the combined onslaught of the monstrous forces of Gog and Mogog, who in turn would be defeated by Christ. According to other sources, before Christ's Second Coming the earth would be dominated by the Antichrist, sometimes identified with Diabo, who would be killed by the Saviour's breath, thus beginning the Final Judgment. The twelfth-century cleric Hildegard of Bingen dreamt that the Antichrist was Diabo: "A Beast with a monstrous head, black as coal, with flaming eyes, wearing asses' ears and with gaping jaws decorated with iron hooks."[440] The medieval encyclopedia the *Liber Floridus* (1090–1120) illustrates the Antichrist with crown and sceptre being triumphantly carried across the seas on the back of Leviathan, a monster with "four sharp teeth which have grown into incurved tusks, a head halfway between a lion and fish, two horns and a crest, the feet of a lion, wings, and a long elegantly swaying tail."[441] In the book of Revelation, Antichrist is represented by the first and second beast; the first is a gigantic red dragon with seven heads and ten horns that rises from the sea or descends from the sky, the second a horned monster that rises out of a bottomless pit in the earth itself—"a gigantic embodiment of anarchic, destructive power," in the words of historian Norman Cohn.[442]

These descriptions fit well the creature depicted in the sixteenth-century mural paintings of the Casas Pintadas in Évora and correspond to a seventeenth-century seven-headed creature painted on a blue vessel in the collection of the Museu Nacional de Arte Antiga. There are also, not surprisingly, close similarities between the Biblical references and the paintings on the dome of the sixteenth-century chapel dedicated to São João in Monsaraz. At the chapel, God sitting in judgment is depicted in the central circular cartouche, surrounded by four other scenes. In the first, São João is seated next to an eagle recording his vision, alongside an apparition of Nossa Senhora. The second scene shows Christ enthroned on clouds and surrounded by terrestrial kings; in the third scene São João, kneeling by an eagle, receives a vision of seven burning candles that surround the body of Christ as He steps down from the clouds. The fourth scene is badly mutilated but depicts a woman dressed in fine clothing riding the seven-headed beast.[443]

The apocalyptic stories reinforced by Sybilline eschatology maintained their fascination in Europe throughout the Middle Ages, becoming, after the Bible and the works of the Church Fathers, the period's most popular literature.[444] They were adapted and manipulated to account for new signs (comets, eclipses, monstrous births) and situations (famines, pestilence, wars, coronations). By the fourteenth century apocalyptic stories had been translated into many European languages, and after the invention of printing they became among the first books to be typeset.[445] They strongly influenced popular culture, such as the *Boat Plays* by Gil Vicente, the founder of modern Portuguese theatre, whose works continue to be performed. Reflecting the persistence of historical memory, Jorge Colaço in 1907 painted the gloomy scenes of the boat to Hell and a more uplifting image of the one to Heaven on tiles decorating the gallery of the Palace Hotel in Buçaco.

By the sixteenth century there emerged a group of Franciscans, the Spirituals or Fraticelli, who longed for the reform of the institutional Church, which they believed had grown corrupt and offensive. The Spanish and Portuguese discoveries of the Americas and the route to Asia, a region

facing, left
Ossuary chapels and niche altars like this, part of Faro's thirteenth-century cathedral, were intended to remind believers that human life was short and that death and divine judgment were inevitable.

facing, right
Ossuary chapel in the fifteenth- to sixteenth-century church of São Francisco in Évora.

top left
JORGE COLAÇO
Demons Collecting the Souls of the Damned, 1907
Palace Hotel, Buçaco

top right
JORGE COLAÇO
The Battle of Ourique, 1922
Pavilion Carlos Lopes, Lisbon
In the centre of the sky can be seen the miraculous cross that promised the Portuguese victory over their adversaries.

bottom left
JORGE COLAÇO
The Boat to Paradise, 1907
Palace Hotel, Buçaco

bottom right
This early twentieth-century *azulejo* at Rua Artur Ravara, Aveiro, represents tradition, industry and progress, embodied by the Roman god Mercury.

associated theologically with the location of the Garden of Eden, seemed to provide new optimism. With the increasing decadence of Europe and the Discoveries, which came to be interpreted as the reappearance of the original Paradise, the Apocalypse was at last believed to be imminent.

Traces of apocalyptic thought survive throughout Europe and, according to Jacob Taubes, provide an original perspective for understanding the world that gave rise to the modern dialectic method: "Kant is the Old Testament and Hegel the New Testament of German idealism."[446] In *Mes Arches de Noé* (1980), the French writer Michel Déon (1919–) counts Portugal as one of the few paradises to have survived the Great Flood and that still lives with ambiguities and paradoxes that, beyond the superficialities of sadness and happiness, evoke adventurism and heroism with a sweet pain and melancholia. Déon's feelings reflect those of Portuguese writers like Teixeira de Pascoaes, Pessoa and Saramago, infusing the country's metaphysical character.

Portuguese history for these authors is a palimpsest, with images, ideas and beliefs from different eras piled one over the other, like the objects in David Gomes's shop or in old museum displays. Often, parts of these imprints are missing or faded and have helped create uncertainty, paradoxes and enigmas that continue to haunt our sensibility. The description of the demons revealed to the shepherd girl, Lucía, in Fátima in 1917 is startlingly similar, though more imaginatively expressed, to medieval sources like that of Hildegard of Bingen. In Fátima the apparitions revealed "demons and souls in human form, like transparent burning embers, all blackened and burnished bronze."[447] Or as Lucía recounted: "The demons could be distinguished by their terrifying and repellent likeness to frightful and unknown animals, black and transparent like burning coals." Lucía spoke of "flames... like sparks in huge fires, without weight or equilibrium."[448] Her description of Hell—similar to those of the Old Testament and Portuguese popular religious notions—provides an intriguing source to enhance the appreciation of the sixteenth-century painting *Inferno*, by an unknown Portuguese artist, in the Museu Nacional de Arte Antiga in Lisbon.

DYSTOPIA AND GNOSIS

Exuberant images of divine intervention, Biblical allegories, the lives and miracles of Christ and divine patrons, the Virgin's Annunciation, Judgment and the burning souls in Purgatory, plus rural allegories of Portugal's regions and peoples, depictions of its overseas adventures, the achievements and portraits of its people, idealizations of its towns and cities and even abstract mathematical concepts (at the University of Coimbra)—all provide subjects usually painted in blue and white on the ceramic tiles or *azulejos* ubiquitous throughout the country. From their origin in the fifteenth century, *azulejos* (from the Arabic *azzelij*, "little polished stones") have been refined and developed as a defining medium for illustrating and spreading a particular image of the country's character, which complements the various conceptualizations of Lusitania's spirit. Many of the interior walls of churches, abbeys, convents and monasteries as well as aristocratic palaces and palacetes, houses, and public and government buildings are decorated by these painted stories. *Azulejos* have been used to decorate gardens and public parks, universities, schools, hospitals, libraries, town halls and, even more ubiquitously, railway and bus stations and the Lisbon Metro. They constitute a massive nationwide program of public education and sensitivization that, after

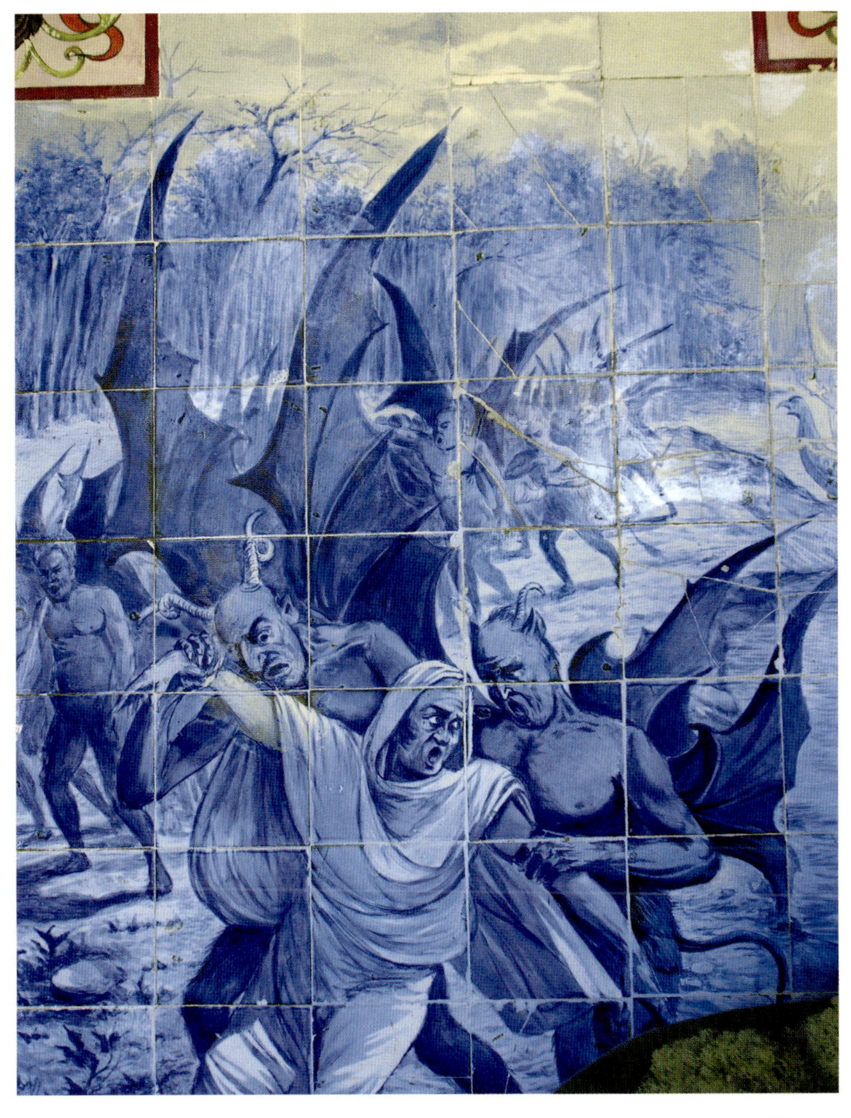
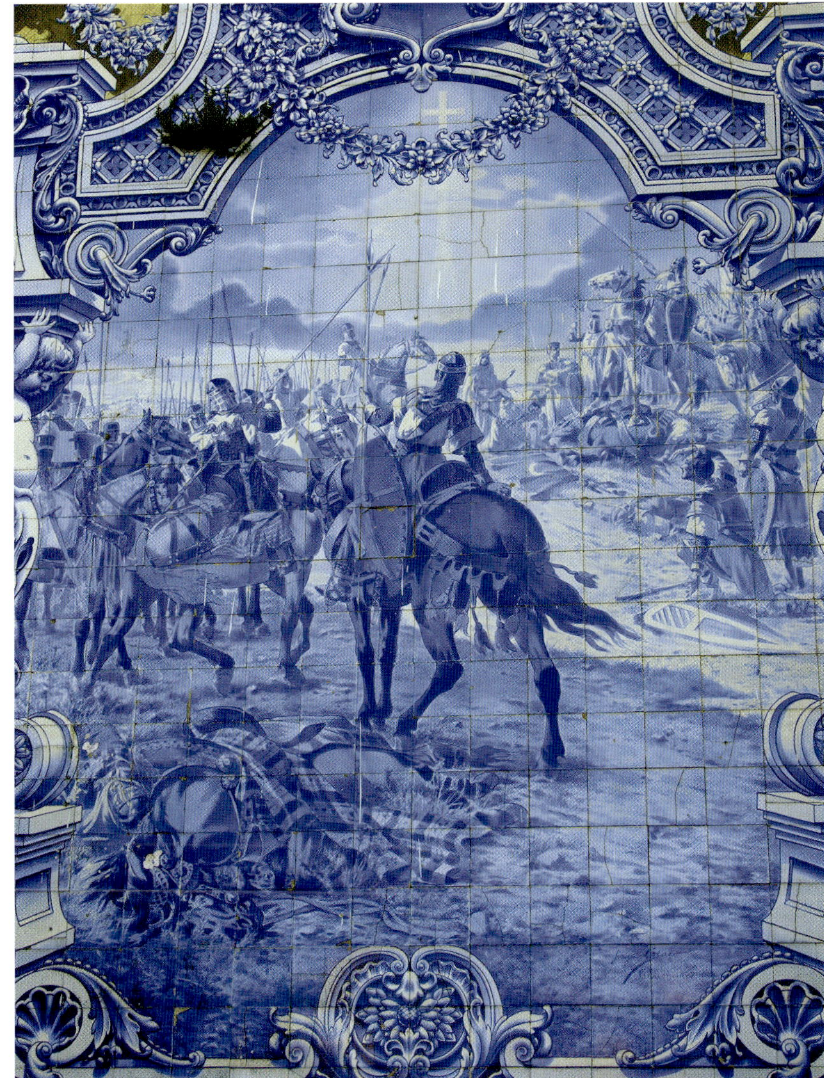
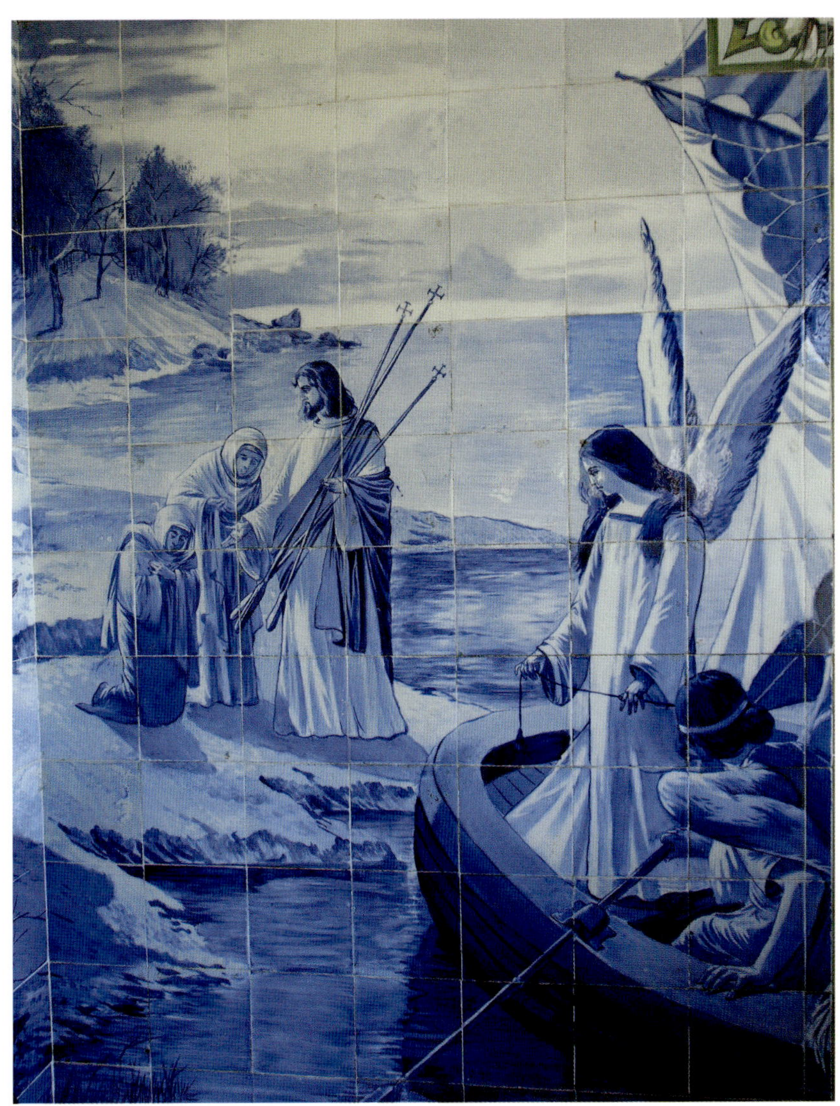
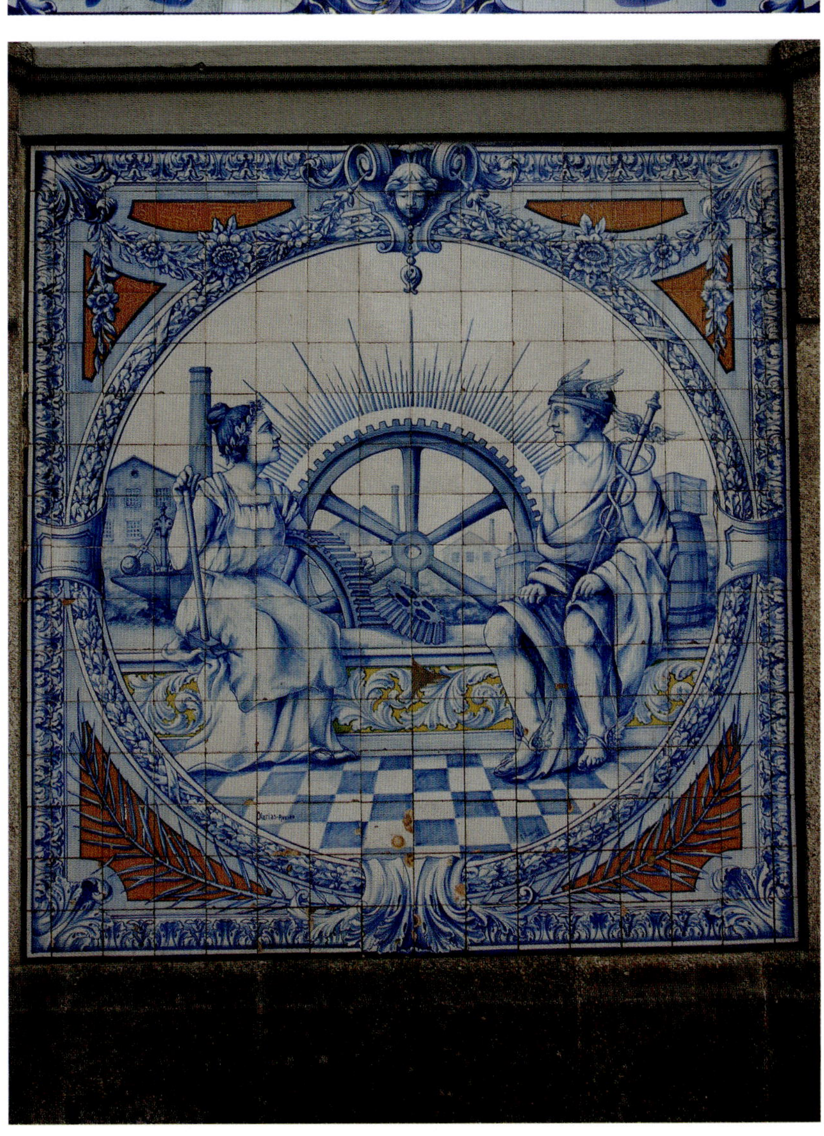

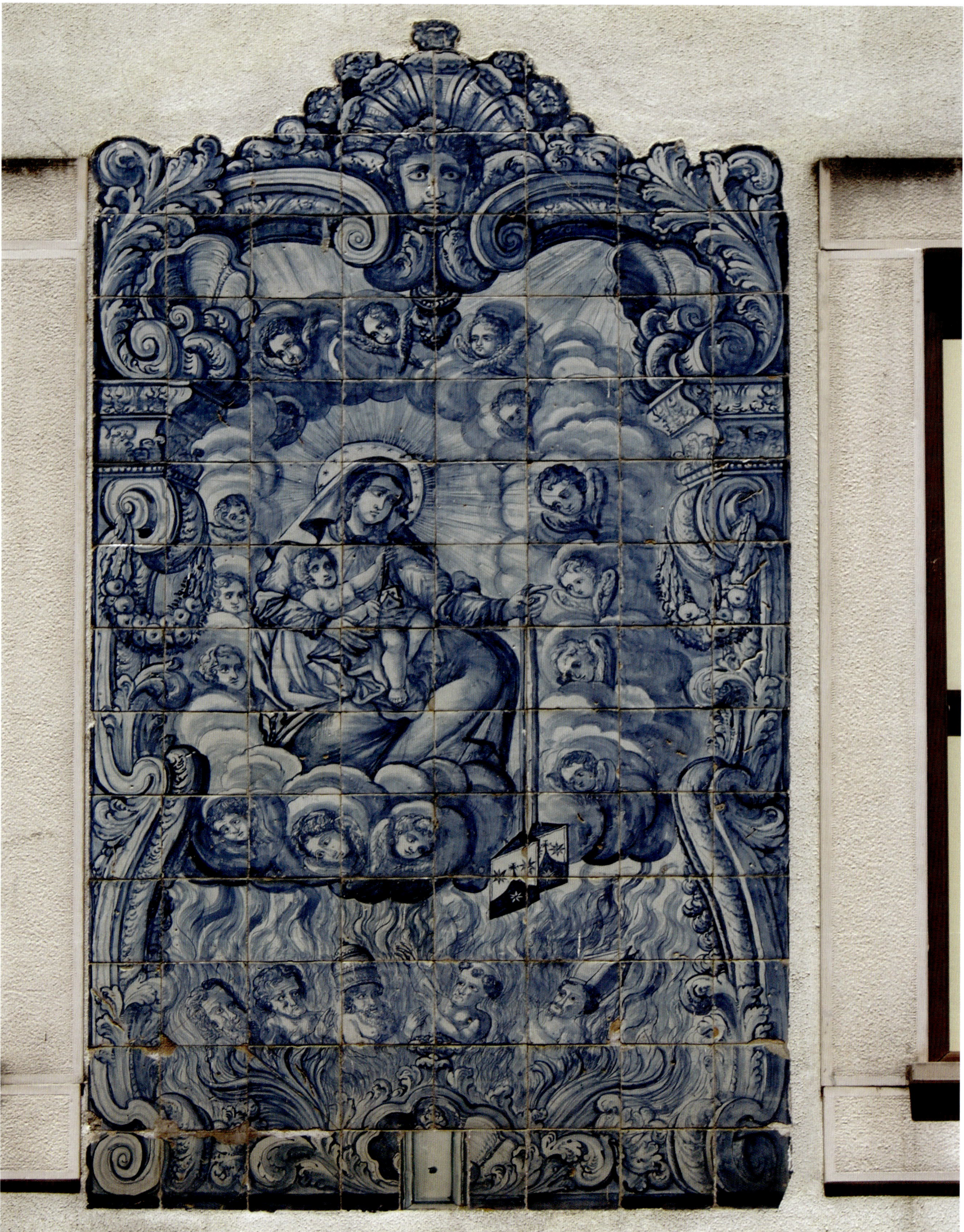

facing
This *azulejo* (tile) showing Nossa Senhora offering succour to the souls burning in Purgatory is located at the confluence of the Rua do Almoxarife with two other narrow streets in the centre of Coimbra.

half a millennium, still continues at a more modest pace today. *Azulejos* do more than visually represent the national character. Their lustrous and iridescent surfaces reflect light, like the white patterned stones of the streets and roads, and give urban environments a luminous quality that invites otherworldly associations.

The decoration of the urban landscape in the late twentieth century has been further augmented by friezes, disjunctured murals and graffiti, often depicting monstrous or imaginative subjects spray-painted onto the walls and doors of buildings and carriages. This was most commonly found in marginal areas such as transport hubs (railway stations, trains, docks, unused buildings, car parks, roadway intersections and overpasses), derelict or abandoned land and nightclub areas, but increasingly they are commissioned for development sites in city centres. Urban murals and graffiti include both clandestine compositions, sprayed without the foreknowledge or approval of site owners, and commissioned works, whose quality varies according to the time expended on them and the resulting composition. Examples of the first category are easily located, but the second category is rarer, associated with unused buildings on major urban thoroughfares and with nightclubs. In 2010, as part of the Crono Urban Art Project supported by the Lisbon municipal government, fourteen international artists decorated the facades of buildings on the Avenida Fontes Pereira de Melo. Three buildings were painted with murals by Sam3, Ericailcane, Os Gêmeos and Lucy Mclauchlan. On Calçada da Glória the city council has erected boards for street artists, and other densely painted facades are located in Amoreiras and along the Rua da Rosa. The end wall of an apartment complex in the northern town of Viseu is decorated by a giant line drawing of a constricted human heart, and in one extraordinary example, Miguel Januário (a.k.a. Kiss My Walls) painted the wall of the platform at Coimbra B Railway Station in 2010 with a giant mural depicting fantastical beings in a dystopic landscape. Regardless of the category, this art shares similarly bleak subject matter that attests to the upsurge of a new visual culture sharply at odds with older national projects, a stark contrast with the religious, idealized or bucolic subjects of *azulejos*.

Most urban art lacks geographically specific identification, referring instead to imaginary anonymous landscapes. Images include fabulous creatures, such as Ericailcane's docile, Godzilla-like lizard about to eat a sardine or Sam3's human shadow weaving in and out of the night sky, both painted on the facades of derelict buildings in central Lisbon, and the house with brightly painted masks in Faro, which is reminiscent of the painted hoardings found in fairgrounds. Other paintings in Caldas da Rainha and elsewhere consist of aliens, robot-like machines, creatures undergoing metamorphoses and futuristic-looking warriors. A building in Lisbon and a train carriage pulling out of Coimbra station provided the mediums for paintings of rather bemused angels and an imbecilic-looking demon.

This emerging visual culture shows little utopian optimism but an internally generated otherness whose origin is not in specific historical or cultural traditions but mediated by virtual and filmic worlds, science fiction and alienation. On their mural on the wall of the block on Avenida Fontes Pereira de Melo, Os Gêmeos (The Twins—these Brazilian artists are identical twin brothers) have painted a red-hooded figure clutching a bespectacled businessman held like a slingshot. The figure wears a badge that reads "I love vandalism." The Italian artist Blu has in the same block painted a massive bloated businessman

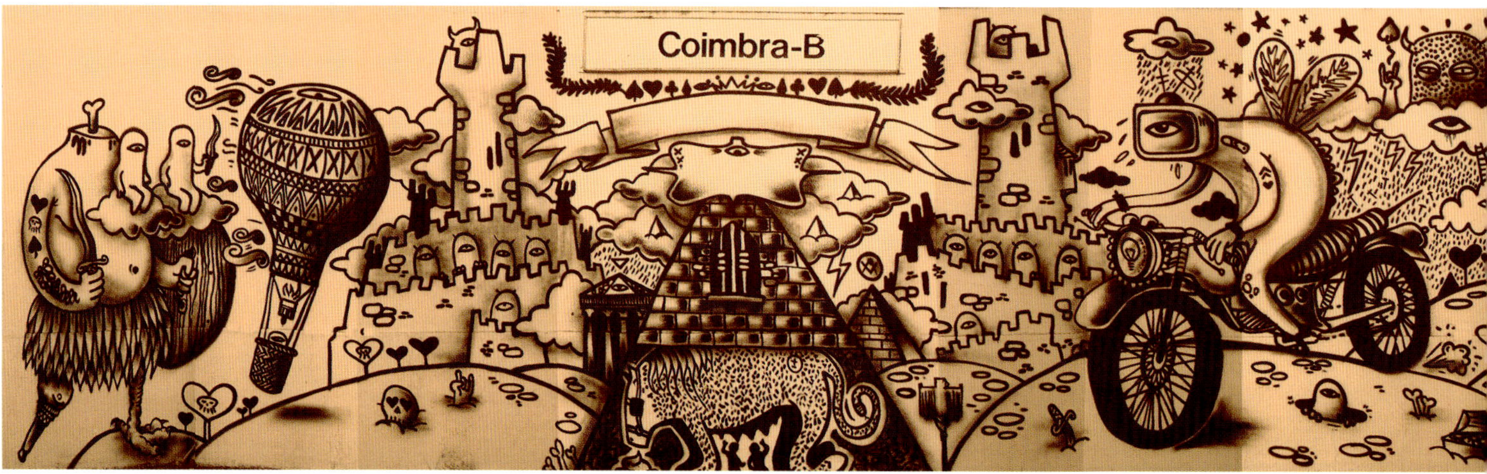

sucking the world dry through a straw. On his head the figure wears a crown decorated by the logos of petroleum companies Esso, Shell, BP, Texaco, Chevron and Agip.

Murals and graffiti are freer of stylistic constraints, historical references and objectivities than other genres of popular art. The rejection of dialogue with society that such an art implies is echoed in its conditions of production, in marginalized spaces, between coming and going, destruction and reconstruction, associated more with the night than the day world. There is no upside down or inversion of the world's condition, as, for example, that which gives Carnival its critical edge; instead there is pure negation, the exposition of a sick art (Ericailcane) or dystopic dreams and visions (Sam3 and Kiss My Walls), a different realm disengaged and sickened by the tropes, intellectual strategies, values and concerns of our overwhelming commodity-driven society. Urban art often turns the skin of humanity inside out to reveal the individual's isolation, fear, alienation and hopelessness, which emerge between the emptiness of words and images and their disengagement with meaning. Diabo, as Manuel Esteves Lima has conjectured, is not a being with discrete form and nature but, as these murals make clear, part of our disfigured humanity under commodity capitalism. Because of the freedom that comes from its often nihilistic detachment and indeterminability, allowed by its relative political and market autonomy—its social emptiness—mural art paradoxically fulfills the role of criticism, like Rosa Ramalho's figures, by gesturing to a space of

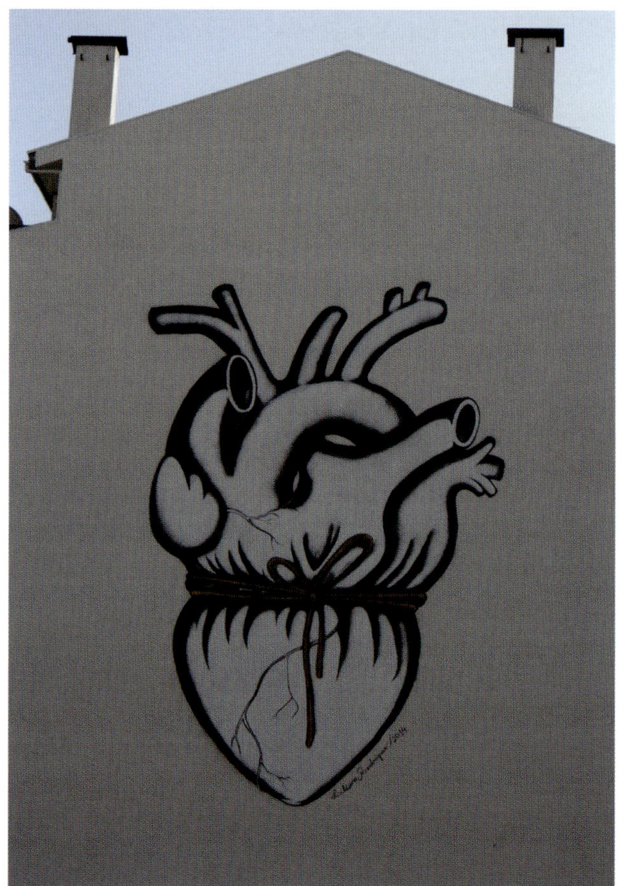

freedom in which to imagine difference. This art confronts the fragmented, meaningless commoditized world from which it emerges by, as Berger writes, expressing large compositional qualities like Hieronymus Bosch gave Hell in his *Millennium* triptych. Bosch's Hell has become everyday existence. "There is no horizon there. There is no continuity between actions, there are no pauses, no paths, no pattern, no past and no future. There

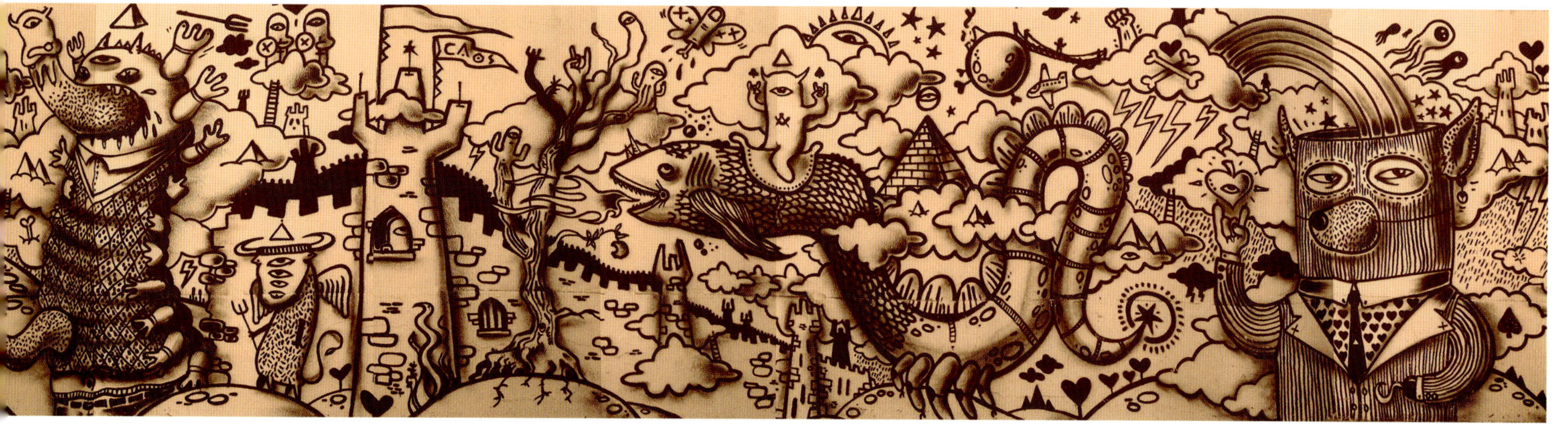

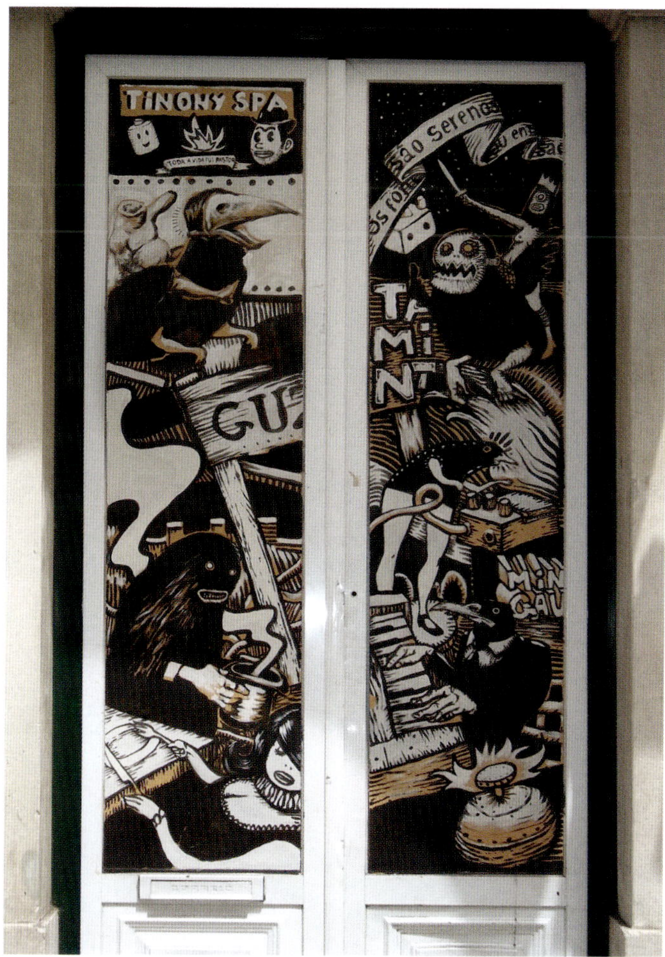

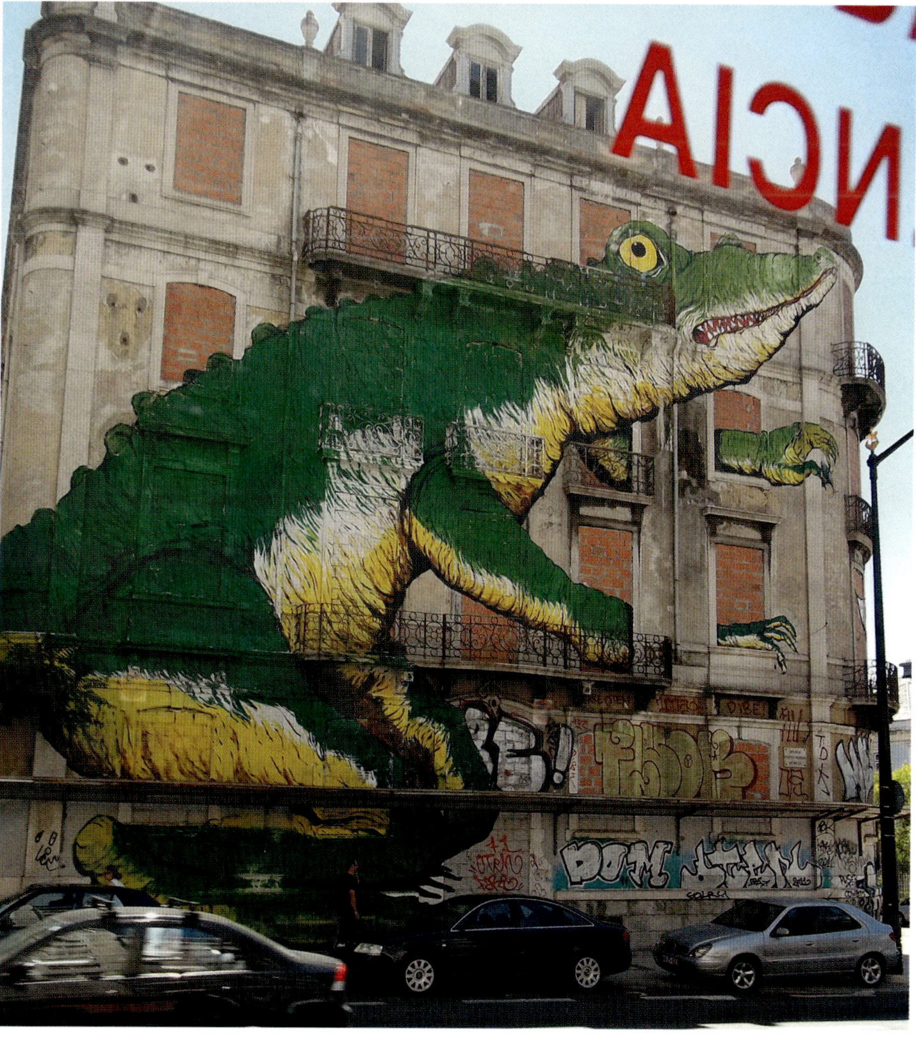

top
MIGUEL JANUÁRIO (A.K.A. KISS MY WALLS)
"Se Numa Noite de Inverno um Viajante" (Italo Calvino), c. 2010
Coimbra B Railway Station

facing, left
Constricted heart wall mural at the end of an apartment block in Viseu.

above left
Tinony Spa door mural, Caldas da Rainha.

above right
ERICAILCANE
The Tear of a Crocodile before It Swallows a Sardine (wall mural), 2011
Avenida Fontes Pereira de Melo, Lisbon

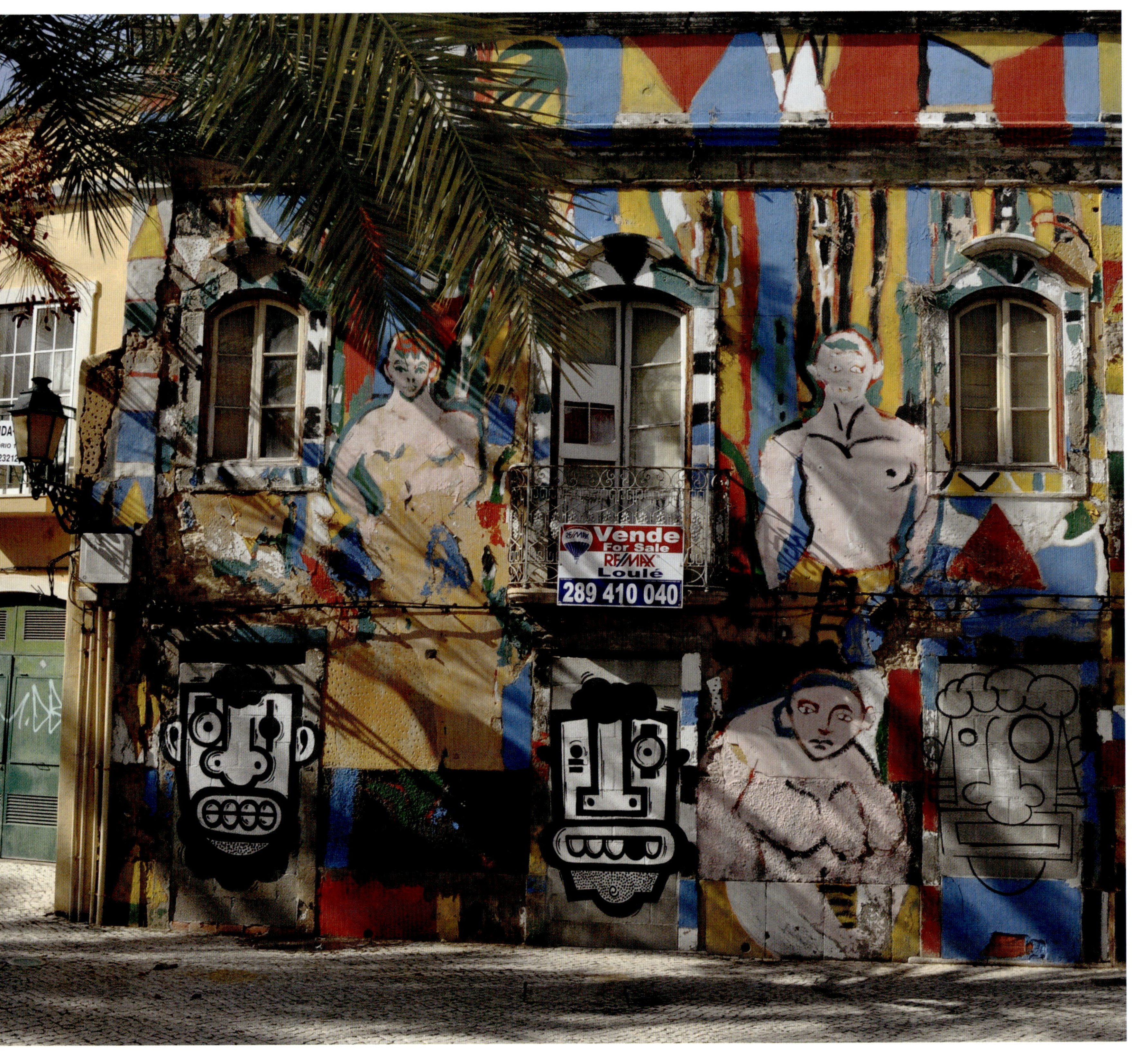
Vende
For Sale
RE/MAX
Loulé
289 410 040

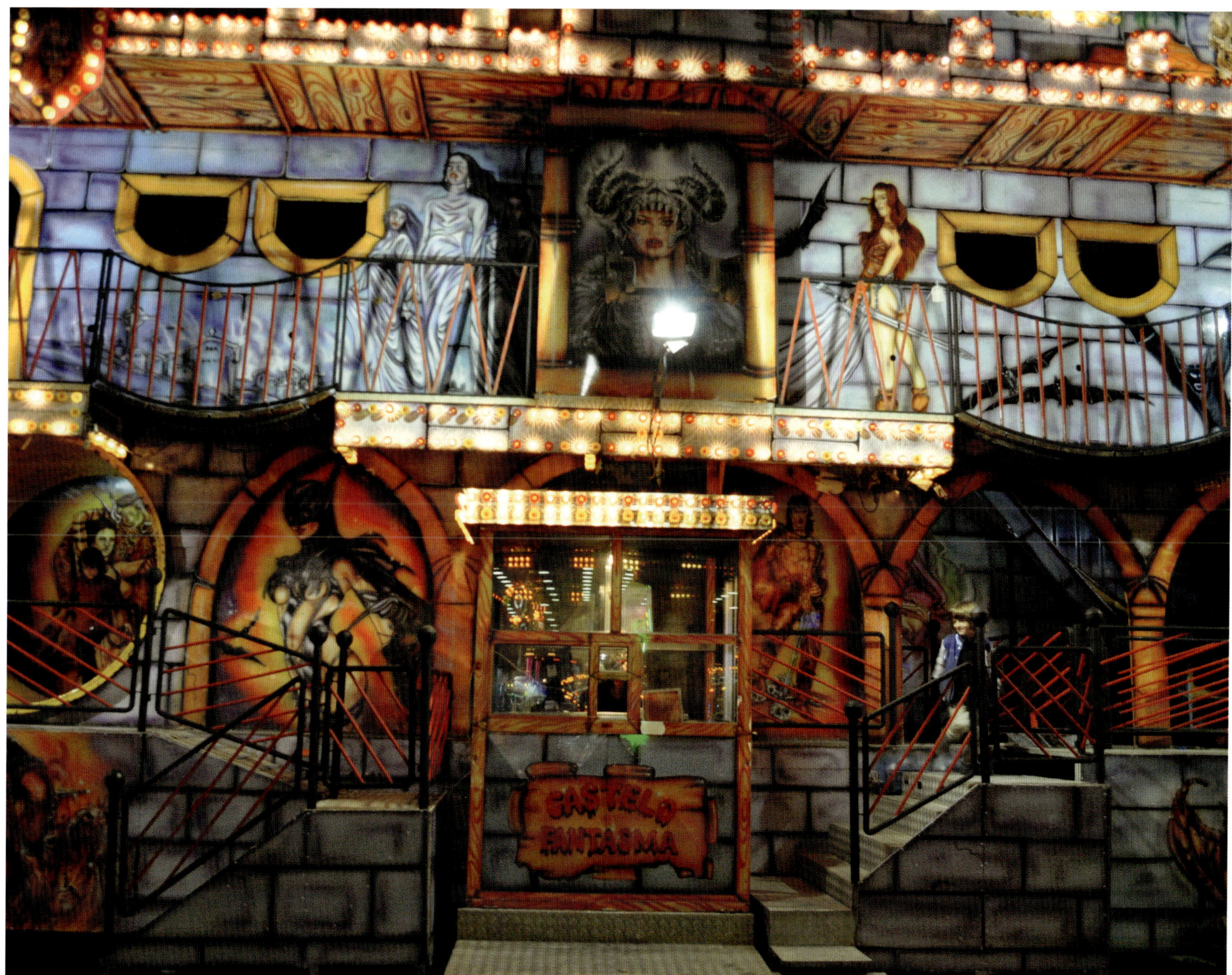

facing
The whole of the front of this house in Faro has been covered by a mural similar to those painted on the facades of fairground stalls.

above
A painted facade of the haunted castle at a fair, Avenida do Brasil, Lisbon, 2010.

is only the clamour of the disparate, fragmentary present. Everywhere there are surprises and sensations, yet nowhere is there any outcome. Nothing flows through; everything interrupts. There is a kind of spatial delirium."[449]

The dystopia alluded to in these compositions is different on four counts from early medieval apocryphal art because of the distinct period under which it was produced. First, the doctrine of apocalypticism was a closed textual or visual exegesis. Manuscript illumination, woodcuts and even paintings were tightly controlled by Biblical and related descriptive texts. Mural art has no such constraints. Second, mural art is not authoritative, either in subject or prophecy. It never sets the date for anything. Third, mural art makes no statements or promises of redemption. It is not usually connected to millenarian prophecy or political programs. Fourth, while millenarian thought is directed at the next world, mural art is resolutely focused on the present, a world in which institutions are seen as losing meaning and authority. There is no New Jerusalem or even an Old Jerusalem, only the self's endurance of the present condition of inanity, a post-humanistic, commoditized present with no apparent hope of salvation or transcendence. The act of painting, such art proposes, takes place in a space of indeterminate, epistemologically varied but contiguous possibilities in which there are no boundaries, no signs and no guides; an infinite non-space independent of structure and meaning, monopolized by artists unencumbered by national identities who suffer a common alienation.

Murals and graffiti demand no response, recognition or understanding. They destabilize social categories by denying dialogical engagement. With its gleaming walls of *azulejos* and crumbling, spray-painted facades, Portugal can sometimes feel caught between the desire for destiny and the promise of nothingness.

PERFORMING DYSTOPIA

Dystopia is not only painted large on walls and carriages, but performed and enacted at specific times during the Christian winter ceremonial cycle. During these months Diabo and his demons break free from Hell, and the souls of the dead temporarily roam the world of the living.

As previously described, the Christian calendar correlates the feast days of the saints to the seasons, divided between the winter and summer solstices (celebrated on 26 December, the Day of Santo Estêvão, and 24 June, the Day of São João, respectively) and the spring and autumn equinoxes. Midday and midnight, and the transition points between these monthly periods, were thought to be ambiguous, dangerous times when the boundaries between temporal periods were at their weakest and they became pervious to evil or frightening supernatural interlopers. At midday and midnight on the Day of São João, for instance, it was believed that Moorish enchantresses might shed their scaly bodies to seduce the unwary, while witches and even Diabo might wander the earth.[450] On the night of the final day of the year, associated with São Silvestre, a saint whose iconography includes a bull and a captive dragon at his feet, huge bonfires were once lit to "burn out the old year," and at Cantar os Reis, a traditional ceremony celebrated at Epiphany (6 January), "masked jinglers, *chocalhadas*, festooned with cow bells once ran through the village raising a deafening noise to exorcise any lingering evil left from the previous year."[451]

During another liminal period of transition, between the commemoration of Christ's crucifixion and resurrection, the membranes between this world and the other again weakened, and Diabo could once more transit into the world unhindered,[452] as he could on the feast day of the exorcist saint São Bartolomeu (24 August).[453]

As the anthropologist Lopes summarizes, specific moral qualities were assigned to the seasons and to the day and night.[454] Like the night, the winter was associated with cold, degeneration, old age and death, while the summer, the same as the day, was commended for its qualities of warmth, light, fertility and life. Carnival represented the symbolic death and reinvigoration of the community, closing the winter period and celebrating the return of fertility and the beginning of a new agricultural cycle.[455] Popular religion synthesized rituals and observations to acknowledge supernatural patrons and ensure the safe transition between dangerous stages in the annual and daily cycles. I shall focus on just two of these pivotal transitions—the Day of Santo Estêvão and Carnival—both of which, it has been argued, parallel the relationship between death and creation that once dominated the thought of rural communities.

The Day of Santo Estêvão and the Carnival period mark the beginning and end of winter and are harbingers of desolation and fertility, respectively. Both days, in the past, were observed in both urban and rural Portugal, but in the cities since the 1950s the Day of Santo Estêvão has increasingly become like Christmas as commonly celebrated elsewhere in Europe. Carnival on the other hand has become more secularized and in some communities, like Mealhada in Beira Litoral, has taken on the traits of its Brazilian counterpart. In the past both these ceremonial periods were associated with loud noises—shouting, screaming, drums, bagpipes, cow and sheep bells, fireworks—intended to expiate evil spirits. Masquerades were, and in some communities remain, common and performed a most important function in mediating and enacting the transition between different forces and expressing the close synergies between vegetative and human life cycles.

The Day of Santo Estêvão is now celebrated with masked performers only in a few northern villages in Trás-os-Montes, including Aveleda, Babe, Baçal, Deilã, Rio de Onor, São Julião, Ousilhão and Vagas, and in Mogadouro in the villages of Vale de Porco and Bemposta. In all but two of the village celebrations in Trás-os-Montes, the day coincides with the *festa dos caretos* or "festival of the masked performers." Even forty years ago this male coming-of-age festival was celebrated more widely in the nearby villages of Mós, Ferreira, Vilarinho de Agrochão,[456] Sacoias,[457] França, Lombada and Terras de Miranda.[458] Elsewhere, in Rio de Onor, the *festa dos caretos* takes place at the time of the Feast of the Kings (6 January).[459] Its moveability strengthens Dias's argument that the masquerade was probably a newer imposition grafted onto earlier localized ceremonies related to growth and the return of the dead.[460] The anthropologist Benjamin Pereira, in the first comprehensive study of Portuguese masks, called attention to the Roman belief in a direct relation between the closure of one year and the opening of another with the return of the souls of the dead.[461] In the Christian calendar, some communities believed souls would return for Christmas, but more commonly the return of the dead coincided with the celebration of All Saints' Day and All Souls' Day on 1 and 2 November.[462] There are differences also in the synchronization of masquerades even with the feast day of Santo Estêvão, but these do not invalidate Dias's and Pereira's interpretations. In Varge and Babe the *festa dos caretos* takes place from 24 to 26 December; in Ousilhão from 25 to 26 December, and in Grijó de Parada on 27 December.

The masked performers in the *festa dos caretos* were nearly all local boys in their teens or younger who performed in successive years. Its interpretation as an initiation or coming-of-age festival is still commonly reiterated,[463] and the requirement for its participants to display strength, daring and fortitude for days at a time favours youthfulness. Costumes and masks vary between villages, but all their wearers use large numbers of increasingly difficult-to-obtain cow, goat and sheep bells to create the unnerving noise associated with their antics and enhance their ability to surprise and frighten young girls, unmarried women and children, who are their chief victims.

In Varge, on 25 and 26 December, after excessive eating and drinking, the *caretos*, accompanied by two stewards, indulge in increasingly ribald behaviour, chasing, leaping, jumping and even somersaulting through the village, accompanied by a racket of bells, bagpipes and drums. Using mimicry, parody and satire, the drunken participants ridicule politicians and professional, wealthy and elderly people and scandalize girls by their unruly and licentious behaviour until, on Christmas Eve, they gather to eat a special supper of calf's meat. On Christmas Day their wild frolics come to a sudden temporary halt as they take time to learn the satirical verses or *loas* that have been prepared for them to read on the twenty-sixth, the Day of Santo Estêvão. The next day begins with masqueraders, accompanied by the stewards, drummers and bagpipe players, visiting households, requesting alms and attempting to gain entrance, accost girls and pretend to steal food and drink. Later they shed their masks to take part in the Mass dedicated to the saint, but then put them back on, impede the congregation from returning home and reassemble the townsfolk to listen to their satires. Local scandal, crime, dissension and bad behaviour form the subjects of these humorous and critical verses that are read aloud, accompanied by mimicry. The ceremony ends the same day after two new stewards have been appointed to organize the next year's ceremony.

The *festa dos caretos* follows a different form in Ousilhão. The stewards who organize the event, and include former *caretos*, dress as a king and two vassals and in the past were sometimes challenged to ritual fights.[464] The ceremony ends with the transfer of power from one king to his successor. Unlike in Varge, there are no *loas* or social criticisms of the villagers, and there is less antagonism between the masqueraders and young girls. Some of these ceremonies incorporate on their final day the burning of two paper images, described as the godfather and godmother or Judas or symbols representing the end of the winter period. In the past, masks and costumes used in the celebrations were also burned as a punishment decreed by Christ, it was said, in revenge for the chaos the *caretos* had provoked with their impersonations of Diabo and their asocial behaviour reminiscent of pre-Creation times, and not to expiate the evil that might still cling to them.[465] This association between the *caretos* and Diabo was also recorded by Pereira in São Pedro in Mogadouro, where, when boys and girls heard the drummers, they would shout, "The *careto* is coming, Diabo is coming!" and take refuge in the most secure houses.[466]

In Podence and Lazarim, the *caretos* make their appearance during Carnival. In Podence they act in similar ways as they do on the Day of Santo Estêvão, as harbingers of disorder, shaking, jumping, running through the village, climbing walls, invading homes and, whenever possible, irritating girls and unmarried women while all the time accompanied by the loud, dull, discordant din made by the clanging noises of their bells. Their unpredictable and inarticulate movement has been compared to that of the medieval dance of São Vito, named after the saint credited with curing seizures and epilepsy. As in other villages, four or so village authorities arrange a mock Carnival marriage between the unmarried girls and boys. The couples are brought together by the authorities, and *loas* joking and criticizing events from the community in the previous year are read out to them by a judge, who also collects a symbolic tribute from each of the boys for the girls' hands in marriage. The tribute is collected on Ash Wednesday, the day Mass is said, and used to buy wine for the boys and *caretos*.[467] Next the four men collect tribute from the girls for the boys they have "married," and the girls prepare their "husbands" a small lunch.

Carnival in Lazarim follows a similar structure to that in Podence, though costumes are makeshift and the masks are wooden and represent a wide range of locally commissioned caricatures. Diabo is ubiquitous, but witches, policemen, kings, Christ, politicians and well-known personalities are also common. The culmination of Carnival is again the reading of the satirical verses related to events that have affected the town during the past year or that the *caretos* have found to be particularly humorous. The verses are written and read by different groups of maskers, both men and women, who compose them weeks before the celebrations begin. Their recitation takes the form of a dialogue in which accusations are made by the women and retorts returned by the men. The recitations have been repeatedly explained by anthropologists as an informal but nevertheless institutionalized mechanism for managing and dissipating social tensions that may have been building throughout the year, and which are finally expiated by the burning of the paper godmother and godfather at the end of the performance.

Not all ceremonies have the same masked protagonists or reproduce the same order of events. In Vinhais, according to Maciel, the streets are again invaded by groups of masked devils on the day after Carnival.[468] Dressed in red costumes with matching cloth masks, the performers rampage throughout the town. Unlike elsewhere, they are accompanied by a figure carrying a mitre and wearing a black suit with a white skeleton painted on it. With his face covered by a handkerchief, the skeleton carries a pitchfork that he commands those he passes to kiss. Pereira reported a figure representing death also appeared in Bragança and Edrosa, part of Vinhais.[469] Coelho discovered a similar suit representing death dating back to 1867 that was kept in the almshouse at Bragança.[470] Demand to wear it was so high during Lent that its rental was restricted to one-hour periods. The masquerader, with accompanying scythe and stirrups, pursued boys and entered houses to chase their inhabitants onto the streets. Early anthropologists interpreted these appearances of Death as a survival from the Middle Ages, when masqueraders walked the street either in penance or to remind the living of their mortality and religious and social responsibilities. However, the final appearance of Death after Carnival may once have expressed the end of winter and the return of the souls of the dead to their usual places of repose.

Carnival, or Entrudo as it is usually called in rural communities, was only introduced into Christianity in the sixteenth century, and its Portuguese version has often been compared to the Roman Saturnalia. According to many mid- and late-twentieth-century ethnographers, Santo Estêvão and Carnival provide pivots on which the seasons alternate between barrenness, death and life's exhaustion and the return of health, growth

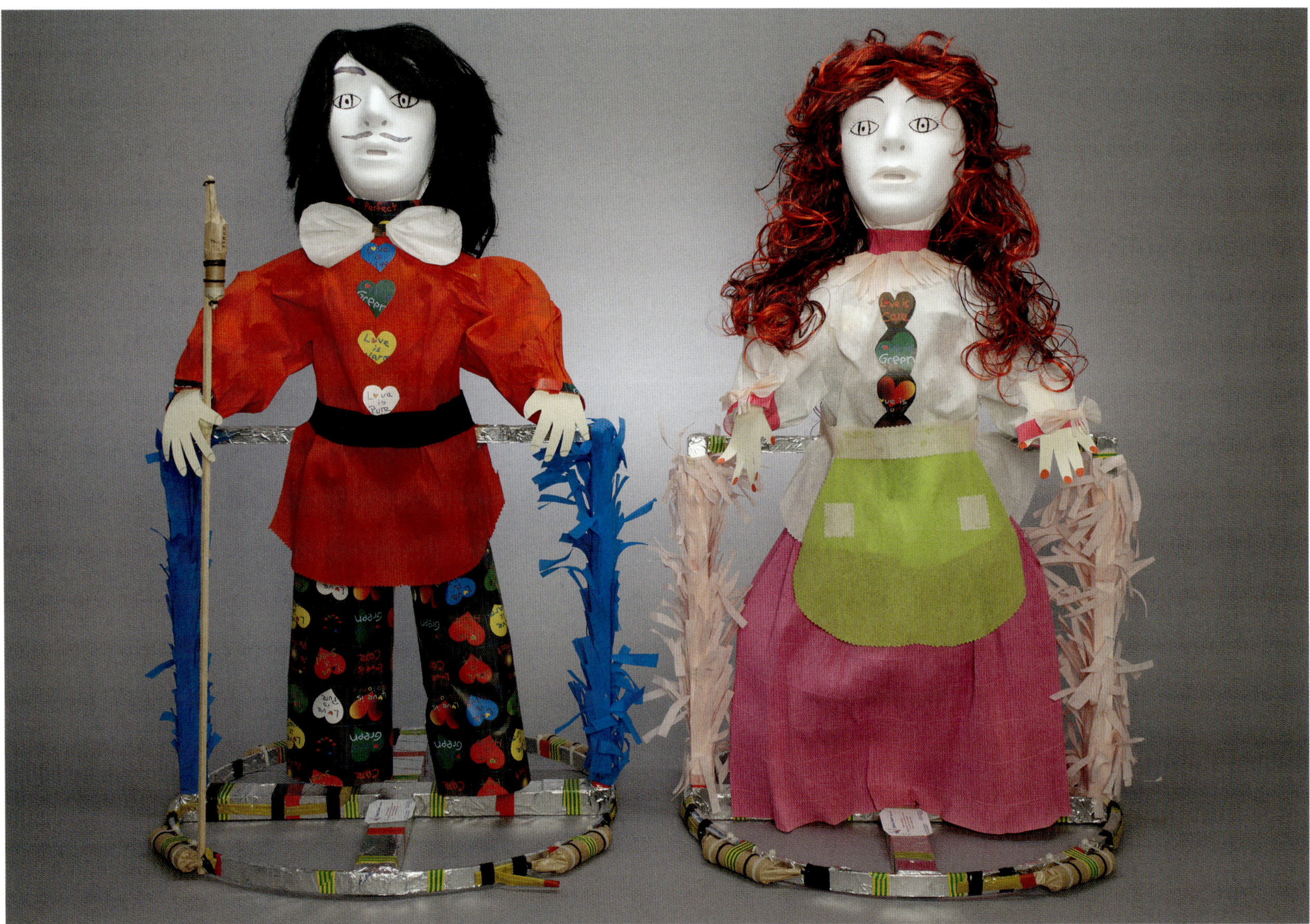

and fertility. In both, the *caretos* play an important role. On the Day of Santo Estêvão they represent the advent of the cold, exhausted, barren world, while at Carnival they enact their defeat and accept expulsion from the world as a prelude to the return of life and growth. The two ceremonies manipulate the membrane separating temporal periods and the moral values and conditions of life and death associated with them. They are based on a view of time as an alternating cyclical movement, whose articulation of life, death and renewal follows a similar logic to that between creation, destruction and rebirth in apocalyptical and eschatological thought.

In the past the appearance of the masked figure of Death, just as much as the infernal din made by the uncontrolled, otherworldly movements and antics of the *caretos*, may have represented a similar act of negation as murals and graffiti do today. Not part of official religion, the *caretos* are organized by their own stewards, which provides them a similar liberty of action outside of social and religious restrictions. Although murals might be more uncompromising in their negation of the world, the *caretos* and other masked performers mark weakened times and spaces in the everyday constituted world and open and close portals in the temporal membrane that separates one from the other. Moreover, these two worlds of dissonant urban mural painters and diabolical impersonators come together annually in Lisbon during the May parade of masqueraders from all over the Iberian Peninsula.

facing
CLODOMIRO FONSECA
Compadre and *comadre* figures, 2011. Figures like these, but with attached fireworks, are made and burnt at the end of the Lazarim Carnival.

These symbolic interpretations of rural ceremonies as agricultural and life-cycle rituals were commonly reproduced by anthropologists until the 1980s, even though in many cases they had a disjunctured history and were, like agriculture, in decline. Such interpretations, rather than losing any of their contemporary relevance, continue to be reproduced in popular writing, including books, promotional literature and Internet pages as well as in television programs and films that have helped reinvigorate new versions of them. A good case in point is Mira, a town in the district of Coimbra, where Carnival masquerades were banned until 1974, repressed again in the 1980s and finally abandoned in the 1990s. Since then they have been revived by a cobbler, Alirio Laranjeiro, who taught children how to make the masks and conical supports for the arcs that surround them. The memory of Carnival, however, was never forgotten, according to one of the mask makers, João Pinho. The loss of young men through emigration or attendance at outside educational institutions was compensated for by opening the masquerade to older men and children, so participants now range from ages three to sixty. The Carnival also dispensed with its secretive protocols, and for fifteen years became formally connected to the Lagonense Football Club, with which it shared offices.

Materials have also changed significantly. In place of the traditional woman's hat that formed the base of the mask's infrastructure, now either a helmet or a traffic cone may be used. Costumes still comprise red skirts and white aprons and shirts—what town dwellers in the past would have thought of as luxury items—but instead of being made out of old clothes by masqueraders themselves, these are now made especially for the performers by their female relatives. Nevertheless the *caretos* share similar behaviour to those in the north, including energetic actions and ribald gestures such as lifting their skirts to young girls, although now, as João Pinho says, the chaos is controlled and always good-humoured. While they no longer function as initiation societies, the Caretos da Lagoa have become a memorable symbol of local identity. In 2014 they established themselves as a separate corporate entity to better organize their increasing activities as representatives of the municipal and regional identities.

The changes to rural life over the last forty years have been profound. Emigration has led to participants in the coming-of-age ceremonies becoming increasingly older,[471] while changes in gender relations, wider educational opportunities and other factors have diversified participants to include girls.[472] These changes in social structure have undermined the original functions of these ceremonies and strengthened their reinvention within an international cultural economy. Local festivals have been emblemized and have become regionalized or even nationalized.[473] This has resulted in international and national participation in rural ceremonies and new opportunities for local participants to perform year-round at events beyond their communities. At the same time, the distance between experiencing a cultivated life and the impoverished public narratives intended to give it sense creates greater alienation and emptiness than ever before.[474] The value of these new commodified cultural expressions is determined by supposed ethnographic criteria based on imaginary factors like rusticity, antiquity and authenticity[475] that create a radical disjuncture between local social relationships and cultural forms. According to some, the Hell imagined in Christian theology has become the hell of worldly existence.

Museologies

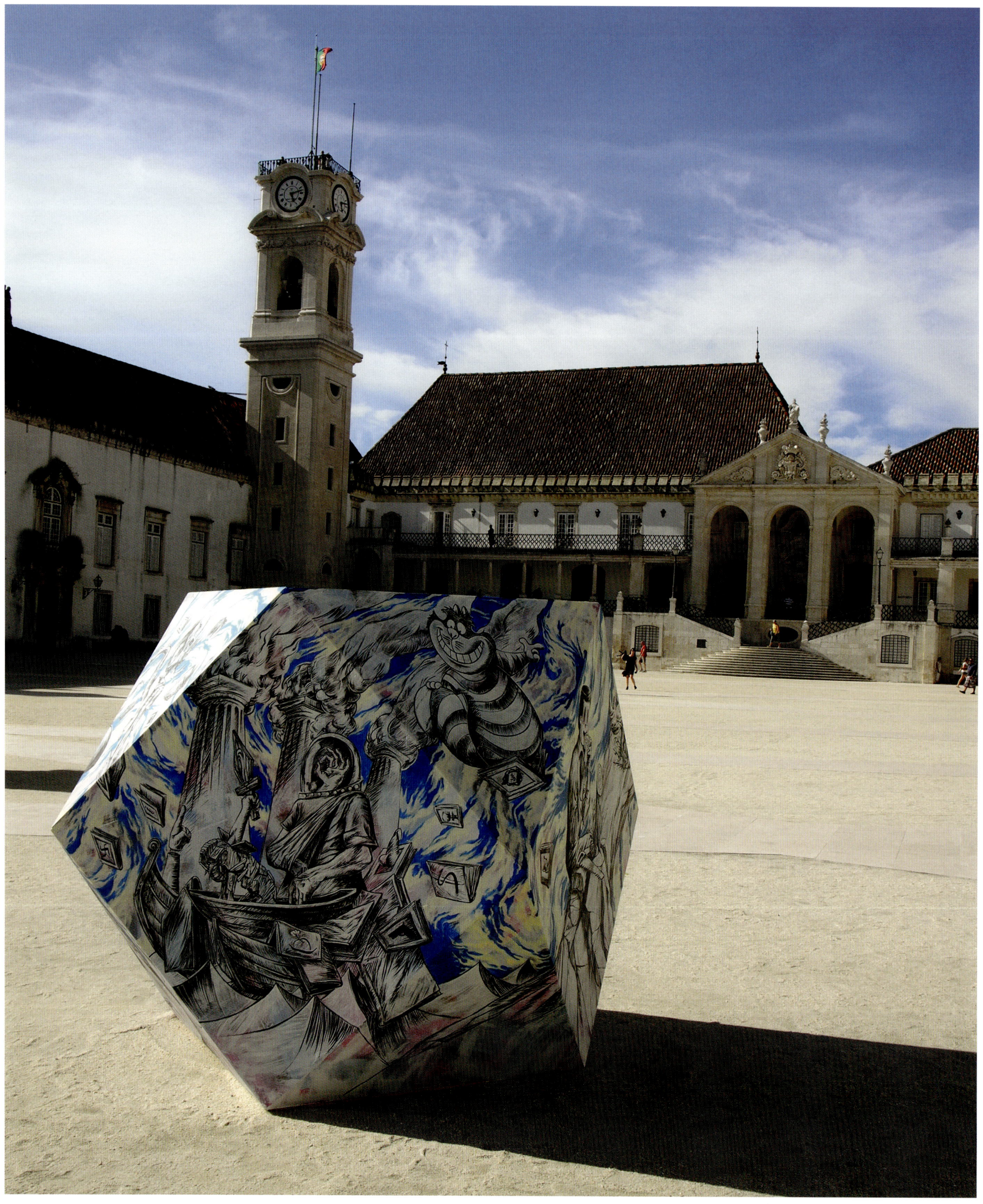

8 A Melancholy History of Portuguese Museums

Colonial culture implies an exercise of power that constricts its own object of domination.

Nuno Porto[476]

BETWEEN THEIR EMERGENCE in the nineteenth century and the mid-twentieth century, public museums were charged by government to organize exhibitions and commemorations intended to strengthen and celebrate the awareness of the antiquity and originality of the Portuguese spirit. Their work was aimed at a small educated social class, which was thought key to mediating the relationship between the governing elite and the mass of urban and rural labourers below them. What connected the philosophy of the "spirit" to the museum movement was Romanticism; the same Romanticism found in the work of the philosopher Pascoaes and, before him, the playwright and writer Almeida Garrett and the historian Alexandre Herculano.

EARLY MODERN COLLECTIONS

The anthropologist Henrique Coutinho Gouveia divided the history of ethnographic collecting in Portugal into five periods.[477] The first encompassed collections made before the devastating 1755 Lisbon earthquake, whereas the second was defined by collections made in the second half of the eighteenth century. This latter period was marked by the vogues for private domestic collections and for the state to sponsor the assemblage of natural history collections to support a paradigm of knowledge based on observation and experimentation. State-sponsored collections included those of, in Lisbon, the Royal Natural History Museum at the Ajuda Palace and the Academy of Sciences and, in Coimbra, the University of Coimbra. Gouveia's third period was dated from 1785 to 1850 and was characterized by foreign appropriation, disuse and sometimes abandonment of collections as a consequence of internal strife and the Peninsular War (1807–14), which led to economic crises resulting in institutional decline and neglect.

The fourth period, 1850 to 1940, saw a general recovery in the organization, breadth and educational utility of museum collections and coincided with the emergence of specialist ethnographic museums and the separation of ethnographic and archaeological material into discrete displays in general-purpose museums. This new impetus to the use and organization of ethnographic collections can be detected in José Leite de Vasconcellos's Museu Etnológico Português and the Museu Municipal Santos Rocha in Figueira da Foz, both of which used ethnographic specimens to

facing
The University of Coimbra, founded in 1290.

illustrate the life of the prehistoric inhabitants of the Peninsula. This was also a period of accelerated museum growth, stimulated by an increasing number of scientific and collecting expeditions and military campaigns in the Portuguese colonies. Other new opportunities to assemble collections were provided by international, colonial and commercial expositions, which on their closure often redistributed their exhibits to museums and scientific institutions. Collections, even when valued and institutionalized in professional museums, were often poorly treated and lacked proper conservation management. For example, the commemorations of Camões in 1880 and Pombal in 1882 included parades and allegorical floats that were decorated with museum collections,[478] while at one stage during the 1940 *Exhibition of the Portuguese World*, the precious *Saint Vincent Panels* were taken from the Museu Nacional de Arte Antiga in Lisbon, attached to poles and paraded through the city's streets by costumed actors. Gouveia's fifth period of Portuguese museum history began with the establishment in 1960 of the Museu de Etnologia do Ultramar (Museum of Overseas Ethnology), which, heavily influenced by modern anthropological fieldwork, adopted an empirical contextual approach to acquiring and displaying ethnographic material culture.

Little if any ethnographic material survives from the earliest period of collecting, a deficiency usually attributed to the disastrous effects of the Great Earthquake and the tsunami and fires that followed it. Surviving documents testify to the richness of the royal and aristocratic collections that had existed, including those assembled in the Royal Palace, the Paço Real, the Palace of the Dukes of Bragança and the Palácio da Anunciada. Other notable collections included those of the archbishop of Braga, Diogo de Sousa; André de Resende, an amateur archaeologist; and the humanist scholar Damião de Góis. According to the chronicles of Góis, the collections of the Casa da Índia, part of the Royal Palace, had been well organized and displayed in an artistic fashion.[479] Brigola describes a number of private eighteenth-century collections, but is unclear whether these had survived the earthquake or were assembled later by aristocrats, traders, businessmen and churchmen.[480] Of particular note was the collection of Father Manuel do Cenáculo, which included local history and archaeological specimens collected from sites at Tróia, Miróbriga and Sines in Alentejo. On becoming bishop of Beja, Cenáculo opened his collection to the public in the São Sisenando chapel, an annex of the Episcopal Palace. The collection, which became the Museu Sisenando Cenaculano Pacense, opened in 1791 and was the first public museum in Portugal.

These early descriptions confirm Simon's observation that the eighteenth century witnessed "a mania to collect things," especially exotic natural history specimens, which were both popular and fashionable.[481] It is this second period of Gouveia's chronological framework that provides greatest insight into the history of the successive institutionalizations of ethnographic collections, including popular art, and the meanings attributed to it in Portugal. Paramount among these were the collections of the Royal Natural History Museum and the botanical gardens of the Ajuda Palace in Belém (1768–1810); the collections and botanical garden of the University of Coimbra (1772); and the collections of the Academy of Sciences in Lisbon (1723–92), which later incorporated the collections of the Museu Maynense and those of the Royal Museum of Ajuda before devolving its natural history collections to the Museu da Escola Politécnica in 1858.[482] These institutions and collections were founded and developed in response to the wide-ranging Pombaline reforms initiated by Sebastião José de Carvalho e Melo, Marquis of Pombal, in the early eighteenth century. They were intended to foster useful knowledge on the economic exploitation of the natural world, not only in Europe but also in the colonies, and to assist in the teaching of natural history, which possessed similar commercial aspirations.[483]

In the last quarter of the eighteenth century the Crown sponsored a series of "philosophical journeys" to Brazil and Portugal's African colonies to report on and collect natural history specimens and establish clarity on Portugal's territorial borders.[484] Here the influence and symbiotic relationship between the University of Coimbra and the Ajuda Palace was essential, with the university training a generation of natural scientists who later carried out research and administration in the palace's laboratories, museum and garden. Part of this newly trained cadre of naturalists was sent on extensive scientific missions, which contributed enormously to the growth of the collections of the two institutions. Of special note were three Brazilian scholars, Alexandre Rodrigues Ferreira, Joaquim José da Silva and Manuel Galvão da Silva, all of whom were trained at the same time at Coimbra and later commissioned by the Crown to undertake scientific missions to Brazil, Angola and the Estado da India, which included Mozambique, Macau, Goa and Timor.[485] The Ajuda Palace Museum was part of an international scientific network and maintained close relations with museums elsewhere in Europe, furnishing them with Brazilian and African specimens.

Parts of the collections amassed by these naturalists, together with their notes and documentation, were sequestered by Napoleon and received by the French National Museum of Natural History in the early nineteenth century.[486] Other collections, including the holdings of the Museu Sisenando Cenaculano Pacense, suffered similar fates. Nevertheless, parts of the Ajuda Palace collections survived intact in Portugal, including ethnographic materials, which were later to enrich the Colonial Museum, the Museum of the Academy of Sciences and the Natural History Museum at the University of Coimbra.

The important Ferreira collection of ethnographic objects, made between 1783 and 1792 from "Pará, Rio Negro, Mato Grasso and Cuyabá," was divided between Coimbra and the Ajuda Palace Museum (later the Academy of Sciences, Lisbon).[487] Arriving in Coimbra in 1806, the Ferreira collection marked the foundation of the university's ethnographic holdings.[488] The University of Coimbra (founded 1290) played a significant role in the Portuguese Enlightenment. Under the educational reforms of 1772 its curriculum in philosophy was notably transformed. Natural history was introduced and divided into two streams, experimental physics and theoretical and practical chemistry, which the university believed would help increase understanding of the natural world. Observation and experimentation became core to teaching and research, with practical skills and techniques honed in the institution's laboratories and museum.[489] According to the university's statutes:

> It is clear that nothing can contribute more to the advance of Natural History than the continual view of the objects, that it comprehends, that produce ideas filled more with strength and truth than all the most precise descriptions and most perfect figures. It is necessary to establish with all due dignity the Study of Nature at the centre of the University and create a Collection of objects that belong to all three of Nature's Kingdoms.[490]

To achieve the education model central to Enlightenment knowledge, Europe's first chemistry laboratory was built, an observatory was constructed and the collections that would provide primary instruction in botany, zoology, geology, mineralogy and, later, anthropology, were assembled in the new Natural History Museum established in 1772.

The end of this period of enlightenment and growth was marked by economic and social crises and widespread institutional dissolution. The Peninsular War ravaged Portugal, claiming up to half a million lives and destroying many of its institutions. In 1836 the dissolution of the Ajuda Palace Museum forced Queen Maria II (reign 1834–53) to transfer its administration, along with that of the botanical garden, to the Royal Academy of Sciences.[491] According to comments made by Émile Cartailhac, a French archaeologist and anthropologist who visited the academy's museum in 1880, its anticipated reform had fallen short of expectations:

> The Royal Academy has objects that one would search in vain for outside the specialist Museums of Leiden, Copenhagen and London; ethnographic treasures that Paris, Berlin, Rome would envy and pay dearly for! And these axes with stone hafts, from South Africa, Oceania and America, these North American masks, Brazilian figurines, these souvenirs from all the Portuguese colonies lie higgledy-piggledy in the dust.[492]

Coimbra fared little better. When King Pedro V (reign 1853–61), a keen naturalist, visited the university's Natural History Museum on two occasions in 1852 before his investiture, he was also notably unimpressed.[493] Yet by the end of the century the museum's fortune had been handsomely reversed.

The regrowth of Portuguese public museums was intimately connected to the rise of liberalism and the appreciation of their educational potential. The period from 1850 to 1940 saw the emergence of new museums and the growth of collections. This was encouraged from the middle of the nineteenth century by government directives requesting that medical doctors and other colonial administrators assist in collecting scientific specimens.[494] When anthropology, human paleontology and prehistoric archaeology were introduced into Coimbra's curriculum in 1885, the new course was firmly centred on the university's museum and laboratory facilities. In 1886–87, a fourth section of the museum dedicated to anthropology was added, under the directorship of Bernardino Machado, the first professor of anthropology at Coimbra.[495] A new relevance was imbued into the teaching of anthropology because of its perceived usefulness in colonial administration. By the end of the nineteenth century, two new universities had been founded in Lisbon and Porto, and in acknowledgement of the teaching and practical benefits of scientific collections, a new Museu Etnológico was established in 1906 at the University of Porto. In the academic year 1912–13 Coimbra offered a new course in colonial ethnography, a development soon emulated by the Geographical Society of Lisbon.

Coimbra's call to colonial administrators to assist in increasing the size and scope of its ethnographic holdings was rewarded by two important gifts. The first, donated in 1882 by José Alberto H. Cunha Corte-Real, the governor of Macau, consisted of 376 Timorese and Macanese objects; the second was presented by Alfredo Pereira de Melo, the governor of the Angolan city of Benguela.[496] In 1896 two collections, principally comprising weapons from Angola and Guinea, were purchased from António E. Ferreira de Mesquita. The following year, the museum bought Alberto Correia's Angolan collection, numbering 517 objects, which had previously been exhibited in Porto's 1895 *Exposição Insular e Colonial* (National and Colonial Exposition).[497] The José Maria Ernesto Carvalho Rogo collection of Mozambique material was purchased in 1902, and in 1903 the museum acquired Fernando Cabral Moncada's Angolan collection. After the First World War, the pace of collecting, not surprisingly, diminished. Smaller though important Angolan collections were acquired from José Pinto Meira (1916–18), Horácio Menano (1923), Eduardo Gomes Martins Cardoso (1927) and Luis Wittnich Carrisso (1927), director of the university's Institute of Botany. Collections from Mozambique included that of José Francisco Nazarette (1924), and in 1933 two small collections from Angola and Guinea were transferred to Coimbra from the Museu Agricola Colonial in Lisbon.[498]

Unfortunately, Eusébio Tamagnini, who replaced Machado and remained director for more than forty years (1907–50), showed little inclination to continue his predecessor's work, preferring instead to focus on building for the museum what became one of the most extensive and important osteological collections in Europe. Not until 1977—with the diversification of the ethnographic collections that now included Portuguese popular art, other ethnographic items and the collection of faience once owned by Fernando Cabral Moncada—did Coimbra's collections begin to grow again appreciably. African collections continued to trickle in, the most notable of which were two Angolan field collections made by Armando Simões between 1922 and 1935, acquired by the museum in 1979, and another put together by Miguel Neves (1984).[499] In 1984 the museum took responsibility for an important loan collection from the Espírito Santo Mission Society, made by José Martins Vaz from the Woyo people in Cabinda, Angola, which included important carved wooden lids depicting proverbs. The focus on Angola has given Coimbra what Rodrigues de Areia referred to as "the best [collections] at a national level and one of the best worldwide."[500]

Elsewhere, ethnographic collections were made by professional associations such as the Portuguese Association of Civic Architects, established in 1863, and the Geographical Society of Lisbon, founded in 1875. The first of these was committed to the preservation of art and monuments and the second to the utilization of the products and resources from the Portuguese colonies. There were also private collections and museums such as that of César Augusto Gomes Ribeiro, comprising 1,200 ethnographic items, which opened in Coimbra in 1892, only to close seven years later; the Museu Luso in Porto, belonging to Augusto Luso da Silva, a schoolteacher; and the Museu Azuaga, now the property of the municipality of Vila Nova de Gaia.[501] The Museu Allen, a private institution founded by a successful British businessman in Porto in 1838, was purchased by the city in 1850 and reopened to the public two years later as the Museu Portuense. It would be another three decades before the first national museum would be opened in Lisbon. Portugal's museums, despite lively interest in the country's folklore, focused on colonial collections rather than Portuguese popular art until the 1930s, when the government, with the help of a small number of ethnographers like Joaquim de Vasconcellos, Luís Chaves, Vergílio Correia and Sebastião Pessanha, attempted a revaluation of their aesthetic significance and their intellectual and ideological worth.[502]

facing
VICENTE GIL
Two Beatified Bishops, C. 1516
Museu de Évora

LATE MODERN COLLECTIONS

Plans for the Museu Nacional de Belas Artes e Arqueologia (National Museum of Fine Art and Archaeology, later renamed the Museu Nacional de Arte Antiga, the National Museum of Ancient Art), the first of Portugal's national museums, were originally submitted to the government in 1876, but their implementation was delayed until 1884, when the museum was installed in the old Palácio de Alvor-Pombal. The museum was entrusted with five functions:

1. To preserve works of art;
2. To stimulate and develop taste, love of Nation, and the appreciation of its monuments;
3. To identify outstanding monuments that were most important for the construction of a Portuguese history of art;
4. To contribute to the teaching of art and industry, and;
5. To combine the arts with industry and promote their common development.[503]

This perceived reciprocal relationship between art and science, it was believed, would be mutually beneficial to both practices. Art, understood as a "synthesis of sensibilities, sentiments or ideals," and science, which was thought to represent a "synthesis of observation, experience, thought, conception, law," should be mutually complementary.[504] Despite the inclusiveness alluded to in its name, the National Museum of Fine Art and Archaeology focused mainly on medieval and Renaissance religious art. This orientation had grown out of the repercussions of Pombal's expulsion of the Jesuits in 1759 and been reinforced by further appropriation of goods and buildings from different religious orders in 1834, which had enriched the state with large amounts of religious paintings, objects, books and manuscripts. These collections were further increased in 1910 following the liberal overthrow of the monarchy, which led to the expropriation of all royal properties and the acquisition of the material wealth of thirty-one suppressed religious orders. Many of these holdings had been stored in deleterious conditions in the ex-convent of São Francisco da Cidade. In 1844 the Portuguese term "museu," far from associated with an institution committed to the care, research or public display of its collections, was more often used to refer to a warehouse for paintings, sculptures or natural history specimens.[505]

Part of the collection that would become the Museu Nacional de Belas Artes e Arqueologia was exhibited in 1859 and again in the 1882 *Retrospective Exhibition of Portuguese and Spanish Ornamental Arts*, both of which drew enthusiastic responses. The opening of the new museum in 1884, however, was a disappointment. António Tomás Fonseca and his curator, Manuel de Macedo, had hung the paintings according to chronology rather than national schools. After Fonseca's death in 1894, his successor, António José Nunes, had the galleries rehung by school, but because he increased the number of paintings on display by including inferior works, criticism was redirected to his lack of connoisseurship. The museum's third director, Carlos Reis, did nothing to correct the criticisms, and it was not until 1911, after the modern collections had been rehoused in a new museum, Museu Nacional de Arte Contemporânea, that the old galleries were again reorganized.

Under the dynamic directorship of José de Figueiredo, the newly named Museu Nacional de Arte Antiga redisplayed the works, with the exception of the Portuguese Primitivist School, according to chronology. The first gallery was

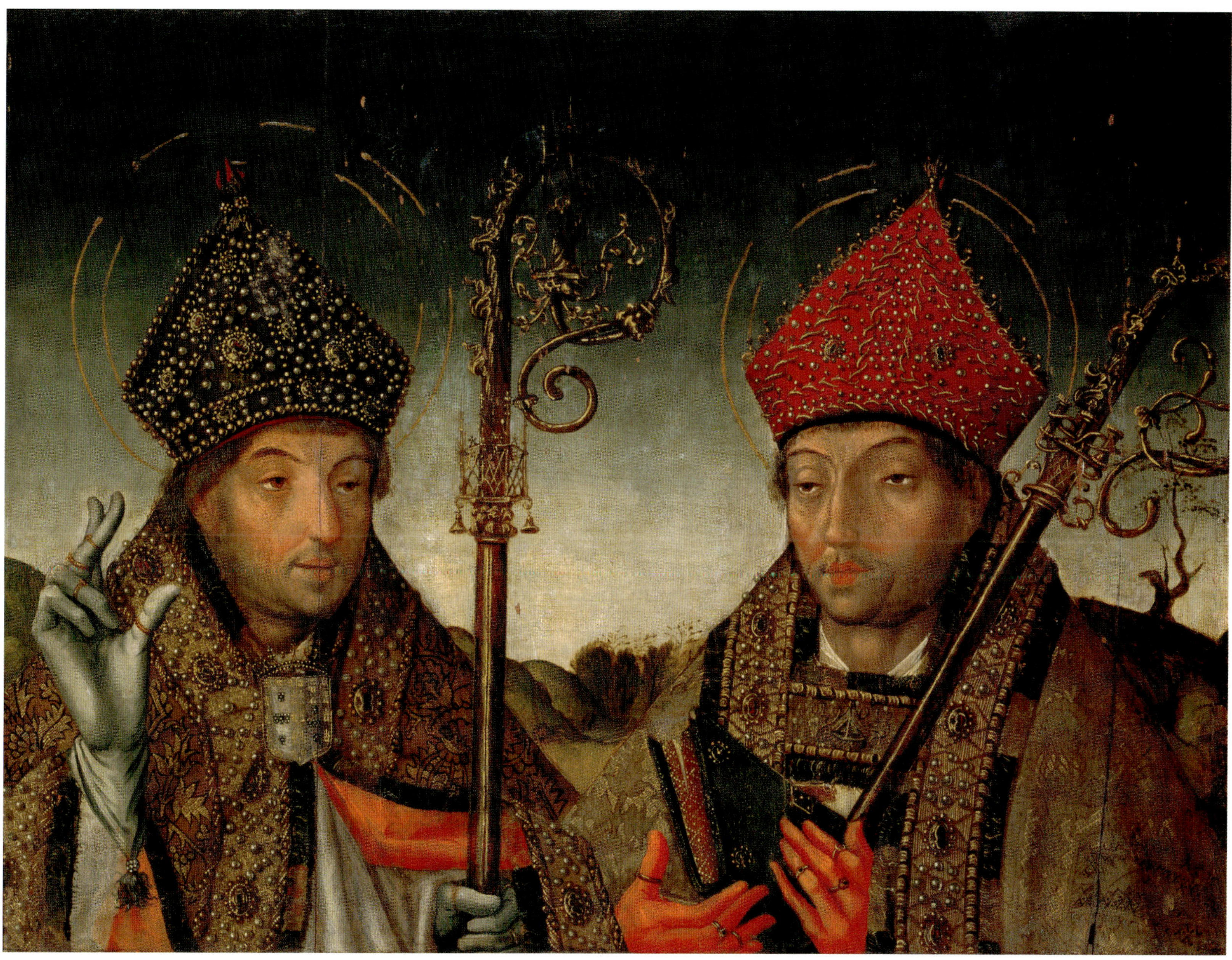

reserved for the then recently conserved *Saint Vincent Panels*, which Figueiredo had identified as being the work of the great fifteenth-century court painter Nuno Gonçalves. The panels, Figueiredo argued, included portraits of many of the most important figures associated with the Discoveries, thereby inscribing them a transcendental national significance that linked the present to the past age of Portuguese power and grandeur. By fronting the gallery with this extraordinary work, Figueiredo made a compelling case on technical and aesthetic grounds for the existence of a distinctive fifteenth-century Portuguese school of painting. Successive galleries that followed on from the Portuguese Primitivist School contained early sixteenth-century Manueline works, divided between regional groupings focused on Évora (south), Viseu (north) and Lisbon (centre), which added to the tight focus on the aesthetic achievements of the works of Portuguese artists active during the nation's Golden Age.

The same cohesive Lusocentric exhibitionary strategy was continued in the three major exhibitions of Portuguese art organized after the 1926 military coup—in Seville (1929), Paris (1937) and London (1955). Figueiredo was replaced as

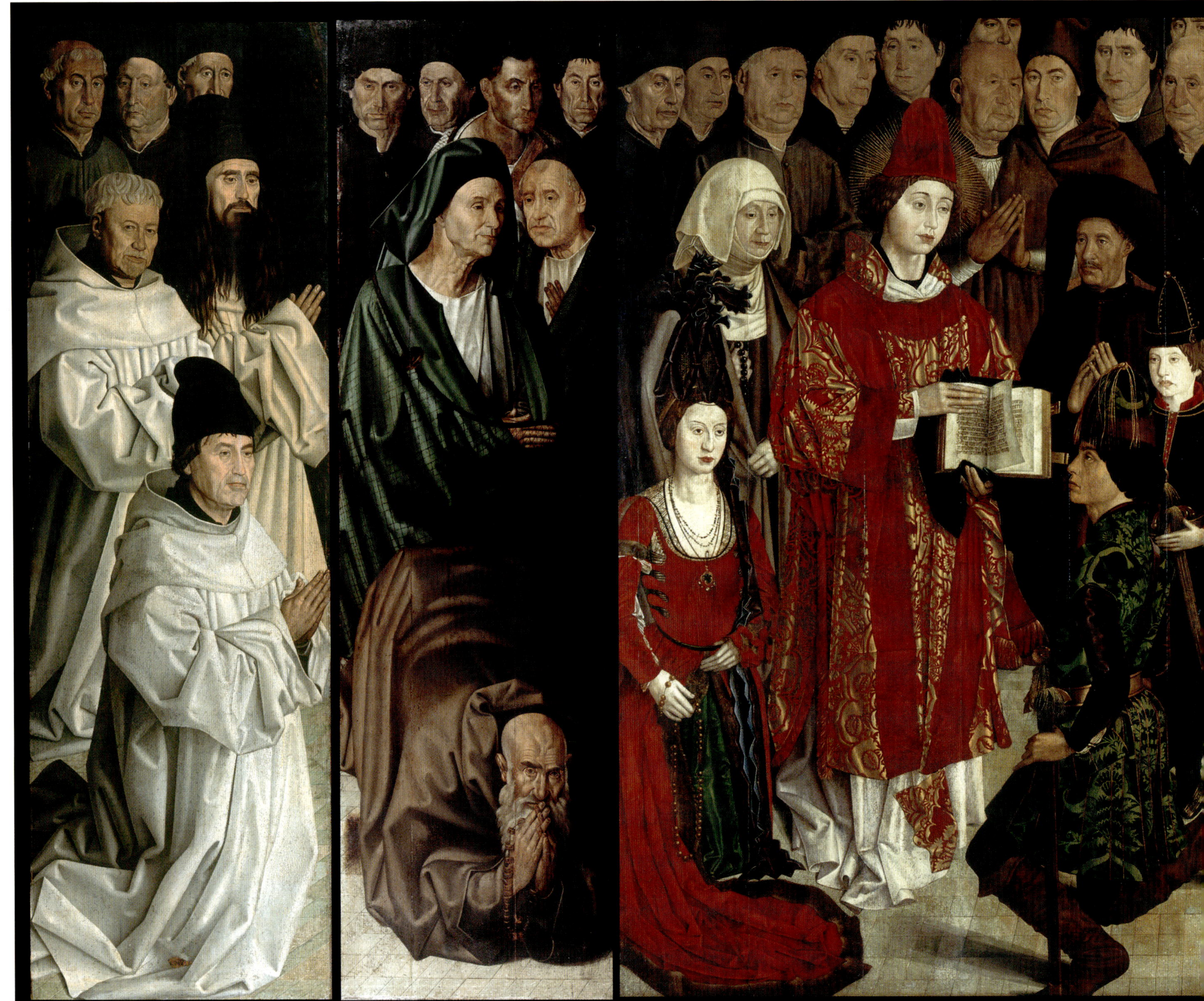

NUNO GONÇALVES
Saint Vincent Panels, C. 1450–90
Museu Nacional de Arte Antiga
Consisting of six panels thought to illustrate leading figures of Portugal's Golden Age, the work is considered to be the most important expression of Portuguese Primitivist art. Originally it belonged to the church of São Vicente de Fora, Lisbon.

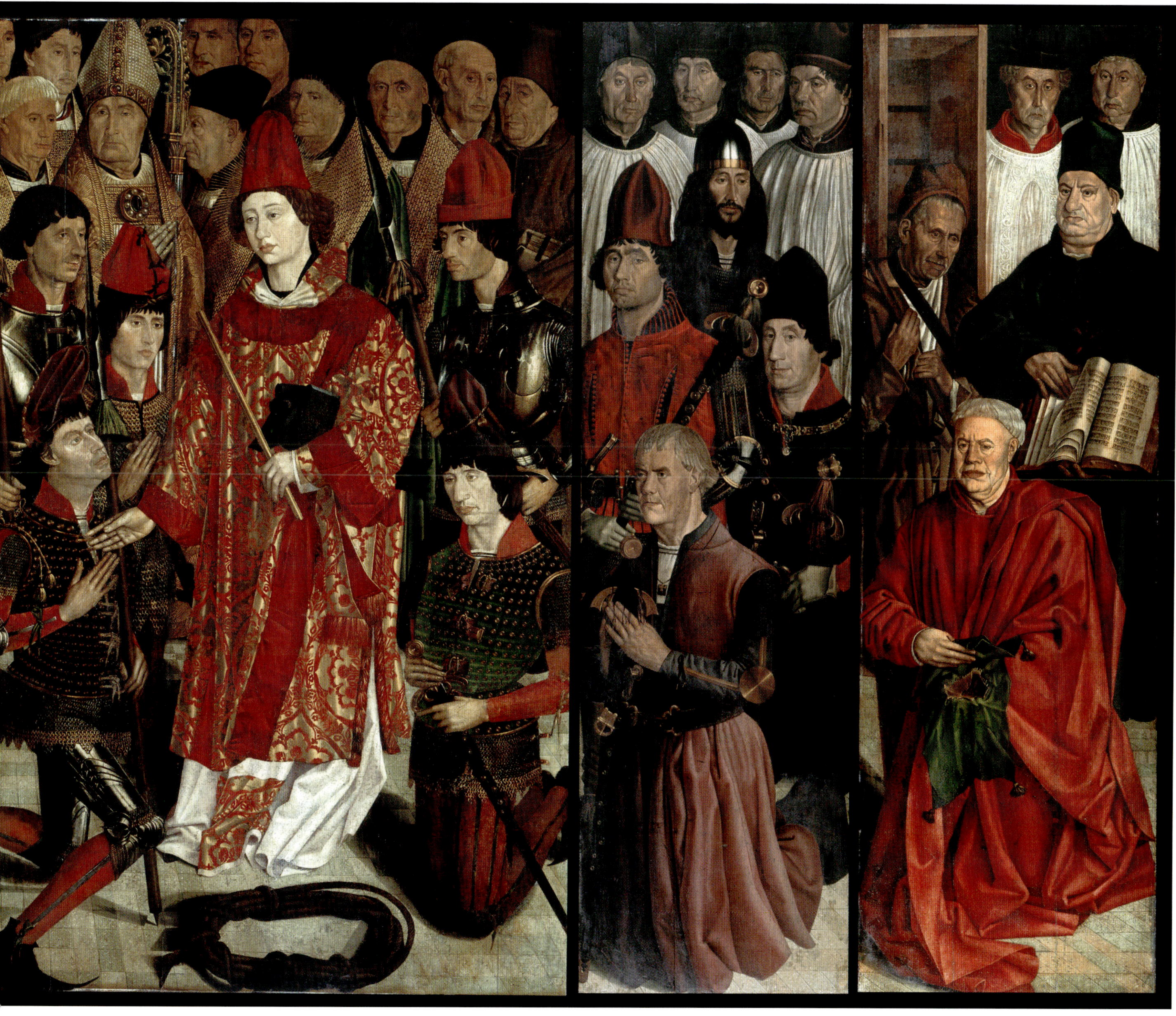

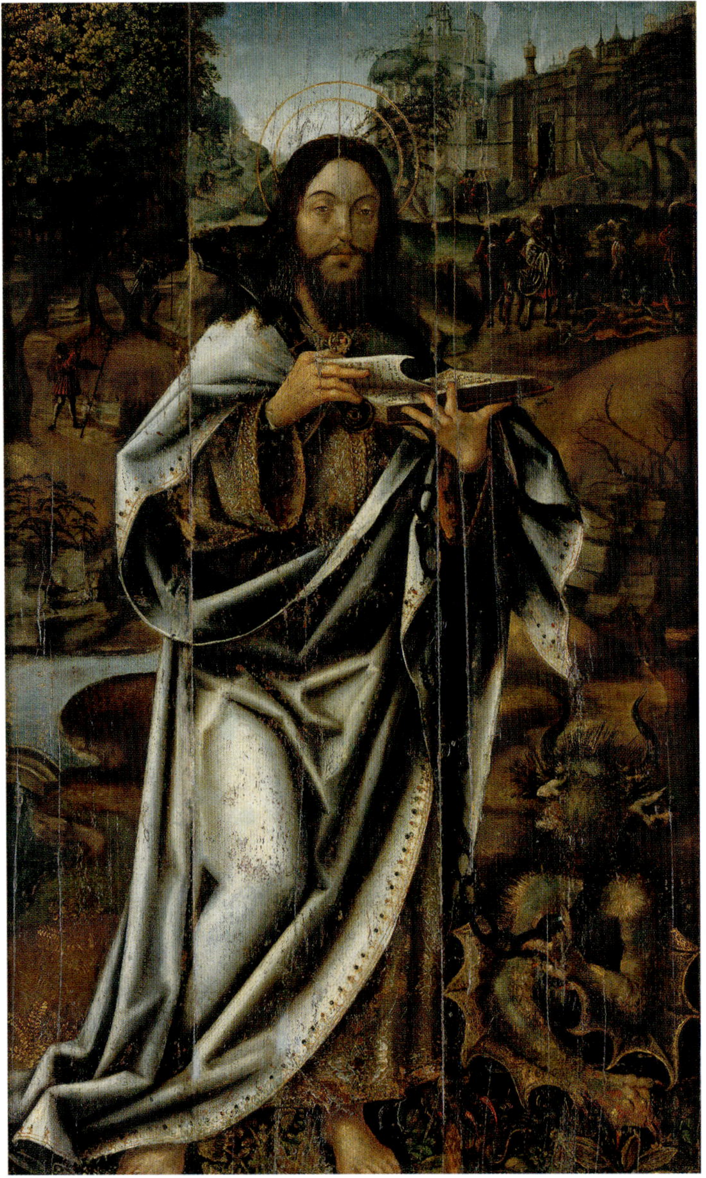

museum director in 1938 by João Couto, under whom the gallery nearly doubled in size. The paintings were reorganized again, primarily by school, though within that scheme they were also arranged chronologically. Portuguese art was divided from other collections and presented in the new annex, thereby enhancing its privileged position within the museum.

The idea of the Lusitanian spirit was inherent to the organization of collections in museums and galleries and their deployment in exhibitions and spectacles. The Portuguese Pavilion curated by Figueiredo for the 1929 Ibero-American Exhibition was designed as a sumptuous Lusitanian sanctuary that included only the finest and most revered Primitivist works: the six *Saint Vincent Panels*, arranged as two triptychs on facing walls, interspersed with tapestries depicting the military conquest of Arzila and Tangier. In the centre of the room stood the *Belém Monstrance* on an Indo-Portuguese table surrounded by the most exquisite fifteenth-century portrait paintings in Portuguese collections. So effective, it was thought, was the aesthetic effect of the arrangement in its conveyance of the essence of the nation that the design was reproduced in the gallery of the Museu Nacional de Arte Antiga and again in the 1931 exhibition of Portuguese art at the Jeu de Paume, Paris.[506] The repetition of the exhibition design, used in the installation of the Portuguese Primitivist works, was intended to express a highly attenuated embodiment of the national spirit prior to the nation's annexation by Spain. In the catalogue to the Paris exhibition the annexation was identified as the catalyst that accelerated the nation's fall and decadence.[507]

The crowning spectacle of the celebration of the Portuguese Primitivists during the time of the Estado Novo took place in 1940. As part of the celebrations commemorating the *Exhibition of the Portuguese World*, the Museu Nacional de Arte Antiga brought together 340 works from more than 600 Primitivist paintings that had been identified in collections throughout the country. These works, from the period 1450–1550, provided the definitive exhibition that established the school's distinctiveness.[508] In his inauguration speech, the then director of the museum, Reynaldo dos Santos, confirmed the school's uniqueness and identified the works as "one of the sources of the sensibility of the Portuguese soul."[509] Santos went on to curate an even more ambitious survey exhibition at London's Royal Academy from 1955 to 1956, *One Thousand Years of Portuguese Art* (800–1800). Through Salazar's

facing
VICENTE GIL
São Bartolomeu, C. 1516
Museu Nacional de Machado de Castro

personal intervention, Santos was able to choose at will the treasures he wanted from both public and private collections, enabling him to assemble six hundred works for the exhibition. The meta-narrative was again the tangible and visual expression of an essentialized, originary aesthetic that distinguished and identified the continuity of the spirit of the Portuguese people.

ANTHROPOLOGICAL COLLECTIONS

Archaeological and ethnographic material objects—identified by early folklorists, ethnographers and archaeologists as vital sources for documenting and illuminating the presence of the Lusitanian spirit and as useful specimens to advance commerce—won government and private funding ahead of that for the arts. This led to the establishment of two quite distinctive institutions: the Colonial Museum and the Geographical Society of Lisbon.

The Ministry of Overseas Territories established the Colonial Museum in the Lisbon Arsenal in 1870, possibly after amalgamating it with the collections of the former Museu de Produções Colonais (Museum of Colonial Products), which had been planned thirty years earlier.[510] The Colonial Museum's mission was to disseminate information about the resources and products of the Portuguese overseas territories to industry and commerce. It was imagined that assembling, classifying and conserving useful specimens and providing limited weekly access to the public would encourage the exploitation of these overseas resources.[511] This ambitious agenda had been inspired by the work of James Hector of the Council of the Royal Colonial Institute, who had elaborated plans for a similar institution in London.[512] The Geographical Society of Lisbon, established in 1875, had also always intended to create a museum of its own. It too was given space to install its galleries in the Lisbon Arsenal, but did not formally open them until 1884.[513]

The collections of the Colonial Museum had been built through the activities of colonial government personnel, while those of the Geographical Society were established through a network of members, missionaries, explorers, and military and commercial personnel and agents.[514] Friction between the two museums and their mutual interest in the colonies predated their later competitive exhibitions.[515] The Colonial Museum existed for just over two decades before it was dissolved in 1892 and its collections combined with those of the Geographical Society to form a new body, the Museu Colonial e Etnográfico (The Colonial and Ethnographic Museum).[516]

The collections of the Geographical Society rapidly increased during the nineteenth century and first quarter of the twentieth century. This period of growth culminated in 1925 with a series of talks on the colonies sponsored by the society to celebrate its fiftieth anniversary. But space limitations, poor conservation and management issues soon pushed the institution into crisis until, by the 1930s and 1940s, it was forced to deaccession its commercial and industrial products and resources collection.[517] In 1890 Adolfo Coelho convinced the society to also begin collecting Portuguese ethnography. It increased its collecting remit even further to incorporate European ethnography more generally and in 1896 acquired the significant Emil Holub collection, which numbered nearly 800 pieces, 120 of which were from Bosnia and Hungary. These were augmented in 1940, after the closure of the *Exhibition of the Portuguese World*, by thirty-seven sets of ethnographic models.[518]

The second major ethnographic collection in Portugal was that of the Museu Nacional de Belas

Artes e Arqueologia, which since its foundation had shown little interest in advancing its ethnographic mandate. This lacuna in the National Museum's collection led to the establishment of the Museu Etnográfico in 1893. The founding of this institution, which embraced both archaeological and contemporary ethnographic objects, was in large part due to the enthusiasm and dedication of the folklorist and archaeologist José Leite de Vasconcellos. Vasconcellos was a close friend of Bernardino Machado, who was not only a keen ethnographer, a disciple of evolutionism and the founder of the country's first anthropology department (at the University of Coimbra), but also minister of public works, commerce and industry and twice president of the Republic.

Through his political offices Machado was able to support the kind of museological institution that Vasconcellos wanted to establish. With the support of other colonialist anthropologists, including Fonseca Cardoso, Rocha Peixoto and Ricardo Severo,[519] Vasconcellos did not hesitate to extol the political advantages of archaeological and ethnographic research in the search for and formulation of a Portuguese national identity, with its particular Lusitanian, regional and colonial inflections. In his writings on the ethnographic museum, Vasconcellos proposed that its first responsibility should be oriented towards the revitalization of a national conscience. By teaching history and inculcating an appreciation of culture, the museum would ensure visitors better appreciated and valued the uniqueness of their own history and culture above those of other nations. Adolfo Coelho, who presided over the commission entrusted to organize the country's first ethnographic exhibition in 1896, expressed a similar position.[520] For Coelho, ethnography's objective was to "deepen knowledge about the Portuguese people" and "awaken human and patriotic interest in our popular classes and develop a reverential sentiment for the sanctity of the nation, the family and work."[521]

Private investors in 1898 organized a popular fair at the site now occupied by the monument to Pombal in Lisbon. The fair displayed various non-Western artifacts and included some eclectic architectural features, such as an Indian pavilion in the shape of an elephant, a Chinese pavilion akin to a pineapple, a theatre, a circus and kiosks selling refreshments and a diverse range of industrial products.[522]

There were more serious aspirations and proposals to found archaeological and ethnographic museums in the last decade of the nineteenth century, but none were ever realized. Estácio da Viega, for example, proposed that an organization for the supervision of art and archaeological patrimony be established under the Ministry of Public Instruction and Fine Arts. Allied to this would be a central museum in Lisbon together with one in each of the country's provinces, all of which would collect ethnographic material. Albino Lopo in 1896 worked on plans for the establishment of an archaeology museum in the northern city of Bragança, the provincial capital of Trás-os-Montes.[523]

The late nineteenth and early twentieth centuries also witnessed a startling growth and interest in folklore studies led by passionate and determined researchers such as Vasconcellos, Machado, Braga, Coelho, Pedroso and Peixoto, who carefully searched for old texts, collected songs and legends and described rituals to help identify surviving remnants of Portugal's ancient past to better map continuities in the expression of the Lusitanian spirit. A similar fascination with the essentialized racial identity of the country was later disclosed by ethnographers like Jorge Dias and

Viega de Oliveira, who focused their research on locating organizational survivals in social structure, political systems and pastoral economy, as well as the ancient technologies still extant in 1930s' and 1950s' rural life. Another group of ethnographers, including Luís Chaves, Vergílio Correia and Sebastião Pessanha, constructed an idealized and general aesthetic sensibility of rural visual culture, "transforming rustic art into icons of national identity"[524] and rebutting the negative characteristics given it by earlier investigators like Braga and Peixoto.[525]

The work of these two generations of ethnographers fortified and enriched the purified evolution of the racialized spirit that first Republican, and later Estado Novo, ideologues identified with the nation.[526] António Ferro, Salazar's minister of national propaganda, saw in popular art and culture Portugal's profound spiritual sovereignty and uniqueness. Popular art, for Ferro, was "a portrait of the soul of a people that wants to renounce neither their grace nor character."[527] The identification of a guiding spiritual evolutionary genius constituted the essentialization of the roots of Portuguese identity. Tracing race to a common ancestry, expressed as much in the works of the Portuguese Primitivists as in popular art, did more than just accrue prestige through antiquity—it also used museums and exhibitions to blend history and ideology to authenticate state ideology and the political apparatus itself.[528] Popular art was regarded not only as a remnant of the past, but, through its live presentation in museums and exhibitions, as an exaltation of the moment.[529] As in Portuguese art historical discourse, the racial ancestors of the present-day Portuguese people were said to be the Lusitanians, who were attributed the uniqueness of spirit that burned in Afonso Henriques and in the other heroes who together had forged the *patria*. This unique Lusitanian spirit, that apparently survived and persisted, was integrated into the political machinations of Salazar's Estado Novo. Vasconcellos had been insistent:

> The people today are still our best artists. They conserve pure traditional forms of our popular pottery, that go back to classical antiquity. They conserve wooden objects and stitching, ornaments fertile in motifs and highly artistic whose origins are lost in even more remote times. They conserve the beautiful lace patterns of the nation. They conserve the secret technical progress, the science of valuable intelligent recipes on important phenomenon, in all innumerable knowledges, that were never written and valued as they deserved. We do not know the value of this perennial source of our national force.[530]

Vasconcellos had divided his ambitious Museu Etnográfico Português into two sections corresponding to archaeology and modern ethnography. Although on its foundation the museum was heavily biased in favour of archaeology, the work of two of its curators, Luís Chaves and Vergílio Correia, had contributed to building an ethnographic collection, including Portuguese popular art, which in 1928 numbered five thousand pieces.[531] In 1897 after the name of the museum was changed to the Museu Etnológico, its collections were rearranged into three sections: prehistoric archaeology and history, ancient and modern anthropology and a comparative section that brought together foreign and national collections to provide models by which the culture of existing races might illuminate archaic society. Such a classification and the uses to which comparisons were put were similar to museological practices elsewhere in Europe. The master narrative nevertheless remained focused on tracing

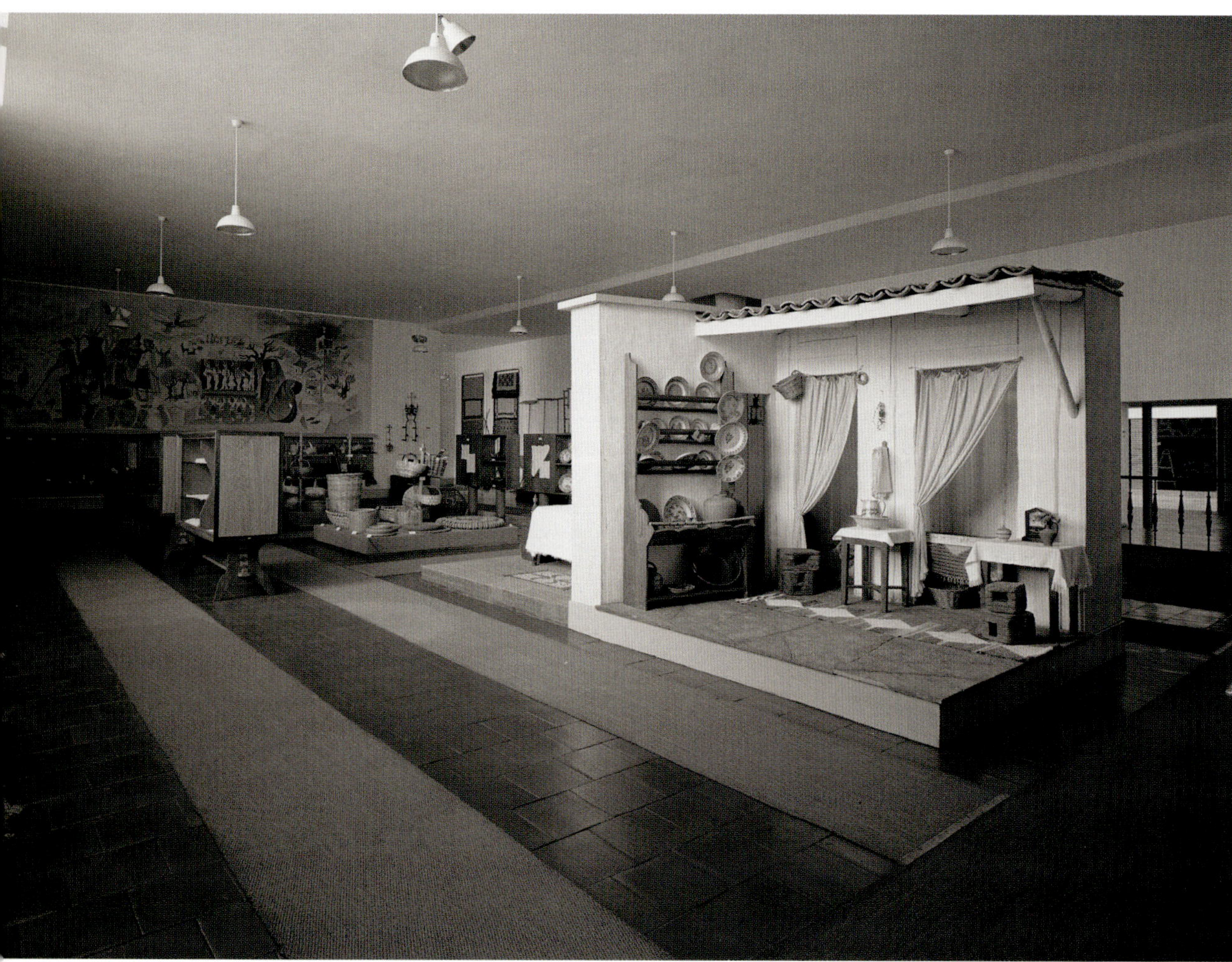

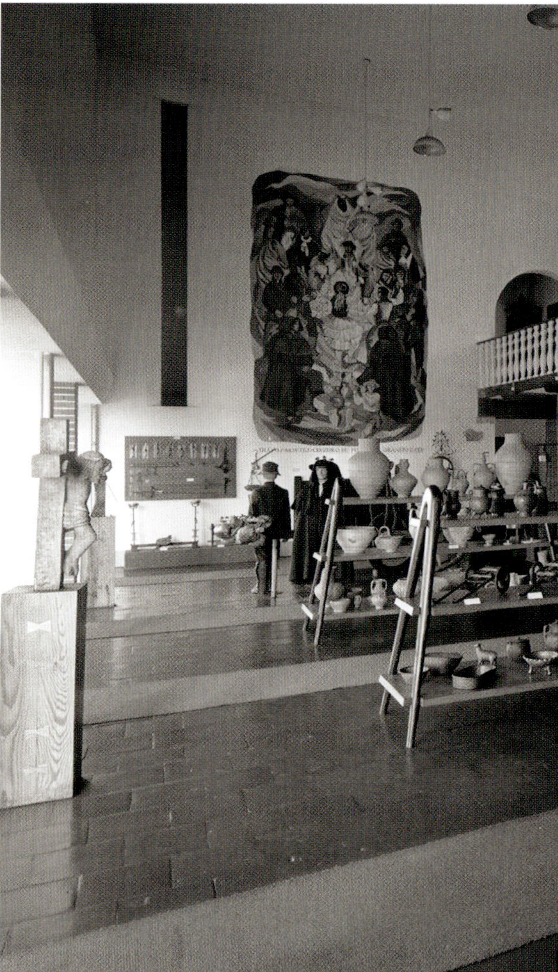

traditional technologies, decoration and beliefs to their neolithic, Roman or pre-Roman or Arabic roots to demonstrate and authenticate the antiquity, vigour and consistency of the Portuguese race. Such a perspective privileged the country's rural population since they were supposedly the ones who had stubbornly clung to archaic cultural and technological practices, like the ceramics of Bisalhães and Barcelos, in which the past could still be seen.

The Museu Etnológico was rehoused in the Jerónimos Monastery in 1903 and reopened three years later. In 1929 Vasconcellos was replaced by Manuel Heleno (1894–1970), a historian who, while keen to demonstrate the antiquity of the race, emphasized archaeological arguments over and above those of ethnography. His disinterest in ethnography led to renewed proposals for an independent, state-sponsored ethnographic museum. Luís Chaves, who worked with Vasconcellos, was a similarly staunch nationalist and proponent of the spiritual unity of the empire. On the occasion of the first national congress on cultural anthropology in 1934, Chaves argued that Portugal had a historical and political obligation to dedicate a museum to its overseas colonies. "The 'collective soul' of the Portuguese people," he insisted, "is exactly tradition, popular culture constructed over a long period of various generations, which is preserved as a cultural phenomenon in constant movement, under the influence of winds from North America, Brazil and the Asian Orient."[532]

Only in 1948 did Portugal create a museum that would focus solely on Portuguese rural ethnography, including that of Madeira and the Azores, which would both fix its profile and address its definitiveness from the material culture of other parts of the world. The Museu de Arte Popular was established under the supervision of the Secretariat of National Propaganda in the last years of António Ferro's leadership. Opened in 1947

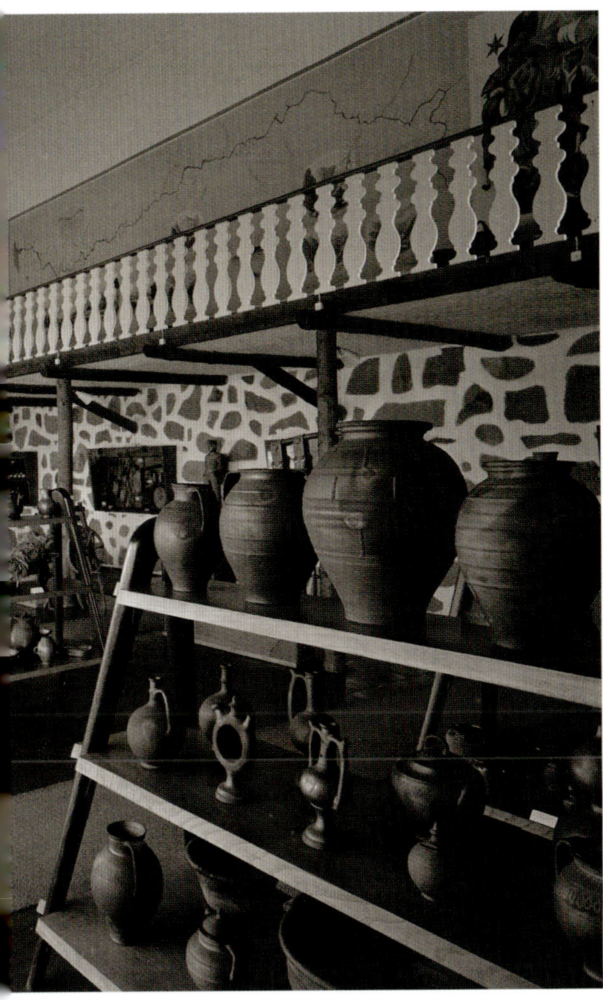

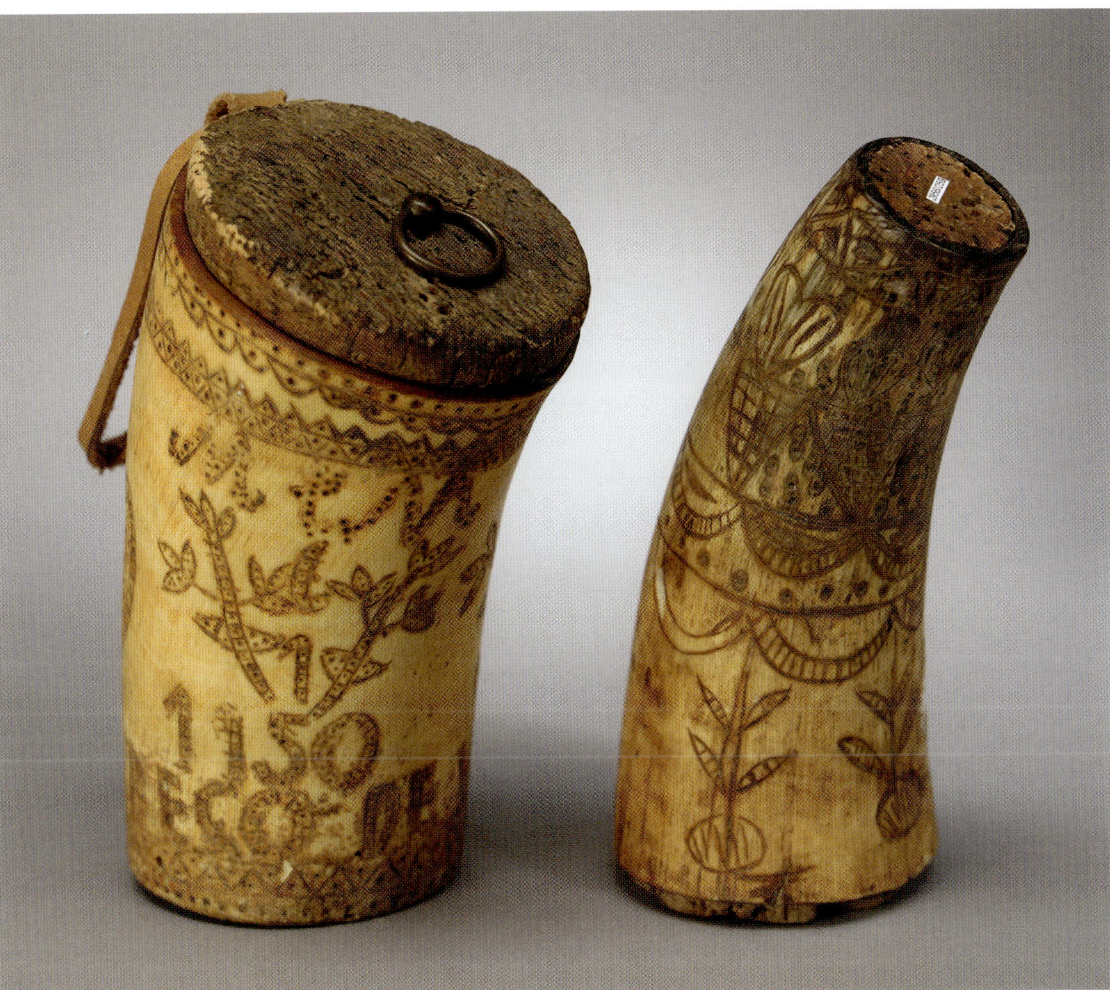

facing, left
The Museum of Popular Art, Alentejo Gallery, 1959.

middle
The Museum of Popular Art, Trás-os-Montes Gallery, 1959.

above
Engraved horns used for carrying foodstuffs: (left) Cabecudo de Vide, 1950; (right) origin unknown, 1898?

under director Jorge Segurado, the Museu de Arte Popular filled its spaces with an array of romanticized images of Portugal's rural cultures. Although heavily influenced by the scenography and exhibitionary strategies employed in the Centro Regional pavilion of the *Exhibition of the Portuguese World*, the museum was arranged not by technologies or material culture but in accordance with José Leite de Vasconcellos's ethnographic classification of Portugal into six cultural regions and ethnic types.[533] The first gallery, devoted to the province of Minho, was dominated by impressive montages, including large assemblages of ceramic dolls in regional costumes—a form of display reproduced in each of the galleries. This first gallery prompted Ferro to describe Minho as "the toybox of Portugal," attributing a kind of infantile characteristic to the region, the people and their culture that had been echoed in earlier exhibitions curated by the Centro Regional pavilion.[534] Exhibits were chosen on the basis of their excessive decoration or miniaturization[535] and included gold and silver filigree jewellery; embroidery; scrimshaw; deeply carved spoons, utensils and furniture; detailed colourful costumes displayed on ceramic dolls; and framed images, *registos*, of saintly figures. The sparkle and colour of the countryside were mixed with material expressions of the ingenuity and technical dexterity of the makers of the handcrafted models, and the supposed naïveté and innocence of the people were conveyed in the faces of dolls, Christmas cribs and the jovial countenances of figures representing the popular saints.

Colourful, naïve, childlike and unspoiled—the life of rural villages expressed a millenarian soul remote from and unconcerned with urban life, what Cardoso Marta described in a different but no less similar context in 1936 as an "epiphany of the marvellous, inventive abilities achieved by our people,"[536] or Augusto Pinto, in the following

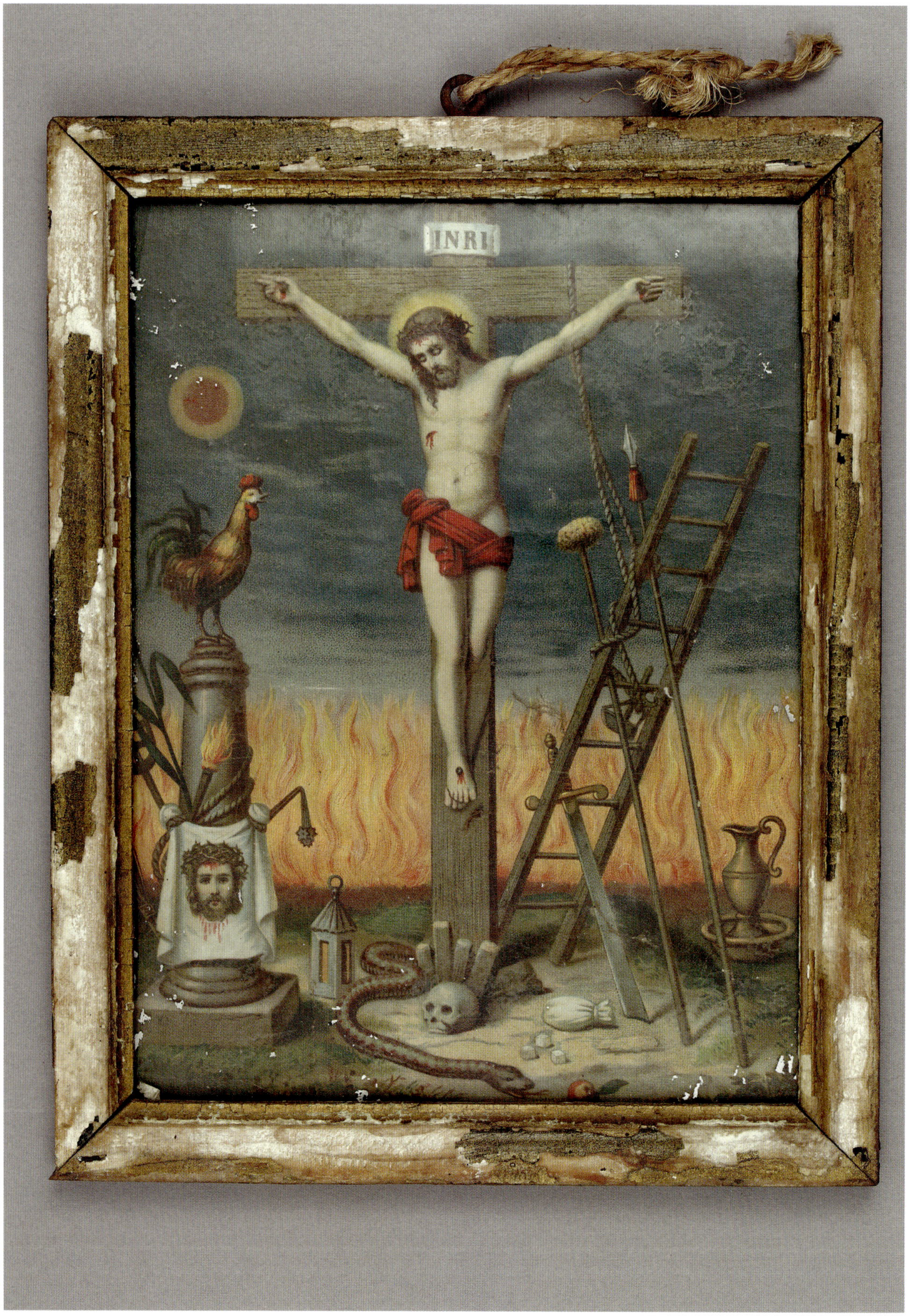

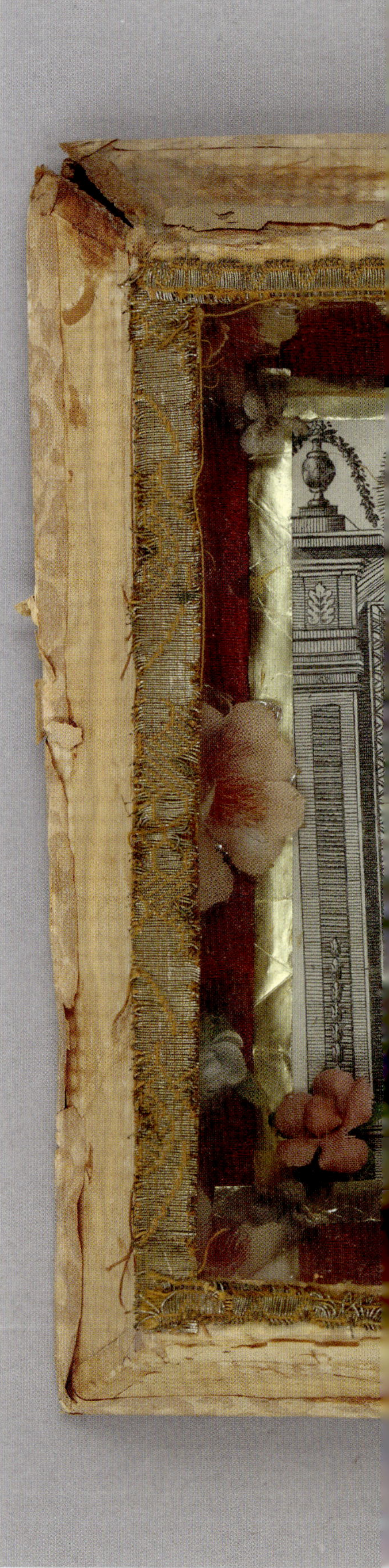

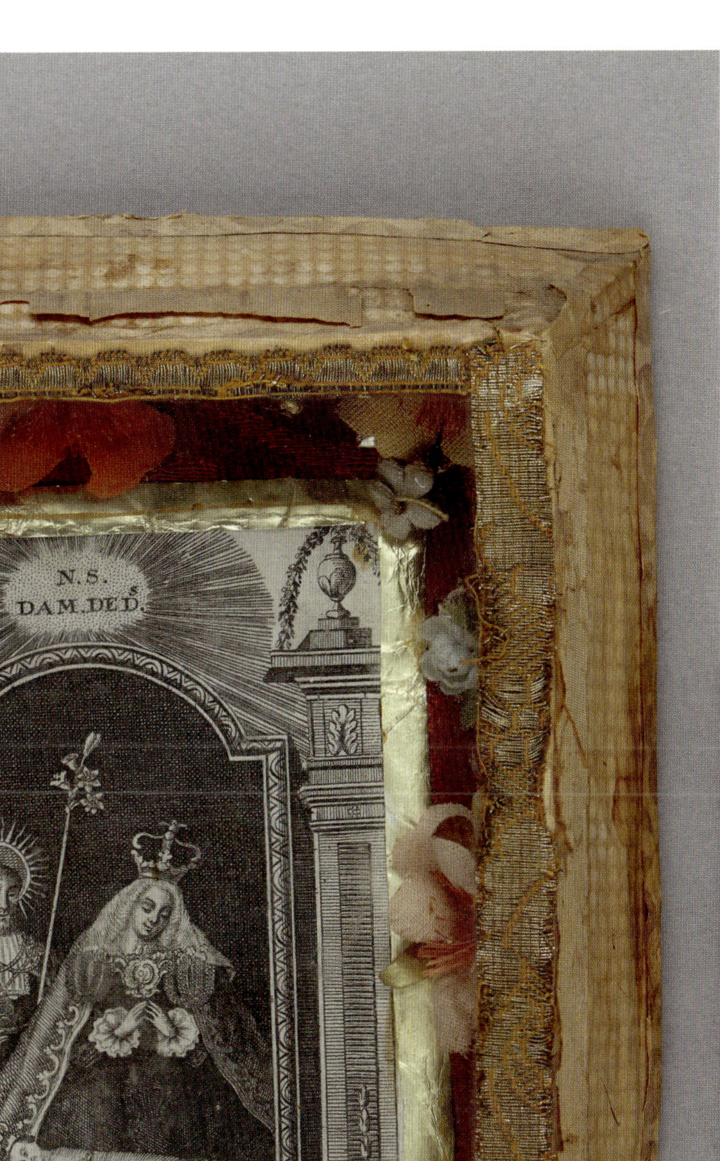

facing
Registo of the Crucifixion, Borba, 1938.

left
Registo of the Holy Family, Borba, c. 1960.

year, referred to as a magical and marvellous world of "precious insignificances."[537] This socially, economically and politically disarticulated and unrealistic image of Salazar's Portugal originated, as the anthropologist Vera Alves has argued, from a perspective that disavowed research and maintained a physical distance from the small settlements and villages the exhibits and their curators pretended to represent. The Museu de Arte Popular built its collections in just a few decades, often through buying at markets, soliciting commissions through rural government agencies, sponsoring the construction of models and acquiring collections from other museums, like the Museu Etnográfico, and from early ethnographers, including Cardoso Marta, Vergílio Correia and Guilherme Felgueiras.[538] To add to the charm of the exhibition design and outstanding collections, the museum commissioned some of Portugal's most accomplished artists, including Tomás de Melo, Carlos Botelho, Manuel Lapa, Eduardo Anahory and Estrela Faria, to depict the cultures characteristic of the country's different provinces on the walls of the various galleries. The museum portrayed a nation of regional contrasts and their social, economic and ceremonial resolutions and reconciliations.[539] This was a vision of a land characterized by an eternal and immutable culture in which the material expressions of toil, hardship and personal insecurity had been transformed into "objects of contemplation and aesthetic pleasure,"[540] a comprehensive materialization of the governmental conception of a folklorized rural Portugal[541] conjured and invoked against the external evils of communism, extreme nationalism, individualism and irreligiosity.

Before the establishment of the Museu de Arte Popular, Chaves had devised an ambitious and comprehensive exhibition plan for a general national ethnological museum, outlining five main display areas. These included a European section, divided between continental mainland (Portugal) and island Europe (Madeira and Azores), and sections dedicated to Africa, especially Morocco; Asia; Oceania, which mainly consisted of Timor; and Brazil.[542] Such a museum, Chaves believed, would map the adventures of the Portuguese and illustrate the story of the dissemination of the Lusitanian spirit over the expanse of the world. Despite his comprehensive purview and determined exhortations, and even ignoring Portugal's position as the third-most important European power in Africa, his proposal was dismissed and the idea not taken up again until 1945.

As the Second World War drew to a close in Europe, the government's Committee for Overseas Research was given responsibility for planning a new museum that would bring together the dispersed and haphazard collections that had grown within the Ministry of Overseas Territories.[543] While various plans were discussed, progress was slow until 1957, when the committee instigated a new organization, the Centro de Estudos Políticos e Sociais (Centre for Political and Social Studies), and established three missions for the study of overseas populations living within Portugal's colonial territories.[544]

This new endeavour coincided with a 1951 law that redefined the colonies as territories within an extended Portuguese nation and granted their peoples the right to representation within the Portuguese Parliament in Lisbon. Despite the lateness of the reforms and the rising racial tensions in Angola and Mozambique, the new research centre was launched under the anthropologist Jorge Dias (1907–73) and his assistants, Margot Dias (1908–2001) and Viegas Guerreiro (1912–97). Regardless of the difficult political conditions, the work undertaken by this small team in Mozambique in 1957 and 1958 gave rise to an impressive set of monographs on the Makonde and a collection of three hundred artifacts, which were exhibited in 1959. This and other smaller collections formed the nucleus of a teaching museum that was inaugurated in 1960 and in 1962 took the name of the Overseas Museum of Ethnology;[545] after several moves it was installed in purpose-built premises in the garden of the Agricultural Museum in Lisbon.[546] From the beginning, Dias envisaged that the museum would focus not only on Portuguese colonial territories but also on other cultures outside the empire as well as the country's rural communities, with a special focus on "Portuguese man."[547]

State support for the acquisition of museum collections increased in the late 1950s and 1960s, at least partly to safeguard the tangible testaments to the spiritual and unique character of the nation's racial origins. As early as 1948 Fernando de Castro Lima claimed,[548] following a now familiar argument instigated by António Ferro, Henrique Galvão and José Leite de Vasconcellos, that

> the folklorist strives to collect oral tradition because the people are a great writer without ever having read a word. It is not enough to archive songs, prayers, tales, stories, divination, but it is also necessary to collect costumes, religious images and objects in popular use. It would be judicious to give great importance to regional museums, which guard all these precious things that demonstrate that the people are also a great artist.... Museums provide live and permanent exhibitions where we can go to find such art and science, [but] which insufficiently document the artistic talent of the people.[549]

From the 1960s, the collections of the Overseas Museum of Ethnology grew much more rapidly than those of any other ethnographic or popular art museum in Portugal. In 1959 it acquired the António de Oliveira collection of 607 items from Angola; in 1960, the Machado Cruz collection of 227 Chokwe artifacts; in 1961, the Françoise and Victor Bandeira collection of 995 pieces from Mali, Cote d'Ivoire, Ghana and Nigeria; in 1963, the Rogado collection of 747 objects from Guinea; and in 1964, 209 pieces from Timor collected by Ruy Cinatti and 283 artifacts brought from Cape Verde by António Carreira. Carreira also participated in five expeditions throughout Africa between 1965 and 1969, returning with 2,761 pieces, while the Bandeiras made another collection in 1964–65 of 738 pieces from the Brazilian Amazon. Other collections came in from different departments within the Ministry of Overseas Territories; a government request was sent to colonial administrators, like similar ones issued previously, to assist in increasing the collections, and further collecting expeditions were sponsored by the Calouste Gulbenkian Foundation (established in 1956). Equal zeal went into acquiring collections from rural Portugal, Madeira and the Azores during the same period.

The museum's early exhibitions, externally staged because of lack of gallery space, included Dias's inspiring *Life and Art of the Makonde* (1959) and another on the West African collection assembled by Victor and Françoise Bandeira, which was displayed at the Superior School of Beaux Arts in Porto before being re-exhibited in Lisbon. The Brazilian embassy and the Calouste Gulbenkian Foundation organized a complementary exhibit of the Bandeiras's Brazilian collection in 1966 and in 1972, while an exhibition of highlights from the museum's collection curated by Dias and Oliveira, *Peoples and Cultures*, opened at the National Gallery of Modern Art in Lisbon. A year after the Carnation Revolution, in 1975 the museum moved to a new purpose-built gallery, but it curated only one further exhibition, *Modernismo e Arte Africana*, before entering a period of crisis that led to its closure until 1985. In 1990 the museum was renamed the Museu Nacional de Etnologia and has since become the country's premier museum of ethnography and Portuguese popular art and culture.

Despite the size of their collections, space limitations and financial difficulties, the Geographical Society of Lisbon and the Overseas Museum of Ethnology were never rationalized to become one institution. As early as 1932 space limitations and lack of collection care resulted in much of the Geographical Society's holdings being returned to storage. In 1934 its curator made a depressing list of the difficulties in adequately displaying the collections, including their poor state of preservation and scarce documentation. As a result of continuing internal concerns and external indifference, the society commissioned its own study on its future sustainability in 1954 and decided to focus solely on foreign ethnographic collections.[550]

REGIONAL AND LOCAL MUSEUMS AND CASAS DO POVO

The number of regional and local museums in Portugal appreciably increased during the first half of the twentieth century until 1965. Growth then levelled out until after the 1974 Carnation Revolution, when they again began to accelerate. By 2010 the Ministry of Culture, a year before its dissolution because of new financial stringencies, was responsible for twenty-nine national museums.

Almost a century earlier, in 1911, the national network of museums had been reorganized into three regional areas with administrative councils in Lisbon, Coimbra and Porto. From 1912 to 1914,

right
The fifteenth-century altars to São Cristóvão and São João Baptista in the Rainha Dona Leonor Museum (Museu Regional de Beja), formerly the convent of Nossa Senhora da Conceição.

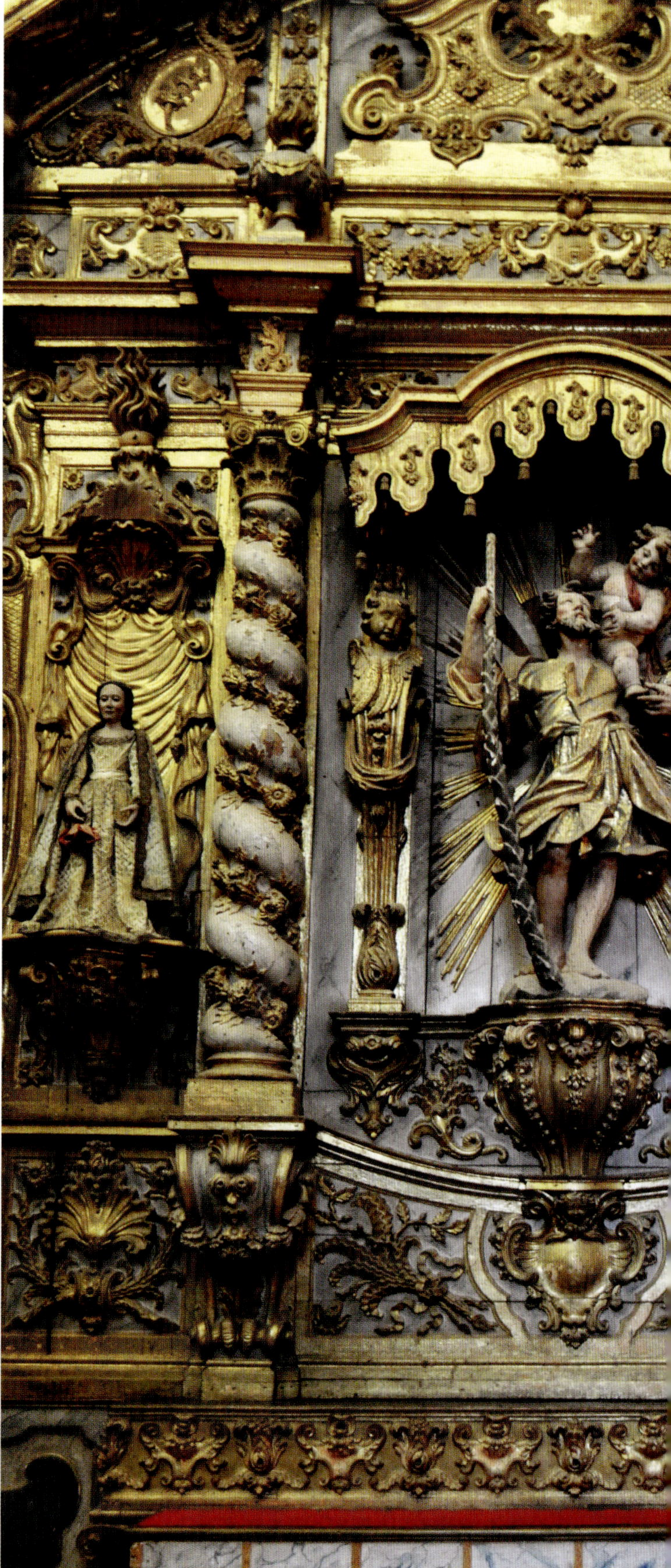

thirteen regional museums designated as museums of art and archaeology were recognized. Later, Salazar abolished the three regional councils, devolved authority to the municipalities and selected six museums to serve as regional centres.[551] The 1932 government paper on museums (*Carta Orgânica dos Museus*) reorganized them as corporate structures and more determinedly linked them to the idea of the philosophy of the spirit. Surprisingly, this form of organizational structure and its attendant philosophy continued to dictate the nature, core values and operations of Portuguese museums until 1986.[552]

In 1948 Portugal had only two national museums, seven regional museums and thirty-three regional collections, administered by municipal, Church and other institutions. From 1933 the domination of the philosophy of the spirit was easily accommodated by the common ideological function that art, archaeology and anthropology were expected to fulfill. Under the Estado Novo the network of museums was administered by the Secretariat of National Propaganda, which, despite claims that it lacked a coherent cultural policy, used museums and galleries as powerful engines in the politicization of culture and the mythologization of the political system.

The network of national museums and regional institutions was supplemented by Casas do Povo, literally "Houses of the People," cultural and educational centres implanted in villages and parishes across the country from 1933 to instill the values and ensure the implementation of the state's social and cultural policy. By 1951 Portugal counted 501 active Casas do Povo, the most inclusive and expansive level of the corporative state that formed a dense network of hubs throughout the country.[553]

From the outset the Casas do Povo were envisioned as corporate bodies made up of community

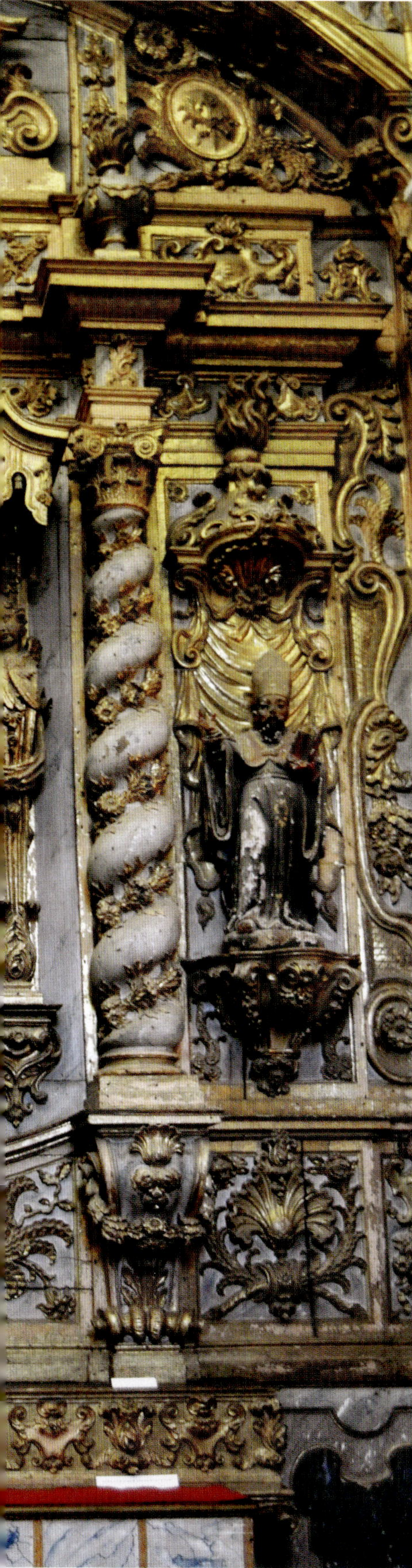

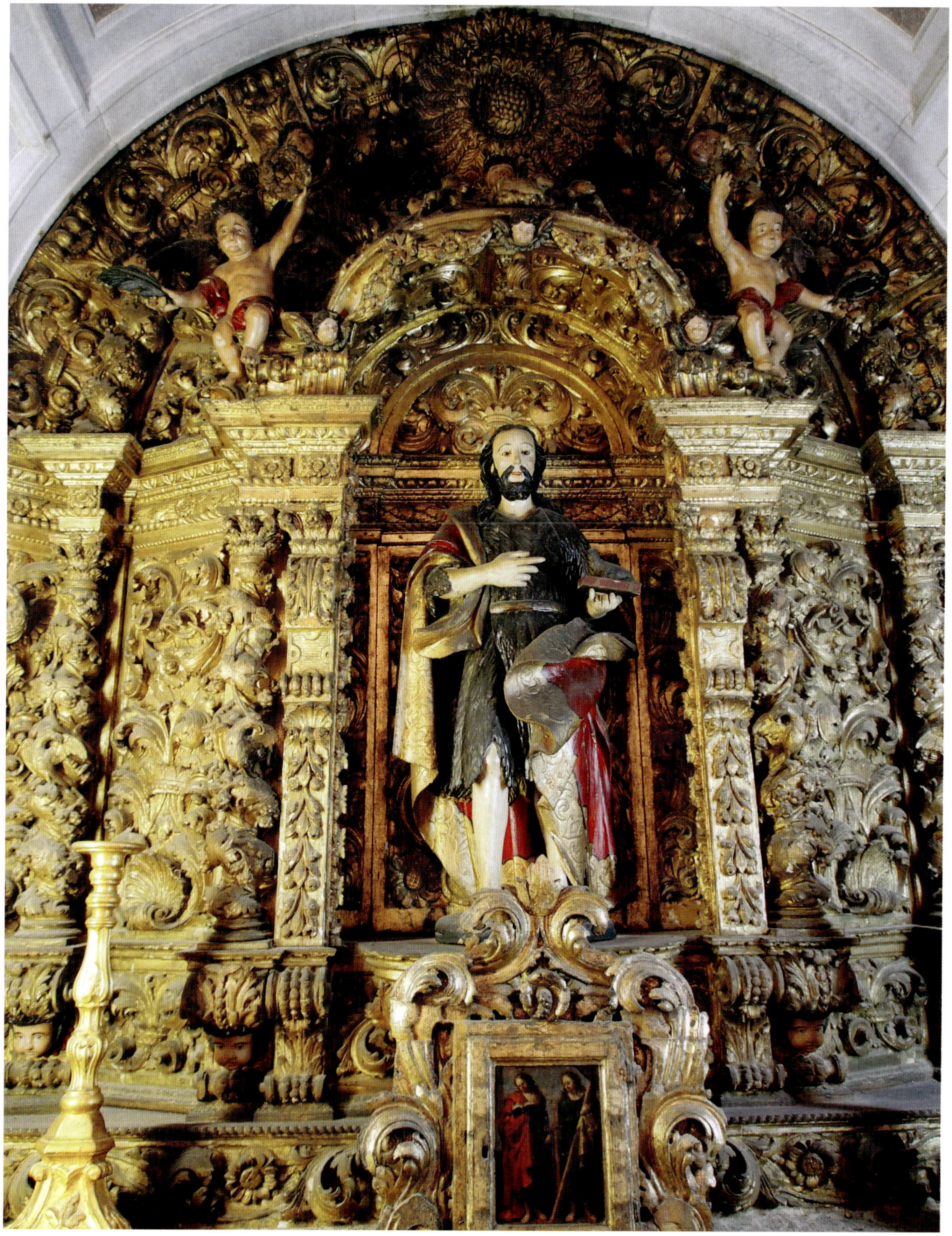

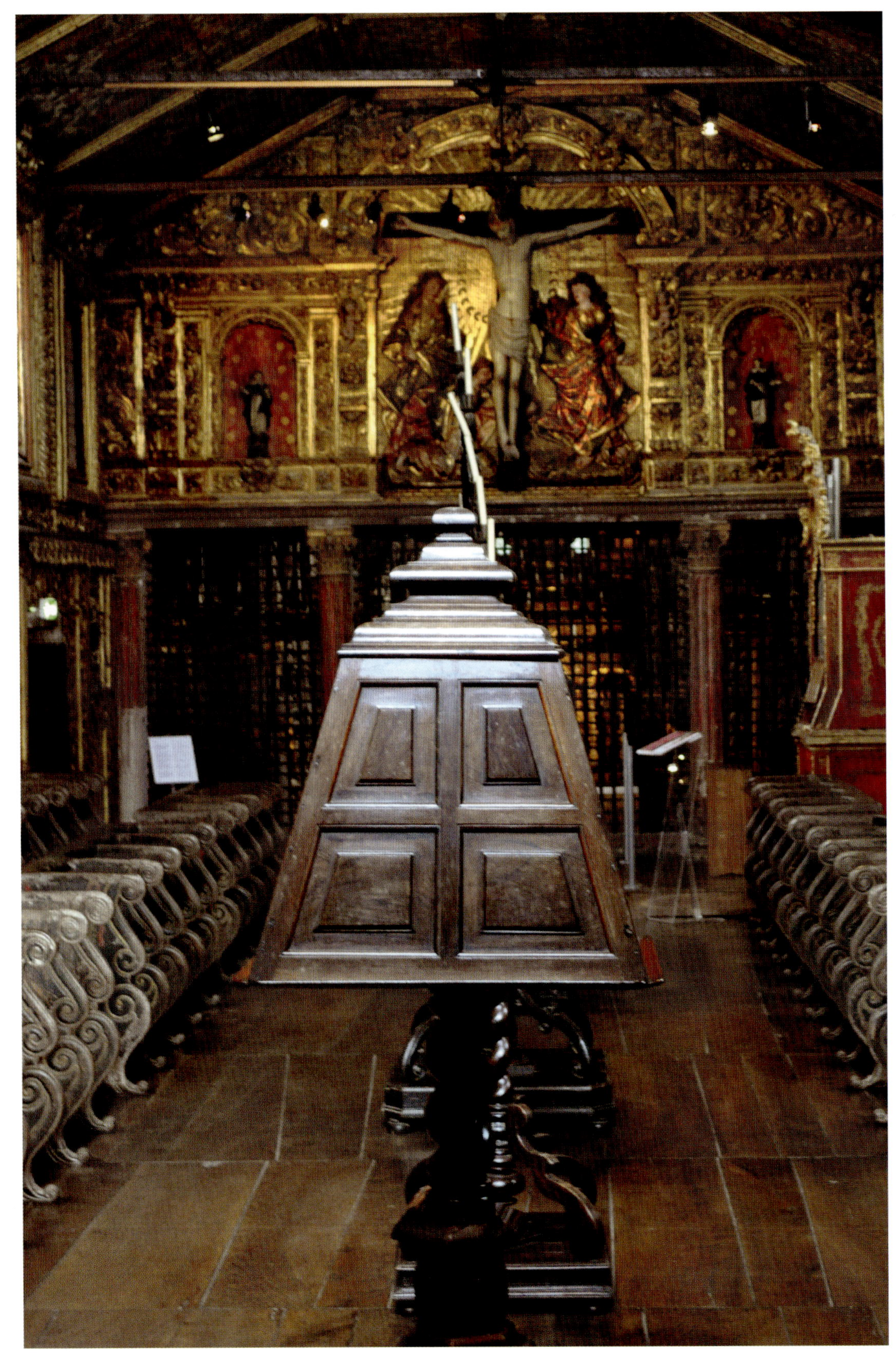

The Santa Joana Museum, Aveiro, formerly the convent of Jesus, built in the fifteenth century.

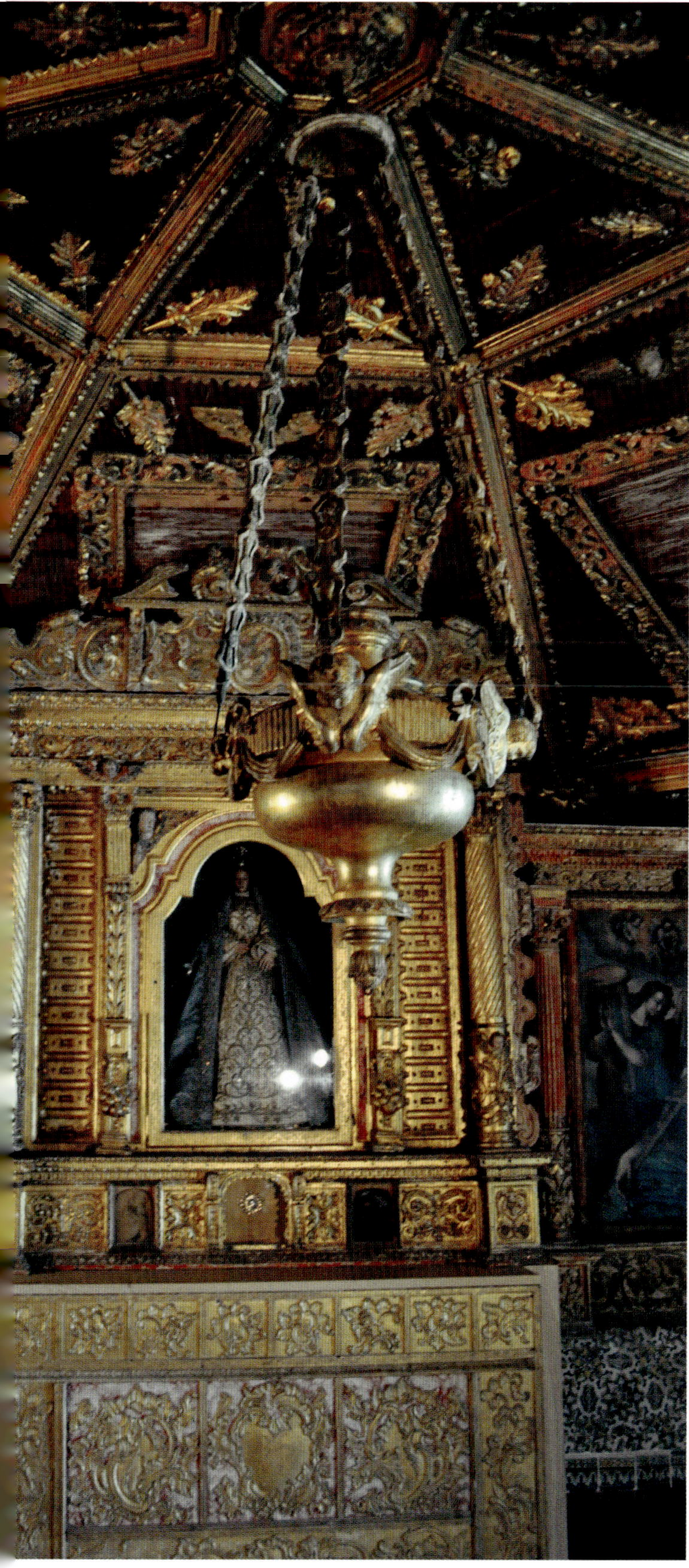

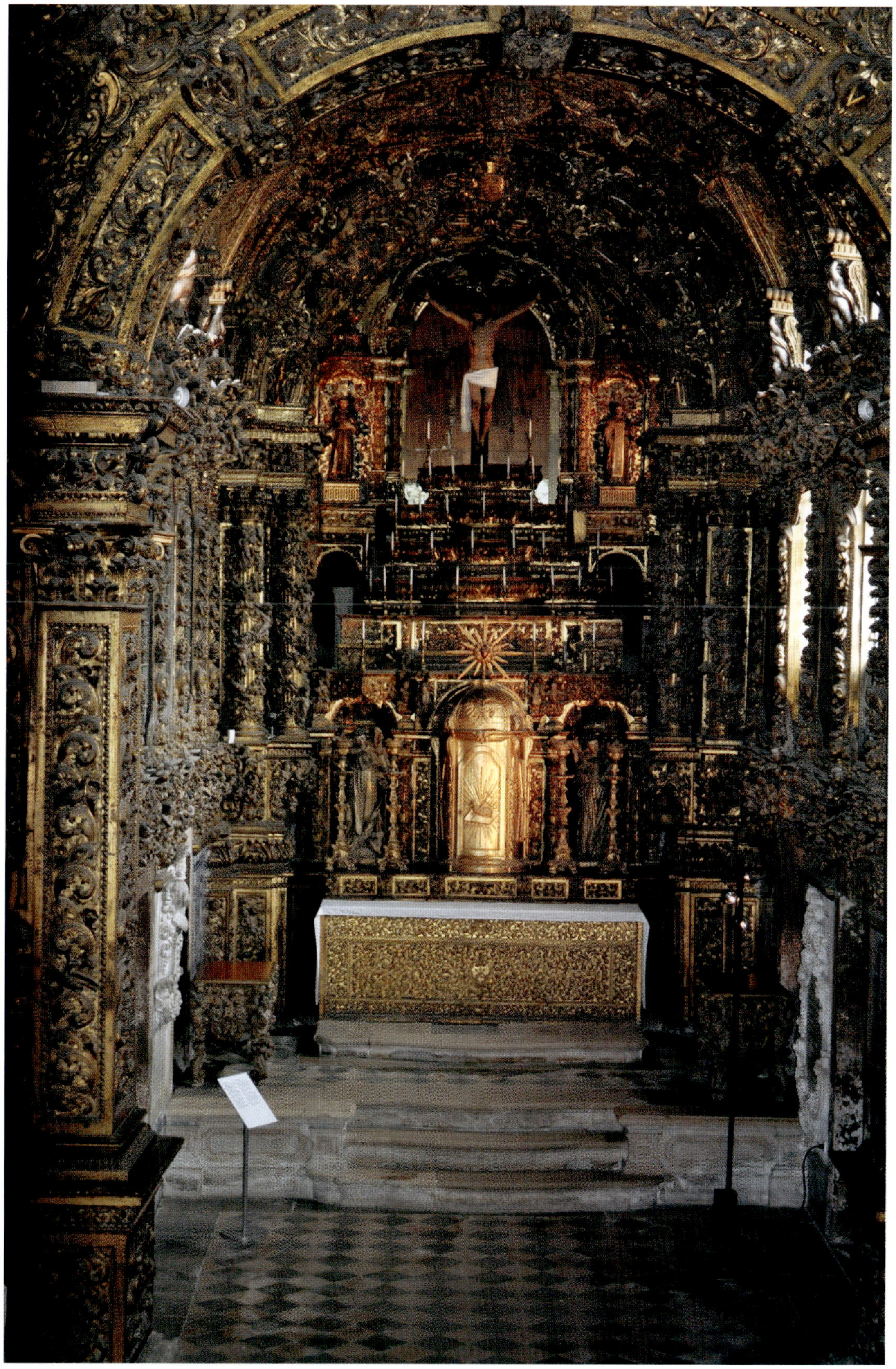

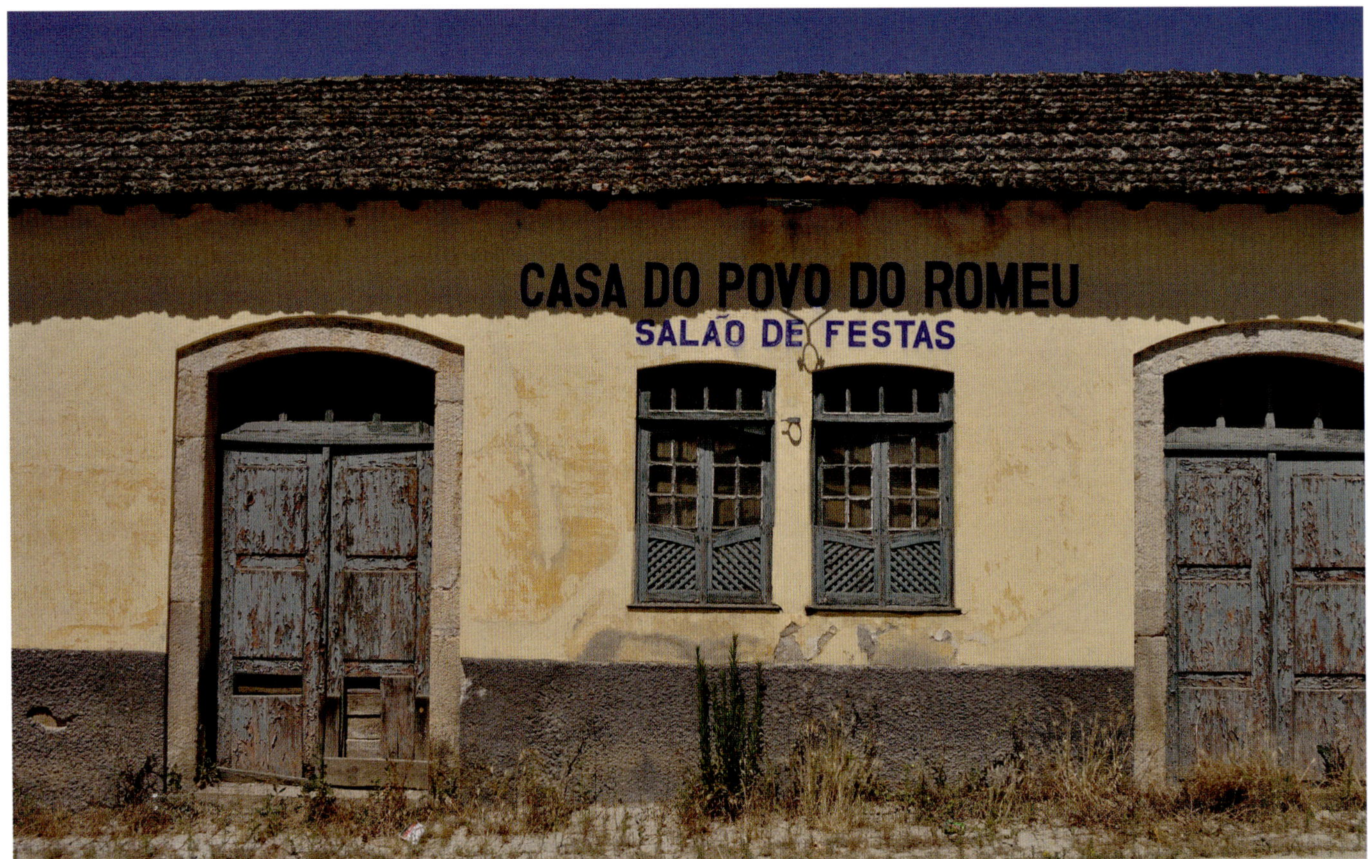

members with a mission to promote adult and child education, sports, games and educational films. Many had small libraries with carefully selected books, and a few had museums as well as sports fields.[554] Through them the Estado Novo purposefully set out to forge a strong character and identity, ensure workers remained active and create citizens entirely devoted to the nation.[555] In pursuit of these ideals the Casas do Povo were charged with the creation of a new aesthetic derived from a pastoral art they extolled as exuberant, polychromatic, rich and vibrant. Every piece encapsulated a poem that expressed the soul of the rural idyll, an exaltation of colour and the picturesque.[556] The Casas do Povo attempted to reformulate taste through competitions, prizes, exhibitions and conferences, but above all they worked ideologically, not only to nourish but to guard and protect the local patrimony from foreign influences.[557]

At times the close ties between three of the principal rural institutions, the Church, schools and Casas do Povo, gave rise to shared projects, such as the preservation of churches and monuments or the rescue of Catholic traditions.[558] Out of a sample of forty-one Casas do Povo operating between 1948 and 1956, Damasceno found ten possessed museums, six had collections but still needed to display them and five had plans to build museums.[559] Ethnography was transformed under Salazar into an official science valued for its ability "to sanction 'superiorization' of a fabricated reality,"[560] and museums became places to celebrate the nation and synthesize and exemplify Portuguese taste.[561] A significant number of ethnographers collaborated with the government from the 1930s to the 1950s,[562] leading Fernando de Castro Lima to call ethnography the most nationalistic of the sciences in Portugal.[563] The museums in the Casas do Povo were designed to encourage awareness of local artistic values, demonstrate ethnic traditions and community industries to local visitors, encourage training in the crafts and help fix an immutable image of community life.[564] They were also considered essential in creating a picturesque image of rural living to attract the development of tourism.[565] This policy also led to the establishment of a network of government inns or *pousadas*, which

facing
One of the few remaining rural Casas do Povo (Houses of the People) built under the dictatorship, in Romeu, Mirandela.

combined modern comforts with Portuguese rustic and folkloric decorative taste, served by staff dressed in the traditional costumes of the region in which they were located.[566]

Not all local museums, such as those attached to the Casas do Povo in Vila Real and Póvoa de Varzim, were sufficiently well ordered, didactically focused or effective to maximize their efficiency as important state apparatuses. Sebastião Pessanha, an ethnographer who contributed to Salazarian cultural policy, lamented that "some of our few specialized museums have fallen into the most shameful abandon and onto the most frightful road to total destruction of the things they have brought together with so much knowledge, work and dedication."[567]

According to Torgal, Mendes and Catroga,[568] this exaltation of rural culture and the revitalization of traditional handicrafts had concrete pragmatic motivations. They allowed the Estado Novo to extol the virtues of the people's natural and spontaneous bonds, creating communities that, from an ideological perspective, stood against the evils of individualism and liberal democratic contractualism. The insularity of Portugal during this period effectively protected a domestic ideology that was propagated through a ubiquitous decentralized museum organization.[569]

In the 1960s new legislation that rationalized museums into specific categories redefined their relations with the state, acknowledged professional subject positions and established a post-graduate qualification in museology. Moreover, in line with international criteria, the Portuguese state also defined the role of museums in terms of their responsibility to conserve, display and interpret collections for public edification. The foundation of museology in Portugal, initially supported both by the International Council of Museums and the Calouste Gulbenkian Foundation, was transferred to the Portuguese Association of Museums in 1965.

This complex and winding history of ethnographic collecting points not to a lack of government policy but to a long-time presupposition that difference was less important than cultural affinities expressed in linguistic and religious commonalities and aesthetics conveyed through decorative art—all Portuguese impositions. When René Pélissier in 1967 expressed his profound disappointment on seeing the small collections that the Overseas Museum of Ethnology had assembled and the few significant collections elsewhere in Portugal, this did not necessarily indicate disinterest but a deliberate avoidance of collecting that was too incommensurate with Portuguese values. Five hundred years of largely ignoring ethnographic collecting and the creation of a related archive had enormous impact in repressing the development of a Portuguese public memory of "otherness."[570]

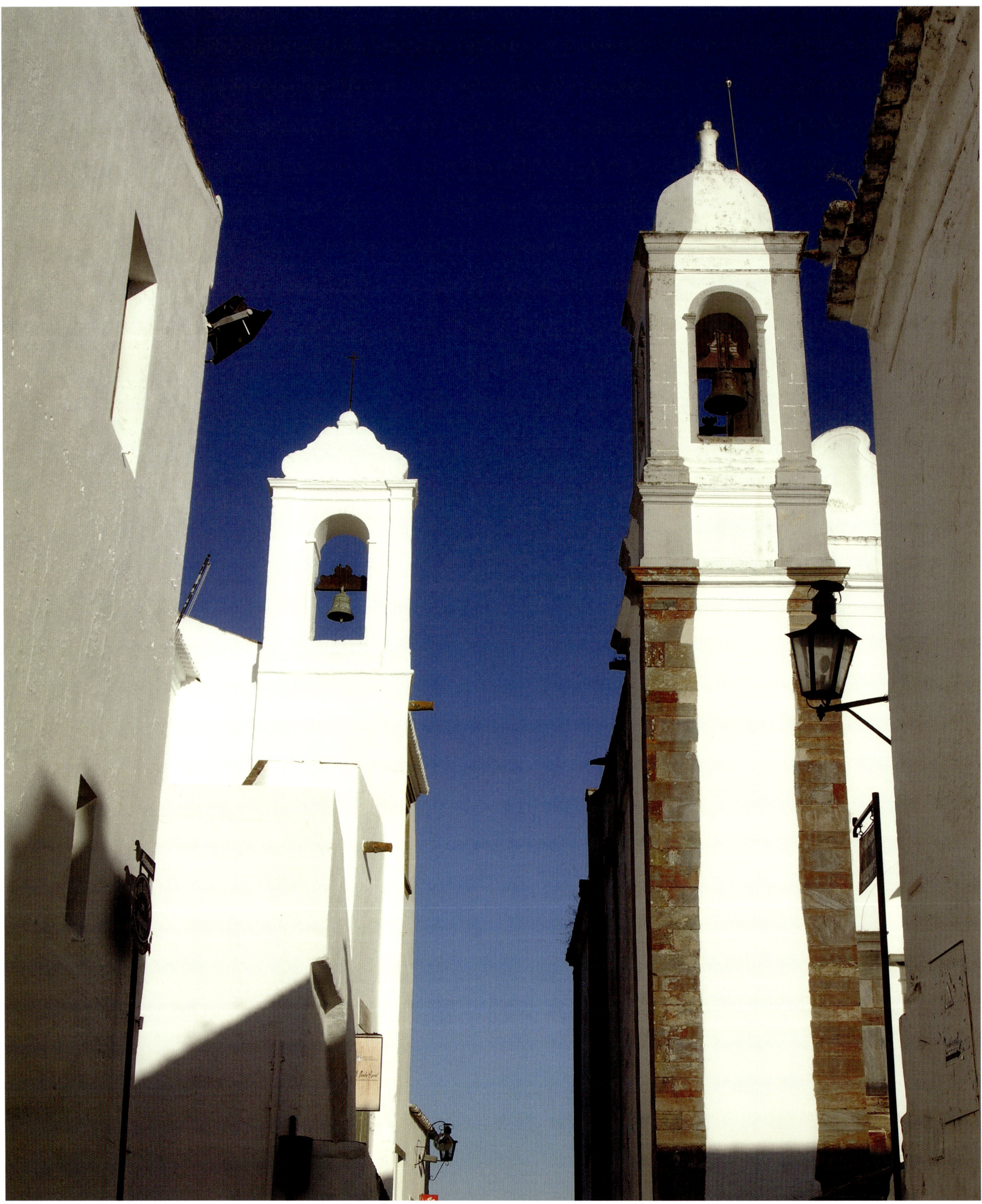

9 The Spectacle of Lusitania

Exhibitions and National Identity

So extensive and fragmented throughout the world is Portugal's territory, so mysterious and diverse is the spirit of this great Atlantic nation, that it becomes very difficult, if not impossible, to quickly grasp the deep meaning and true expression of Portugal.

Introduction, *Catalogue Exposição do Mundo Portugues*, 1940[571]

THE INTELLECTUAL LEGACY that helped shape the Estado Novo's ideologies and part of its policy grew out of the traumatic ferment of Portugal's late nineteenth- and early twentieth-century history. Aspects of these earlier intellectual movements were essentialized and pragmatically rearticulated to legitimate the new government's political, economic and cultural direction. Portuguese philosophy, heavily tainted by nineteenth-century Romanticism, incorporated influential subjectivist and idealistic tendencies, represented by Teixeira de Pascoaes (1877–1952), Leonardo Coimbra (1883–1936) and Jaime Cortesão (1884–1960) and their Renascença Portuguesa (Portuguese Renaissance) movement. Pascoaes's and Coimbra's elaborately constructed philosophies revised the nature and significance of a specifically Lusitanian national spirit, to better define the racial essence and historical trajectory of the Portuguese people. The idea of a national spirit, which Pascoaes believed needed to be cultivated to reanimate Portugal's former glory and the resumption of its apostolic destiny, was clearly distinct from the spirit's earlier positivist formulations. Nevertheless, Pascoaes's philosophy of spirit was selectively subsumed and repoliticized by the Estado Novo to inform a core political ideology. From the 1930s to 1950s, the ideology of the spirit achieved one of its clearest manifestations in state-sponsored exhibitions and spectacles that drew heavily on popular art and rural imagery. Nation and spirit formed the cornerstones of the 1940 *Exhibition of the Portuguese World*, orchestrating a dizzying portrayal of the past and present, the near and far, the cultural diversity and the triumphs of a nation that claimed to be the oldest in Europe.

THE ART OF BEING PORTUGUESE

Both Leonardo Coimbra and Teixeira de Pascoaes began their respective philosophical systems with similar ideas of the moral person. "The individual," wrote Pascoaes, "is the prime material

facing
The seventeenth-century church of Santiago Maior and the sixteenth-century church of Nossa Senhora da Lagoa in Monsaraz.

of all the spiritual beings to which we refer."[572] For Coimbra there could be no development or growth of society without a parallel development of individual conscience. Social revolution, he opined, required an educational revolution, and the advancement of individual conscience to create the moral person was possible only under conditions of unrestricted freedom. Philosophy taught the path to becoming conscious of liberty, while education provided the means for its realization. Having connected the subject of the individual to that of society, Coimbra linked the challenge of society to the nature of the state to insist that the creativity that the education required to shape the moral individual consciousness was not possible without liberty. In his later work he developed his position further to argue that there could be no liberty independent of the democratic state. Creation was itself an act of liberty, but totalitarian states that dominated and controlled personal existence destroyed life by denying the possibility of the growth of the individual's spirit. For Coimbra, an authoritarian state could give rise to only one specific type of knowledge—scientific technological knowledge, which replaced the free creative expression of the spirit by the rules of clockwork. Liberty and spirit are dialectically connected and encourage the growth of culture, while culture nourishes in turn the growth of liberty and the spirit.

Culture, according to Coimbra, shares an identical metaphysic to that of history, making the ability to understand the direction of culture synonymous with the understanding of the direction of history. For Coimbra, history is the arena in which the struggle of the material against the spirit, authority against liberty, takes place, which determines the qualities and expressions of national identities. In the early twentieth century, he argued, Germany and France represented opposing values, the first based on materialism and authority, the second predicated on spirituality and liberty. Independent of society, the individual spirit is benevolent, open, intelligent, free and loving, and although Coimbra acknowledged its propensity to be malevolent, he believed in a determinate principle that always ensured its overall positive qualities. This positive motivation is steered by reason, which led him to believe in the innate superiority of spirit and liberty over materialism and authority. Reason is always in movement and culminates in poetic reason, which, as Pascoaes also asserted, seeks the transcendence of the "real," in search of something greater than itself. By transcending the material world, poetic reason becomes an expression of infinity that culminates in the divine. Poetic reason and grace alone provide the path to the understanding of God and together constitute the sole means of revelation of "the permanent miracle of creation."[573]

From this perspective the maturation of the spirit requires an educational program to cultivate the creative liberty of national-human culture. Education is given purpose and direction by the family, the nation and the person. Education must never be passive, but open and restless, always accepting the guidance of superior knowledge. "The limit of education," for Coimbra, "was the limit of evolution and the limit of evolution is the spiritualization of the cosmos."[574] He believed the purpose of a Portuguese education was to cultivate and bring to fruition a Lusitanian spirit that evolved from cross-fertilizing a cultural spirit with the Portuguese soul, which expresses its deepest nature through language.[575]

In his earlier work, written between 1895 and 1912, the poet and philosopher Teixeira de Pascoaes, a friend and colleague of Coimbra, focused specifically on the growth of the Lusitanian spirit and its relation to the nation, with the specific intention of developing an educational system that could restitute the nation's own authentic spiritual values and restore its vitality.[576]

For Pascoaes, the Portuguese spirit was not dead but had slumbered since the time of the Discoveries. The nation, for Pascoaes, was a moral spiritual being with its own destiny created by the community of moral persons residing within it. The nation does not necessarily coincide with political boundaries, as in the case of Portugal, whose spirit had its origin in the northern heartland of the country between the rivers Douro and Minho. Indeed, Pascoaes suggested the provinces of Trás-os-Montes, with its Jewish legacy, and Alentejo and Algarve, with that of the Moors, amalgamated their spirits to create a synthesis between the Aryan (Greek, Roman, Celtic and Norman) and Semitic (Phoenician, Jewish and Arab) races that seeded Portugal's distinctive identity[577]—a distillation that, as Fernando Clara has commented, has long been used to argue for the country's extra-European identity.[578] Pascoaes and Coimbra counterpoised science and logical reason with poetic reason, insisting upon the superiority of the latter, which they saw as indispensable in the formation of the moral person. Race, Pascoaes argued, develops from a people who have been organized into a nation. It has two attributes: the influence of the natural environment or landscape, and its spiritual legacy, which is passed down through its historical, juridical, economic, literary, artistic and religious thought. Landscape and cultural legacy are therefore related dialectically and mutually shape each other. Pascoaes saw nature as a unidirectional evolutionary process that reveals itself through the movement from simple to complex, superior life forms, which achieve their highest expression in the liberation of the spirit.

In the Portuguese people there live two entities formed by family and racial affinities; every person exists as an individual and as a collective. Character or personality is the sum of those externalized qualities, conserved and transmitted as the inheritance or tradition of a race. For Pascoaes, the life and character of the race can emerge only after these characteristics are visually and materially expressed.

The qualities of the nation are echoed in those of the family, headed by the father, who represents its spiritual manifestation. Of the three types of family that Pascoaes distinguished, only the rural family occupies a privileged position, which he described as "the intimate, indestructible nucleus of the Portuguese motherland."[579] The popular rural classes constitute the blood and soul of the nation, while other classes represent a European hybrid lacking the same character and heritage.[580] Municipal government brings motherland and family spirit together, which give the individual a political means of expression and action. This articulation of the family and the motherland avoids the dysfunctions of political parties, factionalism and clientelism to create the perfect concordance[581] that had been so elusive to the Republican period.

Pascoaes's idea of the "motherland," as we have said, includes race, but race can exist independent of territory. The motherland is bound to the idea of nation, by the personal moral community located in a specific time and distinctive geographical place. The idea of the motherland never stops evolving because it is an ongoing construction remade by successive generations, which always retain the spiritual expression of the race. "Portugal is a race that constitutes a motherland because it acquired a language of its own, a history, art, literature as

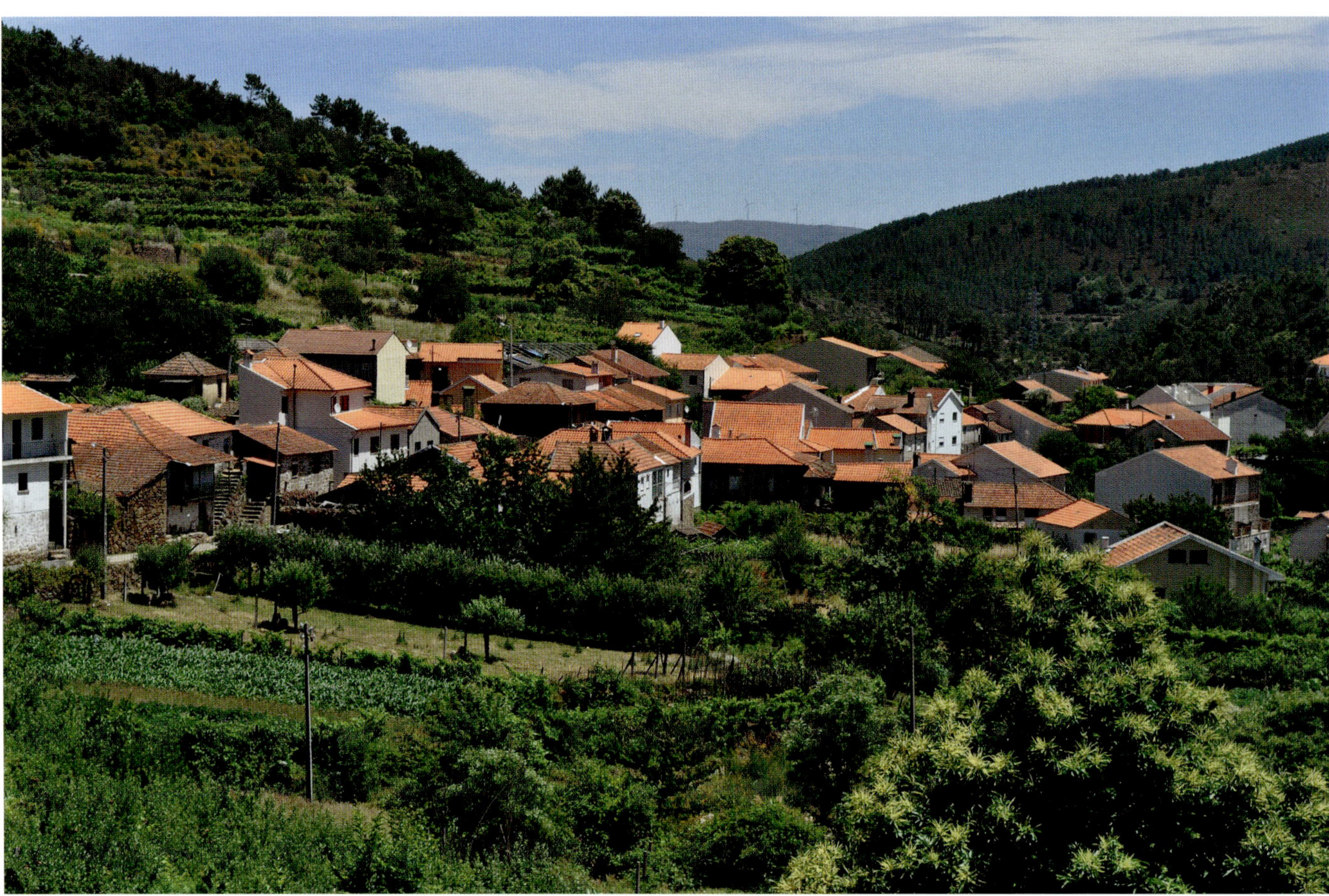

above
The village of Lazarim.

facing
Rural villages like Monsaraz were idealized by the Estado Novo as embodying the essence of the nation.

well as political independence," wrote Pascoaes.[582] History defines and lives within language. Language grasps what individuals see and experience and articulates such perceptions through patterns of thought and sentiment. Language, therefore, Pascoaes insisted, is the expression in verbal form of a people's thoughts and feelings, making it the most important determining characteristic of the motherland and the essence of the people's soul.

Words, Pascoaes argued, are like living beings that are born, transformed, become old and die.[583] The most genuine words, those that give a specific language its uniqueness, are those that are fundamentally untranslatable. In Portuguese these words include *ermo, remoto, ausência, luar, sombra, silêncio, nevoeiro, medo* and, the most important of all, *saudade*.[584] Poets have a special calling, Pascoaes insisted, since they enjoy a more intimate relationship with words than either philosophers or scientists and therefore occupy a privileged position to interpret the soul and destiny of a people to render it visible. The poet was for Pascoaes the veritable priest of the "cult of the mother tongue," who orchestrates the chronicles of the Discoveries, the heroic histories of distinctive royal lines, the legacy of Sebastianism, the Lusitanian Church and the country's municipal organization, laws and customs—in sum, the total spiritualized culture that constitutes the nation's uniqueness.[585] Poets, Pascoaes exhorted, "are the Heroes of our Dream, the Albuquerques and the Nuno Álvares of the infinite; those that burn life, hour after hour, from moment to moment, so the light of the soul is never extinguished."[586]

Within Pascoaes's philosophical world, the word *saudade*, as discussed in Chapter 3, has special significance. It embodies a whole way of thinking and being within and between the contrary categories it binds together: memory and desire, liking and bitterness, sadness and happiness, light and shadow, life and death. *Saudade*, which for Pascoaes represented the perfect Aryan and Semitic synthesis, envelops everything that exists within its indeterminable reach.[587] It constitutes the essence of the Portuguese soul, providing the impetus for exploration, imparting in it a messianic quality (the spiritualization of its adventures and the pressing compulsion to complete the mission of the Renaissance) and driving the indistinguishable desire for liberty and independence.[588] "*Saudade* is the absolute characteristic of the Portuguese.... All novelty that Portugal has to give the world is [contained] within *saudade*," Patrício writes. "*Saudade* is eternal renaissance, eternal human aspiration."[589] It is "the harmony between the Spirit and Material, the principle of Christ and that of Luciferianism or paganism"; it resounds in the intimate bond between Christ and the Father which should, for Pascoaes, always be imprinted on the country's historical evolution.[590] *Saudade* definitively characterizes Portuguese literature and poetry (legend, prose, poetry, song, saga), which, the poet argued, also expresses itself in the parallel florescence of the music of such Portuguese composers as Alfredo Keil, Augusto Machado, Óscar da Silva, Hermínio Nascimento, Arnaldo Martins de Brito, Rui Coelho, Wenceslau Pinto, Margarida Andresen da Costa Roma Machado and Frederico de Freitas. And nowhere, of course, is *saudade* more present than in the literary work of Luís de Camões.

For these authors, then, the function of a Portuguese education is to extrapolate and amplify the local family connection to a specific territory and tradition encapsulated in the municipality with the national spirit of the motherland itself. "The motherland is a spiritual being,"[591] but a being that is itself transcended by humanity and ultimately by God. A Portuguese education, as defined in Pascoaes's *Arte de Ser Português* (1915), is not intended to create a political nationalist but a patriot who is conscious of the national spirit as well as the wider spiritualized humanity of which he or she is part.[592] From this perspective, under the proper conditions, the individual consciousness of Portugueseness inevitably transcends itself

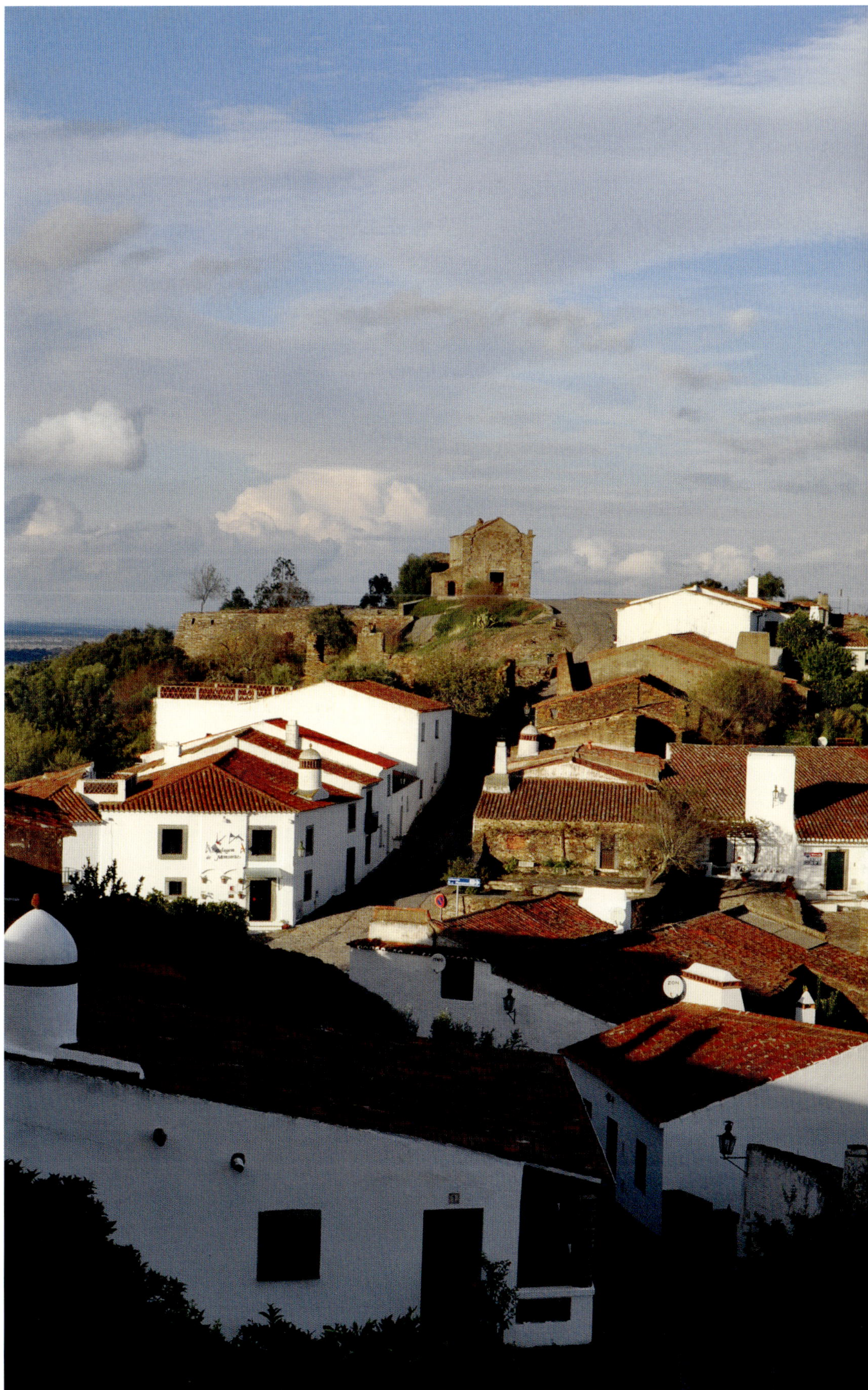

to become universalized with those of all human life forms.[593] Pascoaes's model of the elevated being is not therefore the patriot, but the saint who has achieved transcendence, the Ecco Christ.

Pascoaes's belief that the vocation of the poet is synonymous with the guardianship of the mother tongue justifies the consecration of a hagiography of spirit guardians, beginning with Camões, whose significance collapses the border between poetry, rhetoric and politics. Patrício argues that Pascoaes, Fernando Pessoa and the painter and writer Almada Negreiros (1893–1970) were the twentieth-century creators of a new ontology of Portugal.[594] The spiritualized ontology they constructed was capable of synthesizing a hierarchy between different types of national spirits that enabled Pessoa to speculate on the advent of the Fifth Empire, the dawn of the universal millennium promised in Sebastianist millenarianism, which would unfold under the benign guidance of the Lusitanian spirit. Sebastianist millenarianism is an important expression of *saudade* and, for Pascoaes, symbolically represented the death of material grandeur to allow the resurgence of the spirit. The sleep of the Portuguese spirit is the sleep of Dom Sebastião, who one day will rise again. "In whatever far-off place you lie. Amid shades and rumors, feel us dream of you / And arise from the depths of not being / To your new destiny."[595] *Saudade*, for Pascoaes and Pessoa, was not about remembrance and nostalgia, but about hope and belief in redemption through the universal spirit awaiting its birth.

THE SPECTACLE OF LUSITANIA

There are extensive parallels between the work of Pascoaes and the philosophy of spirit articulated by the Estado Novo between 1933 and 1950, as we shall see in this and the final chapter. The historian Fernando Rosas argues that the Estado Novo strove to create a "new man" who, like Pascoaes's moral individual, would be transfused by the spirit of his race. The being the Estado Novo conceived would subordinate his ego and individualism, be committed to the nation ("everything for the nation, nothing against the nation"), be resolute in accepting a philosophy based on a supposedly natural model of a paternalistic corporate society and be motivated by the moral teachings of the Church under the tutelage of a Catholic God. Rosas synthesizes a sevenfold core mythology that underlay the ideology of the Estado Novo: the myth of regeneration; the myth of a new nationalism based on the revitalization of past grandeur; the imperial myth that legitimated colonialism as a form of civilizing evangelization; the myth of the rural people and rural life providing the repository and lived memory of the nation's past; the myth of honourable poverty, which celebrated the lack of "painful ambitions" and the acceptance of a humble but contented life, described by Salazar as "the vocation of poverty"; the myth of corporate order as having a natural origin; and the myth of Catholicism as providing the essence of national identity.[596] All but the last of these axioms were addressed, though in a widely different context, in Pascoaes's philosophy.

Pascoaes and Coimbra offered a clear articulation of the national spirit, which they associated with a specific historical trajectory and, despite their counter-assertions, with a geographical territory, subordinated to a mystical but Christian theology. Their philosophy subordinated materialism to spirituality, the individual to divine will and the present to the past. Most importantly, it identified the purpose of education in transmitting and concretizing the spirit and in defending the qualities that define the Lusitanian imagination, an imagination that provided the very essence of national identity and the nation's uniqueness and originality. Acknowledgement of the role of education in the mobilization of the forces necessary to create the "new man," a being who was fundamentally old, was shared between both poets and politicians. There remain, of course, fundamental differences between the Pascoaesan model of education that emphasizes the importance of freedom and liberty and the blinded totalitarianism of Salazar and the Estado Novo.

The Education Reform Bill of 1936 was unequivocal in acknowledging that schools alone could not fulfill the state's expectations.[597] Education must, it asserted, envelop the personal life of individuals with that of the nation. School education and the Casas do Povo and Casas dos Pescadores (Houses of the Fishermen) were only part of the extensive organizational network manipulated by the state to disseminate its world view. Educational institutions were supplemented by informal pedagogical agencies that mobilized commemorations and leisure activities that involved a large-scale deployment of popular art and other cultural expressions.

Secular commemorations in Portugal, whether exhibitions, festivals, processions, military parades, conferences or the unveiling of monuments, began to be invented in the late nineteenth century and were part of the strategies employed by earlier political regimes as much as those of the Estado Novo. These civil commemorations were expounded by the French philosopher Auguste Comte and endorsed by leading Portuguese thinkers and politicians, including two presidents with strong anthropological affiliations, Teófilo Braga and Bernardino Machado. They were intended to create a secular hagiography of national heroes and events to counter religious ceremonies and ferment and popularize new values and progressive ideas.[598] Not all agreed on their effectiveness, as evidenced by Oliveira Martins, who acerbically described the cult of great men as a "bureaucratic religion" and the commemorations as a "ministerial mass."[599]

The earliest civic forms and festivities began in 1880. They focused on honouring "great men" and celebrating important events and achievements in the nation's history. Camões was institutionally memorialized through the creation of a special day (10 June). Many others soon followed: the death of the Marquis of Pombal (instituted in 1882); the birth (instituted in 1894) and death (instituted in 1885) of King Afonso Henriques; the celebration of Santo António (beginning 1895); the discovery of the maritime route to India (instituted 1897–98); and the death of Father António Vieira, the seventeenth-century Jesuit writer, philosopher, diplomat and reformist (beginning 1897)—all became the subjects of annual commemorations. This vogue to orchestrate an extensive, but nonetheless selective, national memory also embraced the institutionalization of almshouses, *misericórdias* (instituted in 1898) and the celebration of other historical personages.[600]

Not surprisingly this secular hagiography was closely linked to the cult of the dead that was embraced by the bourgeoisie between 1840 and 1860 and involved elaborate funerary furniture, processions, decorations, flowers and oratory that accompanied worthy ancestors to their final resting place in cemeteries like Prazeres in Lisbon, with its richly symbolic architecture.[601] The funeral processions of Kings Pedro IV (1836) and Pedro V (1861) provided opulent dramatizations of this new cult, which could not have failed to influence the emerging bourgeois vogue. The transfer of the ashes of Camões, da Gama (both 1880), Herculano (1888) and Garrett (1903) to be reburied in the Jerónimos Monastery, which was then consecrated into a pantheon of national heroes, helped incorporate the localized memorialization of specific groups into a unitary national memory theatre that sought to enhance consensus and sociability and even, through its inclusivity, soothe conflicts.[602] By the early twentieth century Portugal had witnessed an epidemic of consecrations, secondary burials, processions and commemorations that had evolved into a hierarchically organized cult of the dead, characterized by Fernando Catroga as religious counter-ceremonies.[603]

The First Republic celebrated, in 1915, the quincentenary of the conquest of Ceuta in North Africa; in 1921, the four-hundred-year anniversaries of the deaths of Afonso de Albuquerque and Fernão de Magalhães; in 1922, the first South Atlantic flight between Portugal and Rio de Janeiro; [604] and in 1924, the four-hundred-year anniversaries of the birth of Camões and the death of Vasco da Gama. The commemorative cycle established a new historical structure of memory and forgetting that strove to articulate a comprehensive reinvention of Portuguese tradition, in which the memory of a new rising social group would be allied to that of the nation itself.

Ceremonies and commemorations were also employed after 1926 by the Estado Novo to shape the "new man" and society they sought to create. The most ambitious of these projections consisted of spectacles, by far the most grandiose of which was the 1940 *Exhibition of the Portuguese World*. The Estado Novo employed a comprehensive range of exhibitionary strategies, including miniaturization, reproduction and reconstruction, live demonstrations and orchestral commissions. These strategies were used in later exhibitions and in the three new museums, which were established as the exhibition's legacy: the Museu de Arte Popular in Lisbon, the Museu Nacional de Etnografia das Províncias do Douro Litoral in Porto and the Museu José Malhoa in Caldas da Rainha.[605] The rustification and folkloricization of the country was undertaken through the commemoration and ritualization of events like the annual blessing and departure of the Cod Fleet described in Chapter 3; competitions like those between folk dance groups or that instigated in 1938 for the most Portuguese village; and adherence to vernacular architectural styles. Legislation was also introduced to protect historical buildings and monuments.[606]

From 1932 to 1946 the state sponsored numerous exhibitions, including the industrial exhibitions held in Lisbon (1932 and 1933), the *Colonial Exhibition* (Porto, 1934), the *Exhibition of Popular Art* (Lisbon, 1936), the *Tenth Year Commemorative Exhibition of the National Revolution* (Lisbon, 1936, celebrating the military coup that led to Salazar's rise to power) and the *Historical Exhibition of the Occupation* (Lisbon, 1937). Other state-sponsored exhibitions focused heavily on "folk" art and culture, such as those on the village of Monsanto (Lisbon, 1942), regional folk costumes of Viana do Castelo (Lisbon, 1945) and woven carpets from Arraiolos (Lisbon, 1946). There were also more heterogeneous exhibitions intended to encourage urban Portuguese to discover Portugal's state-consecrated national history for themselves.[607]

Outside the country, the Estado Novo patronized world fairs, ensuring the country was well represented in the exhibitions of Paris (1931), Geneva (1935 and 1937), London (1935), New York (1939) and San Francisco (1939). The strong predisposition to focus on popular art was further made clear in exhibitions held in Madrid (1943), Valencia (1944), and Seville (1944).[608] Unlike during the Republican period, these exhibitions were administered and tightly controlled and inscribed by government ministries rather than by civic or cultural organizations.[609] Between 1932 and 1960, 76 percent of personnel involved in the organization of all commemorative events were government functionaries or military personnel,[610] who required no more of their public audience than that they be "passive and reverent spectators of the past, tradition and authority."[611]

THE COMMEMORATIONS OF 1940

The *Exhibition of the Portuguese World* recounted and celebrated eight hundred years of national history, from the foundation of the country in 1140 to its subsequent annexation and independence from Spain in 1640 and its second rebirth following the intervention of the Estado Novo in 1940.[612] The first international historical exhibition of its type, it covered 560,000 square metres and included eight pavilions, which were planned by Cottinelli Telmo with the help of twelve architects, nineteen sculptors, forty-three painters and six thousand manual workers on the riverside of Belém, in Lisbon. This area was redolent with associations to the Discoveries and Portugal's empires and encompassed important monuments like the Jerónimos Monastery, now a national pantheon, and the Tower of Belém, part of a medieval river fortification that was made into the ceremonial gateway to Lisbon.[613] The commemorative events were not confined to one site but were dispersed across the country and lasted all year. Concerts, conferences, processions and exhibitions were meticulously coordinated throughout the nation to portray Portugal in full celebration at a time when most of Europe was deeply mired in war.

The exhibition's timing (it opened the day after France's surrender to Germany) provoked its organizers to decry the chaos of Europe as a sign of the continent's decadence, brought about by individualism, nationalist extremism and communism, which Portugal had successfully avoided to create for itself an "oasis of peace."[614] The 1940 exhibition had three core objectives, according to its commissioner general, Augusto de Castro (1883–1971):

> In first place, to project the past so as to make a gallery of heroic images on the nation's foundation and existence: its universal purpose, its Christian and evangelical [mission], the race, and its maritime, colonial and imperial glory. In second place, the affirmation of its present political, creative and moral energy, and in third place, an [affirmation] of faith in its future. These three objectives can be summarized in just one: to provide a testimonial to the apotheosis of the national conscience.[615]

The commemoration's three historical periods—medieval, imperial and the Bragança dynasty (1640–1910)—were each celebrated at different times of the year. The festival was centred on three large-scale programs: the Congress of the Portuguese World (subdivided into nine specialist conferences); *Exhibition of the Portuguese World*, intended to provide a sumptuous representation of the nation's colonial expanse and achievements; and the Procession of the Portuguese World, choreographed to evoke a live synthesis of eight hundred years of history. The summary of the events and programs celebrated throughout the country, presented by the historians Torgal, Mendes and Catroga,[616] gives an impressive indication of the size and magnitude of the "timequake" the Estado Novo sought to spatialize across the nation's geography and convey throughout its empire. To fulfill these ambitions, improvements in infrastructure, such as the construction of roads and hotels and the enlargement of the radio network to include all the countries of the empire

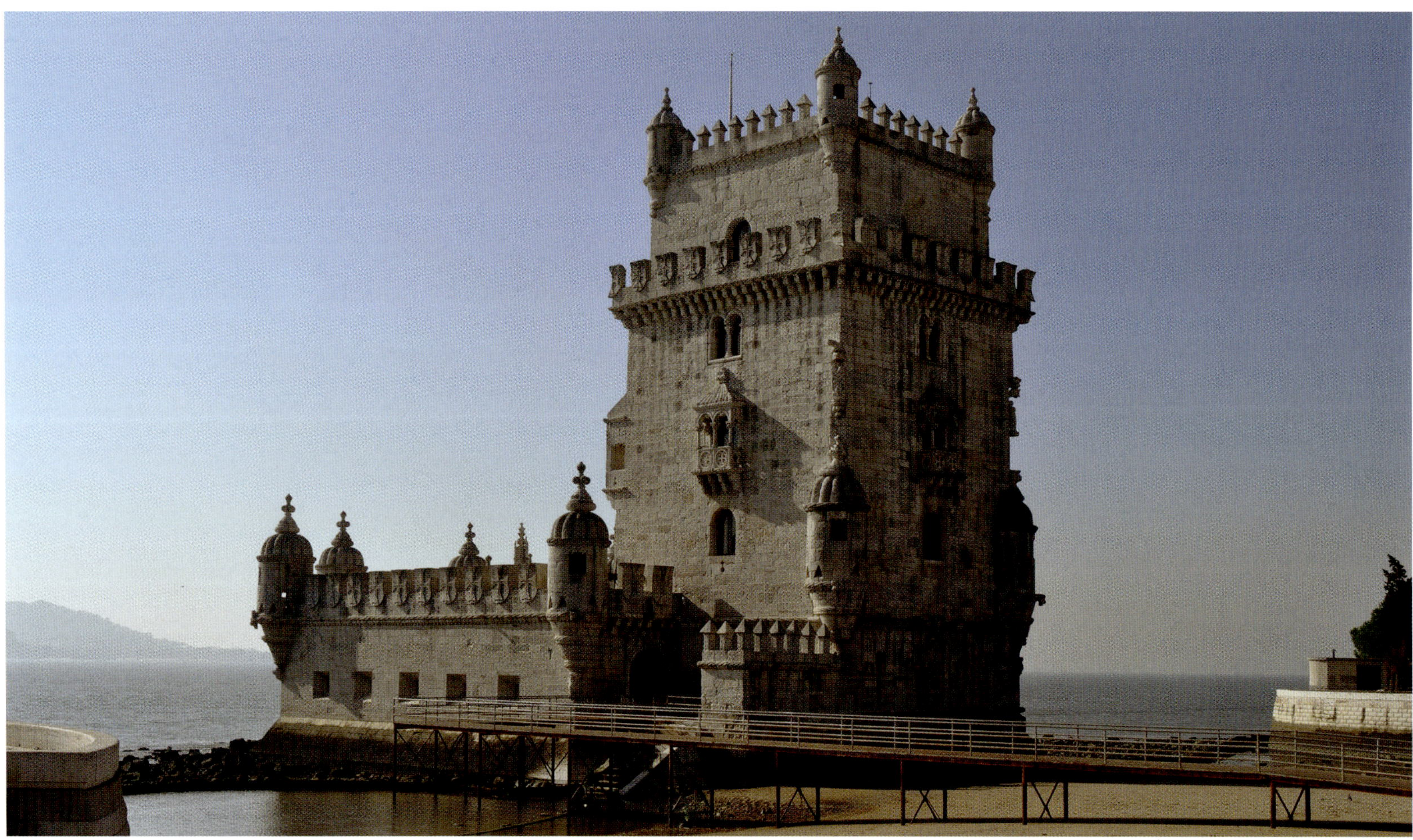

above
The Tower of Belém was part of Lisbon's fifteenth-century maritime fortifications before being made into a ceremonial entrance to the city during the 1940 Exhibition of the Portuguese World.

facing
The fifteenth-century Manueline-style Jerónimos Monastery in Belém contains the tombs of Vasco da Gama and Luís de Camões.

and enable them to "follow the spiritual expressions of the motherland," were essential.[617]

The medieval epoch was the first to be celebrated and was opened with Salazar raising the flag of Afonso Henriques at Guimarães Castle, an act repeated at exactly the same time in all those castles throughout Portugal that had played a decisive mission in the country's creation. The flag-raising ceremony was synchronized with naval and artillery fire, the pealing of church bells in both Portugal and the colonies, and special Masses. During the two weeks of the medieval commemorations (2–15 June), the state organized performances, excursions to symbolically charged sites, religious ceremonies, events celebrating the foundation of judicial and teaching institutions, conferences, concerts, popular parades, street parties and exhibitions, including one on the Portuguese Primitivists curated by the Museu Nacional de Arte Antiga. There was a re-enactment of the Battle of Ourique in Alentejo, and a new monument was installed to commemorate it in São Pedro das Cabeças near Castro Verde.[618]

The imperial epoch, celebrated from 23 June to 14 July, was inaugurated by the *Exhibition of the Portuguese World*, as well as by street celebrations and parades in Lisbon's older neighbourhoods. Exhibitions were held on the realist sculptor, António Soares dos Reis (Porto); cartography (Lisbon); gold work (Coimbra); and the distinguished protagonists of the imperial age. Language, literature and the history of the period were celebrated through academic conferences and events; a special ceremony at Buçaco honoured the fallen in the Peninsular War (1807–14). On 30 June Lisbon was treated to the long and impressive Procession of the Portuguese World, one of the highlights of the year-long celebration.

The third epoch, coinciding with independence from Spain and the installation of the Royal House of Bragança, was commemorated from 10 November to 2 December. It employed celebratory strategies

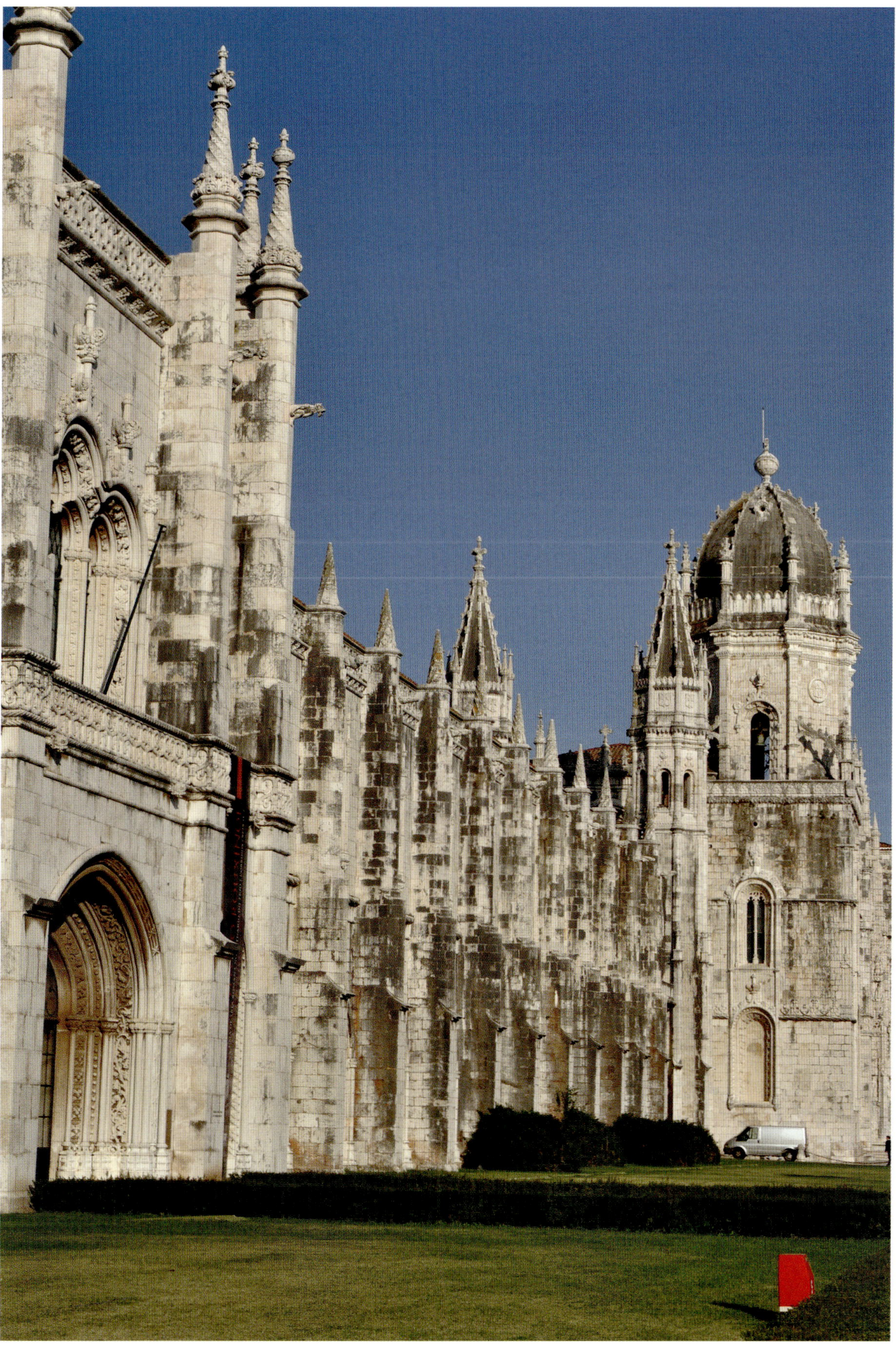

facing
The main entrance of the *Exhibition of the Portuguese World*, 1940.

like those already described: historical excursions, pilgrimages to the tombs of important protagonists, academic conferences, street fairs and parades, concerts and exhibitions. There were a number of commemorations in Alentejo of victories associated with the restoration of independence, including the Battle of Monte Claro of 1665 (Borba), the Battle of Canal of 1663 (Ameixial) and the Battle of Linhâs of 1659 (Elvas). The military museum in Lisbon highlighted the martial strategists and leaders of the era, and the Theatre of São Carlos performed the opera 1640. On 2 December, at Lisbon's municipal hall, President Carmona (1869–1951) officially closed the year-long celebration. The closure ceremony was timed to coincide with similar sessions in town halls throughout the empire and in Portuguese embassies, legations and consulates worldwide.[619]

The year's calendar represented an enormous and impressive coordination of spaces and time not only within the national territory but also throughout the empire on a scale never before contemplated in Portugal. Geography and time were inscribed and manipulated to express spatial and historical coincidences between past and present events, bringing all three different timescapes (medieval, imperial, Bragança dynasty) into confluence, restaging history and legitimating current government ideologies and policies by constructing and invoking their relationships to their historical antecedents. Three different temporal moments were correlated to transform chronological time into duration and place into space and subject the population to a "timequake," which effectively enabled them to relive eight hundred years of history within one year. Historical time was paused while the vast geographical spaces of the Portuguese Empire were impeccably stitched together, the period of decadence erased, the nation and her empire recalibrated with the faultless resumption of the work of the spirit that had always been believed to endow it grandeur. The Lusitanian spirit, through the conspiracy of state and Church,[620] was transhistoricized and universalized.

The organization and elaborate strategic inscriptions behind the celebration moulded the structure of the scriptural apparatus at its centre, the hugely impressive *Exhibition of the Portuguese World*. According to one commentator, "The great objective of the *Exhibition of the Portuguese World* was to project the past onto the present, justifying colonialism as an ecumenical and missionary labour that remained the same in 1940 as it had been during the Discoveries."[621] Augusto de Castro called the exhibition site "a city of illusions" that reflected "the image that the Estado Novo had created for Portugal: heroic, modest, hardworking and faithful to God."[622] Through government direction, the country's rural culture was strategically mobilized to create the folkloric and rustic image of a present that had endured unchanged for centuries, an image whose reassuring stability hid the high child mortality and illiteracy rates, inadequate education, impoverished and unsanitary living conditions and factionalism that afflicted a large part of its population.[623]

The ideology of the spirit was closely inscribed within the Portuguese language and religious faith, as cogently expressed at the opening of the exhibition. On this defining occasion a seamless synthesis was constructed, which combined the recitation of works from some of Portugal's most revered literary figures with the performance of the specially commissioned symphony *Fundação* (Foundation), written using a combination of sacred music from codices preserved in the Cistercian monastery of Alcobaça, musical reconstructions of twelfth- and

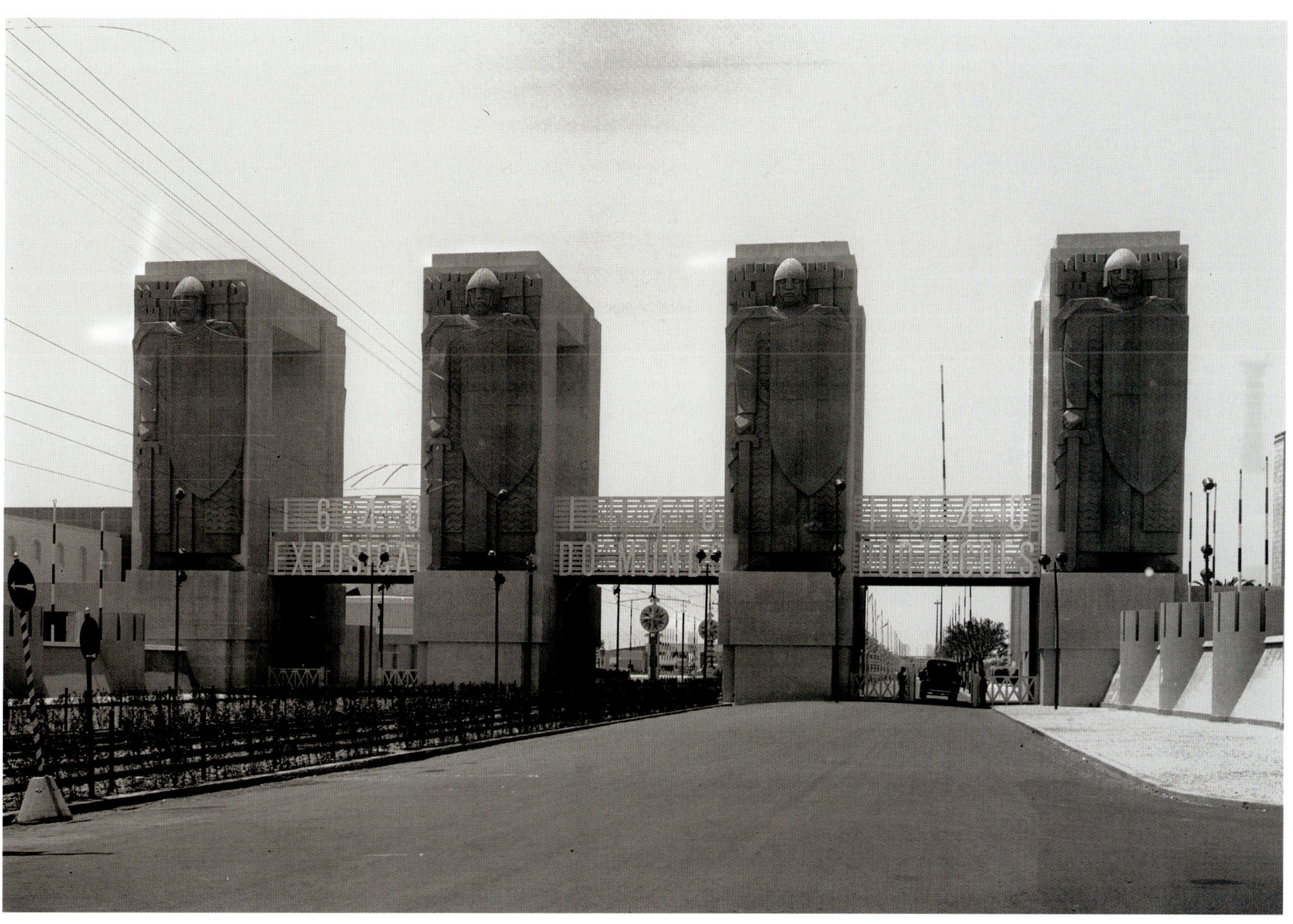

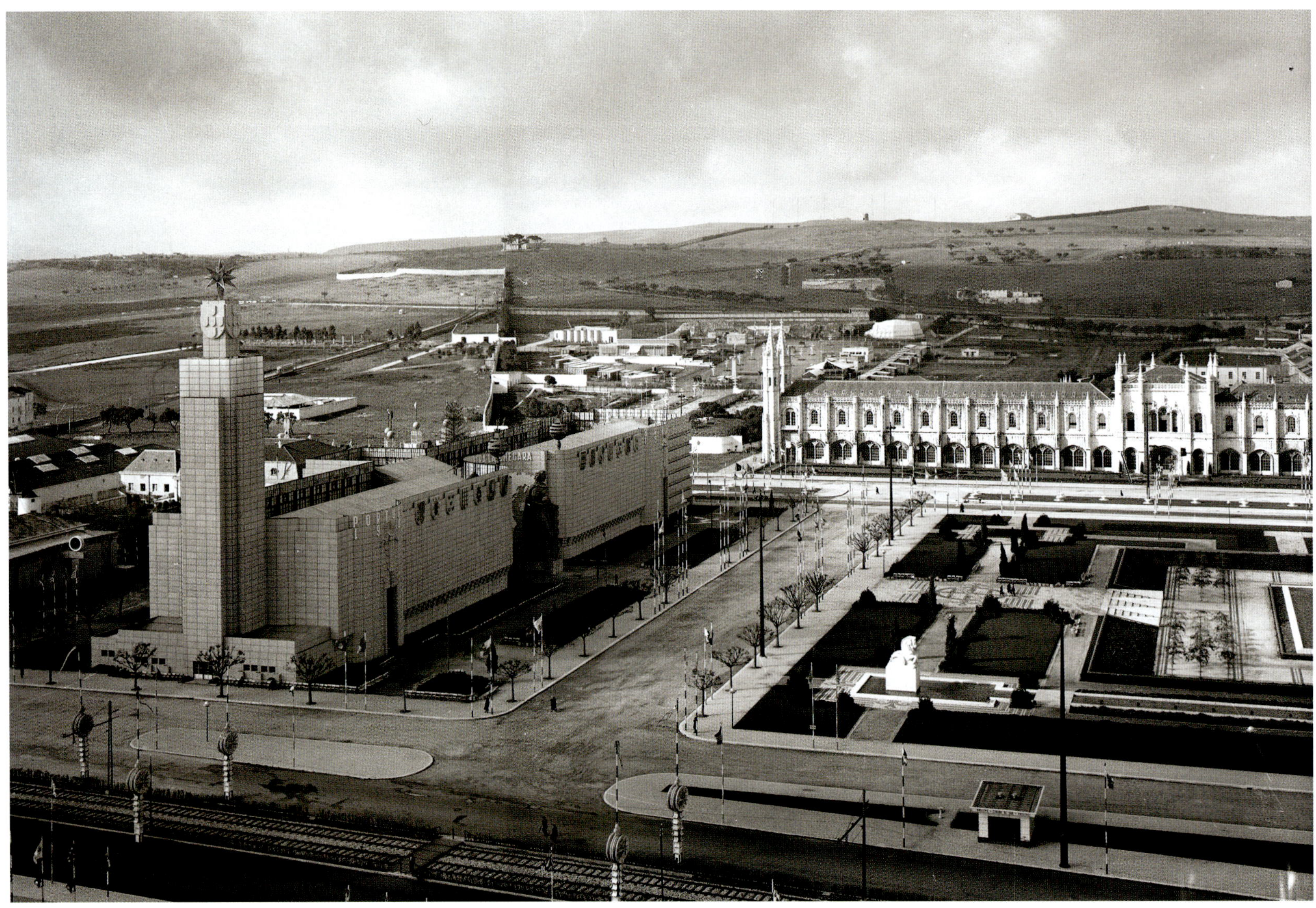

above
The Portuguese in the World Pavilion in Praça do Império during the *Exhibition of the Portuguese World*, 1940. Facing the plaza is the long Jeronimos Monastery.

facing
Pavilion of Honor and the City of Lisbon in Praça do Império during the *Exhibition of the Portuguese World*, 1940. The Jeronimos Monastery flanks the front plaza.

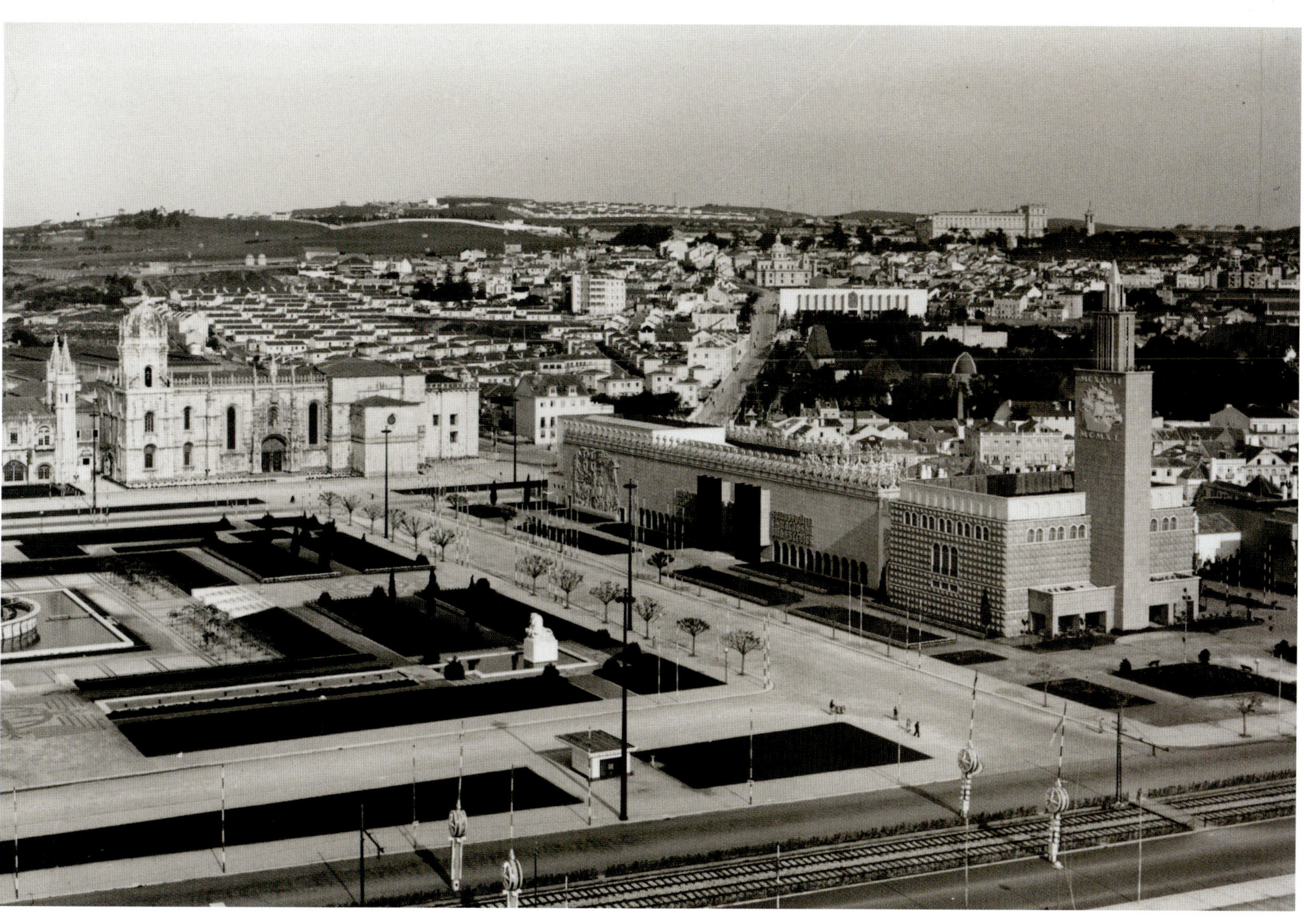

fourteenth-century Galician-Portuguese poetry and a homage to Santo António.[624] The spectacular backdrop of ships and an illuminated galleon on the River Tagus, surmounted by giant figures of King Afonso Henriques and his medieval contemporaries, created an unsurpassed spectacle of monumental effect.

The *Exhibition of the Portuguese World* was intended as an encapsulation of the national spirit, symbolizing and materializing the essence of the Portuguese nation as a modernizing and universal spirit within an ancient soul and affirming it not as the product but as the author of world history.[625] Much of the exhibition evoked the great events of the nation's history as enacted through its eminent protagonists and its earliest kings. In Salazar's opinion the commemoration was intended as a grand exorcism to expel "from us the spirit of sorrow and evil."[626]

The eight pavilions were divided into four separate sections. The site was entered through a ceremonial gateway of four majestic towers decorated with giant Lusitanian knights that cut across the Avenida da Índia and the railway line connecting Lisbon and Cascais. The first pavilion, with its battlement and monumental castellated facade and portico, was dedicated to the nation's foundation, with its statue of King Afonso Henriques, busts of warriors and mural paintings inspired by the medieval paintings in the *Lorvão Apocalypse* and *The Book of Birds*. It focused on Portugal's Roman and Visigothic roots, the Middle Ages and the heroes of the Restoration.

The second pavilion, the Pavilhão da Formação e Conquista (Pavilion of Formation and Conquest), was decorated with panels using graphic elements and themes drawn from medieval codices preserved in the library of the Alcobaça Monastery and the tombs of saints and kings. Its galleries covered the religious orders, a large map of the country, the conquest of the European territories that became Portugal, municipal organization and the internal peopling and historic ethnic composition of the nation. Another pavilion was dedicated to independence and a fourth to the Discoveries: mapping and expeditions across sea and land; documents; figures of the kings, including the Infante, João II and João III; and Camões and the navigators and chroniclers who described the storm-ridden sea and the shipwrecks sacrificed in the construction and rise of its power and empire. Next in the fourth pavilion was a Portuguese galleon.

A fifth pavilion took up the story of colonization and evangelization using maps, paintings, decorative screens, tapestries and carpets, forged iron works and more to recount the establishment of rule in Asia, Africa and the Americas. The representation of the culmination of Portuguese colonial history was divided between two further pavilions, the Portuguese in the World and Brazil. The first recounted the presence of the Portuguese in the Far East, Japan, Ethiopia, Canada and pre-independence Brazil, while the one dedicated to Brazil, the only foreign country with its own pavilion because of its historical and spiritual ties with Portugal, focused on its post-independence history.[627] Despite Salazar's eulogy, "Brazil: The glory of your energy and of your political genius,"[628] and similarities between the Portuguese and Brazilian political systems, the pavilion's modernist design, with its stylized palm trunks and indigenous Amazonian motifs, did nothing to complement its surroundings.

Architecturally and narratively the Brazilian Pavilion stood in sharp contrast to the eighth pavilion, the Centro Regional. While Brazil exhibited a massive diorama of Rio de Janeiro as a modern metropolis, the Centro Regional assembled thirteen reconstructed villages characterized by their distinctive vernacular architectural styles and complemented by "typical" folk art, costumes and artisans representative of the different Portuguese provinces.[629] Other parts of the Portuguese world were assimilated into the exhibition, not inside buildings but as live museums: Macau and Goa by the reconstruction of streets and buildings and Africa through three different village types demonstrative of the lifestyles of the Bijago, Fula and Mandingo peoples, as well as other constructions replete with indigenous inhabitants from Timor, Angola, Mozambique and Cape Verde and São Tomé. Even included was a reproduction of the palace of the king of the Congo, with the royal family in temporary residence.[630]

The folklorist and political consultant to the Secretariat of National Propaganda, Luís Chaves (1888–1975), had envisaged that every aspect of the Portuguese people would be represented in the Centro Regional pavilion: their supposed picturesque lives, costumes and "superstitions" and the beauty of their homes, their work and their soul. António Ferro ensured this whole section of the exhibition remained animated through restaurants and eateries, folkloric dances and craft demonstrations and by a market that sold popular arts. These services and events transformed the area into what he was to later describe as "a live and real theatre of our provinces."[631] The exhibition classified and arranged popular art according to its materials and technical qualities and included a section on sweetbreads. Visitors were welcomed to the exhibition galleries by a display of dolls dressed in distinctive local or regional styles and engaged in "typical" rural activities. Gold work and jewellery were displayed next, followed by a section on land and sea divided into objects used or made by shepherds, hunters and fishermen. Successive sections were devoted to popular saints, lamps, figurative ceramics, basketry, metalwork, carpentry and, lastly, sea and river transport. The pavilion also included cross-sections of reconstructed domestic interiors, a gallery devoted to models and photographs of different house styles and other constructions, and a corridor in which were exhibited a variety of handmade musical instruments.[632]

The Estado Novo folklorized and celebrated rural communities through not only the exhibition but the book that accompanied it, *Vide e Arte do Povo Português* (Life and Art of the Portuguese People), introduced by Ferro and written by various ethnographers and other specialists.[633] Folkloric sentiment was also aroused by the newly founded national folk ballet, the Verde Gaio, which was modelled on the Ballets Russes, much admired by Ferro,[634] and in the following year by the launch of the influential magazine *Panorama: Revista Portuguesa de Arte e Turismo* (Portuguese Magazine of Art and Tourism). The model villages, picturesque backdrops, folk dances, craftspeople and food stores of the Centro Regional provided the backdrop for thousands of photographs that circulated in magazines, books and newspapers, idealizing and romanticizing the Portuguese countryside and likening it to a movie image.[635] Together with the establishment of the Verde Gaio and *Panorama*, the Centro Regional provided an effective apparatus through which the Estado Novo was able to inscribe and disseminate a sanitized, idyllic and rustic image of the country, in which local rural identities were dissolved to become stereotypes and emblems of Salazar's new Portugal.[636] The popular broadsheet *A Voz* aptly described the Centro as respiring "the Biblical peace of rural life from this suave Portuguese earth."[637] Through these apparatuses the material cultures of distinctive communities were neutralized and transformed into a source of artistic and decorative inspiration, a Portuguese taste or *gusto*

facing
HENRIQUE GALVÃO
Portugal não é um país pequeno
(**Portugal Is Not a Small Country**), 1934

perfect for branding hotels, restaurants, homes, gardens, shops, industrial products, books and touristic promotions[638] that retrospectively lacked all conviction. As Augusto de Castro asserted in his grandly worded summation of the exhibition, "Here is the history of what we did and the certainty of who we are. Here is the account of what we dream.... The universality of our historical mission which is not a past fact or the glory of yesterday but our eternal condition."[639]

At the centre of this impressive architectural homage to the bucolic domesticity of Portugal and allegory to empire, the sculptor Salvador Feyo (1899–1990) had created an enormous *Archangel of Victories*, together with statues of Carmona and Salazar. Through sections on culture, religion, trade, politics and warfare, the exhibition took stock of the Portuguese contribution to European civilization and to those countries with sizable Portuguese communities.

The stately visual culture of the exhibition was complemented, reiterated and animated by the grand Procession of the Portuguese World organized by the writer and politician Henrique Galvão (1895–1970). This was divided into three parts: The Portugal of Yesterday, with its chronologically arranged floats (foundation, consolidation, peace, expansion, empire, colonization and splendour), each symbolized by a particular and significant colour; The Portugal of Today, showing the empire's diversity through the presence of different cultural groups, who paraded in traditional costumes; and The Portugal of Tomorrow, represented by an allegorical float and the march of the uniformed fascist youth organization.[640] A review of this immensely popular parade on the front page of the newspaper *Novidades* on 1 July described it as "a dazzling spectacle in which the golden and highest periods of our history passed before us. Our colonies with all their attributes also figured in the parade.... The King of the Congo in all his splendour participated on a float pulled by a zebra."[641]

Exhibitions and spectacle focused not only on history but also on cartography. If the nation, it might be argued, was synonymous with race, then to justify governorship over its territories, this racial definition needed to be expanded and further rationalized to incorporate the empire as a whole. Portugal transmitted the image of itself as having enriched intellectually, morally and economically all four continents and in turn having been enriched by them. To lose part of its empire, for the Estado Novo, was concomitant to losing part of Portugal's integral identity. In 1934 at the time of the *Colonial Exhibition* organized in Porto, a map was circulated that illustrated the land area of Portugal and her then colonies superimposed over a map of Europe. Above the red- and yellow-coloured land areas of Portugal's empire was emblazoned in bold letters, "Portugal is not a small country." Below the map's outline were two tables that provided the statistical confirmation that the empire covered a larger area than Britain, France, Germany, Spain and Italy combined.[642] This map was exhibited in the 1937 Paris exhibition, graphically emphasizing the Portuguese Empire as a "historical cosmopolis"[643] in which race and territories had been conflated. Older people recall that it was later circulated to the nation's schools and used to instill a sense of extra-European identity and Lusocentric geopolitical world order.

THE PHILOSOPHY AND POLITICS OF THE SPIRIT AFTER 1974

When next Portugal commemorated itself in such a comprehensive and extravagant way, it had become a democracy and was fast achieving full membership of the European Union (EU). In 1983, three

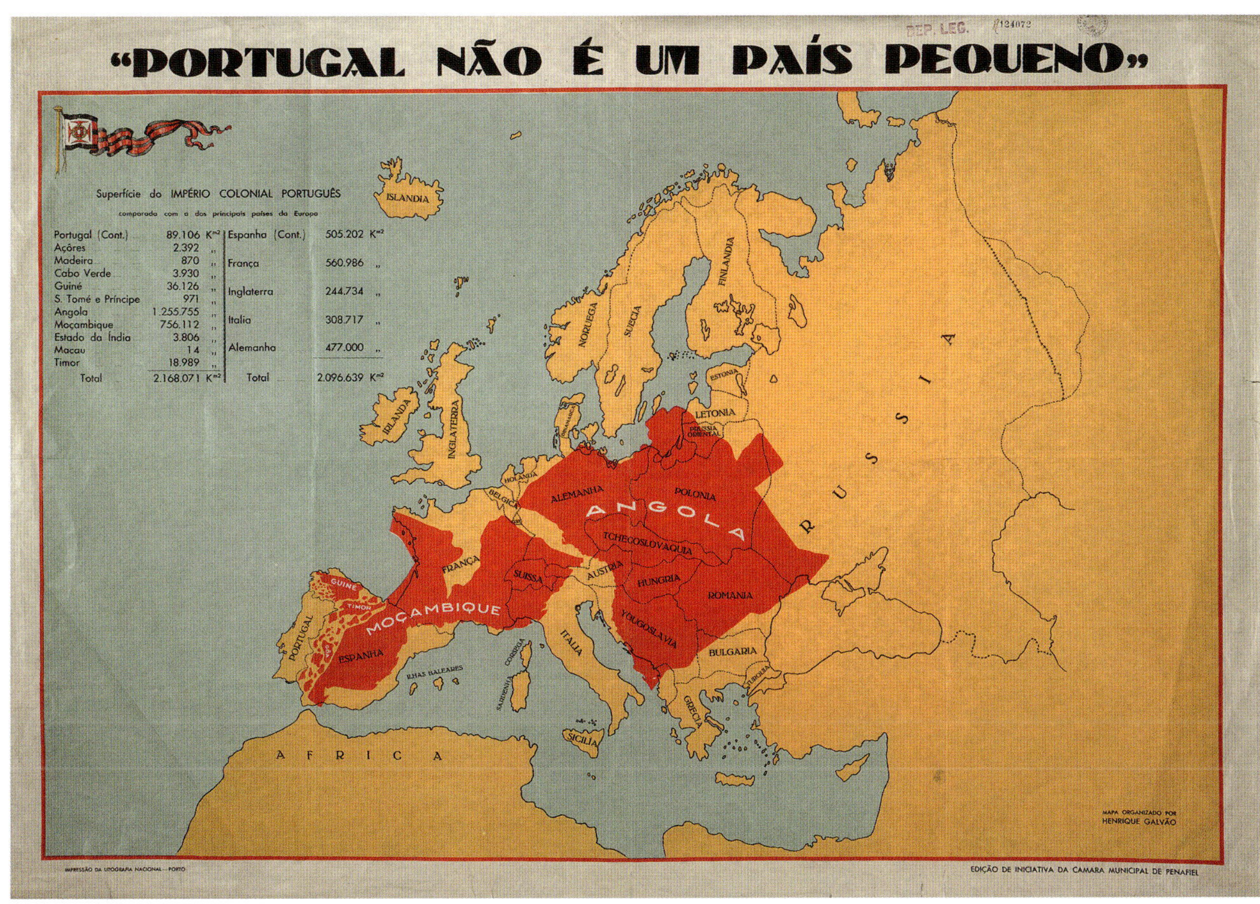

years before the country joined the EU, an ambitious exhibitionary project, *The Portuguese Discoveries and Renaissance Europe*, was inaugurated in Lisbon. The exhibition was part of the cycle of *European Exhibitions of Art, Science and Culture*, which, under the patronage of the Council of Europe, had since 1954 striven to increase "knowledge and appreciation of European art as one of the highest expressions of Europe's culture and common values."[644] More than any time in the past, Portugal was given the opportunity to present itself as a European nation that had contributed to a continental civilization in ways that had relevance for the future of the newly emerging community of nations.

The celebration was made up of five exhibitions that were hosted in separate, recently refurbished historical buildings along the Tagus waterfront: the Casa dos Bicos, the Museu Nacional de Arte Antiga, the Jerónimos Monastery, the convent of Madre de Deus and the Tower of Belém. The focal exhibition, *Blooms the Earth in Sounds and Colours: The Discoveries and the Renaissance, Forms of Coincidence and Culture*, was housed in the newly remodelled Museu Nacional de Arte Antiga from May to October 1983. The arrangement of the exhibition venues and their thematic connections were planned to represent the flow of Portuguese civilization, beginning near the ancient medieval centre of the city and advancing along the banks of the Tagus to the Tower of Belém, the maritime gateway separating Lisbon from the Atlantic Ocean that had done so much to mould the nature of Portuguese civilization. Each of the five venues was conceived as a nucleus, which were "almost simultaneously, moments, phases or results of that essential meeting. Each one of the buildings represents the plastic definition or the creative vocation of the finality it had to embody."[645] The convent of Madre de Deus displayed the ancient cultures prior to the formation of the state, and the Casa dos Bicos focused on the role and patronage of artists and the connections between the themes of their work and everyday life, while the Jerónimos Monastery hosted *A Arte e a Missionação na Rota do Oriente* (Art and Evangelization on the Route to the Orient).

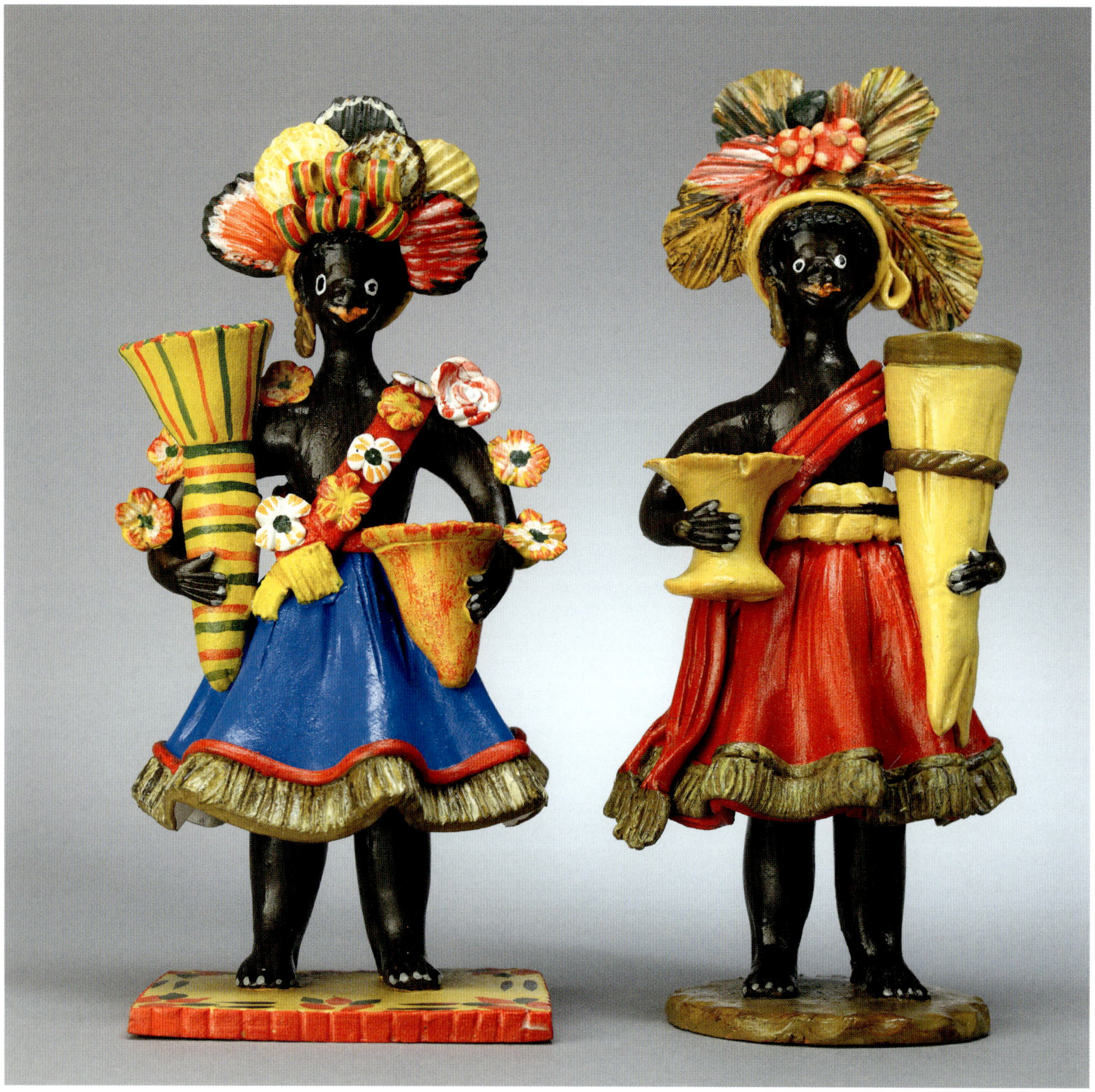

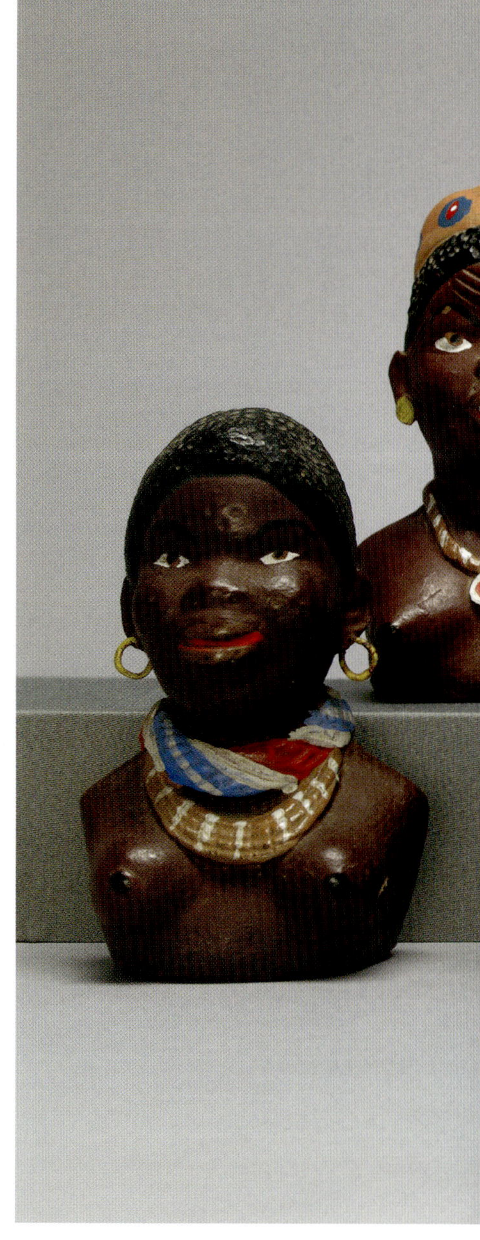

above
PERPÉTUA MATILDE FONSECA SOUSA AND MARIA INÁCIA FONSECA MATEUS
Allegorical figures representing Brazil's cornucopia, 2009.

right
Busts of African racial types from Angola and Mozambique, c. 1940–1950.

Unlike previous projects, the exhibition was not intended to focus solely on Portugal or the Portuguese world. Pedro Canavarro, the exhibition's general commissioner, was adamant that "this exhibition is a significant moment not only on an integrational level in . . . European culture, but also on a national level, for it represents the recovery of urban monuments and the yearned for and proven relation with Europe."[646]

Canavarro insisted that within the politics of European unity, culture provides an essential tool for unification. He acknowledged that "since the most remote ages, the great European centers have foreseen, informed and shaped the beginning of the sea adventure."[647] He added,

> When we undertake this "show" in Portugal we are taking another important step into the inalienable expression of our European cultural identity . . . in a singular and interesting way, for it is the theme itself that suggests and turns real the participation of other countries outside the reach of the European Council. Thus is the compromise of our country as the natural and historical interlocutor between Europe and new worlds.[648]

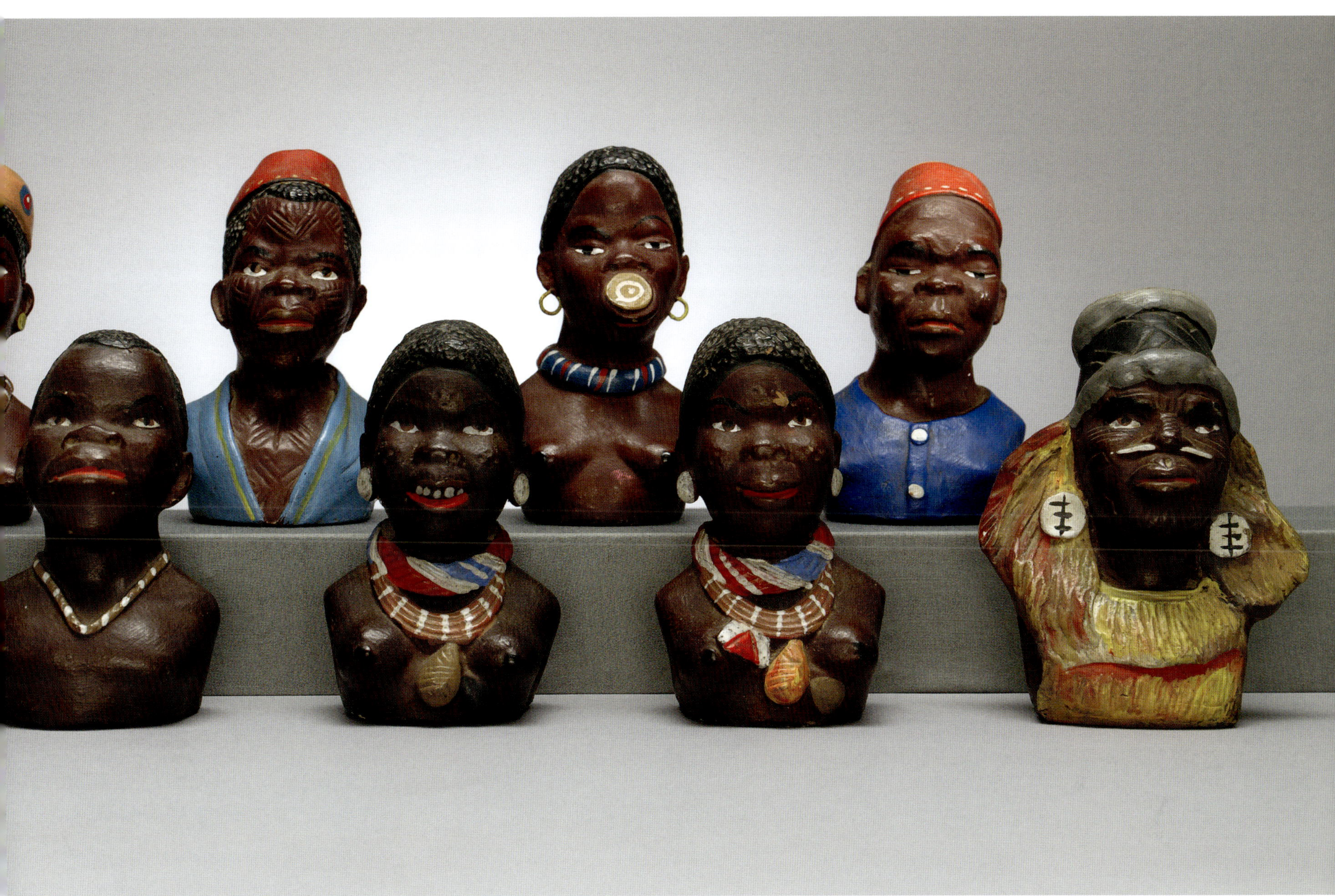

This was no longer an insular or a national history but a project that strove to situate Portuguese history within the wider context of the European continent. Nevertheless, Canavarro did not abandon Portugal's historical relations with its former empire, but used this legacy to support his country's role in promoting a wider dialogue in which it became the interlocutor with Africa and the East in forging new relationships on behalf of the European Union. At the same time, the past legitimation of exploration and colonial activities was subtly shifted away from its older justifications based on civilizing and evangelism, to its contribution to creating spaces for the promotion of cultural and scientific dialogue, which promised reciprocal benefits to former colonizers and colonized alike. The commissioner general's sentiments were not for Portugal to exchange its historical commitments to the Portuguese world for a new set of compromises within the European Union, nor to abandon one national historical ontology for a European historiography, but to encapsulate the Portuguese world, along with Portugal itself, within the wider framework of Europe.

This world's identity is still defined by language and religion, and belief in a spiritualized national identity is also re-acknowledged. But here too there has been a subtle shift in interpretation. The spirit no longer refers to a specific Portuguese way of being but is identified as an expression of scientific knowledge and culture that transcends nation-states and strives to attain the universality that Pascoaes and Coimbra imagined. National identity is maintained within a common European political and economic framework, and neither the fall of the dictatorship nor European membership imply a decisive choice between a European or Lusitanian future.

These subtle but significant shifts in historical ontology and the recasting of identity are endemic to the content and structure of the exhibitions. First, through the network of European institutions mediated by the Council of Europe, Portugal was able to reconstitute the testaments of its patrimony more effectively and to greater effect than at any time in her history, to focus on the impact of the Portuguese Discoveries on the European Renaissance. The content reproduced in past exhibitions, notably those of the Portuguese Primitivists, still occupied a significant position but performed a different function. The exhibition at the Museu Nacional de Arte Antiga was structured around two themes: the reception of the materials, arts and manufactures found or made in the new worlds stemming from the Portuguese encounter and the then contemporary political, social, cultural and intellectual culture, including that of a wider Europe, that had existed and grown in Portugal as a result of this meeting of worlds. According to Macedo, "The Discoveries forced Portugal to spectacularly increase contact with Europe, in all its diversity,"[649] including commerce, fashion, decoration, armaments, literature and art as well as ideas and problems regarding diplomacy, administration and jurisprudence. In this revisionist history, the Discoveries, far from contributing towards Portugal's disinterest in Europe, brokered and accelerated her Europeanization.

"Portugal," according to Macedo, "was acquiring Dürer's masterpieces—and, at the same time, making acquaintances with Congo and India; living the Italian humanism—and, at the same time, meeting the Indian and Chinese ways of life; paying visits to the Brazilian primitives—and, at the same time, sending envoys to Ethiopia. In an apparent incoherence, there was in the same area—Portugal—a confluence of very rich and diverse expressions of a culture so far completely unknown."[650] And later: "In its plastic expression, it is this permeability between Portugal—a bearer of information and news, a creator of new technologies—and Renaissance Europe as bearer of differing cultural attitudes which constituted what was to be seen in the National Museum of Ancient Art."[651]

A Arte e a Missionação na Ruta do Oriente, on the other hand, emphasized the interpenetration of Portuguese culture and the cultures of Africa, Iran, India, Japan and China through displaying hybrid manufactures that these encounters had produced and that Portugal had helped circulate throughout Europe.[652] Portuguese culture of the fifteenth and sixteenth centuries was no longer portrayed as the bearer of an insular genius inherent to itself, but as open and receptive to new ideas from all over Europe as well as from the new worlds it was exploring—what in later exhibitions would be described as its unique "plasticity." Gone was the attitude "that, behind the doors of our cities, in the nearby distance of the countryside, there are vast poetic and 'pagan' pastures where one can still hear songs, myths and the spreading murmur of the *folkelighed*," as Portugal acknowledged that the voices of other cultures might exist now only as captured fragments inscribed within the interior of scriptural systems.[653]

The Portuguese Pavilion in the Universal Exposition of Seville in 1992 further developed this intellectual reorientation, reaffirming the change in world view consistent with the country's full membership in the European Union. The tone of the catalogue texts to this successive exhibitionary complex is more confident, the ideas more decisively formulated and the work as a whole more convincing. The organization of the Seville exhibition moved away from the aesthetic focus of the 1983 *Blooms the Earth* to adopt a more anthropocentric perspective centred on Portugal. Furthermore, the commission responsible for the exhibition expressed their resolute commitment to rethinking the issue of Portuguese identity.[654] The exhibition emphasized four themes—culture, language, cooperation and communication—that allowed Portugal to reiterate its own and its former empire's cultural uniqueness while re-emphasizing its role as a mediator between different cultures. In his preface to the exhibition catalogues, the lawyer, politician and writer Vasco Graça Moura (1942–2014), the first commissioner general of the National Commission for the Commemoration of the Portuguese Discoveries, expands the idea of Portuguese cultural hybridity:

> It is a pre-eminently syncretistic and eclectic originality, approaching reality more in terms of concrete experience than of abstract or generalizing theoreticization; it places great store in cultural crossbreeding as a dignified and essential factor of enrichment at all levels; and it is profoundly interested in attracting and incorporating whatever is different and morphologically heterogeneous. This is true from the Manueline style to the Indo-Portuguese style, from Fernão Mendes Pinto's *Peregrination* to Vasco Fernandes's *Adoration of the Magi* or Father António Vieira's sermons, from the island of Mozambique to Salvador of the Bahia or Goa and Macau.[655]

He also writes, "The dynamics of today's Portugal is above all a dynamics of contact, recovering and reorganizing in contemporary terms a heritage whose tremendous wealth and diversity we hope to be able to demonstrate."[656]

Universalist assumptions are still embedded in these texts, but now they take the form of humanism: "We speak of European roots and origins, but also of our maritime vocation, of the spirit of restless adventure, of cultural and mercantile tradition, of capacity for action, innovation and enterprise, of cultural marks brought back from the world where we ventured, and the traces that we left there that have endured."[657] There is an implicit philosophy of spirit and along with it the romance of adventure, the determination to survive adversity, the epic of valiant deeds and unifying legacy, but without the older politics of insular nationalism or the full recognition of a new scriptural hegemony.

A further shift occurring in the ten years that separated the 1983 from the 1992 exhibitions was the decreased coverage given to religion and its substitution by secular themes. The 1992 exhibition introduced religious works under the rubrics of "The Christian North" and "Portugal in Western Christendom," but these were smaller in number than in previous exhibitions. Here it was not doctrine or spirituality or submission to the calling of God that provided the curators' focus, but the institutional and ideological role of Christendom in constructing Portuguese civilization that was made centre stage. Moreover, the exhibition balanced Christianity with sections on Islam and Judaism, which were and still are usually elided in Portuguese discourses on national identity. Moura acknowledges that "we can only discover what already exists" and reminds his readers that the Discoveries "engendered both splendours and misery," though such contacts might, in time, become both "reciprocal and interactive."[658]

Once a new exhibitionary paradigm was constructed from the fresh research and new methodologies sponsored by the commission, the model was effectively transposed to other institutions. The Museu Nacional de Machado de Castro's 1992 exhibition *De Goa a Lisboa* (From Goa to Lisbon) presented Portugal in relation to other European and Asian countries as a culture in continuous transformation, noting the reciprocal cultural interpenetrations between them and the changes in style and decoration of furniture, ceramics, textiles and other items this engendered. Portugal is positioned alongside Asian civilizations as one of many actors in a transcontinental drama that would later challenge aesthetics, commerce and geopolitical balances throughout Europe. The cosmopolitan, globalized nature of the fifteenth- and sixteenth-century societies on the Indian Ocean that predated Europe's arrival attained in 1992 official acknowledgement, even if the ambiguous nature of the early Portuguese sailors, sometimes described in Asian sources more as pirates than merchants, evaded comment.[659]

This revisionist history further evolved in the exhibitions organized for the 1998 quincentenary commemoration of the Portuguese Discoveries, which most notably included Expo '98, hosted in Lisbon. The Commission for the Commemoration of the Portuguese Discoveries inaugurated an exhibition at the Geographical Society of Lisbon to mark the quincentenary of da Gama's voyage to India: *O centenário da Índia (1898) e a memória da viagem de Vasco da Gama* (The Centenary of India (1898) and the Memory of Vasco da Gama's Voyage). However, unlike the earlier exhibition of 1898, also organized by the Geographical Society, the 1998 show focused not on oceanography, historical biography or the "empirical facts" of the encounter, but on a critical deconstruction of the earlier show. This reflexive, critical engagement with the past also characterized other exhibitions undertaken as part of this program, including *Os Construtores do Oriente Português* (1998), *O Orientalismo em Portugal* (1999) and *Os Índios Nós* (2000).

Nowhere was this revisionism more marked than in the 1998 exhibition *Cultures of the Indian Ocean*. António Manuel Hespanha, the general commissioner of the Commission for the Commemoration of the Portuguese Discoveries, was explicit concerning the commission's intentions: "In our opinion, little can be understood from the history of the Portuguese in the East, if this East—the essence of its history and culture—is not well understood. Understood, that is, from the perspectives of the autonomous ways, categories, sensitivities and images of its diverse cultures."[660] The then director of the Museu Nacional de Arte Antiga, José Luís Porfírio, concurred with the originality of the vision of Hespanha and the exhibit's curator, Rosa Maria Perez. Recalling an earlier meeting with Hespanha and Perez in the museum's gardens overlooking the Tagus, he writes, "I had the immediate perception of a unique initiative that did not repeat schemes already extensively elaborated about the meeting of cultures, but sought instead to reconstruct, through an exhibition, the nature of the differences."[661]

Here it is not India but the Indian Ocean itself that becomes the stage for a complex plurality of encounters, not only between Portugal and India but, predating that, between Islamic and Buddhist cultures and the inhabitants of Africa, the Middle

East and Asia. The Portuguese intruded into a theatre of already hybridized cultures, which, according to Hespanha's over-compensatory and exaggerated determinism,

> dictated the reactions to our arrival and our emigration there. It was with them with whom our diplomacy was involved, improvising formulas unknown in the European tradition. It was they that—in the way in which they permitted the Portuguese to understand them—dictated our political, commercial and missionary strategies. And finally, it was they who stimulated the senses and piqued the imagination, creating a cultural fascination which has survived the disappearance of political hegemony or diminishing economic interests.[662]

Gone from this extraordinary statement are the triumphalism of Camões and the tradition of a century of Portuguese commemorations. The terms of encounter have been reversed, denying the active agency attributed solely to colonizing powers and acknowledging the complex positions taken by those who confronted their Portuguese colonists. This more elaborate, stratified and hybridized approach to the Portuguese encounters with Asia underpinned Hespanha's own exhibition in this series, *O Orientalismo em Portugal* (1999), and Jorge Manuel Flores's earlier show, *Os Construtores do Oriente Português* (1998).

The revisionism in both the 1992 and 1998 exhibitions was not the work of only one or a team of curators but was orchestrated by a powerful, well-funded commission established to oversee and promote the celebration of the Discoveries during the period 1988–2002. Funded by the government, the National Commission for the Commemoration of the Portuguese Discoveries was mandated to direct the "preparation, organization and coordination, at the domestic and international level, of the celebrations of the historical events" related to the Portuguese Discoveries, including those related to the Discoveries Pavilion at Lisbon's Expo '98.[663] First under the directorship of Vasco Graça Moura (1988–95) and later under António Manuel Hespanha (1995–99) and Joaquim Romero de Magalhães (1999–2002), the commission undertook a re-examination, at times controversial, of the scholarship related to the representation of the Discoveries to provide new perspectives for the more than one hundred exhibitions it sponsored during its fifteen-year existence. It sought, in the words of its second commissioner general, that

> da Gama's voyage should not be treated solely as a spectacular symbolic act, that brought the world of the Indian Ocean to Europe and the world of Europe there, five centuries ago. Our intention, above all, was to place the commemorations in a historically correct perspective, correcting the distorted view which, practically since the beginning, has characterized Portuguese images of the East and the reading the Portuguese have given to their own activities there.[664]

In the words of the curator of the exhibition *Cultures of the Indian Ocean*, "Notwithstanding the historical and artistic legitimacy of the 'traditional' Portuguese view of India...this exhibition intends to invert it, taking the voyage of Vasco da Gama as an important cultural route, as the promoter of a sophisticated meeting of civilizations, the fruits of which are very little known to the general Portuguese public."[665] The curator goes on to assert that her exhibition breaks with the traditional Luso-centric approach to examine the effects of contact

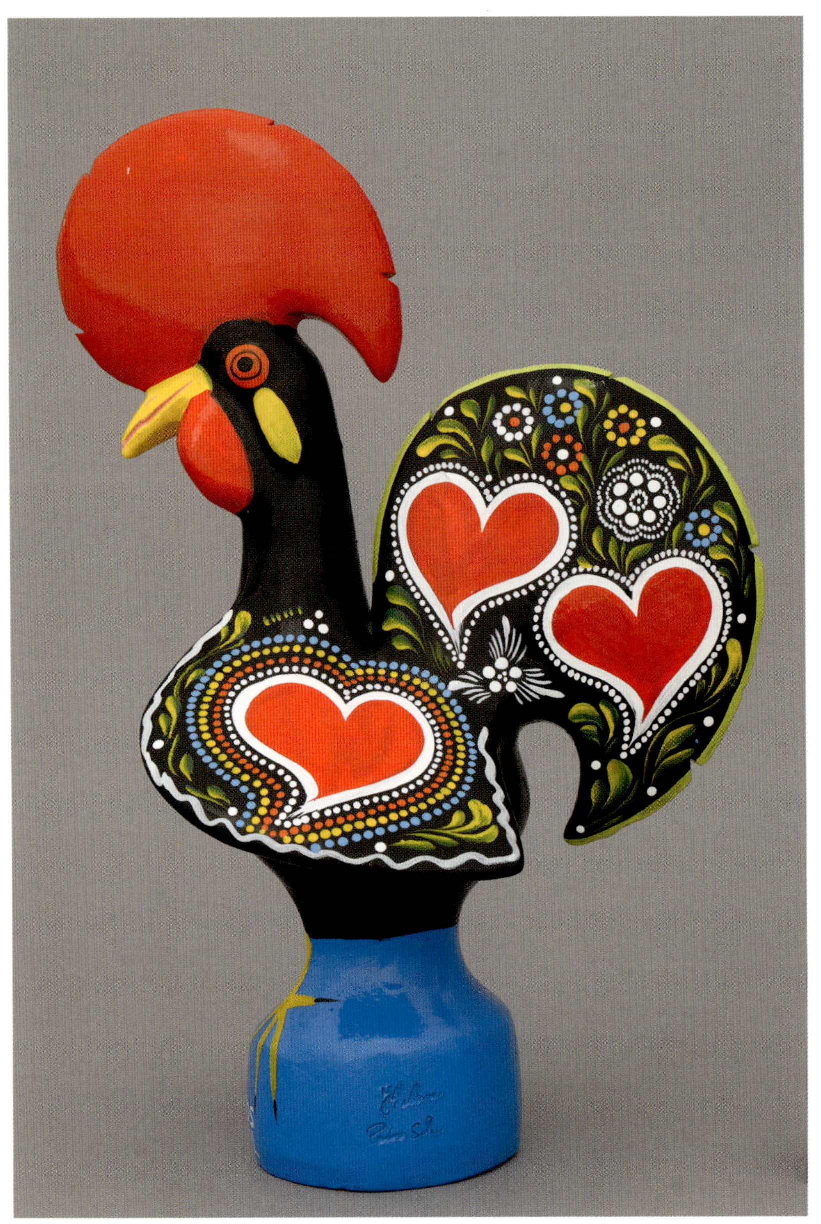

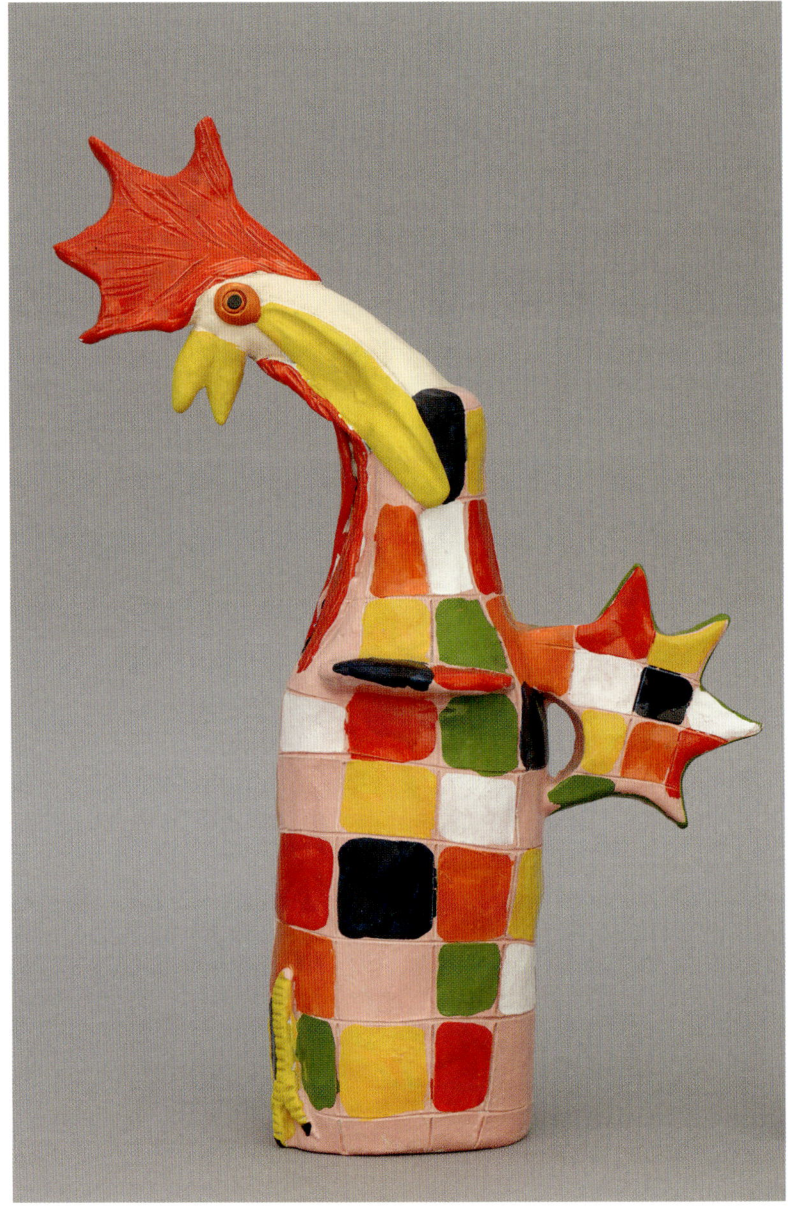

over time, thereby displacing the attention previously focused on da Gama and the voyage itself to the historical contingencies and continuing effects of the encounter he engendered.

The commission mobilized large sectors of the academic and research communities, first establishing a university-level teaching and research centre, the Convent Conferences, later named the Arrábida Conferences, and then the Atlantic University, which included a Department of Atlantic, African and Oriental Studies, areas that had long been ignored by Portuguese universities. It also established new professorial chairs in the European University Institute in Florence, the University of São Paulo (Brazil) and Brown University (USA), supported lectureships and research centres elsewhere and established master's programs in the art faculties of the Universities of Porto, Lisbon, Lisbon Nova and the Azores. The University of Coimbra received funding to introduce courses in colonial art and the art of the Discoveries; new archive centres were established in association with the Torre do Tombo, the national archive in Lisbon, and the Gil Eanes Study Centre in Lagos, in the south of the country. Furthermore, the commission supported fellowships and scholarships in Portuguese history for students all over the world, particularly in Africa. It planned twenty-seven conferences and

facing, left
MARIA HELENA PEDRO SILVA
Rooster, c. 2010
Barcelos
The rooster, Portugal's unofficial national symbol, was first modelled by Domingos Côto in Barcelos in 1935.

facing, right
JOÃO GONÇALVES FERREIRA
Rooster, 2007
Braga
The rooster remains a widely endorsed expression of honesty, integrity, trust and honour.

congresses and, by 2002, had sponsored or had itself published 546 titles and was editing two journals, *Mare Liberum* and *Oceanos*.[666]

The budget and extent of the resources deployed by the commission enabled it to create an international network of scholars and institutions sharing similar commitments towards meticulously revising the sources and interpretations of Portuguese history. Politically, such a project had the potential to stimulate a thorough revision of the country's historical memory and reorient commonly held perceptions of national identity.

The extent of the revision this research made possible is well attested to in two of the exhibitions sponsored by the commission and hosted by the Museu Nacional de Etnologia (National Museum of Ethnography): *Stories from Goa*, curated by Rosa Maria Perez and Susana Sardo in 1997, and *Os Índios Nós* (We, the Indians), coordinated by Joaquim Pais de Brito in 2000.[667] Both followed the interpretive strategies and aspirations Hespanha had championed. *Stories from Goa* deliberately abandoned the temptation towards grand narratives or a reduction and synthesis of local histories within Portuguese narratives of empire, substituting instead micro-histories collected directly from the people of Goa and expressed through prose, paintings, films, objects and songs. This multimedia approach avoided static representations of Goa in favour of attempting to show culture in the very process of its making and continuous reconstruction. Moreover, the stories that were textualized in the exhibition and accompanying catalogue were structured as dialogues between community members and curators, effusing the presentation with vitality, rare in ethnographic exhibitions. The catalogue brought together Indian and Portuguese scholars to unravel the effects and define the differing metropolitan views of Goa and India over the centuries of Portuguese domination. It examined language, the effects of tourism and development and Indo-Portuguese literature and architecture as well as the uses and refractive qualities of different media, travel accounts, religions and political ideologies in identity construction. Pais de Brito elegantly describes the relation between these texts and exhibition in his preface:

> These stories flow together as an approximation of the interwoven and polymorphous space of Goa that the texts of the catalogue of this exhibition analyses. But it is also these that are fragmented in the subjectivities that they evoke or awaken and that are probably the sense that most helps the construction of the readings that each of us make of an exhibition.[668]

Os Índios Nós, which focused on Amazonia, deepened this dialogical approach by inviting non-Indian spectators to contemplate the society they and indigenous people share and the textual and visual strategies deployed to understand this society. It included testaments from early explorers and modern anthropologists in which specific cultural identities were inscribed and indigenous knowledges insinuated into each other's scriptural regimes. The first section, Lessons, contrasted catechists written in indigenous languages and grammar books and vocabularies used by the Portuguese to "educate" Amerindians with the notebooks, diagrams, pictures and maps given to anthropologists by the indigenous peoples themselves to help them understand their societies. The next section, Confrontations and Fear, focused on the collection of watercolours painted by Joaquim José de Miranda in 1771 while among the Xakan Kaingang people in Paraná. This was followed by Knowledge and Wealth, which looked at the "philosophical" voyage of Alexandre Rodrigues Ferreira and included two cabinets, each profiling a different museum collection (*An Old Craftsman* and *War and Peace*). The next section of the exhibition refocused attention on indigenous interpretations of different aspects of Amazonian cultures as these have been written by anthropologists. The final section examined the connections between communities and the Brazilian state in the context of the problematic creation of frontiers. Taken together, the exhibition acknowledged the hybridization and the mutual influences between different cultures and their effect in shaping Brazilian identities as reflected in modern intercultural politics and literature.

The exhibitions sponsored by the Discoveries Commission included reflexive, mainly archival displays such as *O centenário da Índia* and *O Orientalismo em Portugal*; historical exhibitions like that on Dom João V (the last exhibition sponsored by the commission); art exhibitions, including those on ancient art like *Do Mundo antigo aos Novos Mundos: Humanismo, Classicismo e Notícias dos Descobrimentos en Évora* (1516–1624) (From the Old World to the New Worlds: Humanism, Classicism and News of Discovery in Évora, 1516–1624; 1998), and *Francisco Henriques: Um pintor em Évora no tempo de D. Manuel I* (Francisco Henriques: A Painter in Évora in the time of King Manuel I; 1997); as well as contemporary art shows that profiled artists from Portuguese-speaking Africa and Brazil, including an important cycle of four exhibitions under the rubrics of *Trading Images* (Museu da Cidade, Lisbon, 1998) and *Spanning an Entire Ocean* (Culturgest, Lisbon, 2000). The historical exhibitions attempted to avoid the ideological subterfuges of the past and embraced a wider purview than at any previous time, while the contemporary art shows included multimedia artists whose work directly addressed issues around national identity, globalization and the ideological complicities of knowledge.

Despite their critical positioning and diverse disciplinary and interdisciplinary approaches, these commemorations were not without their critics. The anthropologist Miguel Vale de Almeida sees in them a reassertion of essentialized Portuguese racial categorizations based on similar presuppositions as those that underlay previous constructions of national identity.[669] Some of these new textual exegeses and the visual assemblages they informed hid the continued assertions of national character formulated under discourses of Lusotropicalism by the influential Brazilian sociologist Gilberto Freyre (1900–87) and supported by the Portuguese anthropologist Jorge Dias. Lusotropicalism had gained partial acknowledgement by the Estado Novo in the 1950s to quell European hostility towards the regime's continued commitment to colonialism.[670] Freyre's argument,[671] conceived after a year's research trip across Portuguese-speaking Africa, Brazil and Goa, insisted that Portuguese colonialism was different from that administered by other European powers because of its fundamental humanitarianism, racial tolerance and miscegenation, which in the case of Brazil had led to racial democracy. Land, race and tradition, for Freyre as for Pascoaes, Coimbra and others, were the three elements that formed national character. He argued the uniquely Portuguese attitude could be explained by the country's geographical location, tightly wedged against the Atlantic, and the conditions under which the race was formed through its earlier encounter with North Africa and later influence from sub-Saharan Africa. These encounters had, Freyre argued, long made the Portuguese a mestizo nation and helped develop tolerance, openness and adaptability. Such an argument supported the Estado Novo in countering European criticism of its colonial policy by insisting on the specificity of this type of colonialism and its supposedly lofty aspirations to prepare its African states to become "new Brazils."

The absence of racial segregation in colonial Brazil also gave rise to a mestizo population with distinctive racial characteristics that, with the coming and going of peoples between the three continents, further added to Portugal's hybridized nature. Over time, Portugal came to share more commonalities with Brazil and Africa than with other parts of Europe. For Freyre, mestizoization and the conditions under which Brazilian rule had been conducted had encouraged Portugal's more benign colonial model.

As Vale de Almeida and João Leal have astutely argued, the Portuguese racial temperament and expansionist character, which Freyre promulgated, bore striking similarities to those that the influential anthropologist Jorge Dias had identified in his important 1950 essay "Os Elementos Fundamentais da Cultura Portuguesa" (The Fundamental Elements of Portuguese Culture). Furthermore, according to Leal, the majority of these racial characteristics had previously been identified by Teófilo Braga and Adolfo Coelho, who supported a folk psychology that divided Portuguese racial characteristics according to their positive or negative attributes. For Coelho, however, the negative traits stemmed from the perception of the nation's decadence and sudden realization of its waning power. From the late nineteenth to early twentieth centuries, Pascoaes expressed this feeling of decline and decadence in his rejection of material values and cosmopolitanism and his praise for the rural world and the national spirit forged from the miscegenation of Portugal's supposed opposing Aryan and Semitic inheritances.

Dias, like Pascoaes, described the Portuguese character as constituted from a series of contradictions: dream and action; kindness and violence; adaptability and closedness of character; individual liberty and collective solidarity. Freyre argued that these contradictions explain Portuguese history as a series of alternations between periods of greatness and decadence and commitment and indecision and concluded that Brazil and Portugal represented a new type of society that had grown from the miscegenation of their populations and the resulting shared spirit.[672] The Lusitanian spirit could be rethought as having been formed through a long historical process, which reaffirmed the inevitability of Portugal's extraterritorial and pluricultural civilization.

For Vale de Almeida, the problematic and essentialized racial traits that underlie Lusotropicalism and Dias's anthropological definition of national identity continued to be present and reaffirmed through the institutional context in which the quincentenary exhibitions emerged.[673] The radical change in exhibitionary practices that took place from 1983 to 2002 coincided not only with the incorporation of Portugal into the European Union but with the growth and expansion of the social sciences and the adoption by anthropology of more reflexive sociological paradigms. Like Portuguese museums, much of Portuguese anthropology has reoriented itself away from a concern with nation building towards a preoccupation with the nature of national and local identity and the problem of the inscription, reinscription and inventions of culture within a globalized and hypermediated world.

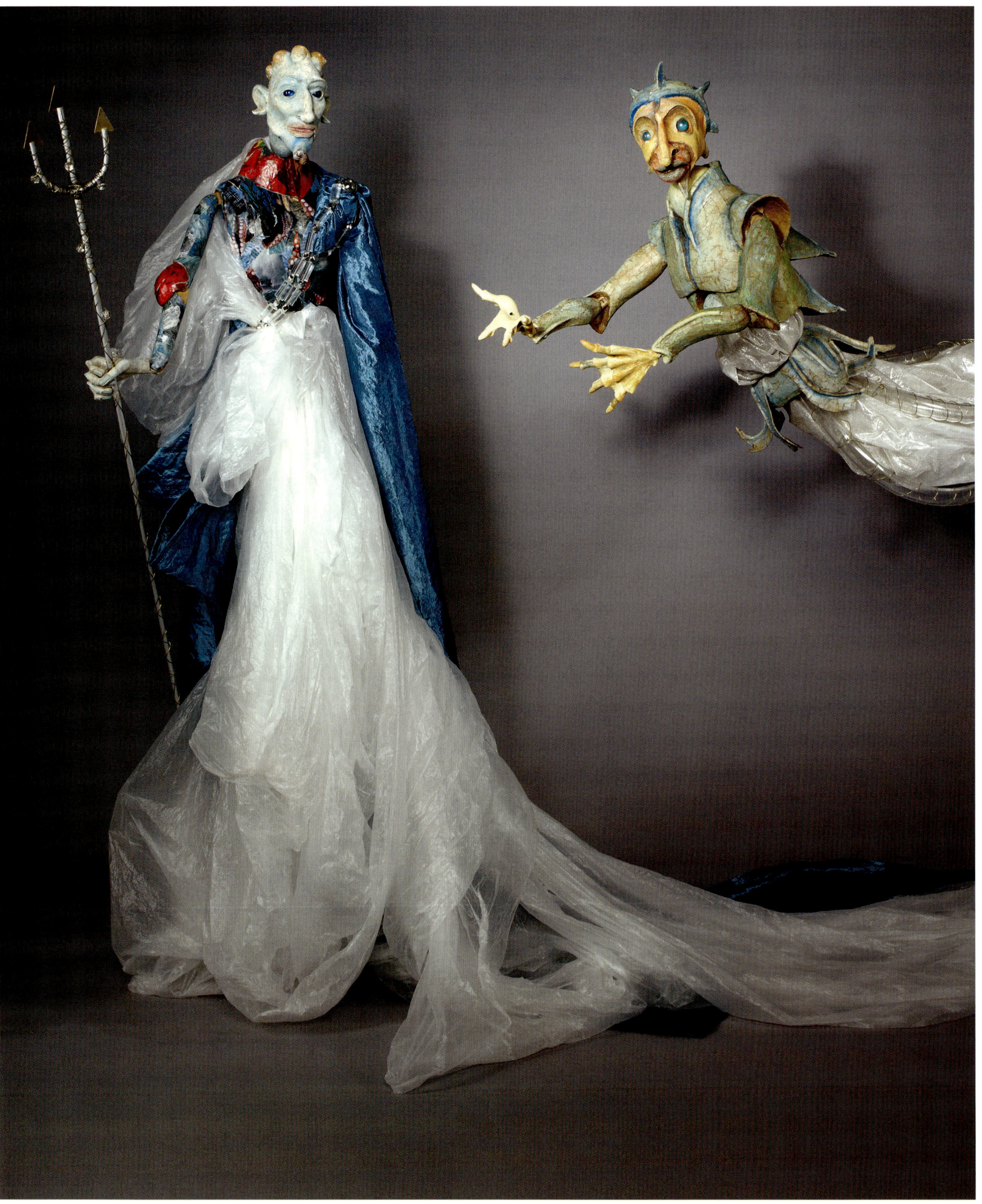

10 House of Dolls

Puppet Theatre and the Rebirth of History

Puppet theatre is unable to describe life as it is because it is aphoristic and prefers metaphorical expressions and forms. Despite being extraordinary, it is in its content realist, because it is destined to reflect life with the objective of transforming it. The realism of marionette theatre is the realism of the imagination.

Henrique Delgado[674]

WITH THE EXCEPTION of Jorge Dias and his small team, the Estado Novo did not conceive ethnography as a field-based inquiry. The collections assembled by the regime's Secretariat of National Propaganda in the 1930s and 1940s for exhibitions both at home and abroad were not made by specialists or teams but ordered by government officials and usually gathered through their local intermediary organizations.[675] Neither were collections built systematically, and the ensuing poor documentation led to objects being divorced from their originating social, economic and political contexts and significances.[676] This was a hands-off ethnography that valued distance over contact, metropolitan interpretation over local exegesis and decorative quality over community function and significance. It preferred ill-defined notions such as "the epiphany of the marvellous"[677] over local knowledge and inspection. Displays of lively, colourful and charming domestic ethnographic objects during the 1930s and 1940s enabled the Estado Novo to focus attention away from the decadence and decline of agriculture, the effects of emigration and urban migration, inequalities in land ownership, poor stewardship and the impoverished conditions in which most of the population lived, towards a more cheerful, manufactured, imaginary Portugal.[678] Moreover, because the popular was equated largely with the rural population and was seldom extended to acknowledge subaltern urban cultures,[679] the everyday art forms of cities and resorts were seldom acknowledged. Rural societies were effectively cordoned off and isolated by governmental practices, and popular expression, including puppet theatre and public masquerades, because they had the propensity to insinuate themselves to disrupt sanctioned optical and ideological regimes, were tightly controlled or prohibited.

Notably absent from governmental ethnographic collections and interpretation was puppetry, a traditional form of entertainment once found in urban areas, seaside resorts and fairs but

facing
JORGE CERQUEIRA
Marionette, 2012
Neptune and Triton from Luís de Camões's *Os Lusíadas*.

facing
Manuel Rosado's Mexican Pavilion, c. 1968.

largely overlooked by the Museu de Arte Popular and exhibition organizers alike.[680]

LIBERTY, SATIRE AND ILLUSION

Puppetry had been performed in Portugal from at least the eighteenth century, as attested to in a note by Alexandre Herculano, who unexpectedly encountered a group of puppets hanging outside a house in Lisbon's Bairro Alto district.[681] Puppetry may have originated in medieval religious ceremonies and Corpus Christi celebrations, which, although prohibited by the Church in 1600, later resurfaced in fairs and other secular entertainments.[682]

There were three types of puppet troupes: first, those that were set up in pavilions during popular fairs by the likes of Joaquim Pinto (1899–1968) of Setúbal, Domingos Moura (19??–1995), António Dias (1920–86) of Lisbon and Manuel Rosado (1909–??), who lived in Almeirim; second, regional companies like the Santo Aleixo puppeteers, whose last director was António Talhinhas and which toured a specific area to take advantage of carnivals, religious fairs, markets and other local gatherings; and third, seaside performers like Jaime "Maluco," Henrique Duarte, Felipe Nunes, Zé Pequeno, Roberto Valente, Augusto Sérgio and contemporary puppeteers who worked or work the beaches between Setúbal and Figueira da Foz.[683] Most puppeteers were itinerant, a style of life disapproved of by the Estado Novo, and performed seasonally; those who worked the *romarias*, fairs and markets were especially active from May to October, while beach puppeteers concentrated their shows in the summer holiday period. Because their members were farm workers, the small regional troupes like the Santo Aleixo puppeteers would tour only in winter after the growing season had ended.

Puppeteers worked alone or with their families, and some were part of relatively large groups that included musicians and bandsmen. Joaquim Pinto's troupe included three puppet manipulators, two assistants and five musicians who played concertina, trombone, saxophone, accordion and trumpet.[684] In some families puppetry was passed from generation to generation. Faustino Duarte, owner of the Guignol Pavilion, passed his profession to his son Henrique Duarte, who in turn trained Joaquim Pinto. Manuel Jaleca traced his descent from six generations of puppeteers, while Augusto Sérgio learned puppetry from his father, António Pereira Guimarães (1895–1961), who worked in one of the Braga pavilions.[685] Puppetry had also been inherited within the Nepomuceno family, the heirs of the Santo Aleixo puppets, until 1940, when a family breakup divided the troupe and its puppet collection.[686] Other renowned puppeteers, such as Manuel Rosado and António Dias, became enthralled after seeing shows in their youth and undertook informal apprenticeships. Clarinda de Azevedo, one of the few women puppeteers, was a circus performer with no family connections to the art who changed her career to be trained as a puppeteer by Manuel Rosado.[687]

Puppeteers inherited or often made their own puppets and scenery. Joaquim Pinto and Manuel Rosado organized their shows in pavilions hastily erected using canvas walls and tin roofs, which at night could easily be used for sleeping. According to Pinto there were tens of thousands of puppet theatre enthusiasts before the 1960s, and many troupes attracted large audiences. Rosado's Mexican Pavilion could accommodate up to 220 spectators. Local rural troupes like the Santo Aleixo puppeteers also drew impressive audiences, but they performed by the light cast by oil lamps in barns and sheds left empty after the harvests had been shipped.

Portuguese puppetry was a participative art not meant for simple contemplation. Many performers

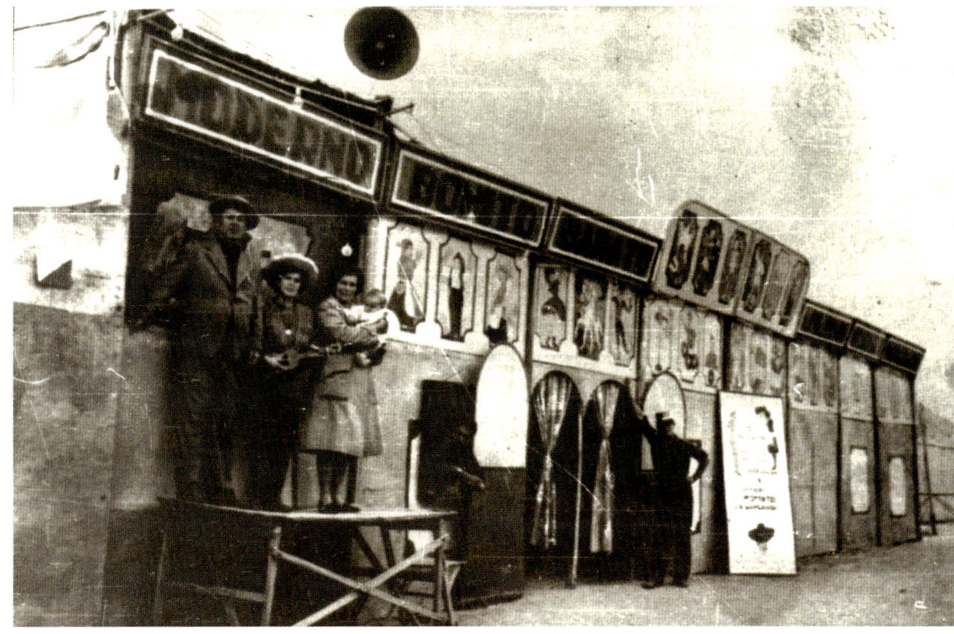

encouraged a close relationship with their audiences. The Santo Aleixo puppet company promoted its audience's active engagement in its shows, and those who knew the performance were not shy about shouting reminders or corrections to the puppeteers' interpretations of their stories. Other puppeteers encouraged banter between their publics and puppets. The Santo Aleixo puppets toured the remote farmlands of the Alto Alentejo and the Spanish province of Extremadura. On arriving at a village, the troupe would parade around beating their drum and loudly announcing their presence and the place of their performance. Shows usually began between 9:00 and 10:00 PM and lasted between five and eight hours.[688] In the popular fairs and markets puppeteers would attract audiences by playing their guitars and singing by their tents until they had sufficient numbers to warrant beginning their shows.

The content of puppet performances varied. Part of the old established repertoire of the Santo Aleixo puppets was preserved in written form and included *The Creation of the World*, which incorporated the popular story of Cain and Abel; *The Birth of Christ*; and *Christ's Martyrdom*.[689] The interludes between the different scenes were filled with puppet dances and vignettes, including banter and comic exchanges between the two lead characters: Father Chanca, a priest, and Mestre-Sala, a master of ceremonies who introduced the plays. These two characters represented the tyrants that embodied Church and civic values and sometimes provided a means to express political criticism and anticlericalism, which had a long history in Alentejo.[690] The Santo Aleixo puppets combined popular religion with scattered humorous, critical social and political commentary, which may have escaped official censure because of the remote locations in which they performed.

The pavilions and seaside booths shared a different theatrical repertoire, which often included performances like *O Barbeiro Diabólico* (The Barber of Seville), *A Tourada* (The Bullfight), *Os Três Namorados* (The Three Lovers) and *O Castelo dos Fantasmas* (The Castle of Ghosts).[691] Pinto's and Rosado's troupes performed *The Marquis of Pombal and the Jesuits* and even, in the latter's case, included a piece on the military struggle in Angola,[692] neither of which endeared them to the military government.[693] Others, like Ernesto de Abreu, incorporated parody into established plays.[694] Even religiously themed plays like those on the death of Saint John the Baptist or the story of Cain and his damnation and subsequent adventures with Diabo retained a satirical and critical content that could easily antagonize government and Church authorities. One record recounts that in 1798, a village priest, Father Vicente Pedro da Rosa, outraged by the disrespectful homilies of Father Chanca and other Santo Aleixo puppets, took revenge by burning some of the characters outside of his house. Pinto's and Rosado's repertoires were more secular than the Santo Aleixo troupe,[695] which Henrique Delgado regarded as the heir to the medieval ecclesiastical tradition. Other troupes also included popular religious stories such as *Os Milagres de Santo António* (The Miracles of Saint Anthony), *O Milagre de Santa Isabel* (The Miracle of Saint Elizabeth) and *Nossa Senhora da Nazaré* (Our Lady of Nazaré).[696]

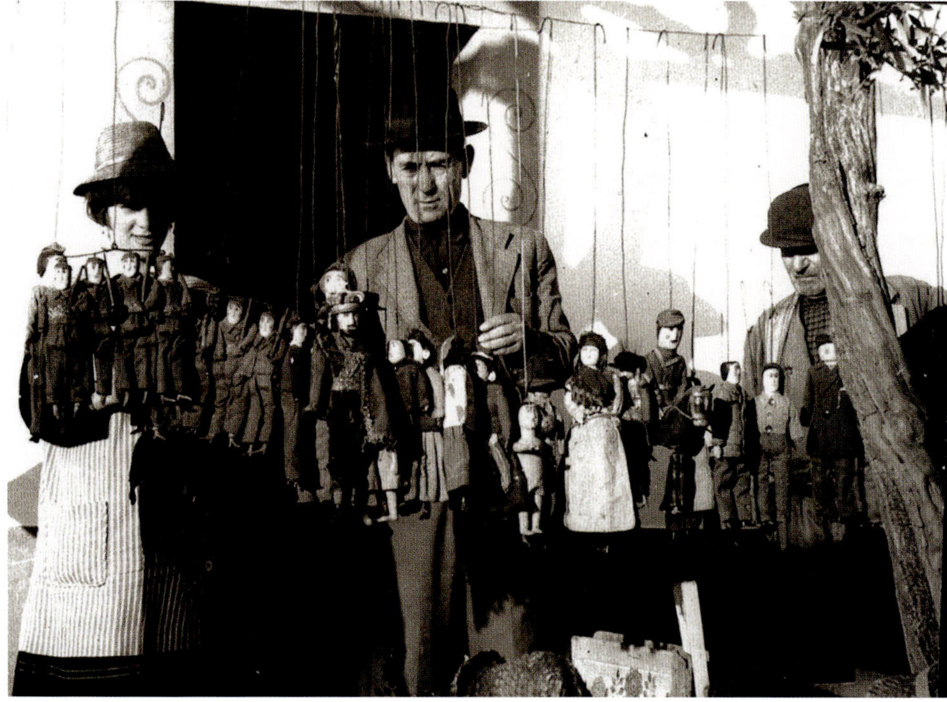

above
The Santo Aleixo puppets with Manuel Jaleca, António Talhinhas and an unidentified woman, c. 1967.

facing
The Santo Aleixo puppets and stage decoration, Museu da Marioneta, Lisbon.

Delgado believed the power of puppetry lay not in copying "the extreme forms of life, but in revealing their essence through the forms born of poetic imagination.... In puppetry, the principal concern is not aesthetic experience but its immediate psychological impact. To give life to an inanimate body is the supreme act of creation. Marionette theatre has two aspects: to give liberty to illusion and the tendency to humanization."[697] Puppets, Delgado believed, should be performed like musical instruments, responding to all the nuances of their manipulators as if they were extensions of their bodies.[698] This close relationship between puppeteers and the puppets they made or inherited sometimes tightly and even tragically tied their destinies together. The old puppeteer Alexandre "Vassourinhas," who had retired close to Braga and who taught Ernesto de Abreu, insisted that on his death his puppets be buried with him,[699] while another story tells that one of the most renowned modern-day puppeteers set fire to his room, both killing himself and burning his puppets. In a similar tragic vein some of the oldest of the Santo Aleixo puppets, part of those that Antónia Maria Nepomuceno had kept after her separation from Manuel Jaleca, were after her death found in a case under her bed, leaving nothing but dust and strings.

These incidents, although illustrating the close affective links between puppeteers and their puppets, were nevertheless unusual; puppets were normally inherited within the family, constantly being repaired and added to along with their repertoires. Troupes sometimes had extensive holdings: Joaquim Pinto had 400 puppets[700] and Rosado had 250,[701] while Talhinhas preserved about a hundred of the Santo Aleixo puppets. José Manuel Gil estimates that by 1958 there were approximately nineteen puppet pavilions operating in Portugal.[702] Pinto retired in 1960, and Rosado's pavilion, the last to tour the fairs, finally succumbed to economic difficulties in 1968, leaving no place where puppet collections like these could be preserved.

Traditional puppetry went into steep decline in the 1960s and 1970s, and Gil is able to recall only two professional performers still working by 1980.[703] The state's support of popular arts and rural culture had, as previously described, always been selective, but after 1950 the cultural politics espoused by the Estado Novo's former secretary of national propaganda, António Ferro, lost its earlier strong focus and impetus. Indifference to puppetry was well established, and it is interesting to note that in 1938, during the competition for the most Portuguese village, the submission from the small village of Orada included a marionette performance by the resident troupe of João Cartaxo and António Sande, which, since the submission was unsuccessful, probably made little impression on the jury. Guilherme Felgueiras wrote an article on Santo Aleixo puppets in *Arte Popular Portuguesa*, which was followed by another note written by Azinhal Abelho in the 1950s in the *Mensário das Casas do Povo*, but since puppetry was slow to catch the imagination of writers and intellectuals and easily courted disdain and hostility from political authorities, it elicited little mention. Not until the end of the

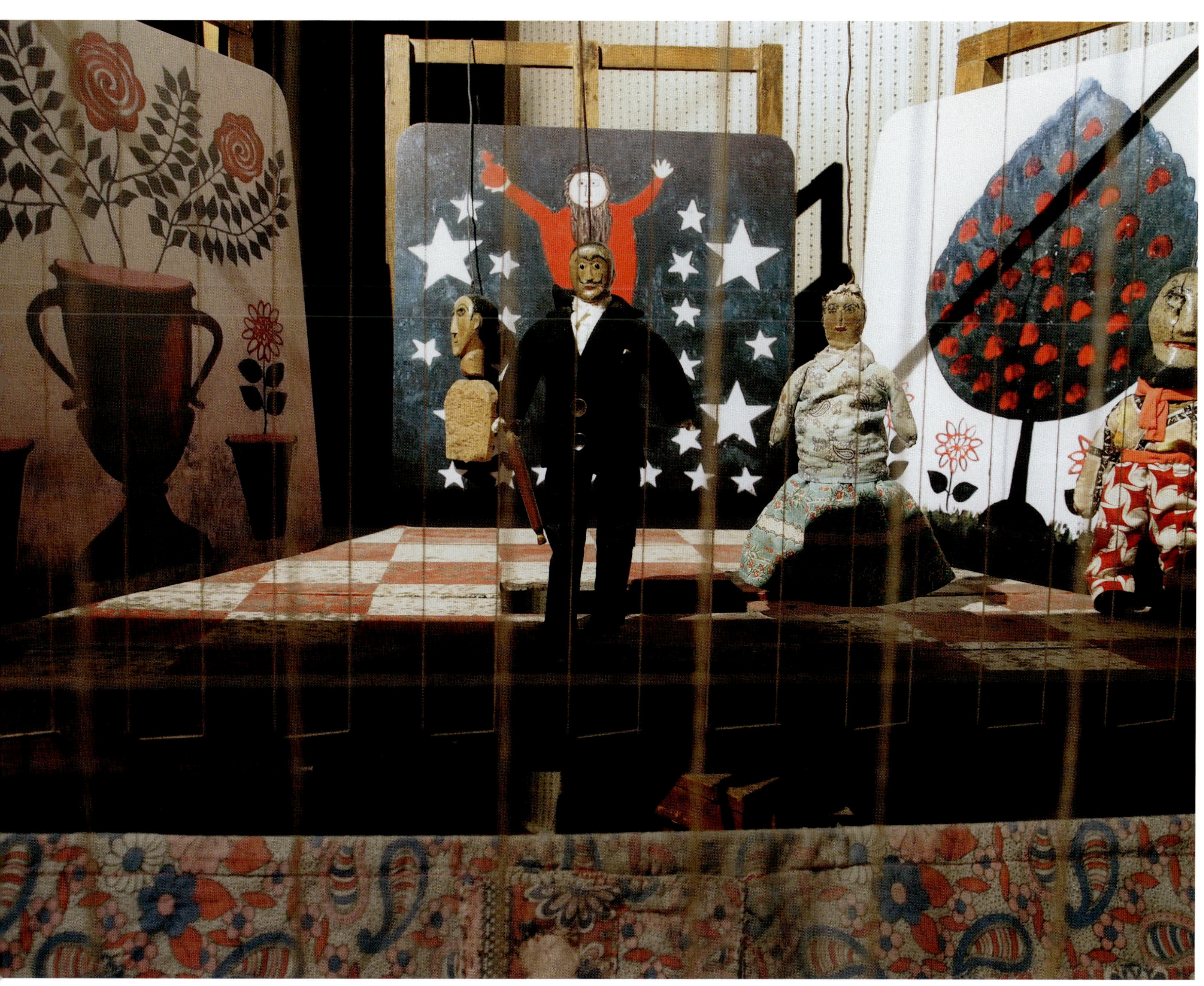

facing, left
Marionette maker Jorge Cerqueira in his workshop in Santa Susana, 2012.

facing, right
Jorge Cerqueira with Jupiter, 2015.

1960s were puppeteers invited to give shows in Lisbon theatres like the Casa da Comédia, but these often drew only small audiences and suffered from inadequate stage design and poor publicity, which often marketed the shows mainly to children.[704]

The Inspecção Geral dos Espectáculos (Inspector General of Performances) supervised the licensing of street performances and had the power to withhold or restrict permissions, leaving those performing without a licence open to arrest.[705] Itinerant puppeteers were persecuted, plays were censored and puppet characters were inspected and sometimes confiscated.[706] Political hostility, together with the declining rate of remuneration—many puppeteers led a poor life and died impoverished—contributed to the decline and disappearance of most troupes. Puppeteers suffered from other trends too. By 1970 popular fairs and markets had changed immeasurably. New and better transport systems meant that people no longer had to walk long distances to attend them, so instead of staying for a few days after their arrival, visitors could return home by bus if they so wished. The cost of renting a space to erect a stall also increased steadily, while the admission costs to performances remained low. Furthermore, puppeteers failed to update their repertoires because of censorship laws and were prevented from extensively commenting on contemporary events, which adversely affected the quality and intensity of their shows.[707] According to Delgado, by the 1960s vestiges of traditional puppetry existed only in Alto Alentejo, Extremadura and Ribatejo.[708] As if to formally mark the passing of Portugal's great puppet era, the distinguished director José Ernesto de Sousa released a highly romanticized film, *História de Dom Roberto* (1962), which included footage of one of the last great puppeteers of the period, António Dias. Lacking government support, the only institutional funding for puppetry during the 1960s and 1970s came from the Calouste Gulbenkian Foundation.

Although traditional puppetry declined significantly in these decades, the period also saw the emergence of a second wave of puppet theatre aimed at child audiences. These theatres were founded in Lisbon and Porto, usually by amateurs with no previous family connection to puppetry, and often included women as puppeteers. The writer Lília da Fonseca established the Teatro de Branca-Flor in 1962. The Teatro Robertoscope, founded in 1963, and the Teatro Lilipute, which opened four years later, were both operated by employees of companies that provided entertainment for children. Lena Perestrelo established her Teatro de Bonifrates before this period, in 1956, but later collaborated with the puppeteer Maria Aurora, who took the Teatro de Polichinelo to the state television network RTP.

From 1966 to 1971, Henrique Delgado (1938–71), the founder of Teatro Lilipute and the pioneer of puppet theatre history, authored numerous newspaper and magazine articles and tirelessly campaigned for the establishment of a puppetry museum and research centre.[709] Repeated calls to found a museum to preserve the puppets of the fast-disappearing troupes were ignored until after the fall of the Estado Novo in 1974, when the theatre company Marionetas de São Lorenço e o Diabo emerged. Founded by Helena Vaz, José Alberto Gill and Fernando Serafim, the company took puppetry back on the road, the performers travelling with their theatre between venues by horse and cart, following the old itineraries of the puppet troupes that had come before them. The collections they assembled enabled them, in 1987 in an old building between São Jorge Castle and Graça in Lisbon, to establish Portugal's first

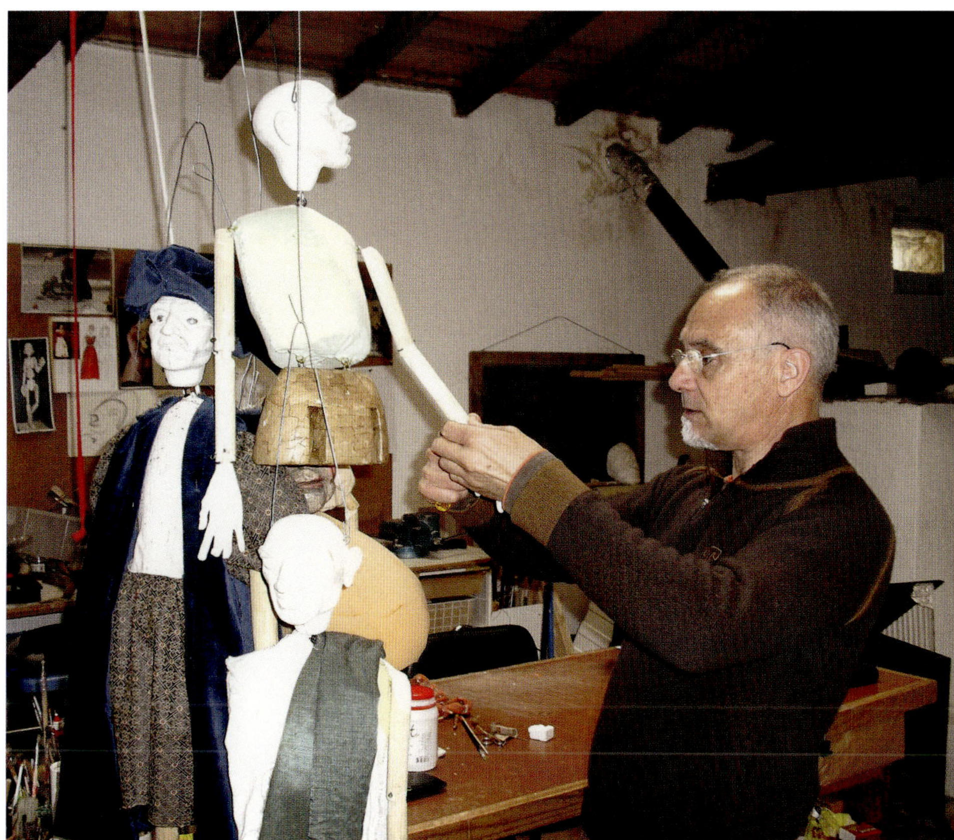

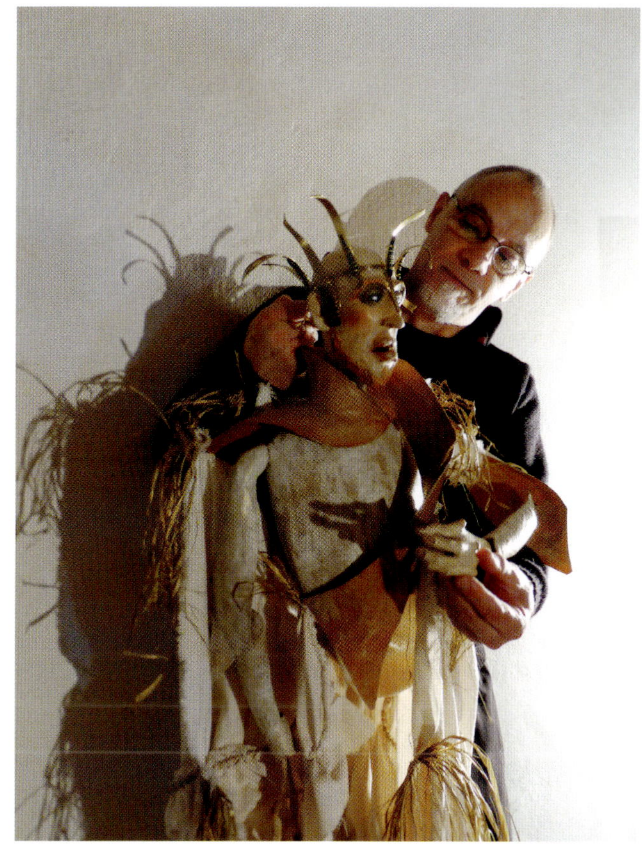

museum of puppetry, the Museu da Marioneta. In 2001 the museum moved to its permanent site at the Bernardas Convent on the Rua da Esperança.

Since the fall of the Estado Novo, Portugal has experienced a resurgence in puppetry and become a European centre for animation. A new generation of puppeteers began performing in the late 1980s and 1990s, including those with beach booths whose puppets are called *robertos*.[710] The pioneering work of the Marionetas de São Lorenço e o Diabo, the Museu da Marioneta in Lisbon and the Teatro de Marionetas do Porto, as well as dedicated artists and writers like João Paulo Seara Cardoso, Isabel Alves Costa, Rute Ribeiro, Luís Vieira and Mónica Almeida, redirected puppetry from its domesticated and constrained focus on children's theatre in the 1960s and 1970s to become a critical interdisciplinary and cross-media art form.

In 2001 the Tarumba Teatro de Marionetas founded the Festival Internacional de Marionetas e Formas Animadas (International Festival of Puppets and Animated Forms; FIMFA). The festival immensely broadened the traditional boundaries of puppetry to incorporate dance, cinema and robotics, creating alternative media and programming strategies, applying new technologies, stretching concepts of aesthetics and serving as an incubator for experimental work, training and audience development. FIMFA has inscribed Portuguese puppetry within an international circuit of practices that has made it one of the country's most radical art forms. Moreover, its strategic alliance with the Museu da Marioneta in Lisbon strengthens the relationship between traditional puppetry and new forms of animation while focusing such diverse forms and potentialities on the ambiguity of the locus between life and the inanimate.

The work of puppet makers like Jorge Cerqueira in Santa Susana and José Carlos Barros in Amadora challenges the boundaries between the real and the fantastic, conjuring essences that are sometimes sensed but seldom visualized. Like the popular artists David Gomes and João Manuel Esteves discussed earlier, Cerqueira, who began making puppets in 1993, explains that he slowly manipulates different languages and techniques until he becomes aware that his creations have been born. His marionettes, like his characters from

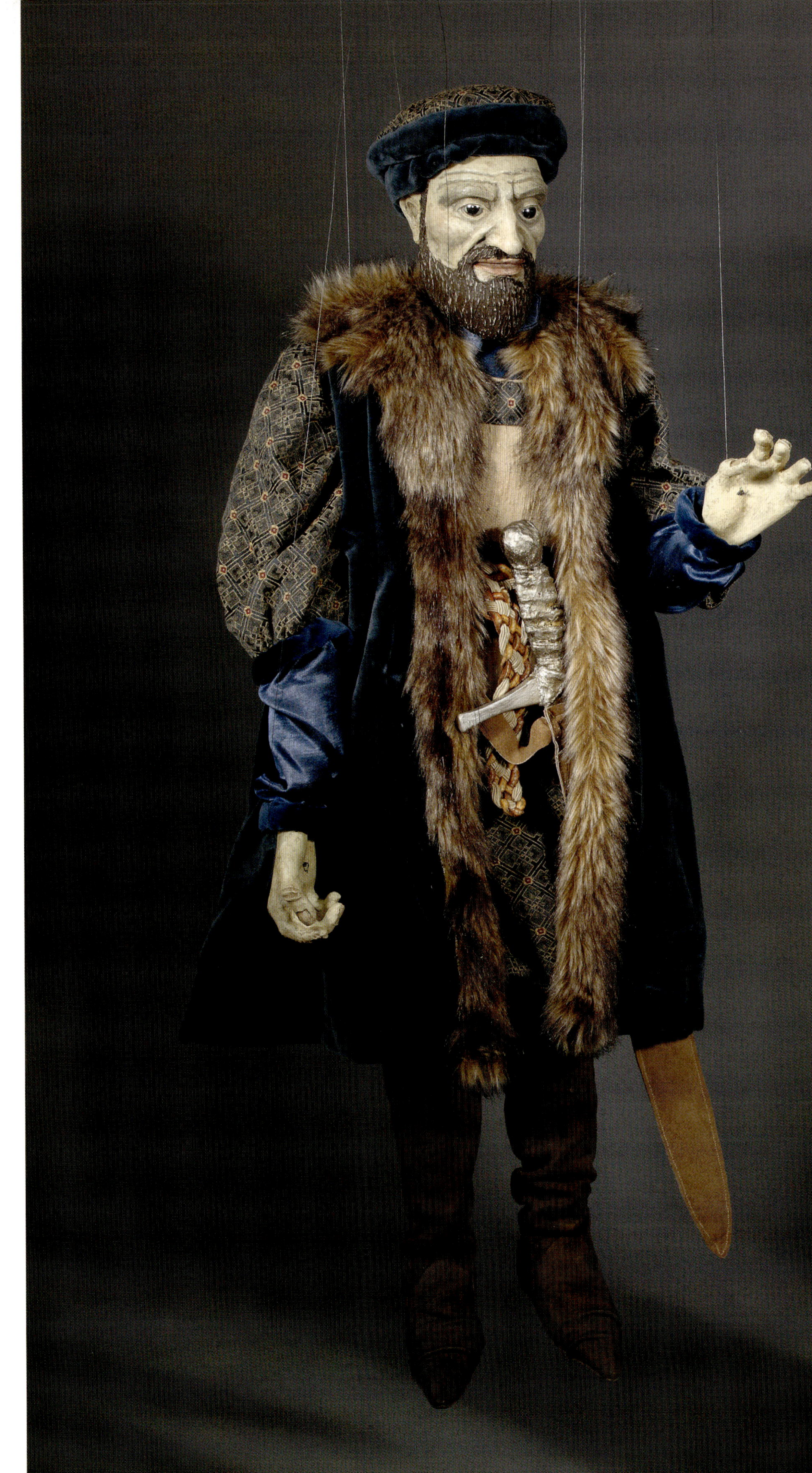

JORGE CERQUEIRA
Three marionettes conveying the characters of, left to right, Vasco da Gama, Infante D. Henrique and Monsayeed, based on Luís de Camões's literary epic *Os Lusíadas*, 2012.

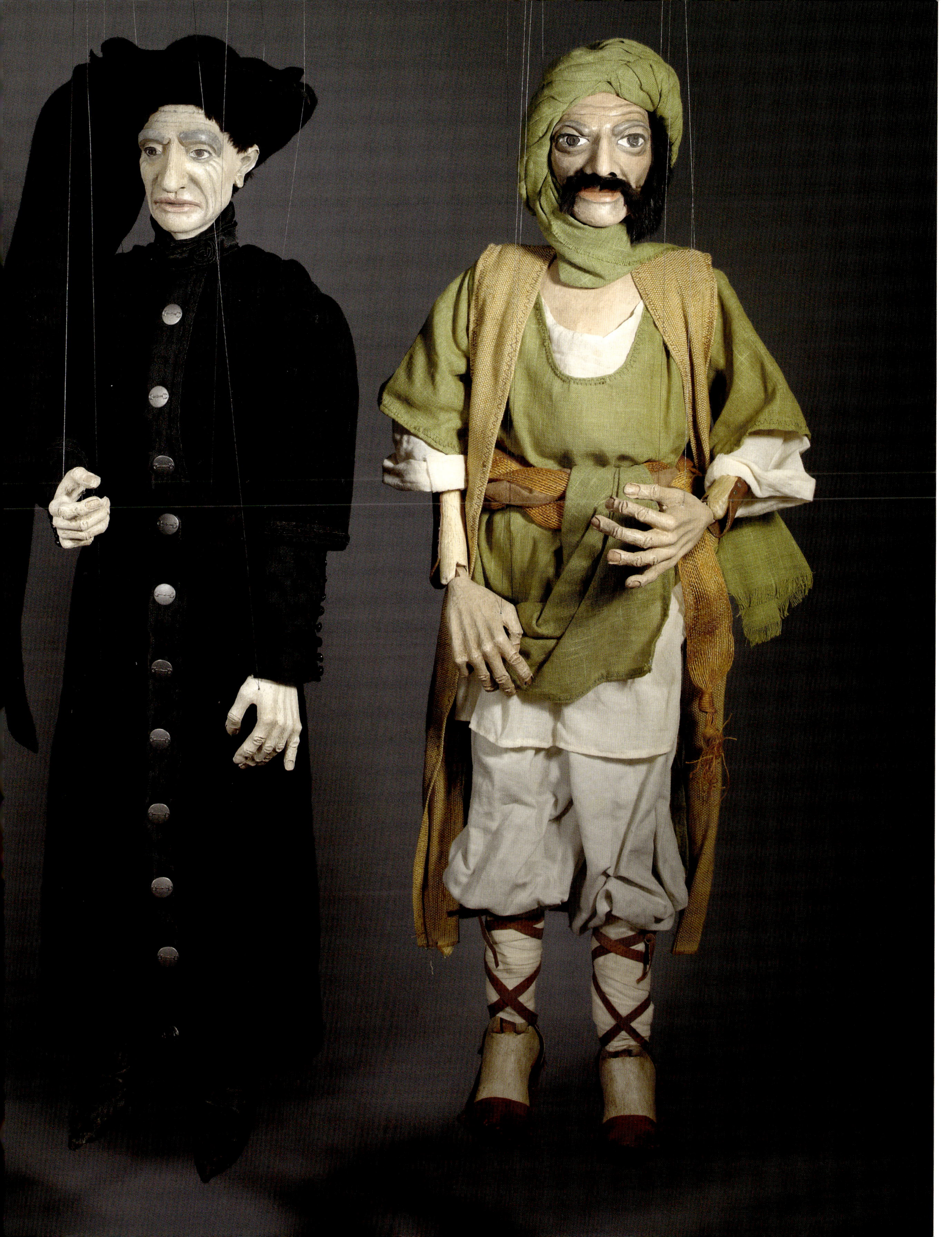

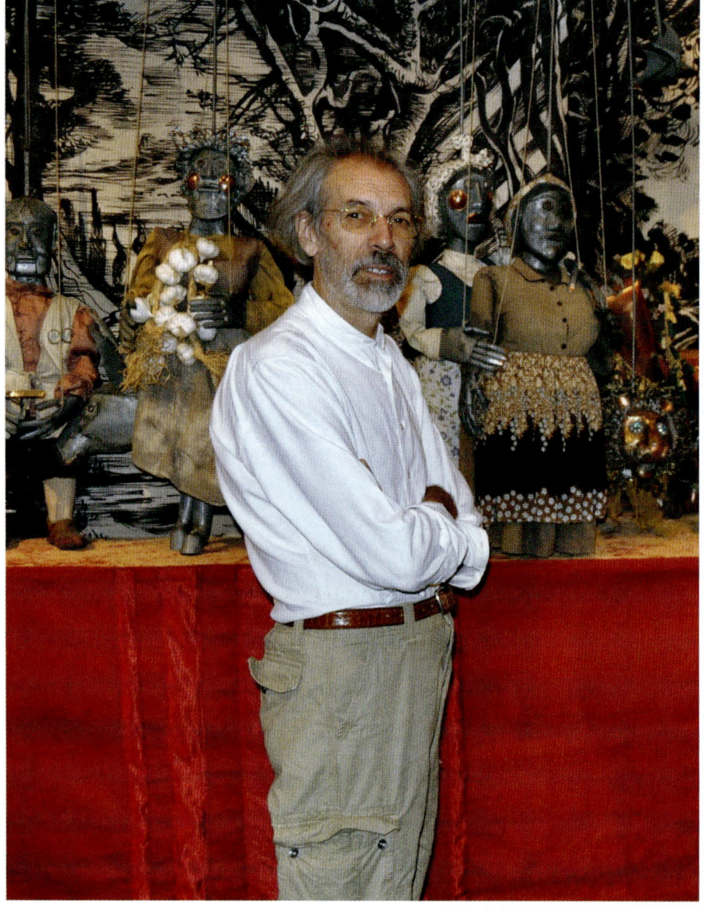

above
Puppet and automaton maker José Carlos Barros with his marionettes in the Museu Nacional do Teatro collection, 2011.

facing
JOSÉ CARLOS BARROS
Marionettes of Don Quixote and Sancho Panza, 2011.

Os Lusíadas, are as effective as Camões's literary style in conjuring the spectral identities of their protagonists and equally capable of enacting their great feats and small deeds alike. The two creative forms, narrative and spectacle, provide hugely contrastive genres through which to express a Portugal at two widely different periods of its history. Camões's work was used to invoke the poetic and heroic spirit that the nineteenth century and the Estado Novo conjured to express a singular millenarian history and closed national identity. Puppet theatre, the only popular art that the agencies of the Estado Novo neither collected, exhibited nor attempted to appropriate and transform into another expression of the national spirit, spluttered and spurted through the twentieth century, more altered by changes in taste than differing political regimes. By the twenty-first century, it conveyed Portugal as a facet of universally shared human paradoxes. Describing FIMFA, the Spanish theatre director Toni Rumbau notes how the mix of popular art, technology, dance, music and cinema

> opens cross-complex spaces of time in the city that welcomes it: fertile dualities of past/present, present/future, familiar/odd, verbal/visual, urban/rural, tradition/modernity. All duality that opens society to the unknown and towards the Other and to our own inner dualities. It transforms the city in[to] a 'double,' ... and I believe Lisbon is one of the capitals of the world that [has] aroused more 'dualities' in everybody.[711]

FIMFA and the Museu da Marioneta, which share the same building, have a symbiotic relationship that sparks from the fictions and frictions between the museum and anti-museum project. Cerqueira's set of ten puppets at MOA provide a very different language for staging our understanding of Camões's *Os Lusíadas* than the commemorations and exhibitions devoted to the great sixteenth-century poet in the nineteenth and twentieth centuries, and Toni Rumbau evokes a very different picture of Lisbon than the travel writers, novelists and cinematographers described in the second chapter of this work.

SPIRITS LAID TO REST

For much of the twentieth century, as we have argued, one version of Portuguese history has shrouded itself in a spiritualized idiom that anchored the present to the past and interpreted specific events, popular art, literature, music, film, museums, spectacles and even architectural decay as manifestations of an essentialized Lusitanian spirit. From the nineteenth to the twenty-first century, this spiritualization of history has assumed different forms, from the positivist-influenced historians and folklorists writing in the nineteenth and early twentieth centuries and the Romantic poets and philosophers of the first half of the twentieth century, to later sociologists and anthropologists implicated in the construction of the cultural policies of the Estado Novo and the governments that succeeded it. Transcendental nationalism was implicit in the work of Alexandre Herculano, the nineteenth-century father of modern Portuguese history, who in his influential account of the Portuguese Middle Ages disputed the authenticity of the apparition of Christ at Ourique only to replace it by a synthesis of Portugal's distinct historical characteristics that, as we have seen, later became re-spiritualized and regarded as the motive force of the nation's future evolution.

A contemporary of Herculano, Teófilo Braga, detected a similar evolutionary trend that disclosed long-time characteristics of Portuguese thought in popular beliefs, literature, song and rural arts and crafts. In conformity with the laws of social evolution, he believed that the true spiritual soul of the nation found its most attenuated expression not in rural cultural survivals, though these were important indicators of the past, but in the erudite work of the sixteenth-century poet and chronicler Luís de Camões. Braga's enthusiastic documentation of the nation's folklore was shared by other and no less encyclopedic collectors, including Pedroso, Coelho, Peixoto and Vasconcellos, who, while lamenting the "primitive" quality of the rural imagination and popular religious practices, nevertheless shared Braga's belief in the welcome inevitability of progress and the superiority of the industrial society that had begun to emerge in Portugal. Some of these writers and politicians, champions of progress and of Comte's humanistic religion, substituted supernaturals and divinities with a state-sanctioned pantheon of the dead constituted by former beings of flesh and bone whose memory was commended for their

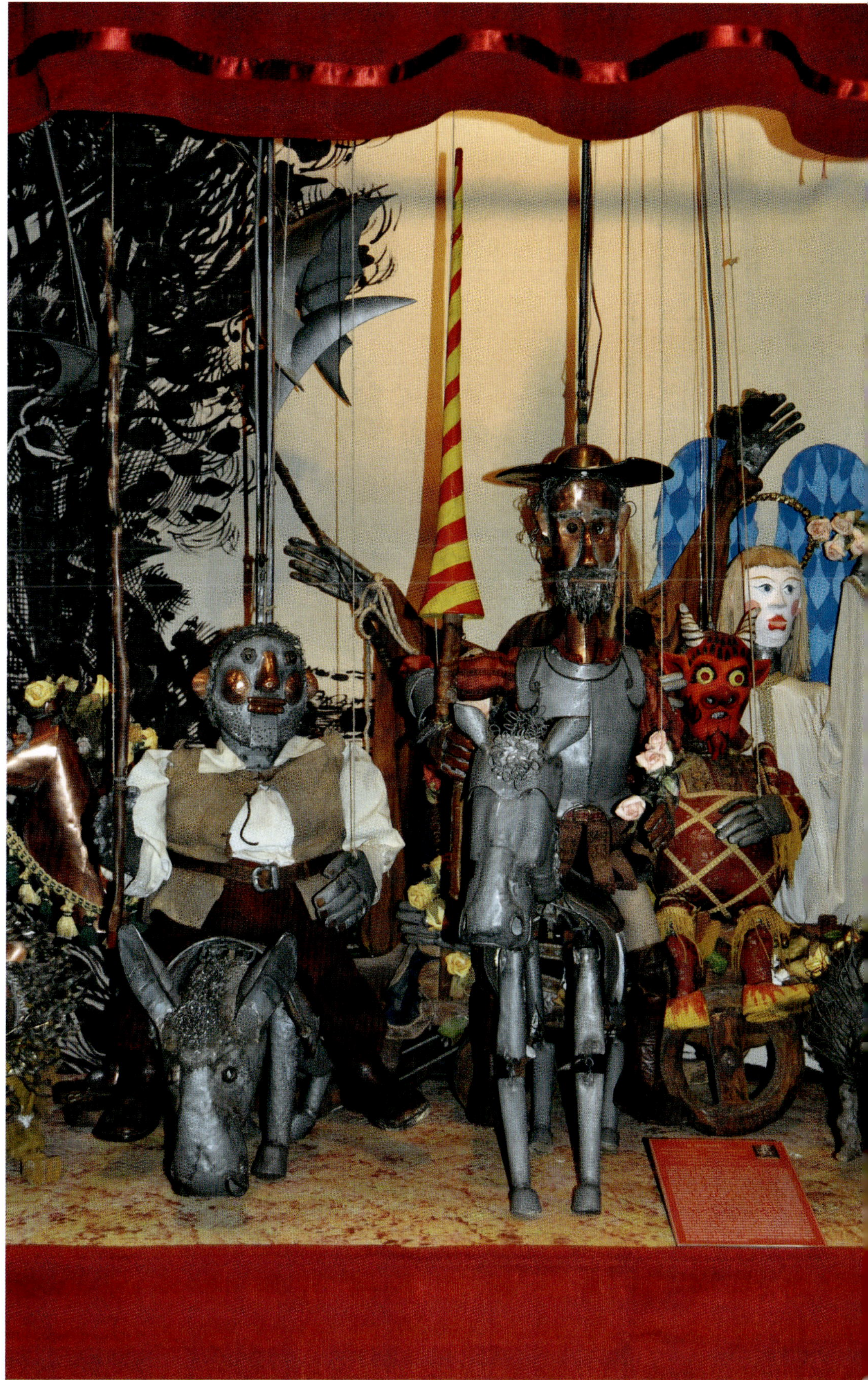

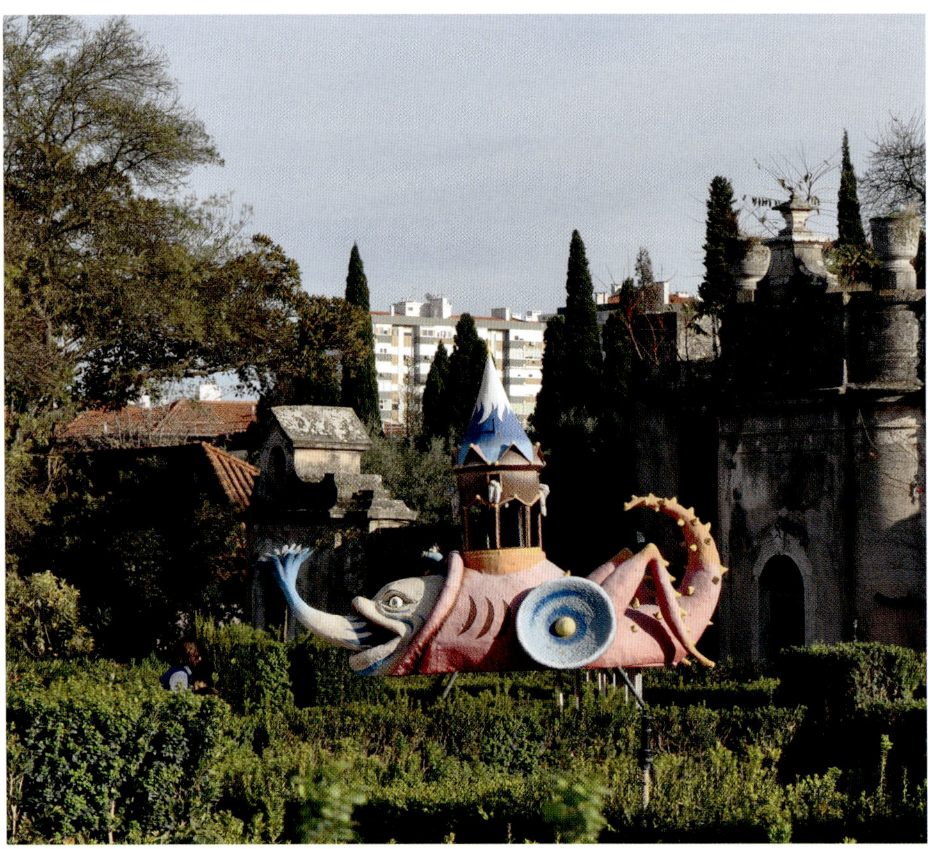
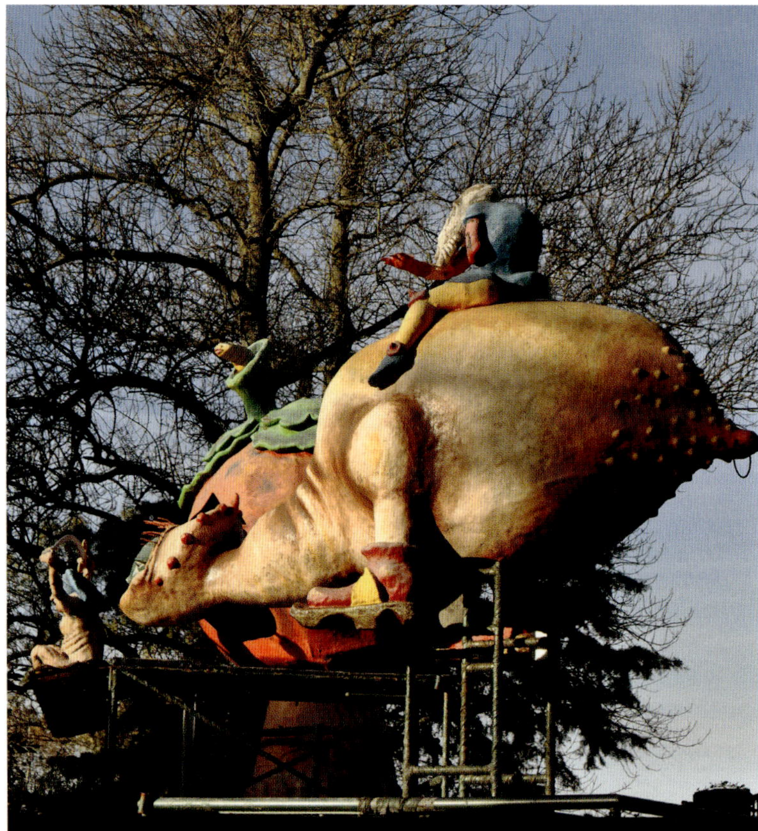

exemplary actions, achievements or moral integrity. There thus emerged in the nineteenth century, against the objections of the Church, an anti-religion predicated on its own conception of the cult of the dead consecrated and evoked through secular ceremonies that strove to dominate the lives of the living every bit as effectively as the priesthood of an omnipotent god.[712]

Competing interpretations of the nature, manifestation and culmination of the nation's evolution, with their own political followings, uneasily coexisted during much of the nineteenth and early twentieth centuries. Liberal thought favoured the secular views of Comte and Braga, the monarchists believed in an ecclesiastic history that never doubted the miraculous interventions of Christ and other divine personages in Portugal's history, while another group, the Cruzada Nuno Álvares, which included António de Oliveira Salazar and a number of early anthropologists, gathered around a mystical nationalistic apostolicism centred on the need for moral unity, social order and the renewal of the traditional family.[713] Between 1910 and 1932, the Portuguese Renacista, led by the philosopher Leonardo Coimbra and the poets and writers Jaime Cortesão and Teixeira de Pascoaes, turned on its head and massively reformulated Comte's secular, materialistic and mechanical view of social evolution into a metaphysical and personal doctrine. For them, if cultivated through liberty and openness, the spirit would grow not only to incorporate the nation and humanity but to reunite a highly spiritualized humankind with God. From the establishment of the Estado Novo in 1933 until his death in 1952, a disappointed Pascoaes abandoned his earlier speculations on the philosophy of spirit and its Lusitanian heritage to focus instead on the spirit's imperfections and the significance of modernism.[714]

Subsequently, philosophers and poets like Coimbra and Pascoaes, anthropologists including Luís Chaves and Jorge Dias and sociologists like Gilberto Freyre implicitly acknowledged the existence of a specific Lusitanian spirit that has survived millennia and shaped the Portuguese way of being and the legacy it has bestowed upon the world.

António Ferro, on becoming the first secretary of Salazar's Secretariat of National Propaganda in

facing, left and right
José Carlos Barros's floats of monstrous beasts inspired by Hieronymus Bosch's *Temptation of Saint Anthony* in the Museu Nacional de Arte Antiga. These floats are displayed in the garden of the Museu Nacional do Teatro.

1933, attempted to mediate these complex intersections, diverse intellectual positions and political imbroglios in inscribing a philosophy of spirit within the totalitarian state. Ferro's intellectual lineage was complex and rendered transparent the larger contradictions in government policy that reflected ideological divisions within the ruling junta. His early writings, particularly *A Idade do Jazz-Band* (The Age of the Jazz Band), had unhesitatingly rejected what he had called the "sickness of *saudades*," tradition, regionalism and the "nostalgia for dead ages" in preference for internationalism, the tonic of African sculpture and an age given over to dissonance and madness.[715] He had been a member of the modernist group Orphée, which had included Fernando Pessoa and Almada Negreiros, neither of whom ever escaped the unresolved contradiction between their intellectual position and their continued nostalgia and longing for spiritual redemption.

This split was writ large in the Estado Novo's attitude to modernization and the reassertion of tradition and apostolic allegiance on which Salazar repeatedly insisted. Early on, Ferro, together with Minister of Public Works Pacheco Duarte, shared their enthusiasm for modernist architecture, but repeatedly felt the need to defend their position against conservative critics. Important and highly visible architectural projects like the pavilions of the 1931 *Paris Colonial Exhibition*, designed by Raul Lino and incorporating accepted historical styles from the fifteenth and sixteenth centuries, including a tower and cross, garnered appreciative support.[716] The Portuguese Pavilion for the 1937 Paris exhibition, however, was not so well received by conservative factions. Salazar and Ferro had wanted the pavilion to present the country's history as well as the changes that had occurred during the dictatorship. Keil do Amaral was appointed architect, while interior design was shared between artists previously used by the regime on similar projects (Paulo Ferreira, Carlos Botelho, José Rocha, Bernardo Marques and Fred Kradolfer) and an untested group more closely identified with the internationalist movement (Eduardo Malta, Lino António, Francis Smith, António Soares dos Reis, Jorge Barradas and sculptors Canto da Maia and Barata Feyo). The modernist design and decoration outraged conservatives and eventually prompted the president of the National Arts Commission, Arnoldo Ressano Garcia, to publicly defend "Christianity, nationalism and normality" against an unprincipled modernism. He called the modernists "social revolutionaries lacking ideals, God and morality," "charlatans" and "paranoids and degenerates" holding communist and Jewish sympathies committed to "beastializing the human spirit."[717]

In fact, since 1922 Ferro had rejected his youthful indulgence in modernism, as he unambiguously admitted in the preface to later editions of *A Idade do Jazz-Band* and reasserted in his 1932 radio interview with Salazar before his governmental appointment. At a literary awards ceremony in 1934 Ferro gave a further unequivocal statement of his understanding of the philosophy of the spirit and its implications to his department (the Secretariat of National Propaganda, or SPN, renamed the SIN in 1941). The SPN would, he insisted, support healthy art but would fight "everything that dirtied the spirit"; "everything that is ugly, coarse and bestial"; "everything that is harmful, hurtful and done for simple sensuality or Satanism." The SPN would attack "certain non-conformist ideas, false liberation"; the "pseudo-vanguards"; certain "corrupt paintings"; "corrosive diabolism"; and "amorality and sickness." It would stop "the renaissance of a sadistic literature" and "Freudian excavations."[718] Instead Ferro advocated a different type of modernity consistent with the eternal qualities and inevitable movement of the spirit that would engender national renovation.[719]

In architecture the style that emerged from the controversy over the 1937 pavilion was a more cautious, simplified classicism decorated using historical national elements and themes. The national continuities referenced in this style are clearly expressed in the buildings that followed, particularly the facades, sculptural details and interior murals of the University of Coimbra. The Mathematics Building (1964) includes two external bas-reliefs designed by Gustavo Bastos—*Mathematics as a Natural Science* and *Mathematics as an Abstract Science*—while the interior contains two frescoes by Almada Negreiros: *Portuguese Mathematics in the Service of the Nation's Epic History* and *Mathematics since Chaldea and Egypt until our Time*. The General Library (1947–56), designed by Alberto Pessoa, contains a decorated faience panel by Jorge Barradas that allegorizes the history of the university and influential figures in the history of the city (1955), while external bas-reliefs, sculpted by António Duarte (1951) and Angélico, represent the sciences and the humanities.

Pessoa was also the architect for the Faculty of Letters, built between 1945 and 1951, which faces his library building. Four statues by Barata Feyo depicting Rhetoric, Philosophy, History and Poetry stand at the front of the building, while inside, the foyer is decorated by two frescoes: Joaquim Rebocho's allegory to classical antiquity and Severo Portela's composition on Portuguese glory and originality. The focus on the history of Portuguese achievements and their relation to the wider evolution of the disciplines, in which carefully demarcated knowledges are depicted synonymously with the unfolding human spirit, is reiterated in other buildings of this period, including the faculties of Medicine and Science. These buildings were constructed along a new tree-lined axis that ends in a square centred on a monumental sculpture of King Dinis (reign 1279–1325), the university's founder. A monumental stairway on the opposite side of the square flanked by two giant armorial spheres connects the campus to the town below it.

The architect in charge of the rebuilding of the University of Coimbra was Cottinelli Telmo (1897–1948). A close friend of Pacheco Duarte and a poet, musician, architect and film producer—he directed the much acclaimed *A Canção de Lisboa* (1933)—Telmo had earlier overseen the overall design of the *Exhibition of the Portuguese World*. He exerted a powerful influence on the visual culture of the Estado Novo, but his work was also inflected by the battle of styles and aesthetic preferences within the regime. Many of his earlier buildings—including the Lisbon ferry terminal, Estação Fluvial Sul e Sueste (1931), and the *Exhibition of the Portuguese World* (1940), especially The Portuguese in the World Pavilion—displayed an uncompromising modernist stance. However, his plan for remodelling the University of Coimbra (1943), although lacking nothing of his predisposition towards monumentalism, adopted a simplified classicism more attuned with the regime's conservative taste. This style was later applied to many court buildings, schools, post offices, government hotels (*pousadas*) and urban housing projects elsewhere in the country.

All twelve architects commissioned by Ferro to work on the *Exhibition of the Portuguese World* had demonstrated their ability to combine classicism with the modern. In the extreme case of the Centro Regional pavilion, the rich collections of popular art gathered from all the country's provinces were integrated into the building's decorative and architectural configuration, fortifying and renewing the old and creating an exhibition intended to appeal to modern sensibilities.[720] Nevertheless, despite these restrained modernist tendencies, the magazine *Arquitectura Portuguesa* estimated that between 1908 and 1958, as many as 99 percent of all new construction could still be classified as traditional.[721] Ferro legitimated his architectural preferences by interpreting them as expressions of the progressive evolution of the spirit, which, fortified by popular art, would achieve the realization of a Portugal that was both different and modern.[722]

FINAL WORDS: THE RETURN OF HISTORY

The contradiction between popular culture and modernism coursed deeply through the ideological veins of the Estado Novo, particularly in the 1930s and 1940s, disclosing its presence in vernacular and international architectural styles and painting and decorative art, and in the exaltation of rural life and the country's rusticized history and a repressed infatuation with industrialization and urbanization. But this distinctively Portuguese form of haunted social existence was not only generated by the contradictions between modernism and the popular, but also created by the reverberations of historical memories and the unresolved counter-projects that insinuated themselves between the practices determined by the state's breathtakingly ambitious vision, a vision that percolated past, present and future; ether and matter; and a pantheon of saints, devils and patriarchs. State-sponsored exhibitions, processions, performances, cultural competitions and written or spoken rhetoric—mobilized to reconsecrate state ideology—only created spaces that visitors to the 1940 commemorations, as well as writers and diarists of the period, sometimes experienced as a strange inquietude, reminding us of Certeau's unnerving observation that "the places people live in are like the presences of diverse absences."[723] The Estado Novo's universe was writ large, but like a ghost theatre it echoed only the absence of those it was meant to engage, accommodate and exalt.

Puppet theatre, on the other hand, is like the contemplative spaces freed and created by the Ramalhos's pottery models, the question of evil raised by the Esteves Lima brothers' familial devils, and astonishment over the nature of divinity prompted by Joaquim Paiva or Zé Augusto's humanized saints—works that are anti-projects that stage or provoke lively incredulity towards established order. Popular art is essentially an outsider art that provides forms of insinuation that carry the potential to disrupt the fields of vision and practices within the spaces delineated and monopolized by the state and its allied institutions. The Estado Novo was politically immobilized between the world as represented in popular art, a relationally stable world of place guaranteed by the state, and the world of tomorrow, a world of "intersections of mobile elements,"[724] which it never succeeded in domesticating and which increasingly interpenetrated and infringed its borders.

The contradiction between subaltern culture and modernity also framed the frictions between popular and institutional religion and the indecision between predicating national identity on a mono-relational Lusitanian world defined by language and religion or a pluricultural globalized world constituted by diverse cultures and languages and overlapping foreign hegemonies.

In 1981 João de Pina-Cabral argued that the pilgrimages, prayers, penances and multitudinous votive offerings piled in churches throughout the country were expressions of complicated relations of exchange and interdependence that connected

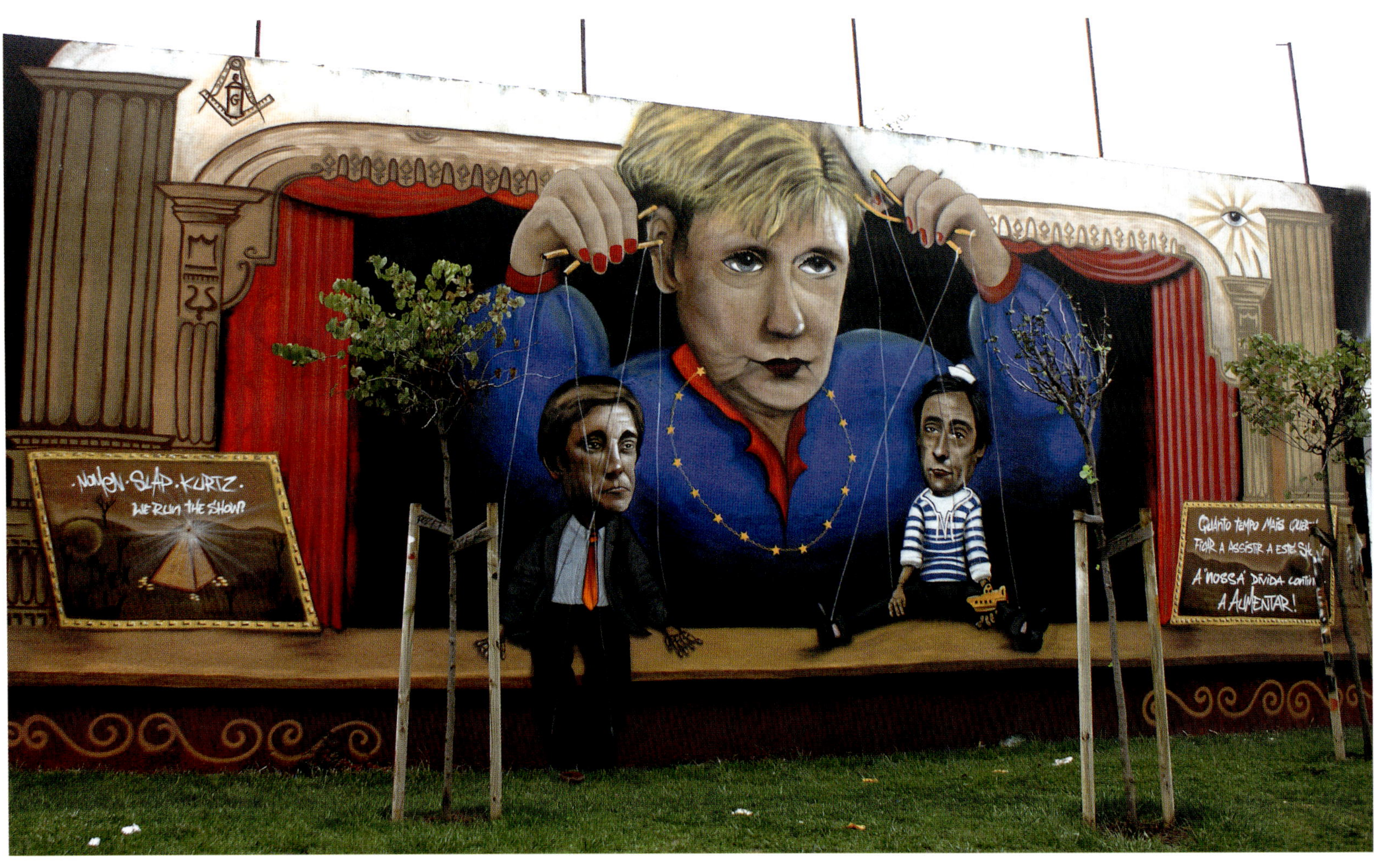

above
NOMEN
As Marionetas de Merkel
(wall mural), 2012
Angela Merkel is shown manipulating puppets of Portugal's prime minister, Pedro Passos Coelho, and deputy prime minister, Paulo Portas.

facing
Remains of the house once belonging to António de Oliveira Salazar at 64 Rua Bernardo Lima, Lisbon.

humans and divinities to constitute the unique fabric of rural society.[725] This view, as we saw in Chapters 4–7, was shared by other commentators of the period, including anthropologists like Ernesto Veiga de Oliveira (1984), Pierre Sanchis (1983) and Moisés Espírito Santo (1984), and was reproduced by both the Museu Nacional de Etnologia and the Museu de Arte Popular. In 1986 Pina-Cabral's seminal monograph *Sons of Adam, Daughters of Eve: The Peasant Worldview of the Alto Minho* revealed the profound changes that had begun to impact the northern Portuguese countryside. Fifteen years after his 1981 paper, he wrote, startlingly, that the integrated and coherent rural society he had attempted to describe in 1979 and the early 1980s no longer existed.[726]

Sons of Adam, Daughters of Eve constitutes the pivotal monograph on Portuguese ethnography that marks the end of one social reality and the inception of another. Within its descriptive pages the strains between a dying social world and the emergence of another test the abilities of a previously robust interpretive framework. Many of the church offerings Pina-Cabral had described originally in his 1981 article—candles, limbs, organs and people and animals made of wax or metal—are still sold in religious shops in Braga, Fátima and elsewhere and are placed or hung above altars. Photographs of the beneficiaries of divine favours are still pinned to church walls, and personal services, especially pilgrimages and prayers, are still rendered, though penitents crawling on bared knees to ascend flights of granite stairs leading to charmed sanctuaries are hardly ever seen. But the focus of all these offerings is no longer social, but individual, according to his revisionist reading: more to do with offering life force through pain and suffering, which the saints can then transform and redouble into happiness and life.[727] A litany of factors, including the injection of capital by returning emigrants, the

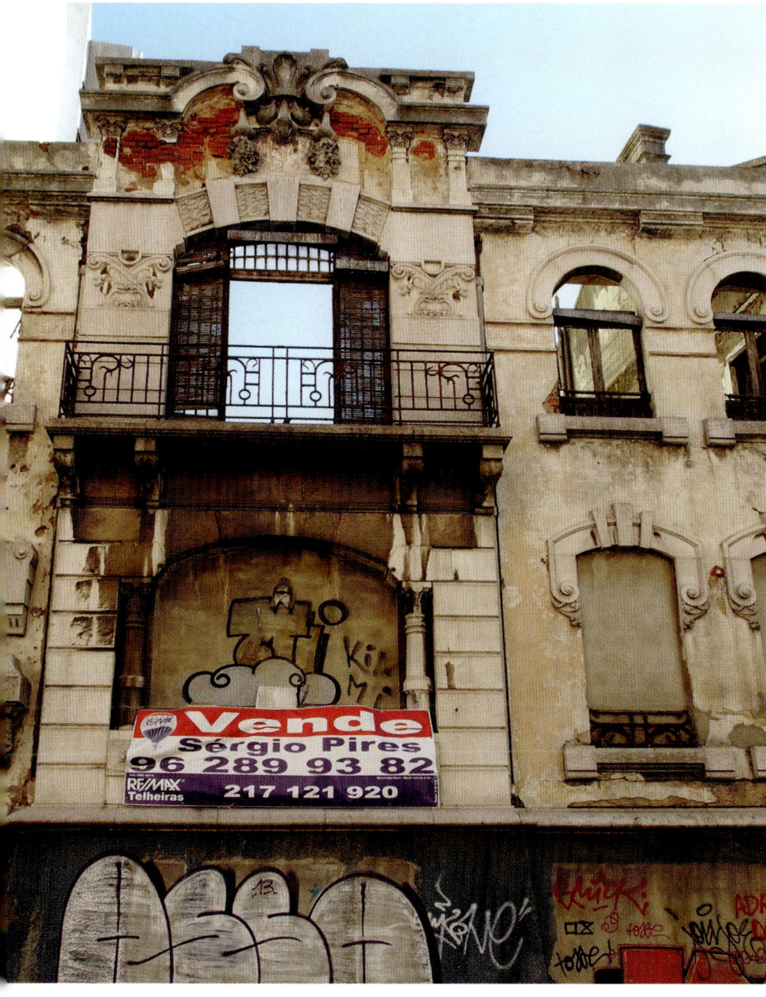

devolution of power to local elites, economic decentralization, improved education, expansion of roads, better communications, commoditization and a consumption-based economy, had transformed rural society beyond all recognition,[728] increasing prosperity and opportunity but helping to dissolve all pretense of its rustic exoticism or religious cohesion.

These tendencies have continued to be mapped and researched by recent fieldworkers, who confirm the complexity and creative restructuring of Portugal's rural social fabric,[729] which, far from eliminating supposedly archaic practices, as Pina-Cabral attests,[730] has repurposed and renewed them.[731] Alongside such well-established and frequently brilliant ethnographic analyses coexists a powerful machinery of writers and authors of promotional literature, tourist guides, books, television programs and films who ignore historical contingencies and reproduce the bucolic and exotic scenography of a 1930s Portugal. If all landscapes are necessarily haunted,[732] the history of the Lusitanian imaginary attests that these hauntings are made up not only of the memories of personal experiences, but of the continuing machinations of the still-unreconciled technologies of spirit mediums and the succession of socio-cultural analysts.

The ideological articulations and strategies that Alves[733] identifies as running through the Estado Novo's mobilization of the country's rural legacy are strikingly similar to the manufactured authenticity and globalized hyperreality that Paulo Raposo describes for masquerades in Podence and, more widely, the visual and performative cultures of the winter ceremonial cycle in Minho and Trás-os-Montes.[734] In conurbations, modern Portuguese puppet theatre has resisted the re-encroachment of popular mythology. Memories transmitted orally through puppet theatre, when renewed by contemporary commentary and enacted in participative arenas, still resist translocalization. Irreducible to inscription, these total social phenomena, like the *loas* recited as part of former male coming-of-age ceremonies,[735] are free of everyday convention and governmental practices, allowing them to preserve what Certeau described as "a kind of anti-museum."[736] To remain animate, popular art needs to adhere to the memories of its makers, users and localities, in a manner not unlike the intimate attachments Antónia Maria Nepomuceno and Alexandre "Vassourinhas" had with their puppets. Portugal is a haunted nation, but its ghosts are not phantoms of the dead; they are the invisible political, financial and intellectual puppeteers who obscure and evade the materialization of the workings of international elites and financial institutions that infringe the autonomy of its history and the liberty of its peoples.

Acknowledgements

Tara Pike, Maria Venne, Cordelia Frewen and Nicky Levell made this publication possible through their selfless work, assistance and support in what must have seemed at times to be an interminable editorial and bibliographic process. In addition, they researched, obtained copyright and organized illustrations, compiled endnotes and commissioned maps, helping to turn a dry academic monograph into a profusely illustrated album of stories, things and museologies. To all four of these extraordinarily committed people, I am immensely grateful. I am similarly indebted to Eduardo Tomé, my research assistant in Portugal, who contributed enormously to discussions with artists and about the interpretation and history of Portuguese anthropology and popular culture and helped commission, pack and dispatch collections of contemporary Portuguese popular art to Canada.

I am especially indebted to David Silva Gomes, whose creative genius and workshop and shop on the Rua do Anjo in Braga inspired both the exhibition and the somewhat unusual interpretive organization of this album. There would have been neither exhibition nor album without the collaboration, goodwill and enthusiasm of all the Portuguese artists who have contributed to my understanding of popular art and the work they do: José Manuel Alves (Podence); João Pinho (Lagoa de Mira); Maria Inácia Fonseca Mateus, Perpétua Matilde Fonseca Sousa, Afonso Ginja and Mário Lagartinho (Estemoz); João Manuel Esteves (Ousilhão); António José Fernandes do Vale (Vila Boa de Ousilhão); Adão de Castro Almeida and José António da Silva Costa (Lazarim); José Augusto Ferreira dos Santos (Aveiro); Sérgio Amaral (Mangualde); José Jorge Correia Cerqueira (Santa Susana) and José Carlos Barros (Amadora). From Barcelos, I would like to thank Júlia Ramalho (Maria Júlia Oliveira Mota), António Ramalho (António Manuel Mota Ferreira), Fernando Baraça (Fernando Gonçaves Pereira), Vitor Baraça (Vitor Manuel Nogueira Gonçalves), Laurinda Pias (Laurinda Macedo Barbosa), Francisco Esteves Lima (Francisco Mistério), Manuel Joaquim Esteves Lima (Manuel Mistério) and Moisés Baraça (Moisés Nogueira Gonçalves). I am deeply saddened that Joaquim Maria Silva Paiva (1930–2010), José Augusto Ferreira dos Santos (1930–2012) and João Manuel Esteves (1938–2014) will not see the album that their work did so much to inspire.

I would also like to thank my esteemed colleague Nuno Porto, who critically reviewed the manuscript and advised on images. Although the text has benefited from his erudite comments, naturally I take sole responsibility for the views here expressed.

I would like to acknowledge the Biblioteca Nacional de Portugal; Biblioteca Nacional de España; the Arquivo Municipal de Lisboa; Turismo de Lisboa; Museu de Olaria, Barcelos; Museu Regional de Beja; Museu da Marioneta, Lisboa and the Fundação Eugénio Almeida, Évora, for graciously acceding to provide illustrations for this work.

It has been a pleasure over the past five years to work with the Consul General of Portugal in Vancouver, first with Carlos Nuno Almeida de Sousa Amaro and more recently with Maria João Boavida Urbano, both of whom have always warmly supported this project. I want also to acknowledge Terry Costas, who led Vancouver's Portuguese Benevolence Society, which welcomed me so graciously when I first arrived in the city, and who first suggested that MOA should present an exhibition on Portuguese popular art. Also I am grateful to Maria Pereira de Cota, Tiago Coen, Paula Filipa Pato Batista, José António Neto, Angela Levell, Nigel Shelton and Tia Mané and family; to Luísa Cruz, who introduced me to Portuguese popular art; and to Ann Stevenson and Alissa Cherry, who tracked down important references.

Skooker Broome and Debbie Cheung orchestrated and translated the ideas expressed in this book into a startling, three-dimensional design concept, replete with light washes and projections, for an exhibition avowedly dedicated to challenging common stereotypes of popular art. Staff and visitors were surprised and bemused at large iron sheets hanging from the museum walls turning shades of red and brown as they rusted under Vancouver's winter weather. Once these rough metallic surfaces, which we found were highly light-absorbent, had been installed and their industrial effect had been tempered by hanging gossamer-thin, unbleached muslin cloth—material intended to evoke the passage of time and the play of light—the diverse collection of popular art, ranging from horn containers and brass bells to carnival costumes and bright polychromatic pottery, was transformed into a series of stunning theatrical assemblages. The success in using these unusual materials owes a great deal to Skooker Broome and to Heidi Swierenga and Mauray Toutloff, our conservators, who ensured the protection of the collection. Krista Bergstrom assisted Kyla Bailey, who shot many of the object photographs in the book. I also want to thank Nancy Bruegeman, Candace Beisel, Teija Dedi, Gerald Lawson and Josh Doherty, who either registered and documented the collection and/or helped install the exhibition, and Moya Waters, Anna Pappalardo, Salma Mawani, Deborah Tibbel, Jill Baird, Celeste Moure and Gwilyn Timmers, who coordinated, organized, marketed and programmed the exhibition and arranged the 2015 members' tour to Portugal.

I am grateful and much indebted to my superlative editors and designers at Figure 1 Publishing, Scott Steedman, Lana Okerlund, Jessica Sullivan and Ingrid Paulson, who with Lara Smith have turned a roughly hewn and perplexing text and a pile of over three thousand photographic images into an album that, without them and all my assistants, would have existed only in my imagination. As always I am indebted to Richard Nadeau, the gracious and ever-patient associate publisher of Figure 1, for believing in this project and supporting our joint publication series. The Audain Foundation for the Visual Arts remains one of MOA's core supporters, and I am indebted and profoundly grateful for its generous support of this publication.

Most of all I want to thank my wife, Nicky Levell, and my children, Marcel, Felix and Lucien, who bestowed me four years of freedom to travel, research, write and do the fieldwork on which this album is based. They accompanied me on some of my trips, meeting makers, participating in and documenting ceremonies, photographing pilgrimage sites, processions and masquarades, and visiting the markets, fairs and pilgrimage centres of Coimbra, Porto, Tomar, Leiria, Braga, Barcelos, Fátima, Viseu and Esposende, among others. Marcel, Felix and Lucien learned to identify popular saints and their miraculous powers, became excited by churches, monasteries, convents and sometimes castles, and grew adept at spotting signs for sites and monuments and forewarning their parents of roadside shrines before we sped past them. To my patient and long-suffering family, I dedicate this album.

This album and the exhibition that accompanies it are based on my long, changing acquaintance with Portugal. I first visited the country in September 1984, a trip entirely prompted by seeing Alain Tanner's film *In the White City*. I found the country and its people no less beguiling, beautiful and exhilarating than the film, and its rural towns and villages, and Lisbon in particular, have never since stopped haunting me.

In 1998 I was invited to a conference on art and anthropology at the Palace of São Marcos, the conference centre of the University of Coimbra, and in 2001 I joined the faculty of the university's anthropology department, where I taught before moving to MOA three years later. Since leaving the country we have spent many of our summers in Portugal, and for seven years I continued to give condensed courses in critical museology at the University of Coimbra. Since 2010–11, when I spent my sabbatical there, I have worked on the research behind this album and the exhibition that accompanies it. I am grateful to the University of Coimbra and the Department of Life Sciences (formerly the Department of Anthropology), which have continued to make their libraries and facilities available to me, and for the friendship of my esteemed colleagues Manuel Rodrigues de Areia, Fernando Florêncio, Nuno Porto, João de Pina-Cabral, Nelia Dias, Susana Viegas, Ana Maria Santos, Paulo Mota de Gama and Alice Semedo, whose friendship and work have helped nourish me. I am similarly indebted to the University of British Columbia, which made my sabbatical possible.

Like many others, my experience of Portugal's singularity has been attenuated through the transparency of her light, the profound blueness of her skies, the warmth and scents of her night air and the stark whiteness of her walls, sometimes festooned with billowing white sheets hung to dry from the windows of the buildings perched on her hillside cities. Every book is written somewhere. The friendships, experiences and family memories I have prized and cherished were first conjoined with the excitement of research in the Bookroom and gardens of our home in Portugal. My final debt of gratitude is to the housekeeper of that home, Sra. Dona Maria Palmira Martins Mota Fernandes, her husband, Sr. Manuel, and family, who care for our books, our children, our dogs and our eccentricities. Thank you.

Image Credits

Courtesy of the Arquivo Municipal de Lisboa
PAULO GUEDES: 217, 218
EDUARDO PORTUGAL: 219
ARMANDO SERÔDIO: 192, 193 (middle)

KYLA BAILEY: 16, 17, 19 (right), 21, 24, 44–45, 56, 66–67, 69, 72, 79–82, 93, 95 (top; bottom left), 96, 99 (right), 100, 107, 109, 111, 113, 114–115, 116, 118 (right), 120, 122–124, 128, 138, 144, 145 (left), 147, 148 (right), 149, 174, 193 (above), 194–195, 224–225, 230, 234, 242–243

COURTESY OF THE BIBLIOTECA NACIONAL DE ESPAÑA: 50, 154, 156, 158

COURTESY OF THE BIBLIOTECA NACIONAL DE PORTUGAL
CARLOS MONTEIRO: 36–37
LUISA OLIVEIRA: 132
LUIS PAVÃO: X
JOSÉ PESSOA: 185, 186–187, 188
PHOTOGRAPHER UNKNOWN: 223

JORGE CERQUEIRA: 241 (right)

TIAGO COEN: 110

COURTESY OF FUNDAÇÃO EUGÉNIO ALMEIDA
JERÓNIMO HEITOR COELHO: 152

NICOLA LEVELL: 105, 118 (left)

COURTESY OF THE MUSEU DA MARIONETA
JOAQUIM LOBO: 238
PHOTOGRAPHER UNKNOWN: 237

COURTESY OF THE MUSEU DE OLARIA ARCHIVE
CARLOS BASTO: 102

COURTESY OF THE MUSEU REGIONAL DE BEJA
ANTÓNIO CUNHA: 26

COURTESY OF NOMEN, WWW.NOMEN1.COM: 250

ANTHONY ALAN SHELTON: front jacket, vi, 10, 12, 14, 15, 19 (left), 29, 30, 39, 40, 41, 42, 46, 48, 52, 53, 55, 61, 62–63, 68, 71, 76, 83 (right), 85 (right), 92, 95 (bottom right), 98, 99 (left), 108, 121 (top right, bottom left and right), 129, 145 (above), 146 (top left and right), 148 (middle), 160, 163, 164, 166 (left), 167 (left and right), 168, 169, 178, 198–199, 200–201, 202, 204, 208, 209, 214, 215, 239, 244, 245, 246

FELIX SHELTON: 251

LUCIEN SHELTON: 83 (left)

MARCEL SHELTON: 85 (left), 142, 146 (bottom)

EDUARDO TOMÉ: 112, 121 (top left), 126, 143, 148 (left), 150, 151, 166–167 (top), 241 (left)

COURTESY OF TURISMO DE LISBOA: 28

Notes

1 Russell, *Groundwaters*, 11.
2 Ibid., 15.
3 Kenny, "'Wallflowers at the Dance of Western Civilization'," 129.
4 Myrone, "Afterword," 135–36.
5 Becker, *Art Worlds*, 247.
6 Danto, "The Artworld and Its Outsiders," 24–25.
7 Kenny, "'Wallflowers at the Dance of Western Civilization'," 127.
8 Ibid., 129.
9 McMillan, "The House that Jack Built," 13.
10 Ibid.
11 Kenny, "'Wallflowers at the Dance of Western Civilization'," 126.
12 Russell, *Groundwaters*, 20.
13 In Bisilliat and Soares, *Edison Carneiro Folklore Museum*, 46.
14 Ibid.
15 Russell, *Groundwaters*, 11.
16 Kenny, "'Wallflowers at the Dance of Western Civilization'," 127.
17 J. Dias, *Rio de Onor*, 23.
18 J. Dias and Ribeiro, *Vilarinho da Furna*, 86–87.
19 Ibid.
20 P. Berger, *The Goddess Obscured*, 5.
21 Silva, *Os nossos santos e beatos e outros*, 13.
22 In Dacosta and Barros, *A escrita do mar*, 60.
23 Vale de Almeida, *Um mar da cor da terra*, 161.
24 Saramago, *Journey to Portugal*, 332.
25 Dacosta and Barros, *A escrita do mar*, 79.
26 Cunha, *Portugal e o mar*, 11.
27 Serrão, "Portugal em ruínas," 43.

CHAPTER 1

28 Pessoa, "O Infante," *Message*.
29 Torga, *Portugal*.
30 Saramago, *Journey to Portugal*.
31 David Gomes, interview with Eduardo Tomé, 11 May 2012.
32 David Gomes, interview with author, 3 October 2008.
33 *Diário do Minho*, 3 October 2008, 9.
34 Gomes, interview with Tomé.
35 Salazar governed Portugal for forty-three years. Since one thousand escudos was approximately the equivilant of five euros at the time, the price of the work was 215 euros. See also Magalhães Costa, "Casas de antiquidades en crise por falta de chertela," *Journal de Notícias Norte*, 23 April 2007, 17.
36 Gomes, interview with Tomé.
37 Gomes, conversation with author.
38 David Gomes and his father had been invited to participate before in concourses and exhibitions of furniture. David had always been resolved that his work was serious and not intended for clients or public display. Gomes, conversation with author.
39 *Diário do Minho*, 3 October 2008, 9.

CHAPTER 2

40 In Buck, *Lisbon*, 88.
41 Déon, *Mes arches de noé*.
42 In 1173, São Vicente was made Lisbon's patron saint.
43 Braga, *Contos tradicionais do povo Português*, 236.
44 Salter, *Introducing Portugal*, 105; Wright and Swift, *Minho and North Portugal*, 3, 28, 135.
45 Sitwell, *Portugal and Madeira*, 42.
46 In Buck, *Lisbon*, 27.
47 In Macaulay, *Fabled Shore*, 145.
48 Macaulay, *They Went to Portugal*, 170.
49 Buck, *Lisbon*, 25–26.
50 Ibid., 11.
51 Eliade, *The Portugal Journal*, 239–46.
52 In Chorão, *Nossa Lisboa dos outros*.
53 Ibid., 28.
54 Ibid., 27.
55 Bridge and Lowndes, *The Selective Traveller in Portugal*, 40.

56 Sitwell, *Portugal and Madeira*, 68.
57 Ibid., 70–71.
58 Pessoa, *The Book of Disquiet*, 15.
59 Pessoa, *Lisboa*, 30.
60 Ricardo Reis is one of Fernando Pessoa's heteronyms.
61 Saramago, *The Year of the Death of Ricardo Reis*, 2.
62 Mercier, *Night Train to Lisbon*, 111.
63 Gallop, *Portugal*, 7–8.
64 In Buck, *Lisbon*, 41.
65 In Chorão, *Nossa Lisboa dos outros*, 38.
66 Mercier, *Night Train to Lisbon*, 60.
67 In Buck, *Lisbon*, 15.
68 In ibid., 36.
69 Cf. Salter, *Introducing Portugal*, 151.
70 J. Leal, "Preface," 19.
71 Cf. ibid., 28.
72 Cf. J. Dias and Ribeiro, *Vilarinho da Furna*, 301, 305.
73 Melo, *Salazarismo e cultura popular*, 39–40.
74 Russell-Wood, *The Portuguese Empire*, 10–11.
75 Bedini, *The Pope's Elephant*, 26, 36.
76 Brigola, *Colecções, gabinetes e museus em Portugal no século* XVIII, 52.
77 Kant's pamphlets were *On the Causes of the Terrestrial Convulsions* (1756), *History and Natural Description of the Most Curious Occurrences associated with the Quake* (1756) and *Further Observation on the Terrestrial Convulsions* (1756).
78 Bridge and Lowndes, *The Selective Traveller in Portugal*, 16.
79 The body of São Francisco Xavier was moved to Goa in 1553 and since 1637 has been encased and publicly displayed in a silver casket in the Basilica of Bom Jesus.
80 The martyrs are also prominently displayed on a pedestal in the monastery of Santa Cruz in Coimbra.
81 Quadros, *Poesia e filosofia do mito Sebastianista*, 23, 187.
82 Dos Passos, *The Portugal Story*, 137–38.
83 Simon, *Scientific Expeditions in the Portuguese Overseas Territories*, 1.
84 Brotton, *Trading Territories*, 83.
85 Simon, *Scientific Expeditions in the Portuguese Overseas Territories*, 1.
86 Eliade, *The Portugal Journal*, 245.
87 Justino, *Loas a Maria*, 37.
88 Quadros, *Poesia e filosofia do mito Sebastianista*, 24.
89 Costa Lobo, *Origens do Sebastianismo*, 95.
90 Pessoa, *Message*, 138.
91 Pedroso, *Contribuições para uma mitologia popular portuguesa*, 85.
92 *Constituições* are ecclesiastical ordinances that carry the power of law to locally enforce the resolutions passed by the Council of Trent (1545–63).
93 Pedroso, *Contribuições para uma mitologia popular portuguesa*, 89.
94 Ibid., 90.
95 Ibid., 89.
96 In Sanchis, *Arraial, festa de um povo*, 205.
97 Ibid., 212.
98 Ibid., 203.
99 In ibid.
100 Ibid., 199.
101 Sanchis, "The Portuguese '*romarias*'," 264.
102 E. Veiga de Oliveira, *Festividades cíclicas em Portugal*, 224.
103 Ibid.; Coelho, *Obra Etnográfica*, 336.
104 Sanchis, *Arraial, festa de um povo*, 87; E. Veiga de Oliviera, *Festividades cíclicas em Portugal*, 242.
105 Pina-Cabral, *Sons of Adam, Daughters of Eve*, 20.
106 Ibid., 20–21.
107 Raposo, *Por detrás da máscara*, 53.
108 Lopes, *A face do caos*, 22; Barros and Costa, *Festas e tradições portuguesas: Novembro e Dezembro*, 197.
109 Gallop, *Portugal*, 105; E. Veiga de Oliveira, *Festividades cíclicas em Portugal*, 38; Barros and Costa, *Festas e tradições portuguesas: Fevereiro*, 59.
110 E. Veiga de Oliveira, *Festividades cíclicas em Portugal*, 109.
111 Sanchis, *Arraial, festa de um povo*, 61.
112 Raposo, *Por detrás da máscara*, 57–58.

CHAPTER 3

113 In Dacosta and Barros, *A escrita do mar*, 91.
114 Mattoso, *Naquele tempo*, 240.
115 Ibid., 225.
116 Genesis 1:2 (Authorized [King James] Version).
117 Genesis 1:20 (AV).
118 Genesis 2:10–14 (AV).
119 Santo, *A religião popular portuguesa*, 35.
120 Ibid., 37.
121 Ibid., 30.
122 Ibid., 35.
123 Coelho, *Obra Etnográfica*, 347–50.
124 Vasconcellos, *Tradições populares de Portugal*, 111–13.
125 Cf. Marques, *Entre a serra e o mar*, 125–26.
126 Gallop, *Portugal*, 144; Santo, *A religião popular portuguesa*, 36.
127 Vasconcellos, *Tradições populares de Portugal*, 118.
128 Mattoso, *Naquele tempo*, 245.
129 Coelho, *Obra Etnográfica*, 334; Santo, *A religião popular portuguesa*, 35; Marques, *Entre a serra e o mar*, 124.
130 Mattoso, *Naquele tempo*, 220.
131 Evans, *Portugal*, 302.
132 Sitwell, *Portugal and Madeira*, 130.
133 Saramago, *Journey to Portugal*, 329.
134 Vasconcellos, *Tradições populares de Portugal*, 118.
135 Macaulay, *Fabled Shore*, 239.

136 Mattoso, *Naquele tempo*, 247.
137 Braga, *Camões*.
138 Mattoso, Daveau and Belo, *Portugal*, 686.
139 Pessoa, *The Book of Disquiet*, 165.
140 J. Dias, *Estudos de antropologia*, 142.
141 Pessoa, *The Book of Disquiet*, 117.
142 Dacosta and Barros, *A escrita do mar*, 28.
143 Ibid., 10.
144 Camões, *The Lusiads*, canto 1, v. 1–3.
145 Ibid., canto 3, v. 20–143.
146 Ibid., canto 8, v. 1–43.
147 Ibid., canto 10.
148 Ibid., canto 7, v. 2–3.
149 Ibid., canto 7, v. 3.
150 Eliade, *The Portugal Journal*, 44.
151 Moura, *Sobre Camões, Gândavo e outras personagens*, 104.
152 Camões, *The Lusiads*, canto 1, v. 3, line 3.
153 Moura, *Sobre Camões, Gândavo e outras personagens*, 97.
154 Dacosta and Barros, *A escrita do mar*, 68.
155 Guerra, *Fado, alma de um povo*, 35–37.
156 In Dacosta and Barros, *A escrita do mar*, 26.
157 Guerra, *Fado, alma de um povo*, 31.
158 Ibid., 35.
159 Ibid.
160 J. Pinto Ribeiro de Carvalho, *História do fado*, 42.
161 Costa and Guerreiro, *O trágico e o contraste*, 47–48.
162 In J. Pinto Ribeiro de Carvalho, *História do fado*, 42.
163 In Patrício, *O messianismo de Teixeira de Pascoaes e a educação dos Portugueses*, 71.
164 Guerra, *Fado, alma de um povo*, 97.
165 Examples include Manuel Maria (father of the ceramicist Rafael Pinheiro), whose bust stands in his grotto in Macau; Simões de Almeida (1844–1926), who modelled a hagiography of national fathers that also included da Gama and the Infante D. Henrique; Álvares Cabral (1467–1520), for the Gabinete Português de Leitura in Rio de Janeiro and the Academia Real de Belas Artes in Lisbon; Francisco José Rensende (1825–93); José Joaquim Teixeira Lopes (1837–1918); António Soares dos Reis (1847–89); and J. de Almeida e Silva, for the city of Viseu in 1913 (João, *Memória e império*, 397–99).
166 Ibid., 356
167 M.M. Cantinho Pereira, *O Museu Etnográfico da Sociedade de Geografia de Lisboa*, 125.
168 In João, *Memória e império*, 540.
169 In ibid., 132.
170 In ibid., 137.
171 Ibid., 541.
172 Caldeira, "Poder e memória nacional," 135.
173 Wright and Swift, *Minho and North Portugal*, 144–45.
174 Sitwell, *Portugal and Madeira*, 137–38.
175 Gallop, *Portugal*, 23; Sitwell, *Portugal and Madeira*, 123–24; Salter, *Introducing Portugal*, 68.
176 Garrido, *A Epopeia do Bacalhau*, 31–33.
177 Garrido, "O Estado Novo e as Pescas," 117.
178 Garrido, *A Epopeia do Bacalhau*, 70.
179 Ibid., 94.
180 Garrido, "O Estado Novo e as Pescas," 106.
181 Garrido, *A Epopeia do Bacalhau*, 103.
182 Mattoso, Daveau and Belo, *Portugal*, 68.
183 Dacosta and Barros, *A escrita do mar*, 52.
184 Ibid., 83.
185 Mattoso, Daveau and Belo, *Portugal*, 12–13.

CHAPTER 4

186 Costa Lobo, *Origens do Sebastianismo*, 13.
187 Gallop, *Portugal*, 80; Sanchis, *Arraial, festa de um povo*, 62–63; Justino, *Loas a Maria*, 23–24; Morais, *Religiosidade popular no Alentejo*, 17.
188 Sanchis, *Arraial, festa de um povo*, 63.
189 Pedroso, *Contribuições para uma mitologia popular portuguesa*, 249.
190 Gallop, *Portugal*, 133.
191 Cortez Pinto, *Santos de Portugal*, 31–35.
192 Sanchis, "The Portuguese *'romarias'*," 264.
193 Cutileiro, *Ricos e pobres no Alentejo*, 360.
194 Sanchis, *Arraial, festa de um povo*, 41–42.
195 E. Veiga de Oliveira, *Festividades cíclicas em Portugal*, 217.
196 Ibid., 219.
197 J. Dias and Ribeiro, *Vilarinho da Furna*, 215.
198 Sanchis, *Arraial, festa de um povo*, 139.
199 Ibid., 143.
200 In Extremadura these are called *círios*, which are different from elsewhere in that they involve people from distant places linked by complex rights and participation in long processions in which the saints are carried on decorated ox carts (Sanchis, *Arraial, festa de um povo*, 83; E. Veiga de Oliveira, *Festividades cíclicas em Portugal*, 220).
201 E. Veiga de Oliveira, *Festividades cíclicas em Portugal*, 217.
202 Sanchis, *Arraial, festa de um povo*, 83.
203 Cutileiro, *Ricos e pobres no Alentejo*, 361.
204 Sanchis, "The Portuguese *'romarias'*," 268.
205 Cutileiro, *Ricos e pobres no Alentejo*, 360.
206 Sanchis, "The Portuguese *'romarias'*," 273.
207 Wright and Swift, *Minho and North Portugal*, 206; Sanchis, *Arraial, festa de um povo*, 39; E. Veiga de Oliveira, *Festividades cíclicas em Portugal*, 222.

208 E. Veiga de Oliveira, *Festividades cíclicas em Portugal*, 242. The use of votive paintings as offerings began in the eighteenth century but had fallen out of fashion by the mid-twentieth century. They were mainly commissioned by more affluent families able to afford them (Pina-Cabral, "O pagamento do santo," 89, 96, 100).
209 Sanchis, *Arraial, festa de um povo*, 93.
210 Cutileiro, *Ricos e pobres no Alentejo*, 377.
211 Sanchis, *Arraial, festa de um povo*, 84; E. Veiga de Oliveira, *Festividades cíclicas em Portugal*, 217.
212 Sanchis, *Arraial, festa de um povo*, 39–40.
213 Gallop, *Portugal*, 80; Wright and Swift, *Minho and North Portugal*, 205; Sanchis, *Arraial, festa de um povo*, 61; Morais, *Religiosidade popular no Alentejo*, 17.
214 Wright and Swift, *Minho and North Portugal*, 207.
215 Santo, *A religião popular portuguesa*, 17.
216 After being flooded in 1972, this village in the municipality of Terras de Bouro (Braga) now lies beneath a reservoir.
217 J. Dias and Ribeiro, *Vilarinho da Furna*, 179–80.
218 Sanchis, *Arraial, festa de um povo*, 82.
219 Pina-Cabral, "Quinze anos depois."
220 Raposo, *Por detrás da máscara*, 25.
221 Sanchis, *Arraial, festa de um povo*, 42.
222 Pina-Cabral and Feijó, "Conflicting Attitudes to Death in Modern Portugal," 26.
223 Cutileiro, *Ricos e pobres no Alentejo*, 347.
224 Sanchis, *Arraial, festa de um povo*, 53; Pina-Cabral and Feijó, "Conflicting Attitudes to Death in Modern Portugal," 28.
225 In Cortez Pinto, *Santos de Portugal*, 5.
226 Rosas, "O Salazarismo e o homem novo," 42.
227 Pimentel, *O sistema museológico Português*, 92.
228 These express the three dominant values during the dictatorship; "Fado" for national stability, "Fátima" for Catholic faith and "Football" for the collective passion.
229 Rosas, "O Salazarismo e o homem novo," 38.
230 Sanchis, *Arraial, festa de um povo*, 201; Torgal, Mendes and Catroga, *História da história*, 274.
231 Caldeira, "Poder e memória nacional," 122; Torgal, Mendes and Catroga, *História da história*, 260; Melo, *Salazarismo e cultura popular*, 30; Rosas, "O Salazarismo e o homem novo," 33.
232 Torgal, Mendes and Catroga, *História da história*, 260–61.
233 Medina, "Ideologia e mentalidade do 'Estado Novo' Salazarista," 184; Damasceno, *Museus para o povo Português*, 118.
234 Torgal, Mendes and Catroga, *História da história*, 261.
235 Ibid., 267.
236 Medina, "Ideologia e mentalidade do 'Estado Novo' Salazarista," 175.
237 Damasceno, *Museus para o povo Português*, 45.
238 In Barros, "Cartazes bem bonitos, modernos, originais," 179.
239 Torgal, Mendes and Catroga, *História da história*, 265.
240 In Medina, "Ideologia e mentalidade do 'Estado Novo' Salazarista," 163; in Torgal, "'O fascismo nunca existiu'," 19.
241 In Torgal, Mendes and Catroga, *História da história*, 261.
242 In Damasceno, *Museus para o povo Português*, 39.
243 Torgal, Mendes and Catroga, *História da história*, 264, 276; Melo, *Salazarismo e cultura popular*, 39–40.
244 Acciaiuoli, *Exposições do Estado Novo*, 127; Torgal, Mendes and Catroga, *História da história*, 264; J. Leal, "Metamorfoses da arte popular," 270.
245 In Damasceno, *Museus para o povo Português*, 29.
246 Torgal, Mendes and Catroga, *História da história*, 261.
247 Ibid., 277; Damasceno, *Museus para o povo Português*, 26.
248 Wright and Swift, *Minho and North Portugal*, 57.
249 They described the pottery decoration as "third century Greek meander design and Halstaat Celtic hatching in between crude ovals" (ibid.).
250 Ibid., 72–73.
251 Bridge and Lowndes, *The Selective Traveller in Portugal*, 2.
252 Melo, *Salazarismo e cultura popular*, 179.
253 Torgal, Mendes and Catroga, *História da história*, 274.
254 Alves, *Arte popular e nação no Estado Novo*, 46.
255 Alves, "'A poesia dos simples'," 67.
256 Rios, Ramos and Régo, *Olaria de Barcelos*, 25–26.
257 Alves, "'A poesia dos simples'," 72; Alves, *Arte popular e nação no Estado Novo*, 18.
258 Medina, "Ideologia e mentalidade do 'Estado Novo' Salazarista," 184.
259 Despite the image portrayed of Salazar's domestic idyll, he also lived in an elegant fin-de-siècle home at 64 Rua Bernardo Lima in the Marquis de Pombal district of Lisbon for five years in the 1930s before taking up residence at the São Bento Palace, which remains the official residence of Portugal's prime minister today.
260 Medina, "Ideologia e mentalidade do 'Estado Novo' Salazarista," 173.
261 J. Dias and Ribeiro, *Vilarinho da Furna*, 69.
262 This image was refuted by Dias's description of rural homes in northern Portugal in the 1940s, which were far from such comforts. According to Dias, rural mountain houses were characterized by the complete absence of aesthetics. Neither the exteriors nor the interiors were decorated, and all comforts were clearly absent (J. Dias and Ribeiro, *Vilarinho da Furna*, 75).
263 Vasconcellos, *Tradições populares de Portugal*.
264 Fernandes, "O 'útil' e o 'inútil'," 31.
265 In Rios, Ramos and Régo, *Olaria de Barcelos*, 18.

266 In Fernandes, "O 'útil' e o 'inútil'," 31.
267 Prado was incorporated into the municipality of Barcelos in 1855.
268 Peixoto, *As Olarias de Prado*, 114.
269 Ibid.
270 Rios, Ramos and Régo, *Olaria de Barcelos*, 26; Alves, "'A poesia dos simples'," 67.
271 Rios, Ramos and Régo, *Olaria de Barcelos*, 38.
272 Ibid., 21.
273 Vermelho, *Barros de Estremoz*, 109.
274 Ibid., 110.
275 Fernandes, "O 'útil' e o 'inútil'," 29; Pais, Pacheco and Coroado, *Cerâmica de Coimbra*, 55.
276 Pais, Pacheco and Coroado, *Cerâmica de Coimbra*, 79–81.
277 In A. de Sousa Dias and Machado, *A cerâmica de Rafael Bordalo Pinheiro*, 16.
278 Ibid., 21.
279 Rios, Ramos and Régo, *Olaria de Barcelos*, 34.
280 Ibid., 35–36.
281 Pina-Cabral, "Tamed Violence," 104.
282 The 1940s–1960s were also a particularly fecund time for other private collectors. Abel de Lacerda assembled an extraordinary, albeit eclectic, collection of automobiles, modern art, tapestries and archaeological pieces that became institutionalized in the museum named after the village Caramulo. Mário Augusto da Silva (1901–77) specialized in scientific instruments and created the collection that formed the National Museum of Science and Technology (now amalgamated with the Science Museum of the University of Coimbra). These collectors were drawn from widely different backgrounds and included poets, artists, medical practitioners and physicists, some of whom were censured by the Estado Novo for their opposition to the regime.
283 Wright and Swift, *Minho and North Portugal*, 11.
284 Ibid., 37.
285 Ibid., 94–95.
286 Wright and Swift, *Algarve*, 53.
287 Wright and Swift, *Minho and North Portugal*, 71.
288 Ibid., 73.
289 Alves, *Arte popular e nação no Estado Novo*, 105.
290 Rios, Ramos and Régo, *Olaria de Barcelos*, 72.
291 Fernandes, "De barro se faz memória," 32; Rios, Ramos and Régo, *Olaria de Barcelos*, 68. Rios mentions Júlia Côta, Rosalina Baraça, Lourdes Ferreira and Fernando Morgado, while the Mistério brothers operate wood- and gas-operated kilns.
292 There is a great variety in painting skills: paint applied when clay is cold, as in work by Mistério and Baraça; thin transparent glaze over polychromatic paints, as in work by Sapateira; monochromatic lead-based glazes like the Ramalhos's; and use of new paints mixed with old materials, like varnishes used by Côta and Lourdes Ferreira. Other artists combine yellow clay from Aveiro with white from Águeda to create contrast (Rios, Ramos and Régo, *Olaria de Barcelos*, 60).
293 Ibid., 37.
294 Cf. A. Alves Costa, "Quando eram rudes e exilados," 9–10; Fernandes, "O 'útil' e o 'inútil'," 40.
295 Cf. Peixoto, *As Olarios de Prado*.
296 Isaiah 64:8 (Authorized [King James] Version).
297 Fernandes, "De barro se faz memória," 18.
298 In Rios, Ramos and Régo, *Olaria de Barcelos*, 37.

CHAPTER 5

299 Saramago, *Baltasar and Blimunda*, 231.
300 Fernandes, "Rosa Ramalho," 19.
301 In Pina-Cabral, *Sons of Adam, Daughters of Eve*, 83.
302 Porto, *O corpo, a razão, o coração*, 21.
303 Ibid., 42.
304 Ibid., 86.
305 Pina-Cabral, *Sons of Adam, Daughters of Eve*, 82.
306 Fernandes, "Rosa Ramalho," 9.
307 Porto, *O corpo, a razão, o coração*, 23.
308 Cutileiro, *Ricos e pobres no Alentejo*, 135–36.
309 Ibid., 137–40.
310 Pina-Cabral, *Sons of Adam, Daughters of Eve*, 8.
311 Fernandes, "Rosa Ramalho," 9.
312 A. de Sousa Dias and Machado, *A cerâmica de Rafael Bordalo Pinheiro*, 25–26.
313 Wright and Swift, *Minho and North Portugal*, 34.
314 Rios, Ramos and Régo, *Olaria de Barcelos*, 27.
315 Fernandes, "O 'útil' e o 'inútil'," 37.
316 Rios, Ramos and Régo, *Olaria de Barcelos*, 27.
317 Fernandes, "O 'útil' e o 'inútil'," 40.
318 Sanchis, "The Portuguese '*romarias*'," 280.
319 Porto, *O corpo, a razão, o coração*, 22.
320 Rios, Ramos and Régo, *Olaria de Barcelos*, 27.
321 Ibid., 74.
322 In ibid., 74.
323 Salter, *Introducing Portugal*, 161.
324 Gallop, *Portugal*, 140.
325 Manuel Gustavo Bordalo Pinheiro, in an early twentieth-century ceramic, depicted this episode in the saint's life.
326 Gallop, *Portugal*, 140.
327 J. Dias and Ribeiro, *Vilarinho da Furna*, 82–83.
328 Cutileiro, *Ricos e pobres no Alentejo*, 376–77.
329 J. Dias, "Os elementos fundamentais da cultura portuguesa," 150.

330 Fernandes, "O 'útil' e o 'inútil'," 39.
331 Alves, "'A poesia dos simples'," 64.
332 Gallop, *Portugal*, 134–35.
333 Sanchis, *Arraial, festa de um povo*, 16; Santo, *A religião popular portuguesa*, 15.
334 Manuel and Francisco Lima, interview with Eduardo Tomé, 2012.
335 Hughes, *Heaven and Hell in Western Art*, 227.
336 Ferguson, *Signs and Symbols in Christian Art*, 19.
337 Ibid., 101.
338 Xavier, "Manuel Gustavo e os jornais humorísticos," 79.
339 A. de Sousa Dias and Machado, *A cerâmica de Rafael Bordalo Pinheiro*, 140.
340 Ibid.
341 Pina-Cabral, "Tamed Violence," 103.
342 Ibid., 113.
343 Five hundred figures were made originally, followed by a further five hundred to satisfy demand.
344 Traditionally, images read "*Queres fiado? Toma!*" (You want credit? Take this!)
345 A. de Sousa Dias and Machado, *A cerâmica de Rafael Bordalo Pinheiro*, 211.
346 In Melo, *Salazarismo e cultura popular*, 76.
347 Ibid., 41; Damasceno, *Museus para o povo Português*, 88–89; Alves, *Arte popular e nação no Estado Novo*, 82.
348 Raposo, *Por detrás da máscara*, 101–2.

CHAPTER 6

349 J. Dias and Ribeiro, *Vilarinho da Furna*, 177.
350 Eliade, *The Portugal Journal*, 232.
351 Gallop, *Portugal*, 58; cf. Coelho, *Obra Etnográfica*, 337.
352 Sanchis, "The Portuguese '*romarias*'," 285.
353 Pedroso, *Contribuições para uma mitologia popular portuguesa*, 229, 295.
354 Pina-Cabral, *Sons of Adam, Daughters of Eve*, 183.
355 Ibid., 242.
356 In Rios, Ramos and Régo, *Olaria de Barcelos*, 45.
357 Gallop, *Portugal*, 58.
358 Coelho, *Obra Etnográfica*, 337.
359 Gallop, *Portugal*, 58.
360 Ibid.
361 Pedroso, *Contribuições para uma mitologia popular portuguesa*, 239.
362 Hughes, *Heaven and Hell in Western Art*, 242.
363 Pedroso, *Contribuições para uma mitologia popular portuguesa*, 240–41; Coelho, *Obra Etnográfica*, 337.
364 Gallop, *Portugal*, 98.
365 Hughes, *Heaven and Hell in Western Art*, 248.
366 Pedroso, *Contribuições para uma mitologia popular portuguesa*, 243.
367 Gil Vicente (1465–c. 1536) was a playwright and the founder of Portuguese theatre.
368 Hughes, *Heaven and Hell in Western Art*, 159.
369 Pedroso, *Contribuições para uma mitologia popular portuguesa*, 242–43; Coelho, *Obra Etnográfica*, 338.
370 Hughes, *Heaven and Hell in Western Art*, 175.
371 J. Dias and Ribeiro, *Vilarinho da Furna*, 181.
372 Pina-Cabral, *Sons of Adam, Daughters of Eve*, 228.
373 Santo, *A religião popular portuguesa*, 184.
374 Pedroso, *Contribuições para uma mitologia popular portuguesa*, 188, 229.
375 Santo, *A religião popular portuguesa*, 134–37.
376 Coelho, *Obra Etnográfica*, 334–35. There is a large collection of these in the cupola of Nossa Senhora da Nazaré and in the cupola of Nossa Senhora da Encarnação near Buarcos. Large collections are also found in the museums of Póvoa and Ilhavo.
377 Santo, *A religião popular portuguesa*, 48.
378 J. Dias and Ribeiro, *Vilarinho da Furna*, 191.
379 Vasconcellos, *Tradições populares de Portugal*, 79.
380 Pedroso, *Contribuições para uma mitologia popular portuguesa*, 249.
381 Sanchis, *Arraial, festa de um povo*, 80.
382 Wright and Swift, *Minho and North Portugal*, 199.
383 Sitwell, *Portugal and Madeira*, 174.
384 Sanchis, *Arraial, festa de um povo*.
385 Vermelho, *Barros de Estremoz*, 92.
386 E. Veiga de Oliveira, *Festividades cíclicas em Portugal*, 224.
387 Wright and Swift, *Minho and North Portugal*, 199.
388 Ibid.
389 Ibid., 81.
390 E. Veiga de Oliveira, *Festividades cíclicas em Portugal*, 224.
391 Pina-Cabral, "Tamed Violence," 108.
392 Ibid., 112.
393 E. Veiga de Oliveira, *Festividades cíclicas em Portugal*, 224.
394 Ibid., 225.
395 Pedroso, *Contribuições para uma mitologia popular portuguesa*, 249; Coelho, *Obra Etnográfica*, 338.
396 Pedroso, *Contribuições para uma mitologia popular portuguesa*, 247.
397 Ibid., 219.
398 Wright and Swift, *Minho and North Portugal*, 206–7.
399 Pedroso, *Contribuições para uma mitologia popular portuguesa*, 296.
400 Santo, *A religião popular portuguesa*, 30.
401 Gallop, *Portugal*, 77; Santo, *A religião popular portuguesa*, 32–34.
402 Vasconcellos, *Tradições populares de Portugal*, 122.
403 Santo, *A religião popular portuguesa*, 38.
404 Gallop, *Portugal*, 78; cf. Pedroso, *Contribuições para uma mitologia popular portuguesa*, 219.

405 Gallop, *Portugal*, 79; Vasconcellos, *Tradições populares de Portugal*, 123; Pedroso, *Contribuições para uma mitologia popular portuguesa*, 224.
406 Vasconcellos, *Tradições populares de Portugal*, 123.
407 Gallop, *Portugal*, 78–79.
408 Ibid., 80; Santo, *A religião popular portuguesa*, 33.
409 Pedroso, *Contribuições para uma mitologia popular portuguesa*, 246, 248.
410 Ibid., 218.
411 Gallop, *Portugal*, 63.
412 Ibid., 84.
413 Pedroso, *Contribuições para uma mitologia popular portuguesa*, 226.
414 J. Dias and Ribeiro, *Vilarinho da Furna*, 209.
415 Pina-Cabral, *Sons of Adam, Daughters of Eve*, 187–88.
416 Ibid., 201; J. Dias and Ribeiro, *Vilarinho da Furna*, 177.
417 Pedroso, *Contribuições para uma mitologia popular portuguesa*, 242.
418 Ibid., 241.
419 Camões, *The Lusiads*, canto 6, v. 17–19:

The hairs of his beard and the hair
Falling from his head to his shoulders
Were all one mass of mud, and visibly
Had never been touched by a comb;
Each dangling dreadlock was a cluster
Of gleaming, blue-black mussels.
On his head, by way of coronet, he wore
The biggest lobster-shell you ever saw.

His body was naked, even his genitals,
So as not to impede his swimming,
But tiny creatures of the sea
Crawled over him by the hundreds;
Crabs and prawns and many others
Which wax with the growing moon,
Cockles and oysters, and the slimy husks
Of convoluted whelks and other mollusks.

In his hand was a huge twisted conch.

420 Gallop, *Portugal*, 58.
421 Peixoto, *As Olarias de Prado*, 114.
422 Maciel, *A máscara de Ousilhão*.
423 The reason MOA was able to purchase so many of these masks was because José Alves had made a large number of pieces for the Mask Association to perform at Disneyland, Paris, fifteen years earlier, and he had more masks than were required for the village-day Carnival celebrations.
424 Pessanha, *Mascarados e máscaras populares de Trás-os-Montes*, 52.
425 Ibid., 109.
426 J. Leal, "Percursos entre festas," 107; Raposo, *Por detrás da máscara*, 19.
427 Ferreira and Perdigão, *Máscaras em Portugal*, 38–43.
428 J. Berger, *The Shape of a Pocket*.

CHAPTER 7

429 Camões, *The Lover and the Beloved*, 67.
430 Cidraes, *A tradição lendária de Afonso Henriques*, 35.
431 Ibid., 35–36.
432 Ibid., 84.
433 Taubes, *Occidental Eschatology*, 32.
434 Revelation 13:1–14 (Authorized [King James] Version).
435 Revelation 20:4–6 (AV).
436 Revelation 21:23 (AV); Le Goff, *The Medieval Imagination*, 188.
437 Taubes, *Occidental Eschatology*, 29.
438 J. Berger, *The Shape of a Pocket*, 209.
439 Le Goff, *The Medieval Imagination*, 190.
440 In ibid., 189.
441 Hughes, *Heaven and Hell in Western Art*, 177.
442 Cohn, *The Pursuit of the Millennium*, 34.
443 Serrão, *As pinturas murais da capela de São João Baptista em Monsaraz*.
444 Ibid., 33.
445 Ibid.; Le Goff, *The Medieval Imagination*, 189.
446 Taubes, *Occidental Eschatology*, 149.
447 Fr. Peter Carota, "Hell Is for Real #5 Our Lady of Fatima," *Traditional Catholic Priest* (blog), 3 February 2015, http://www.traditionalcatholicpriest.com/2015/02/03/hell-real-5-lady-fatima/.
448 In ibid.
449 J. Berger, *The Shape of a Pocket*, 210.
450 E. Veiga de Oliveira, *Festividades cíclicas em Portugal*, 130–31.
451 Tiza, *Inverno mágico*, 27; Barros and Costa, *Festas e tradições portuguesas: Novembro e Dezembro*, 68.
452 Pedroso, *Contribuições para uma mitologia popular portuguesa*, 523; Lopes, *A face do caos*, 24.
453 Pedroso, *Contribuições para uma mitologia popular portuguesa*, 519; Lopes, *A face do caos*, 23.
454 Lopes, *A face do caos*, 37.
455 Santo, *A religião popular portuguesa*, 66.
456 B. Pereira, *Máscaras portuguesas*, 30.
457 Ibid., 32.
458 Ibid., 48.
459 J. Dias, *Rio de Onor*, 179.
460 In B. Pereira, *Máscaras portuguesas*, 24.
461 Ibid., 14.

462 E. Veiga de Oliveira, *Festividades cíclicas em Portugal*, 188.
463 Tiza, *Inverno mágico*, 35.
464 Lopes, *A face do caos*, 111.
465 Ibid., 101.
466 B. Pereira, *Máscaras portuguesas*, 104.
467 Ibid., 126.
468 Maciel, *A máscara de Ousilhão*, 71.
469 B. Pereira, *Máscaras portuguesas*, 134.
470 Coelho, *Obra Etnográfica*, 273.
471 J. Leal, "Percursos entre festas," 106.
472 Vale de Almeida, "Quando a máscara esconde uma mulher," 62.
473 J. Leal, "Percursos entre festas," 107; Raposo, *Por detrás da máscara*, 43.
474 J. Berger, *The Shape of a Pocket*, 176.
475 Raposo, *Por detrás da máscara*, 70–71.

CHAPTER 8

476 Porto, *Modos de objectificação da dominação colonial*, 588.
477 Gouveia, *As colecções etnológicas de origem ultramarina*, 5–14.
478 Ibid., 34.
479 Teixeira, "Portuguese Art Treasures, Medieval Women and Early Museum Collections," 309.
480 Brigola, *Colecções, gabinetes e museus em Portugal no século XVIII*, 365.
481 Simon, *Scientific Expeditions in the Portuguese Overseas Territories*, 20, 113.
482 Gouveia, *As colecções etnológicas de origem ultramarina*, 22; Rodriques de Areia and Miranda, "Profile of a Naturalist."
483 Brigola, *Colecções, gabinetes e museus em Portugal no século XVIII*, 92; Machado and Antunes, "Aniceto Rapozo's Cabinet at the Lisbon Academy of Sciences," 21.
484 Simon, *Scientific Expeditions in the Portuguese Overseas Territories*, 49; Rodrigues de Areia and Miranda, "Profile of a Naturalist," 23.
485 Simon, *Scientific Expeditions in the Portuguese Overseas Territories*, 19.
486 Ibid., 129; Rodrigues de Areia and Miranda, "Profile of a Naturalist," 67–68.
487 Rodrigues de Areia and Miranda, "Profile of a Naturalist," 64–67.
488 M. Martins, "As colecções etnográficas," 117. The collection contains thirteen of the twenty-eight outstanding bark masks collected from the Jurupixunas, from the area of Caldas in the state of Amazonas, as well as a remarkable selection of decorated gourds, pottery, weapons, musical instruments, hammocks, furniture, pestle and mortars, snuff trays, toys and more from other indigenous groups.
489 Gouveia, *Colecções Africanas do Museu e Laboratório Antropológico da Universidade de Coimbra*, 488; Rodrigues de Areia and Tavares da Rocha, "O ensino da antropologia," 14.
490 In Gouveia, *Colecções Africanas do Museu e Laboratório Antropológico da Universidade de Coimbra*, 487.
491 Rodrigues de Areia and Miranda, "Profile of a Naturalist," 68.
492 In ibid., 70–71.
493 Gouveia, *Colecções Africanas do Museu e Laboratório Antropológico da Universidade de Coimbra*, 496.
494 L. Pires Martins, "Ossos do ofício," 115.
495 Rodrigues de Areia and Tavares da Rocha, "O ensino da antropologia," 14.
496 M. Martins, "As colecções etnográficas," 119.
497 Ibid., 122; Gouveia, *As colecções etnológicas de origem ultramarina*, 12.
498 M. Martins, "As colecções etnográficas," 136–39.
499 Ibid., 142–43.
500 Rodrigues de Areia, *A colecções angolanas*, 149.
501 Gouveia, *As colecções etnológicas de origem ultramarina*, 12–13.
502 J. Leal, "Metamorfoses da arte popular," 270; Alves, *Arte popular e nação no Estado Novo*, 195.
503 M.M. Cantinho Pereira, *O Museu Etnográfico da Sociedade de Geografia de Lisboa*, 118.
504 Ibid., 123.
505 Pimentel, *O sistema museológico Português*, 106.
506 Carvalho and Carvalho, "Museus e exposições," 108–9.
507 Ibid., 109.
508 João, *Memória e império*, 370.
509 In Carvalho and Carvalho, "Museus e exposições," 115.
510 M.M. Cantinho Pereira, *O Museu Etnográfico da Sociedade de Geografia de Lisboa*, 84.
511 Ibid., 89.
512 Ibid., 93.
513 M.M. Cantinho Pereira, "O Museu da Sociedade de Geografia de Lisboa nos finais do século XIX"; M.M. Cantinho Pereira, *O Museu Etnográfico da Sociedade de Geografia de Lisboa*, 106.
514 M.M. Cantinho Pereira, *O Museu Etnográfico da Sociedade de Geografia de Lisboa*, 306.
515 Cf. ibid., 281.
516 E. Veiga de Oliveira, "Introduction," 1; Pimentel, *O sistema museológico Português*, 129; M.M. Cantinho Pereira, *O Museu Etnográfico da Sociedade de Geografia de Lisboa*, 416.
517 M.M. Cantinho Pereira, *O Museu Etnográfico da Sociedade de Geografia de Lisboa*, 484.
518 Ibid., 488.
519 Roque, "Colonialidade equívoca," 91.
520 João, *Memória e império*, 359.
521 In Damasceno, *Museus para o povo Português*, 23.

522 João, *Memória e império*, 360.
523 Pimentel, *O sistema museológico Português*, 118–19.
524 J. Leal, "Metamorfoses da arte popular," 270.
525 Alves, *Arte popular e nação no Estado Novo*, 194.
526 E. Castro Leal, "Tópicos sobre os nacionalismos,", 64; Viçosa, "O saudosismo de Teixeira de Pascoaes e a identidade cultural portuguesa," 96; Damasceno, *Museus para o povo Português*, 33.
527 In Alves, *Arte popular e nação no Estado Novo*, 82.
528 J. Leal, *Etnografias portuguesas*, 81.
529 Alves, *Arte popular e nação no Estado Novo*, 83.
530 In Damasceno, *Museus para o povo Português*, 28.
531 Alves, *Arte popular e nação no Estado Novo*, 203.
532 In Damasceno, *Museus para o povo Português*, 31.
533 Alves, *Arte popular e nação no Estado Novo*, 157; Melo, *Salazarismo e cultura popular*, 79–80.
534 Alves, *Arte popular e nação no Estado Novo*, 183.
535 Ibid., 180.
536 In ibid., 187.
537 In ibid., 183.
538 Ibid., 193.
539 Ibid., 100.
540 Rosas, ed., *História de Portugal*, 59; Alves, *Arte popular e nação no Estado Novo*, 110.
541 Melo, *Salazarismo e cultura popular*, 79.
542 Damasceno, *Museus para o povo Português*, 32.
543 E. Veiga de Oliveira, "Introduction," 1; M.M. Cantinho Pereira, *O Museu Etnográfico da Sociedade de Geografia de Lisboa*, 541.
544 Castelo, "*O modo Português de estar no mundo*," 103.
545 E. Veiga de Oliveira, "Introduction," 1.
546 Ibid., 17.
547 Ibid., 16.
548 In the article "Epotome dos Estudos Etnográficos em Portugal," published in the official journal *Mensário das Casas do Povo*.
549 In Damasceno, *Museus para o povo Português*, 27.
550 M.M. Cantinho Pereira, *O Museu Etnográfico da Sociedade de Geografia de Lisboa*, 537–39.
551 Pimentel, *O sistema museológico Português*, 124.
552 Ibid., 89.
553 Melo, *Salazarismo e cultura popular*, 145.
554 Pimentel, *O sistema museológico Português*, 122; Damasceno, *Museus para o povo Português*, 134.
555 Melo, *Salazarismo e cultura popular*, 106.
556 Alves, "'A poesia dos simples'," 72; Alves, *Arte popular e nação no Estado Novo*, 28; Carvalho and Carvalho, "Museus e exposições," 131; Damasceno, *Museus para o povo Português*, 97–98.
557 Damasceno, *Museus para o povo Português*, 136–37.
558 Melo, *Salazarismo e cultura popular*, 128.
559 Damasceno, *Museus para o povo Português*, 140.
560 Melo, *Salazarismo e cultura popular*, 170; Damasceno, *Museus para o povo Português*, 26.
561 Alves, *Arte popular e nação no Estado Novo*, 156.
562 J. Leal, "Metamorfoses da arte popular," 270; Melo, *Salazarismo e cultura popular*, 172; Carvalho and Carvalho, "Museus e exposições," 122; Alves, *Arte popular e nação no Estado Novo*, 232.
563 Damasceno, *Museus para o povo Português*, 26.
564 Melo, *Salazarismo e cultura popular*, 179–80.
565 Damasceno, *Museus para o povo Português*, 142.
566 Alves, *Arte popular e nação no Estado Novo*, 277.
567 In Damasceno, *Museus para o povo Português*, 160.
568 Torgal, Mendes and Catroga, *História da história*, 276.
569 Pimentel, *O sistema museológico Português*, 143.
570 Porto, *Modos de objectificação da dominação colonial*, 45.

CHAPTER 9

571 In Thomaz, "Ecos do Atlântico Sul," 192.
572 In Patrício, *O messianismo de Teixeira de Pascoaes e a educação dos Portugueses*, 31.
573 Patrício, "A filosofia da educação em Portugal no século XX," 91.
574 In ibid.
575 Ibid., 90.
576 Ibid., 80.
577 Patrício, *O messianismo de Teixeira de Pascoaes e a educação dos Portugueses*, 71.
578 Clara, "O fim da Europa," 273.
579 In Patrício, *O messianismo de Teixeira de Pascoaes e a educação dos Portugueses*, 32.
580 Ibid., 68.
581 Ibid., 34–35.
582 In ibid., 21.
583 Ibid., 109.
584 Ibid., 41.
585 Ibid., 22–24; Patrício, "A filosofia da educação em Portugal no século XX," 82.
586 In Patrício, *O messianismo de Teixeira de Pascoaes e a educação dos Portugueses*, 75.
587 Ibid.,71.
588 Ibid., 43.
589 Patrício, "A filosofia da educação em Portugal no século XX," 71.
590 Patrício, *O messianismo de Teixeira de Pascoaes e a educação dos Portuguese*, 45–46.
591 In ibid., 29.

592 Ibid., 36–37.
593 Franco, "As duas leituras de Teixeira de Pascoaes."
594 Patrício, *O messianismo de Teixeira de Pascoaes e a educação dos Portugueses*, 17.
595 Pessoa, *Message*, 114.
596 Rosas, "O Salazarismo e o homem novo," 33–34.
597 Ibid., 40.
598 Catroga, *O céu da memória*, 322; João, *Memória e império*, 50.
599 In João, *Memória e império*, 52.
600 These include Almeida Garrett (1899), Pedro Álvares Cabral (1900), António Feliciano de Castilho (1900), Gil Vicente (1902) and Alexandre Herculano (1910), the founder of modern Portuguese history.
601 Catroga, *O céu da memória*, 155.
602 Ibid., 156.
603 Ibid.
604 The first flight between Lisbon and Rio was piloted by Sacadura Cabral and Gago Coutinho.
605 Pimentel, *O sistema museológico Português*, 141.
606 A park of miniaturized architectural models illustrating the diversity of building styles to be found throughout Portugal and her colonies was also created.
607 These included exhibitions devoted to the discovery of Guinea (1946); the reconquest of Angola from the Netherlands (1948); the births of António Enes (1948), the Mouzinho de Albuquerque (1955), Álvares Cabral (1968) and Vasco da Gama (1969); and the death of the Infante D. Henrique (1960).
608 Cf. Alves, "'A poesia dos simples'," 65.
609 João, *Memória e império*, 92.
610 Ibid., 252.
611 Ibid., 94.
612 Acciaiuoli, *Exposições do Estado Novo*, 107.
613 This was designed by Cottinelli Telmo and António Pardal Monteiro to commemorate the fifth centennial of the death of Henry the Navigator.
614 Acciaiuoli, *Exposições do Estado Novo*, 107; Torgal, Mendes and Catroga, *História da história*, 277; João, *Memória e império*, 104.
615 In Carvalho and Carvalho, "Museus e exposições," 134.
616 Torgal, Mendes and Catroga, *História da história*, 269–71.
617 Acciaiuoli, *Exposições do Estado Novo*, 111.
618 Cidraes, *A tradição lendária de Afonso Henriques*, 116.
619 Torgal, Mendes and Catroga, *História da história*, 271.
620 Thomaz, "Ecos do Atlântico Sul," 193.
621 Damasceno, *Museus para o povo Português*, 55.
622 In ibid., 53.
623 Rosas, ed., *História de Portugal*, 59; Alves, "'A poesia dos simples'," 85.
624 Torgal, Mendes and Catroga, *História da história*, 270; João, *Memória e império*, 349.
625 Carvalho and Carvalho, "Museus e exposições," 134.
626 In Thomaz, "Ecos do Atlântico Sul," 189; Acciaiuoli, *Exposições do Estado Novo*, 120.
627 Thomaz, "Ecos do Atlântico Sul," 196.
628 In ibid., 197.
629 Pimentel, *O sistema museológico Português*, 137–38; Damasceno, *Museus para o povo Português*, 57–58; Alves, *Arte popular e nação no Estado Novo*, 54.
630 Thomaz, "Ecos do Atlântico Sul," 202.
631 In Alves, *Arte popular e nação no Estado Novo*, 73.
632 Ibid., 54–55.
633 Thomaz, "Ecos do Atlântico Sul," 199–200.
634 Alves, *Arte popular e nação no Estado Novo*, 56.
635 Ibid., 270.
636 Ibid., 105.
637 Ibid., 109.
638 Ibid., 58.
639 In Carvalho and Carvalho, "Museus e exposições," 138.
640 Acciaiuoli, *Exposições do Estado Novo*, 208; Torgal, Mendes and Catroga, *História da história*, 271–72.
641 In Henriques, "Africans in Portuguese Society," 85.
642 Sanches, "Introdução," 7.
643 Carvalho and Carvalho, "Museus e exposições," 135.
644 Council of Europe, "Art Exhibition of the Council of Europe," accessed 12 February 2015, http://www.coe.int/t/dg4/cultureheritage/culture/events/exhibitions_en.asp.
645 Macedo, "Blooms the Earth in Sounds and Colours," 97.
646 Canavarro, "Preface," 20.
647 Ibid.
648 Ibid., 19.
649 Macedo, "Blooms the Earth in Sounds and Colours," 97.
650 Ibid., 98.
651 Ibid.
652 Pinto Mendes, "Cumpriu-se o mar," 65–66.
653 Certeau, *The Practice of Everyday Life*, 131–32.
654 A. de Oliveira, "The Activities of the CNCDP," 3.
655 Moura, "Presentation," 17.
656 Ibid., 16.
657 Ibid.
658 Ibid.
659 Gupta, "Movimentações globais das colheitas desde a 'era das descobertas' e transformações das culturas gastrónomicas," 199.
660 Hespanha, "Foreword," 13.
661 Ibid., 15.
662 Ibid., 13.

663 A. de Oliveira, "The Activities of the CNCDP," 1.
664 Hespanha, "Foreword," 13.
665 Perez, *Cultures of the Indian Ocean*, 19.
666 A. de Oliveira, "The Activities of the CNCDP," 5–8.
667 Pais de Brito, *Os índios nós*.
668 Pais de Brito, Perez and Sardo, eds., *Initiation*, 11.
669 Vale de Almeida, *Um mar da cor da terra*, 161.
670 Ibid., 166.
671 Freyre, *The Portuguese and the Tropics*.
672 Vale de Almeida, *Um mar da cor da terra*, 168.
673 Ibid., 181.

CHAPTER 10

674 In Ribeiro, *Henrique Delgado*, 133.
675 Alves, *Arte popular e nação no Estado Novo*, 169.
676 Ibid., 187.
677 Ibid.
678 Rosas, ed., *História de Portugal*, 59.
679 Alves, *Arte popular e nação no Estado Novo*, 107.
680 Delgado in Ribeiro, *Henrique Delgado*, 42.
681 Ibid.
682 Ibid., 56.
683 Ibid., 157; Gil, *Teatro Dom Roberto*, 106–215.
684 Delgado in Ribeiro, *Henrique Delgado*, 138.
685 Ibid., 165.
686 Ibid., 41, 75.
687 Ibid., 163.
688 Ibid., 59.
689 Zurbach, "Os Bonecos de Santo Aleixo," 41; Delgado in Ribeiro, *Henrique Delgado*, 84.
690 Zurbach, "Erudito e popular," 187–88.
691 Gil, *Teatro Dom Roberto*, 77.
692 Delgado in Ribeiro, *Henrique Delgado*, 122.
693 Gil, *Teatro Dom Roberto*, 87.
694 Delgado in Ribeiro, *Henrique Delgado*, 169.
695 Ibid., 133.
696 Ibid., 40, 112.
697 Ibid., 133.
698 Ibid.
699 Ibid., 169.
700 Ibid., 138.
701 Ibid., 116.
702 Gil, *Teatro Dom Roberto*, 72.
703 Ibid., 75.
704 Delgado in Ribeiro, *Henrique Delgado*, 124.
705 Cf. Talhinhas, "Colóquio," 171–74; Gil, *Teatro Dom Roberto*, 69.
706 Delgado in Ribeiro, *Henrique Delgado*, 84, 157.
707 Ibid., 130, 158.
708 Ibid., 30.
709 Ibid., 24.
710 Gil, *Teatro Dom Roberto*, 75–76.
711 Rumbau, "FIMFA Lx," 28.
712 Catroga, *O céu da memória*, 319.
713 J. Leal, *Etnografias portuguesas*, 176, 201; Alves, *Arte popular e nação no Estado Novo*, 214–15.
714 Franco, "As duas leituras de Teixeira de Pascoaes."
715 Rosmaninho, "António Ferro e a propaganda nacional antimoderna," 291.
716 João, *Memória e império*, 98.
717 In Acciaiuoli, *Exposições do Estado Novo*, 121.
718 In Rosmaninho, "António Ferro e a propaganda nacional antimoderna," 295.
719 Ibid., 289.
720 Alves, *Arte popular e nação no Estado Novo*, 83–84.
721 Acciaiuoli, *Exposições do Estado Novo*, 32.
722 Alves, *Arte popular e nação no Estado Novo*, 262.
723 Certeau, *The Practice of Everyday Life*, 108.
724 Ibid., 117.
725 Pina-Cabral, "O pagamento do santo," 84.
726 Pina-Cabral, "Quinze anos depois," 109.
727 Ibid., 116.
728 Ibid., 109.
729 J. Leal, "Percursos entre festas"; Vale de Almeida, "Quando a máscara esconde uma mulher"; Raposo, *Por detrás da máscara*.
730 Pina-Cabral, "Quinze anos depois," 116.
731 B. Pereira, "Rituais de inverno com máscaras," 37.
732 Certeau, *The Practice of Everyday Life*, 108.
733 Alves, *Arte popular e nação no Estado Novo*, 110.
734 Raposo, *Por detrás da máscara*, 73.
735 Godinho, "A 'loas' que contam uma festa," 47.
736 Certeau, *The Practice of Everyday Life*, 108.

Bibliography

Acciaiuoli, M. *Exposições do Estado Novo, 1934–1940*. Lisbon: Livros Horizonte, 1998.

Alves, V.M. "'A poesia dos simples': Arte popular e nação no Estado Novo." *Etnográfica* 11, no. 1 (2007): 63–89.

———. *Arte popular e nação no Estado Novo. A política folclorista do Secretariado da Propaganda Nacional*. Lisbon: Imprensa de Ciências Sociais, 2013.

Araújo, M. da Graça. *Louceiros de Santa Comba. Histórias que o barro escreve*. Barcelos: Museu de Olaria, 2007.

Barros, J. "Cartazes bem bonitos, modernos, originais." In *Os anos de Salazar: O que se contava e o que se ocultava durante o Estado Novo*, vol. 2, edited by A. Simões do Paço, 172–85. Lisbon: Planeta Agostini, 2008.

Barros, J., and S.M. Costa. *Festas e tradições portuguesas: Fevereiro*, vol. 2. Rio de Mouro: Círculo de Leitores, 2003.

———. *Festas e tradições portuguesas: Novembro e Dezembro*, vol. 8. Rio de Mouro: Círculo de Leitores, 2003.

Becker, H.S. *Art Worlds*. Berkeley, Los Angeles and London: University of California Press, 1982.

Bedini, S. *The Pope's Elephant*. Manchester: Carcanet in association with the Calouste Gulbenkian Foundation and the Discoveries Commission, 1997.

Berger, J. *The Shape of a Pocket*. London: Bloomsbury Publishing, 2001.

Berger, P. *The Goddess Obscured: Transformation of the Grain Protectress from Goddess to Saint*. Boston: Beacon Press, 1985.

Bisilliat, M., and R. Soares. *Edison Carneiro Folklore Museum: Sounding the Soul of the People*. São Paulo, Empresa das Artes, 2005.

Braga, T. *Camões. A obra lyrica e épica*. Porto: Livraria Chardron de Lello e Irmao, 1911.

———. *Contos tradicionais do povo Português*, vol. 4. Lisbon: Dom Quixote, 1994.

Bridge, A., and S. Lowndes. *The Selective Traveller in Portugal*. London: Chatto and Windus, 1949.

Brigola, J.C. Pires. *Colecções, gabinetes e museus em Portugal no século XVIII*. Lisbon: Fundação Calouste Gulbenkian, 2003.

Brotton, J. *Trading Territories: Mapping the Early Modern World*. London: Reaktion Books, 1997.

Buck, P. *Lisbon: A Cultural and Literary Companion*. Oxford: Signal Books, 2002.

Caldeira, A.M. "Poder e memória nacional. Heróis e vilões na mitologia salazarista." *Penélope* 15 (1995): 121–42.

Camões, L. de. *The Lover and the Beloved: Poems from Lyric*. Lisbon: Instituto Português do Património Arquitectónico, Mosteiro dos Jerónimos, 2001; originally published 1595.

———. *The Lusiads*. Oxford and New York: Oxford University Press, 1997; originally published 1572.

Canavarro, P. "Preface." In *The Portuguese Discoveries and Renaissance Europe*, vol. 1, 19–20. Lisbon: Presidency of the Council of Ministers, 1983.

Carvalho, J. Pinto Ribeiro de (Tinop). *História do fado*. Lisbon: Dom Quixote, 1982.

Carvalho, J.A. Seabra, and M. Carvalho. "Museus e exposições: Ideias, formas e discursos de representação e celebração da arte portuguesa (do Liberalismo ao Estado Novo)." In *Arte portuguesa: Da pré-história ao século XX*, vol. 20, edited by D. Rodrigues. Vila Nova de Gaia: Fubu, 2009.

Castelo, C.D. *"O modo Português de estar no mundo". O luso-tropicalismo e a ideologia colonial portuguesa (1933–1961)*. Porto: Edições Afrontamento, 1998.

Catroga, F. *O céu da memória: Cemitério romântico e culto civico dos mortos em Portugal (1756–1911)*. Coimbra: Minerva, 1999.

Certeau, M. de. *The Practice of Everyday Life*. Translated by S. Rendall. Berkeley, Los Angeles and London: University of California Press, 1984.

Chorão, J.B. *Nossa Lisboa dos outros*. Lisbon: CTT Correios de Portugal, 1999.

Cidraes, M.L. *A tradição lendária de Afonso Henriques: E as memórias do rei fundador em Castro Verde*. Castro Verde: Câmara Municipal, 2008.

Clara, F. "O fim da Europa. Onde a nação acaba e o império começa." In *Portugal não é um país pequeno: Contar o "império" na pós-colonialidade*, edited by M. R. Sanches, 271–84. Lisbon: Cotovia, 2006.

Coelho, F.A. *Obra Etnográfica*. Vol. 1, *Festas, costumes e outros materiais para uma etnologia de Portugal*. Lisbon: Dom Quixote, 1993.

Cohn, N. *The Pursuit of the Millennium: Revolutionary Millenarians and Mystical Anarchists of the Middle Ages*. London: Paladin, 1970.

Cortez Pinto, A. *Santos de Portugal*. Coimbra: Campanha Nacional de Educação de Adultos, 1956.

Costa, A. Alves. "Quando eram rudes e exilados." In *Rosa Ramalho: A colecção*, edited by A. Alves Costa and I.M. Fernandes, 7–16. Barcelos: Câmara Municipal de Barcelos, Museu de Olaria, 2007.

Costa, A. Alves, and I.M. Fernandes. *Rosa Ramalho: A colecção*. Barcelos: Câmara Municipal de Barcelos, Museu de Olaria, 2007.

Costa, A. Firmino da, and M. Guerreiro. *O trágico e o contraste: O fado no Bairro de Alfama*. Lisbon: Dom Quixote, 1984.

Costa Lobo, A. *Origens do Sebastianismo: História pertiguração dramática*. Alfragide: Texto, 2011.

Cunha, T. Pitta e. *Portugal e o mar: À redescoberta da geografia*. Lisbon: Fundação Francisco Manuel dos Santos, 2011.

Cutileiro, J. *Ricos e pobres no Alentejo: Uma análise de estrutura social*. Lisbon: Sá da Costa Editora, 1977.

Dacosta, F., and J. Barros. *A escrita do mar: Writings of the Sea*. Lisbon: Clube do Coleccionador dos Correios, 1998.

Damasceno, J. *Museus para o povo Português*. Coimbra: Imprensa da Universidade, 2010.

Danto, A. "The Artworld and Its Outsiders." In *Self-Taught Artists of the 20th Century: An American Anthology*, 18–27. San Francisco: Cronicle Books in association with the Museum of American Folk Art, 1998.

Déon, M. *Mes arches de noé*. Paris: La Table Ronde, 1980.

Dias, A. de Sousa, and R. Machado. *A cerâmica de Rafael Bordalo Pinheiro*. Lisbon: Lello Editores, 2009.

Dias, J. *Estudos de antropologia*, vol. 2. Lisbon: Imprensa Nacional/Casa da Moeda, 1993.

———. "Os elementos fundamentais da cultura portuguesa." In *Estudos de antropologia*, vol. 1, edited by J. Dias, 135–58. Lisbon: Imprensa Nacional/Casa da Moeda, 1999.

———. *Rio de Onor: Comunitarismo agro-pastoril*. Porto: Presença, 1984.

Dias, J., and O. Ribeiro. *Vilarinho da Furna: Uma aldeia comunitaria*. Lisbon: Imprensa Nacional/Casa da Moeda, 1981.

Dos Passos, J. *The Portugal Story: Three Centuries of Exploration and Discovery*. London: Hale, 1969.

Eliade, M. *The Portugal Journal*. Albany: State University of New York, 2010.

Evans, D. *Portugal*. London: Cadogan Books, 1990.

Ferguson, G. *Signs and Symbols in Christian Art*. Oxford and New York: Oxford University Press, 1971.

Fernandes, I.M. "De barro se faz memória." In *Olaria portuguesa: do fazer ao usar*, edited by R. Henriques da Silva, I.M. Fernandes and R. Banha da Silva, 17–33. Lisbon: Assírio & Alvim, 2003.

———. "Mistério que se traduz em Domingos, Virgínia, Manuel e Francisco." In *Figurado Português: de santos e diabos está o mundo cheio*, edited by I.M. Fernandes, A.L. Cruz and A. Jorge, 25–33. Porto: Livraria Civilização, 2005.

———. "O 'útil' e o 'inútil': Olaria versus figurado." In *Rosa Ramalho: A colecção*, edited by A. Alves Costa and I.M. Fernandes, 27–43. Barcelos: Câmara Municipal de Barcelos, Museu de Olaria, 2007.

———. "Rosa Ramalho: As minhas mãos são o nosso mundo." In *Figurado Português: De santos e diabos está o mundo cheio*, edited by I.M. Fernandes, A.L. Cruz and A. Jorge, 9–24. Porto: Livraria Civilização, 2005.

Ferreira, H., and T. Perdigão. *Máscaras em Portugal*. Lisbon: Media Livros, 2003.

Franco, A.C. "As duas leituras de Teixeira de Pascoaes." In *Encontro com Teixeira de Pascoaes no cinquentenário da sua morte*, edited by P. Morão and M. das Graças Moreira de Sá, 29–44. Lisbon, Colibri, 2003.

Freyre, G. *The Portuguese and the Tropics: Suggestions Inspired by the Portuguese Methods of Integrating Autochthonous Peoples and Cultures Differing from the European in a New, or Luso-Tropical, Complex of Civilisation*. Lisbon: Executive Committee for the Commemoration of the 5th Centenary of the Death of Prince Henry the Navigator, 1961.

Gallop, R. *Portugal: A Book of Folkways*. Cambridge: Cambridge University Press, 1936.

Garrido, A. *A Epopeia do Bacalhau*. Lisbon: CTT Correios do Portugal, 2011.

———. "O Estado Novo e as Pescas. A recriação historicista de uma 'Tradição Marítima Nacional'." In *Estados autoritários e totalitários e suas representações*, edited by L. Reis Torgal and H. Paulo, 99–118. Coimbra: Imprensa da Universidade de Coimbra, 2008.

Gil, J.M. Valbom. *Teatro Dom Roberto: O Saloio de Alcobaça e os novos Palheta: o teatro tradicional itinerante Português de marionetas*. Lisbon: EGEAC/Museu da Marioneta, 2013.

Godinho, P. "A 'loas' que contam uma festa: Permanência e mudanças na Festa dos Rapazes." In *Rituais de inverno com máscaras: Esposição*, edited by M. Vale de Almeida and V. Mesquita, 39–59. Bragança: Instituto Português de Museus, 2006.

Gouveia, H. Coutinho. *As colecções etnológicas de origem ultramarina no contexto de uma política do património cultural*. Coimbra: Museu e Laboratório Antropológico, Universidade de Coimbra, 1983.

———. *Colecções Africanas do Museu e Laboratório Antropológico da Universidade de Coimbra: Uma perspectiva histórica*. Lisbon: Inst. Port. do Património Cultural, 1985.
Guerra, M.L. *Fado, alma de um povo: Origem histórica*. Lisbon: Imprensa Nacional/Casa da Moeda, 2003.
Gupta, A. "Movimentações globais das colheitas desde a 'era das descobertas' e transformações das culturas gastrónomicas." In *Portugal não é um país pequeno: contar o "império" na pós-colonialidade*, edited by M.R. Sanches, 193–214. Lisbon: Cotovia, 2006.
Hauschild, T. *Power and Magic in Italy*. New York and Oxford: Berghahn Books, 2010.
Henriques, I.C. "Africans in Portuguese Society: Classification Ambiguities and Colonial Realities." In *Imperial Migrations: Colonial Communities and Diaspora in the Portuguese World*, edited by E. Morier-Genoud and M. Cahen, 72–103. Basingstoke and Hampshire: Palgrave Macmillan, 2013.
Hespanha, A. "Foreword." In *Cultures of the Indian Ocean*, edited by R.M. Perez. Lisbon: Comissão Nacional para as Comemorações dos Descobrimentos Portugueses, Instituto Portugués de Museus, 1998.
Hughes, R. *Heaven and Hell in Western Art*. London: Weidenfeld & Nicolson, 1968.
João, M.I. *Memória e império: Comemorações em Portugal (1880–1960)*. Lisbon: Fundação Calouste Gulbenkian, 2002.
Justino, L.J. *Loas a Maria: Religiosidade popular em Portugal*. Lisbon: Colibri, 2004.
Kenny, R. "'Wallflowers at the Dance of Western Civilization': The Limits of Folk Art." In *British Folk Art*, edited by R. Kenny, J. McMillan and M. Myrone, 126–33. London: Tate Publishing, 2014.
Leal, E. Castro. "Tópicos sobre os nacionalismos críticos do demoliberalismo republicano: Moral, religião e politica." In *História do pensamento filosófico Português*, vol. 5, o século XX, vol. 2, edited by P. Calafate, 135–60. Lisbon: Editorial Caminho, 2000.
Leal, J. *Etnografias portuguesas (1870–1970): Cultura popular e identidade nacional*. Lisbon: Dom Quixote, 2000.
———. "Metamorfoses da arte popular: Joaquim de Vasconcellos, Virgílio Correia e Ernesto de Sousa." *Etnográfica* 6, no. 2 (2002): 251–80.
———. "Percursos entre festas." In *Rituais de inverno com mascaras: Esposição*, edited by M. Vale de Almeida and V. Mesquita, 101–10. Bragança: Instituto Português de Museus, 2006.
———. "Preface." In F.A. Coelho and J. Leal, *Obra Etnográfica*. Vol. 1, *Festas, costumes e outros materiais para uma etnologia de Portugal*. Lisbon: Dom Quixote, 1993.
Le Goff, J. *Medieval Civilization 400–1500*. Oxford and New York: Basil Blackwell, 1988.
———. *The Medieval Imagination*. Chicago: University of Chicago Press, 1988.
Lopes, A. *A face do caos: Ritos de subversão na tradição portuguesa*. Alpiarça: Garrido, 2000.
Luis, A. Bessa. *O Mosteiro*. Lisbon: Guimarães, 2009.
Macaulay, R. *Fabled Shore: From the Pyrenees to Portugal*. London: Arrow Books Ltd., 1959; originally published 1949.
———. *They Went to Portugal*. London: Jonathan Cape, 1946.
Macedo, J. Borges de. "Blooms the Earth in Sounds and Colours." In *The Portuguese Discoveries and the Renaissance Europe*, vol. 1, 97–108. Lisbon: Presidency of the Council of Ministers, 1983.
Machado, J.S., and M.T. Antunes. "Aniceto Rapozo's Cabinet at the Lisbon Academy of Sciences: A Window into Brazilian Eighteenth-Century Timber Resources." *Journal of the History of Collections* 26, no. 1 (2014): 21–33.
Maciel, S.A. Araújo Martins. *A máscara de Ousilhão (Vinhais): Uma leitura antropológica e metafísica*. Vinhais: Edição Gabinete de Arqueologia e Património, Câmara Municipal de Vinhais, 1998.
Marques, M. Zulmira Albuquerque Furtado. *Entre a serra e o mar: Etnografia da região de Alcobaça*. Alcobaça: Tipografia Alcobacense, 2002.
Martins, L. Pires. "Ossos do ofício: Antropometria e etnografia no norte de Moçambique (1916–1917)." In *Portugal não é um país pequeno: Contar o "império" na pós-colonialidade*, edited by M.R. Sanches, 113–40. Lisbon: Cotovia, 2006.
Martins, M. "As colecções etnográficas." In *Cem anos de antropologia em Coimbra: 1885–1985*, 117–149. Coimbra: Museu e Laboratório Antropológico, Universidade de Coimbra, 1985.
Mattoso, J. *Naquele tempo: Ensaios de história medieval*. Lisbon: Círculo de Leitores, 2009.
Mattoso, J., S. Daveau, and D. Belo. *Portugal: O sabor da terra: Um retrato histórico e geográfico por regiões*. Lisbon: Círculo de Leitores, 2011.
McMillan, J. "The House that Jack Built: Essay as Sampler." In R. Kenny, J. McMillan and M. Myrone, *British Folk Art*, 10–15. London: Tate Publishing, 2014.
Medina, J. "Ideologia e mentalidade do 'Estado Novo' Salazarista." In *História do pensamento filosófico Português*, vol. 5, o século XX, vol. 2, edited by P. Calafate, 161–94. Lisbon: Editorial Caminho, 2000.
Melo, D. *Salazarismo e cultura popular (1933–1958)*. Lisbon: Instituto de Ciências Sociais da Universidade de Lisboa, 2001.
Mercier, P. *Night Train to Lisbon*. New York: Grove Press, 2008.
Morais, J.A. David de. *Religiosidade popular no Alentejo: A festa de Santa Cruz da Aldeia da Venda e a sua dialéctica con o sagrado*. Lisbon: Colibri, 2010.

Moura, V. G. "Presentation." In *Portugal, Building Up a Country*, edited by J. Mattoso and F. Faria Paulino, 15–17. Lisbon: Comissariado de Portugal for the Seville Universal Exhibition, 1992.
———. *Sobre Camões, Gândavo e outras personagens: Hipóteses de história da cultura*. Porto: Campo das Letras, 2000.
Myrone, M. "Afterword: Reinstituting British Folk Art." In R. Kenny, J. McMillan and M. Myrone, *British Folk Art*, 134–41. London: Tate Publishing, 2014.
Oliveira, A. de. "The Activities of the CNCDP: A Preliminary Assessment." *E-Journal of Portuguese History* 1, no. 1 (2003): 1–11.
Oliveira, E. Veiga de. *Festividades cíclicas em Portugal*. Lisbon: Dom Quixote, 1984.
———. "Introduction." In *Peoples and Cultures: Overseas Museum of Ethnology*, edited by Junta de Investigaçãoes do Ultramar. Lisbon: Junta de Investigaçãoes do Ultramar, 1972.
Pais, A. Nobre, A. Pacheco, and J. Coroado. *Cerâmica de Coimbra: do século XVI–XX*. Lisbon: Edições Inapa/Instituto dos Museus e da Conservação, 2007.
Pais de Brito, J. *Os índios nós*. Lisbon: National Museum of Ethnology, 2001.
Pais de Brito, J., R. Perez, and S. Sardo, eds. *Initiation: Stories of Goa*. Lisbon: National Museum of Ethnology, 1997.
Patrício, M. Ferreira. "A filosofia da educação em Portugal no século XX." In *História do pensamento filosófico Português*, vol. 5, o século XX, vol. 2, edited by P. Calafate, 71–134. Lisbon: Editorial Caminho, 2000.
———. *O messianismo de Teixeira de Pascoaes e a educação dos Portugueses*. Lisbon: Imprensa Nacional/Casa da Moeda, 1996.
Pedroso, C. *Contribuições para uma mitologia popular portuguesa e outros escritos etnográficos*. Lisbon: Dom Quixote, 1988.
Peixoto, R. *As Olarias de Prado*. Barcelos: Câmara Municipal de Barcelos, Museu Regional de Cerâmica, 1966.
Pereira, B. *Máscaras portuguesas*. Lisbon: Museu de Etnologia do Ultramar, 1973.
———. "Rituais de inverno com máscaras." In *Rituais de inverno com máscaras: Esposição*, edited by M. Vale de Almeida and V. Mesquita, 13–37. Bragança: Instituto Português de Museus, 2006.
Pereira, M.M. Cantinho. "O Museu da Sociedade de Geografia de Lisboa nos finais do século XIX." In *Tesouros da Sociedade de Geografia de Lisboa*, edited by L.A. Barros, 81–82. Lisbon: Sociedade de Geografia, 2001.
———. *O Museu Etnográfico da Sociedade de Geografia de Lisboa: Modernidade, colonização, altaridade*. Lisbon: Fundação Calouste Gulbenkian, 2005.
Perez, R.M. *Cultures of the Indian Ocean*. Lisbon: Comissão Nacional para as Comemorações dos Descobrimentos Portugueses and Instituto Português de Museus, 1998.
Pessanha, S. *Mascarados e máscaras populares de Trás-os-Montes*. Lisbon: Livraria Ferin, 1960.
Pessoa, F. *Lisboa: What the Tourist Should See*. Lisbon: Livros Horizonte, 1997.
———. *Message*. Cruz Quebrada: Oficina do Livro, 2008.
———. *The Book of Disquiet*. London: Serpent's Tail, 2010.
Pimentel, C. *O sistema museológico Português (1833–1991): Em direcção a um novo modelo teórico para o seu estudo*. Lisbon: Fundação Calouste Gulbenkian, 2005.
Pina-Cabral, J. de. "O pagamento do santo: Uma tipologia interpretativa dos ex-votos no contexto sócial-cultural do noroeste português." In *Milagre que Fez*, 79–104. Coimbra: Museu Antropológico, Universide de Coimbra, 1997.
———. "Quinze anos depois." In *Milagre que Fez*, 105–20. Coimbra: Museu Antropológico, Universidade de Coimbra, 1997.
———. *Sons of Adam, Daughters of Eve: The Peasant Worldview of the Alto Minho*. New York: Oxford University Press, 1986.
———. "Tamed Violence: Genital Symbolism in Portuguese Popular Culture." *Man*, n.s., 28, no. 1 (1993): 101–20.
Pina-Cabral, J. de, and R. Feijó. "Conflicting Attitudes to Death in Modern Portugal: The Question of Cemeteries." In *Death in Portugal: Studies in Portuguese Anthropology and Modern History*, edited by R. Feijó, H. Martins and J. Pina-Cabral, 17–43. Oxford: Journal of the Anthropological Society of Oxford, 1983.
Pinto Mendes, M.H. "Cumpriu-se o mar." In *Os descobrimentos portugueses e a Europa do Renascimento: XVII exposição o europeia de arte, ciência e cultura*, edited by Council of Europe, Exposição Europaia de Arte, Ciência e Cultura, 65–78. Lisbon: Presidência do conselho de ministros, 1983.
Porto, N. *Modos de objectificação da dominação colonial: O caso do Museu do Dundo, 1940–1970*. Lisbon: Fundação Calouste Gulbenkian, 2009.
———. *O corpo, a razão, o coração: A construção social da sexualidade em Vila Ruiva*. Lisbon: Escher, 1991.
Quadros, A. *Poesia e filosofia do mito Sebastianista*. Lisbon: Guimarães, 2001.
Raposo, P. *Por detrás da máscara: Ensaio de antropologia da performance sobre os caretos de Podence*. Lisbon: Instituto dos Museus e da Conservação, 2010.
Ribeiro, R. *Henrique Delgado: Contributos para a história da marioneta em Portugal*. Lisbon: EGEAC/Museu da Marioneta, 2011.
Rios, C., G. Ramos, and P. Régo. *Olaria de Barcelos: As voltas do Barro*. Barcelos: Câmara Municipal de Barcelos, Museu de Olaria, 2004.
Rodrigues de Areia, M.L. "A colecções angolanas." In *Cem anos de antropologia em Coimbra*, 149–94. Coimbra: Museu e Laboratório Antropólogico, Universidade de Coimbra, 1985.

Rodrigues de Areia, M.L., and M.A. Miranda. "Profile of a Naturalist." In *Memory of Amazonia: Alexandre Rodrigues Ferreira and the Viagem Philosophica in the Captaincies of Grão-Pará, Rio Negro, Mato Grosso and Cuyabá, 1783–1792*, edited by M.L. Rodrigues de Areia, M.A. Miranda and T. Hartmann. Coimbra: Museu e Laboratório Antropológico, Universidade de Coimbra, 1994.

Rodrigues de Areia, M.L., and M.A. Tavares da Rocha. "O ensino da antropologia." In *Cem anos de antropologia em Coimbra*, 13–48. Coimbra: Museu e Laboratório Antropólogico, Universidade de Coimbra, 1985.

Roque, R. "Colonialidade equívoca: Fonseca Cardoso e as origens da antropologia colonial portuguesa." In *Portugal não é um país pequeno: Contar o "império" na pós-colonialidade*, edited by M.R. Sanches, 83–112. Lisbon: Cotovia, 2006.

Rosas, F. "O Salazarismo e o homem novo: Ensaio sobre o Estado Novo e a questão do totalitarismo nos anos 30 e 40." In *Estados autoritários e totalitários e suas representações: propaganda, ideologia, historiografia e memória*, edited by L. Reis Torgal and H. Paulo, 31–48. Coimbra: Imprensa da Universidade, 2008.

———, ed. *História de Portugal: O Estado Novo*, vol. 7. Lisbon: Estampa, 1994.

Rosmaninho, N. "António Ferro e a propaganda nacional antimoderna." In *Estados autoritários e totalitários e suas representações: Propaganda, ideologia, historiografia e memória*, edited by L. Reis Torgal and H. Paulo, 289–300. Coimbra: Imprensa da Universidade, 2008.

Rumbau, T. "FIMFA LX: Dez anos." In FIMFA 10 LX: *Festival internacional de marionetas e formas animadas*, edited by Festival Internacional de Marionetas e Formas Animadas, 24–29. Lisbon: A Tarumba, Teatro de Marionetas, 2010.

Russell, C. *Groundwaters. A Century of Art by Self-Taught and Outsider Artists*. London, Munich and New York: Prestel, 2011.

Russell-Wood, A.J.R. *The Portuguese Empire, 1415–1808: A World on the Move*. Baltimore: Johns Hopkins University Press, 1998.

Salter, C. *Introducing Portugal*. London: Methuen, 1956.

Sanches, M.R. "Introdução." In *Portugal não é um país pequeno: Contar o "império" na pós-colonialidade*, edited by M. R. Sanches, 7–21. Lisbon: Cotovia, 2006.

Sanchis, P. *Arraial, festa de um povo: As romarias portuguesas*. Lisbon: Dom Quixote, 1983.

———. "The Portuguese '*romarias*'." In *Saints and Their Cults: Studies in Religious Sociology, Folklore and History*, edited by S. Wilson, 261–89. Cambridge: Cambridge University Press, 1983.

Santo, M.E. *A religião popular portuguesa*. Lisbon: Assírio e Alvim, 1984.

Saramago, J. *Baltasar and Blimunda*. London: Cape, 1988.

———. *Journey to Portugal: A Pursuit of Portugal's History and Culture*. Translated by A. Hopkinson and N. Caistor. London: Harvill Press, 2000.

———. *The Year of the Death of Ricardo Reis*. San Diego, New York and London: Harcourt Brace Jovanovic, 1991; originally published 1984.

Serrão, V. *As pinturas murais da capela de São João Baptista em Monsaraz (1622)*. Reguengos de Monsaraz: Câmara Municipal, 2010.

———. "Portugal em ruínas. Uma história cripto-antística do património construído." In G. de Brito e Silva, *Portugal em ruínas*, 11–46. Lisbon: Fundação Francisco Manuel dos Santos, 2014.

Silva, A.J. *Os nossos santos e beatos e outros, que Portugal adotou*. Lisbon: A Esfera dos Livros, 2012.

Simon, W.J. *Scientific Expeditions in the Portuguese Overseas Territories, 1783–1808, and the Role of Lisbon in the Intellectual-Scientific Community of the Late Eighteenth Century*. Lisbon: Instituto de Investigação Cientifica Tropical, 1983.

Sitwell, S. *Portugal and Madeira*. London: Batsford, 1954.

Tabucchi, A. *Requiem*. London: Harvill, 1994.

Talhinhas, A. "Colóquio." In *Teatro de marionetas: Tradição e modernidade*, edited by C. Zurbach, 167–74. Évora: Casa do Sul, 2002.

Taubes, J. *Occidental Eschatology*. Stanford: Stanford University Press, 2009.

Teixeira, M.B. "Portuguese Art Treasures, Medieval Women and Early Museum Collections." In *Museums and the Making of "Ourselves": The Role of Objects in National Identity*, edited by F. Kaplan, 291–313. London and New York: Leicester University Press, 1994.

Thomaz, O.R. "Ecos do Atlântico Sul: Representações sobre o terceiro império Português." PhD diss., Universidade de São Paulo, 1997.

Tiza, A.P. *Inverno mágico: Ritos e mistérios transmontanos*. Lisbon: Esquilo, 2004.

Torga, M. *Portugal*. Coimbra: Coimbra Editora, 1954.

Torgal, L. Reis. "'O fascismo nunca existiu...' Reflexões sobre as Representações de Salazar." In *Estados autoritários e totalitários e suas representações: propaganda, ideologia, historiografia e memória*, edited by L. Reis Torgal and H. Paulo, 17–30. Coimbra: Imprensa da Universidade, 2008.

Torgal, L. Reis, J. Mendes, and F. Catroga. *História da história em Portugal séculos XIX–XX. Da historiografia à memória histórica*, vol. 2. Lisbon: Temas e Debates, 1998.

Vale de Almeida, M. "Quando a máscara esconde uma mulher." In *Rituais de inverno com máscaras: Exposição*, edited by M. Vale de Almeida and V. Mesquita, 61–73. Bragança: Instituto Português dos Museus, 2006.

———. *Um mar da cor da terra: Raça, cultura e política da identidade.* Oeiras: Celta, 2000.

Vasconcellos, J. Leite de. *Tradições populares de Portugal.* Lisbon: Imprensa Nacional/Casa da Moeda, 1986.

Vermelho, J.J. *Barros de Estremoz: Contributo monográfico para o estudo da olaria e da barrística.* Estremoz: Pousada Rainha Santa Isabel, 1989.

Vicente, G. *The Boat Plays.* Reading, UK: Arrowhead Books, 1997.

Viçosa, V. "O saudosismo de Teixeira de Pascoaes e a identidade cultural portuguesa." In *Encontro com Teixeira de Pascoaes no cinquentenário da sua morte,* edited by P. Morão and M. das Graças Moreira de Sá, 93–103. Lisbon: Colibri, 2004.

Wright, D., and P. Swift. *Algarve: A Portrait and a Guide.* London: Barrie and Rockliff, 1965.

———. *Minho and North Portugal: A Portrait and a Guide.* London: Barrie and Rockliff, 1968.

Xavier, I. "Manuel Gustavo e os jornais humorísticos." In *Manuel Gustavo Bordalo Pinheiro (1867–1920): obra cerâmica e gráfica,* edited by R. H. da Silva andC. Ramos Horta, 70–83. Caldas da Rainha: Museu de Cerâmica, 2004.

Zurbach, C. "Erudito e popular: A recepção teatral dos Bonecos de Santo Aleixo." In *Teatro de Marionetas: Tradição e modernidade,* edited by C. Zurbach, J.A. Ferreira and P. Saixas, 181–91. Évora: Casa do Sul, 2002.

———. "Os Bonecos de Santo Aleixo: Um repertório teatral." In *Autos, passos e bailinhos: Os textos dos Bonecos de Santo Aleixo,* edited by C. Zurbach, 35–52. Évora: Casa do Sul, 2007.

Index

Page numbers in **bold** refer to image captions. Some illustrations have not been individually identified when they appear within relevant page ranges.

Page references enclosed in square brackets indicate textual references to endnotes.

C

D

E

F

G

H

I

J

N

O

P

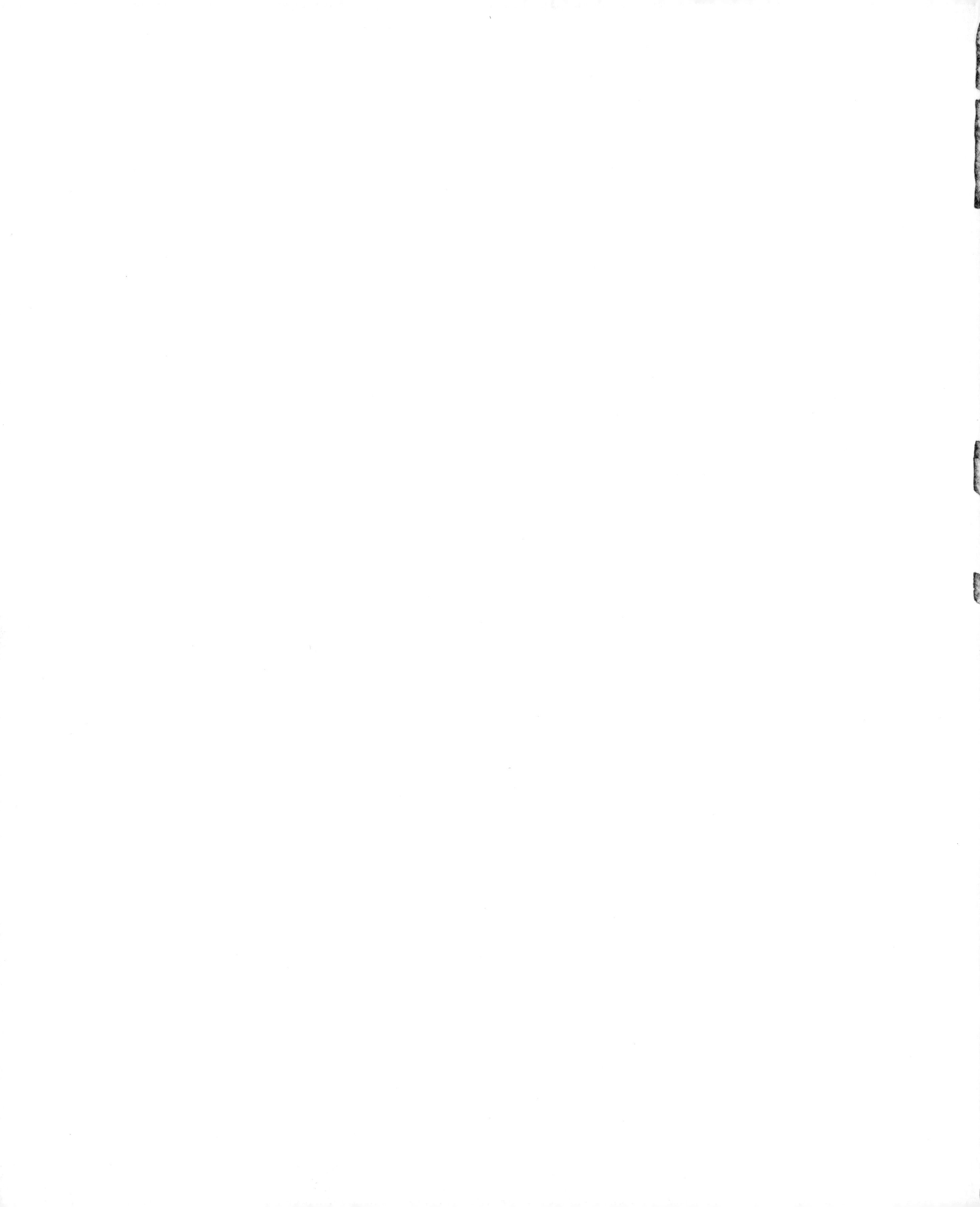